CRIMINAL LAW HANDBOOK OF *NEW YORK*

2020
Interim Supplement

QUESTIONS ABOUT THIS PUBLICATION?

For CUSTOMER SERVICE ASSISTANCE concerning replacement pages, shipments, billing, reprint permission, or other matters, please contact Customer Support at our self-service portal available 24/7 at _support.lexisnexis.com/print_
or call us at 800-833-9844

For EDITORIAL **content questions** concerning this publication,
email: *llp.clp@lexisnexis.com*

For **information on other LEXISNEXIS MATTHEW BENDER publications,**
please call us at (877) 461-8801
or visit our online bookstore at *www.lexisnexis.com/bookstore*

ISBN: 978-1-5221-9037-0 (2020 Edition)

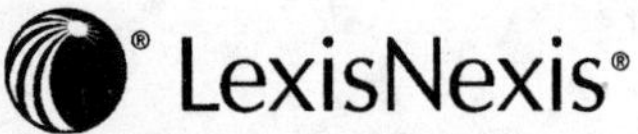

Matthew Bender & Company, Inc.
Editorial Offices
701 E. Water Street
Charlottesville, VA 22902
800-446-3410
www.lexisnexis.com

(Pub. 36858)

PREFACE

CRIMINAL LAW HANDBOOK OF NEW YORK 2020 INTERIM SUPPLEMENT

As publishers of the *New York Consolidated Laws Service*, LexisNexis is pleased to present the 2020 Interim Supplement to the **Criminal Law Handbook of New York**. This interim supplement brings your **2020 Criminal Law Handbook** current through Chapter 88 of the 2020 Regular Session for New York Laws, through May 1, 2020, for New York City Rules and New York City Administrative Code, and through March 13, 2020, for New York Codes, Rules, and Regulations. The interim supplement includes new and amended material from the Penal Law, Criminal Procedure, Correction Law, and related state and city provisions. We are publishing this interim supplement in response to suggestions we have received asking for more frequent updates of the **Criminal Law Handbook** than just the annual edition. Our plan is to offer this interim supplement each summer, and we hope that you will contact us with your feedback about this new reference.

We are committed to providing law enforcement and legal professionals with the most comprehensive, current, and useful publications possible. We welcome your comments and suggestions via email at *llp.clp@lexisnexis.com*. If you have any questions or concerns about your account, please call our Customer Service Department at 800-833-9844. If you are interested in ordering other LexisNexis publications, please call our Sales Department at 877-461-8801 or visit our on-line bookstore at *www.lexisnexis.com*. By providing us with your informed comments, you will be assured of having available a working tool that increases in value each year.

June 2020

TABLE OF CONTENTS

CRIMINAL LAW HANDBOOK OF NEW YORK

2019 Legislative Changes to the Criminal Law Handbook of New York

Alcoholic Beverage Control Law

Section, Effect	*Chap*	*Sec*	*Eff. Date*
64-c, subs 5, 12, 13, 14, 15, 16, 17, 18, 19, amended	655	1	15-Jan-20
100, subs 8, 9, amended	724	1	19-Mar-20
106, subs 13(a)(xii), 13(a)(xiii), 13(a)(xiv), amended	429	2	29-Oct-19
106, subs 13(a)(xii), 13(a)(xiii), amended	549	1	25-Nov-19
106, sub 13(a-1), amended by adding	611	3	06-Dec-19

Correction Law

Section, Effect	*Chap*	*Sec*	*Eff. Date*
29, sub 1, amended	485	2	09-May-20
76, sub 1, amended	385	1	22-Dec-19
803-b, sub 1(c)(ii), amended	723	1	20-Dec-19

Criminal Procedure Law

Section, Effect	*Chap*	*Sec*	*Eff. Date*
1.20, sub 1, amended	450	1	08-Nov-19
2.10, amended by adding	632	1	12-Dec-19
40.51, added	374	1	16-Oct-19
150.50, sub 1, amended	450	2	08-Nov-19
170.15, sub 4, amended	634	1	12-Dec-19
310.10, sub 2, amended	569	1	25-Nov-19
330.20, subs 1(a), 1(b), 1(d), amended	672	63	16-Dec-19
530.11, sub 6, amended	663	2	15-Mar-20
725.15, amended	672	64	16-Dec-19
730.10, subs 3, 4, amended	672	65	16-Dec-19

Executive Law

Section, Effect	*Chap*	*Sec*	*Eff. Date*
624, sub 1(b), amended	690	1	17-Jun-20
624, sub 1-a, amended by adding	690	2	17-Jun-20
626, sub 4, amended by adding	690	3	17-Jun-20
631, sub 13, amended	681	2	15-Jun-20
631-b, added	737	2	22-Mar-20
840, sub 6, amended by adding	552	1	23-Feb-20

Penal Law

Section, Effect	*Chap*	*Sec*	*Eff. Date*
241.00, sub 1, amended	573	4	31-May-20

Penal Law (cont'd)

Section, Effect	*Chap*	*Sec*	*Eff. Date*
241.02, added	573	2	31-May-20
241.05, amended	573	3	31-May-20

Public Health Law

Section, Effect	*Chap*	*Sec*	*Eff. Date*
3309, sub 3-a, amended	504	1	19-Jan-20

Vehicle and Traffic Law

Section, Effect	*Chap*	*Sec*	*Eff. Date*
502, subs 4(a)(i), 4(b), 4(d), 4(c-4), amended	513	1	18-May-20
502, sub 8, amended by adding	740	1	20-Jun-20
504, sub 1(a-1), amended	490	80	12-Nov-20

Administrative Code of the City of New York

Section, Effect	*Eff. Date*
17-315, sub k par 3 amended	17-Nov-19

Rules of the City of New York

Rule, Effect	*Record*	*Eff. Date*
34 RCNY 4-11 (c) par 7 amended	Jan. 4, 2019 §2	15-Feb-19

2020 Legislative Changes to the Criminal Law Handbook of New York

Alcoholic Beverage Control Law

Section, Effect	*Chap*	*Sec*	*Eff. Date*
64-c, sub 5, amended	82	1	15-Jan-20
100, sub 9(a), amended	39	1	19-Mar-20
106, subs 5(a), 5(b), 5(c), amended	55	Part FF, 1	3-Apr-20

Correction Law

Section, Effect	*Chap*	*Sec*	*Eff. Date*
77, repealed	55	Part G, 2	3-Apr-20
80, added	55	Part G, 3	3-Apr-20
803-b, sub 1(c)(ii), amended	35	1	20-Dec-19

Criminal Procedure Law

Section, Effect	*Chap*	*Sec*	*Eff. Date*
95.00, amended	55	Part E, 2	3-Apr-20
140.10, sub 6, amended by adding	55	Part M, 2	1-Nov-20
150.40, sub 1, amended	56	Part UU, 8	2-Jul-20
245.10, sub 1(a), amended	56	Part HHH, 1	3-May-20
245.20, subs 1(c), 1(f), 1(g), 1(j), amended	56	Part HHH, 2	3-May-20
245.25, subs 2, 3, amended	56	Part HHH, 6	3-May-20
245.50, amended	56	Part HHH, 7	3-May-20
245.70, subs 1, 3, amended	56	Part HHH, 3	3-May-20
245.75, amended	56	Part HHH, 5	3-May-20
370.15 subs 1, 2, amended	55	Part Q, 1	3-Apr-20
500.10, sub 3-a, 3-b, amended	56	Part UU, 1	2-Jul-20
510.10, sub 4, amended	56	Part UU, 2	2-Jul-20
510.40, sub 4(c), amended	56	Part UU, 7	2-Jul-20
510.43, amended	56	Part UU, 11	2-Jul-20
530.14, heading, 1(a), 1(b), (1(c), amended	55	Part M, 3	1-Nov-20
530.14, subs 2(a), 2(b), 2(c), amended	55	Part M, 4	1-Nov-20
530.14, sub 3(a), 3(b), 3(c), amended	55	Part M, 5	1-Nov-20
530.14, sub 5(b), 5(d), amended	55	Part M, 6	1-Nov-20
530.14, sub 6, 7, amended	55	Part M, 7	1-Nov-20
530.20, sub 1(b), amended	56	Part UU, 3	2-Jul-20
530.40, sub 4, amended	56	Part UU, 4	2-Jul-20
530.45, sub 2-a, amended by adding	56	Part UU, 9	2-Jul-20
530.50, subs 1, 2, amended	56	Part UU, 10	2-Jul-20

Executive Law

Section, Effect	*Chap*	*Sec*	*Eff. Date*
621, sub 25, amended by adding	70	2	20-Dec-19
624, sub 1-a, amended by repealing	70	1	20-Dec-19
626, sub 1, amended	70	4	17-Jun-20

Executive Law (cont'd)

Section, Effect	*Chap*	*Sec*	*Eff. Date*
626, sub 4, amended by repealing	70	3	17-Jun-20
631, sub 5(e), amended	70	5	17-Jun-20
631, sub 13, amended	55	Part XX, Subpart S, 3	15-June-20
631-b, repealed	55	Part XX, Subpart A, 1	22-Mar-20
837, sub 22, amended by adding	55	Part N, 3	3-Apr-20
837-u, added	56	Part UU, 6	2-Jul-20

Penal Law

Section, Effect	*Chap*	*Sec*	*Eff. Date*
65.10, sub 2(k-2), amended by adding	56	Part VV, 1	2-Jul-20
70.20, sub 4(a-1), amended by repealing	55	Part G, 1	2-Jun-20
265.00, sub 17, amended	55	Part N, 1	3-Apr-21
400.00, sub 1-a, amended by adding	55	Part N, 2	3-Apr-21
485.00, (opening), amended	55	Part R, 2	1-Nov-20
485.05, sub 3, amended	55	Part R, 3	1-Nov-20
490.27, added	55	Part R, 4	1-Nov-20
490.28, added	55	Part R, 4	1-Nov-20

Public Health Law

Section, Effect	*Chap*	*Sec*	*Eff. Date*
3302, sub 21, amended	1	3	8-Mar-20
3306, subs (I)(b)(56), (I)(b)(57), amended	56	Part CC, 1	2-Jul-20
3306, sub (II)(c)(29), amended by adding	56	Part CC, 3	2-Jul-20

Social Services Law

Section, Effect	*Chap*	*Sec*	*Eff. Date*
488, sub 4(a), amended	58	Part RRR, 4	2-Jul-20

Vehicle and Traffic Law

Section, Effect	*Chap*	*Sec*	*Eff. Date*
102-c, added	58	Part XX, 1	3-Apr-20
114-e, added	58	Part XX, 2	3-Apr-20
125, amended	58	Part XX, 3	3-Apr-20
501, amended	6	3	3-Feb-21
501, amended	6	4	3-Feb-21
501-a, sub 1, amended	6	2	3-Feb-21
502, sub 8, amended	31	1	20-Jun-20
507-a, added	2	1	3-Feb-21
510, subs 2(b)(viii), 2(b)(vii), amended	58	Part H, 2	1-Aug-20

Vehicle and Traffic Law (cont'd)

Section, Effect	*Chap*	*Sec*	*Eff. Date*
510, sub 4-g, amended by adding	58	Part H, 3	1-Aug-20
1800, subs (g), (h), (i), amended	58	Part B, 1	30-Sep-20
1809, sub 8, amended	55	Part A, 13	3-Apr-20

Administrative Code of the City of New York

Section, Effect	*Eff. Date*
10-301, subs 21, 22 added	23-Feb-20
10-314 added	23-Feb-20

Rules of the City of New York

Rule, Effect	*Record*	*Eff. Date*
34 RCNY 4-07 (j) par 3 subpar (i) amended	Jan. 10, 2020 §2	9-Feb-20

PENAL LAW

Part TWO
Sentences

Title E
Sentences

Article 65
Sentences of Probation, Conditional Discharge and Unconditional Discharge

§ 65.10. Conditions of probation and of conditional discharge. [Effective until July 2, 2020]

1. In general. The conditions of probation and of conditional discharge shall be such as the court, in its discretion, deems reasonably necessary to insure that the defendant will lead a law-abiding life or to assist him to do so.

2. Conditions relating to conduct and rehabilitation. When imposing a sentence of probation or of conditional discharge, the court shall, as a condition of the sentence, consider restitution or reparation and may, as a condition of the sentence, require that the defendant:

(a) Avoid injurious or vicious habits;

(b) Refrain from frequenting unlawful or disreputable places or consorting with disreputable persons;

(c) Work faithfully at a suitable employment or faithfully pursue a course of study or of vocational training that will equip him for suitable employment;

(d) Undergo available medical or psychiatric treatment and remain in a specified institution, when required for that purpose;

(e) Participate in an alcohol or substance abuse program or an intervention program approved by the court after consultation with the local probation department having jurisdiction, or such other public or private agency as the court determines to be appropriate;

(e-1) Participate in a motor vehicle accident prevention course. The court may require such condition where a person has been convicted of a traffic infraction for a violation of article twenty-six of the vehicle and traffic law where the commission of such violation caused the serious physical injury or death of another person. For purposes of this paragraph, the term "motor vehicle accident prevention course" shall mean a motor vehicle accident prevention course approved by the department of motor vehicles pursuant to article twelve-B of the vehicle and traffic law;

(f) Support his dependents and meet other family responsibilities;

(g) Make restitution of the fruits of his or her offense or make reparation, in an amount he can afford to pay, for the actual out-of-pocket loss caused thereby. When restitution or reparation is a condition of the sentence, the court shall fix the amount thereof, the manner of performance, specifically state the date when restitution is to be paid in full prior to the expiration of the sentence of probation and may establish provisions for the early termination of a sentence of probation or conditional discharge pursuant to the provisions of subdivision three of section 410.90 of the criminal procedure law after the restitution and reparation part of a sentence of probation or conditional discharge has been satisfied. The court shall provide that in the event the person to whom restitution or reparation is to be made dies prior to the completion of said restitution or reparation, the remaining payments shall be made to the estate of the deceased.

(h) Perform services for a public or not-for-profit corporation, association, institution or agency, including but not limited to services for the division of substance abuse services, services in an appropriate community program for removal of graffiti from public or private property, including any property damaged in the underlying offense, or services for the maintenance and repair of real or personal property maintained as a cemetery plot, grave, burial place or other place of interment of human remains. Provided however, that the performance of any such services shall not result in the displacement of employed workers or in the impairment of existing contracts for services, nor shall the performance of any such services be required or permitted in any establishment involved in any labor strike or lockout. The court may establish provisions for the early termination of a sentence of probation or conditional discharge pursuant to the provisions of subdivision three of section 410.90 of the criminal procedure law after such services have been completed. Such sentence may only be imposed upon conviction of a misdemeanor, violation, or class D or class E felony, or a youthful offender finding replacing any such conviction, where the defendant has consented to the amount and conditions of such service;

(i) If a person under the age of twenty-one years,

(i) resides with his parents or in a suitable foster home or hostel as referred to in section two hundred forty-four of the executive law,

(ii) attends school,

(iii) spends such part of the period of the sentence as the court may direct, but not exceeding two years, in a facility made available by the division for youth pursuant to article nineteen-G of the executive law, provided that admission to such facility may be made only with the prior consent of the division for youth,

(iv) attend a non-residential program for such hours and pursuant to a schedule prescribed by the court as suitable for a program of rehabilitation of youth,

(v) contribute to his own support in any home, foster home or hostel;

(j) Post a bond or other security for the performance of any or all conditions imposed;

(k) Observe certain specified conditions of conduct as set forth in an order of protection issued pursuant to section 530.12 or 530.13 of the criminal procedure law.

(k-1) Install and maintain a functioning ignition interlock device, as that term is defined in section one hundred nineteen-a of the vehicle and traffic law, in any vehicle owned or operated by the defendant if the court in its discretion determines that such a condition is necessary to ensure the public safety. The court may require such condition only where a person has been convicted of a violation of subdivision two, two-a or three of section eleven hundred ninety-two of the vehicle and traffic law, or any crime defined by the vehicle and traffic law or this chapter of which an alcohol-related violation of any provision of section eleven hundred ninety-two of the vehicle and traffic law is an essential element. The offender shall be required to install and operate the ignition interlock device only in accordance with section eleven hundred ninety-eight of the vehicle and traffic law.

(l) Satisfy any other conditions reasonably related to his rehabilitation.

3. Conditions relating to supervision. When imposing a sentence of probation the court, in addition to any conditions imposed pursuant to subdivision two of this section, shall require as conditions of the sentence, that the defendant:

(a) Report to a probation officer as directed by the court or the probation officer and permit the probation officer to visit him at his place of abode or elsewhere;

(b) Remain within the jurisdiction of the court unless granted permission to leave by the court or the probation officer. Where a defendant is granted permission to move or travel outside the jurisdiction of the court, the defendant shall sign a written waiver of extradition agreeing to waive extradition proceedings where such proceedings are the result of the issuance of a warrant by the court pursuant to subdivision two of section 410.40 of the criminal procedure law based on an alleged violation of probation. Where any county or the city of New York incurs costs associated with the return of any probationer based on the issuance of a warrant by the court pursuant to subdivision two of section 410.40 of the criminal procedure law, the jurisdiction may collect the reasonable and necessary expenses involved in connection with his or her transport, from the probationer; provided that where the sentence of probation is not revoked pursuant to section 410.70 of the criminal procedure law no such expenses may be collected.

(c) Answer all reasonable inquiries by the probation officer and notify the probation officer prior to any change in address or employment.

4. Electronic monitoring. When imposing a sentence of probation the court may, in addition to any conditions imposed pursuant to subdivisions two and three of this section, require the defendant to submit to the use of an electronic monitoring device and/or to follow a schedule that governs the defendant's daily movement. Such condition may be imposed only where the court, in its discretion, determines that requiring the defendant to comply with such condition will advance public safety, probationer control or probationer surveillance. Electronic monitoring shall be used in accordance with uniform procedures developed by the office of probation and correctional alternatives.

4-a. Mandatory conditions for sex offenders.

(a) When imposing a sentence of probation or conditional discharge upon a person convicted of an offense defined in article one hundred thirty, two hundred thirty-five or two hundred sixty-three of this chapter, or section 255.25, 255.26 or 255.27 of this chapter, and the victim of such offense was under the age of eighteen at the time of such offense or such person has been designated a level three sex offender pursuant to subdivision six of section 168-l of the correction law, the court shall require, as a mandatory condition of such sentence, that such sentenced offender shall refrain from knowingly entering into or upon any school grounds, as that term is defined in subdivision fourteen of section 220.00 of this chapter, or any other facility or institution primarily used for the care or treatment of persons under the age of eighteen while one or more of such persons under the age of eighteen are present, provided however, that when such sentenced offender is a registered student or participant or an employee of such facility or institution or entity contracting therewith or has a family member enrolled in such facility or institution, such sentenced offender may, with the written authorization of his or her probation officer or the court and the superintendent or chief administrator of such facility, institution or grounds, enter such facility, institution or upon such grounds for the limited purposes authorized by the probation officer or the court and superintendent or chief officer. Nothing in this subdivision shall be construed as restricting any lawful condition of supervision that may be imposed on such sentenced offender.

(b) When imposing a sentence of probation or conditional discharge upon a person convicted of an offense for which registration as a sex offender is required pursuant to subdivision two or three of section one hundred sixty-eight-a of the correction law, and the victim of such offense was under the age of eighteen at the time of such offense or such person has been designated a level three sex offender pursuant to subdivision six of section one hundred sixty-eight-l of the correction law or the internet was used to facilitate the commission of the crime, the court shall require, as mandatory conditions of such sentence, that such sentenced offender be prohibited from using the internet to access pornographic material, access a commercial social networking website, communicate with other individuals or groups for the purpose of promoting sexual relations with persons under the age of eighteen, and communicate with a person under the age of eighteen when such offender is over the age of eighteen, provided that the court may permit an offender to use the internet to communicate with a person under the age of eighteen when such offender is the parent of a minor child and is not otherwise prohibited from communicating with such child. Nothing in this subdivision shall be construed as restricting any other lawful condition of supervision that may be imposed on such sentenced offender. As used in this subdivision, a "commercial social networking website" shall mean any business, organization or other entity operating a website that permits persons under eighteen years of age to be registered users for the purpose of establishing personal relationships with other users, where such persons under eighteen years of age may: (i) create web pages or profiles that provide information about themselves where such web pages or profiles are available to the public or to other users; (ii) engage in direct or real time communication with other users, such as a chat room or instant messenger; and (iii) communicate with persons over eighteen years of age; provided, however, that, for purposes of this subdivision, a commercial social networking website shall not include a website that permits users to engage in such other activities as are not enumerated herein.

5. Other conditions. When imposing a sentence of probation the court may, in addition to any conditions imposed pursuant to subdivisions two, three and four of this section, require that the defendant comply with any other reasonable condition as the court shall determine to be necessary or appropriate to ameliorate the conduct which gave rise to the offense or to prevent the incarceration of the defendant.

5-a. Other conditions for sex offenders. When imposing a sentence of probation upon a person convicted of an offense for which registration as a sex offender is required pursuant to subdivision two or three of section one hundred sixty-eight-a of the correction law, in addition to any conditions required under subdivisions two, three, four, four-a and five of this section, the court may require that the defendant comply with a reasonable limitation on his or her use of the internet that the court determines to be necessary or appropriate to ameliorate the conduct which gave rise to the offense or to protect public safety, provided that the court shall not prohibit such sentenced offender from using the internet in connection with education, lawful employment or search for lawful employment.

HISTORY:

Add, L 1965, ch 1030, eff Sept 1, 1967, with substance derived in part from §§ 2188, 2188–b; amd, L 1973, ch 676, § 30; L 1974, ch 930, § 3; L 1975, ch 667, § 35; L 1978, ch 500, § 1; L 1980, ch 270, § 1, eff June 17, 1980; L 1980, ch 284, § 1; L 1980, ch 471, § 22, eff July 23, 1980; L 1980, ch 530, § 16; L 1981, ch 742, § 3, eff Sept 1, 1981; L 1981, ch 583, § 1; L 1982, ch 782, §§ 1, 2; L 1984, ch 335, § 2; L 1984, ch 417, § 1, eff Nov 1, 1984; L 1985, ch 672, §§ 1, 2, eff Sept 30, 1985; L 1986, ch 552, § 1; L 1989, ch 443, § 1; L 1992, ch 465, § 51, eff Jan 13, 1993; L 1992, ch 618, § 15, eff Nov 1, 1992; L 1995, ch 536, § 2; L 1996, ch 186, § 1, eff Nov 1, 1996; L 1996, ch 653, § 1, eff Sept 18, 1996; L 1997, ch 181, § 1, eff July 8, 1997; L 2000, ch 1, § 7, eff Feb 1, 2001; L 2001, ch 508, § 1, eff Jan 20, 2002; L 2005, ch 544, § 1, eff Sept 1, 2006; L 2006, ch 320, § 4, eff Nov 1, 2006; L 2006, ch 571, § 6, eff Nov 1, 2006; L 2007, ch 669, § 1, eff Oct 27, 2007; L 2008, ch 67, §§ 7, 8, eff April 28, 2008; L 2008, ch 406, § 2, eff Aug 5, 2008; L 2010, ch 56, § 46 (Part A), eff June 22, 2010; L 2010, ch 56, § 8 (Part D), eff Sept 20, 2010; L 2018, ch 480, § 2, eff June 26, 2019.

§ 65.10. Conditions of probation and of conditional discharge. [Effective July 2, 2020]

1. In general. The conditions of probation and of conditional discharge shall be such as the court, in its discretion, deems reasonably necessary to insure that the defendant will lead a law-abiding life or to assist him to do so.

2. Conditions relating to conduct and rehabilitation. When imposing a sentence of probation or of conditional discharge, the court shall, as a condition of the sentence, consider restitution or reparation and may, as a condition of the sentence, require that the defendant:

(a) Avoid injurious or vicious habits;

(b) Refrain from frequenting unlawful or disreputable places or consorting with disreputable persons;

(c) Work faithfully at a suitable employment or faithfully pursue a course of study or of vocational training that will equip him for suitable employment;

(d) Undergo available medical or psychiatric treatment and remain in a specified institution, when required for that purpose;

(e) Participate in an alcohol or substance abuse program or an intervention program approved by the court after consultation with the local probation department having jurisdiction, or such other public or private agency as the court determines to be appropriate;

(e-1) Participate in a motor vehicle accident prevention course. The court may require such condition where a person has been convicted of a traffic infraction for a violation of article twenty-six of the vehicle and traffic law where the commission of such violation caused the serious physical injury or death of another person. For purposes of this paragraph, the term "motor vehicle accident prevention course" shall mean a motor vehicle accident prevention course approved by the department of motor vehicles pursuant to article twelve-B of the vehicle and traffic law;

(f) Support his dependents and meet other family responsibilities;

(g) Make restitution of the fruits of his or her offense or make reparation, in an amount he can afford to pay, for the actual out-of-pocket loss caused thereby. When restitution or reparation is a condition of the sentence, the court shall fix the amount thereof, the manner of performance, specifically state the date when restitution is to be paid in full prior to the expiration of the sentence of probation and may establish provisions for the early termination of a sentence of probation or conditional discharge pursuant to the provisions of subdivision three of section 410.90 of the criminal procedure law after the restitution and reparation part of a sentence of probation or conditional discharge has been satisfied. The court shall provide that in the event the person to whom restitution or reparation is to be made dies prior to the completion of said restitution or reparation, the remaining payments shall be made to the estate of the deceased.

(h) Perform services for a public or not-for-profit corporation, association, institution or agency, including but not limited to services for the division of substance abuse services, services in an appropriate community program for removal of graffiti from public or private property, including any property damaged in the underlying offense, or services for the maintenance and repair of real or personal property maintained as a cemetery plot, grave, burial place or other place of interment of human remains. Provided however, that the performance of any such services shall not result in the displacement of employed workers or in the impairment of existing contracts for services, nor shall the performance of any such services be required or permitted in any establishment involved in any labor strike or lockout. The court may establish provisions for the early termination of a sentence of probation or conditional discharge pursuant to the provisions of subdivision three of section 410.90 of the criminal procedure law after such services have been completed. Such sentence may only be imposed upon conviction of a misdemeanor, violation, or class D or class E felony, or a youthful offender finding replacing any such conviction, where the defendant has consented to the amount and conditions of such service;

(i) If a person under the age of twenty-one years,

(i) resides with his parents or in a suitable foster home or hostel as referred to in section two hundred forty-four of the executive law,

(ii) attends school,

(iii) spends such part of the period of the sentence as the court may direct, but not exceeding two years, in a facility made available by the division for youth pursuant to article nineteen-G of the executive law, provided that admission to such facility may be made only with the prior consent of the division for youth,

(iv) attend a non-residential program for such hours and pursuant to a schedule prescribed by the court as suitable for a program of rehabilitation of youth,

(v) contribute to his own support in any home, foster home or hostel;

(j) Post a bond or other security for the performance of any or all conditions imposed;

(k) Observe certain specified conditions of conduct as set forth in an order of protection issued pursuant to section 530.12 or 530.13 of the criminal procedure law.

(k-1) Install and maintain a functioning ignition interlock device, as that term is defined in section one hundred nineteen-a of the vehicle and traffic law, in any vehicle owned or operated by the defendant if the court in its discretion determines that such a condition is necessary to ensure the public safety. The court may require such condition only where a person has been convicted of a violation of subdivision two, two-a or three of section eleven hundred ninety-two of the vehicle and traffic law, or any crime defined by the vehicle and traffic law or this chapter of which an alcohol-related violation of any provision of section eleven hundred ninety-two of the vehicle and traffic law is an essential element. The offender shall be required to install and operate the ignition interlock device only in accordance with section eleven hundred ninety-eight of the vehicle and traffic law.

(k-2)(i) Refrain, upon sentencing for a crime involving unlawful sexual conduct committed against a metropolitan transportation authority passenger, customer, or employee or a crime involving assault against a metropolitan transportation authority employee, committed in or on any facility or conveyance of the metropolitan transportation authority or a subsidiary thereof or the New York city transit authority or a subsidiary thereof, from using or entering any of such authority's subways, trains, buses or other conveyances or facilities specified by the court for a period of up to three years, or a specified period of such probation or conditional discharge, whichever is less. For purposes of this section, a crime involving assault shall mean an offense described in article one hundred twenty of this chapter which has as an element the causing of physical injury or serious physical injury to another as well as the attempt thereof.

(ii) The court may, in its discretion, suspend, modify or cancel a condition imposed under this paragraph in the interest of justice at any time. If the person depends on the authority's subways, trains, buses, or other conveyances or facilities for trips of necessity, including, but not limited to, travel to or from medical or legal appointments, school or training classes or places of employment, obtaining food, clothing or necessary household items, or rendering care to family members, the court may modify such condition to allow for a trip or trips as in its discretion are necessary.

(iii) A person at liberty and subject to a condition under this paragraph who applies, within thirty days after the date such condition becomes effective, for a refund of any prepaid fare amounts rendered unusable in whole or in part by such condition including, but not limited to, a monthly pass, shall be issued a refund of the amounts so prepaid.

(l) Satisfy any other conditions reasonably related to his rehabilitation.

3. Conditions relating to supervision. When imposing a sentence of probation the court, in addition to any conditions imposed pursuant to subdivision two of this section, shall require as conditions of the sentence, that the defendant:

(a) Report to a probation officer as directed by the court or the probation officer and permit the probation officer to visit him at his place of abode or elsewhere;

(b) Remain within the jurisdiction of the court unless granted permission to leave by the court or the probation officer. Where a defendant is granted permission to move or travel outside the jurisdiction of the court, the defendant shall sign a written waiver of extradition agreeing to waive extradition proceedings where such proceedings are the result of the issuance of a warrant by the court pursuant to subdivision two of section 410.40 of the criminal procedure law based on an alleged violation of probation. Where any county or the city of New York incurs costs associated with the return of any probationer based on the issuance of a warrant by the court pursuant to subdivision two of section 410.40 of the criminal procedure law, the jurisdiction may collect the reasonable and necessary expenses involved in connection with his or her transport, from the probationer; provided that where the sentence of probation is not revoked pursuant to section 410.70 of the criminal procedure law no such expenses may be collected.

(c) Answer all reasonable inquiries by the probation officer and notify the probation officer prior to any change in address or employment.

4. Electronic monitoring. When imposing a sentence of probation the court may, in addition to any conditions imposed pursuant to subdivisions two and three of this section, require the defendant to submit to the use of an electronic monitoring device and/or to follow a schedule that governs the defendant's daily movement. Such condition may be imposed only where the court, in its discretion, determines that requiring the defendant to comply with such condition will advance public safety, probationer control or probationer surveillance. Electronic monitoring shall be used in accordance with uniform procedures developed by the office of probation and correctional alternatives.

4-a. Mandatory conditions for sex offenders.

(a) When imposing a sentence of probation or conditional discharge upon a person convicted of an offense defined in article one hundred thirty, two hundred thirty-five or two hundred sixty-three of this chapter, or section 255.25, 255.26 or 255.27 of this chapter, and the victim of such offense was under the age of eighteen at the time of such offense or such person has been designated a level three sex offender pursuant to subdivision six of section 168-l of the correction law, the court shall require, as a mandatory condition of such sentence, that such sentenced offender shall refrain from knowingly entering into or upon any school grounds, as that term is defined in subdivision fourteen of section 220.00 of this chapter, or any other facility or institution primarily used for the care or treatment of persons under the age of eighteen while one or more of such persons under the age of eighteen are present, provided however, that when such sentenced offender is a registered student or participant or an employee of such facility or institution or entity contracting therewith or has a family member enrolled in such facility or institution, such sentenced offender may, with the written authorization of his or her probation officer or the court and the superintendent or chief administrator of such facility, institution or grounds, enter such facility, institution or upon such grounds for the limited purposes authorized by the probation officer or the court and superintendent or chief officer. Nothing in this subdivision shall be construed as restricting any lawful condition of supervision that may be imposed on such sentenced offender.

(b) When imposing a sentence of probation or conditional discharge upon a person convicted of an offense for which registration as a sex offender is required pursuant to subdivision two or three of section one hundred sixty-eight-a of the correction law, and the victim of such offense was under the age of eighteen at the time of such offense or such person has been designated a level three sex offender pursuant to subdivision six of section one hundred sixty-eight-l of the correction law or the internet was used to facilitate the commission of the crime, the court shall require, as mandatory conditions of such sentence, that such sentenced offender be prohibited from using the internet to access pornographic material, access a commercial social networking website, communicate with other individuals or groups for the purpose of promoting sexual relations with persons under the age of eighteen, and communicate with a person under the age of eighteen when such offender is over the age of eighteen, provided that the court may permit an offender to use the internet to communicate with a person under the age of eighteen when such offender is the parent of a minor child and is not otherwise prohibited from communicating with such child. Nothing in this subdivision shall be construed as restricting any other lawful condition of supervision that may be imposed on such sentenced offender. As used in this subdivision, a "commercial social networking website" shall mean any business, organization or other entity operating a website that permits persons under eighteen years of age to be registered users for the purpose of establishing personal relationships with other users, where such persons under eighteen years of age may: (i) create web pages or profiles that provide information about themselves where such web pages or profiles are available to the public or to other users; (ii) engage in direct or real time communication with other users, such as a chat room or instant messenger; and (iii) communicate with persons over eighteen years of age; provided, however, that, for purposes of this subdivision, a commercial social networking website shall not include a website that permits users to engage in such other activities as are not enumerated herein.

5. Other conditions. When imposing a sentence of probation the court may, in addition to any conditions imposed pursuant to subdivisions two, three and four of this section, require that the defendant comply with any other reasonable condition as the court shall determine to be necessary or appropriate to ameliorate the conduct which gave rise to the offense or to prevent the incarceration of the defendant.

5-a. Other conditions for sex offenders. When imposing a sentence of probation upon a person convicted of an offense for which registration as a sex offender is required pursuant to subdivision two or three of section one hundred sixty-eight-a of the correction law, in addition to any conditions required under subdivisions two, three, four, four-a and five of this section, the court may require that the defendant comply with a reasonable limitation on his or her use of the internet that the court determines to be necessary or appropriate to ameliorate the conduct which gave rise to the offense or to protect public safety, provided that the court shall not prohibit such sentenced offender from using the internet in connection with education, lawful employment or search for lawful employment.

HISTORY:
Add, L 1965, ch 1030, eff Sept 1, 1967, with substance derived in part from §§ 2188, 2188–b; amd, L 1973, ch 676, § 30; L 1974, ch 930, § 3; L 1975, ch 667, § 35; L 1978, ch 500, § 1; L 1980, ch 270, § 1, eff June 17, 1980; L 1980, ch 284, § 1; L 1980, ch 471, § 22, eff July 23, 1980; L 1980, ch 530, § 16; L 1981, ch 742, § 3, eff Sept 1, 1981; L 1981, ch 583, § 1; L 1982, ch 782, §§ 1, 2; L 1984, ch 335, § 2; L 1984, ch 417, § 1, eff Nov 1, 1984; L 1985, ch 672, §§ 1, 2, eff Sept 30, 1985; L 1986, ch 552, § 1; L 1989, ch 443, § 1; L 1992, ch 465, § 51, eff Jan 13, 1993; L 1992, ch 618, § 15, eff Nov 1, 1992; L 1995, ch 536, § 2; L 1996, ch 186, § 1, eff Nov 1, 1996; L 1996, ch 653, § 1, eff Sept 18, 1996; L 1997, ch 181, § 1, eff July 8, 1997; L 2000, ch 1, § 7, eff Feb 1, 2001; L 2001, ch 508, § 1, eff Jan 20, 2002; L 2005, ch 544, § 1, eff Sept 1, 2006; L 2006, ch 320, § 4, eff Nov 1, 2006; L 2006, ch 571, § 6, eff Nov 1, 2006; L 2007, ch 669, § 1, eff Oct 27, 2007; L 2008, ch 67, §§ 7, 8, eff April 28, 2008; L 2008, ch 406, § 2, eff Aug 5, 2008; L 2010, ch 56, § 46 (Part A), eff June 22, 2010; L 2010, ch 56, § 8 (Part D), eff Sept 20, 2010; L 2018, ch 480, § 2, eff June 26, 2019; L 2020, ch 56, § 1 (Part VV), eff July 2, 2020.

Article 70
Sentences of Imprisonment

§ 70.20. Place of imprisonment.

1. [Eff until Sept 1, 2021] (a) Indeterminate or determinate sentence. Except as provided in subdivision four of this section, when an indeterminate or determinate sentence of imprisonment is imposed, the court shall commit the defendant to the custody of the state department of corrections and community supervision for the term of his or her sentence and until released in accordance with the law; provided, however, that a defendant sentenced pursuant to subdivision seven of section 70.06 shall be committed to the custody of the state department of corrections and community supervision for immediate delivery to a reception center operated by the department.

(b) The court in committing a defendant who is not yet eighteen years of age to the department of corrections and community supervision shall inquire as to whether the parents or legal guardian of the defendant, if present, will grant to the minor the capacity to consent to routine medical, dental and mental health services and treatment.

(c) Notwithstanding paragraph (b) of this subdivision, where the court commits a defendant who is not yet eighteen years of age to the custody of the department of corrections and community supervision in accordance with this section and no medical consent has been obtained prior to said commitment, the commitment order shall be deemed to grant the capacity to consent to routine medical, dental and mental health services and treatment to the person so committed.

(d) Nothing in this subdivision shall preclude a parent or legal guardian of an inmate who is not yet eighteen years of age from making a motion on notice to the department of corrections and community supervision pursuant to article twenty-two of the civil practice law and rules and section one hundred forty of the correction law, objecting to routine medical, dental or mental health services and treatment being provided to such inmate under the provisions of paragraph (b) of this subdivision.

(e) Nothing in this section shall require that consent be obtained from the parent or legal guardian, where no consent is necessary or where the defendant is authorized by law to consent on his or her own behalf to any medical, dental, and mental health service or treatment.

1. [Eff Sept 1, 2021] (a) Indeterminate sentence. Except as provided in subdivision four of this section, when an indeterminate sentence of imprisonment is imposed, the court shall commit the defendant to the custody of the state department of corrections and community supervision for the term of his or her sentence and until released in accordance with the law.

(b) The court in committing a defendant who is not yet eighteen years of age to the department of corrections and community supervision shall inquire as to whether the parents or legal guardian of the defendant, if present, will grant to the minor the capacity to consent to routine medical, dental and mental health services and treatment.

(c) Notwithstanding paragraph (b) of this subdivision, where the court commits a defendant who is not yet eighteen years of age to the custody of the department of corrections and community supervision in accordance with this section and no medical consent has been obtained prior to said commitment, the commitment order shall be deemed to grant the capacity to consent to routine medical, dental and mental health services and treatment to the person so committed.

(d) Nothing in this subdivision shall preclude a parent or legal guardian of an inmate who is not yet eighteen years of age from making a motion on notice to the department of corrections and community supervision pursuant to article twenty-two of the civil practice law and rules and section one hundred forty of the correction law, objecting to routine medical, dental or mental health services and treatment being provided to such inmate under the provisions of paragraph (b) of this subdivision.

(e) Nothing in this section shall require that consent be obtained from the parent or legal guardian, where no consent is necessary or where the defendant is authorized by law to consent on his or her own behalf to any medical, dental, and mental health service or treatment.

2. Definite sentence. Except as provided in subdivision four of this section, when a definite sentence of imprisonment is imposed, the court shall commit the defendant to the county or regional correctional institution for the term of his sentence and until released in accordance with the law.

2-a. Sentence of life imprisonment without parole. When a sentence of life imprisonment without parole is imposed, the court shall commit the defendant to the custody of the state department of corrections and community supervision for the remainder of the life of the defendant.

3. [Eff until Sept 1, 2021] Undischarged imprisonment in other jurisdiction. When a defendant who is subject to an undischarged term of imprisonment, imposed at a previous time by a court of another jurisdiction, is sentenced to an additional term or terms of imprisonment by a court of this state to run concurrently with such undischarged term, as provided in subdivision four of section 70.25, the return of the defendant to the custody of the appropriate official of the other jurisdiction shall be deemed a commitment for such portion of the term or terms of the sentence imposed by the court of this state as shall not exceed the said undischarged term. The defendant shall be committed to the custody of the state department of corrections and community supervision if the additional term or terms are indeterminate or determinate or to the appropriate county or regional correctional institution if the said term or terms are definite for such portion of the term or terms of the sentence imposed as shall exceed such undischarged term or until released in accordance with law. If such additional term or terms imposed shall run consecutively to the said undischarged term, the defendant shall be committed as provided in subdivisions one and two of this section.

3. [Eff Sept 1, 2021] Undischarged imprisonment in other jurisdiction. When a defendant who is subject to an undischarged term of imprisonment, imposed at a previous time by a court of another jurisdiction, is sentenced to an additional term or terms of imprisonment by a court of this state to run concurrently with such undischarged term, as provided in subdivision four of section 70.25, the return of the defendant to the custody of the appropriate official of the other jurisdiction shall be deemed a commitment for such portion of the term or terms of the sentence imposed by the court of this state as shall not exceed the said undischarged term. The defendant shall be committed to the custody of the state department of corrections and community supervision if the additional term or terms are indeterminate or to the appropriate county or regional correctional institution if the said term or terms are definite for such portion of the term or terms of the sentence imposed as shall exceed such undischarged term or until released in accordance with law. If such additional term or terms imposed shall run consecutively to the said undischarged term, the defendant shall be committed as provided in subdivisions one and two of this section.

4.(a) Notwithstanding any other provision of law to the contrary, a juvenile offender, adolescent offender, or a juvenile offender or adolescent offender who is adjudicated a youthful offender, who is given an indeterminate, determinate or a definite sentence, and who is under the age of twenty-one at the time of sentencing, shall be committed to the custody of the commissioner of the office of children and family services who shall arrange for the confinement of such offender in secure facilities of the office; provided, however if an adolescent offender who committed a crime on or after the youth's sixteenth birthday receives a definite sentence not exceeding one year, the judge may order that the adolescent offender serve such sentence in a specialized secure juvenile detention facility for older youth certified by the office of children and family services in conjunction with the state commission of correction and operated pursuant to section two hundred eighteen-a of the county law. The release or transfer of such juvenile offenders or adolescent offenders from the office of children and family services shall be governed by section five hundred eight of the executive law.

(a-2) Notwithstanding any other provision of law to the contrary, a person sixteen years of age who commits a vehicle and traffic law offense that does not constitute an adolescent offender offense on or after October first, two thousand eighteen and a person seventeen years of age who commits such an offense on or after October first, two thousand nineteen who is sentenced to a term of imprisonment who is under the age of twenty-one at the time he or she is sentenced shall be committed to a specialized secure detention facility for older youth certified by the office of children and family services in conjunction with the state commission of correction.

(b) The court in committing a juvenile offender and youthful offender to the custody of the office of children and family services shall inquire as to whether the parents or legal guardian of the youth, if present, will consent for the office of children and family services to provide routine medical, dental and mental health services and treatment.

(c) Notwithstanding paragraph (b) of this subdivision, where the court commits an offender to the custody of the office of children and family services in accordance with this section and no medical consent has been obtained prior to said commitment, the commitment order shall be deemed to grant consent for the office of children and family services to provide for routine medical, dental and mental health services and treatment to the offender so committed.

(d) Nothing in this subdivision shall preclude a parent or legal guardian of an offender who is not yet eighteen years of age from making a motion on notice to the office of children and family services pursuant to article twenty-two of the civil practice law and rules objecting to routine medical, dental or mental health services and treatment being provided to such offender under the provisions of paragraph (b) of this subdivision.

(e) Nothing in this section shall require that consent be obtained from the parent or legal guardian, where no consent is necessary or where the offender is authorized by law to consent on his or her own behalf to any medical, dental and mental health service or treatment.

5. Subject to regulations of the department of health, routine medical, dental and mental health services and treatment is defined for the purposes of this section to mean any routine diagnosis or treatment, including without limitation the administration of medications or nutrition, the extraction of bodily fluids for analysis, and dental care performed with a local anesthetic. Routine mental health treatment shall not include psychiatric administration of medication unless it is part of an ongoing mental health plan or unless it is otherwise authorized by law.

HISTORY:

Add, L 1965, ch 1030 eff Sept 1, 1967; amd, L 1975, ch 782, § 1; L 1978, ch 268, § 1; L 1981, ch 303, § 2, eff July 22, 1981; L 1992, ch 465, § 52; L 1992, ch 479, § 3, eff July 17, 1992, deemed eff July 15, 1991; L 1995, ch 1, § 6, eff Sept 1, 1995; L 1995, ch 3, § 9, eff Oct 1, 1995; L 1995, ch 516, §§ 2, 3, eff Aug 2, 1995; L 2011, ch 62, §§ 124, 125 (Part C, Subpart B), eff March 31, 2011; L 2013, ch 437, § 1, eff Oct 23, 2013; L 2017, ch 59, §§ 43, 44 (Part WWW), eff Oct 1, 2018; L 2020, ch 55, § 1 (Part G), eff June 2, 2020.

Part THREE
Specific Offenses

Title N
Offenses Against Public Order, Public Sensibilities and the Right to Privacy

Article 241 Harassment of Rent Regulated Tenants

Article 241
Harassment of Rent Regulated Tenants

§ 241.00. Harassment of a rent regulated tenant; definition of terms

As used in this article:

1. "Rent regulated tenant" shall mean a person occupying a housing accommodation or any lawful successor to the tenancy which is subject to the regulations and control of residential rents and evictions pursuant to the emergency housing rent control law, the local emergency housing rent control act, the emergency tenant protection act of nineteen seventy-four, the New York city rent and rehabilitation law or the New York city rent stabilization law of nineteen hundred sixty-nine, and such person is either a party to a lease or rental agreement for such housing accommodation, a statutory tenant or a person who lawfully occupies such housing accommodation with such party to a lease or rental agreement or with such statutory tenant. The definition of "rent regulated tenant" as used in this subdivision shall be applicable only to the provisions of this article and shall not be applicable to any other provision of law.

2. "Housing accommodations" shall mean housing accommodations which are subject to the regulations and control of residential rents and evictions pursuant to the emergency housing rent control law, the local emergency housing rent control act, the emergency tenant protection act of nineteen seventy-four, the New York city rent and rehabilitation law or the New York city rent stabilization law of nineteen hundred sixty-nine.

3. "Owner" shall mean an owner, lessor, sublessor, assignee, net lessee, or a proprietary lessee of a housing accommodation in a structure or premises owned by a cooperative corporation or association, or an owner of a condominium unit or the sponsor of such cooperative corporation or association or condominium development, or any other person or entity receiving or entitled to receive rent for the use or occupation of any housing accommodation, or an agent of or any person acting on behalf of any of the foregoing.

HISTORY:

Add, L 1997, ch 116, § 28, eff July 19, 1997;
amd, L 2019, ch 573, § 4, eff May 31, 2020.

§ 241.02 Harassment of a rent regulated tenant in the second degree.

An owner is guilty of harassment of a rent regulated tenant in the second degree when, with intent to induce a rent regulated tenant to vacate a housing accommodation, such owner intentionally engages in a course of conduct that:

1. impairs the habitability of a housing accommodation; or

2. creates or maintains a condition which endangers the safety or health of the dwelling's tenant; or

3. is reasonably likely to interfere with or disturb, and does interfere with or disturb, the comfort, repose, peace or quiet of such rent regulated tenant in his or her use and occupancy of such housing accommodation including, but not limited to, the interruption or discontinuance of essential services. The good faith commencement and pursuit of a lawful eviction action by an owner against a rent regulated tenant in a court of competent jurisdiction shall not, by itself, constitute a "course of conduct" in violation of this subdivision.

Harassment of a rent regulated tenant in the second degree is a class A misdemeanor.

HISTORY:
L 2019, ch 573, § 2, eff May 31, 2020.

§ 241.05. Harassment of a rent regulated tenant in the first degree.
An owner is guilty of harassment of a rent regulated tenant in the first degree when:

1. With intent to induce a rent regulated tenant to vacate a housing accommodation, such owner:

(a) With intent to cause physical injury to such tenant, causes such injury to such tenant or to a third person; or

(b) Recklessly causes physical injury to such tenant or to a third person; or

2. With intent to induce two or more rent regulated tenants occupying different housing accommodations to vacate such housing accommodations, such owner intentionally engages in a systematic ongoing course of conduct that:

(a) impairs the habitability of such housing accommodations; or

(b) creates or maintains a condition which endangers the safety or health of one or more of the dwellings' rent regulated tenants; or

(c) is reasonably likely to interfere with or disturb, and does interfere with or disturb, the comfort, repose, peace or quiet of one or more of such rent regulated tenants in their use and occupancy of such housing accommodations including, but not limited to, the interruption or discontinuance of essential services; or

3. Such owner commits the crime of harassment of a rent regulated tenant in the second degree as defined in section 241.02 of this article and has previously been convicted within the preceding five years of such crime or the crime of harassment of a rent regulated tenant in the first degree.

The good faith commencement and pursuit of a lawful eviction action by an owner against a rent regulated tenant in a court of competent jurisdiction shall not, by itself, constitute a "systematic ongoing course of conduct" in violation of paragraph (c) of subdivision two of this section.

Harassment of a rent regulated tenant in the first degree is a class E felony.

HISTORY:
Add, L 1997, ch 116, § 28, eff July 19, 1997;
amd, L 2019, ch 573, § 3, eff May 31, 2020.

Title P
Offenses Against Public Safety

Article 265 Firearms and Other Dangerous Weapons

Article 265
Firearms and Other Dangerous Weapons

§ 265.00. Definitions. [Effective until April 3, 2021]
As used in this article and in article four hundred, the following terms shall mean and include:

1. "Machine-gun" means a weapon of any description, irrespective of size, by whatever name known, loaded or unloaded, from which a number of shots or bullets may be rapidly or automatically discharged from a magazine with one continuous pull of the trigger and includes a sub-machine gun.

2. "Firearm silencer" means any instrument, attachment, weapon or appliance for causing the firing of any gun, revolver, pistol or other firearms to be silent, or intended to lessen or muffle the noise of the firing of any gun, revolver, pistol or other firearms.

3. "Firearm" means (a) any pistol or revolver; or (b) a shotgun having one or more

barrels less than eighteen inches in length; or (c) a rifle having one or more barrels less than sixteen inches in length; or (d) any weapon made from a shotgun or rifle whether by alteration, modification, or otherwise if such weapon as altered, modified, or otherwise has an overall length of less than twenty-six inches; or (e) an assault weapon. For the purpose of this subdivision the length of the barrel on a shotgun or rifle shall be determined by measuring the distance between the muzzle and the face of the bolt, breech, or breechlock when closed and when the shotgun or rifle is cocked; the overall length of a weapon made from a shotgun or rifle is the distance between the extreme ends of the weapon measured along a line parallel to the center line of the bore. Firearm does not include an antique firearm.

3-a. "Major component of a firearm, rifle or shotgun" means the barrel, the slide or cylinder, the frame, or receiver of the firearm, rifle, or shotgun.

4. "Switchblade knife" means any knife which has a blade which opens automatically by hand pressure applied to a button, spring or other device in the handle of the knife.

5. "Gravity knife" means any knife which has a blade which is released from the handle or sheath thereof by the force of gravity or the application of centrifugal force which, when released, is locked in place by means of a button, spring, lever or other device.

5-a. "Pilum ballistic knife" means any knife which has a blade which can be projected from the handle by hand pressure applied to a button, lever, spring or other device in the handle of the knife.

5-b. "Metal knuckle knife" means a weapon that, when closed, cannot function as a set of plastic knuckles or metal knuckles, nor as a knife and when open, can function as both a set of plastic knuckles or metal knuckles as well as a knife.

5-c. "Automatic knife" includes a stiletto, a switchblade knife, a cane sword, a pilum ballistic knife, and a metal knuckle knife.

5-d. "Undetectable knife" means any knife or other instrument, which does not utilize materials that are detectable by a metal detector or magnetometer when set at a standard calibration, that is capable of ready use as a stabbing or cutting weapon and was commercially manufactured to be used as a weapon.

6. "Dispose of" means to dispose of, give, give away, lease-loan, keep for sale, offer, offer for sale, sell, transfer and otherwise dispose of.

7. "Deface" means to remove, deface, cover, alter or destroy the manufacturer's serial number or any other distinguishing number or identification mark.

8. "Gunsmith" means any person, firm, partnership, corporation or company who engages in the business of repairing, altering, assembling, manufacturing, cleaning, polishing, engraving or trueing, or who performs any mechanical operation on, any firearm, large capacity ammunition feeding device or machine-gun.

9. "Dealer in firearms" means any person, firm, partnership, corporation or company who engages in the business of purchasing, selling, keeping for sale, loaning, leasing, or in any manner disposing of, any assault weapon, large capacity ammunition feeding device, pistol or revolver.

10. "Licensing officer" means in the city of New York the police commissioner of that city; in the county of Nassau the commissioner of police of that county; in the county of Suffolk the sheriff of that county except in the towns of Babylon, Brookhaven, Huntington, Islip and Smithtown, the commissioner of police of that county; for the purposes of section 400.01 of this chapter the superintendent of state police; and elsewhere in the state a judge or justice of a court of record having his office in the county of issuance.

11. "Rifle" means a weapon designed or redesigned, made or remade, and intended to be fired from the shoulder and designed or redesigned and made or remade to use the energy of the explosive in a fixed metallic cartridge to fire only a single projectile through a rifled bore for each single pull of the trigger.

12. "Shotgun" means a weapon designed or redesigned, made or remade, and intended to be fired from the shoulder and designed or redesigned and made or remade to use the energy of the explosive in a fixed shotgun shell to fire through a smooth bore either a number of ball shot or a single projectile for each single pull of the trigger.

13. "Cane Sword" means a cane or swagger stick having concealed within it a blade that may be used as a sword or stilletto.

14. [There are two subs 14] "Chuka stick" means any device designed primarily as a weapon, consisting of two or more lengths of a rigid material joined together by a thong, rope or chain in such a manner as to allow free movement of a portion of the device while held in the hand and capable of being rotated in such a manner as to inflict serious injury upon a person by striking or choking. These devices are also known as nunchakus and centrifugal force sticks.

14. [There are two subs 14] "Antique firearm" means:

Any unloaded muzzle loading pistol or revolver with a matchlock, flintlock, percussion cap, or similar type of ignition system, or a pistol or revolver which uses fixed cartridges which are no longer available in the ordinary channels of commercial trade.

15. "Loaded firearm" means any firearm loaded with ammunition or any firearm which is possessed by one who, at the same time, possesses a quantity of ammunition which may be used to discharge such firearm.

15-a. "Electronic dart gun" means any device designed primarily as a weapon, the purpose of which is to momentarily stun, knock out or paralyze a person by passing an electrical shock to such person by means of a dart or projectile.

15-b. "Kung Fu star" means a disc-like object with sharpened points on the circumference thereof and is designed for use primarily as a weapon to be thrown.

15-c. "Electronic stun gun" means any device designed primarily as a weapon, the purpose of which is to stun, cause mental disorientation, knock out or paralyze a person by passing a high voltage electrical shock to such person.

16. "Certified not suitable to possess a self-defense spray device, a rifle or shotgun" means that the director or physician in charge of any hospital or institution for mental illness, public or private, has certified to the superintendent of state police or to any organized police department of a county, city, town or village of this state, that a person who has been judicially adjudicated incompetent, or who has been confined to such institution for mental illness pursuant to judicial authority, is not suitable to possess a self-defense spray device, as defined in section 265.20 of this article, or a rifle or shotgun.

17. "Serious offense" means

(a) any of the following offenses defined in the former penal law as in force and effect immediately prior to September first, nineteen hundred sixty-seven: illegally using, carrying or possessing a pistol or other dangerous weapon; making or possessing burglar's instruments; buying or receiving stolen property; unlawful entry of a building; aiding escape from prison; that kind of disorderly conduct defined in subdivisions six and eight of section seven hundred twenty-two of such former penal law; violations of sections four hundred eighty-three, four hundred eighty-three-b, four hundred eighty-four-h and article one hundred six of such former penal law; that kind of criminal sexual act or rape which was designated as a misdemeanor; violation of section seventeen hundred forty-seven-d and seventeen hundred forty-seven-e of such former penal law; any violation of any provision of article thirty-three of the public health law relating to narcotic drugs which was defined as a misdemeanor by section seventeen hundred fifty-one-a of such former penal law, and any violation of any provision of article thirty-three-A of the public health law relating to depressant and stimulant drugs which was defined as a misdemeanor by section seventeen hundred forty-seven-b of such former penal law.

(b) [As amended, L 2010, ch 232, § 2] any of the following offenses defined in the penal law: illegally using, carrying or possessing a pistol or other dangerous weapon; possession of burglar's tools; criminal possession of stolen property in the third degree; escape in the third degree; jostling; fraudulent accosting; endangering the welfare of a child; the offenses defined in article two hundred thirty-five; issuing abortional articles; permitting prostitution; promoting prostitution in the third degree; stalking in the fourth degree; stalking in the third degree; the offenses defined in article one hundred thirty; the offenses defined in article two hundred twenty.

(b) [As amended, L 2010, ch 232, § 3] any of the following offenses defined in the penal law: illegally using, carrying or possessing a pistol or other dangerous weapon; possession of burglar's tools; criminal possession of stolen property in the third degree; escape in the third degree; jostling; fraudulent accosting; endangering the welfare of a child; the offenses defined in article two hundred thirty-five; issuing abortional articles; permitting prostitution; promoting prostitution in the third degree; stalking in the third degree; stalking in the fourth degree; the offenses defined in article one hundred thirty; the offenses defined in article two hundred twenty.

(c) any of the following offenses, where the defendant and the person against whom the offense was committed were members of the same family or household as defined in subdivision one of section 530.11 of the criminal procedure law and as established pursuant to section 370.15 of the criminal procedure law: assault in the third degree; menacing in the third degree; menacing in the second degree; criminal obstruction of breathing or blood circulation; unlawful imprisonment in the second degree; coercion in the third degree; criminal tampering in the third degree; criminal contempt in the second degree; harassment in the first degree; aggravated harassment in the second degree; criminal trespass in the third degree; criminal trespass in the second degree; arson in the fifth degree; or attempt to commit any of the above-listed offenses.

18. "Armor piercing ammunition" means any ammunition capable of being used in pistols or revolvers containing a projectile or projectile core, or a projectile or projectile core for use in such ammunition, that is constructed entirely (excluding the presence of traces of other substances) from one or a combination of any of the following: tungsten alloys, steel, iron, brass, bronze, beryllium copper, or uranium.

19. "Duly authorized instructor" means (a) a duly commissioned officer of the United States army, navy, marine corps or coast guard, or of the national guard of the state of New York; or (b) a duly qualified adult citizen of the United States who has been granted a certificate as an instructor in small arms practice issued by the United States army, navy or marine corps, or by the adjutant general of this state, or by the national rifle association of America, a not-for-profit corporation duly organized under the laws of this state; or (c) by a person duly qualified and designated by the department of environmental conservation under paragraph d of subdivision six of section 11-0713 of the environmental conservation law as its agent in the giving of instruction and the making of certifications of qualification in responsible hunting practices.

20. "Disguised gun" means any weapon or device capable of being concealed on the person from which a shot can be discharged through the energy of an explosive and is designed and intended to appear to be something other than a gun.

21. "Semiautomatic" means any repeating rifle, shotgun or pistol, regardless of barrel or overall length, which utilizes a portion of the energy of a firing cartridge or shell to extract the fired cartridge case or spent shell and chamber the next round, and which requires a separate pull of the trigger to fire each cartridge or shell.

22. "Assault weapon" means

(a) a semiautomatic rifle that has an ability to accept a detachable magazine and has at least one of the following characteristics:

(i) a folding or telescoping stock;

(ii) a pistol grip that protrudes conspicuously beneath the action of the weapon;

(iii) a thumbhole stock;

(iv) a second handgrip or a protruding grip that can be held by the non-trigger hand;

(v) a bayonet mount;

(vi) a flash suppressor, muzzle break, muzzle compensator, or threaded barrel designed to accommodate a flash suppressor, muzzle break, or muzzle compensator;

(vii) a grenade launcher; or

(b) a semiautomatic shotgun that has at least one of the following characteristics:

(i) a folding or telescoping stock;

(ii) a thumbhole stock;

(iii) a second handgrip or a protruding grip that can be held by the non-trigger hand;

(iv) a fixed magazine capacity in excess of seven rounds;

(v) an ability to accept a detachable magazine; or

(c) a semiautomatic pistol that has an ability to accept a detachable magazine and has at least one of the following characteristics:

(i) a folding or telescoping stock;

(ii) a thumbhole stock;

(iii) a second handgrip or a protruding grip that can be held by the non-trigger hand;

(iv) capacity to accept an ammunition magazine that attaches to the pistol outside of the pistol grip;

(v) a threaded barrel capable of accepting a barrel extender, flash suppressor, forward handgrip, or silencer;

(vi) a shroud that is attached to, or partially or completely encircles, the barrel and that permits the shooter to hold the firearm with the non-trigger hand without being burned;

(vii) a manufactured weight of fifty ounces or more when the pistol is unloaded; or

(viii) a semiautomatic version of an automatic rifle, shotgun or firearm;

(d) a revolving cylinder shotgun;

(e) a semiautomatic rifle, a semiautomatic shotgun or a semiautomatic pistol or weapon defined in subparagraph (v) of paragraph (e) of subdivision twenty-two of section 265.00 of this chapter as added by chapter one hundred eighty-nine of the laws of two thousand and otherwise lawfully possessed pursuant to such chapter of the laws of two thousand prior to September fourteenth, nineteen hundred ninety-four;

(f) a semiautomatic rifle, a semiautomatic shotgun or a semiautomatic pistol or weapon defined in paragraph (a), (b) or (c) of this subdivision, possessed prior to the date of enactment of the chapter of the laws of two thousand thirteen which added this paragraph;

(g) provided, however, that such term does not include:

(i) any rifle, shotgun or pistol that (A) is manually operated by bolt, pump, lever or slide action; (B) has been rendered permanently inoperable; or (C) is an antique firearm as defined in 18 U.S.C. 921(a)(16);

(ii) a semiautomatic rifle that cannot accept a detachable magazine that holds more than five rounds of ammunition;

(iii) a semiautomatic shotgun that cannot hold more than five rounds of ammunition in a fixed or detachable magazine; or

(iv) a rifle, shotgun or pistol, or a replica or a duplicate thereof, specified in Appendix A to 18 U.S.C. 922 as such weapon was manufactured on October first, nineteen hundred ninety-three. The mere fact that a weapon is not listed in Appendix A shall not be construed to mean that such weapon is an assault weapon;

(v) any weapon validly registered pursuant to subdivision sixteen-a of section 400.00 of this chapter. Such weapons shall be subject to the provisions of paragraph (h) of this subdivision;

(vi) any firearm, rifle, or shotgun that was manufactured at least fifty years prior to the current date, but not including replicas thereof that is validly registered pursuant to subdivision sixteen-a of section 400.00 of this chapter;

(h) Any weapon defined in paragraph (e) or (f) of this subdivision and any large capacity ammunition feeding device that was legally possessed by an individual prior to the enactment of the chapter of the laws of two thousand thirteen which added this paragraph, may only be sold to, exchanged with or disposed of to a purchaser authorized to possess such weapons or to an individual or entity outside of the state provided that any such transfer to an individual or entity outside of the state must be reported to the entity wherein the weapon is registered within seventy-two hours of such transfer. An individual who transfers any such weapon or large capacity ammunition device to an individual inside New York state or without complying with the provisions of this paragraph shall be guilty of a class A misdemeanor unless such large capacity ammunition feeding device, the possession of which is made illegal by the chapter of the laws of two thousand thirteen which added this paragraph, is transferred within one year of the effective date of the chapter of the laws of two thousand thirteen which added this paragraph.

23. "Large capacity ammunition feeding device" means a magazine, belt, drum, feed strip, or similar device, that (a) has a capacity of, or that can be readily restored or converted to accept, more than ten rounds of ammunition, or [pars (b) and (c) are suspended and not effective as stated in Laws 2013, ch 1, § 58, sub b note below] (b) contains more than seven rounds of ammunition, or (c) is obtained after the effective date of the chapter of the laws of two thousand thirteen which amended this subdivision and has a capacity of, or that can be readily restored or converted to accept, more than seven rounds of ammunition; provided, however, that such term does not include an attached tubular device designed to accept, and capable of

operating only with, .22 caliber rimfire ammunition or a feeding device that is a curio or relic. A feeding device that is a curio or relic is defined as a device that (i) was manufactured at least fifty years prior to the current date, (ii) is only capable of being used exclusively in a firearm, rifle, or shotgun that was manufactured at least fifty years prior to the current date, but not including replicas thereof, (iii) is possessed by an individual who is not prohibited by state or federal law from possessing a firearm and (iv) is registered with the division of state police pursuant to subdivision sixteen-a of section 400.00 of this chapter, except such feeding devices transferred into the state may be registered at any time, provided they are registered within thirty days of their transfer into the state. Notwithstanding paragraph (h) of subdivision twenty-two of this section, such feeding devices may be transferred provided that such transfer shall be subject to the provisions of section 400.03 of this chapter including the check required to be conducted pursuant to such section.

24. "Seller of ammunition" means any person, firm, partnership, corporation or company who engages in the business of purchasing, selling or keeping ammunition.

25. "Qualified retired New York or federal law enforcement officer" means an individual who is a retired police officer as police officer is defined in subdivision thirty-four of section 1.20 of the criminal procedure law, a retired peace officer as peace officer is defined in section 2.10 of the criminal procedure law or a retired federal law enforcement officer as federal law enforcement officer is defined in section 2.15 of the criminal procedure law, who: (a) separated from service in good standing from a public agency located in New York state in which such person served as either a police officer, peace officer or federal law enforcement officer; and (b) before such separation, was authorized by law to engage in or supervise the prevention, detection, investigation, or prosecution of, or the incarceration of any person for, any violation of law, and had statutory powers of arrest, pursuant to their official duties, under the criminal procedure law; and (c) (i) before such separation, served as either a police officer, peace officer or federal law enforcement officer for five years or more and at the time of separation, is such an officer; or (ii) separated from service with such agency, after completing any applicable probationary period of such service, due to a service-connected disability, as determined by such agency at or before the time of separation; and (d)(i) has not been found by a qualified medical professional employed by such agency to be unqualified for reasons relating to mental health; or (ii) has not entered into an agreement with such agency from which the individual is separating from service in which that individual acknowledges he or she is not qualified for reasons relating to mental health; and (e) is not otherwise prohibited by New York or federal law from possessing any firearm.

26. "Rapid-fire modification device" means any bump stock, trigger crank, binary trigger system, burst trigger system, or any other device that is designed to accelerate the rate of fire of a semi-automatic firearm, rifle or shotgun.

27. "Bump stock" means any device or instrument that increases the rate of fire achievable with a semi-automatic firearm, rifle or shotgun by using energy from the recoil of the weapon to generate a reciprocating action that facilitates repeated activation of the trigger.

28. "Trigger crank" means any device or instrument that repeatedly activates the trigger of a semi-automatic firearm, rifle or shotgun through the use of a lever or other part that is turned in a circular motion and thereby accelerates the rate of fire of such firearm, rifle or shotgun, provided, however, that "trigger crank" shall not include any weapon initially designed and manufactured to fire through the use of a crank or lever.

29. "Binary trigger system" means any device that, when installed in or attached to a semi-automatic firearm rifle, or shotgun causes that weapon to fire once when the trigger is pulled and again when the trigger is released.

30. "Burst trigger system" means any device that, when installed in or attached to a semi-automatic firearm, rifle, or shot gun, allows that weapon to discharge two or more shots with a single pull or the trigger by altering the trigger reset.

HISTORY:

Add, L 1965, ch 1030, § 1, eff Sept 1, 1967, with substance derived from § 1896; amd, L 1967, ch 791, § 46; L 1969, ch 123, § 1, eff Sept 1, 1969; L 1972, ch 588, § 1; L 1972, ch 605, § 1; L 1974, ch 179, § 1, eff Sept 1, 1974; L

1974, ch 986, §§ 1, 2; L 1974, ch 1041, § 1, eff Sept 1, 1974; L 1976, ch 217, § 1, eff Sept 1, 1976; L 1982, ch 492, § 1; L 1985, ch 61, § 1, eff Nov 1, 1985; L 1986, ch 328, § 2, eff Nov 1, 1986; L 1986, ch 646, § 1, eff Nov 1, 1986; L 1988, ch 264, § 1; L 1990, ch 264, § 1, eff Nov 1, 1990; L 1995, ch 219, § 2, eff Nov 1, 1995; L 1996, ch 354, § 2, eff Nov 1, 1996; L 1997, ch 446, § 2, eff Aug 25, 1997; L 1998, ch 378, § 1, eff Nov 1, 1998; L 1999, ch 210, § 1, eff Nov 1, 1999; L 1999, ch 635, §§ 11, 15, eff Dec 1, 1999; L 2000, ch 189, §§ 8–10, eff Nov 1, 2000; L 2008, ch 257, § 3, eff Nov 1, 2008; L 2010, ch 232, §§ 2, 3, eff July 30, 2010; L 2013, ch 1, § 37, eff Jan 15, 2013; L 2013, ch 1, § 38, eff April 15, 2013; L 2013, ch 1, § 39, eff March 16, 2013; L 2013, ch 98, § 1, eff July 5, 2013; L 2018, ch 60, § 1, eff June 11, 2018; L 2019, ch 34, § 3, eff May 30, 2019; L 2019, ch 130, § 1, eff July 29, 2019; L 2019, ch 134, § 1, eff Jan 26, 2020; L 2019, ch 146, § 1, eff Nov 1, 2019.

§ 265.00. Definitions. [Effective April 3, 2021]

As used in this article and in article four hundred, the following terms shall mean and include:

1. "Machine-gun" means a weapon of any description, irrespective of size, by whatever name known, loaded or unloaded, from which a number of shots or bullets may be rapidly or automatically discharged from a magazine with one continuous pull of the trigger and includes a sub-machine gun.

2. "Firearm silencer" means any instrument, attachment, weapon or appliance for causing the firing of any gun, revolver, pistol or other firearms to be silent, or intended to lessen or muffle the noise of the firing of any gun, revolver, pistol or other firearms.

3. "Firearm" means (a) any pistol or revolver; or (b) a shotgun having one or more barrels less than eighteen inches in length; or (c) a rifle having one or more barrels less than sixteen inches in length; or (d) any weapon made from a shotgun or rifle whether by alteration, modification, or otherwise if such weapon as altered, modified, or otherwise has an overall length of less than twenty-six inches; or (e) an assault weapon. For the purpose of this subdivision the length of the barrel on a shotgun or rifle shall be determined by measuring the distance between the muzzle and the face of the bolt, breech, or breechlock when closed and when the shotgun or rifle is cocked; the overall length of a weapon made from a shotgun or rifle is the distance between the extreme ends of the weapon measured along a line parallel to the center line of the bore. Firearm does not include an antique firearm.

3-a. "Major component of a firearm, rifle or shotgun" means the barrel, the slide or cylinder, the frame, or receiver of the firearm, rifle, or shotgun.

4. "Switchblade knife" means any knife which has a blade which opens automatically by hand pressure applied to a button, spring or other device in the handle of the knife.

5. "Gravity knife" means any knife which has a blade which is released from the handle or sheath thereof by the force of gravity or the application of centrifugal force which, when released, is locked in place by means of a button, spring, lever or other device.

5-a. "Pilum ballistic knife" means any knife which has a blade which can be projected from the handle by hand pressure applied to a button, lever, spring or other device in the handle of the knife.

5-b. "Metal knuckle knife" means a weapon that, when closed, cannot function as a set of plastic knuckles or metal knuckles, nor as a knife and when open, can function as both a set of plastic knuckles or metal knuckles as well as a knife.

5-c. "Automatic knife" includes a stiletto, a switchblade knife, a cane sword, a pilum ballistic knife, and a metal knuckle knife.

5-d. "Undetectable knife" means any knife or other instrument, which does not utilize materials that are detectable by a metal detector or magnetometer when set at a standard calibration, that is capable of ready use as a stabbing or cutting weapon and was commercially manufactured to be used as a weapon.

6. "Dispose of" means to dispose of, give, give away, lease-loan, keep for sale, offer, offer for sale, sell, transfer and otherwise dispose of.

7. "Deface" means to remove, deface, cover, alter or destroy the manufacturer's serial number or any other distinguishing number or identification mark.

8. "Gunsmith" means any person, firm, partnership, corporation or company who engages in the business of repairing, altering, assembling, manufacturing, cleaning,

polishing, engraving or trueing, or who performs any mechanical operation on, any firearm, large capacity ammunition feeding device or machine-gun.

9. "Dealer in firearms" means any person, firm, partnership, corporation or company who engages in the business of purchasing, selling, keeping for sale, loaning, leasing, or in any manner disposing of, any assault weapon, large capacity ammunition feeding device, pistol or revolver.

10. "Licensing officer" means in the city of New York the police commissioner of that city; in the county of Nassau the commissioner of police of that county; in the county of Suffolk the sheriff of that county except in the towns of Babylon, Brookhaven, Huntington, Islip and Smithtown, the commissioner of police of that county; for the purposes of section 400.01 of this chapter the superintendent of state police; and elsewhere in the state a judge or justice of a court of record having his office in the county of issuance.

11. "Rifle" means a weapon designed or redesigned, made or remade, and intended to be fired from the shoulder and designed or redesigned and made or remade to use the energy of the explosive in a fixed metallic cartridge to fire only a single projectile through a rifled bore for each single pull of the trigger.

12. "Shotgun" means a weapon designed or redesigned, made or remade, and intended to be fired from the shoulder and designed or redesigned and made or remade to use the energy of the explosive in a fixed shotgun shell to fire through a smooth bore either a number of ball shot or a single projectile for each single pull of the trigger.

13. "Cane Sword" means a cane or swagger stick having concealed within it a blade that may be used as a sword or stilletto.

14. [There are two subs 14] "Chuka stick" means any device designed primarily as a weapon, consisting of two or more lengths of a rigid material joined together by a thong, rope or chain in such a manner as to allow free movement of a portion of the device while held in the hand and capable of being rotated in such a manner as to inflict serious injury upon a person by striking or choking. These devices are also known as nunchakus and centrifugal force sticks.

14. [There are two subs 14] "Antique firearm" means:

Any unloaded muzzle loading pistol or revolver with a matchlock, flintlock, percussion cap, or similar type of ignition system, or a pistol or revolver which uses fixed cartridges which are no longer available in the ordinary channels of commercial trade.

15. "Loaded firearm" means any firearm loaded with ammunition or any firearm which is possessed by one who, at the same time, possesses a quantity of ammunition which may be used to discharge such firearm.

15-a. "Electronic dart gun" means any device designed primarily as a weapon, the purpose of which is to momentarily stun, knock out or paralyze a person by passing an electrical shock to such person by means of a dart or projectile.

15-b. "Kung Fu star" means a disc-like object with sharpened points on the circumference thereof and is designed for use primarily as a weapon to be thrown.

15-c. "Electronic stun gun" means any device designed primarily as a weapon, the purpose of which is to stun, cause mental disorientation, knock out or paralyze a person by passing a high voltage electrical shock to such person.

16. "Certified not suitable to possess a self-defense spray device, a rifle or shotgun" means that the director or physician in charge of any hospital or institution for mental illness, public or private, has certified to the superintendent of state police or to any organized police department of a county, city, town or village of this state, that a person who has been judicially adjudicated incompetent, or who has been confined to such institution for mental illness pursuant to judicial authority, is not suitable to possess a self-defense spray device, as defined in section 265.20 of this article, or a rifle or shotgun.

17. "Serious offense" means

(a) any of the following offenses defined in the current penal law and any offense in any jurisdiction or the former penal law that includes all of the essential elements of any of the following offenses: illegally using, carrying or possessing a pistol or other dangerous weapon; possession of burglar's tools; criminal possession of stolen property in the third degree; escape in the third degree; jostling; fraudulent accosting; endangering the welfare of a child; obscenity in the third degree; issuing abortional articles;

permitting prostitution; promoting prostitution in the third degree; stalking in the fourth degree; stalking in the third degree; sexual misconduct; forcible touching; sexual abuse in the third degree; sexual abuse in the second degree; criminal possession of a controlled substance in the seventh degree; criminally possessing a hypodermic instrument; criminally using drug paraphernalia in the second degree; criminal possession of methamphetamine manufacturing material in the second degree; and a hate crime defined in article four hundred eighty-five of this chapter.

(b) any of the following offenses defined in the current penal law and any offense in any jurisdiction or in the former penal law that includes all of the essential elements of any of the following offenses, where the defendant and the person against whom the offense was committed were members of the same family or household as defined in subdivision one of section 530.11 of the criminal procedure law and as established pursuant to section 370.15 of the criminal procedure law: assault in the third degree; menacing in the third degree; menacing in the second degree; criminal obstruction of breathing or blood circulation; unlawful imprisonment in the second degree; coercion in the third degree; criminal tampering in the third degree; criminal contempt in the second degree; harassment in the first degree; aggravated harassment in the second degree; criminal trespass in the third degree; criminal trespass in the second degree; arson in the fifth degree; or attempt to commit any of the above-listed offenses.

(c) any misdemeanor offense in any jurisdiction or in the former penal law that includes all of the essential elements of a felony offense as defined in the current penal law.

18. "Armor piercing ammunition" means any ammunition capable of being used in pistols or revolvers containing a projectile or projectile core, or a projectile or projectile core for use in such ammunition, that is constructed entirely (excluding the presence of traces of other substances) from one or a combination of any of the following: tungsten alloys, steel, iron, brass, bronze, beryllium copper, or uranium.

19. "Duly authorized instructor" means (a) a duly commissioned officer of the United States army, navy, marine corps or coast guard, or of the national guard of the state of New York; or (b) a duly qualified adult citizen of the United States who has been granted a certificate as an instructor in small arms practice issued by the United States army, navy or marine corps, or by the adjutant general of this state, or by the national rifle association of America, a not-for-profit corporation duly organized under the laws of this state; or (c) by a person duly qualified and designated by the department of environmental conservation under paragraph d of subdivision six of section 11-0713 of the environmental conservation law as its agent in the giving of instruction and the making of certifications of qualification in responsible hunting practices.

20. "Disguised gun" means any weapon or device capable of being concealed on the person from which a shot can be discharged through the energy of an explosive and is designed and intended to appear to be something other than a gun.

21. "Semiautomatic" means any repeating rifle, shotgun or pistol, regardless of barrel or overall length, which utilizes a portion of the energy of a firing cartridge or shell to extract the fired cartridge case or spent shell and chamber the next round, and which requires a separate pull of the trigger to fire each cartridge or shell.

22. "Assault weapon" means

(a) a semiautomatic rifle that has an ability to accept a detachable magazine and has at least one of the following characteristics:

(i) a folding or telescoping stock;

(ii) a pistol grip that protrudes conspicuously beneath the action of the weapon;

(iii) a thumbhole stock;

(iv) a second handgrip or a protruding grip that can be held by the non-trigger hand;

(v) a bayonet mount;

(vi) a flash suppressor, muzzle break, muzzle compensator, or threaded barrel designed to accommodate a flash suppressor, muzzle break, or muzzle compensator;

(vii) a grenade launcher; or

(b) a semiautomatic shotgun that has at least one of the following characteristics:

(i) a folding or telescoping stock;

(ii) a thumbhole stock;

(iii) a second handgrip or a protruding grip that can be held by the non-trigger hand;

(iv) a fixed magazine capacity in excess of seven rounds;

(v) an ability to accept a detachable magazine; or

(c) a semiautomatic pistol that has an ability to accept a detachable magazine and has at least one of the following characteristics:

(i) a folding or telescoping stock;

(ii) a thumbhole stock;

(iii) a second handgrip or a protruding grip that can be held by the non-trigger hand;

(iv) capacity to accept an ammunition magazine that attaches to the pistol outside of the pistol grip;

(v) a threaded barrel capable of accepting a barrel extender, flash suppressor, forward handgrip, or silencer;

(vi) a shroud that is attached to, or partially or completely encircles, the barrel and that permits the shooter to hold the firearm with the non-trigger hand without being burned;

(vii) a manufactured weight of fifty ounces or more when the pistol is unloaded; or

(viii) a semiautomatic version of an automatic rifle, shotgun or firearm;

(d) a revolving cylinder shotgun;

(e) a semiautomatic rifle, a semiautomatic shotgun or a semiautomatic pistol or weapon defined in subparagraph (v) of paragraph (e) of subdivision twenty-two of section 265.00 of this chapter as added by chapter one hundred eighty-nine of the laws of two thousand and otherwise lawfully possessed pursuant to such chapter of the laws of two thousand prior to September fourteenth, nineteen hundred ninety-four;

(f) a semiautomatic rifle, a semiautomatic shotgun or a semiautomatic pistol or weapon defined in paragraph (a), (b) or (c) of this subdivision, possessed prior to the date of enactment of the chapter of the laws of two thousand thirteen which added this paragraph;

(g) provided, however, that such term does not include:

(i) any rifle, shotgun or pistol that (A) is manually operated by bolt, pump, lever or slide action; (B) has been rendered permanently inoperable; or (C) is an antique firearm as defined in 18 U.S.C. 921(a)(16);

(ii) a semiautomatic rifle that cannot accept a detachable magazine that holds more than five rounds of ammunition;

(iii) a semiautomatic shotgun that cannot hold more than five rounds of ammunition in a fixed or detachable magazine; or

(iv) a rifle, shotgun or pistol, or a replica or a duplicate thereof, specified in Appendix A to 18 U.S.C. 922 as such weapon was manufactured on October first, nineteen hundred ninety-three. The mere fact that a weapon is not listed in Appendix A shall not be construed to mean that such weapon is an assault weapon;

(v) any weapon validly registered pursuant to subdivision sixteen-a of section 400.00 of this chapter. Such weapons shall be subject to the provisions of paragraph (h) of this subdivision;

(vi) any firearm, rifle, or shotgun that was manufactured at least fifty years prior to the current date, but not including replicas thereof that is validly registered pursuant to subdivision sixteen-a of section 400.00 of this chapter;

(h) Any weapon defined in paragraph (e) or (f) of this subdivision and any large capacity ammunition feeding device that was legally possessed by an individual prior to the enactment of the chapter of the laws of two thousand thirteen which added this paragraph, may only be sold to, exchanged with or disposed of to a purchaser authorized to possess such weapons or to an individual or entity outside of the state provided that any such transfer to an individual or entity outside of the state must be reported to the entity wherein the weapon is registered within seventy-two hours of such transfer. An individual who transfers any such weapon or large capacity ammunition device to an individual inside New York state or without complying with the provisions of this paragraph shall be guilty of a class A misdemeanor unless such large capacity ammunition feeding device, the possession of which is made illegal by the chapter of the laws of two thousand thirteen which added this paragraph, is transferred within one year of the effective date of the chapter of the laws of two thousand thirteen which added this paragraph.

23. "Large capacity ammunition feeding device" means a magazine, belt, drum, feed strip, or similar device, that (a) has a capacity of, or that can be readily restored

or converted to accept, more than ten rounds of ammunition, or [pars (b) and (c) are suspended and not effective as stated in Laws 2013, ch 1, § 58, sub b note below] (b) contains more than seven rounds of ammunition, or (c) is obtained after the effective date of the chapter of the laws of two thousand thirteen which amended this subdivision and has a capacity of, or that can be readily restored or converted to accept, more than seven rounds of ammunition; provided, however, that such term does not include an attached tubular device designed to accept, and capable of operating only with, .22 caliber rimfire ammunition or a feeding device that is a curio or relic. A feeding device that is a curio or relic is defined as a device that (i) was manufactured at least fifty years prior to the current date, (ii) is only capable of being used exclusively in a firearm, rifle, or shotgun that was manufactured at least fifty years prior to the current date, but not including replicas thereof, (iii) is possessed by an individual who is not prohibited by state or federal law from possessing a firearm and (iv) is registered with the division of state police pursuant to subdivision sixteen-a of section 400.00 of this chapter, except such feeding devices transferred into the state may be registered at any time, provided they are registered within thirty days of their transfer into the state. Notwithstanding paragraph (h) of subdivision twenty-two of this section, such feeding devices may be transferred provided that such transfer shall be subject to the provisions of section 400.03 of this chapter including the check required to be conducted pursuant to such section.

24. "Seller of ammunition" means any person, firm, partnership, corporation or company who engages in the business of purchasing, selling or keeping ammunition.

25. "Qualified retired New York or federal law enforcement officer" means an individual who is a retired police officer as police officer is defined in subdivision thirty-four of section 1.20 of the criminal procedure law, a retired peace officer as peace officer is defined in section 2.10 of the criminal procedure law or a retired federal law enforcement officer as federal law enforcement officer is defined in section 2.15 of the criminal procedure law, who: (a) separated from service in good standing from a public agency located in New York state in which such person served as either a police officer, peace officer or federal law enforcement officer; and (b) before such separation, was authorized by law to engage in or supervise the prevention, detection, investigation, or prosecution of, or the incarceration of any person for, any violation of law, and had statutory powers of arrest, pursuant to their official duties, under the criminal procedure law; and (c) (i) before such separation, served as either a police officer, peace officer or federal law enforcement officer for five years or more and at the time of separation, is such an officer; or (ii) separated from service with such agency, after completing any applicable probationary period of such service, due to a service-connected disability, as determined by such agency at or before the time of separation; and (d)(i) has not been found by a qualified medical professional employed by such agency to be unqualified for reasons relating to mental health; or (ii) has not entered into an agreement with such agency from which the individual is separating from service in which that individual acknowledges he or she is not qualified for reasons relating to mental health; and (e) is not otherwise prohibited by New York or federal law from possessing any firearm.

26. "Rapid-fire modification device" means any bump stock, trigger crank, binary trigger system, burst trigger system, or any other device that is designed to accelerate the rate of fire of a semi-automatic firearm, rifle or shotgun.

27. "Bump stock" means any device or instrument that increases the rate of fire achievable with a semi-automatic firearm, rifle or shotgun by using energy from the recoil of the weapon to generate a reciprocating action that facilitates repeated activation of the trigger.

28. "Trigger crank" means any device or instrument that repeatedly activates the trigger of a semi-automatic firearm, rifle or shotgun through the use of a lever or other part that is turned in a circular motion and thereby accelerates the rate of fire of such firearm, rifle or shotgun, provided, however, that "trigger crank" shall not include any weapon initially designed and manufactured to fire through the use of a crank or lever.

29. "Binary trigger system" means any device that, when installed in or attached to a semi-automatic firearm rifle, or shotgun causes that weapon to fire once when the trigger is pulled and again when the trigger is released.

30. "Burst trigger system" means any device that, when installed in or attached to a semi-automatic firearm, rifle, or shot gun, allows that weapon to discharge two or more shots with a single pull or the trigger by altering the trigger reset.

HISTORY:

Add, L 1965, ch 1030, § 1, eff Sept 1, 1967, with substance derived from § 1896; amd, L 1967, ch 791, § 46; L 1969, ch 123, § 1, eff Sept 1, 1969; L 1972, ch 588, § 1; L 1972, ch 605, § 1; L 1974, ch 179, § 1, eff Sept 1, 1974; L 1974, ch 986, §§ 1, 2; L 1974, ch 1041, § 1, eff Sept 1, 1974; L 1976, ch 217, § 1, eff Sept 1, 1976; L 1982, ch 492, § 1; L 1985, ch 61, § 1, eff Nov 1, 1985; L 1986, ch 328, § 2, eff Nov 1, 1986; L 1986, ch 646, § 1, eff Nov 1, 1986; L 1988, ch 264, § 1; L 1990, ch 264, § 1, eff Nov 1, 1990; L 1995, ch 219, § 2, eff Nov 1, 1995; L 1996, ch 354, § 2, eff Nov 1, 1996; L 1997, ch 446, § 2, eff Aug 25, 1997; L 1998, ch 378, § 1, eff Nov 1, 1998; L 1999, ch 210, § 1, eff Nov 1, 1999; L 1999, ch 635, §§ 11, 15, eff Dec 1, 1999; L 2000, ch 189, §§ 8–10, eff Nov 1, 2000; L 2008, ch 257, § 3, eff Nov 1, 2008; L 2010, ch 232, §§ 2, 3, eff July 30, 2010; L 2013, ch 1, § 37, eff Jan 15, 2013; L 2013, ch 1, § 38, eff April 15, 2013; L 2013, ch 1, § 39, eff March 16, 2013; L 2013, ch 98, § 1, eff July 5, 2013; L 2018, ch 60, § 1, eff June 11, 2018; L 2019, ch 34, § 3, eff May 30, 2019; L 2019, ch 130, § 1, eff July 29, 2019; L 2019, ch 134, § 1, eff Jan 26, 2020; L 2019, ch 146, § 1, eff Nov 1, 2019; L 2020, ch 55, § 1 (Part N), eff April 3, 2021.

Part FOUR
Administrative Provisions

Title W
Provisions Relating to Firearms, Fireworks, Pornography Equipment and Vehicles Used in the Transportation of Gambling Records

Article 400 Licensing and Other Provisions Relating to Firearms

Article 400
Licensing and Other Provisions Relating to Firearms

§ 400.00. Licenses to carry, possess, repair and dispose of firearms [Effective until April 3, 2021]

1. Eligibility. No license shall be issued or renewed pursuant to this section except by the licensing officer, and then only after investigation and finding that all statements in a proper application for a license are true. No license shall be issued or renewed except for an applicant (a) twenty-one years of age or older, provided, however, that where such applicant has been honorably discharged from the United States army, navy, marine corps, air force or coast guard, or the national guard of the state of New York, no such age restriction shall apply; (b) of good moral character; (c) who has not been convicted anywhere of a felony or a serious offense or who is not the subject of an outstanding warrant of arrest issued upon the alleged commission of a felony or serious offense; (d) who is not a fugitive from justice; (e) who is not an unlawful user of or addicted to any controlled substance as defined in section 21 U.S.C. 802; (f) who being an alien (i) is not illegally or unlawfully in the United States or (ii) has not been admitted to the United States under a nonimmigrant visa subject to the exception in 18 U.S.C. 922(y)(2); (g) who has not been discharged from the Armed Forces under dishonorable conditions; (h) who, having been a citizen of the United States, has not

renounced his or her citizenship; (i) who has stated whether he or she has ever suffered any mental illness; (j) who has not been involuntarily committed to a facility under the jurisdiction of an office of the department of mental hygiene pursuant to article nine or fifteen of the mental hygiene law, article seven hundred thirty or section 330.20 of the criminal procedure law, section four hundred two or five hundred eight of the correction law, section 322.2 or 353.4 of the family court act, or has not been civilly confined in a secure treatment facility pursuant to article ten of the mental hygiene law; (k) who has not had a license revoked or who is not under a suspension or ineligibility order issued pursuant to the provisions of section 530.14 of the criminal procedure law or section eight hundred forty-two-a of the family court act; (l) in the county of Westchester, who has successfully completed a firearms safety course and test as evidenced by a certificate of completion issued in his or her name and endorsed and affirmed under the penalties of perjury by a duly authorized instructor, except that: (i) persons who are honorably discharged from the United States army, navy, marine corps or coast guard, or of the national guard of the state of New York, and produce evidence of official qualification in firearms during the term of service are not required to have completed those hours of a firearms safety course pertaining to the safe use, carrying, possession, maintenance and storage of a firearm; and (ii) persons who were licensed to possess a pistol or revolver prior to the effective date of this paragraph are not required to have completed a firearms safety course and test; (m) who has not had a guardian appointed for him or her pursuant to any provision of state law, based on a determination that as a result of marked subnormal intelligence, mental illness, incapacity, condition or disease, he or she lacks the mental capacity to contract or manage his or her own affairs; and (n) concerning whom no good cause exists for the denial of the license. No person shall engage in the business of gunsmith or dealer in firearms unless licensed pursuant to this section. An applicant to engage in such business shall also be a citizen of the United States, more than twenty-one years of age and maintain a place of business in the city or county where the license is issued. For such business, if the applicant is a firm or partnership, each member thereof shall comply with all of the requirements set forth in this subdivision and if the applicant is a corporation, each officer thereof shall so comply.

2. Types of licenses. A license for gunsmith or dealer in firearms shall be issued to engage in such business. A license for a pistol or revolver, other than an assault weapon or a disguised gun, shall be issued to (a) have and possess in his dwelling by a householder; (b) have and possess in his place of business by a merchant or storekeeper; (c) have and carry concealed while so employed by a messenger employed by a banking institution or express company; (d) have and carry concealed by a justice of the supreme court in the first or second judicial departments, or by a judge of the New York city civil court or the New York city criminal court; (e) have and carry concealed while so employed by a regular employee of an institution of the state, or of any county, city, town or village, under control of a commissioner of correction of the city or any warden, superintendent or head keeper of any state prison, penitentiary, workhouse, county jail or other institution for the detention of persons convicted or accused of crime or held as witnesses in criminal cases, provided that application is made therefor by such commissioner, warden, superintendent or head keeper; (f) have and carry concealed, without regard to employment or place of possession, by any person when proper cause exists for the issuance thereof; and (g) have, possess, collect and carry antique pistols which are defined as follows: (i) any single shot, muzzle loading pistol with a matchlock, flintlock, percussion cap, or similar type of ignition system manufactured in or before 1898, which is not designed for using rimfire or conventional centerfire fixed ammunition; and (ii) any replica of any pistol described in clause (i) hereof if such replica—

(1) is not designed or redesigned for using rimfire or conventional centerfire fixed ammunition, or

(2) uses rimfire or conventional centerfire fixed ammunition which is no longer manufactured in the United States and which is not readily available in the ordinary channels of commercial trade.

3. Applications.

(a) Applications shall be made and renewed, in the case of a license to carry or possess a pistol or revolver, to the licensing officer in the city or county, as the case may be, where the applicant resides, is principally employed or has his or her principal place of business as merchant or storekeeper; and, in the case of a license as gunsmith or dealer in firearms, to the licensing officer where such place of business is located. Blank applications shall, except in the city of New York, be approved as to form by the superintendent of state police. An application shall state the full name, date of birth, residence, present occupation of each person or individual signing the same, whether or not he or she is a citizen of the United States, whether or not he or she complies with each requirement for eligibility specified in subdivision one of this section and such other facts as may be required to show the good character, competency and integrity of each person or individual signing the application. An application shall be signed and verified by the applicant. Each individual signing an application shall submit one photograph of himself or herself and a duplicate for each required copy of the application. Such photographs shall have been taken within thirty days prior to filing the application. In case of a license as gunsmith or dealer in firearms, the photographs submitted shall be two inches square, and the application shall also state the previous occupation of each individual signing the same and the location of the place of such business, or of the bureau, agency, subagency, office or branch office for which the license is sought, specifying the name of the city, town or village, indicating the street and number and otherwise giving such apt description as to point out reasonably the location thereof. In such case, if the applicant is a firm, partnership or corporation, its name, date and place of formation, and principal place of business shall be stated. For such firm or partnership, the application shall be signed and verified by each individual composing or intending to compose the same, and for such corporation, by each officer thereof.

(b) Application for an exemption under paragraph seven-b of subdivision a of section 265.20 of this chapter. Each applicant desiring to obtain the exemption set forth in paragraph seven-b of subdivision a of section 265.20 of this chapter shall make such request in writing of the licensing officer with whom his application for a license is filed, at the time of filing such application. Such request shall include a signed and verified statement by the person authorized to instruct and supervise the applicant, that has met with the applicant and that he has determined that, in his judgment, said applicant does not appear to be or poses a threat to be, a danger to himself or to others. He shall include a copy of his certificate as an instructor in small arms, if he is required to be certified, and state his address and telephone number. He shall specify the exact location by name, address and telephone number where such instruction will take place. Such licensing officer shall, no later than ten business days after such filing, request the duly constituted police authorities of the locality where such application is made to investigate and ascertain any previous criminal record of the applicant pursuant to subdivision four of this section. Upon completion of this investigation, the police authority shall report the results to the licensing officer without unnecessary delay. The licensing officer shall no later than ten business days after the receipt of such investigation, determine if the applicant has been previously denied a license, been convicted of a felony, or been convicted of a serious offense, and either approve or disapprove the applicant for exemption purposes based upon such determinations. If the applicant is approved for the exemption, the licensing officer shall notify the appropriate duly constituted police authorities and the applicant. Such exemption shall terminate if the application for the license is denied, or at any earlier time based upon any information obtained by the licensing officer or the appropriate police authorities which would cause the license to be denied. The applicant and appropriate police authorities shall be notified of any such terminations.

4. Investigation. Before a license is issued or renewed, there shall be an investigation of all statements required in the application by the duly constituted police authorities of the locality where such application is made, including but not limited to such records as may be accessible to the division of state police or division of criminal justice services pursuant to section 400.02 of this article. For that purpose, the records of the appropriate office of the department of mental hygiene concerning previous or present mental illness of the applicant shall be available for inspection by the investigating officer of the police authority. Where the applicant is domiciled in a foreign state, the investigation shall include inquiry of the foreign state for records concerning the previous or present mental illness of the applicant, and, to the extent

necessary for inspection by the investigating officer, the applicant shall execute a waiver of confidentiality of such record in such form as may be required by the foreign state. In order to ascertain any previous criminal record, the investigating officer shall take the fingerprints and physical descriptive data in quadruplicate of each individual by whom the application is signed and verified. Two copies of such fingerprints shall be taken on standard fingerprint cards eight inches square, and one copy may be taken on a card supplied for that purpose by the federal bureau of investigation; provided, however, that in the case of a corporate applicant that has already been issued a dealer in firearms license and seeks to operate a firearm dealership at a second or subsequent location, the original fingerprints on file may be used to ascertain any criminal record in the second or subsequent application unless any of the corporate officers have changed since the prior application, in which case the new corporate officer shall comply with procedures governing an initial application for such license. When completed, one standard card shall be forwarded to and retained by the division of criminal justice services in the executive department, at Albany. A search of the files of such division and written notification of the results of the search to the investigating officer shall be made without unnecessary delay. Thereafter, such division shall notify the licensing officer and the executive department, division of state police, Albany, of any criminal record of the applicant filed therein subsequent to the search of its files. A second standard card, or the one supplied by the federal bureau of investigation, as the case may be, shall be forwarded to that bureau at Washington with a request that the files of the bureau be searched and notification of the results of the search be made to the investigating police authority. Of the remaining two fingerprint cards, one shall be filed with the executive department, division of state police, Albany, within ten days after issuance of the license, and the other remain on file with the investigating police authority. No such fingerprints may be inspected by any person other than a peace officer, who is acting pursuant to his or her special duties, or a police officer, except on order of a judge or justice of a court of record either upon notice to the licensee or without notice, as the judge or justice may deem appropriate. Upon completion of the investigation, the police authority shall report the results to the licensing officer without unnecessary delay.

4-a. Processing of license applications. Applications for licenses shall be accepted for processing by the licensing officer at the time of presentment. Except upon written notice to the applicant specifically stating the reasons for any delay, in each case the licensing officer shall act upon any application for a license pursuant to this section within six months of the date of presentment of such an application to the appropriate authority. Such delay may only be for good cause and with respect to the applicant. In acting upon an application, the licensing officer shall either deny the application for reasons specifically and concisely stated in writing or grant the application and issue the license applied for.

4-b. Westchester county firearms safety course certificate. In the county of Westchester, at the time of application, the licensing officer to which the license application is made shall provide a copy of the safety course booklet to each license applicant. Before such license is issued, such licensing officer shall require that the applicant submit a certificate of successful completion of a firearms safety course and test issued in his or her name and endorsed and affirmed under the penalties of perjury by a duly authorized instructor.

5. Filing of approved applications.

(a) The application for any license, if granted, shall be filed by the licensing officer with the clerk of the county of issuance, except that in the city of New York and, in the counties of Nassau and Suffolk, the licensing officer shall designate the place of filing in the appropriate division, bureau or unit of the police department thereof, and in the county of Suffolk the county clerk is hereby authorized to transfer all records or applications relating to firearms to the licensing authority of that county. Except as provided in paragraphs (b) through (f) of this subdivision, the name and address of any person to whom an application for any license has been granted shall be a public record. Upon application by a licensee who has changed his place of residence such records or applications shall be transferred to the appropriate officer at the licensee's new place of residence. A duplicate copy of such application shall be filed by the licensing officer in the executive department, division of state police, Albany, within ten days after issuance of the license. The superintendent of state police may designate that such application shall be transmitted to the division of state police electronically. In the event the superintendent of the division of state police determines that it lacks any of the records required to be filed with the division, it may request that such records be provided to it by the appropriate clerk, department or authority and such clerk, department or authority shall provide the division with such records. In the event such clerk, department or authority lacks such records, the division may request the license holder provide information sufficient to constitute such record and such license holder shall provide the division with such information. Such information shall be limited to the license holder's name, date of birth, gender, race, residential address, social security number and firearms possessed by said license holder. Nothing in this subdivision shall be construed to change the expiration date or term of such licenses if otherwise provided for in law. Records assembled or collected for purposes of inclusion in the database established by this section shall be released pursuant to a court order. Records assembled or collected for purposes of inclusion in the database created pursuant to section 400.02 of this chapter shall not be subject to disclosure pursuant to article six of the public officers law.

(b) Each application for a license pursuant to paragraph (a) of this subdivision shall include, on a separate written form prepared by the division of state police within thirty days of the effective date of the chapter of the laws of two thousand thirteen, which amended this section, and provided to the applicant at the same time and in the same manner as the application for a license, an opportunity for the applicant to request an exception from his or her application information becoming public record pursuant to paragraph (a) of this subdivision. Such forms, which shall also be made available to individuals who had applied for or been granted a license prior to the effective date of the chapter of the laws of two thousand thirteen which amended this section, shall notify applicants that, upon discovery that an applicant knowingly provided false information, such applicant may be subject to penalties pursuant to section 175.30 of this chapter, and further, that his or her request for an exception shall be null and void, provided that written notice containing such determination is provided to the applicant. Further, such forms shall provide each applicant an opportunity to specify the grounds on which he or she believes his or her application information should not be publicly disclosed. These grounds, which shall be identified on the application with a box beside each for checking, as applicable, by the applicant, shall be as follows:

(i) the applicant's life or safety may be endangered by disclosure because:

(A) the applicant is an active or retired police officer, peace officer, probation officer, parole officer, or corrections officer;

(B) the applicant is a protected person under a currently valid order of protection;

(C) the applicant is or was a witness in a criminal proceeding involving a criminal charge;

(D) the applicant is participating or previously participated as a juror in a criminal proceeding, or is or was a member of a grand jury; or

(E) the applicant is a spouse, domestic partner or household member of a person identified in this subparagraph or subparagraph (ii) of this paragraph, specifying which subparagraph or subparagraphs and clauses apply.

(ii) the applicant has reason to believe his or her life or safety may be endangered by disclosure due to reasons stated by the applicant.

(iii) the applicant has reason to believe he or she may be subject to unwarranted harassment upon disclosure of such information.

(c) Each form provided for recertification pursuant to paragraph (b) of subdivision ten of this section shall include an opportunity for the applicant to request an exception from the information provided on such form becoming public record pursuant to paragraph (a) of this subdivision. Such forms shall notify applicants that, upon discovery that an applicant knowingly provided false information, such applicant may be subject to penalties pursuant to section 175.30 of this chapter, and further, that his or her request for an exception shall be null and void, provided that written notice containing such determination is provided to the applicant. Further, such forms shall provide each applicant an opportunity to either decline to request the grant or continuation of an exception, or specify the grounds on which he or she believes his or her information should not be publicly disclosed. These grounds, which shall be identified in the application with a box beside each for checking, as applicable, by the applicant, shall be the same as provided in paragraph (b) of this subdivision.

(d) Information submitted on the forms described in paragraph (b) of this subdivision shall be excepted from disclosure and maintained by the entity retaining such information separate and apart from all other records.

(e)(i) Upon receiving a request for exception from disclosure, the licensing officer shall grant such exception, unless the request is determined to be null and void, pursuant to paragraph (b) or (c) of this subdivision.

(ii) A request for an exception from disclosure may be submitted at any time, including after a license or recertification has been granted.

(iii) If an exception is sought and granted pursuant to paragraph (b) of this subdivision, the application information shall not be public record, unless the request is determined to be null and void. If an exception is sought and granted pursuant to paragraph (c) of this subdivision, the information concerning such recertification application shall not be public record, unless the request is determined to be null and void. Notwithstanding the foregoing provisions of this subparagraph, local and state law enforcement shall, upon request, be granted access to and copies of such application information provided that such information obtained by law enforcement pursuant to this subparagraph shall not be considered a public record of such law enforcement agency.

(f) The information of licensees or applicants for a license shall not be disclosed to the public during the first one hundred twenty days following the effective date of the chapter of the laws of two thousand thirteen, which amended this section. After such period, the information of those who had applied for or been granted a license prior to the preparation of the form for requesting an exception, pursuant to paragraph (b) of this subdivision, may be released only if such individuals did not file a request for such an exception during the first sixty days following such preparation; provided, however, that no information contained in an application for licensure or recertification shall be disclosed by an entity that has not completed processing any such requests received during such sixty days.

(g) If a request for an exception is determined to be null and void pursuant to paragraph (b) or (c) of this subdivision, an applicant may request review of such determination pursuant to article seventy-eight of the civil practice laws [law]* and rules. Such proceeding must commence within thirty days after service of the written notice containing the adverse determination. Notice of the right to commence such a petition, and the time period therefor, shall be included in the notice of the determination. Disclosure following such a petition shall not be made prior to the disposition of such review.

6. License: validity. Any license issued pursuant to this section shall be valid notwithstanding the provisions of any local law or ordinance. No license shall be transferable to any other person or premises. A license to carry or possess a pistol or revolver, not otherwise limited as to place or time of possession, shall be effective throughout the state, except that the same shall not be valid within the city of New York unless a special permit granting validity is issued by the police commissioner of that city. Such license to carry or possess shall be valid within the city of New York in the absence of a permit issued by the police commissioner of that city, provided that (a) the firearms covered by such license have been purchased from a licensed dealer within the city of New York and are being transported out of said city forthwith and immediately from said dealer by the licensee in a locked container during a continuous and uninterrupted trip; or provided that (b) the firearms covered by such license are being transported by the licensee in a locked container and the trip through the city of New York is continuous and uninterrupted; or provided that (c) the firearms covered by such license are carried by armored car security guards transporting money or other valuables, in, to, or from motor vehicles commonly known as armored cars, during the course of their employment; or provided that (d) the licensee is a retired police officer as police officer is defined pursuant to subdivision thirty-four of section 1.20 of the criminal

---

*The bracketed word has been inserted by the Publisher.

procedure law or a retired federal law enforcement officer, as defined in section 2.15 of the criminal procedure law, who has been issued a license by an authorized licensing officer as defined in subdivision ten of section 265.00 of this chapter; provided, further, however, that if such license was not issued in the city of New York it must be marked "Retired Police Officer" or "Retired Federal Law Enforcement Officer", as the case may be, and, in the case of a retired officer the license shall be deemed to permit only police or federal law enforcement regulations weapons; or provided that (e) the licensee is a peace officer described in subdivision four of section 2.10 of the criminal procedure law and the license, if issued by other than the city of New York, is marked "New York State Tax Department Peace Officer" and in such case the exemption shall apply only to the firearm issued to such licensee by the department of taxation and finance. A license as gunsmith or dealer in firearms shall not be valid outside the city or county, as the case may be, where issued. Notwithstanding any inconsistent provision of state or local law or rule or regulation, the premises limitation set forth in any license to have and possess a pistol or revolver in the licensee's dwelling or place of business pursuant to paragraph (a) or (b) of subdivision two of this section shall not prevent the transport of such pistol or revolver directly to or from (i) another dwelling or place of business of the licensee where the licensee is authorized to have and possess such pistol or revolver, (ii) an indoor or outdoor shooting range that is authorized by law to operate as such, (iii) a shooting competition at which the licensee may possess such pistol or revolver consistent with the provisions of subdivision a of section 265.20 of this chapter or consistent with the law applicable at the place of such competition, or (iv) any other location where the licensee is lawfully authorized to have and possess such pistol or revolver; provided however, that during such transport to or from a location specified in clauses (i) through (iv) of this paragraph, the pistol or revolver shall be unloaded and carried in a locked container, and the ammunition therefor shall be carried separately; provided further, however, that a license to have and possess a pistol or revolver in the licensee's dwelling or place of business pursuant to paragraph (a) or (b) of subdivision two of this section that is issued by a licensing officer other than the police commissioner of the city of New York shall not authorize transport of a pistol or revolver into the city of New York in the absence of written authorization to do so by the police commissioner of that city. The term "locked container" shall not include the glove compartment or console of a vehicle.

7. License: form. Any license issued pursuant to this section shall, except in the city of New York, be approved as to form by the superintendent of state police. A license to carry or possess a pistol or revolver shall have attached the licensee's photograph, and a coupon which shall be removed and retained by any person disposing of a firearm to the licensee. Such license shall specify the weapon covered by calibre, make, model, manufacturer's name and serial number, or if none, by any other distinguishing number or identification mark, and shall indicate whether issued to carry on the person or possess on the premises, and if on the premises shall also specify the place where the licensee shall possess the same. If such license is issued to an alien, or to a person not a citizen of and usually a resident in the state, the licensing officer shall state in the license the particular reason for the issuance and the names of the persons certifying to the good character of the applicant. Any license as gunsmith or dealer in firearms shall mention and describe the premises for which it is issued and shall be valid only for such premises.

8. License: exhibition and display. Every licensee while carrying a pistol or revolver shall have on his or her person a license to carry the same. Every person licensed to possess a pistol or revolver on particular premises shall have the license for the same on such premises. Upon demand, the license shall be exhibited for inspection to any peace officer, who is acting pursuant to his or her special duties, or police officer. A license as gunsmith or dealer in firearms shall be prominently displayed on the licensed premises. A gunsmith or dealer of firearms may conduct business temporarily at a location other than the location specified on the license if such temporary location is the location for a gun show or event sponsored by any national, state, or local organization, or any affiliate of any such organization devoted to the collection, competitive use or other sporting use of firearms. Any sale or transfer at a gun show must also comply with the provisions of article thirty-nine-DD of the general business law. Records of receipt and disposition of firearms transactions conducted at such temporary location shall

include the location of the sale or other disposition and shall be entered in the permanent records of the gunsmith or dealer of firearms and retained on the location specified on the license. Nothing in this section shall authorize any licensee to conduct business from any motorized or towed vehicle. A separate fee shall not be required of a licensee with respect to business conducted under this subdivision. Any inspection or examination of inventory or records under this section at such temporary location shall be limited to inventory consisting of, or records related to, firearms held or disposed at such temporary locations. Failure of any licensee to so exhibit or display his or her license, as the case may be, shall be presumptive evidence that he or she is not duly licensed.

9. License: amendment. Elsewhere than in the city of New York, a person licensed to carry or possess a pistol or revolver may apply at any time to his or her licensing officer for amendment of his or her license to include one or more such weapons or to cancel weapons held under license. If granted, a record of the amendment describing the weapons involved shall be filed by the licensing officer in the executive department, division of state police, Albany. The superintendent of state police may authorize that such amendment be completed and transmitted to the state police in electronic form. Notification of any change of residence shall be made in writing by any licensee within ten days after such change occurs, and a record of such change shall be inscribed by such licensee on the reverse side of his or her license. Elsewhere than in the city of New York, and in the counties of Nassau and Suffolk, such notification shall be made to the executive department, division of state police, Albany, and in the city of New York to the police commissioner of that city, and in the county of Nassau to the police commissioner of that county, and in the county of Suffolk to the licensing officer of that county, who shall, within ten days after such notification shall be received by him or her, give notice in writing of such change to the executive department, division of state police, at Albany.

10. License: expiration, certification and renewal.

(a) Any license for gunsmith or dealer in firearms and, in the city of New York, any license to carry or possess a pistol or revolver, issued at any time pursuant to this section or prior to the first day of July, nineteen hundred sixty-three and not limited to expire on an earlier date fixed in the license, shall expire not more than three years after the date of issuance. In the counties of Nassau, Suffolk and Westchester, any license to carry or possess a pistol or revolver, issued at any time pursuant to this section or prior to the first day of July, nineteen hundred sixty-three and not limited to expire on an earlier date fixed in the license, shall expire not more than five years after the date of issuance; however, in the county of Westchester, any such license shall be certified prior to the first day of April, two thousand, in accordance with a schedule to be contained in regulations promulgated by the commissioner of the division of criminal justice services, and every such license shall be recertified every five years thereafter. For purposes of this section certification shall mean that the licensee shall provide to the licensing officer the following information only: current name, date of birth, current address, and the make, model, caliber and serial number of all firearms currently possessed. Such certification information shall be filed by the licensing officer in the same manner as an amendment. Elsewhere than in the city of New York and the counties of Nassau, Suffolk and Westchester, any license to carry or possess a pistol or revolver, issued at any time pursuant to this section or prior to the first day of July, nineteen hundred sixty-three and not previously revoked or cancelled, shall be in force and effect until revoked as herein provided. Any license not previously cancelled or revoked shall remain in full force and effect for thirty days beyond the stated expiration date on such license. Any application to renew a license that has not previously expired, been revoked or cancelled shall thereby extend the term of the license until disposition of the application by the licensing officer. In the case of a license for gunsmith or dealer in firearms, in counties having a population of less than two hundred thousand inhabitants, photographs and fingerprints shall be submitted on original applications and upon renewal thereafter only at six year intervals. Upon satisfactory proof that a currently valid original license has been despoiled, lost or otherwise removed from the possession of the licensee and upon application containing an additional photograph of the licensee, the licensing officer shall issue a duplicate license.

(b) All licensees shall be recertified to the division of state police every five years thereafter. Any license issued before the effective date of the chapter of the laws of two thousand thirteen which added this paragraph shall be recertified by the licensee on or before January thirty-first, two thousand eighteen, and not less than one year prior to such date, the state police shall send a notice to all license holders who have not recertified by such time. Such recertification shall be in a form as approved by the superintendent of state police, which shall request the license holder's name, date of birth, gender, race, residential address, social security number, firearms possessed by such license holder, email address at the option of the license holder and an affirmation that such license holder is not prohibited from possessing firearms. The form may be in an electronic form if so designated by the superintendent of state police. Failure to recertify shall act as a revocation of such license. If the New York state police discover as a result of the recertification process that a licensee failed to provide a change of address, the New York state police shall not require the licensing officer to revoke such license.

11. License: revocation and suspension.

(a) The conviction of a licensee anywhere of a felony or serious offense or a licensee at any time becoming ineligible to obtain a license under this section shall operate as a revocation of the license. A license may be revoked or suspended as provided for in section 530.14 of the criminal procedure law or section eight hundred forty-two-a of the family court act. Except for a license issued pursuant to section 400.01 of this article, a license may be revoked and cancelled at any time in the city of New York, and in the counties of Nassau and Suffolk, by the licensing officer, and elsewhere than in the city of New York by any judge or justice of a court of record; a license issued pursuant to section 400.01 of this article may be revoked and cancelled at any time by the licensing officer or any judge or justice of a court of record. The official revoking a license shall give written notice thereof without unnecessary delay to the executive department, division of state police, Albany, and shall also notify immediately the duly constituted police authorities of the locality.

(b) Whenever the director of community services or his or her designee makes a report pursuant to section 9.46 of the mental hygiene law, the division of criminal justice services shall convey such information, whenever it determines that the person named in the report possesses a license issued pursuant to this section, to the appropriate licensing official, who shall issue an order suspending or revoking such license.

(c) In any instance in which a person's license is suspended or revoked under paragraph (a) or (b) of this subdivision, such person shall surrender such license to the appropriate licensing official and any and all firearms, rifles, or shotguns owned or possessed by such person shall be surrendered to an appropriate law enforcement agency as provided in subparagraph (f) of paragraph one of subdivision a of section 265.20 of this chapter. In the event such license, firearm, shotgun, or rifle is not surrendered, such items shall be removed and declared a nuisance and any police officer or peace officer acting pursuant to his or her special duties is authorized to remove any and all such weapons.

12. Records required of gunsmiths and dealers in firearms. Any person licensed as gunsmith or dealer in firearms shall keep a record book approved as to form, except in the city of New York, by the superintendent of state police. In the record book shall be entered at the time of every transaction involving a firearm the date, name, age, occupation and residence of any person from whom a firearm is received or to whom a firearm is delivered, and the calibre, make, model, manufacturer's name and serial number, or if none, any other distinguishing number or identification mark on such firearm. Before delivering a firearm to any person, the licensee shall require him to produce either a license valid under this section to carry or possess the same, or proof of lawful authority as an exempt person pursuant to section 265.20 of this chapter and either (a) the National Instant Criminal Background Check System (NICS) or its successor has issued a "proceed" response to the licensee, or (b) thirty calendar days have elapsed since the date the licensee contacted NICS to initiate a national instant criminal background check and NICS has not notified the licensee that the transfer of the firearm to such person should be denied. In addition, before delivering a firearm to a peace officer, the licensee shall verify that person's status as a peace officer with the

division of state police. After completing the foregoing, the licensee shall remove and retain the attached coupon and enter in the record book the date of such license, number, if any, and name of the licensing officer, in the case of the holder of a license to carry or possess, or the shield or other number, if any, assignment and department, unit or agency, in the case of an exempt person. The original transaction report shall be forwarded to the division of state police within ten days of delivering a firearm to any person, and a duplicate copy shall be kept by the licensee. The superintendent of state police may designate that such record shall be completed and transmitted in electronic form. A dealer may be granted a waiver from transmitting such records in electronic form if the superintendent determines that such dealer is incapable of such transmission due to technological limitations that are not reasonably within the control of the dealer, or other exceptional circumstances demonstrated by the dealer, pursuant to a process established in regulation, and at the discretion of the superintendent. Records assembled or collected for purposes of inclusion in the database created pursuant to section 400.02 of this article shall not be subject to disclosure pursuant to article six of the public officers law. The record book shall be maintained on the premises mentioned and described in the license and shall be open at all reasonable hours for inspection by any peace officer, acting pursuant to his special duties, or police officer. In the event of cancellation or revocation of the license for gunsmith or dealer in firearms, or discontinuance of business by a licensee, such record book shall be immediately surrendered to the licensing officer in the city of New York, and in the counties of Nassau and Suffolk, and elsewhere in the state to the executive department, division of state police.

12-a. State police regulations applicable to licensed gunsmiths engaged in the business of assembling or manufacturing firearms. The superintendent of state police is hereby authorized to issue such rules and regulations as he deems reasonably necessary to prevent the manufacture and assembly of unsafe firearms in the state. Such rules and regulations shall establish safety standards in regard to the manufacture and assembly of firearms in the state, including specifications as to materials and parts used, the proper storage and shipment of firearms, and minimum standards of quality control. Regulations issued by the state police pursuant to this subdivision shall apply to any person licensed as a gunsmith under this section engaged in the business of manufacturing or assembling firearms, and any violation thereof shall subject the licensee to revocation of license pursuant to subdivision eleven of this section.

12-b. [None]

12-c. Firearms records.

(a) Every employee of a state or local agency, unit of local government, state or local commission, or public or private organization who possesses a firearm or machine-gun under an exemption to the licensing requirements under this chapter, shall promptly report in writing to his employer the make, model, calibre and serial number of each such firearm or machine gun. Thereafter, within ten days of the acquisition or disposition of any such weapon, he shall furnish such information to his employer, including the name and address of the person from whom the weapon was acquired or to whom it was disposed.

(b) Every head of a state or local agency, unit of local government, state or local commission, public authority or public or private organization to whom an employee has submitted a report pursuant to paragraph (a) of this subdivision shall promptly forward such report to the superintendent of state police.

(c) Every head of a state or local agency, unit of local government, state or local commission, public authority, or any other agency, firm or corporation that employs persons who may lawfully possess firearms or machine-guns without the requirement of a license therefor, or that employs persons licensed to possess firearms or machine-guns, shall promptly report to the superintendent of state police, in the manner prescribed by him, the make, model, calibre and serial number of every firearm or machine-gun possessed by it on the effective date of this act for the use of such employees or for any other use. Thereafter, within ten days of the acquisition or disposition of any such weapon, such head shall report such information to the superintendent of the state police, including the name and address of the person from whom the weapon was acquired or to whom it was disposed.

13. Expenses. The expense of providing a licensing officer with blank applications, licenses and record books for carrying out the provisions of this section shall be a charge against the county, and in the city of New York against the city.

14. Fees. In the city of New York and the county of Nassau, the annual license fee shall be twenty-five dollars for gunsmiths and fifty dollars for dealers in firearms. In such city, the city council and in the county of Nassau the Board of Supervisors shall fix the fee to be charged for a license to carry or possess a pistol or revolver and provide for the disposition of such fees. Elsewhere in the state, the licensing officer shall collect and pay into the county treasury the following fees: for each license to carry or possess a pistol or revolver, not less than three dollars nor more than ten dollars as may be determined by the legislative body of the county; for each amendment thereto, three dollars, and five dollars in the county of Suffolk; and for each license issued to a gunsmith or dealer in firearms, ten dollars. The fee for a duplicate license shall be five dollars. The fee for processing a license transfer between counties shall be five dollars. The fee for processing a license or renewal thereof for a qualified retired police officer as defined under subdivision thirty-four of section 1.20 of the criminal procedure law, or a qualified retired sheriff, undersheriff, or deputy sheriff of the city of New York as defined under subdivision two of section 2.10 of the criminal procedure law, or a qualified retired bridge and tunnel officer, sergeant or lieutenant of the triborough bridge and tunnel authority as defined under subdivision twenty of section 2.10 of the criminal procedure law, or a qualified retired uniformed court officer in the unified court system, or a qualified retired court clerk in the unified court system in the first and second judicial departments, as defined in paragraphs a and b of subdivision twenty-one of section 2.10 of the criminal procedure law or a retired correction officer as defined in subdivision twenty-five of section 2.10 of the criminal procedure law shall be waived in all counties throughout the state.

15. Any violation by any person of any provision of this section is a class A misdemeanor.

16. Unlawful disposal. No person shall except as otherwise authorized pursuant to law dispose of any firearm unless he is licensed as gunsmith or dealer in firearms.

16-a. Registration.

(a) An owner of a weapon defined in paragraph (e) or (f) of subdivision twenty-two of section 265.00 of this chapter, possessed before the date of the effective date of the chapter of the laws of two thousand thirteen which added this paragraph, must make an application to register such weapon with the superintendent of state police, in the manner provided by the superintendent, or by amending a license issued pursuant to this section within one year of the effective date of this subdivision except any weapon defined under subparagraph (vi) of paragraph (g) of subdivision twenty-two of section 265.00 of this chapter transferred into the state may be registered at any time, provided such weapons are registered within thirty days of their transfer into the state. Registration information shall include the registrant's name, date of birth, gender, race, residential address, social security number and a description of each weapon being registered. A registration of any weapon defined under subparagraph (vi) of paragraph (g) of subdivision twenty-two of section 265.00 or a feeding device as defined under subdivision twenty-three of section 265.00 of this chapter shall be transferable, provided that the seller notifies the state police within seventy-two hours of the transfer and the buyer provides the state police with information sufficient to constitute a registration under this section. Such registration shall not be valid if such registrant is prohibited or becomes prohibited from possessing a firearm pursuant to state or federal law. The superintendent shall determine whether such registrant is prohibited from possessing a firearm under state or federal law. Such check shall be limited to determining whether the factors in 18 USC 922 (g) apply or whether a registrant has been convicted of a serious offense as defined in subdivision sixteen-b of section 265.00 of this chapter, so as to prohibit such registrant from possessing a firearm, and whether a report has been issued pursuant to section 9.46 of the mental hygiene law. All registrants shall recertify to the division of state police every five years thereafter. Failure to recertify shall result in a revocation of such registration.

(a-1) Notwithstanding any inconsistent provisions of paragraph (a) of this subdivision, an owner of an assault weapon as defined in subdivision twenty-two of section 265.00 of this chapter, who is a qualified retired New York or federal law enforcement officer as defined in subdivision twenty-five of section 265.00 of this chapter, where such weapon was issued to or purchased by such officer prior to retirement and in the course of his or her official duties, and for which such officer was qualified by the agency that employed such officer within twelve months prior to his or her retirement, must register such weapon within sixty days of retirement.

(b) The superintendent of state police shall create and maintain an internet website to educate the public as to which semiautomatic rifle, semiautomatic shotgun or semiautomatic pistol or weapon that are illegal as a result of the enactment of the chapter of the laws of two thousand thirteen which added this paragraph, as well as such assault weapons which are illegal pursuant to article two hundred sixty-five of this chapter. Such website shall contain information to assist the public in recognizing the relevant features proscribed by such article two hundred sixty-five, as well as which make and model of weapons that require registration.

(c) A person who knowingly fails to apply to register such weapon, as required by this section, within one year of the effective date of the chapter of the laws of two thousand thirteen which added this paragraph shall be guilty of a class A misdemeanor and such person who unknowingly fails to validly register such weapon within such one year period shall be given a warning by an appropriate law enforcement authority about such failure and given thirty days in which to apply to register such weapon or to surrender it. A failure to apply or surrender such weapon within such thirty-day period shall result in such weapon being removed by an appropriate law enforcement authority and declared a nuisance.

16-b. The cost of the software, programming and interface required to transmit any record that must be electronically transmitted by the dealer or licensing officer to the division of state police pursuant to this chapter shall be borne by the state.

17. Applicability of section. The provisions of article two hundred sixty-five of this chapter relating to illegal possession of a firearm, shall not apply to an offense which also constitutes a violation of this section by a person holding an otherwise valid license under the provisions of this section and such offense shall only be punishable as a class A misdemeanor pursuant to this section. In addition, the provisions of such article two hundred sixty-five of this chapter shall not apply to the possession of a firearm in a place not authorized by law, by a person who holds an otherwise valid license or possession of a firearm by a person within a one year period after the stated expiration date of an otherwise valid license which has not been previously cancelled or revoked shall only be punishable as a class A misdemeanor pursuant to this section.

18. Notice. Upon the issuance of a license, the licensing officer shall issue therewith the following notice in conspicuous and legible twenty-four point type on eight and one-half inches by eleven inches paper stating in bold print the following:

WARNING: RESPONSIBLE FIREARM STORAGE IS THE LAW IN NEW YORK STATE. FIREARMS MUST EITHER BE STORED WITH A GUN LOCKING DEVICE OR IN A SAFE STORAGE DEPOSITORY OR NOT BE LEFT OUTSIDE THE IMMEDIATE POSSESSION AND CONTROL OF THE OWNER OR OTHER LAWFUL POSSESSOR IF A CHILD RESIDES IN THE HOME OR IS PRESENT, OR IF THE OWNER OR POSSESSOR RESIDES WITH A PERSON PROHIBITED FROM POSSESSING A FIREARM UNDER STATE OR FEDERAL LAW. FIREARMS SHOULD BE STORED UNLOADED AND LOCKED IN A LOCATION SEPARATE FROM AMMUNITION. LEAVING FIREARMS ACCESSIBLE TO A CHILD OR OTHER PROHIBITED PERSON MAY SUBJECT YOU TO IMPRISONMENT, FINE, OR BOTH.

Nothing in this subdivision shall be deemed to affect, impair or supersede any special or local law relating to providing notice regarding the safe storage of rifles, shotguns or firearms.

HISTORY:

Add, L 1965, ch 1030, § 1, eff Sept 1, 1967, with substance derived from § 1903; amd, L 1967, ch 791, § 49; L 1971, ch 796; L 1971, ch 1097, §§ 82, 83; L 1973, ch 172; L 1973, ch 546, § 1; L 1973, ch 593, § 1; L 1974, ch 1041, §§ 10, 11; L 1974, ch 1042, § 2, eff Sept 1, 1974; L 1976, ch 584, § 1; L 1977, ch 480, § 1; L 1980, ch 233, §§ 15–17, eff Aug 12, 1980; L 1980, ch 843, §§ 47–50, eff Sept 1, 1980; L 1981, ch 175, § 5; L 1982, ch 71, § 1; L 1984, ch 739, § 1; L 1985, ch 778, § 2, eff Nov 1, 1985; L 1986, ch 539, § 1; L 1988, ch 437, § 1; L 1990, ch 707, § 1; L 1991, ch 414, § 1; L 1992, ch 320, § 1; L 1993, ch 448, §§ 1, 2, eff Nov 1, 1993; L 1993, ch 449, § 1, eff Nov 1, 1993; L 1993, ch 498, § 3; L 1994, ch 332, § 1, eff Nov 1, 1994; L 1994, ch 636, § 1; L 1994, ch 637, § 1, eff Aug 2, 1994; L

1995, ch 236, § 1; L 1995, ch 370, § 1; L 1996, ch 644, § 6; L 1997, ch 446, §§ 3–6; L 1997, ch 447, § 2, eff Aug 25, 1997; L 1998, ch 378, § 8; L 1999, ch 210, §§ 5, 6, eff Nov 1, 1999; L 2000, ch 189, §§ 18–20, eff Nov 1, 2000; L 2002, ch 318, § 5, eff Aug 6, 2002; L 2005, ch 195, § 1, eff July 12, 2005; L 2005, ch 331, § 1, eff July 26, 2005; L 2013, ch 1, § 48; L 2013, ch 98, § 3, eff April 15, 2013; L 2018, ch 60, § 6, eff June 11, 2018; L 2019, ch 104, § 1, eff July 16, 2019; L 2019, ch 129, § 1, eff Sept 12, 2019; L 2019, ch 135, § 3, eff Sept 28, 2019; L 2019, ch 242, § 1, eff Nov 2, 2019; L 2019, ch 244, § 1, eff Sept 3, 2019.

§ 400.00. Licenses to carry, possess, repair and dispose of firearms [Effective April 3, 2021]

1. Eligibility. No license shall be issued or renewed pursuant to this section except by the licensing officer, and then only after investigation and finding that all statements in a proper application for a license are true. No license shall be issued or renewed except for an applicant (a) twenty-one years of age or older, provided, however, that where such applicant has been honorably discharged from the United States army, navy, marine corps, air force or coast guard, or the national guard of the state of New York, no such age restriction shall apply; (b) of good moral character; (c) who has not been convicted anywhere of a felony or a serious offense or who is not the subject of an outstanding warrant of arrest issued upon the alleged commission of a felony or serious offense; (d) who is not a fugitive from justice; (e) who is not an unlawful user of or addicted to any controlled substance as defined in section 21 U.S.C. 802; (f) who being an alien (i) is not illegally or unlawfully in the United States or (ii) has not been admitted to the United States under a nonimmigrant visa subject to the exception in 18 U.S.C. 922(y)(2); (g) who has not been discharged from the Armed Forces under dishonorable conditions; (h) who, having been a citizen of the United States, has not renounced his or her citizenship; (i) who has stated whether he or she has ever suffered any mental illness; (j) who has not been involuntarily committed to a facility under the jurisdiction of an office of the department of mental hygiene pursuant to article nine or fifteen of the mental hygiene law, article seven hundred thirty or section 330.20 of the criminal procedure law, section four hundred two or five hundred eight of the correction law, section 322.2 or 353.4 of the family court act, or has not been civilly confined in a secure treatment facility pursuant to article ten of the mental hygiene law; (k) who has not had a license revoked or who is not under a suspension or ineligibility order issued pursuant to the provisions of section 530.14 of the criminal procedure law or section eight hundred forty-two-a of the family court act; (l) in the county of Westchester, who has successfully completed a firearms safety course and test as evidenced by a certificate of completion issued in his or her name and endorsed and affirmed under the penalties of perjury by a duly authorized instructor, except that: (i) persons who are honorably discharged from the United States army, navy, marine corps or coast guard, or of the national guard of the state of New York, and produce evidence of official qualification in firearms during the term of service are not required to have completed those hours of a firearms safety course pertaining to the safe use, carrying, possession, maintenance and storage of a firearm; and (ii) persons who were licensed to possess a pistol or revolver prior to the effective date of this paragraph are not required to have completed a firearms safety course and test; (m) who has not had a guardian appointed for him or her pursuant to any provision of state law, based on a determination that as a result of marked subnormal intelligence, mental illness, incapacity, condition or disease, he or she lacks the mental capacity to contract or manage his or her own affairs; and (n) concerning whom no good cause exists for the denial of the license. No person shall engage in the business of gunsmith or dealer in firearms unless licensed pursuant to this section. An applicant to engage in such business shall also be a citizen of the United States, more than twenty-one years of age and maintain a place of business in the city or county where the license is issued. For such business, if the applicant is a firm or partnership, each member thereof shall comply with all of the requirements set forth in this subdivision and if the applicant is a corporation, each officer thereof shall so comply.

1-a. For purposes of subdivision one of this section, serious offense shall include an offense in any jurisdiction or the former penal law that includes all of the essential elements of a serious offense as defined by subdivision seventeen of section 265.00 of this chapter. Nothing in this subdivision shall preclude the denial of a license based on the commission of, arrest for or conviction of an offense in any other jurisdiction which does not include all of the essential elements of a serious offense.

2. Types of licenses. A license for gunsmith or dealer in firearms shall be issued to engage in such business. A license for a pistol or revolver, other than an assault weapon or a disguised gun, shall be issued to (a) have and possess in his dwelling by a householder; (b) have and possess in his place of business by a merchant or storekeeper; (c) have and carry concealed while so employed by a messenger employed by a banking institution or express company; (d) have and carry concealed by a justice of the supreme court in the first or second judicial departments, or by a judge of the New York city civil court or the New York city criminal court; (e) have and carry concealed while so employed by a regular employee of an institution of the state, or of any county, city, town or village, under control of a commissioner of correction of the city or any warden, superintendent or head keeper of any state prison, penitentiary, workhouse, county jail or other institution for the detention of persons convicted or accused of crime or held as witnesses in criminal cases, provided that application is made therefor by such commissioner, warden, superintendent or head keeper; (f) have and carry concealed, without regard to employment or place of possession, by any person when proper cause exists for the issuance thereof; and (g) have, possess, collect and carry antique pistols which are defined as follows: (i) any single shot, muzzle loading pistol with a matchlock, flintlock, percussion cap, or similar type of ignition system manufactured in or before 1898, which is not designed for using rimfire or conventional centerfire fixed ammunition; and (ii) any replica of any pistol described in clause (i) hereof if such replica—

(1) is not designed or redesigned for using rimfire or conventional centerfire fixed ammunition, or

(2) uses rimfire or conventional centerfire fixed ammunition which is no longer manufactured in the United States and which is not readily available in the ordinary channels of commercial trade.

3. Applications.

(a) Applications shall be made and renewed, in the case of a license to carry or possess a pistol or revolver, to the licensing officer in the city or county, as the case may be, where the applicant resides, is principally employed or has his or her principal place of business as merchant or storekeeper; and, in the case of a license as gunsmith or dealer in firearms, to the licensing officer where such place of business is located. Blank applications shall, except in the city of New York, be approved as to form by the superintendent of state police. An application shall state the full name, date of birth, residence, present occupation of each person or individual signing the same, whether or not he or she is a citizen of the United States, whether or not he or she complies with each requirement for eligibility specified in subdivision one of this section and such other facts as may be required to show the good character, competency and integrity of each person or individual signing the application. An application shall be signed and verified by the applicant. Each individual signing an application shall submit one photograph of himself or herself and a duplicate for each required copy of the application. Such photographs shall have been taken within thirty days prior to filing the application. In case of a license as gunsmith or dealer in firearms, the photographs submitted shall be two inches square, and the application shall also state the previous occupation of each individual signing the same and the location of the place of such business, or of the bureau, agency, subagency, office or branch office for which the license is sought, specifying the name of the city, town or village, indicating the street and number and otherwise giving such apt description as to point out reasonably the location thereof. In such case, if the applicant is a firm, partnership or corporation, its name, date and place of formation, and principal place of business shall be stated. For such firm or partnership, the application shall be signed and verified by each individual composing or intending to compose the same, and for such corporation, by each officer thereof.

(b) Application for an exemption under paragraph seven-b of subdivision a of section 265.20 of this chapter. Each applicant desiring to obtain the exemption set forth in paragraph seven-b of subdivision a of section 265.20 of this chapter shall make such request in writing of the licensing officer with whom his application for a license is filed, at the time of filing such application. Such request shall include a signed and verified statement by the person authorized to instruct and supervise the applicant, that has met with the applicant and that he has determined that, in his judgment, said applicant does not appear to be or poses a threat to be, a danger to himself or to others. He shall include a copy of his certificate as an instructor in small arms, if he is required to be certified, and state his address and telephone number. He shall specify the exact location by name, address and telephone number where such instruction will take place. Such licensing officer shall, no later than ten business days after such filing, request the duly constituted police authorities of the locality where such application is made to investigate and ascertain any previous criminal record of the applicant pursuant to subdivision four of this section. Upon completion of this investigation, the police authority shall report the results to the licensing officer without unnecessary delay. The licensing officer shall no later than ten business days after the receipt of such investigation, determine if the applicant has been previously denied a license, been convicted of a felony, or been convicted of a serious offense, and either approve or disapprove the applicant for exemption purposes based upon such determinations. If the applicant is approved for the exemption, the licensing officer shall notify the appropriate duly constituted police authorities and the applicant. Such exemption shall terminate if the application for the license is denied, or at any earlier time based upon any information obtained by the licensing officer or the appropriate police authorities which would cause the license to be denied. The applicant and appropriate police authorities shall be notified of any such terminations.

4. Investigation. Before a license is issued or renewed, there shall be an investigation of all statements required in the application by the duly constituted police authorities of the locality where such application is made, including but not limited to such records as may be accessible to the division of state police or division of criminal justice services pursuant to section 400.02 of this article. For that purpose, the records of the appropriate office of the department of mental hygiene concerning previous or present mental illness of the applicant shall be available for inspection by the investigating officer of the police authority. Where the applicant is domiciled in a foreign state, the investigation shall include inquiry of the foreign state for records concerning the previous or present mental illness of the applicant, and, to the extent necessary for inspection by the investigating officer, the applicant shall execute a waiver of confidentiality of such record in such form as may be required by the foreign state. In order to ascertain any previous criminal record, the investigating officer shall take the fingerprints and physical descriptive data in quadruplicate of each individual by whom the application is signed and verified. Two copies of such fingerprints shall be taken on standard fingerprint cards eight inches square, and one copy may be taken on a card supplied for that purpose by the federal bureau of investigation; provided, however, that in the case of a corporate applicant that has already been issued a dealer in firearms license and seeks to operate a firearm dealership at a second or subsequent location, the original fingerprints on file may be used to ascertain any criminal record in the second or subsequent application unless any of the corporate officers have changed since the prior application, in which case the new corporate officer shall comply with procedures governing an initial application for such license. When completed, one standard card shall be forwarded to and retained by the division of criminal justice services in the executive department, at Albany. A search of the files of such division and written notification of the results of the search to the investigating officer shall be made without unnecessary delay. Thereafter, such division shall notify the licensing officer and the executive department, division of state police, Albany, of any criminal record of the applicant filed therein subsequent to the search of its files. A second standard card, or the one supplied by the federal bureau of investigation, as the case may be, shall be forwarded to that bureau at Washington with a request that the files of the bureau be searched and notification of the results of the search be made to the investigating police authority. Of the remaining two fingerprint cards, one shall be filed with the executive department, division of state police, Albany, within ten days after issuance of the license, and the other remain on file with the investigating police authority. No such fingerprints may be inspected by any person other than a peace officer, who is acting pursuant to his or her special duties, or a police officer, except on order of a judge or justice of a court of record either upon notice to the licensee or without notice, as the

judge or justice may deem appropriate. Upon completion of the investigation, the police authority shall report the results to the licensing officer without unnecessary delay.

4-a. Processing of license applications. Applications for licenses shall be accepted for processing by the licensing officer at the time of presentment. Except upon written notice to the applicant specifically stating the reasons for any delay, in each case the licensing officer shall act upon any application for a license pursuant to this section within six months of the date of presentment of such an application to the appropriate authority. Such delay may only be for good cause and with respect to the applicant. In acting upon an application, the licensing officer shall either deny the application for reasons specifically and concisely stated in writing or grant the application and issue the license applied for.

4-b. Westchester county firearms safety course certificate. In the county of Westchester, at the time of application, the licensing officer to which the license application is made shall provide a copy of the safety course booklet to each license applicant. Before such license is issued, such licensing officer shall require that the applicant submit a certificate of successful completion of a firearms safety course and test issued in his or her name and endorsed and affirmed under the penalties of perjury by a duly authorized instructor.

5. Filing of approved applications.

(a) The application for any license, if granted, shall be filed by the licensing officer with the clerk of the county of issuance, except that in the city of New York and, in the counties of Nassau and Suffolk, the licensing officer shall designate the place of filing in the appropriate division, bureau or unit of the police department thereof, and in the county of Suffolk the county clerk is hereby authorized to transfer all records or applications relating to firearms to the licensing authority of that county. Except as provided in paragraphs (b) through (f) of this subdivision, the name and address of any person to whom an application for any license has been granted shall be a public record. Upon application by a licensee who has changed his place of residence such records or applications shall be transferred to the appropriate officer at the licensee's new place of residence. A duplicate copy of such application shall be filed by the licensing officer in the executive department, division of state police, Albany, within ten days after issuance of the license. The superintendent of state police may designate that such application shall be transmitted to the division of state police electronically. In the event the superintendent of the division of state police determines that it lacks any of the records required to be filed with the division, it may request that such records be provided to it by the appropriate clerk, department or authority and such clerk, department or authority shall provide the division with such records. In the event such clerk, department or authority lacks such records, the division may request the license holder provide information sufficient to constitute such record and such license holder shall provide the division with such information. Such information shall be limited to the license holder's name, date of birth, gender, race, residential address, social security number and firearms possessed by said license holder. Nothing in this subdivision shall be construed to change the expiration date or term of such licenses if otherwise provided for in law. Records assembled or collected for purposes of inclusion in the database established by this section shall be released pursuant to a court order. Records assembled or collected for purposes of inclusion in the database created pursuant to section 400.02 of this chapter shall not be subject to disclosure pursuant to article six of the public officers law.

(b) Each application for a license pursuant to paragraph (a) of this subdivision shall include, on a separate written form prepared by the division of state police within thirty days of the effective date of the chapter of the laws of two thousand thirteen, which amended this section, and provided to the applicant at the same time and in the same manner as the application for a license, an opportunity for the applicant to request an exception from his or her application information becoming public record pursuant to paragraph (a) of this subdivision. Such forms, which shall also be made available to individuals who had applied for or been granted a license prior to the effective date of the chapter of the laws of two thousand thirteen which amended this section, shall notify applicants that, upon discovery that an applicant knowingly provided false information, such applicant may be subject to penalties pursuant to section 175.30 of this chapter, and further, that his or her request for an exception shall be null and void, provided that written notice containing such determination is provided to the applicant. Further, such forms shall provide each applicant an opportunity to specify the grounds on which he or she believes his or her application information should not be publicly disclosed. These grounds, which shall be identified on the application with a box beside each for checking, as applicable, by the applicant, shall be as follows:

(i) the applicant's life or safety may be endangered by disclosure because:

(A) the applicant is an active or retired police officer, peace officer, probation officer, parole officer, or corrections officer;

(B) the applicant is a protected person under a currently valid order of protection;

(C) the applicant is or was a witness in a criminal proceeding involving a criminal charge;

(D) the applicant is participating or previously participated as a juror in a criminal proceeding, or is or was a member of a grand jury; or

(E) the applicant is a spouse, domestic partner or household member of a person identified in this subparagraph or subparagraph (ii) of this paragraph, specifying which subparagraph or subparagraphs and clauses apply.

(ii) the applicant has reason to believe his or her life or safety may be endangered by disclosure due to reasons stated by the applicant.

(iii) the applicant has reason to believe he or she may be subject to unwarranted harassment upon disclosure of such information.

(c) Each form provided for recertification pursuant to paragraph (b) of subdivision ten of this section shall include an opportunity for the applicant to request an exception from the information provided on such form becoming public record pursuant to paragraph (a) of this subdivision. Such forms shall notify applicants that, upon discovery that an applicant knowingly provided false information, such applicant may be subject to penalties pursuant to section 175.30 of this chapter, and further, that his or her request for an exception shall be null and void, provided that written notice containing such determination is provided to the applicant. Further, such forms shall provide each applicant an opportunity to either decline to request the grant or continuation of an exception, or specify the grounds on which he or she believes his or her information should not be publicly disclosed. These grounds, which shall be identified in the application with a box beside each for checking, as applicable, by the applicant, shall be the same as provided in paragraph (b) of this subdivision.

(d) Information submitted on the forms described in paragraph (b) of this subdivision shall be excepted from disclosure and maintained by the entity retaining such information separate and apart from all other records.

(e)(i) Upon receiving a request for exception from disclosure, the licensing officer shall grant such exception, unless the request is determined to be null and void, pursuant to paragraph (b) or (c) of this subdivision.

(ii) A request for an exception from disclosure may be submitted at any time, including after a license or recertification has been granted.

(iii) If an exception is sought and granted pursuant to paragraph (b) of this subdivision, the application information shall not be public record, unless the request is determined to be null and void. If an exception is sought and granted pursuant to paragraph (c) of this subdivision, the information concerning such recertification application shall not be public record, unless the request is determined to be null and void. Notwithstanding the foregoing provisions of this subparagraph, local and state law enforcement shall, upon request, be granted access to and copies of such application information provided that such information obtained by law enforcement pursuant to this subparagraph shall not be considered a public record of such law enforcement agency.

(f) The information of licensees or applicants for a license shall not be disclosed to the public during the first one hundred twenty days following the effective date of the chapter of the laws of two thousand thirteen, which amended this section. After such period, the information of those who had applied for or been granted a license prior to the preparation of the form for requesting an exception, pursuant to paragraph (b) of this subdivision, may be released only if such individuals did not file a request for such an exception during the first sixty days following such preparation; provided, however, that no information contained in an application for licensure or recertification shall be disclosed by an entity that has not completed processing any such requests received during such sixty days.

(g) If a request for an exception is determined to be null and void pursuant to paragraph (b) or (c) of this subdivision, an applicant may request review of such determination pursuant to article seventy-eight of the civil practice laws [law]* and rules. Such proceeding must commence within thirty days after service of the written notice containing the adverse determination. Notice of the right to commence such a petition, and the time period therefor, shall be included in the notice of the determination. Disclosure following such a petition shall not be made prior to the disposition of such review.

6. License: validity. Any license issued pursuant to this section shall be valid notwithstanding the provisions of any local law or ordinance. No license shall be transferable to any other person or premises. A license to carry or possess a pistol or revolver, not otherwise limited as to place or time of possession, shall be effective throughout the state, except that the same shall not be valid within the city of New York unless a special permit granting validity is issued by the police commissioner of that city. Such license to carry or possess shall be valid within the city of New York in the absence of a permit issued by the police commissioner of that city, provided that (a) the firearms covered by such license have been purchased from a licensed dealer within the city of New York and are being transported out of said city forthwith and immediately from said dealer by the licensee in a locked container during a continuous and uninterrupted trip; or provided that (b) the firearms covered by such license are being transported by the licensee in a locked container and the trip through the city of New York is continuous and uninterrupted; or provided that (c) the firearms covered by such license are carried by armored car security guards transporting money or other valuables, in, to, or from motor vehicles commonly known as armored cars, during the course of their employment; or provided that (d) the licensee is a retired police officer as police officer is defined pursuant to subdivision thirty-four of section 1.20 of the criminal procedure law or a retired federal law enforcement officer, as defined in section 2.15 of the criminal procedure law, who has been issued a license by an authorized licensing officer as defined in subdivision ten of section 265.00 of this chapter; provided, further, however, that if such license was not issued in the city of New York it must be marked "Retired Police Officer" or "Retired Federal Law Enforcement Officer", as the case may be, and, in the case of a retired officer the license shall be deemed to permit only police or federal law enforcement regulations weapons; or provided that (e) the licensee is a peace officer described in subdivision four of section 2.10 of the criminal procedure law and the license, if issued by other than the city of New York, is marked "New York State Tax Department Peace Officer" and in such case the exemption shall apply only to the firearm issued to such licensee by the department of taxation and finance. A license as gunsmith or dealer in firearms shall not be valid outside the city or county, as the case may be, where issued. Notwithstanding any inconsistent provision of state or local law or rule or regulation, the premises limitation set forth in any license to have and possess a pistol or revolver in the licensee's dwelling or place of business pursuant to paragraph (a) or (b) of subdivision two of this section shall not prevent the transport of such pistol or revolver directly to or from (i) another dwelling or place of business of the licensee where the licensee is authorized to have and possess such pistol or revolver, (ii) an indoor or outdoor shooting range that is authorized by law to operate as such, (iii) a shooting competition at which the licensee may possess such pistol or revolver consistent with the provisions of subdivision a of section 265.20 of this chapter or consistent with the law applicable at the place of such competition, or (iv) any other location where the licensee is lawfully authorized to have and possess such pistol or revolver; provided however, that during such transport to or from a location specified in clauses (i) through (iv) of this paragraph, the pistol or revolver shall be unloaded and carried in a locked container, and the ammunition therefor shall be carried separately; provided further, however, that a license to have and possess a pistol or revolver in the licensee's dwelling or place of business pursuant to paragraph (a) or (b) of subdivision

*The bracketed word has been inserted by the Publisher.

two of this section that is issued by a licensing officer other than the police commissioner of the city of New York shall not authorize transport of a pistol or revolver into the city of New York in the absence of written authorization to do so by the police commissioner of that city. The term "locked container" shall not include the glove compartment or console of a vehicle.

7. License: form. Any license issued pursuant to this section shall, except in the city of New York, be approved as to form by the superintendent of state police. A license to carry or possess a pistol or revolver shall have attached the licensee's photograph, and a coupon which shall be removed and retained by any person disposing of a firearm to the licensee. Such license shall specify the weapon covered by calibre, make, model, manufacturer's name and serial number, or if none, by any other distinguishing number or identification mark, and shall indicate whether issued to carry on the person or possess on the premises, and if on the premises shall also specify the place where the licensee shall possess the same. If such license is issued to an alien, or to a person not a citizen of and usually a resident in the state, the licensing officer shall state in the license the particular reason for the issuance and the names of the persons certifying to the good character of the applicant. Any license as gunsmith or dealer in firearms shall mention and describe the premises for which it is issued and shall be valid only for such premises.

8. License: exhibition and display. Every licensee while carrying a pistol or revolver shall have on his or her person a license to carry the same. Every person licensed to possess a pistol or revolver on particular premises shall have the license for the same on such premises. Upon demand, the license shall be exhibited for inspection to any peace officer, who is acting pursuant to his or her special duties, or police officer. A license as gunsmith or dealer in firearms shall be prominently displayed on the licensed premises. A gunsmith or dealer of firearms may conduct business temporarily at a location other than the location specified on the license if such temporary location is the location for a gun show or event sponsored by any national, state, or local organization, or any affiliate of any such organization devoted to the collection, competitive use or other sporting use of firearms. Any sale or transfer at a gun show must also comply with the provisions of article thirty-nine-DD of the general business law. Records of receipt and disposition of firearms transactions conducted at such temporary location shall include the location of the sale or other disposition and shall be entered in the permanent records of the gunsmith or dealer of firearms and retained on the location specified on the license. Nothing in this section shall authorize any licensee to conduct business from any motorized or towed vehicle. A separate fee shall not be required of a licensee with respect to business conducted under this subdivision. Any inspection or examination of inventory or records under this section at such temporary location shall be limited to inventory consisting of, or records related to, firearms held or disposed at such temporary locations. Failure of any licensee to so exhibit or display his or her license, as the case may be, shall be presumptive evidence that he or she is not duly licensed.

9. License: amendment. Elsewhere than in the city of New York, a person licensed to carry or possess a pistol or revolver may apply at any time to his or her licensing officer for amendment of his or her license to include one or more such weapons or to cancel weapons held under license. If granted, a record of the amendment describing the weapons involved shall be filed by the licensing officer in the executive department, division of state police, Albany. The superintendent of state police may authorize that such amendment be completed and transmitted to the state police in electronic form. Notification of any change of residence shall be made in writing by any licensee within ten days after such change occurs, and a record of such change shall be inscribed by such licensee on the reverse side of his or her license. Elsewhere than in the city of New York, and in the counties of Nassau and Suffolk, such notification shall be made to the executive department, division of state police, Albany, and in the city of New York to the police commissioner of that city, and in the county of Nassau to the police commissioner of that county, and in the county of Suffolk to the licensing officer of that county, who shall, within ten days after such notification shall be received by him or her, give notice in writing of such change to the executive department, division of state police, at Albany.

10. License: expiration, certification and renewal.

(a) Any license for gunsmith or dealer in firearms and, in the city of New York, any license to carry or possess a pistol or revolver, issued at any time pursuant to this section or prior to the first day of July, nineteen hundred sixty-three and not limited to expire on an earlier date fixed in the license, shall expire not more than three years after the date of issuance. In the counties of Nassau, Suffolk and Westchester, any license to carry or possess a pistol or revolver, issued at any time pursuant to this section or prior to the first day of July, nineteen hundred sixty-three and not limited to expire on an earlier date fixed in the license, shall expire not more than five years after the date of issuance; however, in the county of Westchester, any such license shall be certified prior to the first day of April, two thousand, in accordance with a schedule to be contained in regulations promulgated by the commissioner of the division of criminal justice services, and every such license shall be recertified every five years thereafter. For purposes of this section certification shall mean that the licensee shall provide to the licensing officer the following information only: current name, date of birth, current address, and the make, model, caliber and serial number of all firearms currently possessed. Such certification information shall be filed by the licensing officer in the same manner as an amendment. Elsewhere than in the city of New York and the counties of Nassau, Suffolk and Westchester, any license to carry or possess a pistol or revolver, issued at any time pursuant to this section or prior to the first day of July, nineteen hundred sixty-three and not previously revoked or cancelled, shall be in force and effect until revoked as herein provided. Any license not previously cancelled or revoked shall remain in full force and effect for thirty days beyond the stated expiration date on such license. Any application to renew a license that has not previously expired, been revoked or cancelled shall thereby extend the term of the license until disposition of the application by the licensing officer. In the case of a license for gunsmith or dealer in firearms, in counties having a population of less than two hundred thousand inhabitants, photographs and fingerprints shall be submitted on original applications and upon renewal thereafter only at six year intervals. Upon satisfactory proof that a currently valid original license has been despoiled, lost or otherwise removed from the possession of the licensee and upon application containing an additional photograph of the licensee, the licensing officer shall issue a duplicate license.

(b) All licensees shall be recertified to the division of state police every five years thereafter. Any license issued before the effective date of the chapter of the laws of two thousand thirteen which added this paragraph shall be recertified by the licensee on or before January thirty-first, two thousand eighteen, and not less than one year prior to such date, the state police shall send a notice to all license holders who have not recertified by such time. Such recertification shall be in a form as approved by the superintendent of state police, which shall request the license holder's name, date of birth, gender, race, residential address, social security number, firearms possessed by such license holder, email address at the option of the license holder and an affirmation that such license holder is not prohibited from possessing firearms. The form may be in an electronic form if so designated by the superintendent of state police. Failure to recertify shall act as a revocation of such license. If the New York state police discover as a result of the recertification process that a licensee failed to provide a change of address, the New York state police shall not require the licensing officer to revoke such license.

11. License: revocation and suspension.

(a) The conviction of a licensee anywhere of a felony or serious offense or a licensee at any time becoming ineligible to obtain a license under this section shall operate as a revocation of the license. A license may be revoked or suspended as provided for in section 530.14 of the criminal procedure law or section eight hundred forty-two-a of the family court act. Except for a license issued pursuant to section 400.01 of this article, a license may be revoked and cancelled at any time in the city of New York, and in the counties of Nassau and Suffolk, by the licensing officer, and elsewhere than in the city of New York by any judge or justice of a court of record; a license issued pursuant to section 400.01 of this article may be revoked and cancelled at any time by the licensing officer or any judge or justice of a court of record. The official revoking a license shall give written notice thereof without unnecessary delay to the executive department, division of state police, Albany, and shall also notify immediately the duly constituted police authorities of the locality.

(b) Whenever the director of community services or his or her designee makes a report pursuant to section 9.46 of the mental hygiene law, the division of criminal justice services shall convey such information, whenever it determines that the person named in the report possesses a license issued pursuant to this section, to the appropriate licensing official, who shall issue an order suspending or revoking such license.

(c) In any instance in which a person's license is suspended or revoked under paragraph (a) or (b) of this subdivision, such person shall surrender such license to the appropriate licensing official and any and all firearms, rifles, or shotguns owned or possessed by such person shall be surrendered to an appropriate law enforcement agency as provided in subparagraph (f) of paragraph one of subdivision a of section 265.20 of this chapter. In the event such license, firearm, shotgun, or rifle is not surrendered, such items shall be removed and declared a nuisance and any police officer or peace officer acting pursuant to his or her special duties is authorized to remove any and all such weapons.

12. Records required of gunsmiths and dealers in firearms. Any person licensed as gunsmith or dealer in firearms shall keep a record book approved as to form, except in the city of New York, by the superintendent of state police. In the record book shall be entered at the time of every transaction involving a firearm the date, name, age, occupation and residence of any person from whom a firearm is received or to whom a firearm is delivered, and the calibre, make, model, manufacturer's name and serial number, or if none, any other distinguishing number or identification mark on such firearm. Before delivering a firearm to any person, the licensee shall require him to produce either a license valid under this section to carry or possess the same, or proof of lawful authority as an exempt person pursuant to section 265.20 of this chapter and either (a) the National Instant Criminal Background Check System (NICS) or its successor has issued a "proceed" response to the licensee, or (b) thirty calendar days have elapsed since the date the licensee contacted NICS to initiate a national instant criminal background check and NICS has not notified the licensee that the transfer of the firearm to such person should be denied. In addition, before delivering a firearm to a peace officer, the licensee shall verify that person's status as a peace officer with the division of state police. After completing the foregoing, the licensee shall remove and retain the attached coupon and enter in the record book the date of such license, number, if any, and name of the licensing officer, in the case of the holder of a license to carry or possess, or the shield or other number, if any, assignment and department, unit or agency, in the case of an exempt person. The original transaction report shall be forwarded to the division of state police within ten days of delivering a firearm to any person, and a duplicate copy shall be kept by the licensee. The superintendent of state police may designate that such record shall be completed and transmitted in electronic form. A dealer may be granted a waiver from transmitting such records in electronic form if the superintendent determines that such dealer is incapable of such transmission due to technological limitations that are not reasonably within the control of the dealer, or other exceptional circumstances demonstrated by the dealer, pursuant to a process established in regulation, and at the discretion of the superintendent. Records assembled or collected for purposes of inclusion in the database created pursuant to section 400.02 of this article shall not be subject to disclosure pursuant to article six of the public officers law. The record book shall be maintained on the premises mentioned and described in the license and shall be open at all reasonable hours for inspection by any peace officer, acting pursuant to his special duties, or police officer. In the event of cancellation or revocation of the license for gunsmith or dealer in firearms, or discontinuance of business by a licensee, such record book shall be immediately surrendered to the licensing officer in the city of New York, and in the counties of Nassau and Suffolk, and elsewhere in the state to the executive department, division of state police.

12-a. State police regulations applicable to licensed gunsmiths engaged in the business of assembling or manufacturing firearms. The superintendent of state police is hereby authorized to issue such rules and regulations as he deems reasonably necessary to prevent the manufacture and assembly of unsafe firearms in the state. Such rules and regulations shall establish safety standards in regard to the manufacture and assembly of firearms in the state, including specifications as to materials and parts used, the proper storage and shipment of firearms, and minimum standards of quality control. Regulations issued by the state police pursuant to this subdivision shall apply to any person licensed as a gunsmith under this section engaged in the business of manufacturing or assembling firearms, and any violation thereof shall subject the licensee to revocation of license pursuant to subdivision eleven of this section.

12-b. [None]

12-c. Firearms records.

(a) Every employee of a state or local agency, unit of local government, state or local commission, or public or private organization who possesses a firearm or machine-gun under an exemption to the licensing requirements under this chapter, shall promptly report in writing to his employer the make, model, calibre and serial number of each such firearm or machine-gun. Thereafter, within ten days of the acquisition or disposition of any such weapon, he shall furnish such information to his employer, including the name and address of the person from whom the weapon was acquired or to whom it was disposed.

(b) Every head of a state or local agency, unit of local government, state or local commission, public authority or public or private organization to whom an employee has submitted a report pursuant to paragraph (a) of this subdivision shall promptly forward such report to the superintendent of state police.

(c) Every head of a state or local agency, unit of local government, state or local commission, public authority, or any other agency, firm or corporation that employs persons who may lawfully possess firearms or machine-guns without the requirement of a license therefor, or that employs persons licensed to possess firearms or machine-guns, shall promptly report to the superintendent of state police, in the manner prescribed by him, the make, model, calibre and serial number of every firearm or machine-gun possessed by it on the effective date of this act for the use of such employees or for any other use. Thereafter, within ten days of the acquisition or disposition of any such weapon, such head shall report such information to the superintendent of the state police, including the name and address of the person from whom the weapon was acquired or to whom it was disposed.

13. Expenses. The expense of providing a licensing officer with blank applications, licenses and record books for carrying out the provisions of this section shall be a charge against the county, and in the city of New York against the city.

14. Fees. In the city of New York and the county of Nassau, the annual license fee shall be twenty-five dollars for gunsmiths and fifty dollars for dealers in firearms. In such city, the city council and in the county of Nassau the Board of Supervisors shall fix the fee to be charged for a license to carry or possess a pistol or revolver and provide for the disposition of such fees. Elsewhere in the state, the licensing officer shall collect and pay into the county treasury the following fees: for each license to carry or possess a pistol or revolver, not less than three dollars nor more than ten dollars as may be determined by the legislative body of the county; for each amendment thereto, three dollars, and five dollars in the county of Suffolk; and for each license issued to a gunsmith or dealer in firearms, ten dollars. The fee for a duplicate license shall be five dollars. The fee for processing a license transfer between counties shall be five dollars. The fee for processing a license or renewal thereof for a qualified retired police officer as defined under subdivision thirty-four of section 1.20 of the criminal procedure law, or a qualified retired sheriff, undersheriff, or deputy sheriff of the city of New York as defined under subdivision two of section 2.10 of the criminal procedure law, or a qualified retired bridge and tunnel officer, sergeant or lieutenant of the triborough bridge and tunnel authority as defined under subdivision twenty of section 2.10 of the criminal procedure law, or a qualified retired uniformed court officer in the unified court system, or a qualified retired court clerk in the unified court system in the first and second judicial departments, as defined in paragraphs a and b of subdivision twenty-one of section 2.10 of the criminal procedure law or a retired correction officer as defined in subdivision twenty-five of section 2.10 of the criminal procedure law shall be waived in all counties throughout the state.

15. Any violation by any person of any provision of this section is a class A misdemeanor.

16. Unlawful disposal. No person shall except as otherwise authorized pursuant to law dispose of any firearm unless he is licensed as gunsmith or dealer in firearms.

16-a. Registration.

(a) An owner of a weapon defined in paragraph (e) or (f) of subdivision twenty-two of section 265.00 of this chapter, possessed before the date of the effective date of the chapter of the laws of two thousand thirteen which added this paragraph, must make an application to register such weapon with the superintendent of state police, in the manner provided by the superintendent, or by amending a license issued pursuant to this section within one year of the effective date of this subdivision except any weapon defined under subparagraph (vi) of paragraph (g) of subdivision twenty-two of section 265.00 of this chapter transferred into the state may be registered at any time, provided such weapons are registered within thirty days of their transfer into the state. Registration information shall include the registrant's name, date of birth, gender, race, residential address, social security number and a description of each weapon being registered. A registration of any weapon defined under subparagraph (vi) of paragraph (g) of subdivision twenty-two of section 265.00 or a feeding device as defined under subdivision twenty-three of section 265.00 of this chapter shall be transferable, provided that the seller notifies the state police within seventy-two hours of the transfer and the buyer provides the state police with information sufficient to constitute a registration under this section. Such registration shall not be valid if such registrant is prohibited or becomes prohibited from possessing a firearm pursuant to state or federal law. The superintendent shall determine whether such registrant is prohibited from possessing a firearm under state or federal law. Such check shall be limited to determining whether the factors in 18 USC 922 (g) apply or whether a registrant has been convicted of a serious offense as defined in subdivision sixteen-b of section 265.00 of this chapter, so as to prohibit such registrant from possessing a firearm, and whether a report has been issued pursuant to section 9.46 of the mental hygiene law. All registrants shall recertify to the division of state police every five years thereafter. Failure to recertify shall result in a revocation of such registration.

(a-1) Notwithstanding any inconsistent provisions of paragraph (a) of this subdivision, an owner of an assault weapon as defined in subdivision twenty-two of section 265.00 of this chapter, who is a qualified retired New York or federal law enforcement officer as defined in subdivision twenty-five of section 265.00 of this chapter, where such weapon was issued to or purchased by such officer prior to retirement and in the course of his or her official duties, and for which such officer was qualified by the agency that employed such officer within twelve months prior to his or her retirement, must register such weapon within sixty days of retirement.

(b) The superintendent of state police shall create and maintain an internet website to educate the public as to which semiautomatic rifle, semiautomatic shotgun or semiautomatic pistol or weapon that are illegal as a result of the enactment of the chapter of the laws of two thousand thirteen which added this paragraph, as well as such assault weapons which are illegal pursuant to article two hundred sixty-five of this chapter. Such website shall contain information to assist the public in recognizing the relevant features proscribed by such article two hundred sixty-five, as well as which make and model of weapons that require registration.

(c) A person who knowingly fails to apply to register such weapon, as required by this section, within one year of the effective date of the chapter of the laws of two thousand thirteen which added this paragraph shall be guilty of a class A misdemeanor and such person who unknowingly fails to validly register such weapon within such one year period shall be given a warning by an appropriate law enforcement authority about such failure and given thirty days in which to apply to register such weapon or to surrender it. A failure to apply or surrender such weapon within such thirty-day period shall result in such weapon being removed by an appropriate law enforcement authority and declared a nuisance.

16-b. The cost of the software, programming and interface required to transmit any record that must be electronically transmitted by the dealer or licensing officer to the division of state police pursuant to this chapter shall be borne by the state.

17. Applicability of section. The provisions of article two hundred sixty-five of this chapter relating to illegal possession of a firearm, shall not apply to an offense which also constitutes a violation of this section by a person holding an otherwise valid license under the provisions of this section and such offense shall only be punishable as a class A misdemeanor pursuant to this section. In addition, the provisions of such article two

hundred sixty-five of this chapter shall not apply to the possession of a firearm in a place not authorized by law, by a person who holds an otherwise valid license or possession of a firearm by a person within a one year period after the stated expiration date of an otherwise valid license which has not been previously cancelled or revoked shall only be punishable as a class A misdemeanor pursuant to this section.

18. Notice. Upon the issuance of a license, the licensing officer shall issue therewith the following notice in conspicuous and legible twenty-four point type on eight and one-half inches by eleven inches paper stating in bold print the following:

WARNING: RESPONSIBLE FIREARM STORAGE IS THE LAW IN NEW YORK STATE. FIREARMS MUST EITHER BE STORED WITH A GUN LOCKING DEVICE OR IN A SAFE STORAGE DEPOSITORY OR NOT BE LEFT OUTSIDE THE IMMEDIATE POSSESSION AND CONTROL OF THE OWNER OR OTHER LAWFUL POSSESSOR IF A CHILD RESIDES IN THE HOME OR IS PRESENT, OR IF THE OWNER OR POSSESSOR RESIDES WITH A PERSON PROHIBITED FROM POSSESSING A FIREARM UNDER STATE OR FEDERAL LAW. FIREARMS SHOULD BE STORED UNLOADED AND LOCKED IN A LOCATION SEPARATE FROM AMMUNITION. LEAVING FIREARMS ACCESSIBLE TO A CHILD OR OTHER PROHIBITED PERSON MAY SUBJECT YOU TO IMPRISONMENT, FINE, OR BOTH.

Nothing in this subdivision shall be deemed to affect, impair or supersede any special or local law relating to providing notice regarding the safe storage of rifles, shotguns or firearms.

HISTORY:

Add, L 1965, ch 1030, § 1, eff Sept 1, 1967, with substance derived from § 1903; amd, L 1967, ch 791, § 49; L 1971, ch 796; L 1971, ch 1097, §§ 82, 83; L 1973, ch 172; L 1973, ch 546, § 1; L 1973, ch 593, § 1; L 1974, ch 1041, §§ 10, 11; L 1974, ch 1042, § 2, eff Sept 1, 1974; L 1976, ch 584, § 1; L 1977, ch 480, § 1; L 1980, ch 233, §§ 15–17, eff Aug 12, 1980; L 1980, ch 843, §§ 47–50, eff Sept 1, 1980; L 1981, ch 175, § 5; L 1982, ch 71, § 1; L 1984, ch 739, § 1; L 1985, ch 778, § 2, eff Nov 1, 1985; L 1986, ch 539, § 1; L 1988, ch 437, § 1; L 1990, ch 707, § 1; L 1991, ch 414, § 1; L 1992, ch 320, § 1; L 1993, ch 448, §§ 1, 2, eff Nov 1, 1993; L 1993, ch 449, § 1, eff Nov 1, 1993; L 1993, ch 498, § 3; L 1994, ch 332, § 1, eff Nov 1, 1994; L 1994, ch 636, § 1; L 1994, ch 637, § 1, eff Aug 2, 1994; L 1995, ch 236, § 1; L 1995, ch 370, § 1; L 1996, ch 644, § 6; L 1997, ch 446, §§ 3–6; L 1997, ch 447, § 2, eff Aug 25, 1997; L 1998, ch 378, § 8; L 1999, ch 210, §§ 5, 6, eff Nov 1, 1999; L 2000, ch 189, §§ 18–20, eff Nov 1, 2000; L 2002, ch 318, § 5, eff Aug 6, 2002; L 2005, ch 195, § 1, eff July 12, 2005; L 2005, ch 331, § 1, eff July 26, 2005; L 2013, ch 1, § 48; L 2013, ch 98, § 3, eff April 15, 2013; L 2018, ch 60, § 6, eff June 11, 2018; L 2019, ch 104, § 1, eff July 16, 2019; L 2019, ch 129, § 1, eff Sept 12, 2019; L 2019, ch 135, § 3, eff Sept 28, 2019; L 2019, ch 242, § 1, eff Nov 2, 2019; L 2019, ch 244, § 1, eff Sept 3, 2019; L 2020, ch 55, § 2 (Part N), eff April 3, 2021.

Title Y
Hate Crimes Act of 2000

Article 485 Hate Crimes

Article 485
Hate Crimes

§ 485.00. Legislative findings. [Effective until November 1, 2020]

The legislature finds and determines as follows: criminal acts involving violence, intimidation and destruction of property based upon bias and prejudice have become more prevalent in New York state in recent years. The intolerable truth is that in these crimes, commonly and justly referred to as "hate crimes", victims are intentionally selected, in whole or in part, because of their race, color, national origin, ancestry, gender, gender identity or expression, religion, religious practice, age, disability or sexual orientation. Hate crimes do more than threaten the safety and welfare of all citizens. They inflict on victims incalculable physical and emotional damage and tear at the very fabric of free society. Crimes motivated by invidious hatred toward particular groups not only harm individual victims but send a powerful message of intolerance and discrimination to all members of the group to which the victim belongs. Hate crimes can and do intimidate and disrupt entire communities and vitiate the civility that is essential to healthy democratic processes. In a democratic society, citizens cannot be required to approve of the beliefs and practices of others, but must never commit criminal acts on account of them. Current law does not adequately recognize the harm to public order and individual safety that hate crimes cause. Therefore, our laws must be strengthened to provide clear recognition of the gravity of hate crimes and the compelling importance of preventing their recurrence.

Accordingly, the legislature finds and declares that hate crimes should be prosecuted and punished with appropriate severity.

HISTORY:

Add, L 2000, ch 107, § 2, eff Oct 8, 2000;
amd, L 2019, ch 8, § 19, eff Nov 1, 2019.

§ 485.00. Legislative findings. [Effective November 1, 2020]

The legislature finds and determines as follows: criminal acts involving violence, intimidation and destruction of property based upon bias and prejudice have become more prevalent in New York state in recent years. The intolerable truth is that in these crimes, commonly and justly referred to as "hate crimes", victims are intentionally selected, in whole or in part, because of their race, color, national origin, ancestry, gender, gender identity or expression, religion, religious practice, age, disability or sexual orientation. Hate crimes do more than threaten the safety and welfare of all citizens. They inflict on victims incalculable physical and emotional damage and tear at the very fabric of free society. Crimes motivated by invidious hatred toward particular groups not only harm individual victims but send a powerful message of intolerance and discrimination to all members of the group to which the victim belongs. Hate crimes can and do intimidate and disrupt entire communities and vitiate the civility that is essential to healthy democratic processes. In a democratic society, citizens cannot be required to approve of the beliefs and practices of others, but must never commit criminal acts on account of them. However, these criminal acts do occur and are occurring more and more frequently. Quite often, these crimes of hate are also acts of terror. The recent attacks in Monsey, New York as well as the shootings in El Paso, Texas; Pittsburgh, Pennsylvania; Sutherland Springs, Texas; Orlando, Florida; and Charleston, South Carolina illustrate that mass killings are often apolitical, motivated by the hatred of a specific group coupled with a desire to inflict mass casualties. The current law emphasizes the political motivation of an act over its catastrophic effect and does not adequately recognize the harm to public order and individual safety that hate crimes cause. Therefore, our laws must be strengthened to provide clear recognition of the gravity of hate crimes and the compelling importance of preventing their recurrence.

Accordingly, the legislature finds and declares that hate crimes should be prosecuted and punished with appropriate severity.

HISTORY:

Add, L 2000, ch 107, § 2, eff Oct 8, 2000; amd, L 2019, ch 8, § 19, eff Nov 1, 2019; L 2020, ch 55, § 2 (Part R), eff Nov 1, 2020.

§ 485.05. Hate crimes [Effective until November 1, 2020]

1. A person commits a hate crime when he or she commits a specified offense and either:

(a) intentionally selects the person against whom the offense is committed or intended to be committed in whole or in substantial part because of a belief or perception regarding the race, color, national origin, ancestry, gender, gender identity or expression, religion, religious practice, age, disability or sexual orientation of a person, regardless of whether the belief or perception is correct; or

(b) intentionally commits the act or acts constituting the offense in whole or in substantial part because of a belief or perception regarding the race, color, national origin, ancestry, gender, gender identity or expression, religion, religious practice, age, disability or sexual orientation of a person, regardless of whether the belief or perception is correct.

2. Proof of race, color, national origin, ancestry, gender, gender identity or expression, religion, religious practice, age, disability or sexual orientation of the defendant, the victim or of both the defendant and the victim does not, by itself, constitute legally sufficient evidence satisfying the people's burden under paragraph (a) or (b) of subdivision one of this section.

3. A "specified offense" is an offense defined by any of the following provisions of this chapter: section 120.00 (assault in the third degree); section 120.05 (assault in the second degree); section 120.10 (assault in the first degree); section 120.12 (aggravated assault upon a person less than eleven years old); section 120.13 (menacing in the first degree); section 120.14 (menacing in the second degree); section 120.15 (menacing in the third degree); section 120.20 (reckless endangerment in the second degree); section 120.25 (reckless endangerment in the first degree); section 121.12 (strangulation in the second degree); section 121.13 (strangulation in the first degree); subdivision one of section 125.15 (manslaughter in the second degree); subdivision one, two or four of section 125.20 (manslaughter in the first degree); section 125.25 (murder in the second degree); section 120.45 (stalking in the fourth degree); section 120.50 (stalking in the third degree); section 120.55 (stalking in the second degree); section 120.60 (stalking in the first degree); subdivision one of section 130.35 (rape in the first degree); subdivision one of section 130.50 (criminal sexual act in the first degree); subdivision one of section 130.65 (sexual abuse in the first degree); paragraph (a) of subdivision one of section 130.67 (aggravated sexual abuse in the second degree); paragraph (a) of subdivision one of section 130.70 (aggravated sexual abuse in the first degree); section 135.05 (unlawful imprisonment in the second degree); section 135.10 (unlawful imprisonment in the first degree); section 135.20 (kidnapping in the second degree); section 135.25 (kidnapping in the first degree); section 135.60 (coercion in the third degree); section 135.61 (coercion in the second degree); section 135.65 (coercion in the first degree); section 140.10 (criminal trespass in the third degree); section 140.15 (criminal trespass in the second degree); section 140.17 (criminal trespass in the first degree); section 140.20 (burglary in the third degree); section 140.25 (burglary in the second degree); section 140.30 (burglary in the first degree); section 145.00 (criminal mischief in the fourth degree); section 145.05 (criminal mischief in the third degree); section 145.10 (criminal mischief in the second degree); section 145.12 (criminal mischief in the first degree); section 150.05 (arson in the fourth degree); section 150.10 (arson in the third degree); section 150.15 (arson in the second degree); section 150.20 (arson in the first degree); section 155.25 (petit larceny); section 155.30 (grand larceny in the fourth degree); section 155.35 (grand larceny in the third degree); section 155.40 (grand larceny in the second degree); section 155.42 (grand larceny in the first degree); section 160.05 (robbery in the third degree); section 160.10 (robbery in the second degree); section 160.15 (robbery in the first degree); section 240.25 (harassment in the first degree); subdivision one, two or four of section 240.30 (aggravated harassment in the second degree); or any attempt or conspiracy to commit any of the foregoing offenses.

4. For purposes of this section:

(a) the term "age" means sixty years old or more;

(b) the term "disability" means a physical or mental impairment that substantially limits a major life activity;

(c) the term "gender identity or expression" means a person's actual or perceived gender-related identity, appearance, behavior, expression, or other gender-related characteristic regardless of the sex assigned to that person at birth, including, but not limited to, the status of being transgender.

HISTORY:

Add, L 2000, ch 107, § 2, eff Oct 8, 2000; amd, L 2003, ch 264, § 34, eff Nov 1, 2003; L 2010, ch 405, § 13, eff Nov 11, 2010; L 2018, ch 55, § 9 (Part NN), eff Nov 1, 2018; L 2019, ch 8, § 20, eff Nov 1, 2019.

§ 485.05. Hate crimes [Effective November 1, 2020]

1. A person commits a hate crime when he or she commits a specified offense and either:

(a) intentionally selects the person against whom the offense is committed or intended to be committed in whole or in substantial part because of a belief or perception regarding the race, color, national origin, ancestry, gender, gender identity or expression, religion, religious practice, age, disability or sexual orientation of a person, regardless of whether the belief or perception is correct, or

(b) intentionally commits the act or acts constituting the offense in whole or in substantial part because of a belief or perception regarding the race, color, national origin, ancestry, gender, gender identity or expression, religion, religious practice, age, disability or sexual orientation of a person, regardless of whether the belief or perception is correct.

2. Proof of race, color, national origin, ancestry, gender, gender identity or expression, religion, religious practice, age, disability or sexual orientation of the defendant, the victim or of both the defendant and the victim does not, by itself, constitute legally sufficient evidence satisfying the people's burden under paragraph (a) or (b) of subdivision one of this section.

3. A "specified offense" is an offense defined by any of the following provisions of this chapter: section 120.00 (assault in the third degree); section 120.05 (assault in the second degree); section 120.10 (assault in the first degree); section 120.12 (aggravated assault upon a person less than eleven years old); section 120.13 (menacing in the first degree); section 120.14 (menacing in the second degree); section 120.15 (menacing in the third degree); section 120.20 (reckless endangerment in the second degree); section 120.25 (reckless endangerment in the first degree); section 121.12 (strangulation in the second degree); section 121.13 (strangulation in the first degree); subdivision one of section 125.15 (manslaughter in the second degree); subdivision one, two or four of section 125.20 (manslaughter in the first degree); section 125.25 (murder in the second degree); section 120.45 (stalking in the fourth degree); section 120.50 (stalking in the third degree); section 120.55 (stalking in the second degree); section 120.60 (stalking in the first degree); subdivision one of section 130.35 (rape in the first degree); subdivision one of section 130.50 (criminal sexual act in the first degree); subdivision one of section 130.65 (sexual abuse in the first degree); paragraph (a) of subdivision one of section 130.67 (aggravated sexual abuse in the second degree); paragraph (a) of subdivision one of section 130.70 (aggravated sexual abuse in the first degree); section 135.05 (unlawful imprisonment in the second degree); section 135.10 (unlawful imprisonment in the first degree); section 135.20 (kidnapping in the second degree); section 135.25 (kidnapping in the first degree); section 135.60 (coercion in the third degree); section 135.61 (coercion in the second degree); section 135.65 (coercion in the first degree); section 140.10 (criminal trespass in the third degree); section 140.15 (criminal trespass in the second degree); section 140.17 (criminal trespass in the first degree); section 140.20 (burglary in the third degree); section 140.25 (burglary in the second degree); section 140.30 (burglary in the first degree); section 145.00 (criminal mischief in the fourth degree); section 145.05 (criminal mischief in the third degree); section 145.10 (criminal mischief in the second degree); section 145.12 (criminal mischief in the first degree); section 150.05 (arson in the fourth degree); section 150.10 (arson in the third degree); section 150.15 (arson in the second degree); section 150.20 (arson in the first degree); section 155.25 (petit larceny); section 155.30 (grand larceny in the fourth degree); section 155.35 (grand larceny in the third degree); section 155.40 (grand larceny in the second degree); section 155.42 (grand larceny in the first degree); section 160.05 (robbery in the third degree); section 160.10 (robbery in the second degree); section 160.15 (robbery in the first degree); section 240.25 (harassment in the first degree); subdivision one, two or four of section 240.30 (aggravated harassment in the second degree); section 490.10 (soliciting or providing support for an act of terrorism in the second degree); section 490.15 (soliciting or providing support for an act of terrorism in the first degree); section 490.20 (making a terroristic threat); section 490.25 (crime of terrorism); section 490.30 (hindering prosecution of terrorism in the second degree); section 490.35 (hindering prosecution of terrorism in the first degree); section 490.37 (criminal possession of a chemical weapon or biological weapon in the third degree); section 490.40 (criminal possession of a chemical weapon or biological weapon in the second degree); section 490.45 (criminal possession of a chemical weapon or biological weapon in the first degree); section 490.47 (criminal use of a chemical weapon or biological weapon in the third degree); section 490.50 (criminal use of a chemical weapon or biological weapon in

the second degree); section 490.55 (criminal use of a chemical weapon or biological weapon in the first degree); or any attempt or conspiracy to commit any of the foregoing offenses.

4. For purposes of this section:

(a) the term "age" means sixty years old or more;

(b) the term "disability" means a physical or mental impairment that substantially limits a major life activity;

(c) the term "gender identity or expression" means a person's actual or perceived gender-related identity, appearance, behavior, expression, or other gender-related characteristic regardless of the sex assigned to that person at birth, including, but not limited to, the status of being transgender.

HISTORY:

Add, L 2000, ch 107, § 2, eff Oct 8, 2000; amd, L 2003, ch 264, § 34, eff Nov 1, 2003; L 2010, ch 405, § 13, eff Nov 11, 2010; L 2018, ch 55, § 9 (Part NN), eff Nov 1, 2018; L 2019, ch 8, § 20, eff Nov 1, 2019; L 2020, ch 55, § 3 (Part R), eff Nov 1, 2020.

Title Y-1
[Terrorism][*]

Article 490 Terrorism

Article 490
Terrorism

§ 490.27. Domestic act of terrorism motivated by hate in the second degree. [Effective November 1, 2020]

A person is guilty of the crime of domestic act of terrorism motivated by hate in the second degree when, acting with the intent to cause the death of, or serious physical injury to, five or more other persons, in whole or in substantial part because of the perceived race, color, national origin, ancestry, gender, gender identity or expression, religion, religious practice, age, disability, or sexual orientation of such other persons, regardless of whether that belief or perception is correct, he or she, as part of the same criminal transaction, attempts to cause the death of, or serious physical injury to, such five or more persons, provided that the victims are not participants in the criminal transaction.

Domestic act of terrorism motivated by hate in the second degree is a class A-I felony.

HISTORY:

L 2020, ch 55, § 4 (Part R), eff Nov 1, 2020.

§ 490.28. Domestic act of terrorism motivated by hate in the first degree. [Effective November 1, 2020]

A person is guilty of the crime of domestic act of terrorism motivated by hate in the first degree when, acting with the intent to cause the death of, or serious physical injury to, five or more other persons, in whole or in substantial part because of the perceived race, color, national origin, ancestry, gender, gender identity or expression, religion, religious practice, age, disability, or sexual orientation of such other person or persons, regardless of whether that belief or perception is correct, he or she, as part of the same criminal transaction:

[*]The bracketed word has been inserted by the Publisher.

1. causes the death of at least one other person, provided that the victim or victims are not a participant in the criminal transaction; and

2. causes or attempts to cause the death of four or more additional other persons, provided that the victims are not a participant in the criminal transaction; and

3. the defendant was more than eighteen years old at the time of the commission of the crime.

Domestic act of terrorism motivated by hate in the first degree is a class A-I felony.

Notwithstanding any other provision of law, when a person is convicted of domestic act of terrorism motivated by hate in the first degree, the sentence shall be life imprisonment without parole.

HISTORY:

L 2020, ch 55, § 4 (Part R), eff Nov 1, 2020.

CRIMINAL PROCEDURE LAW

Part ONE
General Provisions

Title A
Short Title, Applicability and Definitions

Article 1
Short Title, Applicability and Definitions

§ 1.20. Definitions of terms of general use in this chapter.

Except where different meanings are expressly specified in subsequent provisions of this chapter, the term definitions contained in section 10.00 of the penal law are applicable to this chapter, and, in addition, the following terms have the following meanings:

1. "Accusatory instrument" means: (a) an indictment, an indictment ordered reduced pursuant to subdivision one-a of section 210.20 of this chapter, an information, a simplified information, a prosecutor's information, a superior court information, a misdemeanor complaint or a felony complaint. Every accusatory instrument, regardless of the person designated therein as accuser, constitutes an accusation on behalf of the state as plaintiff and must be entitled "the people of the state of New York" against a designated person, known as the defendant; and

(b) an appearance ticket issued for a parking infraction when (i) such ticket is based on personal knowledge or information and belief of the police officer or other public servant who issues the ticket, (ii) the police officer or other public servant who issues such ticket verifies that false statements made therein are punishable as a class A misdemeanor, (iii) the infraction or infractions contained therein are stated in detail and not in conclusory terms so as to provide the defendant with sufficient notice including, but not limited, to the applicable provision of law allegedly violated, and the date, time and particular place of the alleged infraction, and (iv) such ticket contains: (1) the license plate designation of the ticketed vehicle, (2) the license plate type of the ticketed vehicle, (3) the expiration of the ticketed vehicle's registration, (4) the make or model of the ticketed vehicle, and (5) the body type of the ticketed vehicle, provided, however, that where the plate type or the expiration date are not shown on either the registration plates or sticker of a vehicle or where the registration sticker is covered, faded, defaced or mutilated so that it is unreadable, the plate type or the expiration date may be omitted, provided, further, however, that such condition must be so described and inserted on the instrument.

2. "Local criminal court accusatory instrument" means any accusatory instrument other than an indictment or a superior court information.

3. "Indictment" means a written accusation by a grand jury, more fully defined and described in article two hundred, filed with a superior court, which charges one or

more defendants with the commission of one or more offenses, at least one of which is a crime, and which serves as a basis for prosecution thereof.

3-a. "Superior court information" means a written accusation by a district attorney more fully defined and described in articles one hundred ninety-five and two hundred, filed with a superior court pursuant to article one hundred ninety-five, which charges one or more defendants with the commission of one or more offenses, at least one of which is a crime, and which serves as a basis for prosecution thereof.

4. "Information" means a verified written accusation by a person, more fully defined and described in article one hundred, filed with a local criminal court, which charges one or more defendants with the commission of one or more offenses, none of which is a felony, and which may serve both to commence a criminal action and as a basis for prosecution thereof.

5. [There are two subdivisions 5] "Simplified traffic information" means a written accusation, more fully defined and described in article one hundred, by a police officer or other public servant authorized by law to issue same, filed with a local criminal court, which, being in a brief or simplified form prescribed by the commissioner of motor vehicles, charges a person with one or more traffic infractions or misdemeanors relating to traffic, and which may serve both to commence a criminal action for such offense and as a basis for prosecution thereof.

5. [There are two subdivisions 5]

(a) "Simplified information" means a simplified traffic information, a simplified parks information, or a simplified environmental conservation information.

(b) "Simplified traffic information" means a written accusation by a police officer, or other public servant authorized by law to issue same, more fully defined and described in article one hundred, filed with a local criminal court, which, being in a brief or simplified form prescribed by the commissioner of motor vehicles, charges a person with one or more traffic infractions or misdemeanors relating to traffic, and which may serve both to commence a criminal action for such offense and as a basis for prosecution thereof.

(c) "Simplified parks information" means a written accusation by a police officer, or other public servant authorized by law to issue same, filed with a local criminal court, which, being in a brief or simplified form prescribed by the commissioner of parks and recreation, charges a person with one or more offenses, other than a felony, for which a uniform simplified parks information may be issued pursuant to the parks and recreation law and the navigation law, and which may serve both to commence a criminal action for such offense and as a basis for prosecution thereof.

(d) "Simplified environmental conservation information" means a written accusation by a police officer, or other public servant authorized by law to issue same, filed with a local criminal court, which being in a brief or simplified form prescribed by the commissioner of environmental conservation, charges a person with one or more offenses, other than a felony, for which a uniform simplified environmental conservation simplified* information may be issued pursuant to the environmental conservation law, and which may serve both to commence a criminal action for such offense and as a basis for prosecution thereof.

6. "Prosecutor's information" means a written accusation by a district attorney, more fully defined and described in article one hundred, filed with a local criminal court, which charges one or more defendants with the commission of one or more offenses, none of which is a felony, and which serves as a basis for prosecution thereof.

7. "Misdemeanor complaint" means a verified written accusation by a person, more fully defined and described in article one hundred, filed with a local criminal court, which charges one or more defendants with the commission of one or more offenses, at least one of which is a misdemeanor and none of which is a felony, and which serves to commence a criminal action but which may not, except upon the defendant's consent, serve as a basis for prosecution of the offenses charged therein.

8. "Felony complaint" means a verified written accusation by a person, more fully defined and described in article one hundred, filed with a local criminal court, which charges one or more defendants with the commission of one or more felonies and which serves to commence a criminal action but not as a basis for prosecution thereof.

*So in original.

9. "Arraignment" means the occasion upon which a defendant against whom an accusatory instrument has been filed appears before the court in which the criminal action is pending for the purpose of having such court acquire and exercise control over his person with respect to such accusatory instrument and of setting the course of further proceedings in the action.

10. "Plea," in addition to its ordinary meaning as prescribed in sections 220.10 and 340.20, means, where appropriate, the occasion upon which a defendant enters such a plea to an accusatory instrument.

11. "Trial." A jury trial commences with the selection of the jury and includes all further proceedings through the rendition of a verdict. A non-jury trial commences with the first opening address, if there be any, and, if not, when the first witness is sworn, and includes all further proceedings through the rendition of a verdict.

12. "Verdict" means the announcement by a jury in the case of a jury trial, or by the court in the case of a non-jury trial, of its decision upon the defendant's guilt or innocence of the charges submitted to or considered by it.

13. "Conviction" means the entry of a plea of guilty to, or a verdict of guilty upon, an accusatory instrument other than a felony complaint, or to one or more counts of such instrument.

14. "Sentence" means the imposition and entry of sentence upon a conviction.

15. "Judgment." A judgment is comprised of a conviction and the sentence imposed thereon and is completed by imposition and entry of the sentence.

16. "Criminal action." A criminal action (a) commences with the filing of an accusatory instrument against a defendant in a criminal court, as specified in subdivision seventeen; (b) includes the filing of all further accusatory instruments directly derived from the initial one, and all proceedings, orders and motions conducted or made by a criminal court in the course of disposing of any such accusatory instrument, or which, regardless of the court in which they occurred or were made, could properly be considered as a part of the record of the case by an appellate court upon an appeal from a judgment of conviction; and (c) terminates with the imposition of sentence or some other final disposition in a criminal court of the last accusatory instrument filed in the case.

17. "Commencement of criminal action." A criminal action is commenced by the filing of an accusatory instrument against a defendant in a criminal court, and, if more than one accusatory instrument is filed in the course of the action, it commences when the first of such instruments is filed.

18. "Criminal proceeding" means any proceeding which (a) constitutes a part of a criminal action or (b) occurs in a criminal court and is related to a prospective, pending or completed criminal action, either of this state or of any other jurisdiction, or involves a criminal investigation.

19. "Criminal court" means any court defined as such by section 10.10.

20. "Superior court" means any court defined as such by subdivision two of section 10.10.

21. "Local criminal court" means any court defined as such by subdivision three of section 10.10.

22. "Intermediate appellate court" means any court possessing appellate jurisdiction, other than the court of appeals.

23. "Judge" means any judicial officer who is a member of or constitutes a court, whether referred to in another provision of law as a justice or by any other title.

24. "Trial jurisdiction." A criminal court has "trial jurisdiction" of an offense when an indictment or an information charging such offense may properly be filed with such court, and when such court has authority to accept a plea to, try or otherwise finally dispose of such accusatory instrument.

25. "Preliminary jurisdiction." A criminal court has "preliminary jurisdiction" of an offense when, regardless of whether it has trial jurisdiction thereof, a criminal action for such offense may be commenced therein, and when such court may conduct proceedings with respect thereto which lead or may lead to prosecution and final disposition of the action in a court having trial jurisdiction thereof.

26. "Appearance ticket" means a written notice issued by a public servant, more fully defined in section 150.10, requiring a person to appear before a local criminal court in connection with an accusatory instrument to be filed against him therein.

27. "Summons" means a process of a local criminal court or superior court, more fully defined in section 130.10, requiring a defendant to appear before such court for the purpose of arraignment upon an accusatory instrument filed therewith by which a criminal action against him has been commenced.

28. "Warrant of arrest" means a process of a local criminal court, more fully defined in section 120.10, directing a police officer to arrest a defendant and to bring him before such court for the purpose of arraignment upon an accusatory instrument filed therewith by which a criminal action against him has been commenced.

29. "Superior court warrant of arrest" means a process of a superior court directing a police officer to arrest a defendant and to bring him before such court for the purpose of arraignment upon an indictment filed therewith by which a criminal action against him has been commenced.

30. "Bench warrant" means a process of a criminal court in which a criminal action is pending, directing a police officer, or a uniformed court officer, pursuant to paragraph b of subdivision two of section 530.70 of this chapter, to take into custody a defendant in such action who has previously been arraigned upon the accusatory instrument by which the action was commenced, and to bring him before such court. The function of a bench warrant is to achieve the court appearance of a defendant in a pending criminal action for some purpose other than his initial arraignment in the action.

31. "Prosecutor" means a district attorney or any other public servant who represents the people in a criminal action.

32. "District attorney" means a district attorney, an assistant district attorney or a special district attorney, and, where appropriate, the attorney general, an assistant attorney general, a deputy attorney general, a special deputy attorney general, or the special prosecutor and inspector general for the protection of people with special needs or his or her assistants when acting pursuant to their duties in matters arising under article twenty of the executive law, or the inspector general of New York for transportation or his or her deputies when acting pursuant to article four-B of the executive law.

33. "Peace officer" means a person listed in section 2.10 of this chapter.

34. "Police officer." The following persons are police officers:

(a) A sworn member of the division of state police;

(b) Sheriffs, under-sheriffs and deputy sheriffs of counties outside of New York City;

(c) A sworn officer of an authorized county or county parkway police department;

(d) A sworn officer of an authorized police department or force of a city, town, village or police district;

(e) A sworn officer of an authorized police department of an authority or a sworn officer of the state regional park police in the office of parks and recreation;

(f) A sworn officer of the capital police force of the office of general services;

(g) An investigator employed in the office of a district attorney;

(h) An investigator employed by a commission created by an interstate compact who is, to a substantial extent, engaged in the enforcement of the criminal laws of this state;

(i) The chief and deputy fire marshals, the supervising fire marshals and the fire marshals of the bureau of fire investigation of the New York City fire department;

(j) A sworn officer of the division of law enforcement in the department of environmental conservation;

(k) A sworn officer of a police force of a public authority created by an interstate compact;

(l) Long Island railroad police.

(m) A special investigator employed in the statewide organized crime task force, while performing his assigned duties pursuant to section seventy-a of the executive law.

(n) A sworn officer of the Westchester county department of public safety services who, on or prior to June thirtieth, nineteen hundred seventy-nine was appointed as a sworn officer of the division of Westchester county parkway police or who was appointed on or after July first, nineteen hundred seventy-nine to the title of police officer, sergeant, lieutenant, captain or inspector or who, on or prior to January thirty-first, nineteen hundred eighty-three, was appointed as a Westchester county deputy sheriff.

(o) A sworn officer of the water-supply police employed by the city of New York, appointed to protect the sources, works, and transmission of water supplied to the city of New York, and to protect persons on or in the vicinity of such water sources, works, and transmission.

(p) Persons appointed as railroad police officers pursuant to section eighty-eight of the railroad law.

(q) An employee of the department of taxation and finance (i) assigned to enforcement of the taxes imposed under or pursuant to the authority of article twelve-A of the tax law and administered by the commissioner of taxation and finance, taxes imposed under or pursuant to the authority of article eighteen of the tax law and administered by the commissioner, taxes imposed under article twenty of the tax law, or sales or compensating use taxes relating to petroleum products or cigarettes imposed under article twenty-eight or pursuant to the authority of article twenty-nine of the tax law and administered by the commissioner or (ii) designated as a revenue crimes specialist and assigned to the enforcement of the taxes described in paragraph (c) of subdivision four of section 2.10 of this title, for the purpose of applying for and executing search warrants under article six hundred ninety of this chapter, for the purpose of acting as a claiming agent under article thirteen-A of the civil practice law and rules in connection with the enforcement of the taxes referred to above and for the purpose of executing warrants of arrest relating to the respective crimes specified in subdivision four of section 2.10 of this title.

(r) Any employee of the Suffolk county department of parks who is appointed as a Suffolk county park police officer.

(s) A university police officer appointed by the state university pursuant to paragraph 1 of subdivision two of section three hundred fifty-five of the education law.

(t) A sworn officer of the department of public safety of the Buffalo municipal housing authority who has achieved or been granted the status of sworn police officer and has been certified by the division of criminal justice services as successfully completing an approved basic course for police officers.

(u) Persons appointed as Indian police officers pursuant to section one hundred fourteen of the Indian law.

(v) Supervisor of forest ranger services; assistant supervisor of forest ranger services; forest ranger 3; forest ranger 2; forest ranger 1 employed by the state department of environmental conservation or sworn officer of the division of forest protection and fire management in the department of environmental conservation responsible for wild land search and rescue, wild land fire management in the state as prescribed in subdivision eighteen of section 9-0105 and title eleven of article nine of the environmental conservation law, exercising care, custody and control of state lands administered by the department of environmental conservation.

34-a. "Geographical area of employment." The "geographical area of employment" of certain police officers is as follows:

(a) [Until Sept 1, 2021] Except as provided in paragraph (d) of this subdivision, New York state constitutes the "geographical area of employment" of any police officer employed as such by an agency of the state or by an authority which functions throughout the state, or a police officer designated by the superintendent of state police pursuant to section two hundred twenty-three of the executive law;

(a) [Eff Sept 1, 2021] Except as provided in paragraph (d), New York state constitutes the "geographical area of employment" of any police officer employed as such by an agency of the state or by an authority which functions throughout the state;

(b) A county, city, town or village, as the case may be, constitutes the "geographical area of employment" of any police officer employed as such by an agency of such political subdivision or by an authority which functions only in such political subdivision; and

(c) Where an authority functions in more than one county, the "geographical area of employment" of a police officer employed thereby extends through all of such counties.

(d) The geographical area of employment of a police officer appointed by the state university is the campuses and other property of the state university, including any portion of a public highway which crosses or abuts such property.

(e) The geographical area of employment of a police officer appointed pursuant to section one hundred fourteen of the Indian law is within the county of Franklin, and within that county, only within the boundary of the St. Regis reservation, except that if the superintendent of state police has certified such officer with expanded jurisdiction within the county of Franklin, pursuant to subdivision eight-a of such section, the geographical area of employment of such police officer shall also include the area of expanded jurisdiction set forth in that subdivision.

35. "Commitment to the custody of the sheriff," when referring to an order of a court located in a county or city which has established a department of correction, means commitment to the commissioner of correction of such county or city.

36. "County" ordinarily means (a) any county outside of New York City or (b) New York City in its entirety. Unless the context requires a different construction, New York City, despite its five counties, is deemed a single county within the meaning of the provisions of this chapter in which that term appears.

37. "Lesser included offense." When it is impossible to commit a particular crime without concomitantly committing, by the same conduct, another offense of lesser grade or degree, the latter is, with respect to the former, a "lesser included offense." In any case in which it is legally possible to attempt to commit a crime, an attempt to commit such crime constitutes a lesser included offense with respect thereto.

38. "Oath" includes an affirmation and every other mode authorized by law of attesting to the truth of that which is stated.

39. "Petty offense" means a violation or a traffic infraction.

40. "Evidence in chief" means evidence, received at a trial or other criminal proceeding in which a defendant's guilt or innocence of an offense is in issue, which may be considered as a part of the quantum of substantive proof establishing or tending to establish the commission of such offense or an element thereof or the defendant's connection therewith.

41. "Armed felony" means any violent felony offense defined in section 70.02 of the penal law that includes as an element either:

(a) possession, being armed with or causing serious physical injury by means of a deadly weapon, if the weapon is a loaded weapon from which a shot, readily capable of producing death or other serious physical injury may be discharged; or

(b) display of what appears to be a pistol, revolver, rifle, shotgun, machine gun or other firearm.

42. "Juvenile offender" means (1) a person, thirteen years old who is criminally responsible for acts constituting murder in the second degree as defined in subdivisions one and two of section 125.25 of the penal law, or such conduct as a sexually motivated felony, where authorized pursuant to section 130.91 of the penal law; and (2) a person fourteen or fifteen years old who is criminally responsible for acts constituting the crimes defined in subdivisions one and two of section 125.25 (murder in the second degree) and in subdivision three of such section provided that the underlying crime for the murder charge is one for which such person is criminally responsible; section 135.25 (kidnapping in the first degree); 150.20 (arson in the first degree); subdivisions one and two of section 120.10 (assault in the first degree); 125.20 (manslaughter in the first degree); subdivisions one and two of section 130.35 (rape in the first degree); subdivisions one and two of section 130.50 (criminal sexual act in the first degree); 130.70 (aggravated sexual abuse in the first degree); 140.30 (burglary in the first degree); subdivision one of section 140.25 (burglary in the second degree); 150.15 (arson in the second degree); 160.15 (robbery in the first degree); subdivision two of section 160.10 (robbery in the second degree) of the penal law; or section 265.03 of the penal law, where such machine gun or such firearm is possessed on school grounds, as that phrase is defined in subdivision fourteen of section 220.00 of the penal law; or defined in the penal law as an attempt to commit murder in the second degree or kidnapping in the first degree, or such conduct as a sexually motivated felony, where authorized pursuant to section 130.91 of the penal law.

43. "Judicial hearing officer" means a person so designated pursuant to provisions of article twenty-two of the judiciary law.

44. "Adolescent offender" means a person charged with a felony committed on or after October first, two thousand eighteen when he or she was sixteen years of age or on or after October first, two thousand nineteen, when he or she was seventeen years of age.

45. "Expunge" means, where an arrest and any enforcement activity connected with that arrest, including prosecution and any disposition in any New York state court, is deemed a nullity and the accused is restored, in contemplation of the law, to

the status such individual occupied before the arrest, prosecution and/or disposition; that records of such arrest, prosecution and/or disposition shall be marked as expunged or shall be destroyed as set forth in section 160.50 of this chapter. Neither the arrest nor prosecution and/or disposition, if any, of a matter deemed a nullity shall operate as a disqualification of any person so accused to pursue or engage in any lawful activity, occupation, profession or calling. Except where specifically required or permitted by statute or upon specific authorization of a superior court, no such person shall be required to divulge information pertaining to the arrest, prosecution and/or disposition of such a matter.

HISTORY:

Add, L 1970, ch 996, § 1 eff Sept 1, 1971; amd, L 1970, ch 997, §§ 5– 9, eff Sept 1, 1971; L 1971, ch 544, §§ 1, 2; L 1971, ch 795, § 1; L 1971, ch 884, §§ 1–4; L 1972, ch 315, § 3; L 1972, ch 383, § 2; L 1972, ch 564, § 1; L 1972, ch 589, § 1; L 1972, ch 661, §§ 28, 29; L 1972, ch 662, § 5, eff Sept 1, 1972; L 1972, ch 729, § 2, eff Jan 1, 1973; L 1972, ch 858, § 1, eff June 2, 1972; L 1973, ch 461, § 1; L 1973, ch 780, § 1; L 1973, ch 781, § 1; L 1973, ch 782, § 1; L 1973, ch 948, §§ 1, 2; L 1974, ch 22, § 1, eff Feb 26, 1974; L 1974, ch 250, § 1, eff April 30, 1974; L 1974, ch 281, § 1; L 1974, ch 282, §§ 1, 2; L 1974, ch 467, §§ 1–3, eff June 22, 1974; L 1974, ch 707, §§ 1, 2, eff Sept 1, 1974; L 1974, ch 877, §§ 1, 2, eff Sept 1, 1974; L 1975, ch 509, § 1; L 1975, ch 667, § 13; L 1976, ch 265, § 2, eff Sept 1, 1976; L 1976, ch 590, § 1; L 1977, ch 487, § 1; L 1978, ch 205, § 1; L 1978, ch 481, §§ 8, 32, eff Sept 1, 1978; L 1978, ch 655, § 39; L 1978, ch 756, § 1; L 1979, ch 330, § 1; L 1979, ch 411, § 7; L 1979, ch 533, § 6; L 1980, ch 285, § 1, eff June 19, 1980; L 1980, ch 843, § 1, eff Sept 1, 1980; L 1981, ch 335, § 2, eff Sept 1, 1981; L 1982, ch 658, § 1; L 1983, ch 840, § 9, eff April 1, 1983; L 1984, ch 969, §§ 7, 8, eff Aug 8, 1983; L 1985, ch 65, § 3; L 1986, ch 318, § 1; L 1988, ch 521, § 2; L 1990, ch 209, § 9, eff Sept 1, 1990; L 1991, ch 166, § 340, eff June 12, 1991; L 1991, ch 542, § 1, eff July 23, 1991; L 1993, ch 446, § 1, eff Nov 1, 1993; L 1993, ch 508, § 11, eff Nov 1, 1993; L 1995, ch 2, §§ 68, 69, eff Sept 1, 1995; L 1998, ch 424, §§ 1, 2, eff Jan 1, 1999; L 1998, ch 435, § 1, eff Nov 1, 1998; L 1999, ch 428, § 2, eff Nov 1, 1999; L 2000, ch 599, § 1, eff Dec 20, 2000; L 2001, ch 504, § 5, eff Nov 21, 2001; L 2002, ch 318, §§ 1, 2, eff Aug 6, 2002; L 2003, ch 121, § 1, eff July 1, 2003; L 2003, ch 264, § 35, eff Nov 1, 2003; L 2005, ch 558, § 2, eff Aug 23, 2005; L 2006, ch 693, § 1, eff Sept 13, 2006; L 2007, ch 7, § 46, eff April 13, 2007; L 2011, ch 61, § 55 (Part K), eff Sept 1, 2011; L 2012, ch 501, § 4 (Part A), eff June 30, 2013; L 2017, ch 59, § 2 (Part PPP), eff May 10, 2017; L 2017, ch 59, § 1 (Part WWW), eff Oct 1, 2018; L 2017, ch 96, § 4, eff July 24, 2017; L 2018, ch 476, § 246, eff Dec 28, 2018; L 2019, ch 131, § 6, eff Aug 28, 2019; L 2019, ch 450, § 1, eff Nov 8, 2019.

Article 2
Peace Officers

§ 2.10. Persons designated as peace officers

Notwithstanding the provisions of any general, special or local law or charter to the contrary, only the following persons shall have the powers of, and shall be peace officers:

1. Constables or police constables of a town or village, provided such designation is not inconsistent with local law.

2. The sheriff, undersheriff and deputy sheriffs of New York city and sworn officers of the Westchester county department of public safety services appointed after January thirty-first, nineteen hundred eighty-three to the title of public safety officer and who perform the functions previously performed by a Westchester county deputy sheriff on or prior to such date.

3. Investigators of the office of the state commission of investigation.

4. Employees of the department of taxation and finance designated by the commissioner of taxation and finance as peace officers and assigned by the commissioner of taxation and finance

(a) to the enforcement of any of the criminal or seizure and forfeiture provisions of the tax law relating to (i) taxes imposed under or pursuant to the authority of article twelve-A of the tax law and administered by the commissioner, (ii) taxes imposed under or pursuant to the authority of article eighteen of the tax law and administered by the commissioner, (iii) taxes imposed under article twenty of the tax law, or (iv) sales or compensating use taxes relating to petroleum products or cigarettes imposed under article twenty-eight or pursuant to the authority of article twenty-nine of the tax law and administered by the commissioner or

(b) to the enforcement of any provision of the penal law relating to any of the taxes described in paragraph (a) of this subdivision and relating to crimes effected through the use of a statement or document filed with the department in connection with the administration of such taxes or

(c) as revenue crimes specialist and assigned to the enforcement of any of the criminal provisions of the tax law relating to taxes administered by the commissioner of taxation and finance other than those taxes set forth in paragraph (a) of this subdivision or any provision of the penal law relating to such taxes, and those provisions of the penal law (i) relating to any of the foregoing taxes and (ii) relating to crimes effected through the use of a statement or document filed with the department in connection with the administration of such foregoing taxes or

(d) to the enforcement of any provision of law which is subject to enforcement by criminal penalties and which relates to the performance by persons employed by the department of taxation and finance of the duties of their employment.

Provided, however, that nothing in this subdivision shall be deemed to authorize any such employee designated as a peace officer after November first, nineteen hundred eighty-five to carry, possess, repair or dispose of a firearm unless the appropriate license therefor has been issued pursuant to section 400.00 of the penal law, and further provided that, prior to such designation by the commissioner each such employee shall have successfully completed the training requirements specified in section 2.30 of this article. Provided, further, that any license issued to such employee pursuant to such peace officer designation by the commissioner shall relate only to the firearm issued to such employee by the department of taxation and finance and such permit shall not cover any other firearms. The foregoing sentence shall not be deemed to prohibit such peace officer from applying for a separate permit relating to non-departmental firearms.

5. Employees of the New York city department of finance assigned to enforcement of the tax on cigarettes imposed by title D of chapter forty-six of the administrative code of the city of New York by the commissioner of finance.

6. Confidential investigators and inspectors, as designated by the commissioner, of the department of agriculture and markets, pursuant to rules of the department.

7. Officers or agents of a duly incorporated society for the prevention of cruelty to animals.

7-a. [Expires and repealed Aug 11, 2021] Officers or agents of a duly incorporated society for the prevention of cruelty to children in Rockland county; provided, however, that nothing in this subdivision shall be deemed to authorize such officer or agent to carry, possess, repair, or dispose of a firearm unless the appropriate license therefor has been issued pursuant to section 400.00 of the penal law; and provided further that such officer or agent shall exercise the powers of a peace officer only when he is acting pursuant to his special duties.

8. Inspectors and officers of the New York city department of health when acting pursuant to their special duties as set forth in section 564-11.0 of the administrative code of the city of New York; provided, however, that nothing in this subdivision shall be deemed to authorize such officer to carry, possess, repair or dispose of a firearm unless the appropriate license therefor has been issued pursuant to section 400.00 of the penal law.

9. Park rangers in Suffolk county, who shall be authorized to issue appearance tickets, simplified traffic informations, simplified parks informations and simplified environmental conservation informations.

10. Broome county park rangers who shall be authorized to issue appearance tickets, simplified traffic informations, simplified parks informations, and simplified environmental conservation informations; provided, however, that nothing in this subdivision shall be deemed to authorize such officer to carry, possess, repair or dispose of a firearm unless the appropriate license therefor has been issued pursuant to section 400.00 of the penal law.

11. Park rangers in Onondaga and Cayuga counties, who shall be authorized to issue appearance tickets, simplified traffic informations, simplified parks informations and simplified environmental conservation informations, within the respective counties of Onondaga and Cayuga.

12. Special police officers designated by the commissioner and the directors of in-patient facilities in the office of mental health pursuant to section 7.25 of the mental hygiene law, and special police officers designated by the commissioner and the directors of facilities under his or her jurisdiction in the office for people with developmental disabilities pursuant to section 13.25 of the mental hygiene law; provided, however, that nothing in this subdivision shall be deemed to authorize such officers to carry, possess, repair or dispose of a firearm unless the appropriate license therefor has been issued pursuant to section 400.00 of the penal law.

13. Persons designated as special police officers by the director of a hospital in the department of health pursuant to section four hundred fifty-five of the public health law; provided, however, that nothing in this subdivision shall be deemed to authorize such officer to carry, possess, repair or dispose of a firearm unless the appropriate license therefor has been issued pursuant to section 400.00 of the penal law.

14. [Repealed]

15. Uniformed enforcement forces of the New York state thruway authority, when acting pursuant to subdivision two of section three hundred sixty-one of the public authorities law; provided, however, that nothing in this subdivision shall be deemed to authorize such officer to carry, possess, repair or dispose of a firearm unless the appropriate license therefor has been issued pursuant to section 400.00 of the penal law.

16. Employees of the department of health designated pursuant to section thirty-three hundred eighty-five of the public health law; provided, however, that nothing in this subdivision shall be deemed to authorize such officer to carry, possess, repair or dispose of a firearm unless the appropriate license therefor has been issued pursuant to section 400.00 of the penal law.

17. Uniformed housing guards of the Buffalo municipal housing authority.

18. Bay constable of the city of Rye, the villages of Mamaroneck, South Nyack and bay constables of the towns of East Hampton, Hempstead, Oyster Bay, Riverhead, Southampton, Southold, Islip, Shelter Island, Brookhaven, Babylon, Smithtown, Huntington and North Hempstead; provided, however, that nothing in this subdivision shall be deemed to authorize the bay constables in the city of Rye, the village of South Nyack or the towns of Brookhaven, Babylon, Southold, East Hampton, Riverhead, Islip, other than a bay constable of the town of Islip who prior to April third, nineteen hundred ninety-eight served as harbormaster for such town and whose position was reclassified as bay constable for such town prior to such date, Smithtown, Huntington and Shelter Island to carry, possess, repair or dispose of a firearm unless the appropriate license therefor has been issued pursuant to section 400.00 of the penal law.

19. Harbor masters appointed by a county, city, town or village.

20. Bridge and tunnel officers, sergeants and lieutenants of the Triborough bridge and tunnel authority.

21.a. Uniformed court officers of the unified court system.

b. Court clerks of the unified court system in the first and second departments.

c. Marshall, deputy marshall, clerk or uniformed court officer of a district court.

(d)* Marshalls or deputy marshalls of a city court, provided, however, that nothing in this subdivision shall be deemed to authorize such officer to carry, possess, repair or dispose of a firearm unless the appropriate license therefor has been issued pursuant to section 400.00 of the penal law.

e. Uniformed court officers of the city of Mount Vernon.

f. Uniformed court officers of the city of Jamestown.

22. Patrolmen appointed by the Lake George park commission; provided however that nothing in this subdivision shall be deemed to authorize such officer to carry, possess, repair or dispose of a firearm unless the appropriate license therefor has been issued pursuant to section 400.00 of the penal law.

23. Parole officers or warrant officers in the department of corrections and community supervision.

---

*So in original.

23-a. Parole revocation specialists in the department of corrections and community supervision; provided, however, that nothing in this subdivision shall be deemed to authorize such employee to carry, possess, repair or dispose of a firearm unless the appropriate license therefor has been issued pursuant to section 400.00 of the penal law.

24. Probation officers.

25. Officials, as designated by the commissioner of the department of corrections and community supervision pursuant to rules of the department, and correction officers of any state correctional facility or of any penal correctional institution.

26. Peace officers designated pursuant to the provisions of the New York state defense emergency act, as set forth in chapter seven hundred eighty-four of the laws of nineteen hundred fifty-one, as amended, when acting pursuant to their special duties during a period of attack or imminent attack by enemy forces, or during official drills called to combat natural or man-made disasters, or during official drills in preparation for an attack by enemy forces or in preparation for a natural or man-made disaster; provided, however, that nothing in this subdivision shall be deemed to authorize such officer to carry, possess, repair or dispose of a firearm unless the appropriate license therefor has been issued pursuant to section 400.00 of the penal law; and provided further, that such officer shall have the powers set forth in section 2.20 of this article only during a period of imminent or actual attack by enemy forces and during drills authorized under section twenty-nine-b of article two-B of the executive law, providing for the use of civil defense forces in disasters. Notwithstanding any other provision of law, such officers shall have the power to direct and control traffic during official drills in preparation for an attack by enemy forces or in preparation for combating natural or man-made disasters; however, this grant does not include any of the other powers set forth in section 2.20 of this article.

27. New York city special patrolmen appointed by the police commissioner pursuant to subdivision c or e of section 434a-7.0 or subdivision c or e of section 14-106 of the administrative code of the city of New York; provided, however, that nothing in this subdivision shall be deemed to authorize such officer to carry, possess, repair or dispose of a firearm unless the appropriate license therefor has been issued pursuant to section 400.00 of the penal law and the employer has authorized such officer to possess a firearm during any phase of the officers on-duty employment. Special patrolmen shall have the powers set forth in section 2.20 of this article only when they are acting pursuant to their special duties; provided, however, that the following categories of New York city special patrolmen shall have such powers whether or not they are acting pursuant to their special duties: school safety officers employed by the board of education of the city of New York; parking control specialists, taxi and limousine inspectors, urban park rangers and evidence and property control specialists employed by the city of New York; and further provided that, with respect to the aforementioned categories of New York city special patrolmen, where such a special patrolman has been appointed by the police commissioner and, upon the expiration of such appointment the police commissioner has neither renewed such appointment nor explicitly determined that such appointment shall not be renewed, such appointment shall remain in full force and effect indefinitely, until such time as the police commissioner expressly determines to either renew or terminate such appointment.

28. All officers and members of the uniformed force of the New York city fire department as set forth and subject to the limitations contained in section 487a-15.0 of the administrative code of the city of New York; provided, however, that nothing in this subdivision shall be deemed to authorize such officer to carry, possess, repair or dispose of a firearm unless the appropriate license therefor has been issued pursuant to section 400.00 of the penal law.

29. Special police officers for horse racing, appointed pursuant to the provisions of the pari-mutuel revenue law as set forth in chapter two hundred fifty-four of the laws of nineteen hundred forty, as amended; provided, however, that nothing in this subdivision shall be deemed to authorize such officer to carry, possess, repair or dispose of a firearm unless the appropriate license therefor has been issued pursuant to section 400.00 of the penal law.

30. Supervising fire inspectors, fire inspectors, the fire marshal and assistant fire marshals, all of whom are full-time employees of the county of Nassau fire marshal's office.

31. [Repealed]

32. Investigators of the department of motor vehicles, pursuant to section three hundred ninety-two-b of the vehicle and traffic law; provided, however, that nothing in this subdivision shall be deemed to authorize such officer to carry, possess, repair or dispose of a firearm unless the appropriate license therefor has been issued pursuant to section 400.00 of the penal law.

33. A city marshall of the city of New York who has received training in firearms handling from the federal bureau of investigation or in the New York city police academy, or in the absence of the available training programs from the federal bureau of investigation and the New York city police academy, from another law enforcement agency located in the state of New York, and who has received a firearms permit from the license division of the New York city police department.

34. Waterfront and airport investigators, pursuant to subdivision four of section ninety-nine hundred six of the unconsolidated laws; provided, however, that nothing in this subdivision shall be deemed to authorize such officer to carry, possess, repair or dispose of a firearm unless the appropriate license therefor has been issued pursuant to section 400.00 of the penal law.

35. Special investigators appointed by the state board of elections, pursuant to section 3-107 of the election law.

36. Investigators appointed by the state liquor authority, pursuant to section fifteen of the alcoholic beverage control law; provided, however, that nothing in this subdivision shall be deemed to authorize such officer to carry, possess, repair or dispose of a firearm unless the appropriate license therefor has been issued pursuant to section 400.00 of the penal law.

37. Special patrolmen of a political subdivision, appointed pursuant to section two hundred nine-v of the general municipal law; provided, however, that nothing in this subdivision shall be deemed to authorize such officer to carry, possess, repair or dispose of a firearm unless the appropriate license therefor has been issued pursuant to section 400.00 of the penal law.

38. A special investigator of the New York city department of investigation who has received training in firearms handling in the New York police academy and has received a firearms permit from the license division of the New York city police department.

39. Broome county special patrolman, appointed by the Broome county attorney; provided, however, that nothing in this subdivision shall be deemed to authorize such officer to carry, possess, repair or dispose of a firearm unless the appropriate license therefor has been issued pursuant to section 400.00 of the penal law.

40. Special officers employed by the city of New York or by the New York city health and hospitals corporation; provided, however, that nothing in this subdivision shall be deemed to authorize such officer to carry, possess, repair or dispose of a firearm unless the appropriate license therefor has been issued pursuant to section 400.00 of the penal law. The New York city health and hospitals corporation shall employ peace officers appointed pursuant to this subdivision to perform the patrol, investigation, and maintenance of the peace duties of special officer, senior special officer and hospital security officer, provided however that nothing in this subdivision shall prohibit managerial, supervisory, or state licensed or certified professional employees of the corporation from performing such duties where they are incidental to their usual duties, or shall prohibit police officers employed by the city of New York from performing these duties.

41. Fire police squads organized pursuant to section two hundred nine-c of the general municipal law, at such times as the fire department, fire company or an emergency rescue and first aid squad of the fire department or fire company are on duty, or when, on orders of the chief of the fire department or fire company of which they are members, they are separately engaged in response to a call for assistance pursuant to the provisions of section two hundred nine of the general municipal law; provided, however, that nothing in this subdivision shall be deemed to authorize such officer to carry, possess, repair or dispose of a firearm unless the

appropriate license therefor has been issued pursuant to section 400.00 of the penal law.

42. Special deputy sheriffs appointed by the sheriff of a county within which any part of the grounds of Cornell university or the grounds of any state institution constituting a part of the educational and research plants owned or under the supervision, administration or control of said university are located pursuant to section fifty-seven hundred nine of the education law; provided, however, that nothing in this subdivision shall be deemed to authorize such officer to carry, possess, repair or dispose of a firearm unless the appropriate license therefor has been issued pursuant to section 400.00 of the penal law.

43. Housing patrolmen of the Mount Vernon housing authority, acting pursuant to rules of the Mount Vernon housing authority; provided, however, that nothing in this subdivision shall be deemed to authorize such officer to carry, possess, repair or dispose of a firearm unless the appropriate license therefor has been issued pursuant to section 400.00 of the penal law.

44. The officers, employees and members of the New York city division of fire prevention, in the bureau of fire, as set forth and subject to the limitations contained in subdivision one of section 487a-1.0 of the administrative code of the city of New York; provided, however, that nothing in this subdivision shall be deemed to authorize such officer to carry, possess, repair or dispose of a firearm unless the appropriate license therefor has been issued pursuant to section 400.00 of the penal law.

45. Persons appointed and designated as peace officers by the Niagara frontier transportation authority, pursuant to subdivision thirteen of section twelve hundred ninety-nine-e of the public authorities law.

46. Persons appointed as peace officers by the Sea Gate Association pursuant to the provisions of chapter three hundred ninety-one of the laws of nineteen hundred forty, provided, however, that nothing in this subdivision shall be deemed to authorize such officer to carry, possess, repair or dispose of a firearm unless the appropriate license therefor has been issued pursuant to section 400.00 of the penal law.

47. Employees of the department of financial services when designated as peace officers by the superintendent of financial services and acting pursuant to their special duties as set forth in article four of the financial services law; provided, however, that nothing in this subdivision shall be deemed to authorize such officer to carry, possess, repair or dispose of a firearm unless the appropriate license therefor has been issued pursuant to section 400.00 of the penal law.

48. New York state air base security guards when they are designated as peace officers under military regulations promulgated by the chief of staff to the governor and when performing their duties as air base security guards pursuant to orders issued by appropriate military authority; provided, however, that nothing in this subdivision shall be deemed to authorize such guards to carry, possess, repair or dispose of a firearm unless the appropriate license therefor has been issued pursuant to section 400.00 of the penal law.

49. Members of the army national guard military police and air national guard security personnel belonging to the organized militia of the state of New York when they are designated as peace officers under military regulations promulgated by the adjutant general and when performing their duties as military police officers or air security personnel pursuant to orders issued by appropriate military authority; provided, however, that nothing in this subdivision shall be deemed to authorize such military police or air security personnel to carry, possess, repair or dispose of a firearm unless the appropriate license therefor has been issued pursuant to section 400.00 of the penal law.

50. Transportation supervisors in the city of White Plains appointed by the commissioner of public safety in the city of White Plains; provided, however, that nothing in this subdivision shall be deemed to authorize such officer to carry, possess, repair or dispose of a firearm unless the appropriate license therefor has been issued pursuant to section 400.00 of the penal law.

51. Officers and members of the fire investigation division of the fire department of the city of Rochester, the city of Binghamton and the city of Utica, when acting

pursuant to their special duties in matters arising under the laws relating to fires, the extinguishment thereof and fire perils; provided, however, that nothing in this subdivision shall be deemed to authorize such officer to carry, possess, repair or dispose of a firearm unless the appropriate license therefor has been issued pursuant to section 400.00 of the penal law.

52. Security hospital treatment assistants, as so designated by the commissioner of the office of mental health while performing duties in or arising out of the course of their employment; provided, however, that nothing in this subdivision shall be deemed to authorize such employee to carry, possess, repair or dispose of a firearm unless the appropriate license therefor has been issued pursuant to section 400.00 of the penal law.

53. Authorized agents of the municipal directors of weights and measures in the counties of Suffolk, Nassau and Westchester when acting pursuant to their special duties as set forth in section one hundred eighty-one of the agriculture and markets law; provided, however, that nothing in this subdivision shall be deemed to authorize such officer to carry, possess, repair or dispose of a firearm unless the appropriate license therefor has been issued pursuant to section 400.00 of the penal law.

54. Special police officers appointed pursuant to section one hundred fifty-eight of the town law; provided, however, that nothing in this subdivision shall be deemed to authorize such officer to carry, possess, repair or dispose of a firearm unless the appropriate license therefor has been issued pursuant to section 400.00 of the penal law.

55. [Expired July 1, 1993]

56. Dog control officers of the town of Brookhaven, who at the discretion of the town board may be designated as constables for the purpose of enforcing article twenty-six of the agriculture and markets law and for the purpose of issuing appearance tickets permitted under article seven of such law; provided, however, that nothing in this subdivision shall be deemed to authorize such officer to carry, possess, repair or dispose of a firearm unless the appropriate license therefor has been issued pursuant to section 400.00 of the penal law.

57. Harbor Park rangers employed by the Snug Harbor cultural center in Richmond county and appointed as New York city special patrolmen by the police commissioner pursuant to subdivision c of section 14-106 of the administrative code of the city of New York. Notwithstanding any provision of law, rule or regulation, such officers shall be authorized to issue appearance tickets pursuant to section 150.20 of this chapter, and shall have such other powers as are specified in section 2.20 of this article only when acting pursuant to their special duties. Nothing in this subdivision shall be deemed to authorize such officers to carry, possess, repair or dispose of a firearm unless the appropriate license therefor has been issued pursuant to section 400.00 of the penal law and the employer has authorized such officer to possess a firearm during any phase of the officer's on-duty employment.

57-a. [There are two subdivisions 57-a] Seasonal park rangers of the Westchester county department of public safety while employed as authorized by the commissioner of public safety/sheriff of the county of Westchester; provided, however, that nothing in this subdivision shall be deemed to authorize such officer to carry, possess, repair or dispose of a firearm unless the appropriate license therefor has been issued pursuant to section 400.00 of the penal law.

57-a. [There are two subdivisions 57-a] Officers of the Westchester county public safety emergency force, when activated by the commissioner of public safety/sheriff of the county of Westchester; provided, however that nothing in this subdivision shall be deemed to authorize such officer to carry, possess, repair or dispose of a firearm unless the appropriate license therefor has been issued pursuant to section 400.00 of the penal law.

58. Uniformed members of the security force of the Troy housing authority provided, however, that nothing in this subdivision shall be deemed to authorize such officer to carry, possess, repair or dispose of a firearm unless the appropriate license therefor has been issued pursuant to section 400.00 of the penal law.

59. Officers and members of the sanitation police of the department of sanitation of the city of New York, duly appointed and designated as peace officers by such

department; provided, however, that nothing in this subdivision shall be deemed to authorize such officer to carry, possess, repair or dispose of a firearm unless the appropriate license therefor has been issued pursuant to section 400.00 of the penal law. Provided, further, that nothing in this subdivision shall be deemed to apply to officers and members of the sanitation police regularly and exclusively assigned to enforcement of such city's residential recycling laws.

60. [Repealed]

61. Chief fire marshall, assistant chief fire marshall, fire marshall II and fire marshall I, all of whom are full-time employees of the Suffolk county department of fire, rescue and emergency services, when acting pursuant to their special duties in matters arising under the laws relating to fires, the extinguishment thereof and fire perils; provided, however, that nothing in this subdivision shall be deemed to authorize such officer to carry, possess, repair or dispose of a firearm unless the appropriate license therefor has been issued pursuant to section 400.00 of the penal law.

62. [There are two subdivisions 62] Chief fire marshall, assistant chief fire marshall, fire marshall II and fire marshall I, all of whom are full-time employees of the town of Babylon, when acting pursuant to their special duties in matters arising under the laws relating to fires, the extinguishment thereof and fire perils; provided, however, that nothing in this subdivision shall be deemed to authorize such officer to carry, possess, repair or dispose of a firearm unless the appropriate license therefor has been issued pursuant to section 400.00 of the penal law.

62. [There are two subdivisions 62] Employees of the division for youth assigned to transport and warrants units who are specifically designated by the director in accordance with section five hundred four-b of the executive law, provided, however, that nothing in this subdivision shall be deemed to authorize such employees to carry, possess, repair or dispose of a firearm unless the appropriate license therefor has been issued pursuant to section 400.00 of the penal law.

63. [There are two subdivisions 63] Uniformed members of the fire marshal's office in the town of Southampton and the town of Riverhead, when acting pursuant to their special duties in matters arising under the laws relating to fires, the extinguishment thereof and fire perils; provided, however that nothing in this subdivision shall be deemed to authorize such officer to carry, possess, repair or dispose of a firearm unless the appropriate license therefor has been issued pursuant to section 400.00 of the penal law.

63. [There are two subdivisions 63] Employees of the town court of the town of Greenburgh serving as a security officer; provided, however, that nothing in this subdivision will be deemed to authorize such officer to carry, possess, repair or dispose of a firearm unless the appropriate license therefor has been issued pursuant to section 400.00 of the penal law or to authorize such officer to carry or possess a firearm except while on duty.

64. Cell block attendants employed by the city of Buffalo police department; provided, however, that nothing in this subdivision shall be deemed to authorize such officer to carry, possess, repair or dispose of a firearm unless the appropriate license therefor has been issued pursuant to section 400.00 of the penal law.

65. Chief fire marshall, assistant chief fire marshall, fire marshall II and fire marshall I, all of whom are full-time employees of the town of Brookhaven, when acting pursuant to their special duties in matters arising under the laws relating to fires, the extinguishment thereof and fire perils; provided, however, that nothing in this subdivision shall be deemed to authorize such officer to carry, possess, repair or dispose of a firearm unless the appropriate license thereof has been issued pursuant to section 400.00 of the penal law.

66. Employees of the village court of the village of Spring Valley serving as security officers at such village court; provided, however, that nothing in this subdivision shall be deemed to authorize such officer to carry, possess, repair or dispose of a firearm unless the appropriate license therefor has been issued pursuant to section 400.00 of the penal law.

67. Employees of the town court of the town of Putnam Valley serving as a security officer; provided, however, that nothing in this subdivision will be deemed to authorize such officer to carry, possess, repair or dispose of a firearm unless the

appropriate license therefor has been issued pursuant to section 400.00 of the penal law or to authorize such officer to carry or possess a firearm except while on duty.

68. [There are five subdivisions 68] Employees of the town court of the town of Southampton serving as uniformed court officers at such town court; provided, however, that nothing in this subdivision shall be deemed to authorize such officer to carry, possess, repair or dispose of a firearm unless the appropriate license therefor has been issued pursuant to section 400.00 of the penal law.

68. [There are five subdivisions 68] The state inspector general and investigators designated by the state inspector general; provided, however, that nothing in this subdivision shall be deemed to authorize the state inspector general or such investigators to carry, possess, repair or dispose of a firearm unless the appropriate license therefor has been issued pursuant to section 400.00 of the penal law.

68. [There are five subdivisions 68] Dog control officers of the town of Arcadia, who at the discretion of the town board may be designated as constables for the purpose of enforcing article twenty-six of the agriculture and markets law and for the purpose of issuing appearance tickets permitted under article seven of such law; provided, however, that nothing in this subdivision shall be deemed to authorize such officer to carry, possess, repair or dispose of a firearm unless the appropriate license therefor has been issued pursuant to section 400.00 of the penal law.

68. [There are five subdivisions 68] Employees appointed by the sheriff of Livingston county, when acting pursuant to their special duties serving as uniformed marine patrol officers; provided, however, that nothing in this subdivision shall be deemed to authorize such officer to carry, possess, repair or dispose of a firearm unless the appropriate license has been issued pursuant to section 400.00 of the penal law or to authorize such officer to carry or possess a firearm except while on duty.

68. [There are five subdivisions 68] Persons employed by the Chautauqua county sheriff's office serving as court security officers; provided, however, that nothing in this subdivision shall be deemed to authorize such officer to carry, possess, repair or dispose of a firearm unless the appropriate license therefor has been issued pursuant to section 400.00 of the penal law.

69. Employees of the village court of the village of Amityville serving as uniformed court officers at such village court; provided, however, that nothing in this subdivision shall be deemed to authorize such officer to carry, possess, repair or dispose of a firearm unless the appropriate license therefor has been issued pursuant to section 400.00 of the penal law.

70. Employees appointed by the sheriff of Yates county, pursuant to their special duties serving as uniformed marine patrol officers; provided, however, that nothing in this subdivision shall be deemed to authorize such officer to carry, possess, repair or dispose of a firearm unless the appropriate license has been issued pursuant to section 400.00 of the penal law or to authorize such officer to carry or possess a firearm except while on duty.

71. Town of Smithtown fire marshalls when acting pursuant to their special duties in matters arising under the laws relating to fires, the extinguishment thereof and fire perils; provided, however, that nothing in this subdivision shall be deemed to authorize such officers to carry, possess, repair or dispose of a firearm unless the appropriate license therefor has been issued pursuant to section 400.00 of the penal law.

72. Persons employed by Canisius college as members of the security force of such college; provided, however, that nothing in this subdivision shall be deemed to authorize such officer to carry, possess, repair or dispose of a firearm unless the appropriate license therefor has been issued pursuant to section 400.00 of the penal law.

73. Employees of the town court of the town of Newburgh serving as uniformed court officers at such town court; provided, however, that nothing in this subdivision shall be deemed to authorize such officer to carry, possess, repair or dispose of a firearm unless the appropriate license therefor has been issued pursuant to section 400.00 of the penal law.

74. [There are four subdivisions 74]

a. Special deputy sheriffs appointed by the sheriff of Tompkins county pursuant to paragraphs b and c of this subdivision; provided, however, that nothing in this subdivision shall be deemed to authorize such officer to carry, possess, repair or dispose of a firearm unless the appropriate license therefor has been issued pursuant to section 400.00 of the penal law.

b. For the protection of the grounds, buildings and property of Ithaca college the prevention of crime and the enforcement of law and order, and for the enforcement of such rules and regulations as the board of trustees of Ithaca college shall from time to time make, the sheriff of Tompkins county may appoint and remove following consultation with Ithaca college such number of special deputy sheriffs as is determined by the sheriff to be necessary for the maintenance of public order at Ithaca college, such appointments to be made from persons nominated by the president of Ithaca college. Such special deputy sheriffs shall comply with requirements as established by the sheriff and shall act only within Tompkins county. Such special deputy sheriffs so appointed shall be employees of the college and subject to its supervision and control as outlined in the terms and conditions to be mutually agreed upon between the sheriff and Ithaca college. Such special deputy sheriffs shall have the powers of peace officers and shall act solely within the said grounds or premises owned or administered by Ithaca college, except in those rare and special situations when requested by the sheriff to provide assistance on any public highway which crosses or adjoins such property. Ithaca college will provide legal defense and indemnification, and hold harmless the county of Tompkins, its officers and employees and the Tompkins county sheriff, its officers and employees, from all claims arising out of conduct by or injury to, such personnel while carrying out their law enforcement functions except in those situations when they are acting under the direct supervision and control of the county or sheriff's department.

c. Every special deputy sheriff so appointed shall, before entering upon the duties of his or her office, take and subscribe the oath of office prescribed by article thirteen of the constitution of the state of New York which oath shall be filed in the office of the county clerk of Tompkins county. Every special deputy sheriff appointed under this subdivision when on regular duty shall wear conspicuously a metallic shield with a designating number and the words "Special Deputy Sheriff Ithaca College" thereon.

74. [There are four subdivisions 74] Parks and recreation forest rangers employed by the office of parks, recreation and historic preservation; provided, however, that nothing in this subdivision shall be deemed to authorize such individuals to carry, possess, repair or dispose of a firearm unless the appropriate license therefor has been issued pursuant to section 400.00 of the penal law.

74. [There are four subdivisions 74] Employees of the village court of the village of Quogue, town of Southampton serving as uniformed court officers at such village court; provided, however, that nothing in this subdivision shall be deemed to authorize such officer to carry, possess, repair or dispose of a firearm unless the appropriate license therefor has been issued pursuant to section 400.00 of the penal law.

74. [There are four subdivisions 74] Employees of the town court of the town of East Hampton serving as uniformed court officers at such town court; provided, however, that nothing in this subdivision shall be deemed to authorize such officer to carry, possess, repair or dispose of a firearm unless the appropriate license therefor has been issued pursuant to section 400.00 of the penal law.

75. [There are three subdivisions 75] Dog control officers of the town of Clarence, who at the discretion of the town board may be designated as constables for the purpose of enforcing article twenty-six of the agriculture and markets law and for the purpose of issuing appearance tickets permitted under article seven of the agriculture and markets law; provided, however, that nothing in this subdivision shall be deemed to authorize such officers to carry, possess, repair or dispose of a firearm unless the appropriate license therefor has been issued pursuant to section 400.00 of the penal law.

75. [There are three subdivisions 75] Airport security guards, senior airport security guards, airport security supervisors, retired police officers, and supervisors of same, who are designated by resolution of the town board of the town of Islip to provide security at Long Island MacArthur Airport when acting pursuant to

their duties as such, and such authority being specifically limited to the grounds of the said airport. However, nothing in this subdivision shall be deemed to authorize such officer to carry, possess, repair or dispose of a firearm unless the appropriate license therefor has been issued pursuant to section 400.00 of the penal law.

75. [There are three subdivisions 75] Officers and members of the fire investigation unit of the fire department of the city of Buffalo when acting pursuant to their special duties in matters arising under the laws relating to fires, the extinguishment thereof and fire perils; provided, however, that nothing in this subdivision shall be deemed to authorize such officer to carry, possess, repair or dispose of a firearm unless the appropriate license therefor has been issued pursuant to section 400.00 of the penal law.

76. [There are two subdivisions 76] Employees of the village court of the village of Southampton, town of Southampton serving as uniformed court officers at such village court; provided, however, that nothing in this subdivision shall be deemed to authorize such officer to carry, possess, repair or dispose of a firearm unless the appropriate license therefor has been issued pursuant to section 400.00 of the penal law.

76. [There are two subdivisions 76] Animal control officers employed by the city of Peekskill; provided, however, that nothing in this subdivision shall be deemed to authorize such individuals to carry, possess, repair or dispose of a firearm unless the appropriate license therefor has been issued pursuant to section 400.00 of the penal law.

77. [There are two subdivisions 77]

(a) Syracuse University peace officers appointed by the chief law enforcement officer of the city of Syracuse pursuant to paragraphs (b), (c) and (d) of this subdivision, who shall be authorized to issue appearance tickets and simplified traffic informations; provided, however, that nothing in this subdivision shall be deemed to authorize any such officer to carry, possess, repair or dispose of a firearm unless the appropriate license therefor has been issued pursuant to section 400.00 of the penal law.

(b) For the protection of the grounds, buildings and property of Syracuse University, the prevention of crime and the enforcement of law and order, and for the enforcement of such rules and regulations as Syracuse University shall from time to time establish, the chief law enforcement officer of the city of Syracuse may appoint and remove, following consultations with Syracuse University; such number of Syracuse University peace officers as is determined by the chief law enforcement officer of the city of Syracuse to be necessary for the maintenance of public order at such university, such appointments to be made from persons nominated by the chancellor of Syracuse University. Such peace officers shall comply with such requirements as shall be established by the chief law enforcement officer of the city of Syracuse. Such Syracuse University peace officers so appointed shall be employees of such university, and subject to its supervision and control and the terms and conditions to be mutually agreed upon between the chief law enforcement officer of the city of Syracuse and Syracuse University. Nothing in this paragraph shall limit the authority of Syracuse University to remove such peace officers. Such Syracuse University peace officers shall have the powers of peace officers within the geographical area of employment of the grounds or premises owned, controlled or administrated by Syracuse University within the county of Onondaga, except in those situations when requested by the chief law enforcement officer of the city of Syracuse or his or her designee, including by means of written protocols agreed to by the chief law enforcement officer of the city of Syracuse and Syracuse University, to provide assistance on any public highway which crosses or adjoins such grounds or premises. Syracuse University shall provide legal defense and indemnification, and hold harmless the city of Syracuse, and its officers and employees from all claims arising out of conduct by or injury to, such peace officers while carrying out their law enforcement functions, except in those situations when they are acting under the direct supervision and control of the chief law enforcement officer of the city of Syracuse, or his or her designee.

(c) Every Syracuse University peace officer so appointed shall, before entering upon the duties of his or her office, take and subscribe the oath of office prescribed by article thirteen of the state constitution, which oath shall be filed in the office of the county clerk of the county of Onondaga. Every such peace officer appointed pursuant to this subdivision when on regular duty shall conspicuously wear a metallic shield with a designating number and the words "Syracuse University Peace Officer" engraved thereon.

(d) To become eligible for appointment as a Syracuse University peace officer a candidate shall, in addition to the training requirements as set forth in section 2.30 of this article, complete the course of instruction in public and private law enforcement established pursuant to paragraph (c) of subdivision five of section sixty-four hundred fifty of the education law.

77. [There are two subdivisions 77] Chief fire marshal, assistant chief fire marshal, and fire marshals, all of whom are full-time employees of the town of East Hampton, when acting pursuant to their special duties in matters arising under the laws relating to fires, the extinguishment thereof and fire perils; provided, however, that nothing in this subdivision shall be deemed to authorize such officer to carry, possess, repair or dispose of a firearm unless the appropriate license therefor has been issued pursuant to section 400.00 of the penal law.

78. A security officer employed by a community college who is specifically designated as a peace officer by the board of trustees of a community college pursuant to subdivision five-a of section sixty-three hundred six of the education law, or by a community college regional board of trustees pursuant to subdivision four-a of section sixty-three hundred ten of the education law; provided, however, that nothing in this subdivision shall be deemed to authorize such officer to carry, possess, repair or dispose of a firearm unless the appropriate license therefor has been issued pursuant to section 400.00 of the penal law.

79. [There are four subdivisions 79] Court security officers employed by the Wayne county sheriff's office; provided however, that nothing in this subdivision shall be deemed to authorize such officer to carry, possess, repair or dispose of a firearm unless the appropriate license therefor has been issued pursuant to section 400.00 of the penal law.

79. [There are four subdivisions 79] Supervisors and members of the arson investigation bureau and fire inspection bureau of the office of fire prevention and control when acting pursuant to their special duties in matters arising under the laws relating to fires, their prevention, extinguishment, investigation thereof, and fire perils; provided, however, that nothing in this subdivision shall be deemed to authorize such employees to carry, possess, repair, or dispose of a firearm unless the appropriate license therefor has been issued pursuant to section 400.00 of the penal law.

79. [There are four subdivisions 79] Peace officers appointed by the city university of New York pursuant to subdivision sixteen of section sixty-two hundred six of the education law, who shall have the powers set forth in section 2.20 of this article whether or not they are acting pursuant to their special duties; provided, however, that nothing in this subdivision shall be deemed to authorize such officer to carry, possess, repair or dispose of a firearm unless the appropriate license therefor has been issued pursuant to section 400.00 of the penal law.

79. [There are four subdivisions 79] Animal control officers of the city of Elmira, who at the discretion of the city council of the city of Elmira may be designated as constables for the purpose of enforcing article twenty-six of the agriculture and markets law, and for the purpose of issuing appearance tickets permitted under article seven of such law; provided, however, that nothing in this subdivision shall be deemed to authorize such officer to carry, possess, repair or dispose of a firearm unless the appropriate license therefor has been issued pursuant to section 400.00 of the penal law.

80. Employees of the Onondaga county sheriff's department serving as uniformed court security officers at Onondaga county court facilities; provided, however, that nothing in this subdivision shall be deemed to authorize such officers to carry, possess, repair or dispose of a firearm unless the appropriate license therefor has been issued pursuant to section 400.00 of the penal law.

81. [There are six subdivisions 81] Members of the security force employed by Erie County Medical Center; provided however, that nothing in this subdivision

shall be deemed to authorize such officer to carry, possess, repair or dispose of a firearm unless the appropriate license therefor has been issued pursuant to section 400.00 of the penal law.

81. [There are six subdivisions 81] Employees of the town of Riverhead serving as court officers at town of Riverhead court facilities; provided, however, that nothing in this subdivision shall be deemed to authorize such officers to carry, possess, repair or dispose of a firearm unless the appropriate license therefor has been issued pursuant to section 400.00 of the penal law.

81. [There are six subdivisions 81] Employees of the town court of the town of Southold serving as uniformed court officers at such town court; provided, however, that nothing in this subdivision shall be deemed to authorize such officer to carry, possess, repair or dispose of a firearm unless the appropriate license therefor has been issued pursuant to section 400.00 of the penal law.

81. [There are six subdivisions 81] Commissioners of and court officers in the department of public safety for the town of Rye when acting pursuant to their special duties in matters arising under the laws relating to maintaining the safety and security of citizens, judges and court personnel in the town court, and effecting the safe and secure transport of persons under the custody of said department; provided, however, that nothing in this subdivision shall be deemed to authorize such employees to carry, possess, repair, or dispose of a firearm unless the appropriate license therefor has been issued pursuant to section 400.00 of the penal law.

81. [There are six subdivisions 81] Employees of the town of Yorktown serving as court attendants at town of Yorktown court facilities; provided, however, that nothing in this subdivision shall be deemed to authorize such employees to carry, possess, repair or dispose of a firearm unless the appropriate license therefor has been issued pursuant to section 400.00 of the penal law.

81. [There are six subdivisions 81] Employees of the Lewis county sheriff's department serving as uniformed court security officers at Lewis county court facilities; provided, however, that nothing in this subdivision shall be deemed to authorize such officers to carry, possess, repair or dispose of a firearm unless the appropriate license therefor has been issued pursuant to section 400.00 of the penal law.

82. Employees of the New York city business integrity commission designated as peace officers by the chairperson of such commission; provided, however, that nothing in this subdivision shall be deemed to authorize such officer to carry, possess, repair or dispose of a firearm unless the appropriate license therefor has been issued pursuant to section 400.00 of the penal law.

83. Members of the security force employed by Kaleida Health within and directly adjacent to the hospital buildings on the medical campus located between East North Street, Goodell Street, Main Street and Michigan Avenue. These officers shall only have the powers listed in paragraph (c) of subdivision one of section 2.20 of this article, as well as the power to detain an individual for a reasonable period of time while awaiting the arrival of law enforcement, provided that the officer has actual knowledge, or probable cause to believe, that such individual has committed an offense; provided however, that nothing in this subdivision shall be deemed to authorize such officer to carry, possess, repair or dispose of a firearm unless the appropriate license therefor has been issued pursuant to section 400.00 of the penal law.

84.(a) Public safety officers employed by the University of Rochester who are designated as peace officers by the board of trustees of the University of Rochester pursuant to paragraphs (b), (c), and (d) of this subdivision; provided, however, that nothing in this subdivision shall be deemed to authorize any such officer to carry, possess, repair or dispose of a firearm unless the appropriate license therefor has been issued pursuant to section 400.00 of the penal law.

(b) For the protection of the grounds, buildings and property of the University of Rochester, the prevention of crime and the enforcement of law and order, the board of trustees of the University of Rochester may appoint and remove such number of public safety officers designated as peace officers as is determined by the board of trustees to be necessary for the maintenance of public order consistent with this subdivision. Such peace officers shall comply with such requirements as shall be mutually agreed upon between the chief law enforcement officers of the applicable local law enforcement jurisdictions and the University of Rochester. Such University of Rochester peace officers so appointed shall be employees of the University of Rochester and subject to its supervision and control. Such University of Rochester peace officers shall have the powers of peace officers within the geographic area of employment of the grounds or premises owned, controlled or administered by the University of Rochester within the county of Monroe, on any public street and sidewalk that abuts the grounds, buildings or property of such university, and beyond such geographic area upon the request of the chief law enforcement officer of the local law enforcement jurisdiction or his or her designee, for the purpose of transporting an individual who has been arrested in accordance with section 140.27 of this chapter and when no local law enforcement officer is available for transporting such individual in a timely manner.

(c) The University of Rochester shall provide legal defense and indemnification to applicable municipality and its officers and employees, and hold them harmless, against all claims arising out of conduct by or injury to such peace officers while carrying out their special duties, except in those situations when they are acting as agents of the chief law enforcement officer of the applicable local law enforcement jurisdiction or his or her designee.

(d) To become eligible for designation as a University of Rochester peace officer, a candidate shall, in addition to the training requirements as set forth in section 2.30 of this article, complete the course of instruction in public and private law enforcement established pursuant to subdivision three of section sixty-four hundred thirty-five of the education law.

85. Uniformed members of the bureau of fire prevention of the town of Islip, when acting pursuant to their special duties in matters arising under laws relating to fires, the extinguishment thereof and fire perils; provided, however, that nothing in this subdivision shall be deemed to authorize such members to carry, possess, repair or dispose of a firearm unless the appropriate license therefor has been issued pursuant to section 400.00 of the penal law.

HISTORY:

Add, L 1980, ch 843, § 2, eff Sept 1, 1980; amd, L 1981, ch 175, §§ 6–8, 9, eff July 2, 1981 and applicable to offenses committed on or after such date; L 1981, ch 462, § 1; L 1981, ch 470, § 1; L 1981, ch 523, § 1; L 1981, ch 720, § 5, eff Nov 1, 1981; L 1982, ch 658, § 2, retroactive to and deemed to have been in full force and effect on and after July 1, 1979; L 1983, ch 969, §§ 3–6, 9, eff Aug 8, 1983; L 1984, ch 740, § 1; L 1985, ch 65, § 4, eff April 17, 1985; L 1985, ch 266, § 1; L 1986, ch 318, § 2, eff July 17, 1986; L 1986, ch 364, § 1; L 1987, ch 617, § 11, eff Jan 1, 1988; L 1987, ch 734, §§ 1, 2, eff Nov 1, 1987; L 1988, ch 141, § 70, eff June 20, 1988; L 1988, ch 274, § 1; L 1988, ch 438, § 1, eff July 29, 1988; L 1988, ch 695, § 3, eff Jan 1, 1989; L 1989, ch 188, § 1, eff June 24, 1989; L 1989, ch 189, § 1; L 1989, ch 285, § 1; L 1989, ch 426, § 1; L 1990, ch 931, § 1, eff Oct 15, 1990; L 1991, ch 166, § 341, eff June 12, 1991, expired Nov 1, 1993; L 1992, ch 93, § 1, eff May 17, 1992; L 1992, ch 257, § 1, eff June 30, 1992; L 1992, ch 294, § 1, eff June 30, 1992; L 1992, ch 321, § 4, eff July 17, 1992; L 1992, ch 487, § 1, eff July 17, 1992; L 1992, ch 858, § 1, eff Dec 23, 1992; L 1993, ch 157, § 1, eff July 28, 1993; L 1993, ch 204, § 1, eff July 6, 1993; L 1993, ch 508, § 12; L 1993, ch 687, § 9, eff Dec 2, 1993; L 1994, ch 466, § 1, eff July 20, 1994, expired and repealed Jan 31, 1995; L 1994, ch 519, § 1, eff July 26, 1994; L 1994, ch 620, § 1, eff July 26, 1994; L 1994, ch 665, § 1, eff Aug 2, 1994; L 1994, ch 668, § 1; L 1995, ch 2, §§ 70 and 71, eff Sept 1, 1995; L 1995, ch 206, § 1, eff Sept 24, 1995; L 1995, ch 457, § 1, eff Aug 2, 1995; L 1995, ch 462, § 1, eff Aug 2, 1995; L 1995, ch 521, § 1, eff Aug 2, 1995; L 1995, ch 658, § 1, eff Aug 8, 1995; L 1996, ch 314, § 1, eff July 17, 1996; L 1996, ch 379, § 1, eff July 30, 1996; L 1997, ch 378, § 1, eff Aug 5, 1997; L 1997, ch 555, § 1, eff Sept 10, 1997; L 1997, ch 562, § 1, eff Sept 10, 1997; L 1998, ch 224, § 1, eff July 7, 1998; L 1998, ch 424, § 3, eff Jan 1, 1999; L 1999, ch 212, § 2, eff July 6, 1999; L 1999, ch 584, § 1, eff Nov 1, 1999; L 2000, ch 168, § 1, eff July 18, 2000; L 2000, ch 227, § 1, eff Aug 16, 2000; L 2000, ch 385, § 1, eff Aug 30, 2000; L 2000, ch 393, § 1, Aug 30, 2000; L 2000, ch 404, § 1, eff Aug 30, 2000; L 2001, ch 120, § 1, eff Aug 6, 2001; L 2001, ch 481, § 1, eff Nov 21, 2001; L 2001, ch 548, § 1, eff Dec 12, 2001; L 2002, ch 260, § 1, eff July 30, 2002; L 2002, ch 261, § 1, eff July 30, 2002; L 2002, ch 318, §§ 3, 4, eff Aug 6, 2002; L 2002, ch 320, § 1, Aug 6, 2002; L 2002, ch 321, § 1, Aug 6, 2002; L 2002, ch 623, § 1, eff Oct 2, 2002; L 2003, ch 626, § 1, eff Sept 30, 2003; L 2003, ch 638, § 1, eff Oct 7; L 2003, ch 654, § 1, eff Oct 7, 2003; L 2003, ch 665, § 1, eff Oct 15, 2003; L 2003, ch 671, § 1, eff Oct 15, 2003; L 2003, ch 689, § 3, eff Oct 21, 2003; L 2004, ch 17, § 1, eff March 23, 2004; L

2004, ch 24, § 3, eff April 6, 2004; L 2004, ch 235, § 1, eff July 27, 2004; L 2004, ch 241, § 1, eff July 27, 2004; L 2004, ch 367, § 1, Aug 17, 2004; L 2004, ch 664, §§ 2, 3, eff Oct 26, 2004; L 2004, ch 752, § 1, eff Jan 28, 2005; L 2005, ch 557, § 1, eff Aug 23, 2005; L 2006, ch 438, § 1, eff July 26, 2006, expired and repealed Dec 31, 2006; L 2006, ch 467, § 1, eff Feb 12, 2007; L 2006, ch 482, § 1, eff Aug 16, 2006; L 2006, ch 501, § 1, eff Aug 16, 2006; L 2006, ch 581, § 1, eff Aug 16, 2006; L 2006, ch 584, § 1, eff Aug 16, 2006; L 2006, ch 653, § 1, eff Sept 13, 2006; L 2006, ch 693, § 2, eff Sept 13, 2006; L 2008, ch 564, § 1, eff Sept 4, 2008; L 2009, ch 329, § 7, eff Aug 8, 2009; L 2009, ch 329, § 8, eff Aug 11, 2009; L 2010, ch 56, § 50 (Part B), eff July 1, 2010; L 2011, ch 61, § 56 (Part K), eff Sept 1, 2011; L 2011, ch 62, §§ 78, 78–a (Part A), eff Oct 3, 2011; L 2011, ch 62, § 70 (Part C, Subpart B), eff March 31, 2011; L 2012, ch 502, § 1, eff June 15, 2013; L 2012, ch 504, § 1, eff Dec 17, 2012; L 2014, ch 484, § 1, eff Nov 1, 2015; L 2017, ch 494, § 1, eff Dec 18, 2017; L 2018, ch 476, § 247, eff Dec 28, 2018; L 2019, ch 632, § 1, eff Dec 12, 2019.

Title C
General Principles Relating to Requirements For and Exemptions From Criminal Prosecution

Article 40
Exemption From Prosecution by Reason of Previous Prosecution

§ 40.51 Previous prosecution: presidential reprieve, pardon or other form of clemency.

When a person has been granted a reprieve, pardon or other form of clemency for an offense pursuant to the authority granted in section two of article two of the United States constitution, a separate or subsequent prosecution of an offense is not barred under this article when the people demonstrate, by clear and convincing evidence, that:

1. (a) such person served in or was employed by the executive branch of the government of the United States on the executive staff of the president, in the executive office of the president, or in an acting or confirmed capacity in a position subject to confirmation by the United States senate, at a time when the president granting such reprieve, pardon or other form of clemency served as president or vice-president of the United States; or (b) such person was directly or indirectly employed by, or acted as an agent of, the election, transition or re-election campaign of the president granting such reprieve, pardon or other form of clemency or any for-profit or not-for-profit entity owned or controlled by the president granting such reprieve, pardon or other form of clemency; or

2. such person was, at the time the president granted such reprieve, pardon or other form of clemency, related by consanguinity or affinity within the sixth degree to the president granting such reprieve, pardon or other form of clemency; or

3. such person bears accessorial liability, as defined in section 20.00 of the penal law, or conspiratorial liability, within the meaning of article one hundred five of the penal law, for such offense with one or more persons described in subdivision one or two of this section; or

4. the president who granted such reprieve, pardon or other form of clemency to such person (a) was thereby aided in avoiding potential prosecution or conviction; (b) knowingly obtained a benefit from such offense; or (c) knowingly obtained a tangible, material benefit from or on behalf of such person; or

5. such person possessed or possesses information material to the determination of any criminal or civil investigation, enforcement action or prosecution of the president granting such reprieve, pardon or other form of clemency, or of one or more persons described in subdivision one, two or three of this section.

HISTORY:
L 2019, ch 374, § 1, eff Oct 16, 2019.

Part TWO
The Principal Proceedings

Title H
Preliminary Proceedings in Local Criminal Court

Article 95
Pre-Criminal Proceeding Settlements [Expires and repealed March 31, 2021]

§ 95.00. Pre-criminal proceeding settlement. [Expires and repealed March 31, 2021]

When a county district attorney of a county located in a city of one million or more recovers monies before the filing of an accusatory instrument as defined in subdivision one of section 1.20 of this chapter, after injured parties have been appropriately compensated, the district attorney's office shall retain a percentage of the remaining such monies in recognition that such monies were recovered as a result of investigations undertaken by such office. For each recovery the total amount of such monies to be retained by the county district attorney's office shall equal ten percent of the first twenty-five million dollars received by such office, plus seven and one-half percent of such monies received by such office in excess of twenty-five million dollars but less than fifty million dollars, plus five percent of any such monies received by such office in excess of fifty million dollars but less than one hundred million dollars, plus one percent of such monies received by such office in excess of one hundred million dollars. The remainder of such monies shall be paid by the district attorney's office to the state and to the county in equal amounts within thirty days of receipt, where disposition of such monies is not otherwise prescribed by law. Monies distributed to a county district attorney's office pursuant to this section shall be used to enhance law enforcement efforts within the state of New York. On December first of each year, every district attorney shall provide the governor, temporary president of the senate and speaker of the assembly with an annual report detailing the total amount of monies received as described herein by his or her office, a description of how and where such funds, and an itemization of funds received in the previous ten years, were distributed by his or her office but shall not include a description of the distribution of monies where the disclosure of such information would interfere with a law enforcement investigation or a judicial proceeding, and the current total balance of monies held on deposit for state sanctioned deferred prosecution agreements. The report shall include a detailed description of any entity to which funds are distributed, including but not limited to, whether it is a profit or not-for-profit entity, where it is located, and the intended use of the monies distributed, and shall state the law enforcement purpose.

HISTORY:
L 2018, ch 55, § 1 (Part F), eff April 12, 2018; amd, L 2020, ch 55, § 2 (Part E), eff April 3, 2020.

Article 140
Arrest Without a Warrant

§ 140.10. Arrest without a warrant; by police officer; when and where authorized. [Effective until November 1, 2020]

1. Subject to the provisions of subdivision two, a police officer may arrest a person for:

(a) Any offense when he or she has reasonable cause to believe that such person has committed such offense in his or her presence; and

(b) A crime when he or she has reasonable cause to believe that such person has committed such crime, whether in his or her presence or otherwise.

2. A police officer may arrest a person for a petty offense, pursuant to subdivision one, only when:

(a) Such offense was committed or believed by him or her to have been committed within the geographical area of such police officer's employment or within one hundred yards of such geographical area; and

(b) Such arrest is made in the county in which such offense was committed or believed to have been committed or in an adjoining county; except that the police officer may follow such person in continuous close pursuit, commencing either in the county in which the offense was or is believed to have been committed or in an adjoining county, in and through any county of the state, and may arrest him or her in any county in which he or she apprehends him or her.

3. A police officer may arrest a person for a crime, pursuant to subdivision one, whether or not such crime was committed within the geographical area of such police officer's employment, and he or she may make such arrest within the state, regardless of the situs of the commission of the crime. In addition, he or she may, if necessary, pursue such person outside the state and may arrest him or her in any state the laws of which contain provisions equivalent to those of section 140.55.

4. [Expires and repealed Sept 1, 2021] Notwithstanding any other provisions of this section, a police officer shall arrest a person, and shall not attempt to reconcile the parties or mediate, where such officer has reasonable cause to believe that:

(a) a felony, other than subdivision three, four, nine or ten of section 155.30 of the penal law, has been committed by such person against a member of the same family or household, as member of the same family or household is defined in subdivision one of section 530.11 of this chapter; or

(b) a duly served order of protection or special order of conditions issued pursuant to subparagraph (i) or (ii) of paragraph (o) of subdivision one of section 330.20 of this chapter is in effect, or an order of which the respondent or defendant has actual knowledge because he or she was present in court when such order was issued, where the order appears to have been issued by a court of competent jurisdiction of this or another state, territorial or tribal jurisdiction; and

(i) Such order directs that the respondent or defendant stay away from persons on whose behalf the order of protection or special order of conditions has been issued and the respondent or defendant committed an act or acts in violation of such "stay away" provision of such order; or

(ii) The respondent or defendant commits a family offense as defined in subdivision one of section eight hundred twelve of the family court act or subdivision one of section 530.11 of this chapter in violation of such order of protection or special order of conditions.

The provisions of this subdivision shall apply only to orders of protection issued pursuant to sections two hundred forty and two hundred fifty-two of the domestic relations law, articles four, five, six and eight of the family court act and section 530.12 of this chapter, special orders of conditions issued pursuant to subparagraph (i) or (ii) of paragraph (o) of subdivision one of section 330.20 of this chapter insofar as they involve a victim or victims of domestic violence as defined by subdivision one of section four hundred fifty-nine-a of the social services law or a designated witness or witnesses to such domestic violence, and to orders of protection issued by courts of competent jurisdiction in another state, territorial or tribal jurisdiction. In determining whether reasonable cause exists to make an arrest for a violation of an order issued by a court of another state, territorial or tribal jurisdiction, the officer shall consider, among other factors, whether the order, if available, appears to be valid on its face or whether a record of the order exists on the statewide registry of orders of protection and warrants established pursuant to section two hundred twenty-one-a of the executive law or the protection order file maintained by the national crime information center; provided, however, that entry of the order of protection or special order of conditions into the statewide registry or the national protection order file shall not be required for enforcement of the order. When a special order of conditions is in effect and a defendant or respondent has been taken into custody pursuant to this paragraph, nothing contained in this paragraph shall restrict or impair a police officer from acting pursuant to section 9.41 of the mental hygiene law; or

(c) a misdemeanor constituting a family offense, as described in subdivision one of section 530.11 of this chapter and section eight hundred twelve of the family court act, has been committed by such person against such family or household member, unless the victim requests otherwise. The officer shall neither inquire as to whether the victim seeks an arrest of such person nor threaten the arrest of any person for the purpose of discouraging requests for police intervention. Notwithstanding the foregoing, when an officer has reasonable cause to believe that more than one family or household member has committed such a misdemeanor, the officer is not required to arrest each such person. In such circumstances, the officer shall attempt to identify and arrest the primary physical aggressor after considering: (i) the comparative extent of any injuries inflicted by and between the parties; (ii) whether any such person is threatening or has threatened future harm against another party or another family or household member; (iii) whether any such person has a prior history of domestic violence that the officer can reasonably ascertain; and (iv) whether any such person acted defensively to protect himself or herself from injury. The officer shall evaluate each complaint separately to determine who is the primary physical aggressor and shall not base the decision to arrest or not to arrest on the willingness of a person to testify or otherwise participate in a judicial proceeding.

The protected party in whose favor the order of protection or temporary order of protection is issued may not be held to violate an order issued in his or her favor nor may such protected party be arrested for violating such order.

Nothing contained in this subdivision shall be deemed to (a) require the arrest of any person when the officer reasonably believes the person's conduct is justifiable under article thirty-five of title C of the penal law; or (b) restrict or impair the authority of any municipality, political subdivision, or the division of state police from promulgating rules, regulations and policies requiring the arrest of persons in additional circumstances where domestic violence has allegedly occurred.

No cause of action for damages shall arise in favor of any person by reason of any arrest made by a police officer pursuant to this subdivision, except as provided in sections seventeen and eighteen of the public officers law and sections fifty-k, fifty-l, fifty-m and fifty-n of the general municipal law, as appropriate.

5. Upon investigating a report of a crime or offense between members of the same family or household as such terms are defined in section 530.11 of this chapter and

section eight hundred twelve of the family court act, a law enforcement officer shall prepare, file, and translate, in accordance with section two hundred fourteen-b or eight hundred forty of the executive law, a written report of the incident, on a form promulgated pursuant to section eight hundred thirty-seven of the executive law, including statements made by the victim and by any witnesses, and make any additional reports required by local law enforcement policy or regulations. Such report shall be prepared and filed, whether or not an arrest is made as a result of the officers' investigation, and shall be retained by the law enforcement agency for a period of not less than four years. Where the reported incident involved an offense committed against a person who is sixty-five years of age or older a copy of the report required by this subdivision shall be sent to the New York state committee for the coordination of police services to elderly persons established pursuant to section eight hundred forty-four-b of the executive law. Where the reported incident involved an offense committed by an individual known by the law enforcement officer to be under probation or parole supervision, he or she shall transmit a copy of the report as soon as practicable to the supervising probation department or the department of corrections and community supervision.

HISTORY:

Add, L 1970, ch 996, § 1, eff Sept 1, 1971; amd, L 1970, ch 997, § 1, eff Sept 1, 1971; L 1994, ch 222, § 32, eff Jan 1, 1996; L 1994, ch 224, § 5-a, eff Oct 1, 1995; L 1994, ch 224, § 6, eff Jan 1, 1995; L 1995, ch 349, § 4, eff Jan 1, 1996; L 1996, ch 511, § 1, eff Nov 6, 1996; L 1997, ch 4, §§ 1, 2, eff Jan 12, 1998; L 1997, ch 626, § 1, eff Sept 17, 1997; L 1998, ch 597, § 10, eff Dec 22, 1998; L 2003, ch 300, § 1, eff Nov 1, 2003; L 2004, ch 107, § 5, eff June 8, 2004; L 2004, ch 642, § 4 (repealed, L 2005, ch 87, § 3, eff June 7, 2005, deemed eff Oct 26, 2004), eff Oct 26, 2004; L 2009, ch 476, § 6, eff Dec 15, 2009; L 2011, ch 62, § 72 (Part C, Subpart B), eff March 31, 2011; L 2013, ch 480, § 12, eff Nov 13, 2013; L 2015, ch 432, § 4, eff Feb 18, 2016.

§ 140.10. Arrest without a warrant; by police officer; when and where authorized. [Effective November 1, 2020]

1. Subject to the provisions of subdivision two, a police officer may arrest a person for:

(a) Any offense when he or she has reasonable cause to believe that such person has committed such offense in his or her presence; and

(b) A crime when he or she has reasonable cause to believe that such person has committed such crime, whether in his or her presence or otherwise.

2. A police officer may arrest a person for a petty offense, pursuant to subdivision one, only when:

(a) Such offense was committed or believed by him or her to have been committed within the geographical area of such police officer's employment or within one hundred yards of such geographical area; and

(b) Such arrest is made in the county in which such offense was committed or believed to have been committed or in an adjoining county; except that the police officer may follow such person in continuous close pursuit, commencing either in the county in which the offense was or is believed to have been committed or in an adjoining county, in and through any county of the state, and may arrest him or her in any county in which he or she apprehends him or her.

3. A police officer may arrest a person for a crime, pursuant to subdivision one, whether or not such crime was committed within the geographical area of such police officer's employment, and he or she may make such arrest within the state, regardless of the situs of the commission of the crime. In addition, he or she may, if necessary, pursue such person outside the state and may arrest him or her in any state the laws of which contain provisions equivalent to those of section 140.55.

4. [Expires and repealed Sept 1, 2021] Notwithstanding any other provisions of this section, a police officer shall arrest a person, and shall not attempt to reconcile the parties or mediate, where such officer has reasonable cause to believe that:

(a) a felony, other than subdivision three, four, nine or ten of section 155.30 of the penal law, has been committed by such person against a member of the same family or household, as member of the same family or household is defined in subdivision one of section 530.11 of this chapter; or

(b) a duly served order of protection or special order of conditions issued pursuant to subparagraph (i) or (ii) of paragraph (o) of subdivision one of section 330.20 of this chapter is in effect, or an order of which the respondent or defendant has actual knowledge because he or she was present in court when such order was issued, where the order appears to have been issued by a court of competent jurisdiction of this or another state, territorial or tribal jurisdiction; and

(i) Such order directs that the respondent or defendant stay away from persons on whose behalf the order of protection or special order of conditions has been issued and the respondent or defendant committed an act or acts in violation of such "stay away" provision of such order; or

(ii) The respondent or defendant commits a family offense as defined in subdivision one of section eight hundred twelve of the family court act or subdivision one of section 530.11 of this chapter in violation of such order of protection or special order of conditions.

The provisions of this subdivision shall apply only to orders of protection issued pursuant to sections two hundred forty and two hundred fifty-two of the domestic relations law, articles four, five, six and eight of the family court act and section 530.12 of this chapter, special orders of conditions issued pursuant to subparagraph (i) or (ii) of paragraph (o) of subdivision one of section 330.20 of this chapter insofar as they involve a victim or victims of domestic violence as defined by subdivision one of section four hundred fifty-nine-a of the social services law or a designated witness or witnesses to such domestic violence, and to orders of protection issued by courts of competent jurisdiction in another state, territorial or tribal jurisdiction. In determining whether reasonable cause exists to make an arrest for a violation of an order issued by a court of another state, territorial or tribal jurisdiction, the officer shall consider, among other factors, whether the order, if available, appears to be valid on its face or whether a record of the order exists on the statewide registry of orders of protection and warrants established pursuant to section two hundred twenty-one-a of the executive law or the protection order file maintained by the national crime information center; provided, however, that entry of the order of protection or special order of conditions into the statewide registry or the national protection order file shall not be required for enforcement of the order. When a special order of conditions is in effect and a defendant or respondent has been taken into custody pursuant to this paragraph, nothing contained in this paragraph shall restrict or impair a police officer from acting pursuant to section 9.41 of the mental hygiene law; or

(c) a misdemeanor constituting a family offense, as described in subdivision one of section 530.11 of this chapter and section eight hundred twelve of the family court act, has been committed by such person against such family or household member, unless the victim requests otherwise. The officer shall neither inquire as to whether the victim seeks an arrest of such person nor threaten the arrest of any person for the purpose of discouraging requests for police intervention. Notwithstanding the foregoing, when an officer has reasonable cause to believe that more than one family or household member has committed such a misdemeanor, the officer is not required to arrest each such person. In such circumstances, the officer shall attempt to identify and arrest the primary physical aggressor after considering: (i) the comparative extent of any injuries inflicted by and between the parties; (ii) whether any such person is threatening or has threatened future harm against another party or another family or household member; (iii) whether any such person has a prior history of domestic violence that the officer can reasonably ascertain; and (iv) whether any such person acted defensively to protect himself or herself from injury. The officer shall evaluate each complaint separately to determine who is the primary physical aggressor and shall not base the decision to arrest or not to arrest on the willingness of a person to testify or otherwise participate in a judicial proceeding.

The protected party in whose favor the order of protection or temporary order of protection is issued may not be held to violate an order issued in his or her favor nor may such protected party be arrested for violating such order.

Nothing contained in this subdivision shall be deemed to (a) require the arrest of any person when the officer reasonably believes the person's conduct is justifiable under article thirty-five of title C of the penal law; or (b) restrict or impair the authority of any municipality, political subdivision, or the division of state police from promulgating rules, regulations and policies requiring the arrest of persons in additional circumstances where domestic violence has allegedly occurred.

No cause of action for damages shall arise in favor of any person by reason of any arrest made by a police officer pursuant to this subdivision, except as provided in sections seventeen and eighteen of the public officers law and sections fifty-k, fifty-l, fifty-m and fifty-n of the general municipal law, as appropriate.

5. Upon investigating a report of a crime or offense between members of the same family or household as such terms are defined in section 530.11 of this chapter and section eight hundred twelve of the family court act, a law enforcement officer shall prepare, file, and translate, in accordance with section two hundred fourteen-b or eight hundred forty of the executive law, a written report of the incident, on a form promulgated pursuant to section eight hundred thirty-seven of the executive law, including statements made by the victim and by any witnesses, and make any additional reports required by local law enforcement policy or regulations. Such report shall be prepared and filed, whether or not an arrest is made as a result of the officers' investigation, and shall be retained by the law enforcement agency for a period of not less than four years. Where the reported incident involved an offense committed against a person who is sixty-five years of age or older a copy of the report required by this subdivision shall be sent to the New York state committee for the coordination of police services to elderly persons established pursuant to section eight hundred forty-four-b of the executive law. Where the reported incident involved an offense committed by an individual known by the law enforcement officer to be under probation or parole supervision, he or she shall transmit a copy of the report as soon as practicable to the supervising probation department or the department of corrections and community supervision.

6.(a) A police officer who responds to a report of a family offense as defined in section 530.11 of this chapter and section eight hundred twelve of the family court act may take temporary custody of any firearm, rifle, electronic dart gun, electronic stun gun, disguised gun, imitation weapon, shotgun, antique firearm, black powder rifle, black powder shotgun, or muzzle-loading firearm that is in plain sight or is discovered pursuant to a consensual or other lawful search, and shall take temporary custody of any such weapon that is in the possession of any person arrested for the commission of such family offense or suspected of its commission. An officer who takes custody of any weapon pursuant to this paragraph shall also take custody of any license to carry, possess, repair, and dispose of such weapon issued to the person arrested or suspected of such family offense. The officer shall deliver such weapon and/or license to the appropriate law enforcement officer as provided in subparagraph (f) of paragraph one of subdivision a of section 265.20 of the penal law.

(b) Upon taking custody of weapons or a license described in paragraph (a) of this subdivision, the responding officer shall give the owner or person in possession of such weapons or license a receipt describing such weapons and/or license and indicating any identification or serial number on such weapons. Such receipt shall indicate where the weapons and/or license can be recovered and describe the process for recovery provided in paragraph (e) of this subdivision.

(c) Not less than forty-eight hours after effecting such seizure, and in the absence of (i) an order of protection, an extreme risk protection order, or other court order prohibiting the owner from possessing such a weapon and/or license, or (ii) a pending criminal charge or conviction which prohibits such owner from possessing such a weapon and/or license, and upon a written finding that there is no legal impediment to the owner's possession of such a weapon and/or license, the court or, if no court is involved, licensing authority or custodian of the weapon shall direct return of a weapon not otherwise disposed of in accordance with subdivision one of section 400.05 of the penal law and/or such license taken into custody pursuant to this section.

(d) If any other person demonstrates that such person is the lawful owner of any weapon taken into custody pursuant to this section, and provided that the court or, if no court is involved, licensing authority or custodian of the weapon has made a written finding that there is no legal impediment to the person's possession of such a weapon, such court, licensing authority or custodian of the weapon, as the case may be, shall direct that such weapon be returned to such lawful owner.

(e) All weapons in the possession of a law enforcement official pursuant to this section shall be subject to the provisions of applicable law, including but not limited to subdivision six of section 400.05 of the penal law; provided, however, that any such weapon shall be retained and not disposed of by the law enforcement agency for at least two years unless legally transferred by the owner to an individual permitted by law to own and possess such weapon.

HISTORY:

Add, L 1970, ch 996, § 1, eff Sept 1, 1971; amd, L 1970, ch 997, § 1, eff Sept 1, 1971; L 1994, ch 222, § 32, eff Jan 1, 1996; L 1994, ch 224, § 5-a, eff Oct 1, 1995; L 1994, ch 224, § 6, eff Jan 1, 1995; L 1995, ch 349, § 4, eff Jan 1, 1996; L 1996, ch 511, § 1, eff Nov 6, 1996; L 1997, ch 4, §§ 1, 2, eff Jan 12, 1998; L 1997, ch 626, § 1, eff Sept 17, 1997; L 1998, ch 597, § 10, eff Dec 22, 1998; L 2003, ch 300, § 1, eff Nov 1, 2003; L 2004, ch 107, § 5, eff June 8, 2004; L 2004, ch 642, § 4 (repealed, L 2005, ch 87, § 3, eff June 7, 2005, deemed eff Oct 26, 2004), eff Oct 26, 2004; L 2009, ch 476, § 6, eff Dec 15, 2009; L 2011, ch 62, § 72 (Part C, Subpart B), eff March 31, 2011; L 2013, ch 480, § 12, eff Nov 13, 2013; L 2015, ch 432, § 4, eff Feb 18, 2016; L 2020, ch 55, § 2 (Part M), eff Nov 1, 2020.

Article 150
The Appearance Ticket

§ 150.40. Appearance ticket; where returnable; how and where served [Effective until July 2, 2020]

1. An appearance ticket must be made returnable at a date as soon as possible, but in no event later than twenty days from the date of issuance, or at a later date, with the court's permission due to enrollment in a pre-arraignment diversion program. The appearance ticket shall be made returnable in a local criminal court designated in section 100.55 of this title as one with which an information for the offense in question may be filed.

2. An appearance ticket, other than one issued for a traffic infraction relating to parking, must be served personally, except that an appearance ticket issued for the violation of a local zoning ordinance or local zoning law, or of a building or sanitation code may be served in any manner authorized for service under section three hundred eight of the civil practice law and rules.

3. An appearance ticket may be served anywhere in the county in which the designated offense was allegedly committed or in any adjoining county, and may be served elsewhere as prescribed in subdivision four.

4. A police officer may, for the purpose of serving an appearance ticket upon a person, follow him in continuous close pursuit, commencing either in the county in which the alleged offense was committed or in an adjoining county, in and through any county of the state, and may serve such appearance ticket upon him in any county in which he overtakes him.

HISTORY:

Add, L 1970, ch 996, § 1, eff Sept 1, 1971; amd, L 2004, ch 415, § 1, eff Aug 24, 2004; L 2005, ch 642, § 1, eff Aug 30, 2005; L 2019, ch 59, § 1-c (Part JJJ), eff Jan 1, 2020.

§ 150.40. Appearance ticket; where returnable; how and where served [Effective July 2, 2020]

1. An appearance ticket must be made returnable at a date as soon as possible, but in no event later than twenty days from the date of issuance; or at the next scheduled session of the appropriate local criminal court if such session is scheduled to occur more than twenty days from the date of issuance; or at a later date, with the court's permission due to enrollment in a pre-arraignment diversion program. The appearance ticket shall be made returnable in a local criminal court designated in section 100.55 of this title as one with which an information for the offense in question may be filed.

2. An appearance ticket, other than one issued for a traffic infraction relating to parking, must be served personally, except that an appearance ticket issued for the violation of a local zoning ordinance or local zoning law, or of a building or sanitation

code may be served in any manner authorized for service under section three hundred eight of the civil practice law and rules.

3. An appearance ticket may be served anywhere in the county in which the designated offense was allegedly committed or in any adjoining county, and may be served elsewhere as prescribed in subdivision four.

4. A police officer may, for the purpose of serving an appearance ticket upon a person, follow him in continuous close pursuit, commencing either in the county in which the alleged offense was committed or in an adjoining county, in and through any county of the state, and may serve such appearance ticket upon him in any county in which he overtakes him.

HISTORY:

Add, L 1970, ch 996, § 1, eff Sept 1, 1971; amd, L 2004, ch 415, § 1, eff Aug 24, 2004; L 2005, ch 642, § 1, eff Aug 30, 2005; L 2019, ch 59, § 1-c (Part JJJ), eff Jan 1, 2020; L 2020, ch 56, § 8 (Part UU), eff July 2, 2020.

§ 150.50. Appearance ticket; filing a local criminal court accusatory instrument; dismissal of insufficient instrument

1. A police officer or other public servant who has issued and served an appearance ticket must, at or before the time such appearance ticket is returnable, file or cause to be filed with the local criminal court in which it is returnable a local criminal court accusatory instrument charging the person named in such appearance ticket with the offense specified therein; provided, however, that no separate accusatory instrument shall be required to be filed for an appearance ticket issued for a parking infraction which conforms to the requirements set forth in paragraph (b) of subdivision one of section 1.20 of this chapter. Nothing herein contained shall authorize the use of a simplified information when not authorized by law.

2. If such accusatory instrument is not sufficient on its face, as prescribed in section 100.40, and if the court is satisfied that on the basis of the available facts or evidence it would be impossible to draw and file an accusatory instrument which is sufficient on its face, it must dismiss such accusatory instrument.

HISTORY:

Add, L 1970, ch 996, § 1; amd, L 1972, ch 661, § 37; L 1987, ch 549, § 13, eff Nov 1, 1987; L 2019, ch 450, § 2, eff Nov 8, 2019.

Article 170
Proceedings Upon Information, Simplified Traffic Information, Prosecutor's Information and Misdemeanor Complaint From Arraignment to Plea

§ 170.15. Removal of action from one local criminal court to another

Under circumstances prescribed in this section, a criminal action based upon an information, a simplified information, a prosecutor's information or a misdemeanor complaint may be removed from one local criminal court to another:

1. When a defendant arrested by a police officer for an offense other than a felony, allegedly committed in a city or town, has, owing to special circumstances and pursuant to law, not been brought before the particular local criminal court which by reason of the situs of such offense has trial jurisdiction thereof, but, instead, before a local criminal court which does not have trial jurisdiction thereof, and therein stands charged with such offense by information, simplified information or misdemeanor complaint, such local criminal court must arraign him upon such accusatory instrument. If the defendant desires to enter a plea of guilty thereto immediately following such arraignment, such local criminal court must permit him to do so and must thereafter conduct the action to judgment. Otherwise, it must remit the action, together with all pertinent papers and documents, to the local criminal court which has trial jurisdiction of the action, and the latter court must then conduct such action to judgment or other final disposition.

2. When a defendant arrested by a police officer for an offense other than a felony has been brought before a superior court judge sitting as a local criminal court for

arraignment upon an information, simplified information or misdemeanor complaint charging such offense, such judge must, as a local criminal court, arraign the defendant upon such accusatory instrument. Such judge must then remit the action, together with all pertinent papers and documents, to a local criminal court having trial jurisdiction thereof. The latter court must then conduct such action to judgment or other final disposition.

3. At any time within the period provided by section 255.20, where a defendant is arraigned upon an information, a simplified information, a prosecutor's information or a misdemeanor complaint pending in a city court, town court or a village court having trial jurisdiction thereof, a judge of the county court of the county in which such city court, town court or village court is located may, upon motion of the defendant or the people, order that the action be transferred for disposition from the court in which the matter is pending to another designated local criminal court of the county, upon the ground that disposition thereof within a reasonable time in the court from which removal is sought is unlikely owing to:

(a) Death, disability or other incapacity or disqualification of all of the judges of such court; or

(b) Inability of such court to form a jury in a case, in which the defendant is entitled to and has requested a jury trial.

4. Notwithstanding any provision of this section to the contrary, in any county outside a city having a population of one million or more, upon or after arraignment of a defendant on an information, a simplified information, a prosecutor's information or a misdemeanor complaint pending in a local criminal court, such court may, upon motion of the defendant and after giving the district attorney an opportunity to be heard, order that the action be removed from the court in which the matter is pending to another local criminal court in the same county which has been designated a court formed to address a matter of special concern based upon the status of the defendant or the victim, commonly known as a "problem solving court," including, but not limited to, drug court, domestic violence court, youth court, mental health court, and veterans court, by the chief administrator of the courts, and such problem solving court may then conduct such action to judgment or other final disposition; provided, however, that an order of removal issued under this subdivision shall not take effect until five days after the date the order is issued unless, prior to such effective date, the problem solving court notifies the court that issued the order that:

(a) it will not accept the action, in which event the order shall not take effect, or

(b) it will accept the action on a date prior to such effective date, in which event the order shall take effect upon such prior date.

Upon providing notification pursuant to paragraph (a) or (b) of this subdivision, the problem solving court shall promptly give notice to the defendant, his or her counsel and the district attorney.

Upon providing notification pursuant to paragraph (a) or (b) of this subdivision, the drug court shall promptly give notice to the defendant, his or her counsel and the district attorney.

5.(a) Notwithstanding any provision of this section to the contrary, in any county outside a city having a population of one million or more, upon or after arraignment of a defendant on an information, a simplified information, a prosecutor's information or a misdemeanor complaint pending in a local criminal court, such court may, upon motion of the defendant and after giving the district attorney an opportunity to be heard, order that the action be removed from the court in which the matter is pending to another local criminal court in the same county, or with consent of the district attorney to another court in an adjoining county, that has been designated as a human trafficking court by the chief administrator of the courts, and such human trafficking court may then conduct such action to judgement or other final deposition; provided, however, that an order of removal issued under this subdivision shall not take effect until five days after the date the order is issued unless, prior to such effective date, the human trafficking court notifies the court that issued the order that:

i. it will not accept the action, in which event the order shall not take effect; or

ii. it will accept the action on a date prior to such effective date, in which event the order shall take effect upon such prior date.

(b) Upon providing notification pursuant to subparagraph i or ii of paragraph (a) of this subdivision, the human trafficking court shall promptly give notice to the defendant, his or her counsel, and the district attorney.

HISTORY:

Add, L 1970, ch 996, § 1; amd, L 1972, ch 661, § 39, eff Sept 1, 1972; L 1974, ch 763, § 6; L 1974, ch 837, § 1, eff June 7, 1974; L 1984, ch 695, § 3, eff Aug 1, 1984; L 1998, ch 77, § 1, eff June 2, 1998; L 1999, ch 565, § 1, eff Nov 1, 1999; L 2000, ch 67, § 1, eff Nov 1, 2000; L 2018, ch 191, § 1, eff Aug 15, 2018; L 2019, ch 634, § 1, eff Dec 12, 2019.

Title J
Prosecution of Indictments in Superior Courts—Plea to Sentence

Article 245 Discovery

Article 310 Jury Trial—Deliberation and Verdict of Jury

Article 330 Proceedings from Verdict to Sentence

Article 245
Discovery

§ 245.10. Timing of discovery.

1.(a) Subject to subparagraph (iv) of this paragraph, the prosecution shall perform its initial discovery obligations under subdivision one of section 245.20 of this article as soon as practicable but not later than the time periods specified in subparagraphs (i) and (ii) of this paragraph, as applicable. Portions of materials claimed to be nondiscoverable may be withheld pending a determination and ruling of the court under section 245.70 of this article; but the defendant shall be notified in writing that information has not been disclosed under a particular subdivision of such section, and the discoverable portions of such materials shall be disclosed to the extent practicable. When the discoverable materials, including video footage from body-worn cameras, surveillance cameras, or dashboard cameras, are exceptionally voluminous or, despite diligent, good faith efforts, are otherwise not in the actual possession of the prosecution, the time period in this paragraph may be stayed by up to an additional thirty calendar days without need for a motion pursuant to subdivision two of section 245.70 of this article.

(i) When a defendant is in custody during the pendency of the criminal case, the prosecution shall perform its initial discovery obligations within twenty calendar days after the defendant's arraignment on an indictment, superior court information, prosecutor's information, information, simplified information, misdemeanor complaint or felony complaint.

(ii) When the defendant is not in custody during the pendency of the criminal case, the prosecution shall perform its initial discovery obligations within thirty-five calendar days after the defendant's arraignment on an indictment, superior court information, prosecutor's information, information, simplified information, misdemeanor complaint or felony complaint.

(iii) Notwithstanding the timelines contained in the opening paragraph of this paragraph, the prosecutor's discovery obligation under subdivision one of section 245.20 of this article shall be performed as soon as practicable, but not later than fifteen days before the trial of a simplified information charging a traffic infraction under the vehicle and traffic law, or by an information charging one or more petty offenses as defined by the municipal code of a village, town, city, or county, that do not carry a statutorily authorized sentence of imprisonment, and where the defendant stands charged before the court with no crime or offense, provided however that nothing in this subparagraph shall prevent a defendant from filing a motion for disclosure of such items and information under subdivision one of such section 245.20 of this article at an earlier date.

(iv)

(A) Portions of materials claimed to be non-discoverable may be withheld pending a determination and ruling of the court under section 245.70 of this article; but the defendant shall be notified in writing that information has not been disclosed under a particular subdivision of such section, and the discoverable portions of such materials shall be disclosed to the extent practicable. Information related to or evidencing the identity of a 911 caller, the victim or witness of an offense defined under article one hundred thirty or sections 230.34 and 230.34-a of the penal law, or any other victim or witness of a crime where the defendant has substantiated affiliation with a criminal enterprise as defined in subdivision three of section 460.10 of the penal law may be withheld, provided, however, the defendant may move the court for disclosure.

(B) When the discoverable materials are exceptionally voluminous or, despite diligent, good faith efforts, are otherwise not in the actual possession of the prosecution, the time period in this paragraph may be extended pursuant to a motion pursuant to subdivision two of section 245.70 of this article. For purposes of this article, voluminous materials may include, but are not limited to, video footage from body worn cameras, surveillance cameras or dashboard cameras.

(b) The prosecution shall perform its supplemental discovery obligations under subdivision three of section 245.20 of this article as soon as practicable but not later than fifteen calendar days prior to the first scheduled trial date.

(c) The prosecution shall disclose statements of the defendant as described in paragraph (a) of subdivision one of section 245.20 of this article to any defendant who has been arraigned in a local criminal court upon a currently undisposed of felony complaint charging an offense which is a subject of a prospective or pending grand jury proceeding, no later than forty-eight hours before the time scheduled for the defendant to testify at a grand jury proceeding pursuant to subdivision five of section 190.50 of this part.

2. Defendant's performance of obligations. The defendant shall perform his or her discovery obligations under subdivision four of section 245.20 of this article not later than thirty calendar days after being served with the prosecution's certificate of compliance pursuant to subdivision one of section 245.50 of this article, except that portions of materials claimed to be non-discoverable may be withheld pending a determination and ruling of the court under section 245.70 of this article; but the prosecution must be notified in writing that information has not been disclosed under a particular section.

HISTORY:

L 2019, ch 59, § 2 (Part LLL), eff Jan 1, 2020; amd, L 2020, ch 56, § 1 (Part HHH), eff May 3, 2020.

§ 245.20. Automatic discovery.

1. Initial discovery for the defendant. The prosecution shall disclose to the defendant, and permit the defendant to discover, inspect, copy, photograph and test, all items and information that relate to the subject matter of the case and are in the possession, custody or control of the prosecution or persons under the prosecution's direction or control, including but not limited to:

(a) All written or recorded statements, and the substance of all oral statements, made by the defendant or a co-defendant to a public servant engaged in law enforcement activity or to a person then acting under his or her direction or in cooperation with him or her.

(b) All transcripts of the testimony of a person who has testified before a grand jury, including but not limited to the defendant or a co-defendant. If in the exercise of reasonable diligence, and due to the limited availability of transcription resources, a transcript is unavailable for disclosure within the time period specified in subdivision one of section 245.10 of this article, such time period may be stayed by up to an additional thirty calendar days without need for a motion pursuant to subdivision two of section 245.70 of this article; except that such disclosure shall be made as soon as practicable and not later than thirty calendar days before the first scheduled trial date, unless an order is obtained pursuant to section 245.70 of this article. When the court is required to review grand jury transcripts, the prosecution shall disclose such transcripts to the court expeditiously upon receipt by the prosecutor, notwithstanding the otherwise-applicable time periods for disclosure in this article.

(c) The names and adequate contact information for all persons other than law enforcement personnel whom the prosecutor knows to have evidence or information relevant to any offense charged or to any potential defense thereto, including a designation by the prosecutor as to which of those persons may be called as witnesses. Nothing in this paragraph shall require the disclosure of physical addresses; provided, however, upon a motion and good cause shown the court may direct the disclosure of a physical address. Information under this subdivision relating to the identity of a 911 caller, the victim or witness of an offense defined under article one hundred thirty or section 230.34 or 230.34-a of the penal law, any other victim or witness of a crime where the defendant has substantiated affiliation with a criminal enterprise as defined in subdivision three of section 460.10 of the penal law, or a confidential informant may be withheld, and redacted from discovery materials, without need for a motion pursuant to section 245.70 of this article; but the prosecution shall notify the defendant in writing that such information has not been disclosed, unless the court rules otherwise for good cause shown.

(d) The name and work affiliation of all law enforcement personnel whom the prosecutor knows to have evidence or information relevant to any offense charged or to any potential defense thereto, including a designation by the prosecutor as to which of those persons may be called as witnesses. Information under this subdivision relating to undercover personnel may be withheld, and redacted from discovery materials, without need for a motion pursuant to section 245.70 of this article; but the prosecution shall notify the defendant in writing that such information has not been disclosed, unless the court rules otherwise for good cause shown.

(e) All statements, written or recorded or summarized in any writing or recording, made by persons who have evidence or information relevant to any offense charged or to any potential defense thereto, including all police reports, notes of police and other investigators, and law enforcement agency reports. This provision also includes statements, written or recorded or summarized in any writing or recording, by persons to be called as witnesses at pre-trial hearings.

(f) Expert opinion evidence, including the name, business address, current curriculum vitae, a list of publications, and a list of proficiency tests and results administered or taken within the past ten years of each expert witness whom the prosecutor intends to call as a witness at trial or a pre-trial hearing, and all reports prepared by the expert that pertain to the case, or if no report is prepared, a written statement of the facts and opinions to which the expert is expected to testify and a summary of the grounds for each opinion. This paragraph does not alter or in any way affect the procedures, obligations or rights set forth in section 250.10 of this title. If in the exercise of reasonable diligence this information is unavailable for disclosure within the time period specified in subdivision one of section 245.10 of this article, that period shall be stayed without need for a motion pursuant to subdivision two of section 245.70 of this article; except that the prosecution shall notify the defendant in writing that such information has not been disclosed, and such disclosure shall be made as soon as practicable and not later than sixty calendar days before the first scheduled trial date, unless an order is obtained pursuant to section 245.70 of this article. When the prosecution's expert witness is being called in response to disclosure of an expert witness by the defendant, the court shall alter a scheduled trial date, if necessary, to allow the prosecution thirty calendar days to make the disclosure and the defendant thirty calendar days to prepare and respond to the new materials.

(g) All tapes or other electronic recordings, including all electronic recordings of 911 telephone calls made or received in connection with the alleged criminal incident, and a designation by the prosecutor as to which of the recordings under this paragraph the prosecution intends to introduce at trial or a pre-trial hearing. If the discoverable materials under this paragraph exceed ten hours in total length, the prosecution may disclose only the recordings that it intends to introduce at trial or a pre-trial hearing, along with a list of the source and approximate quantity of other recordings and their general subject matter if known, and the defendant shall have the right upon request to obtain recordings not previously disclosed. The prosecution shall disclose the requested materials as soon as practicable and not less than fifteen calendar days after the defendant's request, unless an order is obtained pursuant to section 245.70 of this article. The prosecution may withhold the names and identifying information of any person who contacted 911 without the need for a protective order pursuant to section 245.70 of this article, provided, however, the defendant may move the court for disclosure. If the prosecution intends to call such person as a witness at a trial or hearing, the prosecution must disclose the name and contact information of such witness no later than fifteen days before such trial or hearing, or as soon as practicable.

(h) All photographs and drawings made or completed by a public servant engaged in law enforcement activity, or which were made by a person whom the prosecutor intends to call as a witness at trial or a pre-trial hearing, or which relate to the subject matter of the case.

(i) All photographs, photocopies and reproductions made by or at the direction of law enforcement personnel of any property prior to its release pursuant to section 450.10 of the penal law.

(j) All reports, documents, records, data, calculations or writings, including but not limited to preliminary tests and screening results and bench notes and analyses performed or stored electronically, concerning physical or mental examinations, or scientific tests or experiments or comparisons, relating to the criminal action or proceeding which were made by or at the request or direction of a public servant engaged in law enforcement activity, or which were made by a person whom the prosecutor intends to call as a witness at trial or a pre-trial hearing, or which the prosecution intends to introduce at trial or a pre-trial hearing. Information under this paragraph also includes, but is not limited to, laboratory information management system records relating to such materials, any preliminary or final findings of non-conformance with accreditation, industry or governmental standards or laboratory protocols, and any conflicting analyses or results by laboratory personnel regardless of the laboratory's final analysis or results. If the prosecution submitted one or more items for testing to, or received results from, a forensic science laboratory or similar entity not under the prosecution's direction or control, the court on motion of a party shall issue subpoenas or orders to such laboratory or entity to cause materials under this paragraph to be made available for disclosure. The prosecution shall not be required to provide information related to the results of physical or mental examinations, or scientific tests or experiments or comparisons, unless and until such examinations, tests, experiments, or comparisons have been completed.

(k) All evidence and information, including that which is known to police or other law enforcement agencies acting on the government's behalf in the case, that tends to: (i) negate the defendant's guilt as to a charged offense; (ii) reduce the degree of or mitigate the defendant's culpability as to a charged offense; (iii) support a potential defense to a charged offense; (iv) impeach the credibility of a testifying prosecution witness; (v) undermine evidence of the defendant's identity as a perpetrator of a charged offense; (vi) provide a basis for a motion to suppress evidence; or (vii) mitigate punishment. Information under this subdivision shall be disclosed whether or not such information is recorded in tangible form and irrespective of whether the prosecutor credits the information. The prosecutor shall disclose the information expeditiously upon its receipt and shall not delay disclosure if it is obtained earlier than the time period for disclosure in subdivision one of section 245.10 of this article.

(l) A summary of all promises, rewards and inducements made to, or in favor of, persons who may be called as witnesses, as well as requests for consideration by persons who may be called as witnesses and copies of all documents relevant to a promise, reward or inducement.

(m) A list of all tangible objects obtained from, or allegedly possessed by, the defendant or a co-defendant. The list shall include a designation by the prosecutor as to which objects were physically or constructively possessed by the defendant and were recovered during a search or seizure by a public servant or an agent thereof, and which tangible objects were recovered by a public servant or an agent thereof after allegedly being abandoned by the defendant. If the prosecution intends to prove the defendant's possession of any tangible objects by means of a statutory presumption of possession, it shall designate such intention as to each such object. If reasonably practicable, the prosecution shall also designate the location from which each tangible object was recovered. There is also a right to inspect, copy, photograph and test the listed tangible objects.

(n) Whether a search warrant has been executed and all documents relating thereto, including but not limited to the warrant, the warrant application, supporting affidavits, a police inventory of all property seized under the warrant, and a transcript of all testimony or other oral communications offered in support of the warrant application.

(o) All tangible property that relates to the subject matter of the case, along with a designation of which items the prosecution intends to introduce in its case-in-chief at trial or a pre-trial hearing. If in the exercise of reasonable diligence the prosecutor has not formed an intention within the time period specified in subdivision one of section 245.10 of this article that an item under this subdivision will be introduced at trial or a pre-trial hearing, the prosecution shall notify the defendant in writing, and the time period in which to designate items as exhibits shall be stayed without need for a motion pursuant to subdivision two of section 245.70 of this article; but the disclosure shall be made as soon as practicable and subject to the continuing duty to disclose in section 245.60 of this article.

(p) A complete record of judgments of conviction for all defendants and all persons designated as potential prosecution witnesses pursuant to paragraph (c) of this subdivision, other than those witnesses who are experts.

(q) When it is known to the prosecution, the existence of any pending criminal action against all persons designated as potential prosecution witnesses pursuant to paragraph (c) of this subdivision.

(r) The approximate date, time and place of the offense or offenses charged and of the defendant's seizure and arrest.

(s) In any prosecution alleging a violation of the vehicle and traffic law, where the defendant is charged by indictment, superior court information, prosecutor's information, information, or simplified information, all records of calibration, certification, inspection, repair or maintenance of machines and instruments utilized to perform any scientific tests and experiments, including but not limited to any test of a person's breath, blood, urine or saliva, for the period of six months prior and six months after such test was conducted, including the records of gas chromatography related to the certification of all reference standards and the certification certificate, if any, held by the operator of the machine or instrument. The time period required by subdivision one of section 245.10 of this article shall not apply to the disclosure of records created six months after a test was conducted, but such disclosure shall be made as soon as practicable and in any event, the earlier of fifteen days following receipt, or fifteen days before the first scheduled trial date.

(t) In any prosecution alleging a violation of section 156.05 or 156.10 of the penal law, the time, place and manner such violation occurred.

(u)(i) A copy of all electronically created or stored information seized or obtained by or on behalf of law enforcement from: (A) the defendant as described in subparagraph (ii) of this paragraph; or (B) a source other than the defendant which relates to the subject matter of the case.

(ii) If the electronically created or stored information originates from a device, account, or other electronically stored source that the prosecution believes the defendant owned, maintained, or had lawful access to and is within the possession, custody or control of the prosecution or persons under the prosecution's direction or control, the prosecution shall provide a complete copy of the electronically created or stored information from the device or account or other source.

(iii) If possession of such electronically created or stored information would be a crime under New York state or federal law, the prosecution shall make those portions of the electronically created or stored information that are not criminal to possess available as specified under this paragraph and shall afford counsel for the defendant access to inspect contraband portions at a supervised location that provides regular and reasonable hours for such access, such as a prosecutor's office, police station, or court.

(iv) This paragraph shall not be construed to alter or in any way affect the right to be free from unreasonable searches and seizures or such other rights a suspect or defendant may derive from the state constitution or the United States constitution. If in the exercise of reasonable diligence the information under this paragraph is not available for disclosure within the time period required by subdivision one of section 245.10 of this article, that period shall be stayed without need for a motion pursuant to subdivision two of section 245.70 of this article, except that the prosecution shall notify the defendant in writing that such information has not been disclosed, and such disclosure shall be made as soon as practicable and not later than forty-five calendar days before the first scheduled trial date, unless an order is obtained pursuant to section 245.70 of this article.

2. Duties of the prosecution. The prosecutor shall make a diligent, good faith effort to ascertain the existence of material or information discoverable under subdivision one of this section and to cause such material or information to be made available for discovery where it exists but is not within the prosecutor's possession, custody or control; provided that the prosecutor shall not be required to obtain by subpoena duces tecum material or information which the defendant may thereby obtain. For purposes of subdivision one of this section, all items and information related to the prosecution of a charge in the possession of any New York state or local police or law enforcement agency shall be deemed to be in the possession of the prosecution. The prosecution shall also identify any laboratory having contact with evidence related to the prosecution of a charge. This subdivision shall not require the prosecutor to ascertain the existence of witnesses not known to the police or another law enforcement agency, or the written or recorded statements thereof, under paragraph (c) or (e) of subdivision one of this section.

3. Supplemental discovery for the defendant. The prosecution shall disclose to the defendant a list of all misconduct and criminal acts of the defendant not charged in the indictment, superior court information, prosecutor's information, information, or simplified information, which the prosecution intends to use at trial for purposes of (a) impeaching the credibility of the defendant, or (b) as substantive proof of any material issue in the case. In addition the prosecution shall designate whether it intends to use each listed act for impeachment and/or as substantive proof.

4. Reciprocal discovery for the prosecution. (a) The defendant shall, subject to constitutional limitations, disclose to the prosecution, and permit the prosecution to discover, inspect, copy or photograph, any material and relevant evidence within the defendant's or counsel for the defendant's possession or control that is discoverable under paragraphs (f), (g), (h), (j), (l) and (o) of subdivision one of this section, which the defendant intends to introduce at trial or a pre-trial hearing, and the names, addresses, birth dates, and all statements, written or recorded or summarized in any writing or recording, of those persons other than the defendant whom the defendant intends to call as witnesses at trial or a pre-trial hearing.

(b) Disclosure of the name, address, birth date, and all statements, written or recorded or summarized in any writing or recording, of a person whom the defendant intends to call as a witness for the sole purpose of impeaching a prosecution witness is not required until after the prosecution witness has testified at trial.

(c) If in the exercise of reasonable diligence the reciprocally discoverable information under paragraph (f) or (o) of subdivision one of this section is unavailable for disclosure within the time period specified in subdivision two of section 245.10 of this article, such time period shall be stayed without need for a motion pursuant to subdivision two of section 245.70 of this article; but the disclosure shall be made as soon as practicable and subject to the continuing duty to disclose in section 245.60 of this article.

5. Stay of automatic discovery; remedies and sanctions. Section 245.10 and subdivisions one, two, three and four of this section shall have the force and effect of a court order, and failure to provide discovery pursuant to such section or subdivision may result in application of any remedies or sanctions permitted for non-compliance with a court order under section 245.80 of this article. However, if in the judgment of either party good cause exists for declining to make any of the disclosures set forth above, such party may move for a protective order pursuant to section 245.70 of this article and production of the item shall be stayed pending a ruling by the court. The opposing party shall be notified in writing that information has not been disclosed under a particular section. When some parts of material or information are discoverable but in the judgment of a party good cause exists for declining to disclose other parts, the discoverable parts shall be disclosed and the disclosing party shall give notice in writing that non-discoverable parts have been withheld.

6. Redactions permitted. Either party may redact social security numbers and tax numbers from disclosures under this article.

7. Presumption of openness. There shall be a presumption in favor of disclosure when interpreting sections 245.10 and 245.25, and subdivision one of section 245.20, of this article.

HISTORY:

L 2019, ch 59, § 2 (Part LLL), eff Jan 1, 2020; amd, L 2020, ch 56, § 2 (Part HHH), eff May 3, 2020.

§ 245.25. Disclosure prior to certain guilty pleas.

1. Pre-indictment guilty pleas. Upon a felony complaint, where the prosecution has made a pre-indictment guilty plea offer requiring a plea to a crime, the prosecutor must disclose to the defense, and permit the defense to discover, inspect, copy, photograph and test, all items and information that would be discoverable prior to trial under subdivision one of section 245.20 of this article and are in the possession, custody or control of the prosecution. The prosecution shall disclose the discoverable items and information not less than three calendar days prior to the expiration date of any guilty plea offer by the prosecution or any deadline imposed by the court for acceptance of the guilty plea offer. If the prosecution does not comply with the requirements of this subdivision, then, on a defendant's motion alleging a violation of this subdivision, the court must consider the impact of any violation on the defendant's decision to accept or reject a plea offer. If the court finds that such violation materially affected the defendant's decision, and if the prosecution declines to reinstate the lapsed or withdrawn plea offer, the court - as a presumptive minimum sanction - must preclude the admission at trial of any evidence not disclosed as required under this subdivision. The court may take other appropriate action as necessary to address the non-compliance. The rights under this subdivision do not apply to items or information that are the subject of a protective order under section 245.70 of this article; but if such information tends to be exculpatory, the court shall reconsider the protective order. A defendant may waive his or her rights under this subdivision; but a guilty plea offer may not be conditioned on such waiver.

2. Other guilty pleas. Upon an indictment, superior court information, prosecutor's information, information, simplified information, or misdemeanor complaint, where the prosecution has made a guilty plea offer requiring a plea to a crime, the prosecutor must disclose to the defense, and permit the defense to discover, inspect, copy, photograph and test, all items and information that would be discoverable prior to trial under subdivision one of section 245.20 of this article and are within the possession, custody or control of the prosecution. The prosecution shall disclose the discoverable items and information not less than seven calendar days prior to the expiration date of any guilty plea offer by the prosecution or any deadline imposed by the court for acceptance of the guilty plea offer. If the prosecution does not comply with the requirements of this subdivision, then, on a defendant's motion alleging a violation of this subdivision, the court must consider the impact of any violation on the defendant's decision to accept or reject a plea offer. If the court finds that such violation materially affected the defendant's decision, and if the prosecution declines to reinstate the lapsed or

withdrawn plea offer, the court - as a presumptive minimum sanction - must preclude the admission at trial of any evidence not disclosed as required under this subdivision. The court may take other appropriate action as necessary to address the non-compliance. The rights under this subdivision do not apply to items or information that are the subject of a protective order under section 245.70 of this article; but if such information tends to be exculpatory, the court shall reconsider the protective order. A defendant may waive his or her rights under this subdivision; but a guilty plea offer may not be conditioned on such waiver. Notwithstanding the timelines contained in the opening paragraph of paragraph (a) of subdivision one of section 245.10 of this article, the prosecutor's discovery obligation under subdivision one of section 245.20 of this article shall be performed as soon as practicable, but not later than fifteen days before the trial of a simplified information charging a traffic infraction under the vehicle and traffic law, or by an information charging one or more petty offenses as defined by the municipal code of a village, town, city, or county, that do not carry a statutorily authorized sentence of imprisonment, and where the defendant stands charged before the court with no crime or offense, provided however that nothing in this subdivision shall prevent a defendant from filing a motion for disclosure of such items and information under subdivision one of such section 245.20 of this article at an earlier date.

3. Repleader. Nothing in this section shall prevent the waiver of discovery from being a condition of a repleader, where the defendant's original conviction is vacated on agreement between the parties pursuant to section 440.10 of this part.

HISTORY:
L 2019, ch 59, § 2 (Part LLL), eff Jan 1, 2020; amd, L 2020, ch 56, § 6 (Part HHH), eff May 3, 2020.

§ 245.50. Certificates of compliance; readiness for trial.

1. By the prosecution. When the prosecution has provided the discovery required by subdivision one of section 245.20 of this article, except for discovery that is lost or destroyed as provided by paragraph (b) of subdivision one of section 245.80 of this article and except for any items or information that are the subject of an order pursuant to section 245.70 of this article, it shall serve upon the defendant and file with the court a certificate of compliance. The certificate of compliance shall state that, after exercising due diligence and making reasonable inquiries to ascertain the existence of material and information subject to discovery, the prosecutor has disclosed and made available all known material and information subject to discovery. It shall also identify the items provided. If additional discovery is subsequently provided prior to trial pursuant to section 245.60 of this article, a supplemental certificate shall be served upon the defendant and filed with the court identifying the additional material and information provided. No adverse consequence to the prosecution or the prosecutor shall result from the filing of a certificate of compliance in good faith and reasonable under the circumstances; but the court may grant a remedy or sanction for a discovery violation as provided in section 245.80 of this article.

2. By the defendant. When the defendant has provided all discovery required by subdivision four of section 245.20 of this article, except for any items or information that are the subject of an order pursuant to section 245.70 of this article, counsel for the defendant shall serve upon the prosecution and file with the court a certificate of compliance. The certificate shall state that, after exercising due diligence and making reasonable inquiries to ascertain the existence of material and information subject to discovery, counsel for the defendant has disclosed and made available all known material and information subject to discovery. It shall also identify the items provided. If additional discovery is subsequently provided prior to trial pursuant to section 245.60 of this article, a supplemental certificate shall be served upon the prosecution and filed with the court identifying the additional material and information provided. No adverse consequence to the defendant or counsel for the defendant shall result from the filing of a certificate of compliance in good faith; but the court may grant a remedy or sanction for a discovery violation as provided in section 245.80 of this article.

3. Trial readiness. Notwithstanding the provisions of any other law, absent an individualized finding of special circumstances in the instant case by the court before which the charge is pending, the prosecution shall not be deemed ready for trial for

purposes of section 30.30 of this chapter until it has filed a proper certificate pursuant to subdivision one of this section. A court may deem the prosecution ready for trial pursuant to section 30.30 of this chapter where information that might be considered discoverable under this article cannot be disclosed because it has been lost, destroyed, or otherwise unavailable as provided by paragraph (b) of subdivision one of section 245.80 of this article, despite diligent and good faith efforts, reasonable under the circumstances. Provided, however, that the court may grant a remedy or sanction for a discovery violation as provided by section 245.80 of this article.

4. Challenges to, or questions related to a certificate of compliance shall be addressed by motion.

HISTORY:

L 2019, ch 59, § 2 (Part LLL), eff Jan 1, 2020; amd, L 2020, ch 56, § 7 (Part HHH), eff May 3, 2020.

§ 245.70. Protective orders.

1. Any discovery subject to protective order. Upon a showing of good cause by either party, the court may at any time order that discovery or inspection of any kind of material or information under this article be denied, restricted, conditioned or deferred, or make such other order as is appropriate, including, for 911 calls, allowing the disclosure of a transcript of an audio recording in lieu of the recording. The court may impose as a condition on discovery to a defendant that the material or information to be discovered be available only to counsel for the defendant; or, alternatively, that counsel for the defendant, and persons employed by the attorney or appointed by the court to assist in the preparation of a defendant's case, may not disclose physical copies of the discoverable documents to a defendant or to anyone else, provided that the prosecution affords the defendant access to inspect redacted copies of the discoverable documents at a supervised location that provides regular and reasonable hours for such access, such as a prosecutor's office, police station, facility of detention, or court. Should the court impose as a condition that some material or information be available only to counsel for the defendant, the court shall inform the defendant on the record that his or her attorney is not permitted by law to disclose such material or information to the defendant. The court may permit a party seeking or opposing a protective order under this section, or another affected person, to submit papers or testify on the record ex parte or in camera. Any such papers and a transcript of such testimony may be sealed and shall constitute a part of the record on appeal. This section does not alter the allocation of the burden of proof with regard to matters at issue, including privilege.

2. Modification of time periods for discovery. Upon motion of a party in an individual case, the court may alter the time periods for discovery imposed by this article upon a showing of good cause.

3. Prompt hearing. Upon request for a protective order, unless the defendant voluntarily consents to the people's request for a protective order, the court shall conduct an appropriate hearing within three business days to determine whether good cause has been shown and when practicable shall render a decision expeditiously. Any materials submitted and a transcript of the proceeding may be sealed and shall constitute a part of the record on appeal. When the defendant is charged with a violent felony offense as defined in section 70.02 of the penal law, or any class A felony other than those defined in article two hundred twenty of the penal law, the court may, at the prosecutor's request, for good cause shown, conduct such hearing in camera and outside the presence of the defendant, provided however that this shall not affect the rights of the court to receive testimony or papers ex-parte or in camera as provided in subdivision one of this section.

4. Showing of good cause. In determining good cause under this section the court may consider: constitutional rights or limitations; danger to the integrity of physical evidence or the safety of a witness; risk of intimidation, economic reprisal, bribery, harassment or unjustified annoyance or embarrassment to any person, and the nature, severity and likelihood of that risk; a risk of an adverse effect upon the legitimate needs of law enforcement, including the protection of the confidentiality of informants, and the nature, severity and likelihood of that risk; the nature and circumstances of the factual allegations in the case; whether the defendant has a history of witness intimidation or tampering and the nature of that history; the nature of the stated

reasons in support of a protective order; the nature of the witness identifying information that is sought to be addressed by a protective order, including the option of employing adequate alternative contact information; danger to any person stemming from factors such as a defendant's substantiated affiliation with a criminal enterprise as defined in subdivision three of section 460.10 of the penal law; and other similar factors found to outweigh the usefulness of the discovery.

5. Successor counsel or pro se defendant. In cases in which the attorney-client relationship is terminated prior to trial for any reason, any material or information disclosed subject to a condition that it be available only to counsel for the defendant, or limited in dissemination by protective order or otherwise, shall be provided only to successor counsel for the defendant under the same condition or conditions or be returned to the prosecution, unless the court rules otherwise for good cause shown or the prosecutor gives written consent. Any work product derived from such material or information shall not be provided to the defendant, unless the court rules otherwise or the prosecutor gives written consent. If the defendant is acting as his or her own attorney, the court may regulate the time, place and manner of access to any discoverable material or information; and it may as appropriate appoint persons to assist the defendant in the investigation or preparation of the case. Upon motion or application of a defendant acting as his or her own attorney, the court may at any time modify or vacate any condition or restriction relating to access to discoverable material or information, for good cause shown.

6. Expedited review of adverse ruling. (a) A party that has unsuccessfully sought, or unsuccessfully opposed the granting of, a protective order under this section relating to the name, address, contact information or statements of a person may obtain expedited review of that ruling by an individual justice of the intermediate appellate court to which an appeal from a judgment of conviction in the case would be taken.

(b) Such review shall be sought within two business days of the adverse or partially adverse ruling, by order to show cause filed with the intermediate appellate court. The order to show cause shall in addition be timely served on the lower court and on the opposing party, and shall be accompanied by a sworn affirmation stating in good faith (i) that the ruling affects substantial interests, and (ii) that diligent efforts to reach an accommodation of the underlying discovery dispute with opposing counsel failed or that no accommodation was feasible; except that service on the opposing party, and a statement regarding efforts to reach an accommodation, are unnecessary where the opposing party was not made aware of the application for a protective order and good cause is shown for omitting service of the order to show cause on the opposing party. The lower court's order subject to review shall be stayed until the appellate justice renders a determination.

(c) The assignment of the individual appellate justice, and the mode of and procedure for the review, shall be determined by rules of the individual appellate courts. The appellate justice may consider any relevant and reliable information bearing on the issue, and may dispense with written briefs other than supporting and opposing materials previously submitted to the lower court. The appellate justice may dispense with the issuance of a written opinion in rendering his or her decision, and when practicable shall render decision and order expeditiously. Such review, decision and order shall not affect the right of a defendant, in a subsequent appeal from a judgment of conviction, to claim as error the ruling reviewed.

7. Compliance with protective order. Any protective order issued under this article is a mandate of the court for purposes of the offense of criminal contempt in subdivision three of section 215.50 of the penal law.

HISTORY:
L 2019, ch 59, § 2 (Part LLL), eff Jan 1, 2020; amd, L 2020, ch 56, § 3 (Part HHH), eff May 3, 2020.

§ 245.75. Waiver of discovery by defendant.

1. A defendant who does not seek discovery from the prosecution under this article shall so notify the prosecution and the court at the defendant's arraignment on an indictment, superior court information, prosecutor's information, information, or simplified information, or expeditiously thereafter but before receiving discovery from the prosecution pursuant to subdivision one of section 245.20 of this article, and the

defendant need not provide discovery to the prosecution pursuant to subdivision four of section 245.20 and section 245.60 of this article. A waiver shall be in writing, signed for the individual case by the counsel for the defendant and filed with the court. The court shall inquire of the defendant on the record to ensure that the defendant understands his or her right to discovery and right to waive discovery. Such a waiver does not alter or in any way affect the procedures, obligations or rights set forth in sections 250.10, 250.20 and 250.30 of this title, or otherwise established or required by law. The prosecution may not condition a guilty plea offer on the defense's execution of a waiver under this section. Counsel for the defendant may advise his or her client about the defendant's right to discovery and right to waive discovery; such advice shall not constitute a condition of a guilty plea.

2. Nothing in this section shall prevent the waiver of discovery from being a condition of the repleader, where the defendant's original conviction is vacated on agreement between the parties pursuant to section 440.10 of this part.

HISTORY:

L 2019, ch 59, § 2 (Part LLL), eff Jan 1, 2020; amd, L 2020, ch 56, § 5 (Part HHH), eff May 3, 2020.

Article 310
Jury Trial—Deliberation and Verdict of Jury

§ 310.10. Jury deliberation; requirement of; where conducted.

1. Following the court's charge, except as otherwise provided by subdivision two of this section, the jury must retire to deliberate upon its verdict in a place outside the courtroom. It must be provided with suitable accommodations therefor and must, except as otherwise provided in subdivision two of this section, be continuously kept together under the supervision of a court officer or court officers. In the event such court officer or court officers are not available, the jury shall be under the supervision of an appropriate public servant or public servants. Except when so authorized by the court or when performing administerial duties with respect to the jurors, such court officers or public servants, as the case may be, may not speak to or communicate with them or permit any other person to do so.

2. At any time after the jury has been charged or commenced its deliberations, and after notice to the parties and affording such parties an opportunity to be heard on the record outside of the presence of the jury, the court may declare the deliberations to be in recess and may thereupon direct the jury to suspend its deliberations and to separate for a reasonable period of time to be specified by the court, not lasting beyond close of business on the second day following such recess or, for good cause shown, beyond close of business on the third day following recess of jury deliberations unless the defendant consents to a longer period of suspension and separation. For the purposes of this section, where a day referred to in this subdivision falls on a Saturday, Sunday or holiday, such day shall mean the next day thereafter during which the courthouse is open for the conduct of trials. Before each recess, the court must admonish the jury as provided in section 270.40 of this title and direct it not to resume its deliberations until all twelve jurors have reassembled in the designated place at the termination of the declared recess.

3. [Repealed]

HISTORY:

Add, L 1970, ch 996, § 1; amd, L 1974, ch 214, § 1; L 1995, ch 83, § 209, eff July 5, 1995; L 2001, ch 47, §§ 2, 3, eff May 30, 2001; L 2019, ch 569, § 1, eff Nov 25, 2019.

Article 330
Proceedings from Verdict to Sentence

§ 330.20. Procedure following verdict or plea of not responsible by reason of mental disease or defect

1. Definition of terms. As used in this section, the following terms shall have the following meanings:

(a) "Commissioner" means the state commissioner of mental health or the state commissioner of the office for people with developmental disabilities.

(b) "Secure facility" means a facility within the state office of mental health or the state office for people with developmental disabilities which is staffed with personnel adequately trained in security methods and is so equipped as to minimize the risk or danger of escapes, and which has been so specifically designated by the commissioner.

(c) "Dangerous mental disorder" means: (i) that a defendant currently suffers from a "mental illness" as that term is defined in subdivision twenty of section 1.03 of the mental hygiene law, and (ii) that because of such condition he currently constitutes a physical danger to himself or others.

(d) "Mentally ill" means that a defendant currently suffers from a mental illness for which care and treatment as a patient, in the in-patient services of a psychiatric center under the jurisdiction of the state office of mental health, is essential to such defendant's welfare and that his judgment is so impaired that he is unable to understand the need for such care and treatment; and, where a defendant is mentally retarded, the term "mentally ill" shall also mean, for purposes of this section, that the defendant is in need of care and treatment as a resident in the in-patient services of a developmental center or other residential facility for the mentally retarded and developmentally disabled under the jurisdiction of the state office for people with developmental disabilities.

(e) "Examination order" means an order directed to the commissioner requiring that a defendant submit to a psychiatric examination to determine whether the defendant has a dangerous mental disorder, or if he does not have dangerous mental disorder, whether he is mentally ill.

(f) "Commitment order" or "recommitment order" means an order committing a defendant to the custody of the commissioner for confinement in a secure facility for care and treatment for six months from the date of the order.

(g) "First retention order" means an order which is effective at the expiration of the period prescribed in a commitment order for a recommitment order, authorizing continued custody of a defendant by the commissioner for a period not to exceed one year.

(h) "Second retention order" means an order which is effective at the expiration of the period prescribed in a first retention order, authorizing continued custody of a defendant by the commissioner for a period not to exceed two years.

(i) "Subsequent retention order" means an order which is effective at the expiration of the period prescribed in a second retention order or a prior subsequent retention order authorizing continued custody of a defendant by the commissioner for a period not to exceed two years.

(j) "Retention order" means a first retention order, a second retention order or a subsequent retention order.

(k) "Furlough order" means an order directing the commissioner to allow a defendant in confinement pursuant to a commitment order, recommitment order or retention order to temporarily leave the facility for a period not exceeding fourteen days, either with or without the constant supervision of one or more employees of the facility.

(l) "Transfer order" means an order directing the commissioner to transfer a defendant from a secure facility to a non-secure facility under the jurisdiction of the commissioner or to any non-secure facility designated by the commissioner.

(m) "Release order" means an order directing the commissioner to terminate a defendant's in-patient status without terminating the commissioner's responsibility for the defendant.

(n) "Discharge order" means an order terminating an order of conditions or unconditionally discharging a defendant from supervision under the provisions of this section.

(o) "Order of conditions" means an order directing a defendant to comply with this prescribed treatment plan, or any other condition which the court determines to be reasonably necessary or appropriate, and, in addition, where a defendant is in custody of the commissioner, not to leave the facility without authorization. In addition to such conditions, when determined to be reasonably necessary or appropriate, an order of conditions may be accompanied by a special order of conditions set forth in a separate document requiring that the defendant: (i) stay away from the home, school, business or place of employment of the victim or victims, or of any witness designated by the court, of such offense; or (ii) refrain from harassing, intimidating, threatening or otherwise interfering with the victim or victims of the offense and such members of the family or household of such victim or victims as shall be specifically named by the court in such special order. An order of conditions or special order of conditions shall be valid for five years from the date of its issuance, except that, for good cause shown, the court may extend the period for an additional five years.

(p) "District attorney" means the office which prosecuted the criminal action resulting in the verdict or plea of not responsible by reason of mental disease or defect.

(q) "Qualified psychiatrist" means a physician who (i) is a diplomate of the American board of psychiatry and neurology or is eligible to be certified by that board; or (ii) is certified by the American osteopathic board of neurology and psychiatry or is eligible to be certified by that board.

(r) "Licensed psychologist" means a person who is registered as a psychologist under article one hundred fifty-three of the education law.

(s) "Psychiatric examiner" means a qualified psychiatrist or a licensed psychologist who has been designated by the commissioner to examine a defendant pursuant to this section, and such designee need not be an employee of the department of mental hygiene.

2. Examination order; psychiatric examiners. Upon entry of a verdict of not responsible by reason of mental disease or defect, or upon the acceptance of a plea of not responsible by reason of mental disease or defect, the court must immediately issue an examination order. Upon receipt of such order, the commissioner must designate two qualified psychiatric examiners to conduct the examination to examine the defendant. In conducting their examination, the psychiatric examiners may employ any method which is accepted by the medical profession for the examination of persons alleged to be suffering from a dangerous mental disorder or to be mentally ill or retarded. The court may authorize a psychiatrist or psychologist retained by a defendant to be present at such examination. The clerk of the court must promptly forward a copy of the examination order to the mental hygiene legal service and such service may thereafter participate in all subsequent proceedings under this section.

In all subsequent proceedings under this section, prior to the issuance of a special order of conditions, the court shall consider whether any order of protection had been issued prior to a verdict of not responsible by reason of mental disease or defect in the case, or prior to the acceptance of a plea of not responsible by reason of mental disease or defect in the case.

2-a. Firearm, rifle or shotgun surrender order. Upon entry of a verdict of not responsible by reason of mental disease or defect, or upon the acceptance of a plea of not responsible by reason of mental disease or defect, or upon a finding that the defendant is an incapacitated person pursuant to article seven hundred thirty of this chapter, the court shall revoke the defendant's firearm license, if any, inquire of the defendant as to the existence and location of any firearm, rifle or shotgun owned or possessed by such defendant and direct the surrender of such firearm, rifle or shotgun pursuant to subparagraph (f) of paragraph one of subdivision a of section 265.20 and subdivision six of section 400.05 of the penal law.

3. Examination order; place of examination. Upon issuing an examination order, the court must, except as otherwise provided in this subdivision, direct that the defendant be committed to a secure facility designated by the commissioner as the place for such

psychiatric examination. The sheriff must hold the defendant in custody pending such designation by the commissioner, and when notified of the designation, the sheriff must promptly deliver the defendant to such secure facility. When the defendant is not in custody at the time of such verdict or plea, because he was previously released on bail or on his own recognizance, the court, in its discretion, may direct that such examination be conducted on an out-patient basis, and at such time and place as the commissioner shall designate. If, however, the commissioner informs the court that confinement of the defendant is necessary for an effective examination, the court must direct that the defendant be confined in a facility designated by the commissioner until the examination is completed.

4. Examination order, duration. Confinement in a secure facility pursuant to an examination order shall be for a period not exceeding thirty days, except that, upon application of the commissioner, the court may authorize confinement for an additional period not exceeding thirty days when a longer period is necessary to complete the examination. If the initial hearing required by subdivision six of this section has not commenced prior to the termination of such examination period, the commissioner shall retain custody of the defendant in such secure facility until custody is transferred to the sheriff in the manner prescribed in subdivision six of this section. During the period of such confinement, the physician in charge of the facility may administer or cause to be administered to the defendant such emergency psychiatric, medical or other therapeutic treatment as in his judgment should be administered. If the court has directed that the examination be conducted on an out-patient basis, the examination shall be completed within thirty days after the defendant has first reported to the place designated by the commissioner, except that, upon application of the commissioner, the court may extend such period for a reasonable time if a longer period is necessary to complete the examination.

5. Examination order; reports. After he has completed his examination of the defendant, each psychiatric examiner must promptly prepare a report of his findings and evaluation concerning the defendant's mental condition, and submit such report to the commissioner. If the psychiatric examiners differ in their opinion as to whether the defendant is mentally ill or is suffering from a dangerous mental disorder, the commissioner must designate another psychiatric examiner to examine the defendant. Upon receipt of the examination reports, the commissioner must submit them to the court that issued the examination order. If the court is not satisfied with the findings of these psychiatric examiners, the court may designate one or more additional psychiatric examiners pursuant to subdivision fifteen of this section. The court must furnish a copy of the reports to the district attorney, counsel for the defendant and the mental hygiene legal service.

6. Initial hearing; commitment order. After the examination reports are submitted, the court must, within ten days of the receipt of such reports, conduct an initial hearing to determine the defendant's present mental condition. If the defendant is in the custody of the commissioner pursuant to an examination order, the court must direct the sheriff to obtain custody of the defendant from the commissioner and to confine the defendant pending further order of the court, except that the court may direct the sheriff to confine the defendant in an institution located near the place where the court sits if that institution has been designated by the commissioner as suitable for the temporary and secure detention of mentally disabled persons. At such initial hearing, the district attorney must establish to the satisfaction of the court that the defendant has a dangerous mental disorder or is mentally ill. If the court finds that the defendant has a dangerous mental disorder, it must issue a commitment order. If the court finds that the defendant does not have a dangerous mental disorder but is mentally ill, the provisions of subdivision seven of this section shall apply.

7. Initial hearing civil commitment and order of conditions. If, at the conclusion of the initial hearing conducted pursuant to subdivision six of this section, the court finds that the defendant is mentally ill but does not have a dangerous mental disorder, the provisions of articles nine or fifteen of the mental hygiene law shall apply at that stage of the proceedings and at all subsequent proceedings. Having found that the defendant is mentally ill, the court must issue an order of conditions and an order committing the defendant to the custody of the commissioner. The latter order shall be deemed an order made pursuant to the mental hygiene law and not pursuant to this section, and further

retention, conditional release or discharge of such defendant shall be in accordance with the provisions of the mental hygiene law. If, at the conclusion of the initial hearing, the court finds that the defendant does not have a dangerous mental disorder and is not mentally ill, the court must discharge the defendant either unconditionally or subject to an order of conditions.

7-a. Whenever the court issues a special order of conditions pursuant to this section, the commissioner shall make reasonable efforts to notify the victim or victims or the designated witness or witnesses that a special order of conditions containing such provisions has been issued, unless such victim or witness has requested that such notice should not be provided.

8. First retention order. When a defendant is in the custody of the commissioner pursuant to a commitment order, the commissioner must, at least thirty days prior to the expiration of the period prescribed in the order, apply to the court that issued the order, or to a superior court in the county where the secure facility is located, for a first retention order or a release order. The commissioner must give written notice of the application to the district attorney, the defendant, counsel for the defendant, and the mental hygiene legal service. Upon receipt of such application, the court may, on its own motion, conduct a hearing to determine whether the defendant has a dangerous mental disorder, and it must conduct such hearing if a demand therefor is made by the district attorney, the defendant, counsel for the defendant, or the mental hygiene legal service within ten days from the date that notice of the application was given to them. If such a hearing is held on an application for retention, the commissioner must establish to the satisfaction of the court that the defendant has a dangerous mental disorder or is mentally ill. The district attorney shall be entitled to appear and present evidence at such hearing. If such a hearing is held on an application for release, the district attorney must establish to the satisfaction of the court that the defendant has a dangerous mental disorder or is mentally ill. If the court finds that the defendant has a dangerous mental disorder it must issue a first retention order. If the court finds that the defendant is mentally ill but does not have a dangerous mental disorder, it must issue a first retention order and, pursuant to subdivision eleven of this section, a transfer order and an order of conditions. If the court finds that the defendant does not have a dangerous mental disorder and is not mentally ill, it must issue a release order and an order of conditions pursuant to subdivision twelve of this section.

9. Second and subsequent retention orders. When a defendant is in the custody of the commissioner pursuant to a first retention order, the commissioner must, at least thirty days prior to the expiration of the period prescribed in the order, apply to the court that issued the order, or to a superior court in the county where the facility is located, for a second retention order or a release order. The commissioner must give written notice of the application to the district attorney, the defendant, counsel for the defendant, and the mental hygiene legal service. Upon receipt of such application, the court may, on its own motion, conduct a hearing to determine whether the defendant has a dangerous mental disorder, and it must conduct such hearing if a demand therefor is made by the district attorney, the defendant, counsel for the defendant, or the mental hygiene legal service within ten days from the date that notice of the application was given to them. If such a hearing is held on an application for retention, the commissioner must establish to the satisfaction of the court that the defendant has a dangerous mental disorder or is mentally ill. The district attorney shall be entitled to appear and present evidence at such hearing. If such a hearing is held on an application for release, the district attorney must establish to the satisfaction of the court that the defendant has a dangerous mental disorder or is mentally ill. If the court finds that the defendant has a dangerous mental disorder it must issue a second retention order. If the court finds that the defendant is mentally ill but does not have a dangerous mental disorder, it must issue a second retention order and, pursuant to subdivision eleven of this section, a transfer order and an order of conditions. If the court finds that the defendant does not have a dangerous mental disorder and is not mentally ill, it must issue a release order and an order of conditions pursuant to subdivision twelve of this section. When a defendant is in the custody of the commissioner prior to the expiration of the period prescribed in a second retention order, the procedures set forth in this subdivision for the issuance of a second retention order shall govern the application for and the issuance of any subsequent retention order.

10. Furlough order. The commissioner may apply for a furlough order, pursuant to this subdivision, when a defendant is in his custody pursuant to a commitment order, recommitment order, or retention order and the commissioner is of the view that, consistent with the public safety and welfare of the community and the defendant, the clinical condition of the defendant warrants a granting of the privileges authorized by a furlough order. The application for a furlough order may be made to the court that issued the commitment order, or to a superior court in the county where the secure facility is located. The commissioner must give ten days written notice to the district attorney, the defendant, counsel for the defendant, and the mental hygiene legal service. Upon receipt of such application, the court may, on its own motion, conduct a hearing to determine whether the application should be granted, and must conduct such hearing if a demand therefor is made by the district attorney. If the court finds that the issuance of a furlough order is consistent with the public safety and welfare of the community and the defendant, and that the clinical condition of the defendant warrants a granting of the privileges authorized by a furlough order, the court must grant the application and issue a furlough order containing any terms and conditions that the court deems necessary or appropriate. If the defendant fails to return to the secure facility at the time specified in the furlough order, then, for purposes of subdivision nineteen of this section, he shall be deemed to have escaped.

11. Transfer order and order of conditions. The commissioner may apply for a transfer order, pursuant to this subdivision, when a defendant is in his custody pursuant to a retention order or a recommitment order, and the commissioner is of the view that the defendant does not have a dangerous mental disorder or that, consistent with the public safety and welfare of the community and the defendant, the clinical condition of the defendant warrants his transfer from a secure facility to a non-secure facility under the jurisdiction of the commissioner or to any non-secure facility designated by the commissioner. The application for a transfer order may be made to the court that issued the order under which the defendant is then in custody, or to a superior court in the county where the secure facility is located. The commissioner must give ten days written notice to the district attorney, the defendant, counsel for the defendant, and the mental hygiene legal service. Upon receipt of such application, the court may, on its own motion, conduct a hearing to determine whether the application should be granted, and must conduct such hearing if the demand therefor is made by the district attorney. At such hearing, the district attorney must establish to the satisfaction of the court that the defendant has a dangerous mental disorder or that the issuance of a transfer order is inconsistent with the public safety and welfare of the community. The court must grant the application and issue a transfer order if the court finds that the defendant does not have a dangerous mental disorder, or if the court finds that the issuance of a transfer order is consistent with the public safety and welfare of the community and the defendant and that the clinical condition of the defendant, warrants his transfer from a secure facility to a non-secure facility. A court must also issue a transfer order when, in connection with an application for a first retention order pursuant to subdivision eight of this section or a second or subsequent retention order pursuant to subdivision nine of this section, it finds that a defendant is mentally ill but does not have a dangerous mental disorder. Whenever a court issues a transfer order it must also issue an order of conditions.

12. Release order and order of conditions. The commissioner may apply for a release order, pursuant to this subdivision, when a defendant is in his custody pursuant to a retention order or recommitment order, and the commissioner is of the view that the defendant no longer has a dangerous mental disorder and is no longer mentally ill. The application for a release order may be made to the court that issued the order under which the defendant is then in custody, or to a superior court in the county where the facility is located. The application must contain a description of the defendant's current mental condition, the past course of treatment, a history of the defendant's conduct subsequent to his commitment, a written service plan for continued treatment which shall include the information specified in subdivision (g) of section 29.15 of the mental hygiene law, and a detailed statement of the extent to which supervision of the defendant after release is proposed. The commissioner must give ten days written notice to the district attorney, the defendant, counsel for the defendant, and the mental hygiene legal service. Upon receipt of such application, the court must promptly

conduct a hearing to determine the defendant's present mental condition. At such hearing, the district attorney must establish to the satisfaction of the court that the defendant has a dangerous mental disorder or is mentally ill. If the court finds that the defendant has a dangerous mental disorder, it must deny the application for a release order. If the court finds that the defendant does not have a dangerous mental disorder but is mentally ill, it must issue a transfer order pursuant to subdivision eleven of this section if the defendant is then confined in a secure facility. If the court finds that the defendant does not have a dangerous mental disorder and is not mentally ill, it must grant the application and issue a release order. A court must also issue a release order when, in connection with an application for a first retention order pursuant to subdivision eight of this section or a second or subsequent retention order pursuant to subdivision nine of this section, it finds that the defendant does not have a dangerous mental disorder and is not mentally ill. Whenever a court issues a release order it must also issue an order of conditions. If the court has previously issued a transfer order and an order of conditions, it must issue a new order of conditions upon issuing a release order. The order of conditions issued in conjunction with a release order shall incorporate a written service plan prepared by a psychiatrist familiar with the defendant's case history and approved by the court, and shall contain any conditions that the court determines to be reasonably necessary or appropriate. It shall be the responsibility of the commissioner to determine that such defendant is receiving the services specified in the written service plan and is complying with any conditions specified in such plan and the order of conditions.

13. Discharge order. The commissioner may apply for a discharge order, pursuant to this subdivision, when a defendant has been continuously on an out-patient status for three years or more pursuant to a release order, and the commissioner is of the view that the defendant no longer has a dangerous mental disorder and is no longer mentally ill and that the issuance of a discharge order is consistent with the public safety and welfare of the community and the defendant. The application for a discharge order may be made to the court that issued the release order, or to a superior court in the county where the defendant is then residing. The commissioner must give ten days written notice to the district attorney, the defendant, counsel for the defendant, and the mental hygiene legal service. Upon receipt of such application, the court may, on its own motion, conduct a hearing to determine whether the application should be granted, and must conduct such hearing if a demand therefor is made by the district attorney. The court must grant the application and issue a discharge order if the court finds that the defendant has been continuously on an out-patient status for three years or more, that he does not have a dangerous mental disorder and is not mentally ill, and that the issuance of the discharge order is consistent with the public safety and welfare of the community and the defendant.

14. Recommitment order. At any time during the period covered by an order of conditions an application may be made by the commissioner or the district attorney to the court that issued such order, or to a superior court in the county where the defendant is then residing, for a recommitment order when the applicant is of the view that the defendant has a dangerous mental disorder. The applicant must give written notice of the application to the defendant, counsel for the defendant, and the mental hygiene legal service, and if the applicant is the commissioner he must give such notice to the district attorney or if the applicant is the district attorney he must give such notice to the commissioner. Upon receipt of such application the court must order the defendant to appear before it for a hearing to determine if the defendant has a dangerous mental disorder. Such order may be in the form of a written notice, specifying the time and place of appearance, served personally upon the defendant, or mailed to his last known address, as the court may direct. If the defendant fails to appear in court as directed, the court may issue a warrant to an appropriate peace officer directing him to take the defendant into custody and bring him before the court. In such circumstance, the court may direct that the defendant be confined in an appropriate institution located near the place where the court sits. The court must conduct a hearing to determine whether the defendant has a dangerous mental disorder. At such hearing, the applicant, whether he be the commissioner or the district attorney must establish to the satisfaction of the court that the defendant has a dangerous mental disorder. If the applicant is the commissioner, the district attorney

shall be entitled to appear and present evidence at such hearing; if the applicant is the district attorney, the commissioner shall be entitled to appear and present evidence at such hearing. If the court finds that the defendant has a dangerous mental disorder, it must issue a recommitment order. When a defendant is in the custody of the commissioner pursuant to a recommitment order, the procedures set forth in subdivisions eight and nine of this section for the issuance of retention orders shall govern the application for and the issuance of a first retention order, a second retention order, and subsequent retention orders.

15. Designation of psychiatric examiners. If, at any hearing conducted under this section to determine the defendant's present mental condition, the court is not satisfied with the findings of the psychiatric examiners, the court may direct the commissioner to designate one or more additional psychiatric examiners to conduct an examination of the defendant and submit a report of their findings. In addition, the court may on its own motion, or upon request of a party, may designate one or more psychiatric examiners to examine the defendant and submit a report of their findings. The district attorney may apply to the court for an order directing that the defendant submit to an examination by a psychiatric examiner designated by the district attorney, and such psychiatric examiner may testify at the hearing.

16. Rehearing and review. Any defendant who is in the custody of the commissioner pursuant to a commitment order, a retention order, or a recommitment order, if dissatisfied with such order, may, within thirty days after the making of such order, obtain a rehearing and review of the proceedings and of such order in accordance with the provisions of section 9.35 or 15.35 of the mental hygiene law.

17. Rights of defendants. Subject to the limitations and provisions of this section, a defendant committed to the custody of the commissioner pursuant to this section shall have the rights granted to patients under the mental hygiene law.

18. Notwithstanding any other provision of law, no person confined by reason of a commitment order, recommitment order or retention order to a secure facility may be discharged or released unless the commissioner shall deliver written notice, at least four days excluding Saturdays, Sundays and holidays, in advance of such discharge or release to all of the following:

(a) the district attorney.

(b) the police department having jurisdiction of the area to which the defendant is to be discharged or released.

(c) any other person the court may designate.

The notices required by this subdivision shall be given by the facility staff physician who was treating the defendant or, if unavailable, by the defendant's treatment team leader, but if neither is immediately available, notice must be given by some other member of the clinical staff of the facility. Such notice must be given by any means reasonably calculated to give prompt actual notice.

19. Escape from custody; notice requirements. If a defendant is in the custody of the commissioner pursuant to an order issued under this section, and such defendant escapes from custody, immediate notice of such escape shall be given by the department facility staff to: (a) the district attorney, (b) the superintendent of state police, (c) the sheriff of the county where the escape occurred, (d) the police department having jurisdiction of the area where the escape occurred, (e) any person the facility staff believes to be in danger, and (f) any law enforcement agency and any person the facility staff believes would be able to apprise such endangered person that the defendant has escaped from the facility. Such notice shall be given as soon as the facility staff know that the defendant has escaped from the facility and shall include such information as will adequately identify the defendant and the person or persons believed to be in danger and the nature of the danger. The notices required by this subdivision shall be given by the facility staff physician who was treating the defendant or, if unavailable, by the defendant's treatment team leader, but if neither is immediately available, notice must be given by some other member of the clinical staff of the facility. Such notice must be given by any means reasonably calculated to give prompt actual notice. The defendant may be apprehended, restrained, transported to, and returned to the facility from which he escaped by any peace officer, and it shall be the duty of the officer to assist any representative of the commissioner to take the defendant into custody upon the request of such representative.

20. Required affidavit. No application may be made by the commissioner under this section without an accompanying affidavit from at least one psychiatric examiner supportive of relief requested in the application, which affidavit shall be served on all parties entitled to receive the notice of application. Such affidavit shall set forth the defendant's clinical diagnosis, a detailed analysis of his or her mental condition which caused the psychiatric examiner to formulate an opinion, and the opinion of the psychiatric examiner with respect to the defendant. Any application submitted without the required affidavit shall be dismissed by the court.

21. Appeals.

(a) A party to proceedings conducted in accordance with the provisions of this section may take an appeal to an intermediate appellate court by permission of the intermediate appellate court as follows:

(i) the commissioner may appeal from any release order, retention order, transfer order, discharge order, order of conditions, or recommitment order, for which he has not applied;

(ii) a defendant, or the mental hygiene legal service on his or her behalf, may appeal from any commitment order, retention order, recommitment order, or, if the defendant has obtained a rehearing and review of any such order pursuant to subdivision sixteen of this section, from an order, not otherwise appealable as of right, issued in accordance with the provisions of section 9.35 or 15.35 of the mental hygiene law authorizing continued retention under the original order, provided, however, that a defendant who takes an appeal from a commitment order, retention order, or recommitment order may not subsequently obtain a rehearing and review of such order pursuant to subdivision sixteen of this section;

(iii) the district attorney may appeal from any release order, transfer order, discharge order, order of conditions, furlough order, or order denying an application for a recommitment order which he opposed.

(b) An aggrieved party may appeal from a final order of the intermediate appellate court to the court of appeals by permission of the intermediate appellate court granted before application to the court of appeals, or by permission of the court of appeals upon refusal by the intermediate appellate court or upon direct application.

(c) An appeal taken under this subdivision shall be deemed civil in nature, and shall be governed by the laws and rules applicable to civil appeals; provided, however, that a stay of the order appealed from must be obtained in accordance with the provisions of paragraph (d) hereof.

(d) The court from or to which an appeal is taken may stay all proceedings to enforce the order appealed from pending an appeal or determination on a motion for permission to appeal, or may grant a limited stay, except that only the court to which an appeal is taken may vacate, limit, or modify a stay previously granted. If the order appealed from is affirmed or modified, the stay shall continue for five days after service upon the appellant of the order of affirmance or modification with notice of its entry in the court to which the appeal was taken. If a motion is made for permission to appeal from such an order, before the expiration of the five days, the stay, or any other stay granted pending determination of the motion for permission to appeal, shall:

(i) if the motion is granted, continue until five days after the appeal is determined; or

(ii) if the motion is denied, continue until five days after the movant is served with the order of denial with notice of its entry.

22. Any special order of conditions issued pursuant to subparagraph (i) or (ii) of paragraph (o) of subdivision one of this section shall bear in a conspicuous manner the term "special order of conditions" and a copy shall be filed by the clerk of the court with the sheriff's office in the county in which anyone intended to be protected by such special order resides, or, if anyone intended to be protected by such special order resides within a city, with the police department of such city. The absence of language specifying that the order is a "special order of conditions" shall not affect the validity of such order. A copy of such special order of conditions may from time to time be filed by the clerk of the court with any other police department or sheriff's office having jurisdiction of the residence, work place, or school of anyone intended to be protected by such special order. A copy of such special order may also be filed by anyone intended to be protected by such

provisions at the appropriate police department or sheriff's office having jurisdiction. Any subsequent amendment or revocation of such special order may be filed in the same manner as provided in this subdivision. Such special order of conditions shall plainly state the date that the order expires.

HISTORY:

Add, L 1980, ch 548, § 11, eff Sept 1, 1980; amd, L 1982, ch 526, §§ 1–4; L 1983, ch 976, § 1, eff Aug 8, 1983; L 1985, ch 789, § 47, eff April 1, 1986; L 1989, ch 693, § 1, eff July 22, 1989; L 1993, ch 330, § 8, eff April 1, 1994; L 2003, ch 525, §§ 1–4, eff Sept 17, 2003; L 2004, ch 107, §§ 1–4, eff June 8, 2004; L 2013, ch 1, § 1, eff March 16, 2013; L 2019, ch 672, § 63, eff Dec 16, 2019.

Title K
Prosecution of Informations in Local Criminal Courts—Plea to Sentence

Article 370
Proceedings from Verdict to Sentence

§ 370.15. Procedure for determining whether certain misdemeanor crimes are serious offenses under the penal law

1. When a defendant has been charged with assault in the third degree, menacing in the third degree, menacing in the second degree, criminal obstruction of breathing or blood circulation, unlawful imprisonment in the second degree, coercion in the third degree, criminal tampering in the third degree, criminal contempt in the second degree, harassment in the first degree, aggravated harassment in the second degree, criminal trespass in the third degree, criminal trespass in the second degree, arson in the fifth degree, or attempt to commit any of the above-listed offenses, the people shall, at arraignment or no later than forty-five days after arraignment, serve on the defendant and file with the court a notice alleging that the defendant and the person alleged to be the victim of such crime were members of the same family or household as defined in subdivision one of section 530.11 of this chapter.

2. Such notice shall include the name of the person alleged to be the victim of such crime and shall specify the nature of the alleged relationship as set forth in subdivision one of section 530.11 of this chapter. Upon conviction of such offense, the court shall advise the defendant that he or she is entitled to a hearing solely on the allegation contained in the notice and, if necessary, an adjournment of the sentencing proceeding in order to prepare for such hearing, and that if such allegation is sustained, that determination and conviction will be reported to the division of criminal justice services. If such allegation is sustained, the court shall report the determination and conviction to the division of criminal justice services within three business days.

3. After having been advised by the court as provided in subdivision two of this section, the defendant may stipulate or admit, orally on the record or in writing, that he or she is related or situated to the victim of such crime in the manner described in subdivision one of this section. In such case, such relationship shall be deemed established. If the defendant denies that he or she is related or situated to the victim of the crime as alleged in the notice served by the people, or stands mute with respect to such allegation, then the people shall bear the burden to prove beyond a reasonable doubt that the defendant is related or situated to the victim in the manner alleged in the notice. The court may consider reliable hearsay evidence submitted by either party provided that it is relevant to the determination of the allegation. Facts previously proven at trial or elicited at the time of entry of a plea of guilty shall be deemed established beyond a reasonable doubt and shall not be relitigated. At the conclusion of the hearing, or upon such a stipulation or admission, as applicable, the court shall make a specific written determination with respect to such allegation.

HISTORY:
Add, L 2011, ch 258, § 1, eff Nov 29, 2011; L 2018, ch 60, § 2, eff June 11, 2018; amd, L 2020, ch 55, § 1 (Part Q), eff April 3, 2020.

Part THREE
Special Proceedings and Miscellaneous Procedures

Title P
Procedures for Securing Attendance at Criminal Actions and Proceedings of Defendants and Witnesses Under Control of Court—Recognizance, Bail and Commitment

Article 500
Recognizance, Bail and Commitment—Definition of Terms

§ 500.10. Recognizance, bail and commitment; definitions of terms. [Effective until July 2, 2020]

As used in this title, and in this chapter generally, the following terms have the following meanings:

1. "Principal" means a defendant in a criminal action or proceeding, or a person adjudged a material witness therein, or any other person so involved therein that the principal may by law be compelled to appear before a court for the purpose of having such court exercise control over the principal's person to secure the principal's future attendance at the action or proceeding when required, and who in fact either is before the court for such purpose or has been before it and been subjected to such control.

2. "Release on own recognizance." A court releases a principal on the principal's own recognizance when, having acquired control over the principal's person, it permits the principal to be at liberty during the pendency of the criminal action or proceeding involved upon condition that the principal will appear thereat whenever the principal's attendance may be required and will at all times render the principal amenable to the orders and processes of the court.

3. "Fix bail." A court fixes bail when, having acquired control over the person of a principal, it designates a sum of money and stipulates that, if bail in such amount is posted on behalf of the principal and approved, it will permit him to be at liberty during the pendency of the criminal action or proceeding involved.

3-a. "Release under non-monetary conditions." A court releases a principal under non-monetary conditions when, having acquired control over a person, it authorizes the person to be at liberty during the pendency of the criminal action or proceeding involved under conditions ordered by the court, which shall be the least restrictive conditions that will reasonably assure the principal's return to court. Such conditions may include, among other conditions reasonable under the circumstances: that the principal be in contact with a pretrial services agency serving principals in that county; that the principal abide by reasonable, specified restrictions on travel that are reasonably related to an actual risk of flight from the jurisdiction; that the principal refrain from possessing a firearm, destructive device or other dangerous weapon; that, when it is shown pursuant to subdivision four of section 510.45 of this title that no other realistic monetary condition or set of non-monetary conditions will suffice to reasonably assure the person's return to court, the person be placed in reasonable pretrial supervision with a pretrial services agency serving principals in that county; that, when it is shown pursuant to paragraph (a) of subdivision four of section 510.40 of this title that no other realistic non-monetary condition or set of non-monetary conditions will suffice to reasonably assure the principal's return to court, the principal's location be monitored with an approved electronic monitoring device, in accordance with such subdivision four of section 510.40 of this title. A principal shall not be required to pay for any part of the cost of release on non-monetary conditions.

4. "Commit to the custody of the sheriff." A court commits a principal to the custody of the sheriff when, having acquired control over the principal's person, it orders that the principal be confined in the custody of the sheriff during the pendency of the criminal action or proceeding involved.

5. "Securing order" means an order of a court committing a principal to the custody of the sheriff or fixing bail, where authorized, or releasing the principal on the principal's own recognizance or releasing the principal under non-monetary conditions.

6. "Order of recognizance or bail" means a securing order releasing a principal on the principal's own recognizance or under non-monetary conditions or, where authorized, fixing bail.

7. "Application for recognizance or bail" means an application by a principal that the court, instead of committing the principal to or retaining the principal in the custody of the sheriff, either release the principal on the principal's own recognizance, release under non-monetary conditions, or, where authorized, fix bail.

8. "Post bail" means to deposit bail in the amount and form fixed by the court, with the court or with some other authorized public servant or agency.

9. "Bail" means cash bail, a bail bond or money paid with a credit card.

10. "Cash bail" means a sum of money, in the amount designated in an order fixing bail, posted by a principal or by another person on his behalf with a court or other authorized public servant or agency, upon the condition that such money will become forfeit to the people of the state of New York if the principal does not comply with the directions of a court requiring his attendance at the criminal action or proceeding involved or does not otherwise render himself amenable to the orders and processes of the court.

11. "Obligor" means a person who executes a bail bond on behalf of a principal and thereby assumes the undertaking described therein. The principal himself may be an obligor.

12. "Surety" means an obligor who is not a principal.

13. "Bail bond" means a written undertaking, executed by one or more obligors, that the principal designated in such instrument will, while at liberty as a result of an order fixing bail and of the posting of the bail bond in satisfaction thereof, appear in a designated criminal action or proceeding when his attendance is required and otherwise render himself amenable to the orders and processes of the court, and that in the event that he fails to do so the obligor or obligors will pay to the people of the state of New York a specified sum of money, in the amount designated in the order fixing bail.

14. "Appearance bond" means a bail bond in which the only obligor is the principal.

15. "Surety bond" means a bail bond in which the obligor or obligors consist of one or more sureties or of one or more sureties and the principal.

16. "Insurance company bail bond" means a surety bond, executed in the form prescribed by the superintendent of financial services, in which the surety-obligor is a corporation licensed by the superintendent of financial services to engage in the business of executing bail bonds.

17. "Secured bail bond" means a bail bond secured by either:

(a) Personal property which is not exempt from execution and which, over and above all liabilities and encumbrances, has a value equal to or greater than the total amount of the undertaking; or

(b) Real property having a value of at least twice the total amount of the undertaking. For purposes of this paragraph, value of real property is determined by either:

(i) dividing the last assessed value of such property by the last given equalization rate or in a special assessing unit, as defined in article eighteen of the real property tax law, the appropriate class ratio established pursuant to section twelve hundred two of such law of the assessing municipality wherein the property is situated and by deducting from the resulting figure the total amount of any liens or other encumbrances upon such property; or

(ii) the value of the property as indicated in a certified appraisal report submitted by a state certified general real estate appraiser duly licensed by the department of state as provided in section one hundred sixty-j of the executive law, and by deducting from the appraised value the total amount of any liens or other encumbrances upon such property. A lien report issued by a title insurance company licensed under article sixty-four of the insurance law, that guarantees the correctness of a lien search conducted by it, shall be presumptive proof of liens upon the property.

18. "Partially secured bail bond" means a bail bond secured only by a deposit of a sum of money not exceeding ten percent of the total amount of the undertaking.

19. "Unsecured bail bond" means a bail bond, other than an insurance company bail bond, not secured by any deposit of or lien upon property.

20. "Court" includes, where appropriate, a judge authorized to act as described in a particular statute, though not as a court.

21. "Qualifies for electronic monitoring," for purposes of subdivision four of section 510.40 of this title, means a person charged with a felony, a misdemeanor crime of domestic violence, a misdemeanor defined in article one hundred thirty of the penal law, a crime and the circumstances of paragraph (b) of subdivision two of section 530.60 of this title apply, or any misdemeanor where the defendant stands previously convicted, within the past five years, of a violent felony offense as defined in section 70.02 of the penal law. For the purposes of this subdivision, in calculating such five year period, any period of time during which the defendant was incarcerated for any reason between the time of the commission of any such previous crime and the time of commission of the present crime shall be excluded and such five year period shall be extended by a period or periods equal to the time served under such incarceration.

22. "Misdemeanor crime of domestic violence," for purposes of subdivision twenty-one of this section, means a misdemeanor under the penal law provisions and circumstances described in subdivision one of section 530.11 of this title.

HISTORY:

Add, L 1970, ch 996, § 1, eff Sept 1, 1971; amd, L 1992, ch 316, § 26, eff Nov 1, 1992; L 2011, ch 62, § 104 (Part A), eff Oct 3, 2011; L 2011, ch 305, § 1, eff Aug 3, 2011; L 2019, ch 59, §§ 1-e, 1-f (Part JJJ), eff Jan 1, 2020.

§ 500.10. Recognizance, bail and commitment; definitions of terms. [Effective July 2, 2020]

As used in this title, and in this chapter generally, the following terms have the following meanings:

1. "Principal" means a defendant in a criminal action or proceeding, or a person adjudged a material witness therein, or any other person so involved therein that the principal may by law be compelled to appear before a court for the purpose of having such court exercise control over the principal's person to secure the principal's future attendance at the action or proceeding when required, and who in fact either is before the court for such purpose or has been before it and been subjected to such control.

2. "Release on own recognizance." A court releases a principal on the principal's own recognizance when, having acquired control over the principal's person, it permits the principal to be at liberty during the pendency of the criminal action or proceeding involved upon condition that the principal will appear thereat whenever the principal's attendance may be required and will at all times render the principal amenable to the orders and processes of the court.

3. "Fix bail." A court fixes bail when, having acquired control over the person of a principal, it designates a sum of money and stipulates that, if bail in such amount is posted on behalf of the principal and approved, it will permit him to be at liberty during the pendency of the criminal action or proceeding involved.

3-a. "Release under non-monetary conditions." A court releases a principal under non-monetary conditions when, having acquired control over a person, it authorizes the person to be at liberty during the pendency of the criminal action or proceeding involved under conditions ordered by the court, which shall be the least restrictive conditions that will reasonably assure the principal's return to court and reasonably assure the principal's compliance with court conditions. A principal shall not be required to pay for any part of the cost of release on non-monetary conditions. Such conditions may include, among other conditions reasonable under the circumstances:

(a) that the principal be in contact with a pretrial services agency serving principals in that county;

(b) that the principal abide by reasonable, specified restrictions on travel that are reasonably related to an actual risk of flight from the jurisdiction, or that the principal surrender his or her passport;

(c) that the principal refrain from possessing a firearm, destructive device or other dangerous weapon;

(d) that, when it is shown pursuant to subdivision four of section 510.45 of this title that no other realistic non-monetary condition or set of non-monetary conditions will suffice to reasonably assure the person's return to court, the person be placed in reasonable pretrial supervision with a pretrial services agency serving principals in that county;

(e) that the principal refrain from associating with certain persons who are connected with the instant charge, including, when appropriate, specified victims, witnesses, or co-defendants;

(f) that the principal be referred to a pretrial services agency for placement in mandatory programming, including counseling, treatment, and intimate partner violence intervention programs. Where applicable, the court may direct the principal be removed to a hospital pursuant to section 9.43 of the mental hygiene law;

(g) that the principal make diligent efforts to maintain employment, housing, or enrollment in school or educational programming;

(h) that the principal obey an order of protection issued by the court, including an order issued pursuant to section 530.11 of this title;

(i) that the principal obey conditions set by the court addressed to the safety of a victim of a family offense as defined in section 530.11 of this title including conditions that may be requested by or on behalf of the victim; and

(j) that, when it is shown pursuant to paragraph (a) of subdivision four of section 510.40 of this title that no other realistic non-monetary condition or set of non-monetary conditions will suffice to reasonably assure the principal's return to court, the principal's location be monitored with an approved electronic monitoring device, in accordance with such subdivision four of section 510.40 of this title.

3-b. Subdivision three-a of this section presents a non-exclusive list of conditions that may be considered and imposed by law, singularly or in combination, when reasonable under the circumstances of the defendant, the case, and the situation of the defendant. The court need not necessarily order one or more specific conditions first before ordering one or more or additional conditions.

4. "Commit to the custody of the sheriff." A court commits a principal to the custody of the sheriff when, having acquired control over the principal's person, it orders that the principal be confined in the custody of the sheriff during the pendency of the criminal action or proceeding involved.

5. "Securing order" means an order of a court committing a principal to the custody of the sheriff or fixing bail, where authorized, or releasing the principal on the principal's own recognizance or releasing the principal under non-monetary conditions.

6. "Order of recognizance or bail" means a securing order releasing a principal on the principal's own recognizance or under non-monetary conditions or, where authorized, fixing bail.

7. "Application for recognizance or bail" means an application by a principal that the court, instead of committing the principal to or retaining the principal in the custody of the sheriff, either release the principal on the principal's own recognizance , release under non-monetary conditions, or, where authorized, fix bail.

8. "Post bail" means to deposit bail in the amount and form fixed by the court, with the court or with some other authorized public servant or agency.

9. "Bail" means cash bail , a bail bond or money paid with a credit card.

10. "Cash bail" means a sum of money, in the amount designated in an order fixing bail, posted by a principal or by another person on his behalf with a court or other authorized public servant or agency, upon the condition that such money will become forfeit to the people of the state of New York if the principal does not comply with the directions of a court requiring his attendance at the criminal action or proceeding involved or does not otherwise render himself amenable to the orders and processes of the court.

11. "Obligor" means a person who executes a bail bond on behalf of a principal and thereby assumes the undertaking described therein. The principal himself may be an obligor.

12. "Surety" means an obligor who is not a principal.

13. "Bail bond" means a written undertaking, executed by one or more obligors, that the principal designated in such instrument will, while at liberty as a result of an order fixing bail and of the posting of the bail bond in satisfaction thereof, appear in a designated criminal action or proceeding when his attendance is required and otherwise render himself amenable to the orders and processes of the court, and that in the event that he fails to do so the obligor or obligors will pay to the people of the

state of New York a specified sum of money, in the amount designated in the order fixing bail.

14. "Appearance bond" means a bail bond in which the only obligor is the principal.

15. "Surety bond" means a bail bond in which the obligor or obligors consist of one or more sureties or of one or more sureties and the principal.

16. "Insurance company bail bond" means a surety bond, executed in the form prescribed by the superintendent of financial services, in which the surety-obligor is a corporation licensed by the superintendent of financial services to engage in the business of executing bail bonds.

17. "Secured bail bond" means a bail bond secured by either:

(a) Personal property which is not exempt from execution and which, over and above all liabilities and encumbrances, has a value equal to or greater than the total amount of the undertaking; or

(b) Real property having a value of at least twice the total amount of the undertaking. For purposes of this paragraph, value of real property is determined by either:

(i) dividing the last assessed value of such property by the last given equalization rate or in a special assessing unit, as defined in article eighteen of the real property tax law, the appropriate class ratio established pursuant to section twelve hundred two of such law of the assessing municipality wherein the property is situated and by deducting from the resulting figure the total amount of any liens or other encumbrances upon such property; or

(ii) the value of the property as indicated in a certified appraisal report submitted by a state certified general real estate appraiser duly licensed by the department of state as provided in section one hundred sixty-j of the executive law, and by deducting from the appraised value the total amount of any liens or other encumbrances upon such property. A lien report issued by a title insurance company licensed under article sixty-four of the insurance law, that guarantees the correctness of a lien search conducted by it, shall be presumptive proof of liens upon the property.

18. "Partially secured bail bond" means a bail bond secured only by a deposit of a sum of money not exceeding ten percent of the total amount of the undertaking.

19. "Unsecured bail bond" means a bail bond, other than an insurance company bail bond, not secured by any deposit of or lien upon property.

20. "Court" includes, where appropriate, a judge authorized to act as described in a particular statute, though not as a court.

21. "Qualifies for electronic monitoring," for purposes of subdivision four of section 510.40 of this title, means a person charged with a felony, a misdemeanor crime of domestic violence, a misdemeanor defined in article one hundred thirty of the penal law, a crime and the circumstances of paragraph (b) of subdivision two of section 530.60 of this title apply, or any misdemeanor where the defendant stands previously convicted, within the past five years, of a violent felony offense as defined in section 70.02 of the penal law. For the purposes of this subdivision, in calculating such five year period, any period of time during which the defendant was incarcerated for any reason between the time of the commission of any such previous crime and the time of commission of the present crime shall be excluded and such five year period shall be extended by a period or periods equal to the time served under such incarceration.

22. "Misdemeanor crime of domestic violence," for purposes of subdivision twenty-one of this section, means a misdemeanor under the penal law provisions and circumstances described in subdivision one of section 530.11 of this title.

HISTORY:

Add, L 1970, ch 996, § 1, eff Sept 1, 1971; amd, L 1992, ch 316, § 26, eff Nov 1, 1992; L 2011, ch 62, § 104 (Part A), eff Oct 3, 2011; L 2011, ch 305, § 1, eff Aug 3, 2011; L 2019, ch 59, §§ 1-e, 1-f (Part JJJ), eff Jan 1, 2020; L 2020, ch 56, § 1 (Part UU), eff July 2, 2020.

Article 510
Recognizance, Bail and Commitment—Determination of Application for Recognizance or Bail, Issuance of Securing Orders, and Related Matters

§ 510.10. Securing order; when required; alternatives available; standard to be applied. [Effective until July 2, 2020]

1. When a principal, whose future court attendance at a criminal action or proceeding is or may be required, comes under the control of a court, such court shall, in accordance with this title, by a securing order release the principal on the principal's own recognizance, release the principal under non-monetary conditions, or, where authorized, fix bail or commit the principal to the custody of the sheriff. In all such cases, except where another type of securing order is shown to be required by law, the court shall release the principal pending trial on the principal's own recognizance, unless it is demonstrated and the court makes an individualized determination that the principal poses a risk of flight to avoid prosecution. If such a finding is made, the court must select the least restrictive alternative and condition or conditions that will reasonably assure the principal's return to court. The court shall explain its choice of release, release with conditions, bail or remand on the record or in writing.

2. A principal is entitled to representation by counsel under this chapter in preparing an application for release, when a securing order is being considered and when a securing order is being reviewed for modification, revocation or termination. If the principal is financially unable to obtain counsel, counsel shall be assigned to the principal.

3. In cases other than as described in subdivision four of this section the court shall release the principal pending trial on the principal's own recognizance, unless the court finds on the record or in writing that release on the principal's own recognizance will not reasonably assure the principal's return to court. In such instances, the court shall release the principal under non-monetary conditions, selecting the least restrictive alternative and conditions that will reasonably assure the principal's return to court. The court shall explain its choice of alternative and conditions on the record or in writing.

4. Where the principal stands charged with a qualifying offense, the court, unless otherwise prohibited by law, may in its discretion release the principal pending trial on the principal's own recognizance or under non-monetary conditions, fix bail, or, where the defendant is charged with a qualifying offense which is a felony, the court may commit the principal to the custody of the sheriff. A principal stands charged with a qualifying offense for the purposes of this subdivision when he or she stands charged with:

(a) a felony enumerated in section 70.02 of the penal law, other than burglary in the second degree as defined in subdivision two of section 140.25 of the penal law or robbery in the second degree as defined in subdivision one of section 160.10 of the penal law;

(b) a crime involving witness intimidation under section 215.15 of the penal law;

(c) a crime involving witness tampering under section 215.11, 215.12 or 215.13 of the penal law;

(d) a class A felony defined in the penal law, other than in article two hundred twenty of such law with the exception of section 220.77 of such law;

(e) a felony sex offense defined in section 70.80 of the penal law or a crime involving incest as defined in section 255.25, 255.26 or 255.27 of such law, or a misdemeanor defined in article one hundred thirty of such law;

(f) conspiracy in the second degree as defined in section 105.15 of the penal law, where the underlying allegation of such charge is that the defendant conspired to commit a class A felony defined in article one hundred twenty-five of the penal law;

(g) money laundering in support of terrorism in the first degree as defined in section 470.24 of the penal law; money laundering in support of terrorism in the second degree as defined in section 470.23 of the penal law; or a felony crime of terrorism as defined in article four hundred ninety of the penal law, other than the crime defined in section 490.20 of such law;

(h) criminal contempt in the second degree as defined in subdivision three of section 215.50 of the penal law, criminal contempt in the first degree as defined in subdivision (b), (c) or (d) of section 215.51 of the penal law or aggravated criminal contempt as defined in section 215.52 of the penal law, and the underlying allegation of such charge of criminal contempt in the second degree, criminal contempt in the first degree or aggravated criminal contempt is that the defendant violated a duly served order of protection where the protected party is a member of the defendant's same family or household as defined in subdivision one of section 530.11 of this article; or

(i) facilitating a sexual performance by a child with a controlled substance or alcohol as defined in section 263.30 of the penal law, use of a child in a sexual performance as defined in section 263.05 of the penal law or luring a child as defined in subdivision one of section 120.70 of the penal law.

5. Notwithstanding the provisions of subdivisions three and four of this section, with respect to any charge for which bail or remand is not ordered, and for which the court would not or could not otherwise require bail or remand, a defendant may, at any time, request that the court set bail in a nominal amount requested by the defendant in the form specified in paragraph (a) of subdivision one of section 520.10 of this title; if the court is satisfied that the request is voluntary, the court shall set such bail in such amount.

6. When a securing order is revoked or otherwise terminated in the course of an uncompleted action or proceeding but the principal's future court attendance still is or may be required and the principal is still under the control of a court, a new securing order must be issued. When the court revokes or otherwise terminates a securing order which committed the principal to the custody of the sheriff, the court shall give written notification to the sheriff of such revocation or termination of the securing order.

HISTORY:

Add, L 1970, ch 996, § 1; amd, L 1984, ch 459, § 1, eff Nov 1, 1984; L 2019, ch 59, § 2 (Part JJJ), eff Jan 1, 2020.

§ 510.10. Securing order; when required; alternatives available; standard to be applied. [Effective July 2, 2020]

1. When a principal, whose future court attendance at a criminal action or proceeding is or may be required, comes under the control of a court, such court shall, in accordance with this title, by a securing order release the principal on the principal's own recognizance, release the principal under non-monetary conditions, or, where authorized, fix bail or commit the principal to the custody of the sheriff. In all such cases, except where another type of securing order is shown to be required by law, the court shall release the principal pending trial on the principal's own recognizance, unless it is demonstrated and the court makes an individualized determination that the principal poses a risk of flight to avoid prosecution. If such a finding is made, the court must select the least restrictive alternative and condition or conditions that will reasonably assure the principal's return to court. The court shall explain its choice of release, release with conditions, bail or remand on the record or in writing.

2. A principal is entitled to representation by counsel under this chapter in preparing an application for release, when a securing order is being considered and when a securing order is being reviewed for modification, revocation or termination. If the principal is financially unable to obtain counsel, counsel shall be assigned to the principal.

3. In cases other than as described in subdivision four of this section the court shall release the principal pending trial on the principal's own recognizance, unless the court finds on the record or in writing that release on the principal's own recognizance will not reasonably assure the principal's return to court. In such instances, the court shall release the principal under non-monetary conditions, selecting the least restrictive alternative and conditions that will reasonably assure the principal's return to court. The court shall explain its choice of alternative and conditions on the record or in writing.

4. Where the principal stands charged with a qualifying offense, the court, unless otherwise prohibited by law, may in its discretion release the principal pending trial on the principal's own recognizance or under non-monetary conditions, fix bail, or, where

the defendant is charged with a qualifying offense which is a felony, the court may commit the principal to the custody of the sheriff. A principal stands charged with a qualifying offense for the purposes of this subdivision when he or she stands charged with:

(a) a felony enumerated in section 70.02 of the penal law, other than robbery in the second degree as defined in subdivision one of section 160.10 of the penal law, provided, however, that burglary in the second degree as defined in subdivision two of section 140.25 of the penal law shall be a qualifying offense only where the defendant is charged with entering the living area of the dwelling;

(b) a crime involving witness intimidation under section 215.15 of the penal law;

(c) a crime involving witness tampering under section 215.11, 215.12 or 215.13 of the penal law;

(d) a class A felony defined in the penal law, provided that for class A felonies under article two hundred twenty of the penal law, only class A-I felonies shall be a qualifying offense;

(e) a sex trafficking offense defined in section 230.34 or 230.34-a of the penal law, or a felony sex offense defined in section 70.80 of the penal law, or a crime involving incest as defined in section 255.25, 255.26 or 255.27 of such law, or a misdemeanor defined in article one hundred thirty of such law;

(f) conspiracy in the second degree as defined in section 105.15 of the penal law, where the underlying allegation of such charge is that the defendant conspired to commit a class A felony defined in article one hundred twenty-five of the penal law;

(g) money laundering in support of terrorism in the first degree as defined in section 470.24 of the penal law; money laundering in support of terrorism in the second degree as defined in section 470.23 of the penal law; money laundering in support of terrorism in the third degree as defined in section 470.22 of the penal law; money laundering in support of terrorism in the fourth degree as defined in section 470.21 of the penal law; or a felony crime of terrorism as defined in article four hundred ninety of the penal law, other than the crime defined in section 490.20 of such law;

(h) criminal contempt in the second degree as defined in subdivision three of section 215.50 of the penal law, criminal contempt in the first degree as defined in subdivision (b), (c) or (d) of section 215.51 of the penal law or aggravated criminal contempt as defined in section 215.52 of the penal law, and the underlying allegation of such charge of criminal contempt in the second degree, criminal contempt in the first degree or aggravated criminal contempt is that the defendant violated a duly served order of protection where the protected party is a member of the defendant's same family or household as defined in subdivision one of section 530.11 of this title;

(i) facilitating a sexual performance by a child with a controlled substance or alcohol as defined in section 263.30 of the penal law, use of a child in a sexual performance as defined in section 263.05 of the penal law or luring a child as defined in subdivision one of section 120.70 of the penal law, promoting an obscene sexual performance by a child as defined in section 263.10 of the penal law or promoting a sexual performance by a child as defined in section 263.15 of the penal law;

(j) any crime that is alleged to have caused the death of another person;

(k) criminal obstruction of breathing or blood circulation as defined in section 121.11 of the penal law, strangulation in the second degree as defined in section 121.12 of the penal law or unlawful imprisonment in the first degree as defined in section 135.10 of the penal law, and is alleged to have committed the offense against a member of the defendant's same family or household as defined in subdivision one of section 530.11 of this title;

(l) aggravated vehicular assault as defined in section 120.04-a of the penal law or vehicular assault in the first degree as defined in section 120.04 of the penal law;

(m) assault in the third degree as defined in section 120.00 of the penal law or arson in the third degree as defined in section 150.10 of the penal law, when such crime is charged as a hate crime as defined in section 485.05 of the penal law;

(n) aggravated assault upon a person less than eleven years old as defined in section 120.12 of the penal law or criminal possession of a weapon on school grounds as defined in section 265.01-a of the penal law;

(o) grand larceny in the first degree as defined in section 155.42 of the penal law, enterprise corruption as defined in section 460.20 of the penal law, or money laundering in the first degree as defined in section 470.20 of the penal law;

(p) failure to register as a sex offender pursuant to section one hundred sixty-eight-t of the correction law or endangering the welfare of a child as defined in subdivision one of section 260.10 of the penal law, where the defendant is required to maintain registration under article six-C of the correction law and designated a level three offender pursuant to subdivision six of section one hundred sixty-eight-l of the correction law;

(q) a crime involving bail jumping under section 215.55, 215.56 or 215.57 of the penal law, or a crime involving escaping from custody under section 205.05, 205.10 or 205.15 of the penal law;

(r) any felony offense committed by the principal while serving a sentence of probation or while released to post release supervision;

(s) a felony, where the defendant qualifies for sentencing on such charge as a persistent felony offender pursuant to section 70.10 of the penal law; or

(t) any felony or class A misdemeanor involving harm to an identifiable person or property, where such charge arose from conduct occurring while the defendant was released on his or her own recognizance or released under conditions for a separate felony or class A misdemeanor involving harm to an identifiable person or property, provided, however, that the prosecutor must show reasonable cause to believe that the defendant committed the instant crime and any underlying crime. For the purposes of this subparagraph, any of the underlying crimes need not be a qualifying offense as defined in this subdivision.

5. Notwithstanding the provisions of subdivisions three and four of this section, with respect to any charge for which bail or remand is not ordered, and for which the court would not or could not otherwise require bail or remand, a defendant may, at any time, request that the court set bail in a nominal amount requested by the defendant in the form specified in paragraph (a) of subdivision one of section 520.10 of this title; if the court is satisfied that the request is voluntary, the court shall set such bail in such amount.

6. When a securing order is revoked or otherwise terminated in the course of an uncompleted action or proceeding but the principal's future court attendance still is or may be required and the principal is still under the control of a court, a new securing order must be issued. When the court revokes or otherwise terminates a securing order which committed the principal to the custody of the sheriff, the court shall give written notification to the sheriff of such revocation or termination of the securing order.

HISTORY:

Add, L 1970, ch 996, § 1; amd, L 1984, ch 459, § 1, eff Nov 1, 1984; L 2019, ch 59, § 2 (Part JJJ), eff Jan 1, 2020; L 2020, ch 56, § 2 (Part UU), eff July 2, 2020.

§ 510.40. Court notification to principal of conditions of release and of alleged violations of conditions of release [Effective until July 2, 2020]

1. Upon ordering that a principal be released on the principal's own recognizance, or released under non-monetary conditions, or, if bail has been fixed, upon the posting of bail, the court must direct the principal to appear in the criminal action or proceeding involved whenever the principal's attendance may be required and to be at all times amenable to the orders and processes of the court. If such principal is in the custody of the sheriff or at liberty upon bail at the time of the order, the court must direct that the principal be discharged from such custody or, as the case may be, that the principal's bail be exonerated.

2. Upon the issuance of an order fixing bail, where authorized, and upon the posting thereof, the court must examine the bail to determine whether it complies with the order. If it does, the court must, in the absence of some factor or circumstance which in law requires or authorizes disapproval thereof, approve the bail and must issue a certificate of release, authorizing the principal to be at liberty, and, if the principal is in the custody of the sheriff at the time, directing the sheriff to discharge the principal therefrom. If the bail fixed is not posted, or is not approved after being posted, the court

must order that the principal be committed to the custody of the sheriff. In the event of any such non-approval, the court shall explain promptly in writing the reasons therefor.

3. Non-monetary conditions of release shall be individualized and established in writing by the court. At future court appearances, the court shall consider a lessening of conditions or modification of conditions to a less burdensome form based on the principal's compliance with such conditions of release. In the event of alleged non-compliance with the conditions of release in an important respect, pursuant to this subdivision, additional conditions may be imposed by the court, on the record or in writing, only after notice of the facts and circumstances of such alleged non-compliance, reasonable under the circumstances, affording the principal and the principal's attorney and the people an opportunity to present relevant, admissible evidence, relevant witnesses and to cross-examine witnesses, and a finding by clear and convincing evidence that the principal violated a condition of release in an important respect. Following such a finding, in determining whether to impose additional conditions for non-compliance, the court shall consider and may select conditions consistent with the court's obligation to impose the least restrictive condition or conditions that will reasonably assure the defendant's return to court. The court shall explain on the record or in writing the reasons for its determination and for any changes to the conditions imposed.

4.(a) Electronic monitoring of a principal's location may be ordered only if the court finds, after notice, an opportunity to be heard and an individualized determination explained on the record or in writing, that the defendant qualifies for electronic monitoring in accordance with subdivision twenty-one of section 500.10 of this title, and no other realistic non-monetary condition or set of non-monetary conditions will suffice to reasonably assure a principal's return to court.

(b) The specific method of electronic monitoring of the principal's location must be approved by the court. It must be the least restrictive procedure and method that will reasonably assure the principal's return to court, and unobtrusive to the greatest extent practicable.

(c) Electronic monitoring of the location of a principal may be conducted only by a public entity under the supervision and control of a county or municipality or a non-profit entity under contract to the county, municipality or the state. A county or municipality shall be authorized to enter into a contract with another county or municipality in the state to monitor principals under non-monetary conditions of release in its county, but counties, municipalities and the state shall not contract with any private for-profit entity for such purposes.

(d) Electronic monitoring of a principal's location may be for a maximum period of sixty days, and may be renewed for such period, after notice, an opportunity to be heard and a de novo, individualized determination in accordance with this subdivision, which shall be explained on the record or in writing.

A defendant subject to electronic location monitoring under this subdivision shall be considered held or confined in custody for purposes of section 180.80 of this chapter and shall be considered committed to the custody of the sheriff for purposes of section 170.70 of the chapter, as applicable.

5. If a principal is released under non-monetary conditions, the court shall, on the record and in an individualized written document provided to the principal, notify the principal, in plain language and a manner sufficiently clear and specific:

(a) of any conditions to which the principal is subject, to serve as a guide for the principal's conduct; and

(b) that the possible consequences for violation of such a condition may include revocation of the securing order and the ordering of a more restrictive securing order.

HISTORY:

Add, L 1970, ch 996, § 1, eff Sept 1, 1971; amd, L 2019, ch 59, § 6 (Part JJJ), eff Jan 1, 2020.

§ 510.40. Court notification to principal of conditions of release and of alleged violations of conditions of release [Effective July 2, 2020]

1. Upon ordering that a principal be released on the principal's own recognizance, or released under non-monetary conditions, or, if bail has been fixed, upon the posting of

bail, the court must direct the principal to appear in the criminal action or proceeding involved whenever the principal's attendance may be required and to be at all times amenable to the orders and processes of the court. If such principal is in the custody of the sheriff or at liberty upon bail at the time of the order, the court must direct that the principal be discharged from such custody or, as the case may be, that the principal's bail be exonerated.

2. Upon the issuance of an order fixing bail, where authorized, and upon the posting thereof, the court must examine the bail to determine whether it complies with the order. If it does, the court must, in the absence of some factor or circumstance which in law requires or authorizes disapproval thereof, approve the bail and must issue a certificate of release, authorizing the principal to be at liberty, and, if the principal is in the custody of the sheriff at the time, directing the sheriff to discharge the principal therefrom. If the bail fixed is not posted, or is not approved after being posted, the court must order that the principal be committed to the custody of the sheriff. In the event of any such non-approval, the court shall explain promptly in writing the reasons therefor.

3. Non-monetary conditions of release shall be individualized and established in writing by the court. At future court appearances, the court shall consider a lessening of conditions or modification of conditions to a less burdensome form based on the principal's compliance with such conditions of release. In the event of alleged non-compliance with the conditions of release in an important respect, pursuant to this subdivision, additional conditions may be imposed by the court, on the record or in writing, only after notice of the facts and circumstances of such alleged non-compliance, reasonable under the circumstances, affording the principal and the principal's attorney and the people an opportunity to present relevant, admissible evidence, relevant witnesses and to cross-examine witnesses, and a finding by clear and convincing evidence that the principal violated a condition of release in an important respect. Following such a finding, in determining whether to impose additional conditions for non-compliance, the court shall consider and may select conditions consistent with the court's obligation to impose the least restrictive condition or conditions that will reasonably assure the defendant's return to court. The court shall explain on the record or in writing the reasons for its determination and for any changes to the conditions imposed.

4.(a) Electronic monitoring of a principal's location may be ordered only if the court finds, after notice, an opportunity to be heard and an individualized determination explained on the record or in writing, that the defendant qualifies for electronic monitoring in accordance with subdivision twenty-one of section 500.10 of this title, and no other realistic non-monetary condition or set of non-monetary conditions will suffice to reasonably assure a principal's return to court.

(b) The specific method of electronic monitoring of the principal's location must be approved by the court. It must be the least restrictive procedure and method that will reasonably assure the principal's return to court, and unobtrusive to the greatest extent practicable.

(c) Electronic monitoring of the location of a principal may be conducted only by a public entity under the supervision and control of a county or municipality or a non-profit entity under contract to the county, municipality or the state. A county or municipality shall be authorized to enter into a contract with another county or municipality in the state to monitor principals under non-monetary conditions of release in its county, but counties, municipalities and the state shall not contract with any private for-profit entity for such purposes. Counties, municipalities and the state may contract with a private for-profit entity to supply electronic monitoring devices or other items, provided that any interaction with persons under electronic monitoring or the data produced by such monitoring shall be conducted solely by employees of a county, municipality, the state, or a non-profit entity under contract with such county, municipality or the state.

(d) Electronic monitoring of a principal's location may be for a maximum period of sixty days, and may be renewed for such period, after notice, an opportunity to be heard and a de novo, individualized determination in accordance with this subdivision, which shall be explained on the record or in writing.

A defendant subject to electronic location monitoring under this subdivision shall be considered held or confined in custody for purposes of section 180.80 of this chapter and shall be considered committed to the custody of the sheriff for purposes of section 170.70 of the chapter, as applicable.

5. If a principal is released under non-monetary conditions, the court shall, on the record and in an individualized written document provided to the principal, notify the principal, in plain language and a manner sufficiently clear and specific:

(a) of any conditions to which the principal is subject, to serve as a guide for the principal's conduct; and

(b) that the possible consequences for violation of such a condition may include revocation of the securing order and the ordering of a more restrictive securing order.

HISTORY:

Add, L 1970, ch 996, § 1, eff Sept 1, 1971; amd, L 2019, ch 59, § 6 (Part JJJ), eff Jan 1, 2020; L 2020, ch 56, § 7 (Part UU), eff July 2, 2020.

§ 510.43. Court appearances: additional notifications. [Effective until July 2, 2020]

The court or, upon direction of the court, a certified pretrial services agency, shall notify all principals released under non-monetary conditions and on recognizance of all court appearances in advance by text message, telephone call, electronic mail or first class mail. The chief administrator of the courts shall, pursuant to subdivision one of section 10.40 of this chapter, develop a form which shall be offered to the principal at court appearances. On such form, which upon completion shall be retained in the court file, the principal may select one such preferred manner of notice.

HISTORY:

L 2019, ch 59, § 7 (Part JJJ), eff Jan 1, 2020.

§ 510.43. Court appearances: additional notifications. [Effective July 2, 2020]

1. The court or, upon direction of the court, a certified pretrial services agency, shall notify all principals released under non-monetary conditions and on recognizance of all court appearances in advance by text message, telephone call, electronic mail or first class mail. The chief administrator of the courts shall, pursuant to subdivision one of section 10.40 of this chapter, develop a form which shall be offered to the principal at court appearances. On such form, which upon completion shall be retained in the court file, the principal may select one such preferred manner of notice.

2. Such form may request the information necessary for the defendant to be provided with notice in accordance with such single, selected manner of notice. After notice of such consequence, a defendant who intentionally declines to provide the information necessary for the defendant to be provided with such notice pursuant to this section shall forfeit the opportunity to receive such notice until such information is timely provided. Any failure by the court or certified pretrial services agency to provide notice of a scheduled court appearance in the manner provided in this section shall not in and of itself constitute grounds or authorization for the defendant to fail to appear for such scheduled court appearance.

HISTORY:

L 2019, ch 59, § 7 (Part JJJ), eff Jan 1, 2020; amd, L 2020, ch 56, § 11 (Part UU), eff July 2, 2020.

Article 530
Orders of Recognizance or Bail With Respect to Defendants in Criminal Actions and Proceedings—When and by What Courts Authorized

§ 530.11. Procedures for family offense matters

1. The family court and the criminal courts shall have concurrent jurisdiction over any proceeding concerning acts which would constitute disorderly conduct, harassment in the first degree, harassment in the second degree, aggravated harassment in the

second degree, sexual misconduct, forcible touching, sexual abuse in the third degree, sexual abuse in the second degree as set forth in subdivision one of section 130.60 of the penal law, stalking in the first degree, stalking in the second degree, stalking in the third degree, stalking in the fourth degree, criminal mischief, menacing in the second degree, menacing in the third degree, reckless endangerment, strangulation in the first degree, strangulation in the second degree, criminal obstruction of breathing or blood circulation, assault in the second degree, assault in the third degree, an attempted assault, identity theft in the first degree, identity theft in the second degree, identity theft in the third degree, grand larceny in the fourth degree, grand larceny in the third degree, coercion in the second degree or coercion in the third degree as set forth in subdivisions one, two and three of section 135.60 of the penal law between spouses or former spouses, or between parent and child or between members of the same family or household except that if the respondent would not be criminally responsible by reason of age pursuant to section 30.00 of the penal law, then the family court shall have exclusive jurisdiction over such proceeding. Notwithstanding a complainant's election to proceed in family court, the criminal court shall not be divested of jurisdiction to hear a family offense proceeding pursuant to this section. For purposes of this section, "disorderly conduct" includes disorderly conduct not in a public place. For purposes of this section, "members of the same family or household" with respect to a proceeding in the criminal courts shall mean the following:

(a) persons related by consanguinity or affinity;

(b) persons legally married to one another;

(c) persons formerly married to one another regardless of whether they still reside in the same household;

(d) persons who have a child in common, regardless of whether such persons have been married or have lived together at any time; and

(e) persons who are not related by consanguinity or affinity and who are or have been in an intimate relationship regardless of whether such persons have lived together at any time. Factors the court may consider in determining whether a relationship is an "intimate relationship" include but are not limited to: the nature or type of relationship, regardless of whether the relationship is sexual in nature; the frequency of interaction between the persons; and the duration of the relationship. Neither a casual acquaintance nor ordinary fraternization between two individuals in business or social contexts shall be deemed to constitute an "intimate relationship".

2. Information to petitioner or complainant. The chief administrator of the courts shall designate the appropriate probation officers, warrant officers, sheriffs, police officers, district attorneys or any other law enforcement officials, to inform any petitioner or complainant bringing a proceeding under this section before such proceeding is commenced, of the procedures available for the institution of family offense proceedings, including but not limited to the following:

(a) That there is concurrent jurisdiction with respect to family offenses in both family court and the criminal courts;

(b) That a family court proceeding is a civil proceeding and is for the purpose of attempting to stop the violence, end family disruption and obtain protection. That referrals for counseling, or counseling services, are available through probation for this purpose;

(c) That a proceeding in the criminal courts is for the purpose of prosecution of the offender and can result in a criminal conviction of the offender;

(d) That a proceeding or action subject to the provisions of this section is initiated at the time of the filing of an accusatory instrument or family court petition, not at the time of arrest, or request for arrest, if any;

(e) [Repealed]

(f) That an arrest may precede the commencement of a family court or a criminal court proceeding, but an arrest is not a requirement for commencing either proceeding.

(g) [Repealed]

(h) At such time as the complainant first appears before the court on a complaint or information, the court shall advise the complainant that the complainant may: continue with the proceeding in criminal court; or have the allegations contained therein heard in a family court proceeding; or proceed concurrently in both criminal and family court. Notwithstanding a complainant's election to proceed in family court, the criminal court shall not be divested of jurisdiction to hear a family offense proceeding pursuant to this section;

(i) Nothing herein shall be deemed to limit or restrict complainant's rights to proceed directly and without court referral in either a criminal or family court, or both, as provided for in section one hundred fifteen of the family court act and section 100.07 of this chapter;

(j) [Repealed]

2-a. Upon the filing of an accusatory instrument charging a crime or violation described in subdivision one of this section between members of the same family or household, as such terms are defined in this section, or as soon as the complainant first appears before the court, whichever is sooner, the court shall advise the complainant of the right to proceed in both the criminal and family courts, pursuant to section 100.07 of this chapter.

3. Official responsibility. No official or other person designated pursuant to subdivision two of this section shall discourage or prevent any person who wishes to file a petition or sign a complaint from having access to any court for that purpose.

4. When a person is arrested for an alleged family offense or an alleged violation of an order of protection or temporary order of protection or arrested pursuant to a warrant issued by the supreme or family court, and the supreme or family court, as applicable, is not in session, such person shall be brought before a local criminal court in the county of arrest or in the county in which such warrant is returnable pursuant to article one hundred twenty of this chapter. Such local criminal court may issue any order authorized under subdivision eleven of section 530.12 of this article, section one hundred fifty-four-d or one hundred fifty-five of the family court act or subdivision three-b of section two hundred forty or subdivision two-a of section two hundred fifty-two of the domestic relations law, in addition to discharging other arraignment responsibilities as set forth in this chapter. In making such order, the local criminal court shall consider de novo the recommendation and securing order, if any, made by the supreme or family court as indicated on the warrant or certificate of warrant. Unless the petitioner or complainant requests otherwise, the court, in addition to scheduling further criminal proceedings, if any, regarding such alleged family offense or violation allegation, shall make such matter returnable in the supreme or family court, as applicable, on the next day such court is in session.

5. Filing and enforcement of out-of-state orders of protection. A valid order of protection or temporary order of protection issued by a court of competent jurisdiction in another state, territorial or tribal jurisdiction shall be accorded full faith and credit and enforced as if it were issued by a court within the state for as long as the order remains in effect in the issuing jurisdiction in accordance with sections two thousand two hundred sixty-five and two thousand two hundred sixty-six of title eighteen of the United States Code.

(a) An order issued by a court of competent jurisdiction in another state, territorial or tribal jurisdiction shall be deemed valid if:

(i) the issuing court had personal jurisdiction over the parties and over the subject matter under the law of the issuing jurisdiction;

(ii) the person against whom the order was issued had reasonable notice and an opportunity to be heard prior to issuance of the order; provided, however, that if the order was a temporary order of protection issued in the absence of such person, that notice had been given and that an opportunity to be heard had been provided within a reasonable period of time after the issuance of the order; and

(iii) in the case of orders of protection or temporary orders of protection issued against both a petitioner, plaintiff or complainant and respondent or defendant, the order or portion thereof sought to be enforced was supported by: (A) a pleading requesting such order, including, but not limited to, a petition, cross-petition or counterclaim; and (B) a judicial finding that the requesting party is entitled to the issuance of the order which may result from a judicial finding of fact, judicial acceptance of an admission by the party against whom the order was issued or judicial finding that the party against whom the order was issued had given knowing, intelligent and voluntary consent to its issuance.

(b) Notwithstanding the provisions of article fifty-four of the civil practice law and rules, an order of protection or temporary order of protection issued by a court of competent jurisdiction in another state, territorial or tribal jurisdiction, accompanied by a sworn affidavit that upon information and belief such order is in effect as written and has not been vacated or modified, may be filed without fee with the clerk of the court, who shall transmit information regarding such order to the statewide registry of orders of protection and warrants established pursuant to section two hundred twenty-one-a of the executive law; provided, however, that such filing and registry entry shall not be required for enforcement of the order.

6. Notice. Every police officer, peace officer or district attorney investigating a family offense under this article shall advise the victim of the availability of a shelter or other services in the community, and shall immediately give the victim written notice of the legal rights and remedies available to a victim of a family offense under the relevant provisions of this chapter and the family court act. Such notice shall be prepared, at minimum, in plain English, Spanish, Chinese and Russian and if necessary, shall be delivered orally, and shall include but not be limited to the information contained in the following statement:

Are you the victim of domestic violence? If you need help now, you can call 911 for the police to come to you. You can also call a domestic violence hotline. You can have a confidential talk with an advocate at the hotline about help you can get in your community including: where you can get treatment for injuries, where you can get shelter, where you can get support, and what you can do to be safe. The New York State 24-hour Domestic & Sexual Violence Hotline number is (insert the statewide multilingual 800 number). They can give you information in many languages. If you are deaf or hard of hearing, call 711.

This is what the police can do:

They can help you and your children find a safe place such as a family or friend's house or a shelter in your community.

You can ask the officer to take you or help you and your children get to a safe place in your community.

They can help connect you to a local domestic violence program.

They can help you get to a hospital or clinic for medical care.

They can help you get your personal belongings.

They must complete a report discussing the incident. They will give you a copy of this police report before they leave the scene. It is free.

They may, and sometimes must, arrest the person who harmed you if you are the victim of a crime. The person arrested could be released at any time, so it is important to plan for your safety.

If you have been abused or threatened, this is what you can ask the police or district attorney to do:

File a criminal complaint against the person who harmed you.

Ask the criminal court to issue an order of protection for you and your child if the district attorney files a criminal case with the court.

Give you information about filing a family offense petition in your local family court.

You also have the right to ask the family court for an order of protection for you and your children.

This is what you can ask the family court to do:

To have your family offense petition filed the same day you go to court.

To have your request heard in court the same day you file or the next day court is open.

Only a judge can issue an order of protection. The judge does that as part of a criminal or family court case against the person who harmed you. An order of protection in family court or in criminal court can say:

That the other person have no contact or communication with you by mail, phone, computer or through other people.

That the other person stay away from you and your children, your home, job or school.

That the other person not assault, harass, threaten, strangle, or commit another family offense against you or your children.

That the other person turn in their firearms and firearms licenses, and not get any more firearms.

That you have temporary custody of your children.

That the other person pay temporary child support.

That the other person not harm your pets or service animals.

If the family court is closed because it is night, a weekend, or a holiday, you can go to a criminal court to ask for an order of protection.

If you do not speak English or cannot speak it well, you can ask the police, the district attorney, or the criminal or family court to get you an interpreter who speaks your language. The interpreter can help you explain what happened.

You can get the forms you need to ask for an order of protection at your local family court (insert addresses and contact information for courts). You can also get them online: www.NYCourts.gov/forms.

You do not need a lawyer to ask for an order of protection.

You have a right to get a lawyer in the family court. If the family court finds that you cannot afford to pay for a lawyer, it must get you one for free.

If you file a complaint or family court petition, you will be asked to swear to its truthfulness because it is a crime to file a legal document that you know is false.

The division of criminal justice services in consultation with the state office for the prevention of domestic violence shall prepare the form of such written notice consistent with provisions of this section and distribute copies thereof to the appropriate law enforcement officials pursuant to subdivision nine of section eight hundred forty-one of the executive law.

Additionally, copies of such notice shall be provided to the chief administrator of the courts to be distributed to victims of family offenses through the criminal court at such time as such persons first come before the court and to the state department of health for distribution to all hospitals defined under article twenty-eight of the public health law. No cause of action for damages shall arise in favor of any person by reason of any failure to comply with the provisions of this subdivision except upon a showing of gross negligence or willful misconduct.

The division of criminal justice services in consultation with the state office for the prevention of domestic violence shall prepare the form of such written notice consistent with provisions of this section and distribute copies thereof to the appropriate law enforcement officials pursuant to subdivision nine of section eight hundred forty-one of the executive law.

Additionally, copies of such notice shall be provided to the chief administrator of the courts to be distributed to victims of family offenses through the criminal court at such time as such persons first come before the court and to the state department of health for distribution to all hospitals defined under article twenty-eight of the public health law. No cause of action for damages shall arise in favor of any person by reason of any failure to comply with the provisions of this subdivision except upon a showing of gross negligence or willful misconduct.

7. Rules of court regarding concurrent jurisdiction. The chief administrator of the courts, pursuant to paragraph (e) of subdivision two of section two hundred twelve of the judiciary law, shall promulgate rules to facilitate record sharing and other communication between the criminal and family courts, subject to applicable provisions of this chapter and the family court act pertaining to the confidentiality, expungement and sealing of records, when such courts exercise concurrent jurisdiction over family offense proceedings.

HISTORY:

Add, L 1980, ch 530, § 15; amd, L 1981, ch 416, § 20; L 1983, ch 925, § 2, eff Aug 8, 1983; L 1984, ch 948, § 13, eff Nov 1, 1984 and applicable to any action and proceeding commenced on or after Nov 1, 1984; L 1986, ch 847, § 2; L 1990, ch 667, § 1; L 1992, ch 345, § 6; L 1994, ch 222, §§ 34–39, eff Jan 1, 1995 (see 1994 note); L 1994, ch 224, § 7, eff Jan 1, 1995; L 1995, ch 349, § 5, eff July 28, 1995; L 1995, ch 440, § 2, eff Nov 1, 1995; L 1997, ch 186, §§ 7–9, eff July 8, 1997; L 1998, ch 597, § 11, eff Dec 22, 1998; L 1999, ch 125, §§ 1, 2, eff June 29, 1999; L 1999, ch 635, § 3, eff Dec 1, 1999; L 2007, ch 541, § 2, eff Nov 13, 2007; L 2008, ch 326, § 11, eff July 21, 2008; L 2009, ch 476, § 3, eff Dec 15, 2009; L 2010, ch 405, § 11, eff Nov 11, 2010; L 2013, ch 526, § 10, eff Dec 18, 2013; L 2018, ch 55, § 4 (Part NN), eff Nov 1, 2018; L 2019, ch 59, § 12 (Part JJJ), eff Jan 1, 2020; L 2019, ch 109, § 2, eff Sept 21, 2019; L 2019, ch 663, § 2, eff March 15, 2020.

§ 530.14. Suspension and revocation of a license to carry, possess, repair or dispose of a firearm or firearms pursuant to section 400.00 of the penal law and ineligibility for such a license; order to surrender firearms [Effective until November 1, 2020]

1. Suspension of firearms license and ineligibility for such a license upon issuance of temporary order of protection. Whenever a temporary order of protection is issued pursuant to subdivision one of section 530.12 or subdivision one of section 530.13 of this article:

(a) the court shall suspend any such existing license possessed by the defendant, order the defendant ineligible for such a license and order the immediate surrender of any or all firearms, rifles and shotguns owned or possessed where the court receives information that gives the court good cause to believe that (i) the defendant has a prior conviction of any violent felony offense as defined in section 70.02 of the penal law; (ii) the defendant has previously been found to have willfully failed to obey a prior order of protection and such willful failure involved (A) the infliction of physical injury, as defined in subdivision nine of section 10.00 of the penal law, (B) the use or threatened use of a deadly weapon or dangerous instrument as those terms are defined in subdivisions twelve and thirteen of section 10.00 of the penal law, or (C) behavior constituting any violent felony offense as defined in section 70.02 of the penal law; or (iii) the defendant has a prior conviction for stalking in the first degree as defined in section 120.60 of the penal law, stalking in the second degree as defined in section 120.55 of the penal law, stalking in the third degree as defined in section 120.50 of the penal law or stalking in the fourth degree as defined in section 120.45 of such law; and

(b) the court shall where the court finds a substantial risk that the defendant may use or threaten to use a firearm, rifle or shotgun unlawfully against the person or persons for whose protection the temporary order of protection is issued, suspend any such existing license possessed by the defendant, order the defendant ineligible for such a license and order the immediate surrender pursuant to subparagraph (f) of paragraph one of subdivision a of section 265.20 and subdivision six of section 400.05 of the penal law, of any or all firearms, rifles and shotguns owned or possessed.

2. Revocation or suspension of firearms license and ineligibility for such a license upon issuance of an order of protection. Whenever an order of protection is issued pursuant to subdivision five of section 530.12 or subdivision four of section 530.13 of this article:

(a) the court shall revoke any such existing license possessed by the defendant, order the defendant ineligible for such a license and order the immediate surrender of any or all firearms, rifles and shotguns owned or possessed where such action is required by section 400.00 of the penal law; and

(b) the court shall where the court finds a substantial risk that the defendant may use or threaten to use a firearm, rifles or shotguns* unlawfully against the person or persons for whose protection the order of protection is issued, (i) revoke any such existing license possessed by the defendant, order the defendant ineligible for such a license and order the immediate surrender of any or all firearms, rifles and shotguns owned or possessed or (ii) suspend or continue to suspend any such existing license possessed by the defendant, order the defendant ineligible for such a license and order the immediate surrender pursuant to subparagraph (f) of paragraph one of subdivision a of section 265.20 and subdivision six of section 400.05 of the penal law, of any or all firearms, rifles and shotguns owned or possessed.

3. Revocation or suspension of firearms license and ineligibility for such a license upon a finding of a willful failure to obey an order of protection. Whenever a defendant has been found pursuant to subdivision eleven of section 530.12 or subdivision eight of section 530.13 of this article to have willfully failed to obey an order of protection issued by a court of competent jurisdiction in this state or another state, territorial or tribal jurisdiction, in addition to any other remedies available pursuant to subdivision eleven of section 530.12 or subdivision eight of section 530.13 of this article:

(a) the court shall revoke any such existing license possessed by the defendant, order the defendant ineligible for such a license and order the immediate surrender

*So in original. ("rifles or shotguns" should be "rifle or shotgun")

of any or all firearms, rifles and shotguns owned or possessed where the willful failure to obey such order involved (i) the infliction of physical injury, as defined in subdivision nine of section 10.00 of the penal law, (ii) the use or threatened use of a deadly weapon or dangerous instrument as those terms are defined in subdivisions twelve and thirteen of section 10.00 of the penal law, (iii) behavior constituting any violent felony offense as defined in section 70.02 of the penal law; or (iv) behavior constituting stalking in the first degree as defined in section 120.60 of the penal law, stalking in the second degree as defined in section 120.55 of the penal law, stalking in the third degree as defined in section 120.50 of the penal law or stalking in the fourth degree as defined in section 120.45 of such law; and

(b) the court shall where the court finds a substantial risk that the defendant may use or threaten to use a firearm, rifle or shotgun unlawfully against the person or persons for whose protection the order of protection was issued, (i) revoke any such existing license possessed by the defendant, order the defendant ineligible for such a license and order the immediate surrender pursuant to subparagraph (f) of paragraph one of subdivision a of section 265.20 and subdivision six of section 400.05 of the penal law, of any or all firearms, rifles and shotguns owned or possessed or (ii) suspend any such existing license possessed by the defendant, order the defendant ineligible for such a license and order the immediate surrender pursuant to subparagraph (f) of paragraph one of subdivision a of section 265.20 and subdivision six of section 400.05 of the penal law, of any or all firearms, rifles and shotguns owned or possessed.

4. Suspension. Any suspension order issued pursuant to this section shall remain in effect for the duration of the temporary order of protection or order of protection, unless modified or vacated by the court.

5. Surrender. (a) Where an order to surrender one or more firearms, rifles and shotguns has been issued, the temporary order of protection or order of protection shall specify the place where such weapons shall be surrendered, shall specify a date and time by which the surrender shall be completed and, to the extent possible, shall describe such weapons to be surrendered, and shall direct the authority receiving such surrendered weapons to immediately notify the court of such surrender.

(b) The prompt surrender of one or more firearms, rifles or shotguns pursuant to a court order issued pursuant to this section shall be considered a voluntary surrender for purposes of subparagraph (f) of paragraph one of subdivision a of section 265.20 of the penal law. The disposition of any such weapons shall be in accordance with the provisions of subdivision six of section 400.05 of the penal law; provided, however, that upon termination of any suspension order issued pursuant to this section or section eight hundred forty-two-a of the family court act, upon written application of the subject of the order, with notice and opportunity to be heard to the district attorney, the county attorney, the protected party, and every licensing officer responsible for issuance of a firearms license to the subject of the order pursuant to article four hundred of the penal law, and upon a written finding that there is no legal impediment to the subject's possession of a surrendered firearm, rifle or shotgun, any court of record exercising criminal jurisdiction may order the return of a firearm, rifle or shotgun not otherwise disposed of in accordance with subdivision six of section 400.05 of the penal law. When issuing such order in connection with any firearm subject to a license requirement under article four hundred of the penal law, if the licensing officer informs the court that he or she will seek to revoke the license, the order shall be stayed by the court until the conclusion of any license revocation proceeding.

(c) The provisions of this section shall not be deemed to limit, restrict or otherwise impair the authority of the court to order and direct the surrender of any or all firearms, rifles and shotguns owned or possessed by a defendant pursuant to sections 530.12 or 530.13 of this article.

6. Notice. (a) Where an order requiring surrender, revocation, suspension or ineligibility has been issued pursuant to this section, any temporary order of protection or order of protection issued shall state that such firearm license has been suspended or revoked or that the defendant is ineligible for such license, as the case may be, and that the defendant is prohibited from possessing any firearm, rifle or shotgun.

(b) The court revoking or suspending the license, ordering the defendant ineligible for such a license, or ordering the surrender of any firearm, rifle or shotgun shall immediately notify the duly constituted police authorities of the locality concerning such action and, in the case of orders of protection and temporary orders of protection issued pursuant to section 530.12 of this article, shall immediately notify the statewide registry of orders of protection.

(c) The court revoking or suspending the license or ordering the defendant ineligible for such a license shall give written notice thereof without unnecessary delay to the division of state police at its office in the city of Albany.

(d) Where an order of revocation, suspension, ineligibility or surrender is modified or vacated, the court shall immediately notify the statewide registry of orders of protection and the duly constituted police authorities of the locality concerning such action and shall give written notice thereof without unnecessary delay to the division of state police at its office in the city of Albany.

7. Hearing. The defendant shall have the right to a hearing before the court regarding any revocation, suspension, ineligibility or surrender order issued pursuant to this section, provided that nothing in this subdivision shall preclude the court from issuing any such order prior to a hearing. Where the court has issued such an order prior to a hearing, it shall commence such hearing within fourteen days of the date such order was issued.

8. Nothing in this section shall delay or otherwise interfere with the issuance of a temporary order of protection or the timely arraignment of a defendant in custody.

HISTORY:

Add, L 1996, ch 644, § 3, eff Nov 1, 1996; amd, L 1998, ch 597, § 13, eff Dec 22, 1998; L 1999, ch 635, § 4, eff Dec 1, 1999; L 2000, ch 434, § 1, eff Oct 20, 2000; L 2007, ch 198, § 1, eff Aug 2, 2007; L 2013, ch 1, §§ 13–15, eff March 16, 2013; L 2018, ch 60, § 4, eff June 11, 2018.

§ 530.14. Suspension and revocation of a license to carry, possess, repair or dispose of a firearm or firearms pursuant to section 400.00 of the penal law and ineligibility for such a license; order to surrender firearms; order to seize firearms. [Effective November 1, 2020]

1. Suspension of firearms license and ineligibility for such a license upon issuance of temporary order of protection. Whenever a temporary order of protection is issued pursuant to subdivision one of section 530.12 or subdivision one of section 530.13 of this article:

(a) the court shall suspend any such existing license possessed by the defendant, order the defendant ineligible for such a license and order the immediate surrender of any or all firearms, rifles and shotguns owned or possessed where the court receives information that gives the court good cause to believe that (i) the defendant has a prior conviction of any violent felony offense as defined in section 70.02 of the penal law; (ii) the defendant has previously been found to have willfully failed to obey a prior order of protection and such willful failure involved (A) the infliction of physical injury, as defined in subdivision nine of section 10.00 of the penal law, (B) the use or threatened use of a deadly weapon or dangerous instrument as those terms are defined in subdivisions twelve and thirteen of section 10.00 of the penal law, or (C) behavior constituting any violent felony offense as defined in section 70.02 of the penal law; or (iii) the defendant has a prior conviction for stalking in the first degree as defined in section 120.60 of the penal law, stalking in the second degree as defined in section 120.55 of the penal law, stalking in the third degree as defined in section 120.50 of the penal law or stalking in the fourth degree as defined in section 120.45 of such law;

(b) the court shall where the court finds a substantial risk that the defendant may use or threaten to use a firearm, rifle or shotgun unlawfully against the person or persons for whose protection the temporary order of protection is issued, suspend any such existing license possessed by the defendant, order the defendant ineligible for such a license and order the immediate surrender pursuant to subparagraph (f) of paragraph one of subdivision a of section 265.20 and subdivision six of section 400.05 of the penal law, of any or all firearms, rifles and shotguns owned or possessed; and

(c) the court may where the defendant willfully refuses to surrender such firearm, rifle or shotgun pursuant to paragraphs (a) and (b) of this subdivision, or for other good cause shown, order the immediate seizure of such firearm, rifle or shotgun, and search therefor, pursuant to an order issued in accordance with article six hundred ninety of this part, consistent with such rights as the defendant may derive from this article or the constitution of this state or the United States.

2. Revocation or suspension of firearms license and ineligibility for such a license upon issuance of an order of protection. Whenever an order of protection is issued pursuant to subdivision five of section 530.12 or subdivision four of section 530.13 of this article:

(a) the court shall revoke any such existing license possessed by the defendant, order the defendant ineligible for such a license and order the immediate surrender of any or all firearms, rifles and shotguns owned or possessed where such action is required by section 400.00 of the penal law;

(b) the court shall where the court finds a substantial risk that the defendant may use or threaten to use a firearm, rifle or shotgun unlawfully against the person or persons for whose protection the order of protection is issued, (i) revoke any such existing license possessed by the defendant, order the defendant ineligible for such a license and order the immediate surrender of any or all firearms, rifles and shotguns owned or possessed or (ii) suspend or continue to suspend any such existing license possessed by the defendant, order the defendant ineligible for such a license and order the immediate surrender pursuant to subparagraph (f) of paragraph one of subdivision a of section 265.20 and subdivision six of section 400.05 of the penal law, of any or all firearms, rifles and shotguns owned or possessed; and

(c) the court may where the defendant willfully refuses to surrender such firearm, rifle or shotgun pursuant to paragraphs (a) and (b) of this subdivision, or for other good cause shown, order the immediate seizure of such firearm, rifle or shotgun, and search therefor, pursuant to an order issued in accordance with article six hundred ninety of this part, consistent with such rights as the defendant may derive from this article or the constitution of this state or the United States.

3. Revocation or suspension of firearms license and ineligibility for such a license upon a finding of a willful failure to obey an order of protection. Whenever a defendant has been found pursuant to subdivision eleven of section 530.12 or subdivision eight of section 530.13 of this article to have willfully failed to obey an order of protection issued by a court of competent jurisdiction in this state or another state, territorial or tribal jurisdiction, in addition to any other remedies available pursuant to subdivision eleven of section 530.12 or subdivision eight of section 530.13 of this article:

(a) the court shall revoke any such existing license possessed by the defendant, order the defendant ineligible for such a license and order the immediate surrender of any or all firearms, rifles and shotguns owned or possessed where the willful failure to obey such order involved (i) the infliction of physical injury, as defined in subdivision nine of section 10.00 of the penal law, (ii) the use or threatened use of a deadly weapon or dangerous instrument as those terms are defined in subdivisions twelve and thirteen of section 10.00 of the penal law, (iii) behavior constituting any violent felony offense as defined in section 70.02 of the penal law; or (iv) behavior constituting stalking in the first degree as defined in section 120.60 of the penal law, stalking in the second degree as defined in section 120.55 of the penal law, stalking in the third degree as defined in section 120.50 of the penal law or stalking in the fourth degree as defined in section 120.45 of such law;

(b) the court shall where the court finds a substantial risk that the defendant may use or threaten to use a firearm, rifle or shotgun unlawfully against the person or persons for whose protection the order of protection was issued, (i) revoke any such existing license possessed by the defendant, order the defendant ineligible for such a license and order the immediate surrender pursuant to subparagraph (f) of paragraph one of subdivision a of section 265.20 and subdivision six of section 400.05 of the penal law, of any or all firearms, rifles and shotguns owned or possessed or (ii) suspend any such existing license possessed by the defendant, order the defendant ineligible for such a license and order the immediate surrender pursuant to subparagraph (f) of paragraph one of subdivision a of section 265.20 and subdivision six of section 400.05 of the penal law, of any or all firearms, rifles and shotguns owned or possessed; and

(c) the court may where the defendant willfully refuses to surrender such firearm, rifle or shotgun pursuant to paragraphs (a) and (b) of this subdivision, or for other good cause shown, order the immediate seizure of such firearm, rifle or shotgun, and search therefor, pursuant to an order issued in accordance with article six hundred ninety of this part, consistent with such rights as the defendant may derive from this article or the constitution of this state or the United States.

4. Suspension. Any suspension order issued pursuant to this section shall remain in effect for the duration of the temporary order of protection or order of protection, unless modified or vacated by the court.

5. Surrender. (a) Where an order to surrender one or more firearms, rifles and shotguns has been issued, the temporary order of protection or order of protection shall specify the place where such weapons shall be surrendered, shall specify a date and time by which the surrender shall be completed and, to the extent possible, shall describe such weapons to be surrendered, and shall direct the authority receiving such surrendered weapons to immediately notify the court of such surrender.

(b) The prompt surrender of one or more firearms, rifles or shotguns pursuant to a court order issued pursuant to this section shall be considered a voluntary surrender for purposes of subparagraph (f) of paragraph one of subdivision a of section 265.20 of the penal law. The disposition of any such weapons, including weapons ordered to be seized pursuant to this section and section eight hundred forty-two-a of the family court act, shall be in accordance with the provisions of subdivision six of section 400.05 of the penal law; provided, however, that upon termination of any suspension order issued pursuant to this section or section eight hundred forty-two-a of the family court act, upon written application of the subject of the order, with notice and opportunity to be heard to the district attorney, the county attorney, the protected party, and every licensing officer responsible for issuance of a firearms license to the subject of the order pursuant to article four hundred of the penal law, and upon a written finding that there is no legal impediment to the subject's possession of a surrendered firearm, rifle or shotgun, any court of record exercising criminal jurisdiction may order the return of a firearm, rifle or shotgun not otherwise disposed of in accordance with subdivision six of section 400.05 of the penal law. When issuing such order in connection with any firearm subject to a license requirement under article four hundred of the penal law, if the licensing officer informs the court that he or she will seek to revoke the license, the order shall be stayed by the court until the conclusion of any license revocation proceeding.

(c) The provisions of this section shall not be deemed to limit, restrict or otherwise impair the authority of the court to order and direct the surrender of any or all firearms, rifles and shotguns owned or possessed by a defendant pursuant to sections 530.12 or 530.13 of this article.

(d) If any other person demonstrates that such person is the lawful owner of any weapon taken into custody pursuant to this section or section eight hundred forty-two-a of the family court act, and provided that the court has made a written finding that there is no legal impediment to the person's possession of such a weapon, such court shall direct that such weapon be returned to such lawful owner.

6. **Notice.**

(a) Where an order requiring surrender, revocation, suspension, seizure or ineligibility has been issued pursuant to this section, any temporary order of protection or order of protection issued shall state that such firearm license has been suspended or revoked or that the defendant is ineligible for such license, as the case may be, and that the defendant is prohibited from possessing any firearm, rifle or shotgun.

(b) The court revoking or suspending the license, ordering the defendant ineligible for such a license, or ordering the surrender or seizure of any firearm, rifle or shotgun shall immediately notify the duly constituted police authorities of the locality concerning such action and, in the case of orders of protection and temporary orders of protection issued pursuant to section 530.12 of this article, shall immediately notify the statewide registry of orders of protection.

(c) The court revoking or suspending the license or ordering the defendant ineligible for such a license shall give written notice thereof without unnecessary delay to the division of state police at its office in the city of Albany.

(d) Where an order of revocation, suspension, ineligibility, surrender or seizure is modified or vacated, the court shall immediately notify the statewide registry of orders of protection and the duly constituted police authorities of the locality concerning such action and shall give written notice thereof without unnecessary delay to the division of state police at its office in the city of Albany.

7. Hearing. The defendant shall have the right to a hearing before the court regarding any revocation, suspension, ineligibility, surrender or seizure order issued pursuant to this section, provided that nothing in this subdivision shall preclude the court from issuing any such order prior to a hearing. Where the court has issued such an order prior to a hearing, it shall commence such hearing within fourteen days of the date such order was issued.

8. Nothing in this section shall delay or otherwise interfere with the issuance of a temporary order of protection or the timely arraignment of a defendant in custody.

HISTORY:

Add, L 1996, ch 644, § 3, eff Nov 1, 1996; amd, L 1998, ch 597, § 13, eff Dec 22, 1998; L 1999, ch 635, § 4, eff Dec 1, 1999; L 2000, ch 434, § 1, eff Oct 20, 2000; L 2007, ch 198, § 1, eff Aug 2, 2007; L 2013, ch 1, §§ 13–15, eff March 16, 2013; L 2018, ch 60, § 4, eff June 11, 2018; L 2020, ch 55, §§ 3–7 (Part M), eff Nov 1, 2020.

§ 530.20. Securing order by local criminal court when action is pending therein. [Effective until July 2, 2020]

When a criminal action is pending in a local criminal court, such court, upon application of a defendant, shall proceed as follows:

1.(a) In cases other than as described in paragraph (b) of this subdivision the court shall release the principal pending trial on the principal's own recognizance, unless the court finds on the record or in writing that release on the principal's own recognizance will not reasonably assure the principal's return to court. In such instances, the court shall release the principal under non-monetary conditions, selecting the least restrictive alternative and conditions that will reasonably assure the principal's return to court. The court shall explain its choice of alternative and conditions on the record or in writing.

(b) Where the principal stands charged with a qualifying offense, the court, unless otherwise prohibited by law, may in its discretion release the principal pending trial on the principal's own recognizance or under non-monetary conditions, fix bail, or, where the defendant is charged with a qualifying offense which is a felony, the court may commit the principal to the custody of the sheriff. The court shall explain its choice of release, release with conditions, bail or remand on the record or in writing. A principal stands charged with a qualifying offense when he or she stands charged with:

(i) a felony enumerated in section 70.02 of the penal law, other than burglary in the second degree as defined in subdivision two of section 140.25 of the penal law or robbery in the second degree as defined in subdivision one of section 160.10 of the penal law;

(ii) a crime involving witness intimidation under section 215.15 of the penal law;

(iii) a crime involving witness tampering under section 215.11, 215.12 or 215.13 of the penal law;

(iv) a class A felony defined in the penal law, other than in article two hundred twenty of such law with the exception of section 220.77 of such law;

(v) a felony sex offense defined in section 70.80 of the penal law or a crime involving incest as defined in section 255.25, 255.26 or 255.27 of such law, or a misdemeanor defined in article one hundred thirty of such law;

(vi) conspiracy in the second degree as defined in section 105.15 of the penal law, where the underlying allegation of such charge is that the defendant conspired to commit a class A felony defined in article one hundred twenty-five of the penal law;

(vii) money laundering in support of terrorism in the first degree as defined in section 470.24 of the penal law; money laundering in support of terrorism in the second degree as defined in section 470.23 of the penal law; or a felony crime of terrorism as defined in article four hundred ninety of the penal law, other than the crime defined in section 490.20 of such law;

(viii) criminal contempt in the second degree as defined in subdivision three of section 215.50 of the penal law, criminal contempt in the first degree as defined in subdivision (b), (c) or (d) of section 215.51 of the penal law or aggravated criminal contempt as defined in section 215.52 of the penal law, and the underlying allegation of such charge of criminal contempt in the second degree, criminal contempt in the first degree or aggravated criminal contempt is that the defendant violated a duly served order of protection where the protected party is a member of the defendant's same family or household as defined in subdivision one of section 530.11 of this article; or

(ix) facilitating a sexual performance by a child with a controlled substance or alcohol as defined in section 263.30 of the penal law, use of a child in a sexual performance as defined in section 263.05 of the penal law or luring a child as defined in subdivision one of section 120.70 of the penal law.

(d) Notwithstanding the provisions of paragraphs (a) and (b) of this subdivision, with respect to any charge for which bail or remand is not ordered, and for which the court would not or could not otherwise require bail or remand, a defendant may, at any time, request that the court set bail in a nominal amount requested by the defendant in the form specified in paragraph (a) of subdivision one of section 520.10 of this title; if the court is satisfied that the request is voluntary, the court shall set such bail in such amount.

2. When the defendant is charged, by felony complaint, with a felony, the court may, in its discretion, order recognizance, release under non-monetary conditions, or, where authorized, bail or commit the defendant to the custody of the sheriff except as otherwise provided in subdivision one of this section or this subdivision:

(a) A city court, a town court or a village court may not order recognizance or bail when (i) the defendant is charged with a class A felony, or (ii) the defendant has two previous felony convictions;

(b) No local criminal court may order recognizance, release under non-monetary conditions or bail with respect to a defendant charged with a felony unless and until:

(i) The district attorney has been heard in the matter or, after knowledge or notice of the application and reasonable opportunity to be heard, has failed to appear at the proceeding or has otherwise waived his right to do so; and

(ii) The court and counsel for the defendant have been furnished with a report of the division of criminal justice services concerning the defendant's criminal record, if any, or with a police department report with respect to the defendant's prior arrest and conviction record, if any. If neither report is available, the court, with the consent of the district attorney, may dispense with this requirement; provided, however, that in an emergency, including but not limited to a substantial impairment in the ability of such division or police department to timely furnish such report, such consent shall not be required if, for reasons stated on the record, the court deems it unnecessary. When the court has been furnished with any such report or record, it shall furnish a copy thereof to counsel for the defendant or, if the defendant is not represented by counsel, to the defendant.

HISTORY:

Add, L 1970, ch 996, § 1; amd, L 1971, ch 762 § 12; L 1972, ch 399, § 23; L 1972, ch 661, § 45, eff Sept 1, 1972; L 1975, ch 531, § 2, eff Aug 28, 1975; L 1979, ch 218, § 1, eff Jan 1, 1980; L 2019, ch 59, § 16 (Part JJJ), eff Jan 1, 2020.

§ 530.20. Securing order by local criminal court when action is pending therein. [Effective July 2, 2020]

When a criminal action is pending in a local criminal court, such court, upon application of a defendant, shall proceed as follows:

1.(a) In cases other than as described in paragraph (b) of this subdivision the court shall release the principal pending trial on the principal's own recognizance, unless the court finds on the record or in writing that release on the principal's own recognizance will not reasonably assure the principal's return to court. In such instances, the court shall release the principal under non-monetary conditions, selecting the least restrictive alternative and conditions that will reasonably assure the principal's return to court. The court shall explain its choice of alternative and conditions on the record or in writing.

(b) Where the principal stands charged with a qualifying offense, the court, unless otherwise prohibited by law, may in its discretion release the principal pending trial on the principal's own recognizance or under non-monetary conditions, fix bail, or, where the defendant is charged with a qualifying offense which is a felony, the court may commit the principal to the custody of the sheriff. The court shall explain its choice of release, release with conditions, bail or remand on the record or in writing. A principal stands charged with a qualifying offense when he or she stands charged with:

(i) a felony enumerated in section 70.02 of the penal law, other than robbery in the second degree as defined in subdivision one of section 160.10 of the penal law, provided, however, that burglary in the second degree as defined in subdivision two of section 140.25 of the penal law shall be a qualifying offense only where the defendant is charged with entering the living area of the dwelling;

(ii) a crime involving witness intimidation under section 215.15 of the penal law;

(iii) a crime involving witness tampering under section 215.11, 215.12 or 215.13 of the penal law;

(iv) a class A felony defined in the penal law, provided, that for class A felonies under article two hundred twenty of such law, only class A-I felonies shall be a qualifying offense;

(v) a sex trafficking offense defined in section 230.34 or 230.34-a of the penal law, or a felony sex offense defined in section 70.80 of the penal law or a crime involving incest as defined in section 255.25, 255.26 or 255.27 of such law, or a misdemeanor defined in article one hundred thirty of such law;

(vi) conspiracy in the second degree as defined in section 105.15 of the penal law, where the underlying allegation of such charge is that the defendant conspired to commit a class A felony defined in article one hundred twenty-five of the penal law;

(vii) money laundering in support of terrorism in the first degree as defined in section 470.24 of the penal law; money laundering in support of terrorism in the second degree as defined in section 470.23 of the penal law; money laundering in support of terrorism in the third degree as defined in section 470.22 of the penal law; money laundering in support of terrorism in the fourth degree as defined in section 470.21 of the penal law; or a felony crime of terrorism as defined in article four hundred ninety of the penal law, other than the crime defined in section 490.20 of such law;

(viii) criminal contempt in the second degree as defined in subdivision three of section 215.50 of the penal law, criminal contempt in the first degree as defined in subdivision (b), (c) or (d) of section 215.51 of the penal law or aggravated criminal contempt as defined in section 215.52 of the penal law, and the underlying allegation of such charge of criminal contempt in the second degree, criminal contempt in the first degree or aggravated criminal contempt is that the defendant violated a duly served order of protection where the protected party is a member of the defendant's same family or household as defined in subdivision one of section 530.11 of this article;

(ix) facilitating a sexual performance by a child with a controlled substance or alcohol as defined in section 263.30 of the penal law, use of a child in a sexual performance as defined in section 263.05 of the penal law or luring a child as defined in subdivision one of section 120.70 of the penal law, promoting an obscene sexual performance by a child as defined in section 263.10 of the penal law or promoting a sexual performance by a child as defined in section 263.15 of the penal law;

(x) any crime that is alleged to have caused the death of another person;

(xi) criminal obstruction of breathing or blood circulation as defined in section 121.11 of the penal law, strangulation in the second degree as defined in section 121.12 of the penal law or unlawful imprisonment in the first degree as defined in section 135.10 of the penal law, and is alleged to have committed the offense against a member of the defendant's same family or household as defined in subdivision one of section 530.11 of this article;

(xii) aggravated vehicular assault as defined in section 120.04-a of the penal law or vehicular assault in the first degree as defined in section 120.04 of the penal law;

(xiii) assault in the third degree as defined in section 120.00 of the penal law or arson in the third degree as defined in section 150.10 of the penal law, when such crime is charged as a hate crime as defined in section 485.05 of the penal law;

(xiv) aggravated assault upon a person less than eleven years old as defined in section 120.12 of the penal law or criminal possession of a weapon on school grounds as defined in section 265.01-a of the penal law;

(xv) grand larceny in the first degree as defined in section 155.42 of the penal law, enterprise corruption as defined in section 460.20 of the penal law, or money laundering in the first degree as defined in section 470.20 of the penal law;

(xvi) failure to register as a sex offender pursuant to section one hundred sixty-eight-t of the correction law or endangering the welfare of a child as defined in subdivision one of section 260.10 of the penal law, where the defendant is required to maintain registration under article six-C of the correction law and designated a level three offender pursuant to subdivision six of section one hundred sixty-eight-l of the correction law;

(xvii) a crime involving bail jumping under section 215.55, 215.56 or 215.57 of the penal law, or a crime involving escaping from custody under section 205.05, 205.10 or 205.15 of the penal law;

(xviii) any felony offense committed by the principal while serving a sentence of probation or while released to post release supervision;

(xix) a felony, where the defendant qualifies for sentencing on such charge as a persistent felony offender pursuant to section 70.10 of the penal law; or

(xx) any felony or class A misdemeanor involving harm to an identifiable person or property, where such charge arose from conduct occurring while the defendant was released on his or her own recognizance or released under conditions for a separate felony or class A misdemeanor involving harm to an identifiable person or property, provided, however, that the prosecutor must show reasonable cause to believe that the defendant committed the instant crime and any underlying crime. For the purposes of this subparagraph, any of the underlying crimes need not be a qualifying offense as defined in this subdivision.

(d) Notwithstanding the provisions of paragraphs (a) and (b) of this subdivision, with respect to any charge for which bail or remand is not ordered, and for which the court would not or could not otherwise require bail or remand, a defendant may, at any time, request that the court set bail in a nominal amount requested by the defendant in the form specified in paragraph (a) of subdivision one of section 520.10 of this title; if the court is satisfied that the request is voluntary, the court shall set such bail in such amount.

2. When the defendant is charged, by felony complaint, with a felony, the court may, in its discretion, order recognizance, release under non-monetary conditions, or, where authorized, bail or commit the defendant to the custody of the sheriff except as otherwise provided in subdivision one of this section or this subdivision:

(a) A city court, a town court or a village court may not order recognizance or bail when (i) the defendant is charged with a class A felony, or (ii) the defendant has two previous felony convictions;

(b) No local criminal court may order recognizance, release under non-monetary conditions or bail with respect to a defendant charged with a felony unless and until:

(i) The district attorney has been heard in the matter or, after knowledge or notice of the application and reasonable opportunity to be heard, has failed to appear at the proceeding or has otherwise waived his right to do so; and

(ii) The court and counsel for the defendant have been furnished with a report of the division of criminal justice services concerning the defendant's criminal record, if any, or with a police department report with respect to the defendant's prior arrest and conviction record, if any. If neither report is available, the court, with the consent of the district attorney, may dispense with this requirement; provided, however, that in an emergency, including but not limited to a substantial impairment in the ability of such division or police department to timely furnish such report, such consent shall not be required if, for reasons stated on the record, the court deems it unnecessary. When the court has been furnished with any such report or record, it shall furnish a copy thereof to counsel for the defendant or, if the defendant is not represented by counsel, to the defendant.

HISTORY:

Add, L 1970, ch 996, § 1; amd, L 1971, ch 762 § 12; L 1972, ch 399, § 23; L 1972, ch 661, § 45, eff Sept 1, 1972; L 1975, ch 531, § 2, eff Aug 28, 1975; L 1979, ch 218, § 1, eff Jan 1, 1980; L 2019, ch 59, § 16 (Part JJJ), eff Jan 1, 2020; L 2020, ch 56, § 3 (Part UU), eff July 2, 2020.

§ 530.40. Order of recognizance, release under non-monetary conditions or bail; by superior court when action is pending therein [Effective until July 2, 2020]

When a criminal action is pending in a superior court, such court, upon application of a defendant, must or may order recognizance or bail as follows:

1. When the defendant is charged with an offense or offenses of less than felony grade only, the court must, unless otherwise provided by law, order recognizance or release under non-monetary conditions in accordance with this section.

2. When the defendant is charged with a felony, the court may, unless otherwise provided by law in its discretion, order recognizance, release under non-monetary conditions or, where authorized, bail. In any such case in which an indictment (a) has resulted from an order of a local criminal court holding the defendant for the action of the grand jury, or (b) was filed at a time when a felony complaint charging the same conduct was pending in a local criminal court, and in which such local criminal court or a superior court judge has issued an order of recognizance, release under non-monetary conditions or, where authorized, bail which is still effective, the superior court's order may be in the form of a direction continuing the effectiveness of the previous order.

3. In cases other than as described in subdivision four of this section the court shall release the principal pending trial on the principal's own recognizance, unless the court finds on the record or in writing that release on the principal's own recognizance will not reasonably assure the principal's return to court. In such instances, the court shall release the principal under non-monetary conditions, selecting the least restrictive alternative and conditions that will reasonably assure the principal's return to court. The court shall explain its choice of alternative and conditions on the record or in writing.

4. Where the principal stands charged with a qualifying offense, the court, unless otherwise prohibited by law, may in its discretion release the principal pending trial on the principal's own recognizance or under non-monetary conditions, fix bail, or, where the defendant is charged with a qualifying offense which is a felony, the court may commit the principal to the custody of the sheriff. The court shall explain its choice of release, release with conditions, bail or remand on the record or in writing. A principal stands charged with a qualifying offense for the purposes of this subdivision when he or she stands charged with:

(a) a felony enumerated in section 70.02 of the penal law, other than burglary in the second degree as defined in subdivision two of section 140.25 of the penal law or robbery in the second degree as defined in subdivision one of section 160.10 of the penal law;

(b) a crime involving witness intimidation under section 215.15 of the penal law;

(c) a crime involving witness tampering under section 215.11, 215.12 or 215.13 of the penal law;

(d) a class A felony defined in the penal law, other than in article two hundred twenty of such law with the exception of section 220.77 of such law;

(e) a felony sex offense defined in section 70.80 of the penal law or a crime involving incest as defined in section 255.25, 255.26 or 255.27 of such law, or a misdemeanor defined in article one hundred thirty of such law;

(f) conspiracy in the second degree as defined in section 105.15 of the penal law, where the underlying allegation of such charge is that the defendant conspired to commit a class A felony defined in article one hundred twenty-five of the penal law;

(g) money laundering in support of terrorism in the first degree as defined in section 470.24 of the penal law; money laundering in support of terrorism in the second degree as defined in section 470.23 of the penal law; or a felony crime of terrorism as defined in article four hundred ninety of the penal law, other than the crime defined in section 490.20 of such law;

(h) criminal contempt in the second degree as defined in subdivision three of section 215.50 of the penal law, criminal contempt in the first degree as defined in subdivision (b), (c) or (d) of section 215.51 of the penal law or aggravated criminal contempt as defined in section 215.52 of the penal law, and the underlying allegation of such charge of criminal contempt in the second degree, criminal contempt in the first degree or aggravated criminal contempt is that the defendant violated a duly served order of protection where the protected party is a member of the defendant's same family or household as defined in subdivision one of section 530.11 of this article; or

(i) facilitating a sexual performance by a child with a controlled substance or alcohol as defined in section 263.30 of the penal law, use of a child in a sexual performance as defined in section 263.05 of the penal law or luring a child as defined in subdivision one of section 120.70 of the penal law.

5. Notwithstanding the provisions of subdivisions three and four of this section, with respect to any charge for which bail or remand is not ordered, and for which the court would not or could not otherwise require bail or remand, a defendant may, at any time, request that the court set bail in a nominal amount requested by the defendant in the form specified in paragraph (a) of subdivision one of section 520.10 of this title; if the court is satisfied that the request is voluntary, the court shall set such bail in such amount.

6. Notwithstanding the provisions of subdivisions two, three and four of this section, a superior court may not order recognizance, release under non-monetary conditions or, where authorized, bail, or permit a defendant to remain at liberty pursuant to an existing order, after the defendant has been convicted of either: (a) a class A felony or (b) any class B or class C felony as defined in article one hundred thirty of the penal law committed or attempted to be committed by a person eighteen years of age or older against a person less than eighteen years of age. In either case the court must commit or remand the defendant to the custody of the sheriff.

7. Notwithstanding the provisions of subdivisions two, three and four of this section, a superior court may not order recognizance, release under non-monetary conditions or, where authorized, bail when the defendant is charged with a felony unless and until the district attorney has had an opportunity to be heard in the matter and such court and counsel for the defendant have been furnished with a report as described in subparagraph (ii) of paragraph (b) of subdivision two of section 530.20 of this article.

HISTORY:

Add, L 1970, ch 996, § 1, eff Sept 1, 1971; amd, L 1971, ch 762, § 14, eff Sept 1, 1971; L 2000, ch 1, § 12, eff Feb 1, 2001 (see 2000 note); L 2003, ch 264, § 46, eff Nov 1, 2003; L 2019, ch 59, § 18 (Part JJJ), eff Jan 1, 2020.

§ 530.40. Order of recognizance, release under non-monetary conditions or bail; by superior court when action is pending therein [Effective July 2, 2020]

When a criminal action is pending in a superior court, such court, upon application of a defendant, must or may order recognizance or bail as follows:

1. When the defendant is charged with an offense or offenses of less than felony grade only, the court must, unless otherwise provided by law, order recognizance or release under non-monetary conditions in accordance with this section.

2. When the defendant is charged with a felony, the court may, unless otherwise provided by law in its discretion, order recognizance , release under non-monetary conditions or, where authorized, bail. In any such case in which an indictment (a) has resulted from an order of a local criminal court holding the defendant for the action of the grand jury, or (b) was filed at a time when a felony complaint charging the same conduct was pending in a local criminal court, and in which such local criminal court or a superior court judge has issued an order of recognizance , release under non-monetary conditions or, where authorized, bail which is still effective, the superior court's order may be in the form of a direction continuing the effectiveness of the previous order.

3. In cases other than as described in subdivision four of this section the court shall release the principal pending trial on the principal's own recognizance, unless the court finds on the record or in writing that release on the principal's own recognizance will not reasonably assure the principal's return to court. In such instances, the court shall release the principal under non-monetary conditions, selecting the least restrictive alternative and conditions that will reasonably assure the principal's return to court. The court shall explain its choice of alternative and conditions on the record or in writing.

4. Where the principal stands charged with a qualifying offense, the court, unless otherwise prohibited by law, may in its discretion release the principal pending trial

on the principal's own recognizance or under non-monetary conditions, fix bail, or, where the defendant is charged with a qualifying offense which is a felony, the court may commit the principal to the custody of the sheriff. The court shall explain its choice of release, release with conditions, bail or remand on the record or in writing. A principal stands charged with a qualifying offense for the purposes of this subdivision when he or she stands charged with:

(a) a felony enumerated in section 70.02 of the penal law, other than robbery in the second degree as defined in subdivision one of section 160.10 of the penal law, provided, however, that burglary in the second degree as defined in subdivision two of section 140.25 of the penal law shall be a qualifying offense only where the defendant is charged with entering the living area of the dwelling;

(b) a crime involving witness intimidation under section 215.15 of the penal law;

(c) a crime involving witness tampering under section 215.11, 215.12 or 215.13 of the penal law;

(d) a class A felony defined in the penal law, provided that for class A felonies under article two hundred twenty of such law, only class A-I felonies shall be a qualifying offense;

(e) a sex trafficking offense defined in section 230.34 or 230.34-a of the penal law, or a felony sex offense defined in section 70.80 of the penal law or a crime involving incest as defined in section 255.25, 255.26 or 255.27 of such law, or a misdemeanor defined in article one hundred thirty of such law;

(f) conspiracy in the second degree as defined in section 105.15 of the penal law, where the underlying allegation of such charge is that the defendant conspired to commit a class A felony defined in article one hundred twenty-five of the penal law;

(g) money laundering in support of terrorism in the first degree as defined in section 470.24 of the penal law; money laundering in support of terrorism in the second degree as defined in section 470.23 of the penal law; money laundering in support of terrorism in the third degree as defined in section 470.22 of the penal law; money laundering in support of terrorism in the fourth degree as defined in section 470.21 of the penal law; or a felony crime of terrorism as defined in article four hundred ninety of the penal law, other than the crime defined in section 490.20 of such law;

(h) criminal contempt in the second degree as defined in subdivision three of section 215.50 of the penal law, criminal contempt in the first degree as defined in subdivision (b), (c) or (d) of section 215.51 of the penal law or aggravated criminal contempt as defined in section 215.52 of the penal law, and the underlying allegation of such charge of criminal contempt in the second degree, criminal contempt in the first degree or aggravated criminal contempt is that the defendant violated a duly served order of protection where the protected party is a member of the defendant's same family or household as defined in subdivision one of section 530.11 of this article;

(i) facilitating a sexual performance by a child with a controlled substance or alcohol as defined in section 263.30 of the penal law, use of a child in a sexual performance as defined in section 263.05 of the penal law or luring a child as defined in subdivision one of section 120.70 of the penal law, promoting an obscene sexual performance by a child as defined in section 263.10 of the penal law or promoting a sexual performance by a child as defined in section 263.15 of the penal law;

(j) any crime that is alleged to have caused the death of another person;

(k) criminal obstruction of breathing or blood circulation as defined in section 121.11 of the penal law, strangulation in the second degree as defined in section 121.12 of the penal law or unlawful imprisonment in the first degree as defined in section 135.10 of the penal law, and is alleged to have committed the offense against a member of the defendant's same family or household as defined in subdivision one of section 530.11 of this article;

(l) aggravated vehicular assault as defined in section 120.04-a of the penal law or vehicular assault in the first degree as defined in section 120.04 of the penal law;

(m) assault in the third degree as defined in section 120.00 of the penal law or arson in the third degree as defined in section 150.10 of the penal law, when such crime is charged as a hate crime as defined in section 485.05 of the penal law;

(n) aggravated assault upon a person less than eleven years old as defined in section 120.12 of the penal law or criminal possession of a weapon on school grounds as defined in section 265.01-a of the penal law;

(o) grand larceny in the first degree as defined in section 155.42 of the penal law, enterprise corruption as defined in section 460.20 of the penal law, or money laundering in the first degree as defined in section 470.20 of the penal law;

(p) failure to register as a sex offender pursuant to section one hundred sixty-eight-t of the correction law or endangering the welfare of a child as defined in subdivision one of section 260.10 of the penal law, where the defendant is required to maintain registration under article six-C of the correction law and designated a level three offender pursuant to subdivision six of section one hundred sixty-eight-l of the correction law;

(q) a crime involving bail jumping under section 215.55, 215.56 or 215.57 of the penal law, or a crime involving escaping from custody under section 205.05, 205.10 or 205.15 of the penal law;

(r) any felony offense committed by the principal while serving a sentence of probation or while released to post release supervision;

(s) a felony, where the defendant qualifies for sentencing on such charge as a persistent felony offender pursuant to section 70.10 of the penal law; or

(t) any felony or class A misdemeanor involving harm to an identifiable person or property, where such charge arose from conduct occurring while the defendant was released on his or her own recognizance or released under conditions for a separate felony or class A misdemeanor involving harm to an identifiable person or property, provided, however, that the prosecutor must show reasonable cause to believe that the defendant committed the instant crime and any underlying crime. For the purposes of this subparagraph, any of the underlying crimes need not be a qualifying offense as defined in this subdivision.

5. Notwithstanding the provisions of subdivisions three and four of this section, with respect to any charge for which bail or remand is not ordered, and for which the court would not or could not otherwise require bail or remand, a defendant may, at any time, request that the court set bail in a nominal amount requested by the defendant in the form specified in paragraph (a) of subdivision one of section 520.10 of this title; if the court is satisfied that the request is voluntary, the court shall set such bail in such amount.

6. Notwithstanding the provisions of subdivisions two, three and four of this section, a superior court may not order recognizance, release under non-monetary conditions or, where authorized, bail, or permit a defendant to remain at liberty pursuant to an existing order, after the defendant has been convicted of either: (a) a class A felony or (b) any class B or class C felony as defined in article one hundred thirty of the penal law committed or attempted to be committed by a person eighteen years of age or older against a person less than eighteen years of age. In either case the court must commit or remand the defendant to the custody of the sheriff.

7. Notwithstanding the provisions of subdivisions two, three and four of this section, a superior court may not order recognizance, release under non-monetary conditions or, where authorized, bail when the defendant is charged with a felony unless and until the district attorney has had an opportunity to be heard in the matter and such court and counsel for the defendant have been furnished with a report as described in subparagraph (ii) of paragraph (b) of subdivision two of section 530.20 of this article.

HISTORY:

Add, L 1970, ch 996, § 1, eff Sept 1, 1971; amd, L 1971, ch 762, § 14, eff Sept 1, 1971; L 2000, ch 1, § 12, eff Feb 1, 2001 (see 2000 note); L 2003, ch 264, § 46, eff Nov 1, 2003; L 2019, ch 59, § 18 (Part JJJ), eff Jan 1, 2020; L 2020, ch 56, § 4 (Part UU), eff July 2, 2020.

§ 530.45. Order of recognizance or bail; after conviction and before sentence. [Effective until July 2, 2020]

1. When the defendant is at liberty in the course of a criminal action as a result of a prior order of recognizance, release under non-monetary conditions or bail and the court revokes such order and then, where authorized, fixes no bail or fixes bail in a greater amount or in a more burdensome form than was previously fixed and remands or commits defendant to the custody of the sheriff, or issues a more restrictive securing order, a judge designated in subdivision two of this section, upon application of the

defendant following conviction of an offense other than a class A felony or a class B or class C felony offense as defined in article one hundred thirty of the penal law committed or attempted to be committed by a person eighteen years of age or older against a person less than eighteen years of age, and before sentencing, may issue a securing order and release the defendant on the defendant's own recognizance, release the defendant under non-monetary conditions, or, where authorized, fix bail or fix bail in a lesser amount or in a less burdensome form, or issue a less restrictive securing order, than fixed by the court in which the conviction was entered.

2. An order as prescribed in subdivision one may be issued by the following judges in the indicated situations:

(a) If the criminal action was pending in supreme court or county court, such order may be issued by a justice of the appellate division of the department in which the conviction was entered.

(b) If the criminal action was pending in a local criminal court, such order may be issued by a judge of a superior court holding a term thereof in the county in which the conviction was entered.

3. An application for an order specified in this section must be made upon reasonable notice to the people, and the people must be accorded adequate opportunity to appear in opposition thereto. Not more than one application may be made pursuant to this section. Defendant must allege in his application that he intends to take an appeal to an intermediate appellate court immediately after sentence is pronounced.

4. Notwithstanding the provisions of subdivision one, if within thirty days after sentence the defendant has not taken an appeal to an intermediate appellate court from the judgment or sentence, the operation of such order terminates and the defendant must surrender himself to the criminal court in which the judgment was entered in order that execution of the judgment be commenced.

5. Notwithstanding the provisions of subdivision one, if within one hundred twenty days after the filing of the notice of appeal such appeal has not been brought to argument in or submitted to the intermediate appellate court, the operation of such order terminates and the defendant must surrender himself to the criminal court in which the judgment was entered in order that execution of the judgment be commenced or resumed; except that this subdivision does not apply where the intermediate appellate court has (a) extended the time for argument or submission of the appeal to a date beyond the specified period of one hundred twenty days, and (b) upon application of the defendant, expressly ordered that the operation of the order continue until the date of the determination of the appeal or some other designated future date or occurrence.

6. Where the defendant is at liberty during the pendency of an appeal as a result of an order issued pursuant to this section, the intermediate appellate court, upon affirmance of the judgment, must by appropriate certificate remit the case to the criminal court in which such judgment was entered. The criminal court must, upon at least two days notice to the defendant, his surety and his attorney, promptly direct the defendant to surrender himself to the criminal court in order that execution of the judgment be commenced or resumed, and if necessary the criminal court may issue a bench warrant to secure his appearance.

HISTORY:

Add, L 1974, ch 435, § 1, eff Sept 1, 1974; amd, L 2000, ch 1, § 13, eff Feb 1, 2001; L 2003, ch 264, § 47, eff Nov 1, 2003; L 2019, ch 59, § 19 (Part JJJ), eff Jan 1, 2020.

§ 530.45. Order of recognizance or bail; after conviction and before sentence. [Effective July 2, 2020]

1. When the defendant is at liberty in the course of a criminal action as a result of a prior order of recognizance, release under non-monetary conditions or bail and the court revokes such order and then, where authorized, fixes no bail or fixes bail in a greater amount or in a more burdensome form than was previously fixed and remands or commits defendant to the custody of the sheriff, or issues a more restrictive securing order, a judge designated in subdivision two of this section, upon application of the defendant following conviction of an offense other than a class A felony or a class B or class C felony offense as defined in article one hundred thirty of the penal law

committed or attempted to be committed by a person eighteen years of age or older against a person less than eighteen years of age, and before sentencing, may issue a securing order and release the defendant on the defendant's own recognizance, release the defendant under non-monetary conditions, or, where authorized, fix bail or fix bail in a lesser amount or in a less burdensome form, or issue a less restrictive securing order, than fixed by the court in which the conviction was entered.

2. An order as prescribed in subdivision one may be issued by the following judges in the indicated situations:

(a) If the criminal action was pending in supreme court or county court, such order may be issued by a justice of the appellate division of the department in which the conviction was entered.

(b) If the criminal action was pending in a local criminal court, such order may be issued by a judge of a superior court holding a term thereof in the county in which the conviction was entered.

2-a. Notwithstanding the provisions of subdivision four of section 510.10, paragraph (b) of subdivision one of section 530.20 and subdivision four of section 530.40 of this title, when a defendant charged with an offense that is not such a qualifying offense is convicted, whether by guilty plea or verdict, in such criminal action or proceeding of an offense that is not a qualifying offense, the court may, in accordance with law, issue a securing order: releasing the defendant on the defendant's own recognizance or under non-monetary conditions where authorized, fix bail, or remand the defendant to the custody of the sheriff where authorized.

3. An application for an order specified in this section must be made upon reasonable notice to the people, and the people must be accorded adequate opportunity to appear in opposition thereto. Not more than one application may be made pursuant to this section. Defendant must allege in his application that he intends to take an appeal to an intermediate appellate court immediately after sentence is pronounced.

4. Notwithstanding the provisions of subdivision one, if within thirty days after sentence the defendant has not taken an appeal to an intermediate appellate court from the judgment or sentence, the operation of such order terminates and the defendant must surrender himself to the criminal court in which the judgment was entered in order that execution of the judgment be commenced.

5. Notwithstanding the provisions of subdivision one, if within one hundred twenty days after the filing of the notice of appeal such appeal has not been brought to argument in or submitted to the intermediate appellate court, the operation of such order terminates and the defendant must surrender himself to the criminal court in which the judgment was entered in order that execution of the judgment be commenced or resumed; except that this subdivision does not apply where the intermediate appellate court has (a) extended the time for argument or submission of the appeal to a date beyond the specified period of one hundred twenty days, and (b) upon application of the defendant, expressly ordered that the operation of the order continue until the date of the determination of the appeal or some other designated future date or occurrence.

6. Where the defendant is at liberty during the pendency of an appeal as a result of an order issued pursuant to this section, the intermediate appellate court, upon affirmance of the judgment, must by appropriate certificate remit the case to the criminal court in which such judgment was entered. The criminal court must, upon at least two days notice to the defendant, his surety and his attorney, promptly direct the defendant to surrender himself to the criminal court in order that execution of the judgment be commenced or resumed, and if necessary the criminal court may issue a bench warrant to secure his appearance.

HISTORY:

Add, L 1974, ch 435, § 1, eff Sept 1, 1974; amd, L 2000, ch 1, § 13, eff Feb 1, 2001; L 2003, ch 264, § 47, eff Nov 1, 2003; L 2019, ch 59, § 19 (Part JJJ), eff Jan 1, 2020; L 2020, ch 56, § 9 (Part UU), eff July 2, 2020.

§ 530.50. Order of recognizance or bail; during pendency of appeal. [Effective until July 2, 2020]

A judge who is otherwise authorized pursuant to section 460.50 or section 460.60 to issue an order of recognizance or bail pending the determination of an appeal, may do so unless the defendant received a class A felony sentence or a sentence for any class B or class C felony offense defined in article one hundred thirty of the penal law committed or attempted to be committed by a person eighteen years of age or older against a person less than eighteen years of age.

HISTORY:

Add, L 1970, ch 996, § 1, eff Sept 1, 1971; amd, L 2000, ch 1, § 14, eff Feb 1, 2001; L 2003, ch 264, § 48, eff Nov 1, 2003.

§ 530.50. Order of recognizance or bail; during pendency of appeal. [Effective July 2, 2020]

1. A judge who is otherwise authorized pursuant to section 460.50 or section 460.60 to issue an order of recognizance or bail pending the determination of an appeal, may do so unless the defendant received a class A felony sentence or a sentence for any class B or class C felony offense defined in article one hundred thirty of the penal law committed or attempted to be committed by a person eighteen years of age or older against a person less than eighteen years of age.

2. Notwithstanding the provisions of subdivision four of section 510.10, paragraph (b) of subdivision one of section 530.20 and subdivision four of section 530.40 of this title, when a defendant charged with an offense that is not such a qualifying offense applies, pending determination of an appeal, for an order of recognizance or release on non-monetary conditions, where authorized, or fixing bail, a judge identified in subdivision two of section 460.50 or paragraph (a) of subdivision one of section 460.60 of this chapter may, in accordance with law, and except as otherwise provided by law, issue a securing order: releasing the defendant on the defendant's own recognizance or under non-monetary conditions where authorized, fixing bail, or remanding the defendant to the custody of the sheriff where authorized.

HISTORY:

Add, L 1970, ch 996, § 1, eff Sept 1, 1971; amd, L 2000, ch 1, § 14, eff Feb 1, 2001; L 2003, ch 264, § 48, eff Nov 1, 2003; L 2020, ch 56, § 10 (Part UU), eff July 2, 2020.

Title U
Special Proceedings Which Replace, Suspend or Abate Criminal Actions

Article 725
Removal of Proceeding Against Juvenile Offender to Family Court

§ 725.15. Sealing of records.

Except where specifically required or permitted by statute or upon specific authorization of the court that directed removal of an action to the family court all official records and papers of the action up to and including the order of removal, whether on file with the court, a police agency or the division of criminal justice services, are confidential and must not be made available to any person or public or private agency, provided however that availability of copies of any such records and papers on file with the family court shall be governed by provisions that apply to family court records, and further provided that all official records and papers of the action shall be included in those records and reports that may be obtained upon request by the commissioner of mental health or commissioner of the office for people with developmental disabilities, as appropriate; the case review panel; and the attorney general pursuant to section 10.05 of the mental hygiene law.

HISTORY:
Add, L 1978, ch 481, § 44, eff Sept 1, 1978; amd, L 2007, ch 7, § 15, eff April 13, 2007; L 2019, ch 672, § 64, eff Dec 16, 2019.

Article 730
Mental Disease or Defect Excluding Fitness to Proceed

§ 730.10. Fitness to proceed; definitions.

As used in this article, the following terms have the following meanings:

1. "Incapacitated person" means a defendant who as a result of mental disease or defect lacks capacity to understand the proceedings against him or to assist in his own defense.

2. "Order of examination" means an order issued to an appropriate director by a criminal court wherein a criminal action is pending against a defendant or by a court evaluating the capacity of an alleged violator in a parole revocation proceeding pursuant to subparagraph (xii) of paragraph (f) of subdivision three of section two hundred fifty-nine-i of the executive law, or by a family court pursuant to section 322.1 of the family court act wherein a juvenile delinquency proceeding is pending against a juvenile, directing that such person be examined for the purpose of determining if he is an incapacitated person.

3. "Commissioner" means the state commissioner of mental health or the state commissioner of the office for people with developmental disabilities.

4. "Director" means (a) the director of a state hospital operated by the office of mental health or the director of a developmental center operated by the office for people with developmental disabilities, or (b) the director of a hospital operated by any local government of the state that has been certified by the commissioner as having adequate facilities to examine a defendant to determine if he is an incapacitated person, or (c) the director of community mental health services.

5. "Qualified psychiatrist" means a physician who:

(a) is a diplomate of the American board of psychiatry and neurology or is eligible to be certified by that board; or,

(b) is certified by the American osteopathic board of neurology and psychiatry or is eligible to be certified by that board.

6. "Certified psychologist" means a person who is registered as a certified psychologist under article one hundred fifty-three of the education law.

7. "Psychiatric examiner" means a qualified psychiatrist or a certified psychologist who has been designated by a director to examine a defendant pursuant to an order of examination.

8. "Examination report" means a report made by a psychiatric examiner wherein he sets forth his opinion as to whether the defendant is or is not an incapacitated person, the nature and extent of his examination and, if he finds that the defendant is an incapacitated person, his diagnosis and prognosis and a detailed statement of the reasons for his opinion by making particular reference to those aspects of the proceedings wherein the defendant lacks capacity to understand or to assist in his own defense. The state administrator and the commissioner must jointly adopt the form of the examination report; and the state administrator shall prescribe the number of copies thereof that must be submitted to the court by the director.

9. "Appropriate institution" means: (a) a hospital operated by the office of mental health or a developmental center operated by the office for people with developmental disabilities; or (b) a hospital licensed by the department of health which operates a psychiatric unit licensed by the office of mental health, as determined by the commissioner provided, however, that any such hospital that is not operated by the state shall qualify as an "appropriate institution" only pursuant to the terms of an agreement between the commissioner and the hospital. Nothing in this article shall be construed as requiring a hospital to consent to providing care and treatment to an incapacitated person at such hospital.

HISTORY:

Add, L 1970, ch 996, § 1, eff Sept 1, 1971; amd, L 1973, ch 195, § 11; L 1974, ch 629, §§ 5, 6; L 1976, ch 435, § 4, eff June 23, 1976; L 1987, ch 440, § 1, eff April 1, 1988; L 1994, ch 566, § 1, eff July 26, 1994; L 2012, ch 56, § 1 (Part Q), eff March 30, 2012; L 2015, ch 545, § 3, eff June 8, 2016; L 2019, ch 672, § 65, eff Dec 16, 2019.

CORRECTION LAW

Article 2—Department of Corrections and Community Supervision

§ 29. Department statistics

1. The department shall continue to collect, maintain, and analyze statistical and other information and data with respect to persons subject to the jurisdiction of the department, including but not limited to: (a) the number of such persons: placed in the custody of the department, assigned to a specific department program, accorded community supervision and declared delinquent, recommitted to a state correctional institution upon revocation of community supervision, or discharged upon maximum expiration of sentence; (b) the criminal history of such persons; (c) the social, educational, and vocational circumstances of any such persons; (d) the institutional and community supervision programs and the behavior of such persons; and, (e) the military background and circumstances, if such person served in the United States armed forces. Provided, however, in the event any statistical information on the ethnic background of the inmate population of a correctional facility or facilities is collected by the department, such statistical information shall contain, but not be limited to, the following ethnic categories: (i) Caucasian; (ii) Asian; (iii) American Indian; (iv) Afro-American/Black; and (v) Spanish speaking/Hispanic which category shall include, but not be limited to, the following subcategories consisting of: (1) Puerto Ricans; (2) Cubans; (3) Dominicans; and (4) other Hispanic nationalities.

2. The commissioner shall make rules as to the privacy of records, statistics and other information collected, obtained and maintained by the department, its institutions or the board of parole and information obtained in an official capacity by officers, employees or members thereof.

3. The commissioner shall have access to records and criminal statistics collected by the division of criminal justice services and the commissioner of criminal justice services shall have access to records and criminal statistics collected by the department of corrections and community supervision, as the commissioner of corrections and community supervision and the commissioner of criminal justice services shall mutually determine.

4.(a) The commissioner shall provide an annual report to the legislature on the staffing of correction officers and correction sergeants in state correctional facilities. Such report shall include, but not be limited to the following factors: the number of security posts on the current plot plan for each facility that have been closed on a daily basis, by correctional facility security classification (minimum, medium and maximum); the number of security positions eliminated by correctional facility since two thousand compared to the number of inmates incarcerated in each such facility; a breakdown by correctional facility security classification (minimum, medium, and maximum) of the staff hours of overtime worked, by year since two thousand and the annual aggregate costs related to this overtime. In addition, such report shall be delineated by correctional facility security classification, the annual number of security positions eliminated, the number of closed posts and amount of staff hours of overtime accrued as well as the overall overtime expenditures that resulted. Such report shall be provided to the chairs of the senate finance, assembly ways and means, senate crime and corrections and assembly correction committees, and posted on the department's website, annually by February first.

(b) Such report shall also include but not be limited to: the total number of correctional facilities in operation which are maintained by the department, the security level of each facility, the number of beds at each facility as of December thirty-first of the prior year, as classified by the department, and the number of empty beds, if any, by such classification as of such date.

HISTORY:

Add, L 1974, ch 654, § 1, eff May 30, 1974, with substance derived from §§ 15–a, 615; amd, L 1989, ch 411, § 1; L 1990, ch 598, § 1, eff July 18, 1990 and deemed eff Aug 15, 1989; L 2003, ch 62, § 4 (Part H); L 2004, ch 56, § 1 (Part N); L 2005, ch 56, § 1 (Part R), eff April 12, 2005, deemed eff on and after April 1, 2005; L 2011, ch 62, § 12 (Part C, Subpart A), eff March 31, 2011; L 2012, ch 55, § 1 (Part U), eff March 30, 2012; L 2019, ch 485, § 2, eff May 9, 2020.

Article 4—Establishment of Correctional Facilities, Commitment to Department and Custody of Inmates

§ 76. Notice of transitional services for inmates released from correctional facilities

1.(a) Prior to the release of an inmate from a correctional facility, the department shall provide such inmate with information on transitional services available in the county or city where such inmate is scheduled to be released. Such information shall include programs designed to promote the successful and productive reentry and reintegration of an inmate into society including medical and mental health services, HIV/AIDS services, educational, vocational and employment services, alcohol or substance abuse treatment and housing services. The department shall maintain a current list of transitional services which shall be updated regularly in order to effectuate the purposes of this section. Where appropriate, the department shall provide assistance to an inmate in contacting a program or service provider prior to such inmate's release to the community.

(b) Upon discharge of an inmate from a correctional facility, the department shall provide such inmate with educational information about the prevention of human immunodeficiency virus (HIV) infection, instructions about how to obtain free HIV testing upon release, including contact information for HIV counseling and testing service providers located in the county or city in which such inmate intends to reside upon release, and referrals to community-based HIV prevention, education and counseling resources located in the county or city in which such inmate intends to reside upon release.

2. The commissioner shall consult with, and be entitled to receive the assistance of, the commissioners of education, labor, health, mental health and the office of temporary and disability assistance in the implementation of this section.

HISTORY:

L 2014, ch 506, § 1, eff April 16, 2015; amd, L 2015, ch 5, § 1, eff April 16, 2015; L 2019, ch 385, § 1, eff Dec 22, 2019.

§ 77. Adolescent offender facilities [Repealed effective October 1, 2020]

1.(a) The state shall establish one or more facilities with enhanced security features and specially trained staff to serve the adolescent offenders sentenced to a determinate or indeterminate sentence for committing offenses on or after their sixteenth birthday who are determined to need an enhanced level of secure care which shall be managed by the department with the office of children and family services assistance, and services or programs.

(b) A council comprised of the commissioner, and the office of children and family services, the commissioner of the state commission of correction, and the commissioner of the division of criminal justice services shall be established to assess the operation of the facility. The governor shall designate the chair of the council. The council shall have the power to perform all acts necessary to carry out its duties including making unannounced visits and inspections of the facility at any time. Notwithstanding any other provision of state law to the contrary, the council may request and the department shall submit to the council, to the extent permitted by federal law, all information in the form and manner and at such times as the council may require that is appropriate to the purposes and operation of the council. The council shall be subject to the same laws as apply to the department regarding the protection and confidentiality of the information made available to the council and shall prevent access thereto by, or the distribution thereof to, persons not authorized by law.

(c) Appropriate staff working in such facilities shall receive specialized training to address working with the types of youth placed in the facility, which shall include but not be limited to, training on tactical responses and de-escalation techniques. All staff of the facility shall be subject to random drug tests.

2. The office of children and family services shall assign an assistant commissioner to assist the department, on a permanent basis, with programs or services provided within such facilities.

3. The department, the state commission of correction and the office of children and family services shall jointly establish a placement classification protocol to be used to determine the appropriate level of care for each adolescent offender in such facility. The protocol shall include, but not necessarily be limited to, consideration of the nature of the youth's offense and the youth's history and service needs.

4. Any new facilities developed by the department in consultation with the office of children and family services to serve the youth committed as adolescent offenders as a result of raising the age of juvenile jurisdiction shall, to the extent practicable, consist of smaller, more home-like facilities located near the youths' homes and families that provide gender-responsive programming, services and treatment in small, closely supervised groups that offer extensive and on-going individual attention and encourage supportive peer relationships.

5. Adolescent offenders committed or transferred to the facility, as defined in this section for committing a crime on or after their sixteenth birthday who still have time left on their sentences of imprisonment shall be transferred to a non-adolescent offender facility in the department for confinement pursuant to this chapter after completing two years in an adolescent offender facility unless they are within four months of completing the imprisonment portion of their sentence and the department determines, in its discretion, on a case-by-case basis that the youth should be permitted to remain in such facility for the additional short period of time necessary to enable them to complete their sentence. In making such a determination, the factors the department may consider include, but are not limited to, the age of the youth, the amount of time remaining on the youth's sentence of imprisonment, the level of the youth's participation in the program, the youth's educational and vocational progress, the opportunities available to the youth through the department, and the length of any applicable post-release supervision sentence. Nothing in this subdivision shall authorize a youth to remain in such facility beyond his or her twenty-third birthday.

HISTORY:

L 2017, ch 59, § 81-a (Part WWW), eff April 10, 2017; repealed, L 2020, ch 55, § 2 (Part G), eff Oct 1, 2020.

§ 80. Transfer of adolescents from the department.

The department and the office of children and family services shall jointly establish a transition plan and protocol to be used in transferring custody of all adolescent offenders and individuals under the age of eighteen from the custody of the department to the custody of the office of children and family services on or before October first, two thousand twenty. The plan and protocol shall be completed on or before July first, two thousand twenty.

HISTORY:
L 2020, ch 55, § 3 (Part G), eff April 3, 2020.

Article 24—Provisions Applicable to Sentences Imposed Under the [the]* Revised Penal Plan

§ 803-b. Limited credit time allowances for inmates serving indeterminate or determinate sentences imposed for specified offenses

1. Definitions. As used in this section the following terms shall have the following meanings:

(a) "eligible offender" means a person under the custody of the department or confined in a facility in the department of mental hygiene, other than a person who is subject to a sentence imposed for murder in the first degree as defined in section 125.27 of the penal law, an offense defined in article one hundred thirty of such law, or an attempt or a conspiracy to commit any such offense, who is otherwise subject to:

(i) an indeterminate sentence imposed for any class A-I felony offense other than criminal possession of a controlled substance in the first degree as defined in section 220.21 of the penal law or criminal sale of a controlled substance in the first degree as defined in section 220.43 of such law or an attempt or a conspiracy to commit such controlled substance offense; or

(ii) an indeterminate or determinate sentence imposed for an offense listed in subdivision one of section 70.02 of the penal law; or

(iii) an indeterminate or determinate sentence imposed for an offense defined in article one hundred twenty-five of the penal law.

(b) "limited credit time benefit" means:

(i) in the case of an eligible offender who is subject to an indeterminate sentence with a maximum term of life imprisonment, such offender shall be eligible for release six months before the completion of the controlling minimum period of imprisonment as defined by subdivision one of section 70.40 of the penal law; or

(ii)(A) in the case of an eligible offender who is not subject to an indeterminate sentence with a maximum term of life imprisonment, such offender shall be eligible for conditional release six months earlier than as provided by paragraph (b) of subdivision one of section 70.40 of the penal law, provided that the department determines such offender has earned the full amount of good time authorized by section eight hundred three of this article; the withholding of any good behavior time credit by the department shall render an inmate ineligible for the credit defined herein;

(B) in the event the limited credit time benefit defined herein causes such conditional release date to precede the parole eligibility date as calculated pursuant to subdivision one of section 70.40 of the penal law, a limited credit time benefit shall also be applied to the parole eligibility date, but only to the extent necessary to cause such parole eligibility date to be the same date as the conditional release date;

(C) an inmate shall not be eligible for the credit defined herein if he or she is returned to the department pursuant to a revocation of presumptive release, parole, conditional release, or post-release supervision and has not been sentenced to an additional indeterminate or determinate term of imprisonment.

(iii) Regardless of the number of sentences to which an eligible offender is subject, the limited credit time benefit authorized pursuant to this section shall be limited to a single six-month credit applied to such person's parole eligibility date pursuant to subparagraph (i) of this paragraph or to such person's conditional release date pursuant to subparagraph (ii) of this paragraph. Except as provided in clause (B) of subparagraph (ii) of this paragraph, the limited credit time benefit authorized pursuant to this section shall not be applied to an eligible offender's parole eligibility date and conditional release date.

(c) "significant programmatic accomplishment" means that the inmate:

(i) participates in no less than two years of college programming; or

(ii) obtains an associate degree, bachelor's degree, master's degree or doctoral degree by completing a registered program from a New York state degree-granting institution,

*Brackets have been inserted by the Publisher around this word as it is superfluous.

or a program offered by an out-of-state institution of higher education authorized to offer post-secondary distance education in New York state pursuant to applicable rules and regulations promulgated by the education department of the state of New York; or

(iii) successfully participates as an inmate program associate for no less than two years; or

(iv) receives a certification from the state department of labor for his or her successful participation in an apprenticeship program; or

(v) successfully works as an inmate hospice aid for a period of no less than two years; or

(vi) successfully works in the division of correctional industries' optical program for no less than two years and receives a certification as an optician from the American board of opticianry; or

(vii) receives an asbestos handling certificate from the department of labor upon successful completion of the training program and then works in the division of correctional industries' asbestos abatement program as a hazardous materials removal worker or group leader for no less than eighteen months; or

(viii) successfully completes the course curriculum and passes the minimum competency screening process performance examination for sign language interpreter, and then works as a sign language interpreter for deaf inmates for no less than one year; or

(ix) successfully works in the puppies behind bars program for a period of no less than two years; or

(x) successfully participates in a vocational culinary arts program for a period of no less than two years and earns a servsafe certificate that is recognized by the national restaurant association; or

(xi) successfully completes the four hundred ninety hour training program while assigned to a department of motor vehicles call center, and continues to work at such call center for an additional twenty-one months; or

(xii) receives a certificate from the food production center in an assigned position following the completion of no less than eight hundred hours of work in such position, and continues to work for an additional eighteen months at the food production center.

(d) "serious disciplinary infraction" or "overall poor institutional record" shall be defined in regulations promulgated by the commissioner and need not be the same as the regulations promulgated for the meaning of serious disciplinary infraction pursuant to paragraph (d) of subdivision one of section eight hundred three of this article.

(e) "disqualifying judicial determination" means a judicial determination that the person, while an inmate, commenced or continued a civil action or proceeding or claim that was found to be frivolous as defined in subdivision (c) of section eight thousand three hundred three-a of the civil practice law and rules, or an order of a federal court pursuant to rule 11 of the federal rules of civil procedure imposing sanctions in an action commenced by a person while an inmate against a state agency, officer or employee.

2. Every eligible offender under the custody of the department or confined in a facility in the department of mental hygiene may earn a limited credit time allowance if such offender successfully participates in the work and treatment program assigned pursuant to section eight hundred five of this article and:

(a) successfully completes one or more significant programmatic accomplishments; and

(b) has not committed a serious disciplinary infraction or maintained an overall negative institutional record as defined in rules and regulations promulgated by the commissioner; and

(c) has not received a disqualifying judicial determination.

3. No person shall have the right to demand or require the credit authorized by this section. The commissioner may revoke at any time such credit for any disciplinary infraction committed by the inmate or for any failure to continue to participate successfully in any assigned work and treatment program after the certificate of earned eligibility has been awarded. Any action by the commissioner pursuant to this section shall be deemed a judicial function and shall not be reviewable if done in accordance with law.

HISTORY:

Add, L 2009, ch 56, § 4 (Part L), eff April 7, 2009; amd, L 2010, ch 412, § 1, eff Aug 13, 2010; L 2017, ch 55, § 1 (Part E), eff April 1, 2017; L 2019, ch 723, § 1, eff Dec 20, 2019; L 2020, ch 35, § 1, eff Dec 20, 2019.

VEHICLE AND TRAFFIC LAW

Title I
Words and Phrases Defined

Article 1 Words and Phrases Defined

Article 1
Words and Phrases Defined

§ 102-c. Bicycle with electric assist.

A bicycle which is no more than thirty-six inches wide and has an electric motor of less than seven hundred fifty watts, equipped with operable pedals, meeting the equipment and manufacturing requirements for bicycles adopted by the Consumer Product Safety Commission under 16 C.F.R. Part 1512.1 et seq. and meeting the requirements of one of the following three classes:

(a) "Class one bicycle with electric assist." A bicycle with electric assist having an electric motor that provides assistance only when the person operating such bicycle is pedaling, and that ceases to provide assistance when such bicycle reaches a speed of twenty miles per hour.

(b) "Class two bicycle with electric assist." A bicycle with electric assist having an electric motor that may be used exclusively to propel such bicycle, and that is not capable of providing assistance when such bicycle reaches a speed of twenty miles per hour.

(c) "Class three bicycle with electric assist." Solely within a city having a population of one million or more, a bicycle with electric assist having an electric motor that may be used exclusively to propel such bicycle, and that is not capable of providing assistance when such bicycle reaches a speed of twenty-five miles per hour.

HISTORY:

L 2020, ch 58, § 1 (Part XX), eff April 3, 2020.

§ 114-e. Electric scooter.

Every device weighing less than one hundred pounds that (a) has handlebars, a floorboard or a seat that can be stood or sat upon by the operator, and an electric motor, (b) can be powered by the electric motor and/or human power, and (c) has a maximum speed of no more than twenty miles per hour on a paved level surface when powered solely by the electric motor.

HISTORY:

L 2020, ch 58, § 2 (Part XX), eff April 3, 2020.

§ 125. Motor vehicles.

Every vehicle operated or driven upon a public highway which is propelled by any power other than muscular power, except (a) electrically-driven mobility assistance devices operated or driven by a person with a disability, (a-1) electric personal assistive mobility devices operated outside a city with a population of one million or more, (b) vehicles which run only upon rails or tracks, (c) snowmobiles as defined in article forty-seven of this chapter, (d) all terrain vehicles as defined in article forty-eight-B of this chapter, (e) bicycles with electric assist as defined in section one hundred two-c of this article, and (f) electric scooters as defined in section one hundred fourteen-e of this article. For the purposes of title four of this chapter, the term motor vehicle shall exclude fire and police vehicles other than ambulances. For the purposes of titles four and five of this chapter the term motor vehicles shall exclude farm type tractors and all terrain type vehicles used exclusively for agricultural purposes, or for snow plowing, other than for hire, farm equipment, including self-propelled machines used exclusively in growing, harvesting or handling farm produce, and self-propelled caterpillar or crawler-type equipment while being operated on the contract site.

HISTORY:

Add, L 1959, ch 775, with substance transferred from former § 125; amd, L 1960, ch 300, § 3; L 1960, ch 608, § 2; L 1962, ch 290; L 1962, ch 708; L 1962, ch 930; L 1964, ch 757; L 1967, ch 706; L 1970, ch 459, § 1; L 1972, ch 661, § 25; L 1973, ch 839, § 1; L 1985, ch 346, § 1; L 1985, ch 671, § 1; L 1987, ch 15, § 1; L 1991, ch 374, § 2, eff Jan 1, 1992; L 2008, ch 365, § 2, eff July 21, 2008; L 2020, ch 58, § 3 (Part XX), eff April 3, 2020.

Title V
Drivers' Licenses

Article 19
Licensing of Drivers

§ 501. Drivers' licenses and learners' permits [Effective until February 3, 2021]

1. The commissioner shall issue classified drivers' licenses as provided in this article. Any such license shall be valid only for the operation of the type of vehicles specified for each such class of license but shall not be valid for the operation of any type of vehicle for which an endorsement is required by this section or regulations promulgated hereunder unless the license contains such endorsement and shall be subject to any restrictions contained thereon.

2. Driver license classifications, endorsements and restrictions and exceptions.

(a) License classifications.

(i) Class A. Such license shall be valid to operate any motor vehicle or any combination of vehicles except it shall not be valid to operate a motorcycle other than a class B or C limited use motorcycle.

(ii) Class B. Such license shall be valid to operate any vehicle or combination of vehicles which may be operated with a class E license and shall be valid to operate any motor vehicle or any such vehicle, other than a tractor, towing a vehicle having a GVWR of not more than ten thousand pounds except it shall not be valid to operate a motorcycle other than a class B or C limited use motorcycle.

(iii) Class C. Such license shall be valid to operate any vehicle or combination of vehicles which may be operated with a class E license and shall be valid to operate any motor vehicle with a GVWR of not more than twenty-six thousand pounds and any such vehicle towing another vehicle with a GVWR of not more than ten thousand pounds except it shall not be valid to operate a tractor or a motorcycle other than a class B or C limited use motorcycle.

(iv) Class D. Such license shall be valid to operate any passenger or limited use automobile or any truck with a GVWR of not more than twenty-six thousand pounds or any such vehicle towing a vehicle with a GVWR of not more than ten thousand pounds, or any such vehicle towing another vehicle with a GVWR of more than ten thousand pounds provided such combination of vehicles has a GCWR of not more than twenty-six thousand pounds, or any personal use vehicle with a GVWR of not more than twenty-six thousand pounds or any such vehicle towing a vehicle with a GVWR of not more than ten thousand pounds, except it shall not be valid to operate a tractor, a motorcycle other than a class B or C limited use motorcycle, a vehicle used to transport passengers for hire or for which a hazardous materials endorsement is required, or a vehicle defined as a bus in subdivision one of section five hundred nine-a of this title.

(v) Class E. Such license shall be valid to operate only vehicles which may be operated with a class D license, except that in addition it shall be valid to operate any such motor vehicle, other than a vehicle defined as a bus in subdivision one of section five hundred nine-a of this chapter, used to transport up to fourteen passengers for hire.

(vi) Class DJ. Such license shall be valid to operate only vehicles which may be operated with a class D license by a person under eighteen years of age, except it shall not be valid to operate a motor vehicle with an unladen weight or a GVWR of more than ten thousand pounds or any motor vehicle towing another vehicle with an unladen weight or GVWR of more than three thousand pounds. Such license shall automatically become a class D license when the holder becomes eighteen years of age.

(vii) Class M. Such license shall be valid to operate any motorcycle, or any motorcycle, other than a limited use motorcycle, towing a trailer.

(viii) Class MJ. Such license shall be valid to operate any motorcycle or limited use motorcycle by a person under eighteen years of age. Such license shall automatically become a class M license when the holder becomes eighteen years of age.

(b) Endorsements. The following endorsements shall be required to operate vehicles as set forth herein. In addition the commissioner by regulation may provide for further endorsements.

(i) T endorsement. Shall be required to operate double and triple trailers.

(ii) H endorsement. Shall be required to transport hazardous materials as defined in section one hundred three of the hazardous materials transportation act, public law 93-633, title I, when the vehicle transporting such materials is required to be placarded under the hazardous materials regulation, 49 CFR part 172, subpart F or is transporting any quantity of material listed as a select agent or toxin in 42 CFR part 73. An applicant for a commercial driver's license in this state who wishes to transport hazardous materials must obtain a New York state hazardous materials endorsement even if such applicant holds a valid hazardous materials endorsement issued by another state. A farm vehicle shall be exempt from the requirement for such endorsement when transporting hazardous materials within one hundred fifty miles of the person's farm. However, a separate non-commercial endorsement shall be required for such exempted transportation. In order to obtain such endorsement, the license holder must submit fingerprints for purposes of a criminal history record check pursuant to subdivision six of this section.

(iii) N endorsement. Shall be required to operate tank vehicles.

(iv) P endorsement. Shall be required to operate a bus as defined in sections one hundred four and five hundred nine-a of this chapter or any motor vehicle with a gross vehicle weight or gross vehicle weight rating of more than twenty-six thousand pounds which is designed to transport passengers in commerce. For the purposes of this subparagraph the gross vehicle weight of a vehicle shall mean the actual weight of the vehicle and the load.

(v) X endorsement. Shall be an endorsement combining H and N endorsements.

(vi) [Repealed]

(vii) Personal use vehicle endorsement. Shall be required to operate a personal use vehicle or a combination of personal use vehicles which may not be operated with a class C, D or E license. The identification and scope of any such endorsement or endorsements shall be as prescribed by regulation of the commissioner, but no such endorsement shall permit the operation of a rental truck towing a vehicle with a GVWR of more than ten thousand pounds.

(viii) W endorsement. Shall be required to operate a tow truck.

(ix) Metal coil endorsement. Shall be required to operate any commercial motor vehicle, as defined in subdivision four of section five hundred one-a of this article, carrying metal coils. The identification and scope of such endorsement shall be as prescribed by regulation of the commissioner.

(x) S endorsement. Shall be required to operate a school bus, as defined in section one hundred forty-two of this chapter, which is designed or used to transport fifteen or more passengers.

(c) Restrictions. Notwithstanding the foregoing provisions of this subdivision, the operation of vehicles may be limited by a restriction or restrictions placed on a license. The following restrictions may be issued by the commissioner based upon the representative vehicle in which the road test was taken, or if the license is issued based on driving experience, the vehicle in which the experience was gained. In addition, the commissioner may by regulation provide for additional restrictions based upon other types of vehicles or other factors deemed appropriate by the commissioner.

(i) A restriction prohibiting the operation of a vehicle with air brakes.

(ii) A restriction limiting the operation of a combination of vehicles to truck-trailer combinations.

(iii) A restriction limiting operation to vehicles of not more than a specified GVWR.

(d) Exceptions. (i) Notwithstanding the foregoing provisions of this subdivision, a motor vehicle or combination of vehicles, other than a motorcycle, that is (A) a military vehicle operated by a member of the armed forces, or (B) a police vehicle or fire vehicle during its use in an emergency operation as defined in section one hundred fourteen-b of this chapter, or in the performance of official duties, or activities related to the execution of emergency governmental functions pursuant to section 383.3 (d)(2) of title 49 of the code of federal regulations, or (C) a vehicle owned and identified as being owned by the state or a political subdivision thereof or an ambulance service as defined in subdivision two of section three thousand one of the public health law or a voluntary ambulance service as defined in subdivision three of such section and used to provide emergency medical service as defined in section three thousand one of the public health law, or to perform official duties, or activities related to the execution of emergency governmental functions pursuant to section 383.3 (d)(2) of title 49 of the code of federal regulations, may be operated with any class license other than a class DJ, M or MJ license. For the purposes of this paragraph the term "member of the armed forces" shall include active duty military personnel; members of the reserve components of the armed forces; members of the national guard on active duty, including personnel on full time active guard duty, personnel on part-time national guard training, and national guard military technicians (civilians who are required to wear military uniforms); and active duty United States coast guard personnel. The term shall not include United States reserve technicians. Notwithstanding the provisions of section one hundred fourteen-b of this chapter, for the purposes of this subparagraph, the term "emergency operation" shall include returning from emergency service.

(ii) Notwithstanding the foregoing provisions of this subdivision, a motor vehicle or combination of vehicles which is designed and primarily used for purposes other than the transportation of persons or property which is excluded from the definition of commercial motor vehicle pursuant to the provisions of subparagraph (iv) of paragraph (a) of subdivision four of section five hundred one-a of this chapter may be operated with any class license other than a class DJ, M or MJ license.

3. Restrictions on use of class DJ and class MJ licenses. A class DJ or class MJ license shall permit the holder to operate a vehicle in accordance with the following restrictions:

(a) in the counties of Nassau and Suffolk:

(i) for the purpose of driving to and from a state-approved cooperative work-study educational program, or to or from an approved program for credit in a post-secondary institution, or to or from a state-approved registered evening high school or while engaged in farm employment, or to or from an approved driver education course; or

(ii) from five o'clock in the morning to nine o'clock in the evening, to and from a place of business where the holder is regularly employed, or when accompanied by a duly licensed parent, guardian, person in a position of loco parentis, driver education teacher, or driving school instructor.

(b) in all other areas of the state, except for the city of New York:

(i) from five o'clock in the morning to nine o'clock in the evening; or

(ii) from nine o'clock in the evening to five o'clock in the morning when going to or from school, or to or from a place of business where the holder is employed on a regularly scheduled basis, or when accompanied by a duly licensed parent, guardian or one in a position of loco parentis to the licensee.

(c) in the city of New York, driving shall be prohibited.

(d) for the purpose of this subdivision, the term "school" shall mean instruction, education or training licensed or approved by a department or agency of the state or training conducted by the armed forces of the United States except it shall not include extra-curricular activities or social events for which scholastic credits are not given.

(e) any person operating a motor vehicle to or from school or to or from a place of business as authorized by this subdivision must possess documentation signed by such person's instructor or employer. The commissioner shall, by regulation, prescribe the form and content of such documentation.

4. Probationary licenses. Any driver's license, other than a class DJ and class MJ license, shall be considered probationary until the expiration of six months following the date of issuance thereof, and thereafter as provided in section five hundred ten-b of this title, but this subdivision shall not apply to renewals of a license, or, unless so provided by the commissioner, to a license for which a road test has been waived by the commissioner.

5. Learners' permits.

(a) The commissioner shall issue learner's permits as provided in this article. Such permit shall be valid only

(i) for the operation of a motor vehicle of a type which could be operated by the holder of the class of license for which application is being made;

(ii) when the holder is under the immediate supervision and control of a person at least twenty-one years of age who holds a license valid in this state for the operation of the type of vehicle being operated; and

(iii) in accordance with any additional restrictions prescribed by the commissioner and noted on such permit.

(b) In addition to the restrictions contained in paragraph (a) of this subdivision, a learner's permit issued to a person applying for a class DJ or class MJ license shall be subject to the restrictions contained in section five hundred one-b of this article and shall not be valid for the operation of any motor vehicle:

(i) within the city of New York, except that the holder of such permit may operate a motor vehicle within the city of New York from five o'clock in the morning to nine o'clock in the evening when such person is under the immediate supervision and control of a person at least twenty-one years of age who is such holder's parent, guardian, person in a position of loco parentis, driver education teacher for the purpose of certification pursuant to section eight hundred six-a of the education law or driving school instructor for the purpose of certification pursuant to subdivision seven-a of section three hundred ninety-four of this chapter and such vehicle is equipped with dual controls as prescribed by the commissioner;

(ii) in the counties of Nassau and Suffolk, except that the holder of such permit may operate a motor vehicle within the counties of Nassau and Suffolk from five o'clock in the morning to nine o'clock in the evening when such person is under the immediate supervision and control of a person at least twenty-one years of age who is such holder's licensed parent, guardian, person in a position of loco parentis, driver education teacher for the purpose of certification pursuant to section eight hundred six-a of the education law, or driving school instructor for the purpose of certification pursuant to subdivision seven-a of section three hundred ninety-four of this chapter, or a person at least twenty-one years of age who holds a license valid in this state for the operation of the type of vehicle being operated, for the purpose of certification pursuant to subdivision two of section five hundred two of this article, and who has been designated by such holder's parent, guardian or person in a position of loco parentis to accompany such holder, as evidenced by a written statement to that effect;

(iii) from nine o'clock in the evening to five o'clock in the morning, unless the holder of such permit is under the immediate supervision and control of a person at least twenty-one years of age who is such holder's licensed parent, guardian, person in a position of loco parentis, driver education teacher for the purpose of certification pursuant to section eight hundred six-a of the education law, or driving school instructor for the purpose of certification pursuant to subdivision seven-a of section three hundred ninety-four of this chapter.

(c) The restrictions contained in paragraphs (a) and (b) of this subdivision shall apply to a learner's permit which has been issued to a person who has made application for a class M or class MJ license, except that the required supervising driver need exercise only general supervision and control over the learner as prescribed by regulation of the commissioner when the learner is operating a motorcycle, provided, however, a person who possesses a learner's permit and who has made application for a class M or class MJ license, shall not operate a motorcycle while there is another person on such motorcycle unless such other person possesses a valid class M license.

6. H endorsement criminal history record check. Upon receipt of an application and completion of all other requirements imposed by the commissioner for an H endorsement to permit the operator to transport hazardous materials as defined in section one hundred three of the hazardous materials transportation act, public law 93-633, title I, when the vehicle transporting such materials is required to be placarded under the hazardous materials regulation, 49 CFR part 172, subpart F, or is transporting any quantity of material listed as a select agent or toxin in 42 CFR part 73, the commissioner, subject to the rules and regulations of the division of criminal justice services, shall initiate a criminal history record check of the person making the application. The commissioner shall obtain from each applicant two sets of fingerprints and the division of criminal justice services processing fee imposed pursuant to subdivision eight-a of section eight hundred thirty-seven of the executive law and any fee imposed by the federal bureau of investigation. The commissioner shall promptly transmit such fingerprints and fees to the division of criminal justice services for processing. The federal bureau of investigation and the division of criminal justice services shall forward such criminal history record, if any, to the commissioner. All such criminal history records processed and sent pursuant to this section shall be confidential pursuant to the applicable federal and state laws, rules and regulations, and shall not be published or in any way disclosed to persons other than authorized personnel, unless otherwise authorized by law. No cause of action against the commissioner, the department or the division of criminal justice services for damages related to the dissemination of criminal history records pursuant to this section shall exist when the commissioner, department or division of criminal justice services has reasonably and in good faith relied upon the accuracy and completeness of criminal history information furnished to it by qualified agencies. The provision of such information by the division of criminal justice services shall be subject to the provisions of subdivision sixteen of section two hundred ninety-six of the executive law. The consideration of such criminal history record by the commissioner shall be subject to article twenty-three-A of the correction law. The commissioner shall review such criminal history record for a conviction within the previous ten years for: (i) any violent felony offense, as defined in section 70.02 of the penal law; or (ii) any felony defined in article one hundred twenty, one hundred twenty-five, one hundred thirty, one hundred thirty-five, one hundred forty, one hundred forty-five, one hundred fifty, one hundred fifty-five, one hundred sixty, one hundred seventy, one hundred seventy-five, two hundred, two hundred ten, two hundred twenty, two hundred twenty-one, two hundred forty, two hundred sixty-five, four hundred sixty, four hundred seventy, four hundred eighty-five, or four hundred ninety of the penal law or section fifty-three-e of the railroad law; or (iii) any offense in another jurisdiction which includes all of the essential elements of such offenses described in paragraphs (i) and (ii) of this subdivision and for which a sentence of imprisonment for more than one year was authorized in the other jurisdiction and is authorized in this state, regardless of whether such sentence was imposed; or any of the

following federal offenses: improper transportation of a hazardous material, as defined in 49 U.S.C. 46312, conveying false information or threats, as defined in 49 U.S.C. 46507, espionage, as defined in 18 U.S.C. 793, 794 or 3077, sedition, as defined in 18 U.S.C. 2384, 2385 or section 4 of the subversive activities control act of 1950, treason, as defined in 18 U.S.C. 2381 or conspiracy or solicitation, as defined in 18 U.S.C. 371 or 373; or (iv) an attempt or conspiracy to commit any of the offenses specified in paragraphs (i), (ii), or (iii) of this subdivision. In calculating such ten year period, any period of time during which the person was incarcerated for any reason between the time of commission of the previous felony and the time of commission of the present felony shall be excluded and such ten year period shall be extended by a period or periods equal to the time served under such incarceration. After receipt of a criminal history record from the division of criminal justice services, if any, and review of such record, the commissioner shall promptly notify the applicant whether he or she will be granted an H endorsement based upon the applicant's criminal history and promptly notify such applicant of the determination and the procedure for requesting a hearing pursuant to this subdivision. If the commissioner denies an applicant an H endorsement based either in whole or in part on such applicant's criminal record, the commissioner must notify such applicant of the basis for such denial, and afford such applicant notice and an opportunity to be heard and offer proof in opposition to such determination. If the applicant requests a hearing to contest the commissioner's determination, such hearing must be requested no later than thirty days after the applicant's receipt of the determination and must be scheduled by the commissioner within sixty days of such request. Upon request and pursuant to the rules and regulations of the division of criminal justice services, any applicant may obtain, review and seek correction of his or her criminal history record.

HISTORY:

Add, L 1972, ch 780, § 9, eff April 1, 1973; amd, L 1973, ch 77, § 1; L 1974, ch 102, § 1; L 1974, ch 380, § 1; L 1977, ch 931, §§ 5, 7, 8; L 1979, ch 193, § 1; L 1980, ch 382, §§ 1, 2; L 1983, ch 312, § 1; L 1983, ch 894, § 1; L 1983, ch 999, § 2; L 1984, ch 111, § 1; L 1985, ch 692, § 1, eff April 1, 1986; L 1986, ch 540, § 1; L 1987, ch 87, § 1; L 1989, ch 449, §§ 1, 2, eff Jan 1, 1990; L 1990, ch 84, § 1, eff April 13, 1990; L 1990, ch 173, §§ 35–38, eff Feb 19, 1991; L 1990, ch 696, § 3, eff Feb 19, 1990; L 1992, ch 84, § 1, eff May 10, 1992, deemed eff April 1, 1992; L 1994, ch 552, §§ 5, 6, eff Jan 22, 1995; L 1998, ch 382, § 1, eff July 14, 1998; L 2000, ch 604, § 2, eff Dec 27, 2000; L 2001, ch 260, § 2, eff March 4, 2002; L 2002, ch 63, § 1, eff May 7, 2002; L 2002, ch 644, §§ 2–6, eff Sept 1, 2003; L 2003, ch 62, §§ 1, 2 (Part I), eff May 15, 2003; L 2005, ch 60, §§ 3, 4, 6, 7 (Part E), eff April 12, 2005; L 2005, ch 60, § 5 (Part E), eff Sept 30, 2005; L 2005, ch 339, § 1, eff July 26, 2005; L 2009, ch 36, § 1, eff May 21, 2009; L 2009, ch 59, § 4 (Part K), eff April 7, 2009; L 2009, ch 403, § 1, eff Feb 22, 2010; L 2016, ch 58, §§ 1, 4 (Part E), eff July 11, 2016.

§ 501. Drivers' licenses and learners' permits [Effective February 3, 2021]

1. The commissioner shall issue classified drivers' licenses as provided in this article. Any such license shall be valid only for the operation of the type of vehicles specified for each such class of license but shall not be valid for the operation of any type of vehicle for which an endorsement is required by this section or regulations promulgated hereunder unless the license contains such endorsement and shall be subject to any restrictions contained thereon.

2. Driver license classifications, endorsements and restrictions and exceptions.

(a) License classifications.

(i) Class A. Such license shall be valid to operate any motor vehicle or any combination of vehicles except it shall not be valid to operate a motorcycle other than a class B or C limited use motorcycle.

(ii) Class B. Such license shall be valid to operate any vehicle or combination of vehicles which may be operated with a class E license and shall be valid to operate any motor vehicle or any such vehicle, other than a tractor, towing a vehicle having a GVWR of not more than ten thousand pounds and shall be valid to operate any altered motor vehicle commonly referred to as a "stretch limousine" having a seating capacity of nine or more passengers including the driver except it shall not be valid to operate a motorcycle other than a class B or C limited use motorcycle.

(iii) Class C. Such license shall be valid to operate any vehicle or combination of vehicles which may be operated with a class E license and shall be valid to operate any motor vehicle with a GVWR of not more than twenty-six thousand pounds and any such vehicle towing another vehicle with a GVWR of not more than ten thousand pounds except it shall not be valid to operate a tractor or a motorcycle other than a class B or C limited use motorcycle.

(iv) Class D. Such license shall be valid to operate any passenger or limited use automobile or any truck with a GVWR of not more than twenty-six thousand pounds or any such vehicle towing a vehicle with a GVWR of not more than ten thousand pounds, or any such vehicle towing another vehicle with a GVWR of more than ten thousand pounds provided such combination of vehicles has a GCWR of not more than twenty-six thousand pounds, or any personal use vehicle with a GVWR of not more than twenty-six thousand pounds or any such vehicle towing a vehicle with a GVWR of not more than ten thousand pounds, except it shall not be valid to operate a tractor, a motorcycle other than a class B or C limited use motorcycle, a vehicle used to transport passengers for hire or for which a hazardous materials endorsement is required, or a vehicle defined as a bus in subdivision one of section five hundred nine-a of this title.

(v) Class E. Such license shall be valid to operate only vehicles which may be operated with a class D license, except that in addition it shall be valid to operate any such motor vehicle, other than a vehicle defined as a bus in subdivision one of section five hundred nine-a of this chapter, used to transport up to fourteen passengers for hire and other than an altered motor vehicle commonly referred to as a "stretch limousine" having a seating capacity of nine or more passengers including the driver.

(vi) Class DJ. Such license shall be valid to operate only vehicles which may be operated with a class D license by a person under eighteen years of age, except it shall not be valid to operate a motor vehicle with an unladen weight or a GVWR of more than ten thousand pounds or any motor vehicle towing another vehicle with an unladen weight or GVWR of more than three thousand pounds. Such license shall automatically become a class D license when the holder becomes eighteen years of age.

(vii) Class M. Such license shall be valid to operate any motorcycle, or any motorcycle, other than a limited use motorcycle, towing a trailer.

(viii) Class MJ. Such license shall be valid to operate any motorcycle or limited use motorcycle by a person under eighteen years of age. Such license shall automatically become a class M license when the holder becomes eighteen years of age.

(b) Endorsements. The following endorsements shall be required to operate vehicles as set forth herein. In addition the commissioner by regulation may provide for further endorsements.

(i) T endorsement. Shall be required to operate double and triple trailers.

(ii) H endorsement. Shall be required to transport hazardous materials as defined in section one hundred three of the hazardous materials transportation act, public law 93-633, title I, when the vehicle transporting such materials is required to be placarded under the hazardous materials regulation, 49 CFR part 172, subpart F or is transporting any quantity of material listed as a select agent or toxin in 42 CFR part 73. An applicant for a commercial driver's license in this state who wishes to transport hazardous materials must obtain a New York state hazardous materials endorsement even if such applicant holds a valid hazardous materials endorsement issued by another state. A farm vehicle shall be exempt from the requirement for such endorsement when transporting hazardous materials within one hundred fifty miles of the person's farm. However, a separate non-commercial endorsement shall be required for such exempted transportation. In order to obtain such endorsement, the license holder must submit fingerprints for purposes of a criminal history record check pursuant to subdivision six of this section.

(iii) N endorsement. Shall be required to operate tank vehicles.

(iv) P endorsement. Shall be required to operate a bus as defined in sections one hundred four and five hundred nine-a of this chapter, any altered motor vehicle commonly referred to as a "stretch limousine" having a seating capacity of nine or more passengers including the driver or any motor vehicle with a gross vehicle weight or gross vehicle weight rating of more than twenty-six thousand pounds which is designed to transport passengers in commerce. For the purposes of this subparagraph the gross vehicle weight of a vehicle shall mean the actual weight of the vehicle and the load.

(v) X endorsement. Shall be an endorsement combining H and N endorsements.

(vi) [Repealed]

(vii) Personal use vehicle endorsement. Shall be required to operate a personal use vehicle or a combination of personal use vehicles which may not be operated with a class C, D or E license. The identification and scope of any such endorsement or endorsements shall be as prescribed by regulation of the commissioner, but no such endorsement shall permit the operation of a rental truck towing a vehicle with a GVWR of more than ten thousand pounds.

(viii) W endorsement. Shall be required to operate a tow truck.

(ix) Metal coil endorsement. Shall be required to operate any commercial motor vehicle, as defined in subdivision four of section five hundred one-a of this article, carrying metal coils. The identification and scope of such endorsement shall be as prescribed by regulation of the commissioner.

(x) S endorsement. Shall be required to operate a school bus, as defined in section one hundred forty-two of this chapter, which is designed or used to transport fifteen or more passengers.

(c) Restrictions. Notwithstanding the foregoing provisions of this subdivision, the operation of vehicles may be limited by a restriction or restrictions placed on a license. The following restrictions may be issued by the commissioner based upon the representative vehicle in which the road test was taken, or if the license is issued based on driving experience, the vehicle in which the experience was gained. In addition, the commissioner may by regulation provide for additional restrictions based upon other types of vehicles or other factors deemed appropriate by the commissioner.

(i) A restriction prohibiting the operation of a vehicle with air brakes.

(ii) A restriction limiting the operation of a combination of vehicles to truck-trailer combinations.

(iii) A restriction limiting operation to vehicles of not more than a specified GVWR.

(d) Exceptions. (i) Notwithstanding the foregoing provisions of this subdivision, a motor vehicle or combination of vehicles, other than a motorcycle, that is (A) a military vehicle operated by a member of the armed forces, or (B) a police vehicle or fire vehicle during its use in an emergency operation as defined in section one hundred fourteen-b of this chapter, or in the performance of official duties, or activities related to the execution of emergency governmental functions pursuant to section 383.3 (d)(2) of title 49 of the code of federal regulations, or (C) a vehicle owned and identified as being owned by the state or a political subdivision thereof or an ambulance service as defined in subdivision two of section three thousand one of the public health law or a voluntary ambulance service as defined in subdivision three of such section and used to provide emergency medical service as defined in section three thousand one of the public health law, or to perform official duties, or activities related to the execution of emergency governmental functions pursuant to section 383.3 (d)(2) of title 49 of the code of federal regulations, may be operated with any class license other than a class DJ, M or MJ license. For the purposes of this paragraph the term "member of the armed forces" shall include active duty military personnel; members of the reserve components of the armed forces; members of the national guard on active duty, including personnel on full time active guard duty, personnel on part-time national guard training, and national guard military technicians (civilians who are required to wear military uniforms); and active duty United States coast guard personnel. The term shall not include United States reserve technicians. Notwithstanding the provisions of section one hundred fourteen-b of this chapter, for the purposes of this subparagraph, the term "emergency operation" shall include returning from emergency service.

(ii) Notwithstanding the foregoing provisions of this subdivision, a motor vehicle or combination of vehicles which is designed and primarily used for purposes other than the transportation of persons or property which is excluded from the definition of commercial motor vehicle pursuant to the provisions of subparagraph (iv) of paragraph (a) of subdivision four of section five hundred one-a of this chapter may be operated with any class license other than a class DJ, M or MJ license.

3. Restrictions on use of class DJ and class MJ licenses. A class DJ or class MJ license shall permit the holder to operate a vehicle in accordance with the following restrictions:

(a) in the counties of Nassau and Suffolk:

(i) for the purpose of driving to and from a state-approved cooperative work-study educational program, or to or from an approved program for credit in a post-secondary institution, or to or from a state-approved registered evening high school or while engaged in farm employment, or to or from an approved driver education course; or

(ii) from five o'clock in the morning to nine o'clock in the evening, to and from a place of business where the holder is regularly employed, or when accompanied by a duly licensed parent, guardian, person in a position of loco parentis, driver education teacher, or driving school instructor.

(b) in all other areas of the state, except for the city of New York:

(i) from five o'clock in the morning to nine o'clock in the evening; or

(ii) from nine o'clock in the evening to five o'clock in the morning when going to or from school, or to or from a place of business where the holder is employed on a regularly scheduled basis, or when accompanied by a duly licensed parent, guardian or one in a position of loco parentis to the licensee.

(c) in the city of New York, driving shall be prohibited.

(d) for the purpose of this subdivision, the term "school" shall mean instruction, education or training licensed or approved by a department or agency of the state or training conducted by the armed forces of the United States except it shall not include extra-curricular activities or social events for which scholastic credits are not given.

(e) any person operating a motor vehicle to or from school or to or from a place of business as authorized by this subdivision must possess documentation signed by such person's instructor or employer. The commissioner shall, by regulation, prescribe the form and content of such documentation.

4. Probationary licenses. Any driver's license, other than a class DJ and class MJ license, shall be considered probationary until the expiration of six months following the date of issuance thereof, and thereafter as provided in section five hundred ten-b of this title, but this subdivision shall not apply to renewals of a license, or, unless so provided by the commissioner, to a license for which a road test has been waived by the commissioner.

5. Learners' permits.

(a) The commissioner shall issue learner's permits as provided in this article. Such permit shall be valid only

(i) for the operation of a motor vehicle of a type which could be operated by the holder of the class of license for which application is being made;

(ii) when the holder is under the immediate supervision and control of a person at least twenty-one years of age who holds a license valid in this state for the operation of the type of vehicle being operated; and

(iii) in accordance with any additional restrictions prescribed by the commissioner and noted on such permit.

(b) In addition to the restrictions contained in paragraph (a) of this subdivision, a learner's permit issued to a person applying for a class DJ or class MJ license shall be subject to the restrictions contained in section five hundred one-b of this article and shall not be valid for the operation of any motor vehicle:

(i) within the city of New York, except that the holder of such permit may operate a motor vehicle within the city of New York from five o'clock in the morning to nine o'clock in the evening when such person is under the immediate supervision and control of a person at least twenty-one years of age who is such holder's parent, guardian, person in a position of loco parentis, driver education teacher for the purpose of certification pursuant to section eight hundred six-a of the education law or driving school instructor for the purpose of certification pursuant to subdivision seven-a of section three hundred ninety-four of this chapter and such vehicle is equipped with dual controls as prescribed by the commissioner;

(ii) in the counties of Nassau and Suffolk, except that the holder of such permit may operate a motor vehicle within the counties of Nassau and Suffolk from five o'clock in the morning to nine o'clock in the evening when such person is under the immediate supervision and control of a person at least twenty-one years of age who is such holder's licensed parent, guardian, person in a position of loco parentis, driver education teacher for the purpose of certification pursuant to section eight hundred six-a of the education law, or driving school instructor for the purpose of certification pursuant to subdivision seven-a of section three hundred ninety-four of this chapter, or a person at least twenty-one years of age who holds a license valid in this state for the operation of the type of vehicle being operated, for the purpose of certification pursuant to subdivision two of section five hundred two of this article, and who has been designated by such holder's parent, guardian or person in a position of loco parentis to accompany such holder, as evidenced by a written statement to that effect;

(iii) from nine o'clock in the evening to five o'clock in the morning, unless the holder of such permit is under the immediate supervision and control of a person at least twenty-one years of age who is such holder's licensed parent, guardian, person in a position of loco parentis, driver education teacher for the purpose of certification pursuant to section eight hundred six-a of the education law, or driving school instructor for the purpose of certification pursuant to subdivision seven-a of section three hundred ninety-four of this chapter.

(c) The restrictions contained in paragraphs (a) and (b) of this subdivision shall apply to a learner's permit which has been issued to a person who has made application for a class M or class MJ license, except that the required supervising driver need exercise only general supervision and control over the learner as prescribed by regulation of the commissioner when the learner is operating a motorcycle, provided, however, a person who possesses a learner's permit and who has made application for a class M or class MJ license, shall not operate a motorcycle while there is another person on such motorcycle unless such other person possesses a valid class M license.

6. H endorsement criminal history record check. Upon receipt of an application and completion of all other requirements imposed by the commissioner for an H endorsement to permit the operator to transport hazardous materials as defined in section one hundred three of the hazardous materials transportation act, public law 93-633, title I, when the vehicle transporting such materials is required to be placarded under the hazardous materials regulation, 49 CFR part 172, subpart F, or is transporting any quantity of material listed as a select agent or toxin in 42 CFR part 73, the commissioner, subject to the rules and regulations of the division of criminal justice services, shall initiate a criminal history record check of the person making the application. The commissioner shall obtain from each applicant two sets of fingerprints and the division of criminal justice services processing fee imposed pursuant to subdivision eight-a of section eight hundred thirty-seven of the executive law and any fee imposed by the federal bureau of investigation. The commissioner shall promptly transmit such fingerprints and fees to the division of criminal justice services for processing. The federal bureau of investigation and the division of criminal justice services shall forward such criminal history record, if any, to the commissioner. All such criminal history records processed and sent pursuant to this section shall be confidential pursuant to the applicable federal and state laws, rules and regulations, and shall not be published or in any way disclosed to persons other than authorized personnel, unless otherwise authorized by law. No cause of action against the commissioner, the department or the division of criminal justice services for damages related to the dissemination of criminal history records pursuant to this section shall exist when the commissioner, department or division of criminal justice services has reasonably and in good faith relied upon the accuracy and completeness of criminal history information furnished to it by qualified agencies. The provision of such information by the division of criminal justice services shall be subject to the provisions of subdivision sixteen of section two hundred ninety-six of the executive law. The consideration of such criminal history record by the commissioner shall be subject to article twenty-three-A of the correction law. The commissioner shall review such criminal history record for a conviction within the previous ten years for: (i) any violent felony offense, as defined in section 70.02 of the penal law; or (ii) any felony defined in article one hundred twenty, one hundred twenty-five, one hundred thirty, one hundred thirty-five, one hundred forty, one hundred forty-five, one hundred fifty, one hundred fifty-five, one hundred sixty, one hundred seventy, one hundred seventy-five, two hundred, two hundred ten, two hundred twenty, two hundred twenty-one, two hundred forty, two hundred sixty-five, four hundred sixty, four hundred seventy, four hundred eighty-five, or four hundred ninety of the penal law or section fifty-three-e of the railroad law; or (iii) any offense in another jurisdiction which includes all of the essential elements of such

offenses described in paragraphs (i) and (ii) of this subdivision and for which a sentence of imprisonment for more than one year was authorized in the other jurisdiction and is authorized in this state, regardless of whether such sentence was imposed; or any of the following federal offenses: improper transportation of a hazardous material, as defined in 49 U.S.C. 46312, conveying false information or threats, as defined in 49 U.S.C. 46507, espionage, as defined in 18 U.S.C. 793, 794 or 3077, sedition, as defined in 18 U.S.C. 2384, 2385 or section 4 of the subversive activities control act of 1950, treason, as defined in 18 U.S.C. 2381 or conspiracy or solicitation, as defined in 18 U.S.C. 371 or 373; or (iv) an attempt or conspiracy to commit any of the offenses specified in paragraphs (i), (ii), or (iii) of this subdivision. In calculating such ten year period, any period of time during which the person was incarcerated for any reason between the time of commission of the previous felony and the time of commission of the present felony shall be excluded and such ten year period shall be extended by a period or periods equal to the time served under such incarceration. After receipt of a criminal history record from the division of criminal justice services, if any, and review of such record, the commissioner shall promptly notify the applicant whether he or she will be granted an H endorsement based upon the applicant's criminal history and promptly notify such applicant of the determination and the procedure for requesting a hearing pursuant to this subdivision. If the commissioner denies an applicant an H endorsement based either in whole or in part on such applicant's criminal record, the commissioner must notify such applicant of the basis for such denial, and afford such applicant notice and an opportunity to be heard and offer proof in opposition to such determination. If the applicant requests a hearing to contest the commissioner's determination, such hearing must be requested no later than thirty days after the applicant's receipt of the determination and must be scheduled by the commissioner within sixty days of such request. Upon request and pursuant to the rules and regulations of the division of criminal justice services, any applicant may obtain, review and seek correction of his or her criminal history record.

HISTORY:

Add, L 1972, ch 780, § 9, eff April 1, 1973; amd, L 1973, ch 77, § 1; L 1974, ch 102, § 1; L 1974, ch 380, § 1; L 1977, ch 931, §§ 5, 7, 8; L 1979, ch 193, § 1; L 1980, ch 382, §§ 1, 2; L 1983, ch 312, § 1; L 1983, ch 894, § 1; L 1983, ch 999, § 2; L 1984, ch 111, § 1; L 1985, ch 692, § 1, eff April 1, 1986; L 1986, ch 540, § 1; L 1987, ch 87, § 1; L 1989, ch 449, §§ 1, 2, eff Jan 1, 1990; L 1990, ch 84, § 1, eff April 13, 1990; L 1990, ch 173, §§ 35–38, eff Feb 19, 1991; L 1990, ch 696, § 3, eff Feb 19, 1990; L 1992, ch 84, § 1, eff May 10, 1992, deemed eff April 1, 1992; L 1994, ch 552, §§ 5, 6, eff Jan 22, 1995; L 1998, ch 382, § 1, eff July 14, 1998; L 2000, ch 604, § 2, eff Dec 27, 2000; L 2001, ch 260, § 2, eff March 4, 2002; L 2002, ch 63, § 1, eff May 7, 2002; L 2002, ch 644, §§ 2–6, eff Sept 1, 2003; L 2003, ch 62, §§ 1, 2 (Part I), eff May 15, 2003; L 2005, ch 60, §§ 3, 4, 6, 7 (Part E), eff April 12, 2005; L 2005, ch 60, § 5 (Part E), eff Sept 30, 2005; L 2005, ch 339, § 1, eff July 26, 2005; L 2009, ch 36, § 1, eff May 21, 2009; L 2009, ch 59, § 4 (Part K), eff April 7, 2009; L 2009, ch 403, § 1, eff Feb 22, 2010; L 2016, ch 58, §§ 1, 4 (Part E), eff July 11, 2016; L 2020, ch 6, §§ 3, 4, eff Feb 3, 2021.

§ 501-a. Definitions [Effective until February 3, 2021]

The following terms when used in this article and in articles twenty and thirty-one of this chapter, shall have the following meanings:

1. Commercial driver's license or CDL. A class A or B driver's license or a class C driver's license which bears an H, P or X endorsement, which licenses contain the legend commercial driving license or CDL thereon and which is issued in accordance with the commercial motor vehicle safety act of 1986, public law 99-570, title XII, and this article which authorizes a person to operate a commercial motor vehicle.

2. Gross vehicle weight rating or GVWR. The weight of a vehicle consisting of the unladen weight and the maximum carrying capacity recommended by the manufacturer of such vehicle. The GVWR of a combination of vehicles (commonly referred to as the "Gross Combination Weight Rating" or GCWR) is the GVWR of the power unit plus the GVWR of each vehicle in the combination.

3. Hazardous materials. Any material that has been designated as hazardous under 49 U.S.C. 5103 and is required to be placarded under subpart F of 49 CFR part 172 or any quantity of a material listed as a select agent or toxin in 42 CFR part 73.

4. Commercial motor vehicle.

(a) A motor vehicle or combination of vehicles designed or used to transport passengers or property:

(i) which has a GVWR of more than twenty-six thousand pounds; or

(ii) which has a GCWR of more than twenty-six thousand pounds, including any towed unit with a GVWR of more than ten thousand pounds; or

(iii) designed or used to transport fifteen or more passengers, in addition to the driver; or

(iv) defined as a bus in subdivision one of section five hundred nine-a of this chapter; or

(v) of any size, other than a farm vehicle operated within one hundred fifty miles of the operator's farm, used in the transportation of materials found by the United States secretary of transportation to be hazardous under the hazardous materials transportation act and which requires the motor vehicle transporting such materials to be placarded under the hazardous materials regulation, 49 CFR part 172, subpart F or is transporting any quantity of a material listed as a select agent or toxin in 42 CFR part 73.

(b) However, a commercial motor vehicle shall not include: (i) a personal use vehicle or a covered farm vehicle or a combination of such vehicles; (ii) any motor vehicle or combination of motor vehicles operated by a member of the armed forces for military purposes; (iii) a police vehicle or fire vehicle, or combination of such vehicles during its use in an emergency operation as defined in section one hundred fourteen-b of this chapter, or in the performance of official duties, or activities related to the execution of emergency governmental functions pursuant to section 383.3 (d)(2) of title 49 of the code of federal regulations; (iv) a vehicle or combination of vehicles owned and identified as being owned by the state or a political subdivision thereof or an ambulance service as defined in subdivision two of section three thousand one of the public health law or a voluntary ambulance service as defined in subdivision three of such section and used to provide emergency medical service as defined in section three thousand one of the public health law, or to perform official duties, or activities related to the execution of emergency governmental functions pursuant to section 383.3 (d)(2) of title 49 of the code of federal regulations; or (v) a vehicle or combination of vehicles which is designed and primarily used for purposes other than the transportation of persons or property and which is operated on a public highway only occasionally for the purpose of being transported to a construction or off-highway site at which its primary purpose is to be performed except as may otherwise be specifically provided by regulation of the commissioner. For the purposes of this paragraph, the term "member of the armed forces" shall include active duty military personnel; members of the reserve components of the armed forces; members of the national guard on active duty, including personnel on full time active guard duty, personnel on part-time national guard training, and national guard military technicians (civilians who are required to wear military uniforms); and active duty United States coast guard personnel. The term shall not include United States reserve technicians. Notwithstanding the provisions of section one hundred fourteen-b of this chapter, for the purposes of this paragraph, the term "emergency operation" shall include returning from emergency service.

(c) [Repealed]

5. Representative vehicle. The type of motor vehicle or combination of vehicles specified by regulation of the commissioner that an applicant for a driver's license must operate during a road test in order to receive a specific class of license or endorsement.

6. Tank vehicle. Any commercial motor vehicle designed to transport any liquid or gaseous material within a tank or tanks having an individual rated capacity of more than one hundred nineteen gallons and an aggregate rated capacity of one thousand gallons or more that is either permanently or temporarily attached to the vehicle or the chassis. Such term shall not include a commercial motor vehicle transporting an empty storage container tank, not designed for transportation, with a rated capacity of one thousand gallons or more that is temporarily attached to a flatbed trailer.

7. Personal use vehicle. A vehicle constructed or altered to be used for recreational purposes which is exclusively used to transport family members and/or personal possessions of such family members for non-business recreational purposes by the

operator, or a rental truck which is exclusively used to transport personal possessions of the person who has rented the truck for non-business purposes.

8. Covered farm vehicle. (a) A vehicle or combination of vehicles registered in this state, which (i) displays a covered farm vehicle designation issued by the commissioner, (ii) is operated by the owner or operator of a farm or ranch, or an employee or family member of an owner or operator of a farm or ranch, (iii) is used to transport agricultural commodities, livestock, machinery or supplies to or from a farm or ranch, (iv) is not used in for-hire motor carrier operations, exclusive of operation by a tenant pursuant to a crop share farm lease agreement to transport the landlord's portion of the crops under that agreement; and (v) is not used for the transportation of hazardous materials.

(b) A covered farm vehicle with a gross vehicle weight or gross vehicle weight rating, whichever is greater, of more than twenty-six thousand pounds may only be operated within one hundred fifty air miles of the farm or ranch.

(c) The commissioner shall, by regulation, designate an endorsement or endorsements for the operation of covered farm vehicles with a gross vehicle weight or gross vehicle weight rating of more than twenty-six thousand pounds. Such endorsement or endorsements shall be required to operate such a covered farm vehicle or combination of covered farm vehicles. The identification and scope of such endorsement or endorsements shall, at a minimum, include a distinction between the operation of a covered farm vehicle having a gross vehicle weight or gross vehicle weight rating of more than twenty-six thousand pounds and the operation of a combination of covered farm vehicles having a gross vehicle weight or gross vehicle weight rating of more than twenty-six thousand pounds.

(d) For the purposes of this subdivision, the gross vehicle weight of a vehicle shall mean the actual weight of the vehicle and the load.

HISTORY:

Add, L 1990, ch 173, § 39, eff Feb 19, 1991; amd, L 1990, ch 696, § 4, eff Feb 19, 1991; L 1992, ch 84, § 2, eff May 10, 1992, deemed eff April 1, 1992; L 1993, ch 550, § 1, eff Jan 24, 1994; L 1998, ch 382, § 2, eff July 14, 1998; L 2005, ch 60, §§ 8–10 (Part E), eff April 12, 2005; L 2007, ch 251, § 2, eff July 18, 2007; L 2009, ch 36, § 2, eff May 21, 2009; L 2009, ch 59, § 5 (Part K), eff April 7, 2009; L 2015, ch 58, § 2 (Part I), eff July 8, 2015; L 2016, ch 58, §§ 2, 3 (Part E), eff July 11, 2016.

§ 501-a. Definitions [Effective February 3, 2021]

The following terms when used in this article and in articles twenty and thirty-one of this chapter, shall have the following meanings:

1. Commercial driver's license or CDL. A class A or B driver's license or a class C driver's license which bears an H, P or X endorsement, which licenses contain the legend commercial driving license or CDL thereon and which is issued in accordance with the commercial motor vehicle safety act of 1986, public law 99-570, title XII, and this article which authorizes a person to operate a commercial motor vehicle and an altered motor vehicle commonly referred to as a "stretch limousine" having a seating capacity of nine or more passengers including the driver.

2. Gross vehicle weight rating or GVWR. The weight of a vehicle consisting of the unladen weight and the maximum carrying capacity recommended by the manufacturer of such vehicle. The GVWR of a combination of vehicles (commonly referred to as the "Gross Combination Weight Rating" or GCWR) is the GVWR of the power unit plus the GVWR of each vehicle in the combination.

3. Hazardous materials. Any material that has been designated as hazardous under 49 U.S.C. 5103 and is required to be placarded under subpart F of 49 CFR part 172 or any quantity of a material listed as a select agent or toxin in 42 CFR part 73.

4. Commercial motor vehicle.

(a) A motor vehicle or combination of vehicles designed or used to transport passengers or property:

(i) which has a GVWR of more than twenty-six thousand pounds; or

(ii) which has a GCWR of more than twenty-six thousand pounds, including any towed unit with a GVWR of more than ten thousand pounds; or

(iii) designed or used to transport fifteen or more passengers, in addition to the driver; or

(iv) defined as a bus in subdivision one of section five hundred nine-a of this chapter; or

(v) of any size, other than a farm vehicle operated within one hundred fifty miles of the operator's farm, used in the transportation of materials found by the United States secretary of transportation to be hazardous under the hazardous materials transportation act and which requires the motor vehicle transporting such materials to be placarded under the hazardous materials regulation, 49 CFR part 172, subpart F or is transporting any quantity of a material listed as a select agent or toxin in 42 CFR part 73.

(b) However, a commercial motor vehicle shall not include: (i) a personal use vehicle or a covered farm vehicle or a combination of such vehicles; (ii) any motor vehicle or combination of motor vehicles operated by a member of the armed forces for military purposes; (iii) a police vehicle or fire vehicle, or combination of such vehicles during its use in an emergency operation as defined in section one hundred fourteen-b of this chapter, or in the performance of official duties, or activities related to the execution of emergency governmental functions pursuant to section 383.3 (d)(2) of title 49 of the code of federal regulations; (iv) a vehicle or combination of vehicles owned and identified as being owned by the state or a political subdivision thereof or an ambulance service as defined in subdivision two of section three thousand one of the public health law or a voluntary ambulance service as defined in subdivision three of such section and used to provide emergency medical service as defined in section three thousand one of the public health law, or to perform official duties, or activities related to the execution of emergency governmental functions pursuant to section 383.3 (d)(2) of title 49 of the code of federal regulations; or (v) a vehicle or combination of vehicles which is designed and primarily used for purposes other than the transportation of persons or property and which is operated on a public highway only occasionally for the purpose of being transported to a construction or off-highway site at which its primary purpose is to be performed except as may otherwise be specifically provided by regulation of the commissioner. For the purposes of this paragraph, the term "member of the armed forces" shall include active duty military personnel; members of the reserve components of the armed forces; members of the national guard on active duty, including personnel on full time active guard duty, personnel on part-time national guard training, and national guard military technicians (civilians who are required to wear military uniforms); and active duty United States coast guard personnel. The term shall not include United States reserve technicians. Notwithstanding the provisions of section one hundred fourteen-b of this chapter, for the purposes of this paragraph, the term "emergency operation" shall include returning from emergency service.

(c) [Repealed]

5. Representative vehicle. The type of motor vehicle or combination of vehicles specified by regulation of the commissioner that an applicant for a driver's license must operate during a road test in order to receive a specific class of license or endorsement.

6. Tank vehicle. Any commercial motor vehicle designed to transport any liquid or gaseous material within a tank or tanks having an individual rated capacity of more than one hundred nineteen gallons and an aggregate rated capacity of one thousand gallons or more that is either permanently or temporarily attached to the vehicle or the chassis. Such term shall not include a commercial motor vehicle transporting an empty storage container tank, not designed for transportation, with a rated capacity of one thousand gallons or more that is temporarily attached to a flatbed trailer.

7. Personal use vehicle. A vehicle constructed or altered to be used for recreational purposes which is exclusively used to transport family members and/or personal possessions of such family members for non-business recreational purposes by the operator, or a rental truck which is exclusively used to transport personal possessions of the person who has rented the truck for non-business purposes.

8. Covered farm vehicle. (a) A vehicle or combination of vehicles registered in this state, which (i) displays a covered farm vehicle designation issued by the commissioner, (ii) is operated by the owner or operator of a farm or ranch, or an employee or family member of an owner or operator of a farm or ranch, (iii) is used to transport agricultural commodities, livestock, machinery or supplies to or from a farm or ranch, (iv) is not used in for-hire motor carrier operations, exclusive of operation by a tenant

pursuant to a crop share farm lease agreement to transport the landlord's portion of the crops under that agreement; and (v) is not used for the transportation of hazardous materials.

(b) A covered farm vehicle with a gross vehicle weight or gross vehicle weight rating, whichever is greater, of more than twenty-six thousand pounds may only be operated within one hundred fifty air miles of the farm or ranch.

(c) The commissioner shall, by regulation, designate an endorsement or endorsements for the operation of covered farm vehicles with a gross vehicle weight or gross vehicle weight rating of more than twenty-six thousand pounds. Such endorsement or endorsements shall be required to operate such a covered farm vehicle or combination of covered farm vehicles. The identification and scope of such endorsement or endorsements shall, at a minimum, include a distinction between the operation of a covered farm vehicle having a gross vehicle weight or gross vehicle weight rating of more than twenty-six thousand pounds and the operation of a combination of covered farm vehicles having a gross vehicle weight or gross vehicle weight rating of more than twenty-six thousand pounds.

(d) For the purposes of this subdivision, the gross vehicle weight of a vehicle shall mean the actual weight of the vehicle and the load.

HISTORY:

Add, L 1990, ch 173, § 39, eff Feb 19, 1991; amd, L 1990, ch 696, § 4, eff Feb 19, 1991; L 1992, ch 84, § 2, eff May 10, 1992, deemed eff April 1, 1992; L 1993, ch 550, § 1, eff Jan 24, 1994; L 1998, ch 382, § 2, eff July 14, 1998; L 2005, ch 60, §§ 8–10 (Part E), eff April 12, 2005; L 2007, ch 251, § 2, eff July 18, 2007; L 2009, ch 36, § 2, eff May 21, 2009; L 2009, ch 59, § 5 (Part K), eff April 7, 2009; L 2015, ch 58, § 2 (Part I), eff July 8, 2015; L 2016, ch 58, §§ 2, 3 (Part E), eff July 11, 2016; L 2020, ch 6, § 2, eff Feb 3, 2021.

§ 502. Requirements for licensing [Effective June 30, 2020]

1. Application for license. Application for a driver's license shall be made to the commissioner. The fee prescribed by law may be submitted with such application. The applicant shall furnish such proof of identity, age, and fitness as may be required by the commissioner. With respect to a non-commercial driver's license or learner's permit which does not meet federal standards for identification, in addition to the acceptable proofs of age and identity approved by the commissioner as of January first, two thousand nineteen, acceptable proof of identity shall also include, but not be limited to, a valid, unexpired foreign passport issued by the applicant's country of citizenship (which shall also be eligible as proof of age), a valid, unexpired consular identification document issued by a consulate from the applicant's country of citizenship, or a valid foreign driver's license that includes a photo image of the applicant and which is unexpired or expired for less than twenty-four months of its date of expiration, as primary forms of such proof. Nothing contained in this subdivision shall be deemed to preclude the commissioner from approving additional proofs of identity and age. The commissioner may also provide that the application procedure shall include the taking of a photo image or images of the applicant in accordance with rules and regulations prescribed by the commissioner. In addition, the commissioner also shall require that the applicant provide his or her social security number or, in lieu thereof, with respect to an application for a non-commercial driver's license or learner's permit which does not meet federal standards for identification, an affidavit signed by such applicant that they have not been issued a social security number. The commissioner also shall provide space on the application so that the applicant may register in the New York state organ and tissue donor registry under section forty-three hundred ten of the public health law with the following stated on the application in clear and conspicuous type:

"You must fill out the following section: Would you like to be added to the Donate Life Registry? Check box for 'yes' or 'skip this question'."

The commissioner of health shall not maintain records of any person who checks "skip this question". Except where the application is made in person or electronically, failure to check a box shall not impair the validity of an application, and failure to check "yes" or checking "skip this question" shall not be construed to imply a wish not to donate. In the case of an applicant under eighteen years of age, checking "yes" shall not constitute consent to make an anatomical gift or registration in the donate life registry, except as otherwise provided pursuant to the provisions of paragraph (b) of subdivision one of section forty-three hundred one of the public health law. Where an applicant has previously consented to make an anatomical gift or registered in the donate life registry, checking "skip this question" or failing to check a box shall not impair that consent or registration. In addition, an applicant for a commercial driver's license who will operate a commercial motor vehicle in interstate commerce shall certify that such applicant meets the requirements to operate a commercial motor vehicle, as set forth in public law 99-570, title XII, and title 49 of the code of federal regulations, and all regulations promulgated by the United States secretary of transportation under the hazardous materials transportation act. In addition, an applicant for a commercial driver's license shall submit a medical certificate at such intervals as required by the federal motor carrier safety improvement act of 1999 and Part 383.71(h) of title 49 of the code of federal regulations relating to medical certification and in a manner prescribed by the commissioner. For purposes of this section and sections five hundred three, five hundred ten-a, and five hundred ten-aa of this title, the terms "medical certificate" and "medical certification" shall mean a form substantially in compliance with the form set forth in Part 391.43(h) of title 49 of the code of federal regulations. Upon a determination that the holder of a commercial driver's license has made any false statement, with respect to the application for such license, the commissioner shall revoke such license.

2. Age.

(a) An applicant for a class A license or for a commercial driver's license which contains an H or an X endorsement or which is valid for operation in interstate commerce shall be at least twenty-one years of age.

(b) Except as provided in paragraph (a) of this subdivision an applicant for a class B, C or E license shall be at least eighteen years of age.

(c) An applicant for a class D or M license shall be at least eighteen years of age, except that an application shall be accepted if the applicant is at least seventeen years of age and submits acceptable proof of successful completion of a driver education course, approved by the state education department and the commissioner, and proof of completion of the minimum hours of supervised driving as required in paragraph (d) of this subdivision.

(d) [Eff until June 30, 2025] An applicant for a class DJ or MJ license shall be at least sixteen years of age and such applicant must submit written consent to the issuance of such license by the applicant's parent or guardian. Upon receipt of withdrawal of such consent, any class DJ or MJ license, learner's permit or license application shall be cancelled. No class DJ or MJ license shall be issued unless the applicant presents, at the time of the road test administered pursuant to paragraph (b) of subdivision four of this section, a written certification by the applicant's parent or guardian: (i) that such applicant has operated a motor vehicle for no less than fifty hours, at least fifteen hours of which shall be after sunset, under the immediate supervision of a person as authorized pursuant to subparagraph (ii) of paragraph (a) or paragraph (b) of subdivision five of section five hundred one of this article, a driver education teacher pursuant to section eight hundred six-a of the education law or a driving school instructor pursuant to subdivision seven-a of section three hundred ninety-four of this chapter; and (ii) if such applicant completed an internet delivered pre-licensing course approved by the commissioner pursuant to article twelve-d of this chapter, that such applicant participated throughout such course.

(d) [Eff June 30, 2025] An applicant for a class DJ or MJ license shall be at least sixteen years of age and such applicant must submit written consent to the issuance of such license by the applicant's parent or guardian. Upon receipt of withdrawal of such consent, any class DJ or MJ license, learner's permit or license application shall be cancelled. No class DJ or MJ license shall be issued unless the applicant presents, at the time of the road test administered pursuant to paragraph (b) of subdivision four of this section, a written certification by the applicant's parent or guardian that such applicant has operated a motor vehicle for no less than fifty hours, at least fifteen hours of which shall be after sunset, under the immediate supervision of a person as authorized pursuant to subparagraph (ii) of paragraph (a) or paragraph (b) of subdivision five of section five hundred one of this article, a driver education teacher pursuant to section eight hundred six-a of the education law or a driving school instructor pursuant to subdivision seven-a of section three hundred ninety-four of this chapter.

3. Application for learner's permit. An application for a learner's permit shall be included in the application for a license. A learner's permit shall be issued in such form as the commissioner shall determine but shall not be issued unless the applicant has successfully passed the vision test required by this section and the test set forth in paragraph (a) of subdivision four of this section with respect to laws relating to traffic and ability to read and comprehend traffic signs and symbols and has satisfactorily completed any course required pursuant to paragraph (a) of subdivision four of this section. Upon acceptance of an application for a learner's permit the commissioner shall provide the applicant with a driver's manual which includes but is not limited to the laws relating to traffic, the laws relating to and physiological effects of driving while ability impaired and driving while intoxicated, the law for exercising due care to avoid colliding with a parked, stopped or standing vehicle pursuant to section eleven hundred forty-four-a of this chapter, explanations of traffic signs and symbols and such other matters as the commissioner may prescribe.

4. Examinations.

(a)(i) Upon submission of an application for a driver's license, the applicant shall be required to take and pass a test, or submit evidence of passage of a test, with respect to the laws relating to traffic, the laws relating to driving while ability is impaired and while intoxicated, under the overpowering influence of "Road Rage", "Work Zone Safety" awareness and "Motorcycle Safety" awareness as defined by the commissioner, "School Bus Safety" awareness, the law relating to exercising due care to avoid colliding with a parked, stopped or standing authorized emergency vehicle or hazard vehicle pursuant to section eleven hundred forty-four-a of this chapter, the ability to read and comprehend traffic signs and symbols and such other matters as the commissioner may prescribe, and to satisfactorily complete a course prescribed by the commissioner of not less than four hours and not more than five hours, consisting of classroom driver training and highway safety instruction or the equivalent thereof. Such test shall include at least seven written questions concerning the effects of consumption of alcohol or drugs on the ability of a person to operate a motor vehicle and the legal and financial consequences resulting from violations of section eleven hundred ninety-two of this chapter, prohibiting the operation of a motor vehicle while under the influence of alcohol or drugs. Such test shall include one or more written questions concerning the devastating effects of "Road Rage" on the ability of a person to operate a motor vehicle and the legal and financial consequences resulting from assaulting, threatening or interfering with the lawful conduct of another person legally using the roadway. Such test shall include one or more questions concerning the potential dangers to persons and equipment resulting from the unsafe operation of a motor vehicle in a work zone. Such test may include one or more questions concerning motorcycle safety. Such test may include one or more questions concerning the law for exercising due care to avoid colliding with a parked, stopped or standing vehicle pursuant to section eleven hundred forty-four-a of this chapter. Such test may include one or more questions concerning school bus safety. Such test shall be administered by the commissioner. The commissioner shall cause the applicant to take a vision test and a test for color blindness. Upon passage of the vision test, the application may be accepted and the application fee shall be payable.

(ii) The commissioner shall promulgate rules and regulations establishing eligibility standards for the taking and passing of knowledge tests in other than written form.

(b) Upon successful completion of the requirements set forth in paragraph (a) of this subdivision which shall include an alcohol and drug education component as described in paragraph (c) of this subdivision, a "Road Rage" awareness component as described in paragraph (c-1) of this subdivision and a "Work Zone Safety" awareness component as described in paragraph (c-2) of this subdivision, a "Motorcycle Safety" awareness component as described in paragraph (c-3) of this subdivision, and a "School Bus Safety" awareness component as described in paragraph (c-4) of this subdivision the commissioner shall cause the applicant to take a road test in a representative vehicle of a type prescribed by the commissioner which shall be appropriate to the type of license for which application is made, except that the commissioner may waive the road test requirements for certain classes of applicants.

The commissioner shall have the power to establish a program to allow persons other than employees of the department to conduct road tests in representative vehicles when such tests are required for applicants to obtain a class A, B or C license. If she chooses to do so, she shall set forth her reasons in writing and conduct a public hearing on the matter. She shall only establish such a program after holding the public hearing.

(c) Alcohol and drug education component. The commissioner shall provide in the pre-licensing course, set forth in paragraph (b) of this subdivision a mandatory component in alcohol and drug education of not less than two hours as a prerequisite for obtaining a license to operate a motor vehicle. The purpose of the component is to educate prospective licensees on the effects that ingestion of alcohol and other drugs have on a person's ability to operate a motor vehicle. The commissioner shall establish a curriculum for the alcohol and drug education component which shall include but not be limited to: instruction describing the hazards of driving while impaired or intoxicated; the penalties for alcohol related motor vehicle violations including sanctions set forth in the penal law that apply to homicides and assaults arising out of the operation of a motor vehicle while intoxicated and those sanctions set forth in the vehicle and traffic law relating to driving while intoxicated; and the medical, biological and physiological effects of the consumption of alcohol and their impact on the operation of a motor vehicle.

(c-1) "Road Rage" awareness component. The commissioner shall provide in the pre-licensing course, set forth in paragraph (b) of this subdivision a mandatory component in "Road Rage" awareness education as a prerequisite for obtaining a license to operate a motor vehicle. The purpose of the component is to educate prospective licensees on the effects that the development and expression of "Road Rage", as defined by the commissioner, have on a person's ability to operate a motor vehicle. The commissioner shall establish a curriculum for the "Road Rage" component which shall include but not be limited to: instruction describing the hazards of driving and exiting the vehicle while under the influence of "Road Rage"; the penalties for "Road Rage"-related motor vehicle or other violations including sanctions set forth in the penal law that apply to homicides and assaults arising out of the operation of a motor vehicle while expressing "Road Rage", and any sanctions set forth in law relating to driving while under the influence of "Road Rage"; and the medical, biological and physiological effects of the development and expression of "Road Rage", and their impact on the operation of a motor vehicle. The commissioner is charged with the responsibility for defining the term "Road Rage", as used in this paragraph, in consultation with law enforcement personnel, medical professionals, representatives of the court system, highway safety officials, and any other group that the commissioner believes can contribute to a comprehensive statement of the issue.

(c-2) "Work Zone Safety" awareness component.

(i) The commissioner shall provide in the pre-licensing course, set forth in paragraph (b) of this subdivision, a mandatory component in "Work Zone Safety" awareness education as a prerequisite for obtaining a license to operate a motor vehicle. The purpose of the component is to educate prospective licensees on the potential dangers to construction workers, construction equipment operators and operators of motor vehicles in a highway work zone. For the purposes of this paragraph, the term "work zone" shall include "work area" as defined by section one hundred sixty of this chapter, and "restricted highway" as authorized in section sixteen hundred twenty-five of this chapter.

(ii) The commissioner shall establish a curriculum for the "Work Zone Safety" component which shall include but not be limited to: instruction describing the potential hazards of driving through a work zone, whether or not work, maintenance or other related construction is being undertaken therein, and information on the provisions of law relating to driving within a work zone and sanctions for violations of such provisions, including speeding in a work zone.

(iii) In developing such curriculum, the commissioner shall consult with the commissioner of transportation, the superintendent of the state police, representatives of the highway construction industry, representatives of highway construction workers, highway safety officials, and any other group that the commissioner believes can contribute to a comprehensive presentation of the issue.

(c-3) "Motorcycle Safety" awareness component. The commissioner shall provide in the pre-licensing course, set forth in paragraph (b) of this subdivision, a mandatory component in "Motorcycle Safety" awareness education as a prerequisite for obtaining a license to operate a motor vehicle. The purpose of the component is to educate prospective licensees on the potential dangers to persons operating motorcycles on the roadway.

(c-4) "School Bus Safety" awareness component.

(i) The commissioner shall provide in the pre-licensing course, set forth in paragraph (b) of this subdivision, a mandatory component in "School Bus Safety" awareness education as a prerequisite for obtaining a license to operate a motor vehicle. The purpose of the component is to educate prospective licensees on the dangers of passing a school bus in violation of section eleven hundred seventy-four of this chapter, to reduce the number of such incidents, and to promote school bus safety.

(ii) The commissioner shall establish a curriculum for the "School Bus Safety" awareness component which shall include, but shall not be limited to, an overview of traffic laws governing overtaking and passing school buses, including but not limited to section eleven hundred seventy-one and section eleven hundred seventy-four of this chapter.

(iii) In developing such curriculum, the commissioner shall consult with the commissioner of transportation.

(d) The commissioner shall make available for distribution upon registration at each location where the pre-licensing course will be given, instructional handbooks outlining the content of the entire curriculum of the pre-licensing course including the information required to be included in the course pursuant to paragraphs (c), (c-1), (c-2), (c-3) and (c-4) of this subdivision. The commissioner shall also provide for the additional training of the instructors necessary for the competent instruction of the alcohol and drug education, "Road Rage" awareness, "Work Zone Safety" awareness, "Motorcycle Safety" awareness and "School Bus Safety" awareness subject matters of the pre-licensing course.

(e) The commissioner shall make available to each applicant for a commercial driver's license instructional handbooks outlining the requirements necessary to qualify for such license, and containing a discussion of the offenses which will result in disqualification from operating a commercial motor vehicle as defined in section five hundred one-a of this chapter. Such handbooks shall be available in both English and Spanish language versions.

(f) The commissioner shall promulgate such rules and regulations as are necessary to carry out the provisions of this section.

(g) The commissioner may, in his discretion, waive the requirement for passage of a test with respect to the laws relating to traffic, the laws relating to driving while ability is impaired and while intoxicated and the ability to read and comprehend traffic signs and symbols, and the requirement for completion of the course set forth in paragraph (a) of this subdivision for applicants who hold a valid or renewable driver's license issued by another jurisdiction or the United States government.

(h) [Eff until June 30, 2025] Course completion certificate fee. The fee for a course completion certificate provided by the department to an entity that is approved by the commissioner to offer the pre-licensing course, required by this subdivision, for issuance by such entity to students upon their completion of such pre-licensing course shall be one dollar. Such fee shall be paid by such entity and shall not be charged to a person who takes the course in any manner. The provisions of this paragraph shall not apply to a pre-licensing course established pursuant to article twelve-D of this chapter.

(h) [Eff June 30, 2025] Course completion certificate fee. The fee for a course completion certificate provided by the department to an entity that is approved by the commissioner to offer the pre-licensing course, required by this subdivision, for issuance by such entity to students upon their completion of such pre-licensing course shall be one dollar. Such fee shall be paid by such entity and shall not be charged to a person who takes the course in any manner.

5. Issuance of license.

(a) Upon successful completion of the requirements set forth in subdivision four of this section, and upon payment of the fee prescribed by law, the commissioner shall issue an appropriate license to the applicant, except that the commissioner may refuse to issue such license

(i) if the applicant is the holder of a currently valid or renewable license to drive issued by another state or foreign country unless the applicant surrenders such license, or

(ii) if such issuance would be inconsistent with the provisions of section five hundred sixteen of this chapter.

(b) The commissioner shall, with respect to the issuance of a hazardous materials endorsement, comply with the requirements imposed upon states pursuant to sections 383.141 and 1572.13 of title 49 of the code of federal regulations.

(c) The commissioner shall not issue a commercial driver's license to a person while such person would be subject to disqualification from operating a commercial motor vehicle for any cause set forth in the commercial motor vehicle safety act of nineteen hundred eighty-six, public law 99-570, title XII and regulations promulgated thereunder. In addition, the commissioner shall suspend a commercial driver's license for the period of time in which such driver is determined to constitute an imminent hazard and is disqualified pursuant to 49 C.F.R 383.52.

6. Renewal of license.

(a) A license issued pursuant to subdivision five of this section shall be valid until the expiration date contained thereon, unless such license is suspended, revoked or cancelled. Such license may be renewed by submission of an application for renewal, the fee prescribed by law, proofs of prior licensing, fitness and acceptable vision prescribed by the commissioner, the applicant's social security number or, in lieu thereof, with respect to an application for a non-commercial driver's license or learner's permit which does not meet federal standards for identification, an affidavit signed by such applicant that they have not been issued a social security number, and if required by the commissioner, a photo image of the applicant in such numbers and form as the commissioner shall prescribe. In addition, an applicant for renewal of a license containing a hazardous material endorsement shall pass an examination to retain such endorsement. The commissioner shall, with respect to the renewal of a hazardous materials endorsement, comply with the requirements imposed upon states by sections 383.141 and 1572.13 of title 49 of the code of federal regulations. A renewal of such license shall be issued by the commissioner upon approval of such application, except that no such license shall be issued if its issuance would be inconsistent with the provisions of section five hundred sixteen of this title, and except that the commissioner may refuse to renew such license if the applicant is the holder of a currently valid or renewable license to drive issued by another state or foreign country unless the applicant surrenders such license.

(b) Time for renewal. A renewal license may only be issued if an application for such license is filed within two years from the date of expiration of the prior license. Such application may be filed prior to the expiration of the license being renewed for a period of time as provided by regulation of the commissioner.

7. Selective service act. The commissioner shall provide separate space on the application for a learner's permit, driver's license, nondriver identification card, or renewal thereof so that any person who is at least eighteen years of age but less than twenty-six years of age who applies to the commissioner for such permit, license, or card or renewal thereof may opt to register with the selective service in accordance with 50 U.S.C. App 451 et. seq., as amended, if such person is subject to such act, and consent to have the commissioner forward the necessary personal information in accordance with this subdivision. Such consent shall be separate from any other certification or signature on such application. The commissioner shall include on the application a brief statement about the requirement of the law, a citation of the act, and the consequences for failing to meet the same. The commissioner shall forward to the selective service system, in an electronic format, the necessary personal information required for registration only of individuals who have affirmatively opted and consented, pursuant to this subdivision, to authorize the commissioner to forward such information to the selective service system.

8. [There are two subs 8] Non-commercial drivers' licenses and learners' permits which do not meet federal standards for identification.

(a) Non-commercial drivers' licenses and learners' permits which do not meet federal standards for identification shall be issued in such form as the commissioner shall determine, provided that such licenses and permits shall be visually identical to non-commercial drivers' licenses and learners' permits which do meet federal standards for identification except that such licenses and permits may state "Not for Federal Purposes". Provided, however, that the commissioner may promulgate regulations providing for additional design or color indicators for both such non-commercial drivers' licenses and learners' permits if required to comply with federal law.

(b) Applicants for a non-commercial driver's license or learner's permit or a renewal thereof shall not be required to prove that they are lawfully present in the United States.

(c) Application forms for non-commercial drivers' licenses and learners' permits which do not meet federal standards for identification or for renewal thereof shall not state (i) the documents an applicant used to prove age or identity, or (ii) an applicant's ineligibility for a social security number where applicable, or (iii) an applicant's citizenship or immigration status.

(d) The commissioner and any agent or employee of the commissioner shall not retain the documents or copies of documents presented by applicants for non-commercial drivers' licenses or learners' permits which do not meet federal standards for identification to prove age or identity except for a limited period necessary to ensure the validity and authenticity of such documents.

(e) (i) A non-commercial driver's license or learner's permit which does not meet federal standards for identification shall not be used as evidence of a person's citizenship or immigration status, and shall not be the basis for investigating, arresting, or detaining a person. (ii) Neither the commissioner nor any agent or employee of the commissioner shall inquire about the citizenship or immigration status of any applicant for a non-commercial driver's license or learner's permit which does not meet federal standards for identification.

8. [There are two subs 8] Loss of consciousness. a. This subdivision shall apply to any applicant for an original driver's license in this state who has ever suffered a loss of consciousness, to any applicant for a renewal driver's license who has suffered a loss of consciousness since his or her last license was issued in this state, to any person who is required to submit physicians', physician assistants', or nurse practitioners' statements, in such form as the commissioner may require, as a condition for continuing licensing, and to persons holding a driver's license concerning whom the commissioner has received evidence of loss of consciousness.

b. As used in this subdivision, the following terms shall have the following meanings: "loss of consciousness" shall mean the condition of not being aware of one's surroundings or of one's existence and the inability to receive, interpret or react to sensory impressions as the result of epilepsy, syncope, cataplexy, narcolepsy and other disorders affecting consciousness and control; and "evidence of loss of consciousness" shall mean a police accident report filed pursuant to section six hundred three of this chapter indicating a loss of consciousness, no matter how denominate, as the cause of an accident, or admission by an applicant or licensee, or a complaint alleging loss of consciousness received from police agencies and others.

c. A person to whom this part is applicable shall be deemed to be fit for licensing only as determined by the commissioner in accordance with section 9.3 of part 9 of title 15 of the codes, rules and regulations of the state of New York as prescribed by the commissioner.

d.(i) Upon receipt of an application for an original driver's license, or for renewal of a driver's license, or upon a scheduled review of evidence confirmed by a department hearing or investigation that a licensee has experienced a lack of consciousness, or if the commissioner has not received an acceptable physician's, physician assistant's or nurse practitioner's statement as defined in subparagraph (ii) of this paragraph, or, if such a statement is received but the commissioner's medical consultant finds grounds to disagree with or to question a recommendation of such physician, physician assistant or nurse practitioner made in accordance with the provisions of section 9.3 of part 9 of title 15 of the codes, rules and regulations of the state of New York, the commissioner shall deny or suspend such license, whichever is appropriate, and offer to hold a department hearing to review such action, upon written request of such person. If such request for hearing is not made within thirty days of such denial or suspension, the offer to hold a hearing shall be deemed to be withdrawn.

(ii) A physician's, physician assistant's or nurse practitioner's statement shall not be acceptable unless such licensed physician, physician assistant or nurse practitioner has attended or examined the patient within one hundred twenty days of the date of such statement, and if required by the commissioner, may be required to be submitted by a physician licensed in a specialty appropriate to the condition in question.

e. The commissioner may require the submission of physicians', physician assistants' or nurse practitioners' statements on a scheduled basis as a condition of licensing in those cases in which a person has experienced loss of consciousness but meets standards of fitness as set forth in rules and regulations prescribed by the commissioner, and the physician's, physician assistant's or nurse practitioner's statement indicates that medication is being taken to meet such standards and, in the opinion of either the submitting physician, physician assistant or nurse practitioner or the medical consultant to the commissioner, the submission of such scheduled physician's, physician assistant's or nurse practitioner's statements is considered necessary or desirable. However, the provisions of this subdivision shall not be applicable in any case where a person has been seizure free without medication for a minimum period of one year and submits a physician's, physician assistant's or nurse practitioner's statement.

f. Any hearing held pursuant to this subdivision shall be conducted in conformity with the provisions of the state administrative procedure act and any regulations promulgated by the commissioner thereunder. Judicial review of a determination made by the commissioner after a hearing held pursuant to this subdivision may be had without an administrative appeal being made pursuant to article three-A of this chapter.

HISTORY:

Add, L 1972, ch 780, § 9, eff April 1, 1973; amd, L 1973, ch 168, § 4; L 1973, ch 229, §§ 2–4; L 1977, ch 931, § 10, eff Aug 11, 1977; L 1979, ch 436, § 1; L 1980, ch 381, § 3; L 1981, ch 138, § 1, eff Aug 24, 1981; L 1983, ch 719, §§ 2–5; L 1985, ch 692, §§ 2–4, eff April 1, 1986; L 1987, ch 342, § 1; L 1987, ch 857, § 1, eff April 21, 1988; L 1990, ch 173, §§ 40–46, eff Feb 19, 1991; L 1991, ch 520, § 1, eff July 19, 1991; L 1993, ch 60, § 47, eff April 15, 1993, deemed eff April 1, 1993; L 1995, ch 81, §§ 209, 210, eff Oct 1, 1995; L 1996, ch 309, §§ 83–87, eff July 13, 1996; L 2001, ch 536, §§ 1, 2, eff Sept 1, 2002; L 2002, ch 533, § 1, eff March 16, 2003; L 2002, ch 585, §§ 1, 2, eff Sept 1, 2002; L 2002, ch 644, § 8, eff Sept 1, 2003; L 2005, ch 60, § 11 (Part E), eff Sept 30, 2005; L 2006, ch 639, § 4, eff Feb 12, 2007; L 2009, ch 59, §§ 2, 3 (Part K), eff April 7, 2009; L 2009, ch 59, § 1 (Part L), eff July 6, 2009; L 2009, ch 403, § 5, eff Feb 22, 2010; L 2010, ch 215, § 1, eff Aug 14, 2010; L 2010, ch 387, §§ 2, 3, eff Sept 1, 2010; L 2011, ch 58, § 2 (Part CC), eff Jan 30, 2012; L 2011, ch 458, §§ 1, 2, eff Sept 1, 2011; L 2012, ch 58, § 1 (Part D), eff March 30, 2012; L 2012, ch 465, § 5, eff Oct 3, 2013; L 2012, ch 487, § 2, eff Oct 3, 2013; L 2015, ch 405, § 3, eff Oct 26, 2015; L 2016, ch 97, §§ 1, 2, eff Jan 17, 2017; L 2016, ch 248, § 4, eff Feb 14, 2017; L 2017, ch 355, §§ 1, 2, eff April 21, 2018; L 2019, ch 37, §§ 3–5, eff Dec 14, 2019; L 2019, ch 513, § 1, eff May 18, 2020; L 2019, ch 368, §§ 2, 3, eff June 30, 2020.

§ 502. Requirements for licensing [Effective June 20, 2020]

1. Application for license. Application for a driver's license shall be made to the commissioner. The fee prescribed by law may be submitted with such application. The applicant shall furnish such proof of identity, age, and fitness as may be required by the commissioner. With respect to a non-commercial driver's license or learner's permit which does not meet federal standards for identification, in addition to the acceptable proofs of age and identity approved by the commissioner as of January first, two thousand nineteen, acceptable proof of identity shall also include, but not be limited to, a valid, unexpired foreign passport issued by the applicant's country of citizenship (which shall also be eligible as proof of age), a valid, unexpired consular identification document issued by a consulate from the applicant's country of citizenship, or a valid foreign driver's license that includes a photo image of the applicant and which is unexpired or expired for less than twenty-four months of its date of expiration, as primary forms of such proof. Nothing contained in this subdivision shall be deemed to preclude the commissioner from approving additional proofs of identity and age. The

commissioner may also provide that the application procedure shall include the taking of a photo image or images of the applicant in accordance with rules and regulations prescribed by the commissioner. In addition, the commissioner also shall require that the applicant provide his or her social security number or, in lieu thereof, with respect to an application for a non-commercial driver's license or learner's permit which does not meet federal standards for identification, an affidavit signed by such applicant that they have not been issued a social security number. The commissioner also shall provide space on the application so that the applicant may register in the New York state organ and tissue donor registry under section forty-three hundred ten of the public health law with the following stated on the application in clear and conspicuous type:

"You must fill out the following section: Would you like to be added to the Donate Life Registry? Check box for 'yes' or 'skip this question'."

The commissioner of health shall not maintain records of any person who checks "skip this question". Except where the application is made in person or electronically, failure to check a box shall not impair the validity of an application, and failure to check "yes" or checking "skip this question" shall not be construed to imply a wish not to donate. In the case of an applicant under eighteen years of age, checking "yes" shall not constitute consent to make an anatomical gift or registration in the donate life registry, except as otherwise provided pursuant to the provisions of paragraph (b) of subdivision one of section forty-three hundred one of the public health law. Where an applicant has previously consented to make an anatomical gift or registered in the donate life registry, checking "skip this question" or failing to check a box shall not impair that consent or registration. In addition, an applicant for a commercial driver's license who will operate a commercial motor vehicle in interstate commerce shall certify that such applicant meets the requirements to operate a commercial motor vehicle, as set forth in public law 99-570, title XII, and title 49 of the code of federal regulations, and all regulations promulgated by the United States secretary of transportation under the hazardous materials transportation act. In addition, an applicant for a commercial driver's license shall submit a medical certificate at such intervals as required by the federal motor carrier safety improvement act of 1999 and Part 383.71(h) of title 49 of the code of federal regulations relating to medical certification and in a manner prescribed by the commissioner. For purposes of this section and sections five hundred three, five hundred ten-a, and five hundred ten-aa of this title, the terms "medical certificate" and "medical certification" shall mean a form substantially in compliance with the form set forth in Part 391.43(h) of title 49 of the code of federal regulations. Upon a determination that the holder of a commercial driver's license has made any false statement, with respect to the application for such license, the commissioner shall revoke such license.

2. Age.

(a) An applicant for a class A license or for a commercial driver's license which contains an H or an X endorsement or which is valid for operation in interstate commerce shall be at least twenty-one years of age.

(b) Except as provided in paragraph (a) of this subdivision an applicant for a class B, C or E license shall be at least eighteen years of age.

(c) An applicant for a class D or M license shall be at least eighteen years of age, except that an application shall be accepted if the applicant is at least seventeen years of age and submits acceptable proof of successful completion of a driver education course, approved by the state education department and the commissioner, and proof of completion of the minimum hours of supervised driving as required in paragraph (d) of this subdivision.

(d) An applicant for a class DJ or MJ license shall be at least sixteen years of age and such applicant must submit written consent to the issuance of such license by the applicant's parent or guardian. Upon receipt of withdrawal of such consent, any class DJ or MJ license, learner's permit or license application shall be cancelled. No class DJ or MJ license shall be issued unless the applicant presents, at the time of the road test administered pursuant to paragraph (b) of subdivision four of this section, a written certification by the applicant's parent or guardian that such applicant has operated a motor vehicle for no less than fifty hours, at least fifteen hours of which shall be after sunset, under the immediate supervision of a person as authorized pursuant to subparagraph (ii) of paragraph (a) or paragraph (b) of subdivision five of section five hundred one of this article, a driver education teacher pursuant to section eight hundred six-a of the education law or a driving school instructor pursuant to subdivision seven-a of section three hundred ninety-four of this chapter.

3. Application for learner's permit. An application for a learner's permit shall be included in the application for a license. A learner's permit shall be issued in such form as the commissioner shall determine but shall not be issued unless the applicant has successfully passed the vision test required by this section and the test set forth in paragraph (a) of subdivision four of this section with respect to laws relating to traffic and ability to read and comprehend traffic signs and symbols and has satisfactorily completed any course required pursuant to paragraph (a) of subdivision four of this section. Upon acceptance of an application for a learner's permit the commissioner shall provide the applicant with a driver's manual which includes but is not limited to the laws relating to traffic, the laws relating to and physiological effects of driving while ability impaired and driving while intoxicated, the law for exercising due care to avoid colliding with a parked, stopped or standing vehicle pursuant to section eleven hundred forty-four-a of this chapter, explanations of traffic signs and symbols and such other matters as the commissioner may prescribe.

4. Examinations.

(a)(i) Upon submission of an application for a driver's license, the applicant shall be required to take and pass a test, or submit evidence of passage of a test, with respect to the laws relating to traffic, the laws relating to driving while ability is impaired and while intoxicated, under the overpowering influence of "Road Rage", "Work Zone Safety" awareness and "Motorcycle Safety" awareness as defined by the commissioner, "School Bus Safety" awareness, the law relating to exercising due care to avoid colliding with a parked, stopped or standing authorized emergency vehicle or hazard vehicle pursuant to section eleven hundred forty-four-a of this chapter, the ability to read and comprehend traffic signs and symbols and such other matters as the commissioner may prescribe, and to satisfactorily complete a course prescribed by the commissioner of not less than four hours and not more than five hours, consisting of classroom driver training and highway safety instruction or the equivalent thereof. Such test shall include at least seven written questions concerning the effects of consumption of alcohol or drugs on the ability of a person to operate a motor vehicle and the legal and financial consequences resulting from violations of section eleven hundred ninety-two of this chapter, prohibiting the operation of a motor vehicle while under the influence of alcohol or drugs. Such test shall include one or more written questions concerning the devastating effects of "Road Rage" on the ability of a person to operate a motor vehicle and the legal and financial consequences resulting from assaulting, threatening or interfering with the lawful conduct of another person legally using the roadway. Such test shall include one or more questions concerning the potential dangers to persons and equipment resulting from the unsafe operation of a motor vehicle in a work zone. Such test may include one or more questions concerning motorcycle safety. Such test may include one or more questions concerning the law for exercising due care to avoid colliding with a parked, stopped or standing vehicle pursuant to section eleven hundred forty-four-a of this chapter. Such test may include one or more questions concerning school bus safety. Such test shall be administered by the commissioner. The commissioner shall cause the applicant to take a vision test and a test for color blindness. Upon passage of the vision test, the application may be accepted and the application fee shall be payable.

(ii) The commissioner shall promulgate rules and regulations establishing eligibility standards for the taking and passing of knowledge tests in other than written form.

(b) Upon successful completion of the requirements set forth in paragraph (a) of this subdivision which shall include an alcohol and drug education component as described in paragraph (c) of this subdivision, a "Road Rage" awareness component as described in paragraph (c-1) of this subdivision and a "Work Zone Safety" awareness component as described in paragraph (c-2) of this subdivision, a "Motorcycle Safety" awareness component as described in paragraph (c-3) of this subdivision, and a "School Bus Safety" awareness component as described in paragraph (c-4) of this subdivision the commissioner shall cause the applicant to take a road test in a representative vehicle of a type prescribed by the commissioner which shall be appropriate to the type of license for which application is made, except that the commissioner may waive the road test requirements for certain classes of applicants.

The commissioner shall have the power to establish a program to allow persons other than employees of the department to conduct road tests in representative vehicles when such tests are required for applicants to obtain a class A, B or C license. If she chooses to do so, she shall set forth her reasons in writing and conduct a public hearing on the matter. She shall only establish such a program after holding the public hearing.

(c) Alcohol and drug education component. The commissioner shall provide in the pre-licensing course, set forth in paragraph (b) of this subdivision a mandatory component in alcohol and drug education of not less than two hours as a prerequisite for obtaining a license to operate a motor vehicle. The purpose of the component is to educate prospective licensees on the effects that ingestion of alcohol and other drugs have on a person's ability to operate a motor vehicle. The commissioner shall establish a curriculum for the alcohol and drug education component which shall include but not be limited to: instruction describing the hazards of driving while impaired or intoxicated; the penalties for alcohol related motor vehicle violations including sanctions set forth in the penal law that apply to homicides and assaults arising out of the operation of a motor vehicle while intoxicated and those sanctions set forth in the vehicle and traffic law relating to driving while intoxicated; and the medical, biological and physiological effects of the consumption of alcohol and their impact on the operation of a motor vehicle.

(c-1) "Road Rage" awareness component. The commissioner shall provide in the pre-licensing course, set forth in paragraph (b) of this subdivision a mandatory component in "Road Rage" awareness education as a prerequisite for obtaining a license to operate a motor vehicle. The purpose of the component is to educate prospective licensees on the effects that the development and expression of "Road Rage", as defined by the commissioner, have on a person's ability to operate a motor vehicle. The commissioner shall establish a curriculum for the "Road Rage" component which shall include but not be limited to: instruction describing the hazards of driving and exiting the vehicle while under the influence of "Road Rage"; the penalties for "Road Rage"-related motor vehicle or other violations including sanctions set forth in the penal law that apply to homicides and assaults arising out of the operation of a motor vehicle while expressing "Road Rage", and any sanctions set forth in law relating to driving while under the influence of "Road Rage"; and the medical, biological and physiological effects of the development and expression of "Road Rage", and their impact on the operation of a motor vehicle. The commissioner is charged with the responsibility for defining the term "Road Rage", as used in this paragraph, in consultation with law enforcement personnel, medical professionals, representatives of the court system, highway safety officials, and any other group that the commissioner believes can contribute to a comprehensive statement of the issue.

(c-2) "Work Zone Safety" awareness component.

(i) The commissioner shall provide in the pre-licensing course, set forth in paragraph (b) of this subdivision, a mandatory component in "Work Zone Safety" awareness education as a prerequisite for obtaining a license to operate a motor vehicle. The purpose of the component is to educate prospective licensees on the potential dangers to construction workers, construction equipment operators and operators of motor vehicles in a highway work zone. For the purposes of this paragraph, the term "work zone" shall include "work area" as defined by section one hundred sixty of this chapter, and "restricted highway" as authorized in section sixteen hundred twenty-five of this chapter.

(ii) The commissioner shall establish a curriculum for the "Work Zone Safety" component which shall include but not be limited to: instruction describing the potential hazards of driving through a work zone, whether or not work, maintenance or other related construction is being undertaken therein, and information on the provisions of law relating to driving within a work zone and sanctions for violations of such provisions, including speeding in a work zone.

(iii) In developing such curriculum, the commissioner shall consult with the commissioner of transportation, the superintendent of the state police, representatives of the highway construction industry, representatives of highway construction workers, highway safety officials, and any other group that the commissioner believes can contribute to a comprehensive presentation of the issue.

(c-3) "Motorcycle Safety" awareness component. The commissioner shall provide in the pre-licensing course, set forth in paragraph (b) of this subdivision, a mandatory component in "Motorcycle Safety" awareness education as a prerequisite for obtaining a license to operate a motor vehicle. The purpose of the component is to educate prospective licensees on the potential dangers to persons operating motorcycles on the roadway.

(c-4) "School Bus Safety" awareness component.

(i) The commissioner shall provide in the pre-licensing course, set forth in paragraph (b) of this subdivision, a mandatory component in "School Bus Safety" awareness education as a prerequisite for obtaining a license to operate a motor vehicle. The purpose of the component is to educate prospective licensees on the dangers of passing a school bus in violation of section eleven hundred seventy-four of this chapter, to reduce the number of such incidents, and to promote school bus safety.

(ii) The commissioner shall establish a curriculum for the "School Bus Safety" awareness component which shall include, but shall not be limited to, an overview of traffic laws governing overtaking and passing school buses, including but not limited to section eleven hundred seventy-one and section eleven hundred seventy-four of this chapter.

(iii) In developing such curriculum, the commissioner shall consult with the commissioner of transportation.

(d) The commissioner shall make available for distribution upon registration at each location where the pre-licensing course will be given, instructional handbooks outlining the content of the entire curriculum of the pre-licensing course including the information required to be included in the course pursuant to paragraphs (c), (c-1), (c-2), (c-3) and (c-4) of this subdivision. The commissioner shall also provide for the additional training of the instructors necessary for the competent instruction of the alcohol and drug education, "Road Rage" awareness, "Work Zone Safety" awareness, "Motorcycle Safety" awareness and "School Bus Safety" awareness subject matters of the pre-licensing course.

(e) The commissioner shall make available to each applicant for a commercial driver's license instructional handbooks outlining the requirements necessary to qualify for such license, and containing a discussion of the offenses which will result in disqualification from operating a commercial motor vehicle as defined in section five hundred one-a of this chapter. Such handbooks shall be available in both English and Spanish language versions.

(f) The commissioner shall promulgate such rules and regulations as are necessary to carry out the provisions of this section.

(g) The commissioner may, in his discretion, waive the requirement for passage of a test with respect to the laws relating to traffic, the laws relating to driving while ability is impaired and while intoxicated and the ability to read and comprehend traffic signs and symbols, and the requirement for completion of the course set forth in paragraph (a) of this subdivision for applicants who hold a valid or renewable driver's license issued by another jurisdiction or the United States government.

(h) Course completion certificate fee. The fee for a course completion certificate provided by the department to an entity that is approved by the commissioner to offer the pre-licensing course, required by this subdivision, for issuance by such entity to students upon their completion of such pre-licensing course shall be one dollar. Such fee shall be paid by such entity and shall not be charged to a person who takes the course in any manner.

5. Issuance of license.

(a) Upon successful completion of the requirements set forth in subdivision four of this section, and upon payment of the fee prescribed by law, the commissioner shall issue an appropriate license to the applicant, except that the commissioner may refuse to issue such license

(i) if the applicant is the holder of a currently valid or renewable license to drive issued by another state or foreign country unless the applicant surrenders such license, or

(ii) if such issuance would be inconsistent with the provisions of section five hundred sixteen of this chapter.

(b) The commissioner shall, with respect to the issuance of a hazardous materials endorsement, comply with the requirements imposed upon states pursuant to sections 383.141 and 1572.13 of title 49 of the code of federal regulations.

(c) The commissioner shall not issue a commercial driver's license to a person while such person would be subject to disqualification from operating a commercial motor vehicle for any cause set forth in the commercial motor vehicle safety act of nineteen hundred eighty-six, public law 99-570, title XII and regulations promulgated thereunder. In addition, the commissioner shall suspend a commercial driver's license for the period of time in which such driver is determined to constitute an imminent hazard and is disqualified pursuant to 49 C.F.R 383.52.

6. Renewal of license.

(a) A license issued pursuant to subdivision five of this section shall be valid until the expiration date contained thereon, unless such license is suspended, revoked or cancelled. Such license may be renewed by submission of an application for renewal, the fee prescribed by law, proofs of prior licensing, fitness and acceptable vision prescribed by the commissioner, the applicant's social security number or, in lieu thereof, with respect to an application for a non-commercial driver's license or learner's permit which does not meet federal standards for identification, an affidavit signed by such applicant that they have not been issued a social security number, and if required by the commissioner, a photo image of the applicant in such numbers and form as the commissioner shall prescribe. In addition, an applicant for renewal of a license containing a hazardous material endorsement shall pass an examination to retain such endorsement. The commissioner shall, with respect to the renewal of a hazardous materials endorsement, comply with the requirements imposed upon states by sections 383.141 and 1572.13 of title 49 of the code of federal regulations. A renewal of such license shall be issued by the commissioner upon approval of such application, except that no such license shall be issued if its issuance would be inconsistent with the provisions of section five hundred sixteen of this title, and except that the commissioner may refuse to renew such license if the applicant is the holder of a currently valid or renewable license to drive issued by another state or foreign country unless the applicant surrenders such license.

(b) Time for renewal. A renewal license may only be issued if an application for such license is filed within two years from the date of expiration of the prior license. Such application may be filed prior to the expiration of the license being renewed for a period of time as provided by regulation of the commissioner.

7. Selective service act. The commissioner shall provide separate space on the application for a learner's permit, driver's license, nondriver identification card, or renewal thereof so that any person who is at least eighteen years of age but less than twenty-six years of age who applies to the commissioner for such permit, license, or card or renewal thereof may opt to register with the selective service in accordance with 50 U.S.C. App 451 et. seq., as amended, if such person is subject to such act, and consent to have the commissioner forward the necessary personal information in accordance with this subdivision. Such consent shall be separate from any other certification or signature on such application. The commissioner shall include on the application a brief statement about the requirement of the law, a citation of the act, and the consequences for failing to meet the same. The commissioner shall forward to the selective service system, in an electronic format, the necessary personal information required for registration only of individuals who have affirmatively opted and consented, pursuant to this subdivision, to authorize the commissioner to forward such information to the selective service system.

8. Non-commercial drivers' licenses and learners' permits which do not meet federal standards for identification.

(a) Non-commercial drivers' licenses and learners' permits which do not meet federal standards for identification shall be issued in such form as the commissioner shall determine, provided that such licenses and permits shall be visually identical to non-commercial drivers' licenses and learners' permits which do meet federal standards for identification except that such licenses and permits may state "Not for Federal Purposes". Provided, however, that the commissioner may promulgate regulations providing for additional design or color indicators for both such non-commercial drivers' licenses and learners' permits if required to comply with federal law.

(b) Applicants for a non-commercial driver's license or learner's permit or a renewal thereof shall not be required to prove that they are lawfully present in the United States.

(c) Application forms for non-commercial drivers' licenses and learners' permits which do not meet federal standards for identification or for renewal thereof shall not state (i) the documents an applicant used to prove age or identity, or (ii) an applicant's ineligibility for a social security number where applicable, or (iii) an applicant's citizenship or immigration status.

(d) The commissioner and any agent or employee of the commissioner shall not retain the documents or copies of documents presented by applicants for non-commercial drivers' licenses or learners' permits which do not meet federal standards for identification to prove age or identity except for a limited period necessary to ensure the validity and authenticity of such documents.

(e) (i) A non-commercial driver's license or learner's permit which does not meet federal standards for identification shall not be used as evidence of a person's citizenship or immigration status, and shall not be the basis for investigating, arresting, or detaining a person. (ii) Neither the commissioner nor any agent or employee of the commissioner shall inquire about the citizenship or immigration status of any applicant for a non-commercial driver's license or learner's permit which does not meet federal standards for identification.

8. Loss of consciousness.

a. This subdivision shall apply to any applicant for an original driver's license in this state who has ever suffered a loss of consciousness, to any applicant for a renewal driver's license who has suffered a loss of consciousness since his or her last license was issued in this state, to any person who is required to submit physicians', physician assistants', or nurse practitioners' statements, in such form as the commissioner may require, as a condition for continuing licensing, and to persons holding a driver's license concerning whom the commissioner has received evidence of loss of consciousness.

b. As used in this subdivision, the following terms shall have the following meanings: "loss of consciousness" shall mean the condition of not being aware of one's surroundings or of one's existence and the inability to receive, interpret or react to sensory impressions as the result of epilepsy, syncope, cataplexy, narcolepsy and other disorders affecting consciousness and control; and "evidence of loss of consciousness" shall mean a police accident report filed pursuant to section six hundred three of this chapter indicating a loss of consciousness, no matter how denominated, as the cause of an accident, or admission by an applicant or licensee, or a complaint alleging loss of consciousness received from police agencies and others.

c. A person to whom this part is applicable shall be deemed to be fit for licensing only as determined by the commissioner in accordance with section 9.3 of part 9 of title 15 of the codes, rules and regulations of the state of New York as prescribed by the commissioner.

d.(i) Upon a scheduled review of a statement as required under paragraph e of this section or upon receipt of evidence from a police agency, police accident report or physician, physician assistant or nurse practitioner confirmed by a department hearing or investigation that a licensee has experienced a lack of consciousness, or if the commissioner has not received an acceptable physician's, physician assistant's or nurse practitioner's statement as defined in subparagraph (iii) of this paragraph, or, if such a statement is received but the commissioner's medical consultant finds grounds to disagree with or to question a recommendation of such physician, physician assistant or nurse practitioner made in accordance with the provisions of section 9.3 of part 9 of title 15 of the codes, rules and regulations of the state of New York, the commissioner shall deny or suspend such license, whichever is appropriate, and offer to hold a department hearing to review such action, upon written request of such person. If such request for hearing is not made within thirty days of such denial or suspension, the offer to hold a hearing shall be deemed to be withdrawn. Notwithstanding the offer to hold a department hearing to review the denial or suspension, a department hearing will not be held until such time as the motorist submits to the commissioner a physician,

physician assistant or nurse practitioner statement as required under the provisions of part 9 of title 15 of the codes, rules and regulations of the state of New York and the commissioner and the commissioner's medical consultants have reviewed such statements within a reasonable period of time. The denial or suspension shall remain in effect until a department hearing is held to review such denial or suspension or after review of the physician, physician assistant or nurse practitioner statement the commissioner and his or her medical consultants finds no grounds to disagree with or to question the physician's, physician assistant's or nurse practitioner's statement.

(ii) Notwithstanding the provisions of subparagraph (i) of this section, upon receipt of an application for an original driver's license, or for renewal of a driver's license, or upon receipt of evidence from a source other than a police agency, police accident report or physician, physician assistant or nurse practitioner, confirmed by a department hearing or investigation that a licensee has experienced a loss of consciousness, the commissioner shall, unless he or she deems such person's operation of a motor vehicle on a public highway to be an immediate hazard, send to such person a proposed denial or suspension of license, whichever is appropriate, with an offer to withhold such action until after a department hearing, if such hearing is requested by such person. The failure of such person to reply to the commissioner, either accepting the denial or suspension or requesting a hearing, within thirty days of the date of such notice, shall result in the imposition of the denial or suspension. If the commissioner deems any such person's operation of a motor vehicle on a public highway to be an immediate hazard, he or she shall deny or suspend such license as required under subparagraph (i) of this paragraph and such denial or suspension shall be subject to the provisions of such subparagraph (i). For the purposes of this subparagraph, a person's operation of a motor vehicle on a public highway shall be deemed to constitute an immediate hazard if the commissioner has received evidence that such person's loss of consciousness has caused or contributed to a motor vehicle accident.

(iii) A physician's, physician assistant's or nurse practitioner's statement shall not be acceptable unless such licensed physician, physician assistant or nurse practitioner has attended or examined the patient within one hundred twenty days of the date of such statement, and if required by the commissioner, may be required to be submitted by a physician licensed in a specialty appropriate to the condition in question.

e. The commissioner may require the submission of physicians', physician assistants' or nurse practitioners' statements on a scheduled basis as a condition of licensing in those cases in which a person has experienced loss of consciousness but meets standards of fitness as set forth in rules and regulations prescribed by the commissioner, and the physician's, physician assistant's or nurse practitioner's statement indicates that medication is being taken to meet such standards and, in the opinion of either the submitting physician, physician assistant or nurse practitioner or the medical consultant to the commissioner, the submission of such scheduled physician's, physician assistant's or nurse practitioner's statements is considered necessary or desirable. However, the provisions of this subdivision shall not be applicable in any case where a person has been seizure free without medication for a minimum period of one year and submits a physician's, physician assistant's or nurse practitioner's statement.

f. Any hearing held pursuant to this subdivision shall be conducted in conformity with the provisions of the state administrative procedure act and any regulations promulgated by the commissioner thereunder. Judicial review of a determination made by the commissioner after a hearing held pursuant to this subdivision may be had without an administrative appeal being made pursuant to article three-A of this chapter.

HISTORY:

Add, L 1972, ch 780, § 9, eff April 1, 1973; amd, L 1973, ch 168, § 4; L 1973, ch 229, §§ 2–4; L 1977, ch 931, § 10, eff Aug 11, 1977; L 1979, ch 436, § 1; L 1980, ch 381, § 3; L 1981, ch 138, § 1, eff Aug 24, 1981; L 1983, ch 719, §§ 2–5; L 1985, ch 692, §§ 2–4, eff April 1, 1986; L 1987, ch 342, § 1; L 1987, ch 857, § 1, eff April 21, 1988; L 1990, ch 173, §§ 40–46, eff Feb 19, 1991; L 1991, ch 520, § 1, eff July 19, 1991; L 1993, ch 60, § 47, eff April 15, 1993, deemed eff April 1, 1993; L 1995, ch 81, §§ 209, 210, eff Oct 1, 1995; L 1996, ch 309, §§ 83–87, eff July 13, 1996; L 2001, ch 536, §§ 1, 2, eff Sept 1, 2002; L 2002, ch 533, § 1, eff March 16, 2003; L 2002, ch 585, §§ 1, 2, eff Sept 1, 2002; L 2002, ch 644, § 8, eff Sept 1, 2003; L 2005, ch 60, § 11 (Part E), eff Sept 30, 2005; L 2006, ch

639, § 4, eff Feb 12, 2007; L 2009, ch 59, §§ 2, 3 (Part K), eff April 7, 2009; L 2009, ch 59, § 1 (Part L), eff July 6, 2009; L 2009, ch 403, § 5, eff Feb 22, 2010; L 2010, ch 215, § 1, eff Aug 14, 2010; L 2010, ch 387, §§ 2, 3, eff Sept 1, 2010; L 2011, ch 58, § 2 (Part CC), eff Jan 30, 2012; L 2011, ch 458, §§ 1, 2, eff Sept 1, 2011; L 2012, ch 58, § 1 (Part D), eff March 30, 2012; L 2012, ch 465, § 5, eff Oct 3, 2013; L 2012, ch 487, § 2, eff Oct 3, 2013; L 2015, ch 405, § 3, eff Oct 26, 2015; L 2016, ch 97, §§ 1, 2, eff Jan 17, 2017; L 2016, ch 248, § 4, eff Feb 14, 2017; L 2017, ch 355, §§ 1, 2, eff April 21, 2018; L 2019, ch 37, §§ 3–5, eff Dec 14, 2019; L 2019, ch 513, § 1, eff May 18, 2020; L 2020, ch 31, § 1, eff June 20, 2020.

§ 504. Form of license [Effective until November 12, 2020]

1.(a) [As amended L 2006, ch 568, § 1 and L 2006, ch 639, § 5] Every license or renewal thereof shall contain a distinguishing mark and adequate space upon which an anatomical gift, pursuant to section forty-three hundred ten of the public health law, by the licensee shall be recorded and shall contain such other information and shall be issued in such form as the commissioner shall determine; provided, however, every license or renewal thereof issued to a person under the age of twenty-one years shall have prominently imprinted upon it the statement "UNDER 21 YEARS OF AGE" in notably distinctive print or format; provided further, however, every license or renewal thereof issued to a person making an anatomical gift shall have prominently printed upon the front of such license or renewal thereof the statement "ORGAN DONOR" in notably distinctive print or format. The commissioner shall not require fees for the issuance of such licenses or renewals thereof to persons under twenty-one years of age or to persons making an anatomical gift which are different from the fees required for the issuance of licenses or renewals thereof to persons twenty-one years of age or over or to persons not making an anatomical gift.

(a-1) Every license or renewal thereof issued to an applicant who was a member of the armed forces of the United States and received an honorable discharge or was released therefrom under honorable conditions shall, upon his or her request and submission of proof as set forth herein, contain a distinguishing mark, in such form as the commissioner shall determine, indicating that he or she is a veteran. Such proof shall consist of a certificate of release or discharge from active duty including but not limited to a DD Form 214 or other proof satisfactory to the commissioner. The commissioner shall not require fees for the issuance of such licenses or renewals thereof to persons requesting a veteran distinguishing mark which are different from fees otherwise required; provided, however, that notwithstanding the provisions of this section, the commissioner shall not require fees for a duplication or amendment of a license prior to its renewal if such duplication or amendment was solely for the purpose of adding a veteran distinguishing mark to such license.

(b) The commissioner may by regulation provide that every driver's license contain the photo image of the licensee. The learner's permit may also contain the photo image of the permittee pursuant to regulations established by the commissioner.

2. Whenever an applicant for a license has successfully met the requirements for the issuance of a license, the license issued by the commissioner may be a temporary license which shall be valid until the license provided in subdivision one of this section is issued or until forty-five days from the date such temporary license is issued, whichever occurs first. The commissioner may in his discretion extend the period of validity of such temporary license. Such temporary license shall be in such form as the commissioner shall determine.

3. Notwithstanding any other provision of law, any photo image taken as part of the application procedure for a learner's permit or an original, duplicate, renewal or amended driver's license shall not be a public record.

HISTORY:

Add, L 1972, ch 780, § 9, eff April 1, 1973; amd, L 1975, ch 315, § 1; L 1979, ch 433, §§ 3, 4; L 1980, ch 843, § 96, eff Sept 1, 1980; L 1989, ch 600, § 2; L 1990, ch 173, § 50, eff Feb 19, 1991; L 2001, ch 406, § 1, eff Jan 29, 2002; L 2006, ch 568, § 1, eff Oct 15, 2006; L 2006, ch 639, § 5, eff Feb 12, 2007; L 2012, ch 487, § 3, eff Oct 3, 2013; L 2014, ch 429, § 2, eff Nov 7, 2014.

§ 504. Form of license [Effective November 12, 2020]

1.(a) [As amended L 2006, ch 568, § 1 and L 2006, ch 639, § 5] Every license or renewal thereof shall contain a distinguishing mark and adequate space upon which an anatomical gift, pursuant to section forty-three hundred ten of the public health law, by the licensee shall be recorded and shall contain such other information and shall be issued in such form as the commissioner shall determine; provided, however, every license or renewal thereof issued to a person under the age of twenty-one years shall have prominently imprinted upon it the statement "UNDER 21 YEARS OF AGE" in notably distinctive print or format; provided further, however, every license or renewal thereof issued to a person making an anatomical gift shall have prominently printed upon the front of such license or renewal thereof the statement "ORGAN DONOR" in notably distinctive print or format. The commissioner shall not require fees for the issuance of such licenses or renewals thereof to persons under twenty-one years of age or to persons making an anatomical gift which are different from the fees required for the issuance of licenses or renewals thereof to persons twenty-one years of age or over or to persons not making an anatomical gift.

(a-1) Every license or renewal thereof issued to an applicant who was a member of the armed forces of the United States and who (i) received an honorable discharge or was released therefrom under honorable conditions, or (ii) has a qualifying condition, as defined in section three hundred fifty of the executive law, and has received a discharge other than bad conduct or dishonorable from such service, or (iii) is a discharged LGBT veteran, as defined in section three hundred fifty of the executive law, and has received a discharge other than bad conduct or dishonorable from such service, shall, upon his or her request and submission of proof as set forth herein, contain a distinguishing mark, in such form as the commissioner shall determine, indicating that he or she is a veteran. Such proof shall consist of a certificate of release or discharge from active duty including but not limited to a DD Form 214 or other proof satisfactory to the commissioner. The commissioner shall not require fees for the issuance of such licenses or renewals thereof to persons requesting a veteran distinguishing mark which are different from fees otherwise required; provided, however, that notwithstanding the provisions of this section, the commissioner shall not require fees for a duplication or amendment of a license prior to its renewal if such duplication or amendment was solely for the purpose of adding a veteran distinguishing mark to such license.

(b) The commissioner may by regulation provide that every driver's license contain the photo image of the licensee. The learner's permit may also contain the photo image of the permittee pursuant to regulations established by the commissioner.

2. Whenever an applicant for a license has successfully met the requirements for the issuance of a license, the license issued by the commissioner may be a temporary license which shall be valid until the license provided in subdivision one of this section is issued or until forty-five days from the date such temporary license is issued, whichever occurs first. The commissioner may in his discretion extend the period of validity of such temporary license. Such temporary license shall be in such form as the commissioner shall determine.

3. Notwithstanding any other provision of law, any photo image taken as part of the application procedure for a learner's permit or an original, duplicate, renewal or amended driver's license shall not be a public record.

HISTORY:

Add, L 1972, ch 780, § 9, eff April 1, 1973; amd, L 1975, ch 315, § 1; L 1979, ch 433, §§ 3, 4; L 1980, ch 843, § 96, eff Sept 1, 1980; L 1989, ch 600, § 2; L 1990, ch 173, § 50, eff Feb 19, 1991; L 2001, ch 406, § 1, eff Jan 29, 2002; L 2006, ch 568, § 1, eff Oct 15, 2006; L 2006, ch 639, § 5, eff Feb 12, 2007; L 2012, ch 487, § 3, eff Oct 3, 2013; L 2014, ch 429, § 2, eff Nov 7, 2014; L 2019, ch 490, § 80, eff Nov 12, 2020.

§ 507-a. Special requirements for for-hire vehicle motor carriers and drivers; drugs and alcohol. [Effective February 3, 2021]

1.(a) All motor carriers shall be required to conduct pre-employment and random drug and alcohol testing in accordance with the provisions and requirements of Part 382 of Title 49 of the Code of Federal Regulations on all drivers of any for-hire vehicle having a seating capacity of nine or more passengers, including the driver, regardless of a commercial driver's license endorsement. Every such driver shall be included in the random testing pool from which drivers are randomly selected for testing, and every such driver shall submit to such testing when selected, as required in Part 382 of Title 49 of the Code of Federal Regulations.

(b) Drug testing administered pursuant to this subdivision shall, at a minimum, be in conformance with drug testing procedures as set forth in Part 382 of Title 49 of the Code of Federal Regulations.

2. No person shall:

(a) consume a drug, controlled substance or an intoxicating liquor, regardless of its alcoholic content, or be under the influence of an intoxicating liquor or drug, within eight hours before going on duty or operating, or having physical control of a for-hire vehicle having a seating capacity of nine or more passengers, including the driver; or

(b) consume a drug, controlled substance or an intoxicating liquor, regardless of its alcoholic content while on duty, or operating, or in physical control of a for-hire vehicle having a seating capacity of nine or more passengers, including the driver; or

(c) possess a drug, controlled substance or an intoxicating liquor, regardless of its alcoholic content, while on duty, operating or in physical control of a for-hire vehicle having a seating capacity of nine or more passengers, including the driver. However, this paragraph shall not apply to possession of a drug, controlled substance or an intoxicating liquor which is transported as part of a shipment or personal effects of a passenger or to alcoholic beverages which are in sealed containers.

3. No motor carrier shall require or permit a driver to:

(a) violate any provision of subdivision two of this section; or

(b) be on duty or operate a for-hire vehicle having a seating capacity of nine or more passengers, including the driver, if by such person's general appearance or by such person's conduct or by other substantiating evidence, such person appears to have consumed a drug, controlled substance or an intoxicating liquor within the preceding eight hours before such driver operates such for-hire vehicle.

4.(a) Every motor carrier shall submit an affidavit to the commissioner attesting to compliance with this section. Such affidavit shall be submitted annually beginning no later than six months after the effective date of this subdivision, in a manner prescribed by regulations established by the commissioner.

(b) Where an affidavit is not submitted pursuant to this section, the commissioner may, in his or her discretion, suspend the registration of the for-hire vehicle or vehicles or deny registration or renewal to the for-hire vehicle or vehicles owned or operated by the motor carrier. Such suspension or denial shall only remain in effect as long as the motor carrier fails to submit such affidavit.

(c) The commissioner may require any motor carrier to pay to the people of this state a civil penalty, if after the motor carrier has had an opportunity to be heard, the commissioner finds that the motor carrier has violated any provision of this section or regulations promulgated pursuant to this section, or has made any false statement or misrepresentation on any affidavit of compliance filed with the commissioner. Any civil penalty assessed for a first violation shall not be less than five hundred dollars nor greater than two thousand five hundred dollars for each violation, false statement or misrepresentation found to have been made or committed, and for a second or subsequent violation, not arising out of the same incident, all of which were committed within a period of eighteen months, shall not be less than five hundred dollars nor greater than five thousand dollars for each violation, false statement or misrepresentation found to have been made or committed. If the registrant fails to pay such penalty within twenty days after the mailing of such order, postage prepaid, certified and addressed to the last known place of business of such registrant, unless such order is stayed by an order of a court of competent jurisdiction, the commissioner may revoke the for-hire vehicle registrations or out of state registration privilege of operation in the state of such motor carrier or may suspend the same for such periods as the commissioner may determine. Civil penalties assessed under this subdivision shall be paid to the commissioner for deposit into the dedicated highway and bridge trust fund established pursuant to section eighty-nine-b of the state finance law after reimbursing the department for the actual costs of public education activities undertaken by the department to implement this section, and unpaid civil penalties may be recovered by the commissioner in a civil action in the name of the commissioner.

(d) Upon the suspension of a vehicle registration pursuant to paragraph (b) or (c) of this subdivision, the commissioner shall have the authority to deny a registration or renewal application to any other person for the same for-hire vehicle and may deny a registration or renewal application for any other for-hire motor vehicle registered in the name of the applicant where the commissioner has reasonable grounds to believe that such registration or renewal will have the effect of defeating the purposes of this section. Such suspension or denial shall remain in effect only as long as the suspension entered pursuant to paragraph (b) or (c) of this subdivision remains in effect.

5. For purposes of this section, the term "motor carrier" shall mean any person, firm, corporation, association or entity which directs one or more drivers of a for-hire vehicle or vehicles, having a seating capacity of nine or more passengers, including the driver, and which operates such for-hire vehicle or vehicles in the business of transporting passengers for compensation, and the term "for-hire vehicle" shall mean a taxicab or livery having a seating capacity of nine or more passengers, including the driver, including an altered motor vehicle commonly referred to as a "stretch limousine" having a seating capacity of nine or more passengers, including the driver.

HISTORY:

L 2020, ch 2, § 1, eff Feb 3, 2021.

Article 20
Suspension and Revocation

§ 510. Suspension, revocation and reissuance of licenses and registrations. [Effective until August 1, 2020]

1. Who may suspend or revoke. Any magistrate, justice or judge, in a city, in a town, or in a village, any supreme court justice, any county judge, any judge of a district court, the superintendent of state police and the commissioner of motor vehicles or any person deputized by him, shall have power to revoke or suspend the license to drive a motor vehicle or motorcycle of any person, or in the case of an owner, the registration, as provided herein.

A learner's permit, or a license which has expired but is renewable, shall be deemed a license within the meaning of this section.

2. Mandatory revocations and suspensions.

a. Mandatory revocations. Such licenses shall be revoked and such registrations may also be revoked where the holder is convicted:

(i) of homicide or assault arising out of the operation of a motor vehicle or motorcycle or criminal negligence in the operation of a motor vehicle or motorcycle resulting in death, whether the conviction was had in this state or elsewhere;

(ii) pursuant to section twenty-three hundred eighty-five of title eighteen of the United States code, of the crime of advocating the overthrow of government, whether the conviction was had in this state or elsewhere;

(iii) of any violation of subdivision two of section six hundred or section three hundred ninety-two or of a local law or ordinance making it unlawful to leave the scene of an accident without reporting;

(iv) of a third or subsequent violation, committed within a period of eighteen months, of any provision of section eleven hundred eighty of this chapter, any ordinance or regulation limiting the speed of motor vehicles and motorcycles or any provision constituted a misdemeanor by this chapter, not included in subparagraphs (i) or (iii) of this paragraph, except violations of subdivision one of section three hundred seventy-five of this chapter or of subdivision one of section four hundred one of this chapter and similar violations under any local law, ordinance or regulation committed by an employed driver if the offense occurred while operating, in the course of his employment, a vehicle not owned by said driver, whether such three or more violations were repetitions of the same offense or were different offenses;

(v) of a violation for the conviction of which any such license is subject to revocation under subdivision two of section five hundred ten-b;

(vi) of a violation of any provision of section eleven hundred eighty-two of this chapter;

(vii) of a second violation of any provision of section eleven hundred eighty-two committed within a period of three years of a previous violation of the aforesaid section shall result in a license revocation of one year;

(viii) of a third violation, committed within a period of three years, of any provision of subdivision a of section eleven hundred seventy-four of this chapter;

(ix) of a violation of section twelve hundred twenty-four of this chapter, other than a violation adjudicated by the environmental control board of a city having a population of one million or more pursuant to subdivision seven of such section, and fails to pay the fine imposed thereon pursuant to subdivision seven of such section;

(x) of a traffic infraction for a subsequent violation of article twenty-six of this chapter and the commission of such violation caused serious physical injury to another person and such subsequent violation occurred within eighteen months of a prior violation of any provision of article twenty-six of this chapter where the commission of such prior violation caused the serious physical injury or death of another person;

(xi) of a traffic infraction for a subsequent violation of article twenty-six of this chapter and the commission of such violation caused the death of another person and such subsequent violation occurred within eighteen months of a prior violation of any provision of article twenty-six of this chapter where the commission of such prior violation caused the serious physical injury or death of another person;

(xii) of a second or subsequent conviction of a violation of section twelve hundred twenty-five-c or section twelve hundred twenty-five-d of this chapter committed where such person is the holder of a probationary license, as defined in subdivision four of section five hundred one of this title, at the time of the commission of such violation and such second or subsequent violation was committed within six months following the restoration or issuance of such probationary license; or

(xiii) of a second or subsequent conviction of a violation of section twelve hundred twenty-five-c or section twelve hundred twenty-five-d of this chapter committed where such person is the holder of a class DJ or MJ learner's permit or a class DJ or MJ license at the time of the commission of such violation and such second or subsequent violation was committed within six months following the restoration of such permit or license.

b. Mandatory suspensions. Such licenses shall be suspended, and such registrations may also be suspended:

(i) for a period of sixty days where the holder is convicted of a violation for the conviction of which such license is subject to suspension pursuant to subdivision one of section five hundred ten-b;

(ii) when the holder forfeits bail given upon being charged with any of the offenses mentioned in this subdivision, until the holder submits to the jurisdiction of the court in which he forfeited bail; and

(iii) such registrations shall be suspended when necessary to comply with subdivision nine of section one hundred forty or subdivision four of section one hundred forty-five of the transportation law or with an out of service order issued by the United States department of transportation. The commissioner shall have the authority to deny a registration or renewal application to any other person for the same vehicle and may deny a registration or renewal application for any other motor vehicle registered in the name of the applicant where it has been determined that such registrant's intent has been to evade the purposes of this subdivision and where the commissioner has reasonable grounds to believe that such registration or renewal will have the effect of defeating the purposes of this subdivision. Any suspension issued pursuant to this subdivision by reason of an out of service order issued by the United States department of transportation shall remain in effect until such time as the commissioner is notified by the United States department of transportation or the commissioner of transportation that the order resulting in the suspension is no longer in effect.

(iv) For a period of not less than thirty nor greater than one hundred eighty days where the holder is convicted of the crime of assault in the first, second or third degree as defined in article one hundred twenty of the penal law, where such offense was committed against a traffic enforcement agent employed by the city of New York or the city of Buffalo while such agent was enforcing or attempting to enforce the traffic regulations of such city.

(v) [Repealed.]

(vi) [Repealed.]

(vii) [Repealed.]

(viii) for a period of sixty days where the holder is convicted of a violation of section twelve hundred twenty-b of this chapter within a period of eighteen months of a previous violation of such section.

(ix) For a period of three months where the holder is sentenced to a license suspension pursuant to paragraph (a) of subdivision five of section sixty-five-b of the alcoholic beverage control law, provided however, that, in accordance with such subdivision five, such suspension shall be only a license suspension.

(x) For a period of six months where the holder is sentenced to a license suspension pursuant to paragraph (b) of subdivision five of section sixty-five-b of the alcoholic beverage control law, provided however, that, in accordance with such subdivision five, such suspension shall be only a license suspension.

(xi) For a period of one year or until the holder reaches the age of twenty-one, whichever is the greater period of time, where the holder is sentenced to a license suspension pursuant to paragraph (c) of subdivision five of section sixty-five-b of the alcoholic beverage control law, provided however, that, in accordance with such subdivision five, such suspension shall be only a license suspension.

(xii) for [For]* a period of one year where the holder is convicted of, or receives a youthful offender or juvenile delinquency adjudication in connection with a violation of section 240.62 or subdivision five of section 240.60 of the penal law.

(xiii) for a period of sixty days where the holder is convicted of two or more violations of paragraph two of subdivision (d) or subdivision (f) of section eleven hundred eighty of this chapter.

(xiv) for a period of forty-five days where the holder is convicted of a traffic infraction for a first violation of article twenty-six of this chapter and the commission of such violation caused serious physical injury to another person, except: (A) where the holder is convicted of a traffic infraction for a first violation of section eleven hundred forty-six of this chapter and the commission of such violation caused serious physical injury to another person, the suspension shall be for a period of six months; and (B) where the holder is convicted of a traffic infraction for a second violation of section eleven hundred forty-six of this chapter and the commission of such violation caused serious physical injury to another person, and such person has previously been convicted of a traffic infraction for a violation of section eleven hundred forty-six of this chapter and the commission of such violation caused serious physical injury to another person within five years, the suspension shall be for a period of one year.

(xv) for a period of seventy-five days where the holder is convicted of a traffic infraction for a first violation of article twenty-six of this chapter and the commission of such violation caused the death of another person.

(xvi) for a period of one hundred twenty days where the holder is convicted of a violation of section twelve hundred twenty-five-c or section twelve hundred twenty-five-d of this chapter when such violation was committed while such holder had a probationary license, as defined in subdivision four of section five hundred one of this title.

(xvii) for a period of one hundred twenty days where the holder is convicted of a violation of section twelve hundred twenty-five-c or section twelve hundred twenty-five-d of this chapter when such violation was committed while such holder had a class DJ or MJ learner's permit or a class DJ or MJ license.

c. Application of mandatory revocations and suspensions to non-residents and to unlicensed persons. Whenever a non-resident or a person who is unlicensed is convicted of any violation or receives a youthful offender or juvenile delinquency adjudication in conjunction with a violation of section 240.62 or subdivision five of section 240.60 of the penal law, which would require the revocation or suspension of a license, pursuant to the provisions of this chapter, if the person so convicted or adjudicated was the holder of a license issued by the commissioner, such non-resident's privilege of operating a motor vehicle in this state or such unlicensed person's privilege of obtaining a license issued by the commissioner shall be revoked or suspended, and such non-resident's privilege of operation within this state of any

*The bracketed word has been inserted by the Publisher.

motor vehicle owned by such person or such unlicensed person's privilege of obtaining a registration issued by the commissioner may be suspended as if such non-resident or unlicensed person was the holder of a license issued by the commissioner. The provisions of subdivisions six and seven of this section shall be applicable to any such suspension or revocation.

d. Mandatory suspensions; vehicles over eighteen thousand pounds. A license or privilege shall be suspended by the commissioner for a period of sixty days, where the holder is convicted of a violation of subdivision (g) of section eleven hundred eighty of this chapter, and (i) the recorded or entered speed upon which the conviction was based exceeded the applicable speed limit by more than twenty miles per hour or (ii) the recorded or entered speed upon which the conviction was based exceeded the applicable speed limit by more than ten miles per hour and the vehicle was either (A) in violation of any rules or regulations involving an out-of-service defect relating to brake systems, steering components and/or coupling devices, or (B) transporting flammable gas, radioactive materials or explosives. Whenever a license is suspended pursuant to this paragraph, the commissioner shall immediately issue a restricted license provided the holder of such license is otherwise eligible to receive such restricted license, except that no such restricted license shall be valid for the operation of a vehicle with a GVWR of more than eighteen thousand pounds and further provided that issuing a license to such person does not create a substantial traffic safety hazard.

2-a. Mandatory suspension and revocation of a license and registration in certain cases. (a) Within seven days after conviction for a violation of any local law which prohibits the knowing operation or offering to operate or permitting the operation for hire of any vehicle as a taxicab, livery, as defined in section one hundred twenty-one-e of this chapter, coach, limousine, van or wheelchair accessible van or tow truck within the state without first having obtained an appropriate license therefor from the appropriate licensing authority and appropriate for-hire insurance from the appropriate insurance agency, the taxi and limousine commission or other local body having jurisdiction over such offenses with respect to such vehicles shall provide notice of such conviction to the commissioner in a manner agreed upon between any such local body and the commissioner. Upon receipt of such notice, the commissioner shall suspend the license of such operator and the registration of such vehicle for a period of sixty days.

(b) Within seven days after conviction for a violation of any local law which prohibits the knowing operation or offering to operate or permitting the operation for hire of any vehicle as a taxicab, livery, as defined in section one hundred twenty-one-e of this chapter, coach, limousine, van or wheelchair accessible van or tow truck within the state without first having obtained an appropriate license therefor from the appropriate licensing authority and appropriate for-hire insurance from the appropriate insurance agency where the operator has, within the previous five years, been convicted of any such violation, the taxi and limousine commission or other local body having jurisdiction over such offenses with respect to such vehicles shall provide notice to the commissioner in a manner agreed upon between any such local body and the commissioner. Upon receipt of such notice, the commissioner shall revoke the license of such operator.

(c) Within seven days after conviction for a violation of any local law which prohibits the knowing operation or offering to operate or permitting the operation for hire of any vehicle as a taxicab, livery, as defined in section one hundred twenty-one-e of this chapter, coach, limousine, van or wheelchair accessible van or tow truck within the state without first having obtained an appropriate license therefor from the appropriate licensing authority and appropriate for-hire insurance from the appropriate insurance agency where the registrant has, within the previous five years, been convicted of any such violation, the taxi and limousine commission or other local body having jurisdiction over such offenses with respect to such vehicles shall provide notice to the commissioner in a manner agreed upon between any such local body and the commissioner. Upon receipt of such notice, the commissioner shall revoke the registration of such vehicle, and no new registration shall be issued for at least six months, nor thereafter, except in the discretion of the commissioner.

(d) The provisions of this subdivision shall not apply to any taxicab or livery as defined in section one hundred twenty-one-e of this chapter, coach, limousine, van or wheelchair accessible van or tow truck licensed or permitted for such operation by the appropriate local body of any other municipality, the department of transportation, the metropolitan transportation authority or the interstate commerce commission.

3. Permissive suspensions and revocations. Such licenses and registrations and the privilege of a non-resident of operating a motor vehicle in this state and of operation within this state of any motor vehicle owned by him and the privilege of an unlicensed person of obtaining a license issued by the commissioner and of obtaining a registration issued by the commissioner may be suspended or revoked:

a. for any violation of the provisions of this chapter, except section eleven hundred ninety-two, or for any violation of a local ordinance or regulation prohibiting dangerous driving as shall, in the discretion of the officer acting hereunder, justify such revocation or suspension;

b. because of some physical or mental disability of the holder, the court commitment of the holder to an institution under the jurisdiction of the department of mental hygiene or the disability of the holder by reason of intoxication or the use of drugs;

c. because of the conviction of the holder at any time of a felony;

d. for habitual or persistent violation of any of the provisions of this chapter, or of any lawful ordinance, rule or regulation made by local authorities in relation to traffic;

e. for gross negligence in the operation of a motor vehicle or motorcycle or operating a motor vehicle or motorcycle in a manner showing a reckless disregard for life or property of others;

f. for knowingly permitting or suffering any motor vehicle or motorcycle under the direction or control of the holder to be used in aid or furtherance of the commission of any crime;

g. for preventing lawful identification of any motor vehicle or motorcycle under the holder's direction or control, or evading lawful arrest or prosecution while operating such motor vehicle or motorcycle;

h. for wilfully evading lawful prosecution in this state or in another state or jurisdiction for an offense committed therein against the motor vehicle or traffic laws thereof;

i. for habitual or persistent violation of any provisions of this chapter, and/or any lawful ordinance, rule or regulation made by local authorities in relation to traffic, and/or violations committed in a commercial motor vehicle of any law, statute, ordinance, rule or regulation in relation to traffic made by any other state, District of Columbia, Canadian province or local authority of such state, district or province;

j. except as provided in subdivision one herein or section eleven hundred ninety-three of this chapter upon the conviction of a person under eighteen years of age of any crime or in the case of an adjudication of youthful offender under nineteen years of age, such license or registration may be suspended or revoked for a maximum period of one year by the judge or justice sentencing him;

k. for a period of up to ninety days because of the conviction of the holder of the offenses of menacing as defined in section 120.15 of the penal law, where such offense was committed against a traffic enforcement agent employed by the city of New York or the city of Buffalo while such agent was enforcing or attempting to enforce the traffic regulations of such city.

3-a. Opportunity to be heard and temporary suspensions. Where revocation or suspension is permissive, the holder, unless he shall waive such right, shall have an opportunity to be heard except where such revocation or suspension is based solely on a court conviction or convictions or on a court commitment to an institution under the jurisdiction of the department of mental hygiene. A license or registration, or the privilege of a non-resident of operating a motor vehicle in this state or of the operation within this state of any motor vehicle owned by him, may, however, be temporarily suspended without notice, pending any prosecution, investigation or hearing.

4. Administrative action pursuant to interstate compact.

a. Such licenses may be suspended where pursuant to any compact or agreement authorized by section five hundred seventeen of this chapter the holder thereof is issued a summons for a moving traffic violation, is not detained or required to furnish bail or collateral and fails to appear in response to such summons. Such suspension shall remain in effect only until such holder submits to the jurisdiction of the court in which such summons is returnable.

b. If notification is received by the commissioner pursuant to any compact or agreement authorized by section five hundred sixteen-b of this article that the holder of a New York license or an unlicensed New York resident has been convicted of an offense set forth in such compact or agreement, such conviction, for the purpose of administrative action which must or may be taken by the commissioner pursuant to the provisions of this section, shall be deemed to be a conviction of an offense committed within this state in accordance with the provisions of such compact or agreement.

4-a. Suspension for failure to answer an appearance ticket or to pay a fine.

(a) Upon receipt of a court notification of the failure of a person to appear within sixty days of the return date or new subsequent adjourned date, pursuant to an appearance ticket charging said person with a violation of any of the provisions of this chapter (except one for parking, stopping, or standing), of any violation of the tax law or of the transportation law regulating traffic or of any lawful ordinance or regulation made by a local or public authority, relating to traffic (except one for parking, stopping, or standing) or the failure to pay a fine imposed by a court the commissioner or his or her agent may suspend the driver's license or privileges of such person pending receipt of notice from the court that such person has appeared in response to such appearance ticket or has paid such fine. Such suspension shall take effect no less than thirty days from the day upon which notice thereof is sent by the commissioner to the person whose driver's license or privileges are to be suspended. Any suspension issued pursuant to this paragraph shall be subject to the provisions of paragraph (j-l) of subdivision two of section five hundred three of this chapter.

(b) The provisions of paragraph (a) of this subdivision shall not apply to a registrant who was not operating a vehicle, but who was issued a summons or an appearance ticket for a violation of section three hundred eighty-five, section four hundred one or section five hundred eleven-a of this chapter. Upon the receipt of a court notification of the failure of such person to appear within sixty days of the return date or a new subsequent adjourned date, pursuant to an appearance ticket charging said person with such violation, or the failure of such person to pay a fine imposed by a court, the commissioner or his or her agent may suspend the registration of the vehicle or vehicles involved in such violation or privilege of operation of any motor vehicle owned by the registrant pending receipt of notice from the court that such person has appeared in response to such appearance ticket or has paid such fine. Such suspension shall take effect no less than thirty days from the day upon which notice thereof is sent by the commissioner to the person whose registration or privilege is to be suspended. Any suspension issued pursuant to this paragraph shall be subject to the provisions of paragraph (j-1) of subdivision two of section five hundred three of this chapter.

(c) Upon receipt of notification from a traffic and parking violations agency or a traffic violations agency of the failure of a person to appear within sixty days of the return date or new subsequent adjourned date, pursuant to an appearance ticket charging said person with a violation of:

(i) any of the provisions of this chapter except one for parking, stopping or standing and except those violations described in paragraphs (a), (b), (d), (e) and (f) of subdivision two and in paragraphs (a), (b), (d), (e), (f) and (g) of subdivision two-a and in paragraphs (a), (b), (d), (e), (f) and (g) of subdivision two-b of section three hundred seventy-one of the general municipal law;

(ii) section five hundred two or subdivision (a) of section eighteen hundred fifteen of the tax law;

(iii) section fourteen-f (except paragraph (b) of subdivision four of section fourteen-f), two hundred eleven or two hundred twelve of the transportation law; or

(iv) any lawful ordinance or regulation made by a local or public authority relating to traffic (except one for parking, stopping or standing) or the failure to pay a fine imposed for such a violation by a traffic and parking violations agency or a traffic violations agency, the commissioner or his or her agent may suspend the driver's license or privileges of such person pending receipt of notice from the agency that such person has appeared in response to such appearance ticket or has paid such fine. Such suspension shall take effect no less than thirty days from the day upon which notice thereof is sent by the commissioner to the person whose driver's license or privileges are to be suspended. Any suspension issued pursuant to this paragraph shall be subject to the provisions of paragraph (j-1) of subdivision two of section five hundred three of this chapter.

4-b. Suspension of registration for failure to answer or to pay fines with respect to certain violations. Upon receipt of certification from a court or administrative tribunal of appropriate jurisdiction that the owner of a motor vehicle or his representative failed to appear on the return date or dates or any subsequent adjourned date or dates or failed to comply with the rules and regulations of an administrative tribunal following entry of a final decision or decisions in response to twenty-five or more summonses or other process, issued within an eighteen month period charging that such motor vehicle is parked, stopped or standing in violation of any of the provisions of this chapter or of any law, ordinance, rule or regulation made by a local authority, the commissioner shall suspend the registration of such motor vehicle. Such suspension shall take effect no less than thirty days from the date on which notice thereof is sent by the commissioner to the person whose registration is to be suspended and shall remain in effect as long as the summmons [summons]* or summonses remain unanswered, or in the case of an administrative tribunal, the registrant fails to comply with the rules and regulations following the entry of a final decision or decisions.

4-c. [Repealed Sept 1, 2021] Suspension of registration for failure to answer or to pay fines with respect to parking, stopping and standing violations. Upon receipt of certification from a court or administrative tribunal of appropriate jurisdiction in a city with a population in excess of one hundred thousand persons according to the nineteen hundred eighty United States census that the owner of a motor vehicle or his representative following compliance by such city with the notice provisions of subdivision two of section two hundred thirty-five of this chapter, failed to appear on the return date or dates or any subsequent adjourned date or dates or failed to comply with the rules and regulations of an administrative tribunal following entry of a final decision or decisions, in response to five or more summonses or other process, issued within a twelve month period charging that such motor vehicle is parked, stopped or standing in violation of any of the provisions of this chapter or of any law, ordinance, rule or regulation made by a local authority, the commissioner shall suspend the registration of such motor vehicle. Such suspension shall take effect no less than thirty days from the date on which notice thereof is sent by the commissioner to the person whose registration is to be suspended and shall remain in effect as long as the summons or summonses remain unanswered, or in the case of an administrative tribunal, the registrant fails to comply with the rules and regulations following the entry of a final decision or decisions.

4-d. Suspension of registration for failure to answer or pay penalties with respect to certain violations. Upon the receipt of a notification from a court or an administrative tribunal that an owner of a motor vehicle failed to appear on the return date or dates or a new subsequent adjourned date or dates or failed to pay any penalty imposed by a court or failed to comply with the rules and regulations of an administrative tribunal following entry of a final decision or decisions, in response to five or more notices of liability or other process, issued within an eighteen month period charging such owner with a violation of toll collection regulations in accordance with the provisions of section two thousand nine hundred eighty-five of the public authorities law or sections sixteen-a, sixteen-b and sixteen-c of chapter seven hundred seventy-four of the laws of nineteen hundred fifty, the commissioner or his agent shall suspend the registration of the vehicle or vehicles involved in the violation or the privilege of operation of any motor vehicle owned by the registrant. Such suspension shall take effect no less than thirty days from the date on which notice thereof is sent by the commissioner to the person whose registration or privilege is suspended and shall remain in effect until such registrant has appeared in response to such notices of liability or has paid such penalty or in the case of an administrative tribunal, the registrant has complied with the rules and regulations following the entry of a final decision or decisions.

*The bracketed word has been inserted by the Publisher.

4-e. [Expires and repealed August 31, 2021] Suspension and disqualification for failure to make child support payments or failure to comply with a summons, subpoena or warrant relating to a paternity or child support proceeding.

(1) The commissioner, on behalf of the department, shall enter into a written agreement with the commissioner of the office of temporary and disability assistance, on behalf of the office of temporary and disability assistance, which shall set forth the procedures for suspending the driving privileges of individuals who have failed to make payments of child support or combined child and spousal support.

(2) Such agreement shall include:

(i) the procedure under which the office of temporary and disability assistance shall notify the department of an individual's liability for support arrears;

(ii) the procedure under which the department shall be notified by the office of temporary and disability assistance that an individual has satisfied or commenced payment of his or her support arrears; or has made satisfactory payment arrangements thereon and shall have the suspension of his or her driving privileges terminated;

(iii) the procedure for reimbursement of the department and its agents by the office of temporary and disability assistance for the full additional costs of carrying out the procedures authorized by this section, and may include, subject to the approval of the director of the budget, a procedure for reimbursement of necessary additional costs of collecting social security numbers pursuant to section five hundred two of this title;

(iv) provision for the publicizing of sanctions for nonpayment of child support including the potential for the suspension of delinquent support obligors' driving privileges if they fail to pay child support or combined child and spousal support; and

(v) such other matters as the parties to such agreement shall deem necessary to carry out provisions of this section.

(3) Upon receipt of notification from the office of temporary and disability assistance of a person's failure to satisfy support arrears or to make satisfactory payment arrangements thereon pursuant to paragraph (e) of subdivision twelve of section one hundred eleven-b of the social services law or notification from a court issuing an order pursuant to section four hundred fifty-eight-a of the family court act or section two hundred forty-four-b of the domestic relations law, the commissioner or his or her agent shall suspend the license of such person to operate a motor vehicle. In the event such person is unlicensed, such person's privilege of obtaining a license shall be suspended. Such suspension shall take effect no later than fifteen days from the date of the notice thereof to the person whose license or privilege of obtaining a license is to be suspended, and shall remain in effect until such time as the commissioner is advised that the person has satisfied the support arrears or has made satisfactory payment arrangements thereon pursuant to paragraph (e) of subdivision twelve of section one hundred eleven-b of the social services law or until such time as the court issues an order to terminate such suspension;

(4) From the time the commissioner is notified by the office of temporary and disability assistance of a person's liability for support arrears under this section, the commissioner shall be relieved from all liability to such person which may otherwise arise under this section, and such person shall have no right to commence a court action or proceeding or to any other legal recourse against the commissioner to recover such driving privileges as authorized by this section. In addition, notwithstanding any other provision of law, such person shall have no right to a hearing or appeal pursuant to this chapter with respect to a suspension of driving privileges as authorized by this section. However, nothing herein shall be construed to prohibit such person from proceeding against the support collection unit pursuant to article seventy-eight of the civil practice law and rules.

(5) Any person whose license has been suspended pursuant to subdivision three of this section may apply for the issuance of a restricted use license as provided in section five hundred thirty of this title.

4-f. Suspension for failure to pay past-due tax liabilities.

(1) The commissioner shall enter into a written agreement with the commissioner of taxation and finance, as provided in section one hundred seventy-one-v of the tax law, which shall set forth the procedures for suspending the drivers' licenses of individuals who have failed to satisfy past-due tax liabilities as such terms are defined in such section.

(2) Upon receipt of notification from the department of taxation and finance that an individual has failed to satisfy past-due tax liabilities, or to otherwise make payment arrangements satisfactory to the commissioner of taxation and finance, or has failed to comply with the terms of such payment arrangements more than once within a twelve month period, the commissioner or his or her agent shall suspend the license of such person to operate a motor vehicle. In the event such person is unlicensed, such person's privilege of obtaining a license shall be suspended. Such suspension shall take effect no later than fifteen days from the date of the notice thereof provided to the person whose license or privilege of obtaining a license is to be suspended, and shall remain in effect until such time as the commissioner is advised that the person has satisfied his or her past-due tax liabilities, or has otherwise made payment arrangements satisfactory to the commissioner of taxation and finance.

(3) From the time the commissioner is notified by the department of taxation and finance under this section, the commissioner shall be relieved from all liability to such person which may otherwise arise under this section, and such person shall have no right to commence a court action or proceeding or to any other legal recourse against the commissioner to recover such driving privileges as authorized by this section. In addition, notwithstanding any other provision of law, such person shall have no right to a hearing or appeal pursuant to this chapter with respect to a suspension of driving privileges as authorized by this section.

(4) Notwithstanding any provision of law to the contrary, the department shall furnish the department of taxation and finance with the information necessary for the proper identification of an individual referred to the department for the purpose of driver's license suspension pursuant to this section and section one hundred seventy-one-v of the tax law. This shall include the individual's name, social security number and any other information the commissioner of motor vehicles deems necessary.

(5) Any person whose driver's license is suspended pursuant to paragraph two of this subdivision may apply for the issuance of a restricted use license as provided in section five hundred thirty of this title.

5. Restoration. A license or registration may be restored by direction of the commissioner but not otherwise. Reversal on appeal, of any conviction because of which any license or registration has been revoked or suspended, shall entitle the holder to restoration thereof forthwith. The privileges of a non-resident may be restored by direction of the commissioner in his discretion but not otherwise.

6. Restrictions.

a. Where revocation is mandatory hereunder, no new license shall be issued for at least six months or, in certain cases a longer period as specified in this chapter, nor thereafter, except in the discretion of the commissioner of motor vehicles.

b. Except as otherwise provided in paragraph c of this subdivision, where revocation is mandatory pursuant to subparagraph (iii) of paragraph a of subdivision two of this section, no new commercial driver's license shall be issued for at least one year nor thereafter except in the discretion of the commissioner, except that if such person has previously been found to have refused a chemical test pursuant to section eleven hundred ninety-four of this chapter or has a prior conviction of any of the following offenses: any violation of section eleven hundred ninety-two of this chapter; any violation of subdivision one or two of section six hundred of this chapter; or has a prior conviction of any felony involving the use of a motor vehicle pursuant to paragraph (a) of subdivision one of section five hundred ten-a of this article, then such commercial driver's license revocation shall be permanent.

c. Where revocation is mandatory pursuant to subdivision one of section five hundred ten-a of this chapter or subparagraph (iii) of paragraph a of subdivision two of this section and the violation of subdivision two of section six hundred of this chapter was committed while operating a commercial motor vehicle transporting hazardous materials, no new commercial driver's license shall be issued for at least three years nor thereafter except in the discretion of the commissioner, except that if such person has previously been found to have refused a chemical test pursuant to section eleven hundred ninety-four of this chapter or has a prior conviction of any of the following offenses: any violation of section eleven hundred ninety-two of this chapter; any violation of subdivision one or two of section six hundred of this chapter;

or has a prior conviction of any felony involving the use of a motor vehicle pursuant to paragraph (a) of subdivision one of section five hundred ten-a of this article, then such commercial driver's license revocation shall be permanent.

d. The permanent commercial driver's license revocation required by paragraphs b and c of this subdivision may be waived by the commissioner after a period of ten years has expired from such sentence provided:

(i) that during such ten year period such person has not been found to have refused a chemical test pursuant to section eleven hundred ninety-four of this chapter and has not been convicted of any one of the following offenses: any violation of section eleven hundred ninety-two of this chapter; any violation of subdivision one or two of section six hundred of this chapter; or has a prior conviction of any felony involving the use of a motor vehicle pursuant to paragraph (a) of subdivision one of section five hundred ten-a of this article;

(ii) if any of the grounds upon which the permanent commercial driver's license revocation is based involved a finding of refusal to submit to a chemical test pursuant to section eleven hundred ninety-four of this chapter or a conviction of a violation of any subdivision of section eleven hundred ninety-two of this chapter, that such person provides acceptable documentation to the commissioner that such person has voluntarily enrolled in and successfully completed an appropriate rehabilitation program; and

(iii) after such documentation, if required, is accepted, that such person is granted a certificate of relief from disabilities or a certificate of good conduct pursuant to article twenty-three of the correction law by the court in which such person was last penalized.

e. Upon a third finding of refusal and/or conviction of any of the offenses which require a permanent commercial driver's license revocation, such permanent revocation may not be waived by the commissioner under any circumstances.

f. Where revocation is mandatory hereunder, based upon a conviction had outside this state, no new license shall be issued until after sixty days from the date of such revocation, nor thereafter, except in the discretion of the commissioner.

g. Except as provided in paragraph k of this subdivision, where revocation is permissive, no new license or certificate shall be issued by such commissioner to any person until after thirty days from the date of such revocation, nor thereafter, except in the discretion of the commissioner after an investigation or upon a hearing, provided, however, that where the revocation is based upon a failure in a reexamination pursuant to section five hundred six of this chapter, a learner's permit may be issued immediately and provided further, that where revocation is based upon a conviction of a felony, other than a felony relating to the operation of a motor vehicle or motorcycle, a license shall be issued immediately, if the applicant is otherwise qualified and if the application for such license is accompanied by consent in writing issued by the parole or probation authority having jurisdiction over such applicant.

h. The provisions of this subdivision shall not apply to revocations issued pursuant to sections eleven hundred ninety-three and eleven hundred ninety-four of this chapter.

i. [Repealed]

j. [Repealed]

k. Where revocation is permissive hereunder, based upon a finding of a violation of section three hundred ninety-two or section three hundred ninety-two-a of this chapter, no new license or certificate shall be issued until after one year from the date of such revocation, nor thereafter, except in the discretion of the commissioner.

l. Where revocation is mandatory pursuant to subparagraph (x) of paragraph a of subdivision two of this section, no new license shall be issued for at least seventy-five days, nor thereafter except in the discretion of the commissioner.

m. Where revocation is mandatory pursuant to subparagraph (xi) of paragraph a of subdivision two of this section, no new license shall be issued for at least one hundred twenty days, nor thereafter except in the discretion of the commissioner.

n. Notwithstanding the provisions of paragraph a of this subdivision, subdivision two of section five hundred ten-b of this article or paragraph (b) of subdivision one of section five hundred ten-c of this article, where revocation is mandatory pursuant to subparagraph (xii) or subparagraph (xiii) of paragraph a of subdivision two of this section, no new license shall be issued for at least one year, nor thereafter except in the discretion of the commissioner.

o. Notwithstanding the provisions of paragraph a of this subdivision, where revocation is mandatory pursuant to subparagraph (iii) of paragraph a of subdivision two of this section involving a violation of section three hundred ninety-two of this chapter in relation to an application for the commercial driver's license or the commercial learner's permit being revoked, no new commercial driver's license or commercial learner's permit shall be issued for at least one year, nor thereafter except in the discretion of the commissioner.

7. Miscellaneous provisions. Except as expressly provided, a court conviction shall not be necessary to sustain a revocation or suspension. Revocation or suspension hereunder shall be deemed an administrative act reviewable by the supreme court as such. Notice of revocation or suspension, as well as any required notice of hearing, where the holder is not present, may be given by mailing the same in writing to him or her at the address contained in his or her license, certificate of registration or at the current address provided by the United States postal service, as the case may be. Proof of such mailing by certified mail to the holder shall be presumptive evidence of the holder's receipt and actual knowledge of such notice. Attendance of witnesses may be compelled by subpoena. Failure of the holder or any other person possessing the license card or number plates, to deliver the same to the suspending or revoking officer is a misdemeanor. Suspending or revoking officers shall place such license cards and number plates in the custody of the commissioner except where the commissioner shall otherwise direct. If any person shall fail to deliver a license card or number plates as provided herein, any police officer, bridge and tunnel officer of the Triborough bridge and tunnel authority, or agent of the commissioner having knowledge of such facts shall have the power to secure possession thereof and return the same to the commissioner, and the commissioner may forthwith direct any police officer, bridge and tunnel officer of the Triborough bridge and tunnel authority, acting pursuant to his or her special duties, or agent of the commissioner to secure possession thereof and to return the same to the commissioner. Failure of the holder or of any person possessing the license card or number plates to deliver to any police officer, bridge and tunnel officer of the Triborough bridge and tunnel authority, or agent of the commissioner who requests the same pursuant to this subdivision shall be a misdemeanor. Notice of revocation or suspension of any license or registration shall be transmitted forthwith by the commissioner to the chief of police of the city or prosecuting officer of the locality in which the person whose license or registration so revoked or suspended resides. In case any license or registration shall expire before the end of any period for which it has been revoked or suspended, and before it shall have been restored as provided in this chapter, then and in that event any renewal thereof may be withheld until the end of such period of suspension or until restoration, as the case may be.

The revocation of a learner's permit shall automatically cancel the application for a license of the holder of such permit.

No suspension or revocation of a license or registration shall be made because of a judgment of conviction if the suspending or revoking officer is satisfied that the magistrate who pronounced the judgment failed to comply with subdivision one of section eighteen hundred seven of this chapter. In case a suspension or revocation has been made and the commissioner is satisfied that there was such failure, the commissioner shall restore the license or registration or both as the case may be.

8. Cancellation. Upon receipt of a license which has been surrendered to the licensing authority of any other jurisdiction as a prerequisite to the issuance of a license by such other jurisdiction in accordance with the provisions of the Driver License Compact or any other laws of such jurisdiction, the commissioner shall cancel such license. Provided, however, that such license shall not be cancelled if the licensee is a resident of this state.

9. Railroad vehicle violations. Upon certification by the commissioner of transportation that there has been a violation of section seventy-six-b of the railroad law, the commissioner of motor vehicles may rescind, cancel or suspend the registration of any motor vehicle described in subdivision one of section seventy-six-b of the railroad law and may rescind, cancel, suspend or take possession of the current registration certificate and number plates of any such motor vehicle.

10. Where a youth is determined to be a youthful offender, following a conviction of a violation for which a license suspension or revocation is mandatory or where a youth receives a juvenile delinquency adjudication in conjunction with a violation of section 240.62 or subdivision five of section 240.60 of the penal law, the court shall impose such suspension or revocation as is otherwise required upon conviction and, further, shall notify the commissioner of said suspension or revocation and its finding that said violator is granted youthful offender status as is required pursuant to section five hundred thirteen of this chapter or received a juvenile delinquency adjudication.

11. Notwithstanding any contrary provision of law, the division of criminal justice services is authorized to share with the commissioner such criminal history information in its possession as may be necessary to effect the provisions of this chapter.

HISTORY:

Add, L 1959, ch 775, with substance transferred from former § 71; amd, L 1960, ch 184, §§ 3–5; L 1961 ch 962, § 1; L 1962, ch 779, § 1; L 1963, ch 869, § 3; L 1964, ch 447, § 1; L 1964, ch 905, § 1; L 1965, ch 651, § 2; L 1966, ch 86 § 1; L 1966, ch 759, § 1; L 1966, ch 963, § 2; L 1967, ch 79, § 1, eff Oct 1, 1967; L 1968, ch 36, § 1; L 1969, ch 445, § 3, eff Jan 1, 1970; L 1970, ch 275, § 1; L 1971, ch 1106, § 1; L 1972, ch 99, § 3; L 1972, ch 243, § 2; L 1973, ch 156, § 1; L 1973, ch 168, § 5; L 1973, ch 541, § 2; L 1974, ch 129, § 1; L 1974, ch 772, § 1; L 1975, ch 143, § 3; L 1976, ch 282, § 1; L 1976, ch 404, §§ 1, 2; L 1976, ch 670, § 2; L 1977, ch 163, § 1; L 1979, ch 195, § 1, eff June 4, 1979; L 1979, ch 594, § 2; L 1980, ch 381, § 2; L 1980, ch 722, § 2, eff June 30, 1980; L 1980, ch 806, §§ 2, 3; L 1980, ch 807, § 1; L 1980, ch 843, § 98; L 1981, ch 428, § 1; L 1981, ch 477, § 1; L 1981, ch 912, § 1; L 1982, ch 861, § 1; L 1982, ch 888, §§ 1, 2; L 1983, ch 802, § 1; L 1983, ch 890, § 2; L 1983, ch 892, §§ 1–3; L 1984, ch 192, § 1; L 1984, ch 977, §§ 1, 2; L 1984, ch 978, § 2, eff Nov 1, 1984; L 1985, ch 707, § 1; L 1985, ch 718, § 1; L 1986, ch 132, §§ 5–11, eff June 2, 1986; L 1986, ch 411, § 20; L 1986, ch 492, §§ 1, 2; L 1986, ch 649, § 4; L 1986, ch 731, § 1, eff July 30, 1986; L 1987, ch 188, § 1; L 1987, ch 338, § 3, eff Jan 1, 1988; L 1987, ch 594, §§ 2, 3; L 1987, ch 687, §§ 1, 2; L 1988, ch 47, §§ 5–9, eff Nov 1, 1988; L 1988, ch 183, §§ 1–5, eff Nov 1, 1988; L 1988, ch 197, § 3, eff Nov 1, 1988; L 1988, ch 254, § 2; L 1989, ch 625, § 1, eff Nov 1, 1989; L 1989, ch 703, § 1, eff Sept 22, 1989; L 1989, ch 779, §§ 3, 4, eff July 1, 1990; L 1990, ch 173, §§ 23, 51–a, eff Aug 19, 1990; L 1990, ch 173, §§ 52, 53, eff Feb 19, 1991; L 1990, ch 173, § 54, eff April 1, 1991; L 1990, ch 496, § 6, eff July 18, 1990; L 1991, ch 166, § 373, eff June 12, 1991; L 1992, ch 124, §§ 1, 2, eff Nov 1, 1992; L 1992, ch 379, § 15, eff July 17, 1992; L 1992, ch 605, § 2, eff Nov 21, 1992; L 1993, ch 349, § 3, eff July 21, 1993; L 1993, ch 533, §§ 1–3, eff Sept 30, 1993; L 1993, ch 606, § 1, eff Nov 1, 1993; L 1994, ch 307, §§ 5, 6, eff Sept 18, 1994; L 1994, ch 313, § 2, eff Nov 1, 1994; L, 1994, ch 429, § 2, eff July 20, 1994; L 1995, ch 3, § 72, eff June 10, 1995 and deemed eff on and after April 1, 1995; L 1995, ch 81, § 211, eff July 1, 1995; L 1997, ch 398, § 133, eff Jan 1, 1998; L 1997, ch 505, § 1, eff Oct 3, 1997; L 1998, ch 383, § 9, eff April 1, 1999; L 1998, ch 652, § 1, eff April 1, 1999; L 1999, ch 412, § 5 (Part J), eff Aug 9, 1999, deemed eff on and after April 1, 1999; L 1999, ch 561, §§ 6–8, eff Dec 1, 1999; L 2003, ch 62, § 10 (Part J), eff Sept 12, 2003; L 2005, ch 60, § 12 (Part E), eff Sept 30, 2005; L 2005, ch 223, § 2, eff Nov 1, 2005; L 2006, ch 571, §§ 1–4, eff Nov 1, 2006; L 2007, ch 601, § 23, eff Aug 15, 2007; L 2010, ch 56, § 29 (Part LL), eff June 22, 2010; L 2010, ch 59, § 5 (Part K), eff June 22, 2010; L 2010, ch 409, § 2, eff Aug 13, 2010; L 2013, ch 59, § 2 (Part P), eff March 28, 2013; L 2014, ch 55, §§ 1–3 (Part B), eff Nov 1, 2014; L 2015, ch 58, § 4 (Part I), eff July 8, 2015; L 2015, ch 58, § 11 (Part CC), eff July 1, 2015; L 2017, ch 157, § 12, eff April 21, 2018; L 2018, ch 58, § 1 (Part A), eff April 12, 2018; L 2019, ch 55, §§ 1, 2 (Part II, Subpart J), eff April 12, 2019.

§ 510. Suspension, revocation and reissuance of licenses and registrations. [Effective August 1, 2020]

1. Who may suspend or revoke. Any magistrate, justice or judge, in a city, in a town, or in a village, any supreme court justice, any county judge, any judge of a district court, the superintendent of state police and the commissioner of motor vehicles or any person deputized by him, shall have power to revoke or suspend the license to drive a motor vehicle or motorcycle of any person, or in the case of an owner, the registration, as provided herein.

A learner's permit, or a license which has expired but is renewable, shall be deemed a license within the meaning of this section.

2. Mandatory revocations and suspensions.

a. Mandatory revocations. Such licenses shall be revoked and such registrations may also be revoked where the holder is convicted:

(i) of homicide or assault arising out of the operation of a motor vehicle or motorcycle or criminal negligence in the operation of a motor vehicle or motorcycle resulting in death, whether the conviction was had in this state or elsewhere;

(ii) pursuant to section twenty-three hundred eighty-five of title eighteen of the United States code, of the crime of advocating the overthrow of government, whether the conviction was had in this state or elsewhere;

(iii) of any violation of subdivision two of section six hundred or section three hundred ninety-two or of a local law or ordinance making it unlawful to leave the scene of an accident without reporting;

(iv) of a third or subsequent violation, committed within a period of eighteen months, of any provision of section eleven hundred eighty of this chapter, any ordinance or regulation limiting the speed of motor vehicles and motorcycles or any provision constituted a misdemeanor by this chapter, not included in subparagraphs (i) or (iii) of this paragraph, except violations of subdivision one of section three hundred seventy-five of this chapter or of subdivision one of section four hundred one of this chapter and similar violations under any local law, ordinance or regulation committed by an employed driver if the offense occurred while operating, in the course of his employment, a vehicle not owned by said driver, whether such three or more violations were repetitions of the same offense or were different offenses;

(v) of a violation for the conviction of which any such license is subject to revocation under subdivision two of section five hundred ten-b;

(vi) of a violation of any provision of section eleven hundred eighty-two of this chapter;

(vii) of a second violation of any provision of section eleven hundred eighty-two committed within a period of three years of a previous violation of the aforesaid section shall result in a license revocation of one year;

(viii) of a third violation, committed within a period of three years, of any provision of subdivision a of section eleven hundred seventy-four of this chapter;

(ix) of a violation of section twelve hundred twenty-four of this chapter, other than a violation adjudicated by the environmental control board of a city having a population of one million or more pursuant to subdivision seven of such section, and fails to pay the fine imposed thereon pursuant to subdivision seven of such section;

(x) of a traffic infraction for a subsequent violation of article twenty-six of this chapter and the commission of such violation caused serious physical injury to another person and such subsequent violation occurred within eighteen months of a prior violation of any provision of article twenty-six of this chapter where the commission of such prior violation caused the serious physical injury or death of another person;

(xi) of a traffic infraction for a subsequent violation of article twenty-six of this chapter and the commission of such violation caused the death of another person and such subsequent violation occurred within eighteen months of a prior violation of any provision of article twenty-six of this chapter where the commission of such prior violation caused the serious physical injury or death of another person;

(xii) of a second or subsequent conviction of a violation of section twelve hundred twenty-five-c or section twelve hundred twenty-five-d of this chapter committed where such person is the holder of a probationary license, as defined in subdivision four of section five hundred one of this title, at the time of the commission of such violation and such second or subsequent violation was committed within six months following the restoration or issuance of such probationary license; or

(xiii) of a second or subsequent conviction of a violation of section twelve hundred twenty-five-c or section twelve hundred twenty-five-d of this chapter committed where such person is the holder of a class DJ or MJ learner's permit or a class DJ or MJ license at the time of the commission of such violation and such second or subsequent violation was committed within six months following the restoration of such permit or license.

b. Mandatory suspensions. Such licenses shall be suspended, and such registrations may also be suspended:

(i) for a period of sixty days where the holder is convicted of a violation for the conviction of which such license is subject to suspension pursuant to subdivision one of section five hundred ten-b;

(ii) when the holder forfeits bail given upon being charged with any of the offenses mentioned in this subdivision, until the holder submits to the jurisdiction of the court in which he forfeited bail; and

(iii) such registrations shall be suspended when necessary to comply with subdivision nine of section one hundred forty or subdivision four of section one hundred forty-five of the transportation law or with an out of service order issued by the United States department of transportation. The commissioner shall have the authority to deny a registration or renewal application to any other person for the same vehicle and may deny a registration or renewal application for any other motor vehicle registered in the name of the applicant where it has been determined that such registrant's intent has been to evade the purposes of this subdivision and where the commissioner has reasonable grounds to believe that such registration or renewal will have the effect of defeating the purposes of this subdivision. Any suspension issued pursuant to this subdivision by reason of an out of service order issued by the United States department of transportation shall remain in effect until such time as the commissioner is notified by the United States department of transportation or the commissioner of transportation that the order resulting in the suspension is no longer in effect.

(iv) For a period of not less than thirty nor greater than one hundred eighty days where the holder is convicted of the crime of assault in the first, second or third degree as defined in article one hundred twenty of the penal law, where such offense was committed against a traffic enforcement agent employed by the city of New York or the city of Buffalo while such agent was enforcing or attempting to enforce the traffic regulations of such city.

(v) [Repealed.]

(vi) for a period of sixty days where the holder is convicted of a violation of subdivision one of section twelve hundred twenty-b of this chapter within a period of eighteen months of a previous violation of such subdivision.

(vii) for a period of ninety days where the holder is convicted of a violation of subdivision one of section twelve hundred twenty-b of this chapter within a period of eighteen months of two or more previous violations of such subdivision.

(ix) For a period of three months where the holder is sentenced to a license suspension pursuant to paragraph (a) of subdivision five of section sixty-five-b of the alcoholic beverage control law, provided however, that, in accordance with such subdivision five, such suspension shall be only a license suspension.

(x) For a period of six months where the holder is sentenced to a license suspension pursuant to paragraph (b) of subdivision five of section sixty-five-b of the alcoholic beverage control law, provided however, that, in accordance with such subdivision five, such suspension shall be only a license suspension.

(xi) For a period of one year or until the holder reaches the age of twenty-one, whichever is the greater period of time, where the holder is sentenced to a license suspension pursuant to paragraph (c) of subdivision five of section sixty-five-b of the alcoholic beverage control law, provided however, that, in accordance with such subdivision five, such suspension shall be only a license suspension.

(xii) for [For]* a period of one year where the holder is convicted of, or receives a youthful offender or juvenile delinquency adjudication in connection with a violation of section 240.62 or subdivision five of section 240.60 of the penal law.

(xiii) for a period of sixty days where the holder is convicted of two or more violations of paragraph two of subdivision (d) or subdivision (f) of section eleven hundred eighty of this chapter.

(xiv) for a period of forty-five days where the holder is convicted of a traffic infraction for a first violation of article twenty-six of this chapter and the commission of such violation caused serious physical injury to another person, except: (A) where the holder is convicted of a traffic infraction for a first violation of section eleven hundred forty-six of this chapter and the commission of such violation caused serious physical injury to another person, the suspension shall be for a period of six months; and (B) where the holder is convicted of a traffic infraction for a second violation of section eleven hundred forty-six of this chapter and the commission of such violation caused serious physical injury to another person, and such person has previously been convicted of a traffic infraction for a violation of section eleven hundred forty-six of this chapter and the commission of such violation caused serious physical injury to another person within five years, the suspension shall be for a period of one year.

*The bracketed word has been inserted by the Publisher.

(xv) for a period of seventy-five days where the holder is convicted of a traffic infraction for a first violation of article twenty-six of this chapter and the commission of such violation caused the death of another person.

(xvi) for a period of one hundred twenty days where the holder is convicted of a violation of section twelve hundred twenty-five-c or section twelve hundred twenty-five-d of this chapter when such violation was committed while such holder had a probationary license, as defined in subdivision four of section five hundred one of this title.

(xvii) for a period of one hundred twenty days where the holder is convicted of a violation of section twelve hundred twenty-five-c or section twelve hundred twenty-five-d of this chapter when such violation was committed while such holder had a class DJ or MJ learner's permit or a class DJ or MJ license.

c. Application of mandatory revocations and suspensions to non-residents and to unlicensed persons. Whenever a non-resident or a person who is unlicensed is convicted of any violation or receives a youthful offender or juvenile delinquency adjudication in conjunction with a violation of section 240.62 or subdivision five of section 240.60 of the penal law, which would require the revocation or suspension of a license, pursuant to the provisions of this chapter, if the person so convicted or adjudicated was the holder of a license issued by the commissioner, such non-resident's privilege of operating a motor vehicle in this state or such unlicensed person's privilege of obtaining a license issued by the commissioner shall be revoked or suspended, and such non-resident's privilege of operation within this state of any motor vehicle owned by such person or such unlicensed person's privilege of obtaining a registration issued by the commissioner may be suspended as if such non-resident or unlicensed person was the holder of a license issued by the commissioner. The provisions of subdivisions six and seven of this section shall be applicable to any such suspension or revocation.

d. Mandatory suspensions; vehicles over eighteen thousand pounds. A license or privilege shall be suspended by the commissioner for a period of sixty days, where the holder is convicted of a violation of subdivision (g) of section eleven hundred eighty of this chapter, and (i) the recorded or entered speed upon which the conviction was based exceeded the applicable speed limit by more than twenty miles per hour or (ii) the recorded or entered speed upon which the conviction was based exceeded the applicable speed limit by more than ten miles per hour and the vehicle was either (A) in violation of any rules or regulations involving an out-of-service defect relating to brake systems, steering components and/or coupling devices, or (B) transporting flammable gas, radioactive materials or explosives. Whenever a license is suspended pursuant to this paragraph, the commissioner shall immediately issue a restricted license provided the holder of such license is otherwise eligible to receive such restricted license, except that no such restricted license shall be valid for the operation of a vehicle with a CVWR of more than eighteen thousand pounds and further provided that issuing a license to such person does not create a substantial traffic safety hazard.

2-a. Mandatory suspension and revocation of a license and registration in certain cases. (a) Within seven days after conviction for a violation of any local law which prohibits the knowing operation or offering to operate or permitting the operation for hire of any vehicle as a taxicab, livery, as defined in section one hundred twenty-one-e of this chapter, coach, limousine, van or wheelchair accessible van or tow truck within the state without first having obtained an appropriate license therefor from the appropriate licensing authority and appropriate for-hire insurance from the appropriate insurance agency, the taxi and limousine commission or other local body having jurisdiction over such offenses with respect to such vehicles shall provide notice of such conviction to the commissioner in a manner agreed upon between any such local body and the commissioner. Upon receipt of such notice, the commissioner shall suspend the license of such operator and the registration of such vehicle for a period of sixty days.

(b) Within seven days after conviction for a violation of any local law which prohibits the knowing operation or offering to operate or permitting the operation for hire of any vehicle as a taxicab, livery, as defined in section one hundred twenty-one-e of this chapter, coach, limousine, van or wheelchair accessible van or tow truck within the state without first having obtained an appropriate license therefor from the appropriate licensing authority and appropriate for-hire insurance from the appropriate insurance agency where the operator has, within the previous five years, been convicted of any such violation, the taxi and limousine commission or other local body having jurisdiction over such offenses with respect to such vehicles shall provide notice to the commissioner in a manner agreed upon between any such local body and the commissioner. Upon receipt of such notice, the commissioner shall revoke the license of such operator.

(c) Within seven days after conviction for a violation of any local law which prohibits the knowing operation or offering to operate or permitting the operation for hire of any vehicle as a taxicab, livery, as defined in section one hundred twenty-one-e of this chapter, coach, limousine, van or wheelchair accessible van or tow truck within the state without first having obtained an appropriate license therefor from the appropriate licensing authority and appropriate for-hire insurance from the appropriate insurance agency where the registrant has, within the previous five years, been convicted of any such violation, the taxi and limousine commission or other local body having jurisdiction over such offenses with respect to such vehicles shall provide notice to the commissioner in a manner agreed upon between any such local body and the commissioner. Upon receipt of such notice, the commissioner shall revoke the registration of such vehicle, and no new registration shall be issued for at least six months, nor thereafter, except in the discretion of the commissioner.

(d) The provisions of this subdivision shall not apply to any taxicab or livery as defined in section one hundred twenty-one-e of this chapter, coach, limousine, van or wheelchair accessible van or tow truck licensed or permitted for such operation by the appropriate local body of any other municipality, the department of transportation, the metropolitan transportation authority or the interstate commerce commission.

3. Permissive suspensions and revocations. Such licenses and registrations and the privilege of a non-resident of operating a motor vehicle in this state and of operation within this state of any motor vehicle owned by him and the privilege of an unlicensed person of obtaining a license issued by the commissioner and of obtaining a registration issued by the commissioner may be suspended or revoked:

a. for any violation of the provisions of this chapter, except section eleven hundred ninety-two, or for any violation of a local ordinance or regulation prohibiting dangerous driving as shall, in the discretion of the officer acting hereunder, justify such revocation or suspension;

b. because of some physical or mental disability of the holder, the court commitment of the holder to an institution under the jurisdiction of the department of mental hygiene or the disability of the holder by reason of intoxication or the use of drugs;

c. because of the conviction of the holder at any time of a felony;

d. for habitual or persistent violation of any of the provisions of this chapter, or of any lawful ordinance, rule or regulation made by local authorities in relation to traffic;

e. for gross negligence in the operation of a motor vehicle or motorcycle or operating a motor vehicle or motorcycle in a manner showing a reckless disregard for life or property of others;

f. for knowingly permitting or suffering any motor vehicle or motorcycle under the direction or control of the holder to be used in aid or furtherance of the commission of any crime;

g. for preventing lawful identification of any motor vehicle or motorcycle under the holder's direction or control, or evading lawful arrest or prosecution while operating such motor vehicle or motorcycle;

h. for wilfully evading lawful prosecution in this state or in another state or jurisdiction for an offense committed therein against the motor vehicle or traffic laws thereof;

i. for habitual or persistent violation of any provisions of this chapter, and/or any lawful ordinance, rule or regulation made by local authorities in relation to traffic, and/or violations committed in a commercial motor vehicle of any law, statute, ordinance, rule or regulation in relation to traffic made by any other state, District of Columbia, Canadian province or local authority of such state, district or province;

j. except as provided in subdivision one herein or section eleven hundred ninety-three of this chapter upon the conviction of a person under eighteen years of age of any crime or in the case of an adjudication of youthful offender under nineteen years of age, such license or registration may be suspended or revoked for a maximum period of one year by the judge or justice sentencing him;

k. for a period of up to ninety days because of the conviction of the holder of the offenses of menacing as defined in section 120.15 of the penal law, where such offense was committed against a traffic enforcement agent employed by the city of New York or the city of Buffalo while such agent was enforcing or attempting to enforce the traffic regulations of such city.

3-a. Opportunity to be heard and temporary suspensions. Where revocation or suspension is permissive, the holder, unless he shall waive such right, shall have an opportunity to be heard except where such revocation or suspension is based solely on a court conviction or convictions or on a court commitment to an institution under the jurisdiction of the department of mental hygiene. A license or registration, or the privilege of a non-resident of operating a motor vehicle in this state or of the operation within this state of any motor vehicle owned by him, may, however, be temporarily suspended without notice, pending any prosecution, investigation or hearing.

4. Administrative action pursuant to interstate compact.

a. Such licenses may be suspended where pursuant to any compact or agreement authorized by section five hundred seventeen of this chapter the holder thereof is issued a summons for a moving traffic violation, is not detained or required to furnish bail or collateral and fails to appear in response to such summons. Such suspension shall remain in effect only until such holder submits to the jurisdiction of the court in which such summons is returnable.

b. If notification is received by the commissioner pursuant to any compact or agreement authorized by section five hundred sixteen-b of this article that the holder of a New York license or an unlicensed New York resident has been convicted of an offense set forth in such compact or agreement, such conviction, for the purpose of administrative action which must or may be taken by the commissioner pursuant to the provisions of this section, shall be deemed to be a conviction of an offense committed within this state in accordance with the provisions of such compact or agreement.

4-a. Suspension for failure to answer an appearance ticket or to pay a fine.

(a) Upon receipt of a court notification of the failure of a person to appear within sixty days of the return date or new subsequent adjourned date, pursuant to an appearance ticket charging said person with a violation of any of the provisions of this chapter (except one for parking, stopping, or standing), of any violation of the tax law or of the transportation law regulating traffic or of any lawful ordinance or regulation made by a local or public authority, relating to traffic (except one for parking, stopping, or standing) or the failure to pay a fine imposed by a court the commissioner or his or her agent may suspend the driver's license or privileges of such person pending receipt of notice from the court that such person has appeared in response to such appearance ticket or has paid such fine. Such suspension shall take effect no less than thirty days from the day upon which notice thereof is sent by the commissioner to the person whose driver's license or privileges are to be suspended. Any suspension issued pursuant to this paragraph shall be subject to the provisions of paragraph (j-l) of subdivision two of section five hundred three of this chapter.

(b) The provisions of paragraph (a) of this subdivision shall not apply to a registrant who was not operating a vehicle, but who was issued a summons or an appearance ticket for a violation of section three hundred eighty-five, section four hundred one or section five hundred eleven-a of this chapter. Upon the receipt of a court notification of the failure of such person to appear within sixty days of the return date or a new subsequent adjourned date, pursuant to an appearance ticket charging said person with such violation, or the failure of such person to pay a fine imposed by a court, the commissioner or his or her agent may suspend the registration of the vehicle or vehicles involved in such violation or privilege of operation of any motor vehicle owned by the registrant pending receipt of notice from the court that such person has appeared in response to such appearance ticket or has paid such fine. Such suspension shall take effect no less than thirty days from the day upon which notice thereof is sent by the commissioner to the person whose registration or privilege is to be suspended. Any suspension issued pursuant to this paragraph shall be subject to the provisions of paragraph (j-1) of subdivision two of section five hundred three of this chapter.

(c) Upon receipt of notification from a traffic and parking violations agency or a traffic violations agency of the failure of a person to appear within sixty days of the return date or new subsequent adjourned date, pursuant to an appearance ticket charging said person with a violation of:

(i) any of the provisions of this chapter except one for parking, stopping or standing and except those violations described in paragraphs (a), (b), (d), (e) and (f) of subdivision two and in paragraphs (a), (b), (d), (e), (f) and (g) of subdivision two-a and in paragraphs (a), (b), (d), (e), (f) and (g) of subdivision two-b of section three hundred seventy-one of the general municipal law;

(ii) section five hundred two or subdivision (a) of section eighteen hundred fifteen of the tax law;

(iii) section fourteen-f (except paragraph (b) of subdivision four of section fourteen-f), two hundred eleven or two hundred twelve of the transportation law; or

(iv) any lawful ordinance or regulation made by a local or public authority relating to traffic (except one for parking, stopping or standing) or the failure to pay a fine imposed for such a violation by a traffic and parking violations agency or a traffic violations agency, the commissioner or his or her agent may suspend the driver's license or privileges of such person pending receipt of notice from the agency that such person has appeared in response to such appearance ticket or has paid such fine. Such suspension shall take effect no less than thirty days from the day upon which notice thereof is sent by the commissioner to the person whose driver's license or privileges are to be suspended. Any suspension issued pursuant to this paragraph shall be subject to the provisions of paragraph (j-1) of subdivision two of section five hundred three of this chapter.

4-b. Suspension of registration for failure to answer or to pay fines with respect to certain violations. Upon receipt of certification from a court or administrative tribunal of appropriate jurisdiction that the owner of a motor vehicle or his representative failed to appear on the return date or dates or any subsequent adjourned date or dates or failed to comply with the rules and regulations of an administrative tribunal following entry of a final decision or decisions in response to twenty-five or more summonses or other process, issued within an eighteen month period charging that such motor vehicle is parked, stopped or standing in violation of any of the provisions of this chapter or of any law, ordinance, rule or regulation made by a local authority, the commissioner shall suspend the registration of such motor vehicle. Such suspension shall take effect no less than thirty days from the date on which notice thereof is sent by the commissioner to the person whose registration is to be suspended and shall remain in effect as long as the summmons [summons]* or summonses remain unanswered, or in the case of an administrative tribunal, the registrant fails to comply with the rules and regulations following the entry of a final decision or decisions.

4-c. [Repealed Sept 1, 2021] Suspension of registration for failure to answer or to pay fines with respect to parking, stopping and standing violations. Upon receipt of certification from a court or administrative tribunal of appropriate jurisdiction in a city with a population in excess of one hundred thousand persons according to the nineteen hundred eighty United States census that the owner of a motor vehicle or his representative following compliance by such city with the notice provisions of subdivision two of section two hundred thirty-five of this chapter, failed to appear on the return date or dates or any subsequent adjourned date or dates or failed to comply with the rules and regulations of an administrative tribunal following entry of a final decision or decisions, in response to five or more summonses or other process, issued within a twelve month period charging that such motor vehicle is parked, stopped or standing in violation of any of the provisions of this chapter or of any law, ordinance, rule or regulation made by a local authority, the commissioner shall suspend the registration of such motor vehicle. Such suspension shall take effect no less than thirty days from

*The bracketed word has been inserted by the Publisher.

the date on which notice thereof is sent by the commissioner to the person whose registration is to be suspended and shall remain in effect as long as the summons or summonses remain unanswered, or in the case of an administrative tribunal, the registrant fails to comply with the rules and regulations following the entry of a final decision or decisions.

4-d. Suspension of registration for failure to answer or pay penalties with respect to certain violations. Upon the receipt of a notification from a court or an administrative tribunal that an owner of a motor vehicle failed to appear on the return date or dates or a new subsequent adjourned date or dates or failed to pay any penalty imposed by a court or failed to comply with the rules and regulations of an administrative tribunal following entry of a final decision or decisions, in response to five or more notices of liability or other process, issued within an eighteen month period charging such owner with a violation of toll collection regulations in accordance with the provisions of section two thousand nine hundred eighty-five of the public authorities law or sections sixteen-a, sixteen-b and sixteen-c of chapter seven hundred seventy-four of the laws of nineteen hundred fifty, the commissioner or his agent shall suspend the registration of the vehicle or vehicles involved in the violation or the privilege of operation of any motor vehicle owned by the registrant. Such suspension shall take effect no less than thirty days from the date on which notice thereof is sent by the commissioner to the person whose registration or privilege is suspended and shall remain in effect until such registrant has appeared in response to such notices of liability or has paid such penalty or in the case of an administrative tribunal, the registrant has complied with the rules and regulations following the entry of a final decision or decisions.

4-e. [Expires and repealed August 31, 2021] Suspension and disqualification for failure to make child support payments or failure to comply with a summons, subpoena or warrant relating to a paternity or child support proceeding.

(1) The commissioner, on behalf of the department, shall enter into a written agreement with the commissioner of the office of temporary and disability assistance, on behalf of the office of temporary and disability assistance, which shall set forth the procedures for suspending the driving privileges of individuals who have failed to make payments of child support or combined child and spousal support.

(2) Such agreement shall include:

(i) the procedure under which the office of temporary and disability assistance shall notify the department of an individual's liability for support arrears;

(ii) the procedure under which the department shall be notified by the office of temporary and disability assistance that an individual has satisfied or commenced payment of his or her support arrears; or has made satisfactory payment arrangements thereon and shall have the suspension of his or her driving privileges terminated;

(iii) the procedure for reimbursement of the department and its agents by the office of temporary and disability assistance for the full additional costs of carrying out the procedures authorized by this section, and may include, subject to the approval of the director of the budget, a procedure for reimbursement of necessary additional costs of collecting social security numbers pursuant to section five hundred two of this title;

(iv) provision for the publicizing of sanctions for nonpayment of child support including the potential for the suspension of delinquent support obligors' driving privileges if they fail to pay child support or combined child and spousal support; and

(v) such other matters as the parties to such agreement shall deem necessary to carry out provisions of this section.

(3) Upon receipt of notification from the office of temporary and disability assistance of a person's failure to satisfy support arrears or to make satisfactory payment arrangements thereon pursuant to paragraph (e) of subdivision twelve of section one hundred eleven-b of the social services law or notification from a court issuing an order pursuant to section four hundred fifty-eight-a of the family court act or section two hundred forty-four-b of the domestic relations law, the commissioner or his or her agent shall suspend the license of such person to operate a motor vehicle. In the event such person is unlicensed, such person's privilege of obtaining a license shall be suspended. Such suspension shall take effect no later than fifteen days from the date of the notice thereof to the person whose license or privilege of obtaining a license is to be suspended, and shall remain in effect until such time as the commissioner is advised that the person has satisfied the support arrears or has made satisfactory

payment arrangements thereon pursuant to paragraph (e) of subdivision twelve of section one hundred eleven-b of the social services law or until such time as the court issues an order to terminate such suspension;

(4) From the time the commissioner is notified by the office of temporary and disability assistance of a person's liability for support arrears under this section, the commissioner shall be relieved from all liability to such person which may otherwise arise under this section, and such person shall have no right to commence a court action or proceeding or to any other legal recourse against the commissioner to recover such driving privileges as authorized by this section. In addition, notwithstanding any other provision of law, such person shall have no right to a hearing or appeal pursuant to this chapter with respect to a suspension of driving privileges as authorized by this section. However, nothing herein shall be construed to prohibit such person from proceeding against the support collection unit pursuant to article seventy-eight of the civil practice law and rules.

(5) Any person whose license has been suspended pursuant to subdivision three of this section may apply for the issuance of a restricted use license as provided in section five hundred thirty of this title.

4-f. Suspension for failure to pay past-due tax liabilities.

(1) The commissioner shall enter into a written agreement with the commissioner of taxation and finance, as provided in section one hundred seventy-one-v of the tax law, which shall set forth the procedures for suspending the drivers' licenses of individuals who have failed to satisfy past-due tax liabilities as such terms are defined in such section.

(2) Upon receipt of notification from the department of taxation and finance that an individual has failed to satisfy past-due tax liabilities, or to otherwise make payment arrangements satisfactory to the commissioner of taxation and finance, or has failed to comply with the terms of such payment arrangements more than once within a twelve month period, the commissioner or his or her agent shall suspend the license of such person to operate a motor vehicle. In the event such person is unlicensed, such person's privilege of obtaining a license shall be suspended. Such suspension shall take effect no later than fifteen days from the date of the notice thereof provided to the person whose license or privilege of obtaining a license is to be suspended, and shall remain in effect until such time as the commissioner is advised that the person has satisfied his or her past-due tax liabilities, or has otherwise made payment arrangements satisfactory to the commissioner of taxation and finance.

(3) From the time the commissioner is notified by the department of taxation and finance under this section, the commissioner shall be relieved from all liability to such person which may otherwise arise under this section, and such person shall have no right to commence a court action or proceeding or to any other legal recourse against the commissioner to recover such driving privileges as authorized by this section. In addition, notwithstanding any other provision of law, such person shall have no right to a hearing or appeal pursuant to this chapter with respect to a suspension of driving privileges as authorized by this section.

(4) Notwithstanding any provision of law to the contrary, the department shall furnish the department of taxation and finance with the information necessary for the proper identification of an individual referred to the department for the purpose of driver's license suspension pursuant to this section and section one hundred seventy-one-v of the tax law. This shall include the individual's name, social security number and any other information the commissioner of motor vehicles deems necessary.

(5) Any person whose driver's license is suspended pursuant to paragraph two of this subdivision may apply for the issuance of a restricted use license as provided in section five hundred thirty of this title.

4-g. Suspension of registration for unlawful solicitation of ground transportation services at an airport. Upon the receipt of a notification from a court or an administrative tribunal that an owner of a motor vehicle was convicted of a second conviction of unlawful solicitation of ground transportation services at an airport in violation of subdivision one of section twelve hundred twenty-b of this chapter both of which were committed within a period of eighteen months, the commissioner or his agent shall suspend the registration of the vehicle involved in the violation for a period of ninety days; upon the receipt of such notification of a third or subsequent conviction for a violation of such subdivision all of which were committed within a period of eighteen months, the commissioner or his agent shall suspend such registration for a period of one hundred eighty days. Such suspension shall take effect no less than thirty days from the date on which notice thereof is sent by the commissioner to the person whose registration or privilege is suspended. The commissioner shall have the authority to deny a registration or renewal application to any other person for the same vehicle, where it has been determined that such registrant's intent has been to evade the purposes of this subdivision and where the commissioner has reasonable grounds to believe that such registration or renewal will have the effect of defeating the purposes of this subdivision.

5. Restoration. A license or registration may be restored by direction of the commissioner but not otherwise. Reversal on appeal, of any conviction because of which any license or registration has been revoked or suspended, shall entitle the holder to restoration thereof forthwith. The privileges of a non-resident may be restored by direction of the commissioner in his discretion but not otherwise.

6. Restrictions.

a. Where revocation is mandatory hereunder, no new license shall be issued for at least six months or, in certain cases a longer period as specified in this chapter, nor thereafter, except in the discretion of the commissioner of motor vehicles.

b. Except as otherwise provided in paragraph c of this subdivision, where revocation is mandatory pursuant to subparagraph (iii) of paragraph a of subdivision two of this section, no new commercial driver's license shall be issued for at least one year nor thereafter except in the discretion of the commissioner, except that if such person has previously been found to have refused a chemical test pursuant to section eleven hundred ninety-four of this chapter or has a prior conviction of any of the following offenses: any violation of section eleven hundred ninety-two of this chapter; any violation of subdivision one or two of section six hundred of this chapter; or has a prior conviction of any felony involving the use of a motor vehicle pursuant to paragraph (a) of subdivision one of section five hundred ten-a of this article, then such commercial driver's license revocation shall be permanent.

c. Where revocation is mandatory pursuant to subdivision one of section five hundred ten-a of this chapter or subparagraph (iii) of paragraph a of subdivision two of this section and the violation of subdivision two of section six hundred of this chapter was committed while operating a commercial motor vehicle transporting hazardous materials, no new commercial driver's license shall be issued for at least three years nor thereafter except in the discretion of the commissioner, except that if such person has previously been found to have refused a chemical test pursuant to section eleven hundred ninety-four of this chapter or has a prior conviction of any of the following offenses: any violation of section eleven hundred ninety-two of this chapter; any violation of subdivision one or two of section six hundred of this chapter; or has a prior conviction of any felony involving the use of a motor vehicle pursuant to paragraph (a) of subdivision one of section five hundred ten-a of this article, then such commercial driver's license revocation shall be permanent.

d. The permanent commercial driver's license revocation required by paragraphs b and c of this subdivision may be waived by the commissioner after a period of ten years has expired from such sentence provided:

(i) that during such ten year period such person has not been found to have refused a chemical test pursuant to section eleven hundred ninety-four of this chapter and has not been convicted of any one of the following offenses: any violation of section eleven hundred ninety-two of this chapter; any violation of subdivision one or two of section six hundred of this chapter; or has a prior conviction of any felony involving the use of a motor vehicle pursuant to paragraph (a) of subdivision one of section five hundred ten-a of this article;

(ii) if any of the grounds upon which the permanent commercial driver's license revocation is based involved a finding of refusal to submit to a chemical test pursuant to section eleven hundred ninety-four of this chapter or a conviction of a violation of any subdivision of section eleven hundred ninety-two of this chapter, that such person provides acceptable documentation to the commissioner that such person has voluntarily enrolled in and successfully completed an appropriate rehabilitation program; and

(iii) after such documentation, if required, is accepted, that such person is granted a certificate of relief from disabilities or a certificate of good conduct pursuant to article twenty-three of the correction law by the court in which such person was last penalized.

e. Upon a third finding of refusal and/or conviction of any of the offenses which require a permanent commercial driver's license revocation, such permanent revocation may not be waived by the commissioner under any circumstances.

f. Where revocation is mandatory hereunder, based upon a conviction had outside this state, no new license shall be issued until after sixty days from the date of such revocation, nor thereafter, except in the discretion of the commissioner.

g. Except as provided in paragraph k of this subdivision, where revocation is permissive, no new license or certificate shall be issued by such commissioner to any person until after thirty days from the date of such revocation, nor thereafter, except in the discretion of the commissioner after an investigation or upon a hearing, provided, however, that where the revocation is based upon a failure in a reexamination pursuant to section five hundred six of this chapter, a learner's permit may be issued immediately and provided further, that where revocation is based upon a conviction of a felony, other than a felony relating to the operation of a motor vehicle or motorcycle, a license shall be issued immediately, if the applicant is otherwise qualified and if the application for such license is accompanied by consent in writing issued by the parole or probation authority having jurisdiction over such applicant.

h. The provisions of this subdivision shall not apply to revocations issued pursuant to sections eleven hundred ninety-three and eleven hundred ninety-four of this chapter.

i. [Repealed]

j. [Repealed]

k. Where revocation is permissive hereunder, based upon a finding of a violation of section three hundred ninety-two or section three hundred ninety-two-a of this chapter, no new license or certificate shall be issued until after one year from the date of such revocation, nor thereafter, except in the discretion of the commissioner.

l. Where revocation is mandatory pursuant to subparagraph (x) of paragraph a of subdivision two of this section, no new license shall be issued for at least seventy-five days, nor thereafter except in the discretion of the commissioner.

m. Where revocation is mandatory pursuant to subparagraph (xi) of paragraph a of subdivision two of this section, no new license shall be issued for at least one hundred twenty days, nor thereafter except in the discretion of the commissioner.

n. Notwithstanding the provisions of paragraph a of this subdivision, subdivision two of section five hundred ten-b of this article or paragraph (b) of subdivision one of section five hundred ten-c of this article, where revocation is mandatory pursuant to subparagraph (xii) or subparagraph (xiii) of paragraph a of subdivision two of this section, no new license shall be issued for at least one year, nor thereafter except in the discretion of the commissioner.

o. Notwithstanding the provisions of paragraph a of this subdivision, where revocation is mandatory pursuant to subparagraph (iii) of paragraph a of subdivision two of this section involving a violation of section three hundred ninety-two of this chapter in relation to an application for the commercial driver's license or the commercial learner's permit being revoked, no new commercial driver's license or commercial learner's permit shall be issued for at least one year, nor thereafter except in the discretion of the commissioner.

7. Miscellaneous provisions. Except as expressly provided, a court conviction shall not be necessary to sustain a revocation or suspension. Revocation or suspension hereunder shall be deemed an administrative act reviewable by the supreme court as such. Notice of revocation or suspension, as well as any required notice of hearing, where the holder is not present, may be given by mailing the same in writing to him or her at the address contained in his or her license, certificate of registration or at the current address provided by the United States postal service, as the case may be. Proof of such mailing by certified mail to the holder shall be presumptive evidence of the holder's receipt and actual knowledge of such notice. Attendance of witnesses may be compelled by subpoena. Failure of the holder or any other person possessing the license

card or number plates, to deliver the same to the suspending or revoking officer is a misdemeanor. Suspending or revoking officers shall place such license cards and number plates in the custody of the commissioner except where the commissioner shall otherwise direct. If any person shall fail to deliver a license card or number plates as provided herein, any police officer, bridge and tunnel officer of the Triborough bridge and tunnel authority, or agent of the commissioner having knowledge of such facts shall have the power to secure possession thereof and return the same to the commissioner, and the commissioner may forthwith direct any police officer, bridge and tunnel officer of the Triborough bridge and tunnel authority, acting pursuant to his or her special duties, or agent of the commissioner to secure possession thereof and to return the same to the commissioner. Failure of the holder or of any person possessing the license card or number plates to deliver to any police officer, bridge and tunnel officer of the Triborough bridge and tunnel authority, or agent of the commissioner who requests the same pursuant to this subdivision shall be a misdemeanor. Notice of revocation or suspension of any license or registration shall be transmitted forthwith by the commissioner to the chief of police of the city or prosecuting officer of the locality in which the person whose license or registration so revoked or suspended resides. In case any license or registration shall expire before the end of any period for which it has been revoked or suspended, and before it shall have been restored as provided in this chapter, then and in that event any renewal thereof may be withheld until the end of such period of suspension or until restoration, as the case may be.

The revocation of a learner's permit shall automatically cancel the application for a license of the holder of such permit.

No suspension or revocation of a license or registration shall be made because of a judgment of conviction if the suspending or revoking officer is satisfied that the magistrate who pronounced the judgment failed to comply with subdivision one of section eighteen hundred seven of this chapter. In case a suspension or revocation has been made and the commissioner is satisfied that there was such failure, the commissioner shall restore the license or registration or both as the case may be.

8. Cancellation. Upon receipt of a license which has been surrendered to the licensing authority of any other jurisdiction as a prerequisite to the issuance of a license by such other jurisdiction in accordance with the provisions of the Driver License Compact or any other laws of such jurisdiction, the commissioner shall cancel such license. Provided, however, that such license shall not be cancelled if the licensee is a resident of this state.

9. Railroad vehicle violations. Upon certification by the commissioner of transportation that there has been a violation of section seventy-six-b of the railroad law, the commissioner of motor vehicles may rescind, cancel or suspend the registration of any motor vehicle described in subdivision one of section seventy-six-b of the railroad law and may rescind, cancel, suspend or take possession of the current registration certificate and number plates of any such motor vehicle.

10. Where a youth is determined to be a youthful offender, following a conviction of a violation for which a license suspension or revocation is mandatory or where a youth receives a juvenile delinquency adjudication in conjunction with a violation of section 240.62 or subdivision five of section 240.60 of the penal law, the court shall impose such suspension or revocation as is otherwise required upon conviction and, further, shall notify the commissioner of said suspension or revocation and its finding that said violator is granted youthful offender status as is required pursuant to section five hundred thirteen of this chapter or received a juvenile delinquency adjudication.

11. Notwithstanding any contrary provision of law, the division of criminal justice services is authorized to share with the commissioner such criminal history information in its possession as may be necessary to effect the provisions of this chapter.

HISTORY:

Add, L 1959, ch 775, with substance transferred from former § 71; amd, L 1960, ch 184, §§ 3–5; L 1961 ch 962, § 1; L 1962, ch 779, § 1; L 1963, ch 869, § 3; L 1964, ch 447, § 1; L 1964, ch 905, § 1; L 1965, ch 651, § 2; L 1966, ch 86 § 1; L 1966, ch 759, § 1; L 1966, ch 963, § 2; L 1967, ch 79, § 1, eff Oct 1, 1967; L 1968, ch 36, § 1; L 1969, ch 445, § 3, eff Jan 1, 1970; L 1970, ch 275, § 1; L 1971, ch 1106, § 1; L 1972, ch 99, § 3; L 1972, ch 243, § 2; L 1973, ch 156, § 1; L 1973, ch 168, § 5; L 1973, ch 541, § 2; L 1974, ch 129, § 1; L 1974, ch 772, § 1; L 1975, ch 143, § 3; L 1976, ch 282, § 1; L 1976, ch 404, §§ 1, 2; L 1976, ch 670, § 2; L 1977, ch 163, § 1; L 1979, ch 195, § 1, eff June 4, 1979; L 1979, ch

594, § 2; L 1980, ch 381, § 2; L 1980, ch 722, § 2, eff June 30, 1980; L 1980, ch 806, §§ 2, 3; L 1980, ch 807, § 1; L 1980, ch 843, § 98; L 1981, ch 428, § 1; L 1981, ch 477, § 1; L 1981, ch 912, § 1; L 1982, ch 861, § 1; L 1982, ch 888, §§ 1, 2; L 1983, ch 802, § 1; L 1983, ch 890, § 2; L 1983, ch 892, §§ 1–3; L 1984, ch 192, § 1; L 1984, ch 977, §§ 1, 2; L 1984, ch 978, § 2, eff Nov 1, 1984; L 1985, ch 707, § 1; L 1985, ch 718, § 1; L 1986, ch 132, §§ 5–11, eff June 2, 1986; L 1986, ch 411, § 20; L 1986, ch 492, §§ 1, 2; L 1986, ch 649, § 4; L 1986, ch 731, § 1, eff July 30, 1986; L 1987, ch 188, § 1; L 1987, ch 338, § 3, eff Jan 1, 1988; L 1987, ch 594, §§ 2, 3; L 1987, ch 687, §§ 1, 2; L 1988, ch 47, §§ 5–9, eff Nov 1, 1988; L 1988, ch 183, §§ 1–5, eff Nov 1, 1988; L 1988, ch 197, § 3, eff Nov 1, 1988; L 1988, ch 254, § 2; L 1989, ch 625, § 1, eff Nov 1, 1989; L 1989, ch 703, § 1, eff Sept 22, 1989; L 1989, ch 779, §§ 3, 4, eff July 1, 1990; L 1990, ch 173, §§ 23, 51–a, eff Aug 19, 1990; L 1990, ch 173, §§ 52, 53, eff Feb 19, 1991; L 1990, ch 173, § 54, eff April 1, 1991; L 1990, ch 496, § 6, eff July 18, 1990; L 1991, ch 166, § 373, eff June 12, 1991; L 1992, ch 124, §§ 1, 2, eff Nov 1, 1992; L 1992, ch 379, § 15, eff July 17, 1992; L 1992, ch 605, § 2, eff Nov 21, 1992; L 1993, ch 349, § 3, eff July 21, 1993; L 1993, ch 533, §§ 1–3, eff Sept 30, 1993; L 1993, ch 606, § 1, eff Nov 1, 1993; L 1994, ch 307, §§ 5, 6, eff Sept 18, 1994; L 1994, ch 313, § 2, eff Nov 1, 1994; L, 1994, ch 429, § 2, eff July 20, 1994; L 1995, ch 3, § 72, eff June 10, 1995 and deemed eff on and after April 1, 1995; L 1995, ch 81, § 211, eff July 1, 1995; L 1997, ch 398, § 133, eff Jan 1, 1998; L 1997, ch 505, § 1, eff Oct 3, 1997; L 1998, ch 383, § 9, eff April 1, 1999; L 1998, ch 652, § 1, eff April 1, 1999; L 1999, ch 412, § 5 (Part J), eff Aug 9, 1999, deemed eff on and after April 1, 1999; L 1999, ch 561, §§ 6–8, eff Dec 1, 1999; L 2003, ch 62, § 10 (Part J), eff Sept 12, 2003; L 2005, ch 60, § 12 (Part E), eff Sept 30, 2005; L 2005, ch 223, § 2, eff Nov 1, 2005; L 2006, ch 571, §§ 1–4, eff Nov 1, 2006; L 2007, ch 601, § 23, eff Aug 15, 2007; L 2010, ch 56, § 29 (Part LL), eff June 22, 2010; L 2010, ch 59, § 5 (Part K), eff June 22, 2010; L 2010, ch 409, § 2, eff Aug 13, 2010; L 2013, ch 59, § 2 (Part P), eff March 28, 2013; L 2014, ch 55, §§ 1–3 (Part B), eff Nov 1, 2014; L 2015, ch 58, § 4 (Part I), eff July 8, 2015; L 2015, ch 58, § 11 (Part CC), eff July 1, 2015; L 2017, ch 157, § 12, eff April 21, 2018; L 2018, ch 58, § 1 (Part A), eff April 12, 2018; L 2019, ch 55, §§ 1, 2 (Part II, Subpart J), eff April 12, 2019; L 2020, ch 58, §§ 2, 3 (Part H), eff Aug 1, 2020.

Title IX
Penalties and Disposition of Fines and Forfeitures

Article 45 Penalties and Disposition of Fines and Forfeitures

Article 45
Penalties and Disposition of Fines and Forfeitures

§ 1800. Penalties for traffic infractions [Effective until September 30, 2020]

(a) It is a traffic infraction for any person to violate any of the provisions of this chapter or of any local law, ordinance, order, rule or regulation adopted pursuant to this chapter, unless such violation is by this chapter or other law of this state declared to be a misdemeanor or a felony.

(b)1. Every person convicted of a traffic infraction for a violation of any of the provisions of this chapter or of any ordinance, order, rule or regulation adopted pursuant to section sixteen hundred thirty or sixteen hundred thirty-one of this chapter for which another penalty is not provided shall for a first conviction thereof be punished by a fine of not more than one hundred fifty dollars or by imprisonment for not more than fifteen days or by both such fine and imprisonment; for a conviction of a second violation, both of which were committed within a period of eighteen months, such person shall be punished by a fine of not more than three hundred dollars or by imprisonment for not more than forty-five days or by both such fine and imprisonment; upon a conviction of a third or subsequent violation, all of which were committed within a period of eighteen months, such person shall be punished by a fine of not more than four hundred fifty dollars or by imprisonment for not more than ninety days or by both such fine and imprisonment, except that a person convicted of a traffic infraction for a violation of paragraph one of subdivision (d) of section one thousand one hundred eleven of this chapter outside of a city having a population of one million or more shall, for a first conviction thereof, be punished by a fine of not less than seventy-five dollars nor more than two hundred twenty-five dollars or by imprisonment for not more than fifteen days or by both such fine and imprisonment; for a conviction of a second violation, both of which were committed within a period of eighteen months, such person shall be punished by a fine of not less than one hundred fifty dollars nor more than three hundred seventy-five dollars or by imprisonment for not more than forty-five days or by both such fine and imprisonment; upon a conviction of a third or subsequent violation, all of which were committed within a period of eighteen months, such person shall be punished by a fine of not less than three hundred seventy-five dollars nor more than six hundred seventy-five dollars or by imprisonment for not more than ninety days or by both such fine and imprisonment except that a person convicted for a violation of paragraph one of subdivision (d) of section one thousand one hundred eleven of this chapter shall, for a first conviction thereof, be punished by a fine of not less than one hundred fifty dollars nor more than four hundred fifty dollars or by imprisonment for not more than fifteen days or by both such fine and imprisonment; for a conviction of a second violation, both of which were committed within a period of eighteen months, such person shall be punished by a fine of not less than three hundred dollars nor more than seven hundred fifty dollars or by imprisonment for not more than forty-five days or by both such fine and imprisonment; upon a conviction of a third or subsequent violation, all of which were committed within a period of eighteen months, such person shall be punished by a fine of not less than seven hundred fifty dollars nor more than one thousand five hundred dollars or by imprisonment for not more than ninety days or by both such fine and imprisonment.

2. Notwithstanding the provisions of paragraph one of this subdivision, a person convicted of a traffic infraction for a violation of paragraph two of subdivision (b) of section twelve hundred two of this chapter shall for a first conviction thereof be punished by a fine of not more than four hundred dollars or by imprisonment for not more than fifteen days or by both such fine and imprisonment. Upon a conviction for a second violation, both of which were committed within a period of eighteen months, such person shall be punished by a fine of not more than six hundred dollars or by imprisonment for not more than forty-five days or by both such fine and imprisonment; upon a conviction of a third or subsequent violation, all of which were committed within a period of eighteen months, such person shall be punished by a fine of not more than seven hundred fifty dollars or by imprisonment for not more than ninety days or by both such fine and imprisonment.

(c) Every person convicted of a traffic infraction for a violation of any local law, ordinance, order, rule, regulation or administrative code provision adopted pursuant to this chapter by any local authority or continued in effect by this chapter, except those adopted pursuant to sections sixteen hundred thirty and sixteen hundred thirty-one, shall be punished in the same manner as has heretofore been prescribed by law unless or until otherwise prescribed by local law, ordinance or state statute.

(d) A conviction of violation of any provision of this chapter shall not be a bar to a prosecution for an assault or for a homicide committed by any person in operating a motor vehicle or motorcycle.

(e) Every person convicted of a violation of the provisions of section eleven hundred forty-four of this chapter shall for a first conviction thereof be punished by a fine of not more than two hundred seventy-five dollars or by imprisonment for not more than fifteen days or by both such fine and imprisonment. For a conviction of a second violation, both of which were committed within a period of eighteen months, such person shall be punished by a fine of not more than four hundred fifty dollars or by imprisonment for not more than forty-five days or by both such fine and imprisonment. For a conviction of a third violation and all subsequent violations, all of which were committed within a period of eighteen months, such person shall be punished by a fine of not more than seven hundred fifty dollars or by imprisonment for not more than ninety days or by both such fine and imprisonment.

(f) Every person convicted of operating a truck, tractor or tractor-trailer combination having a total gross weight in excess of ten thousand pounds in violation of a local law, ordinance, rule or regulation enacted by the legislative body of any city with a population in excess of one million pursuant to the provisions of paragraph ten of subdivision (a) of section sixteen hundred forty of this chapter shall, for a first offense thereof, be punished by a fine of not less than two hundred dollars nor more than five hundred dollars or by imprisonment for not more than fifteen days or by both such fine and imprisonment. For a conviction of a second violation, both of which were committed within a period of eighteen months, such person shall be punished by a fine of not less than five hundred dollars nor more than one thousand dollars or by imprisonment for not more than forty-five days or by both such fine and imprisonment. For a conviction of a third violation and all subsequent violations, all of which were committed within a period of eighteen months, such person shall be punished by a fine of not less than one thousand dollars nor more than two thousand dollars, or by imprisonment for not more than ninety days or by both such fine and imprisonment.

(g) Notwithstanding the provisions of subdivisions (b) and (c) of this section, a person convicted of a traffic infraction for a violation of any ordinance, order, rule, regulation or local law adopted pursuant to one or more of the following provisions of this chapter: paragraphs two and nine of subdivision (a) of section sixteen hundred twenty-one; subdivision three of section sixteen hundred thirty; or subdivision five of section seventy-one of the transportation law, prohibiting the operation on a highway or parkway of a motor vehicle registered as a commercial vehicle and having a gross vehicle weight rating of less than twenty-six thousand pounds shall, for a first conviction thereof, be punished by a fine of not more than two hundred fifty dollars or by imprisonment of not more than fifteen days or by both such fine and imprisonment; for a conviction of a second violation, both of which were committed within a period of eighteen months, such person shall be punished by a fine of not more than five hundred dollars or by imprisonment for not more than forty-five days or by both such fine and imprisonment; upon a conviction of a third or subsequent violation, all of which were committed within a period of eighteen months, such person shall be punished by a fine of not more than seven hundred fifty dollars or by imprisonment of not more than ninety days or by both such fine and imprisonment. Provided, however, the provisions of this subdivision shall not apply to a commercial motor vehicle as such term is defined in paragraph (a) of subdivision four of section five hundred one-a of this chapter.

(h) Notwithstanding the provisions of subdivisions (b) and (c) of this section, a person convicted of a traffic infraction for a violation of any ordinance, order, rule, regulation or local law adopted pursuant to one or more of the following provisions of this chapter: paragraphs two and nine of subdivision (a) of section sixteen hundred twenty-one; subdivision three of section sixteen hundred thirty; or subdivision five of section seventy-one of the transportation law, prohibiting the operation on a highway or parkway of a commercial motor vehicle as defined in paragraph (a) of subdivision four of section five hundred one-a of this chapter, for a first conviction thereof, be punished by a fine of not more than three hundred fifty dollars or by imprisonment of not more than fifteen days or by both such fine and imprisonment; for a conviction of a second violation, both of which were committed within a period of eighteen months, such person shall be punished by a fine of not more than seven hundred dollars or by imprisonment for not more than forty-five days or by both such fine and imprisonment; upon a conviction of a third or subsequent violation, all of which were committed within a period of eighteen months, such person shall be punished by a fine of not more than one thousand dollars or by imprisonment of not more than ninety days or by both such fine and imprisonment.

HISTORY:

Add, L 1959, ch 775, eff Oct 1, 1960, with substance transferred from former §§ 70(12), 1800; amd, L 1967, ch 783, § 3; L 1968, ch 186, § 1; L 1969, ch 1075, § 2; L 1970, ch 337, § 8, eff July 1, 1970; L 1981, ch 162, § 2; L 1983, ch 926, § 1; L 1983, ch 927, § 1; L 1989, ch 61, § 48, effective and applicable to violations committed on and after May 19, 1989; L 1993, ch 540, § 1, eff Nov 1, 1993; L 1995, ch 202, § 1, eff Aug 25, 1995; L 2003, ch 62, § 1 (Part C), eff May 15, 2003; L 2003, ch 203, § 1, eff Nov 1, 2003; L 2006, ch 574, § 2, eff Nov 1, 2006; L 2008, ch 221, § 1, eff Nov 1, 2008.

§ 1800. Penalties for traffic infractions [Effective September 30, 2020]

(a) It is a traffic infraction for any person to violate any of the provisions of this chapter or of any local law, ordinance, order, rule or regulation adopted pursuant to this chapter, unless such violation is by this chapter or other law of this state declared to be a misdemeanor or a felony.

(b)1. Every person convicted of a traffic infraction for a violation of any of the provisions of this chapter or of any ordinance, order, rule or regulation adopted pursuant to section sixteen hundred thirty or sixteen hundred thirty-one of this chapter for which another penalty is not provided shall for a first conviction thereof be punished by a fine of not more than one hundred fifty dollars or by imprisonment for not more than fifteen days or by both such fine and imprisonment; for a conviction of a second violation, both of which were committed within a period of eighteen months, such person shall be punished by a fine of not more than three hundred dollars or by imprisonment for not more than forty-five days or by both such fine and imprisonment; upon a conviction of a third or subsequent violation, all of which were committed within a period of eighteen months, such person shall be punished by a fine of not more than four hundred fifty dollars or by imprisonment for not more than ninety days or by both such fine and imprisonment, except that a person convicted of a traffic infraction for a violation of paragraph one of subdivision (d) of section one thousand one hundred eleven of this chapter outside of a city having a population of one million or more shall, for a first conviction thereof, be punished by a fine of not less than seventy-five dollars nor more than two hundred twenty-five dollars or by imprisonment for not more than fifteen days or by both such fine and imprisonment; for a conviction of a second violation, both of which were committed within a period of eighteen months, such person shall be punished by a fine of not less than one hundred fifty dollars nor more than three hundred seventy-five dollars or by imprisonment for not more than forty-five days or by both such fine and imprisonment; upon a conviction of a third or subsequent violation, all of which were committed within a period of eighteen months, such person shall be punished by a fine of not less than three hundred seventy-five dollars nor more than six hundred seventy-five dollars or by imprisonment for not more than ninety days or by both such fine and imprisonment except that a person convicted for a violation of paragraph one of subdivision (d) of section one thousand one hundred eleven of this chapter shall, for a first conviction thereof, be punished by a fine of not less than one hundred fifty dollars nor more than four hundred fifty dollars or by imprisonment for not more than fifteen days or by both such fine and imprisonment; for a conviction of a second violation, both of which were committed within a period of eighteen months, such person shall be punished by a fine of not less than three hundred dollars nor more than seven hundred fifty dollars or by imprisonment for not more than forty-five days or by both such fine and imprisonment; upon a conviction of a third or subsequent violation, all of which were committed within a period of eighteen months, such person shall be punished by a fine of not less than seven hundred fifty dollars nor more than one thousand five hundred dollars or by imprisonment for not more than ninety days or by both such fine and imprisonment.

2. Notwithstanding the provisions of paragraph one of this subdivision, a person convicted of a traffic infraction for a violation of paragraph two of subdivision (b) of section twelve hundred two of this chapter shall for a first conviction thereof be punished by a fine of not more than four hundred dollars or by imprisonment for not more than fifteen days or by both such fine and imprisonment. Upon a conviction for a second violation, both of which were committed within a period of eighteen months, such person shall be punished by a fine of not more than six hundred dollars or by imprisonment for not more than forty-five days or by both such fine and imprisonment; upon a conviction of a third or subsequent violation, all of which were committed within a period of eighteen months, such person shall be punished by a fine of not more than seven hundred fifty dollars or by imprisonment for not more than ninety days or by both such fine and imprisonment.

(c) Every person convicted of a traffic infraction for a violation of any local law, ordinance, order, rule, regulation or administrative code provision adopted pursuant to this chapter by any local authority or continued in effect by this chapter, except those adopted pursuant to sections sixteen hundred thirty and sixteen hundred thirty-one, shall be punished in the same manner as has heretofore been prescribed by law unless or until otherwise prescribed by local law, ordinance or state statute.

(d) A conviction of violation of any provision of this chapter shall not be a bar to a prosecution for an assault or for a homicide committed by any person in operating a motor vehicle or motorcycle.

(e) Every person convicted of a violation of the provisions of section eleven hundred forty-four of this chapter shall for a first conviction thereof be punished by a fine of not more than two hundred seventy-five dollars or by imprisonment for not more than fifteen days or by both such fine and imprisonment. For a conviction of a second violation, both of which were committed within a period of eighteen months, such person shall be punished by a fine of not more than four hundred fifty dollars or by imprisonment for not more than forty-five days or by both such fine and imprisonment. For a conviction of a third violation and all subsequent violations, all of which were committed within a period of eighteen months, such person shall be punished by a fine of not more than seven hundred fifty dollars or by imprisonment for not more than ninety days or by both such fine and imprisonment.

(f) Every person convicted of operating a truck, tractor or tractor-trailer combination having a total gross weight in excess of ten thousand pounds in violation of a local law, ordinance, rule or regulation enacted by the legislative body of any city with a population in excess of one million pursuant to the provisions of paragraph ten of subdivision (a) of section sixteen hundred forty of this chapter shall, for a first offense thereof, be punished by a fine of not less than two hundred dollars nor more than five hundred dollars or by imprisonment for not more than fifteen days or by both such fine and imprisonment. For a conviction of a second violation, both of which were committed within a period of eighteen months, such person shall be punished by a fine of not less than five hundred dollars nor more than one thousand dollars or by imprisonment for not more than forty-five days or by both such fine and imprisonment. For a conviction of a third violation and all subsequent violations, all of which were committed within a period of eighteen months, such person shall be punished by a fine of not less than one thousand dollars nor more than two thousand dollars, or by imprisonment for not more than ninety days or by both such fine and imprisonment.

(g) Notwithstanding the provisions of subdivisions (b) and (c) of this section, a person convicted of a traffic infraction for a violation of any ordinance, order, rule, regulation or local law adopted pursuant to one or more of the following provisions of this chapter: paragraphs two and nine of subdivision (a) of section sixteen hundred twenty-one; subdivision three of section sixteen hundred thirty; or subdivision five of section seventy-one of the transportation law, prohibiting the operation on a highway or parkway of a motor vehicle registered as a commercial vehicle and having a gross vehicle weight rating of less than ten thousand pounds shall, for a first conviction thereof, be punished by a fine of not more than two hundred fifty dollars or by imprisonment of not more than fifteen days or by both such fine and imprisonment; for a conviction of a second violation, both of which were committed within a period of eighteen months, such person shall be punished by a fine of not more than five hundred dollars or by imprisonment for not more than forty-five days or by both such fine and imprisonment; upon a conviction of a third or subsequent violation, all of which were committed within a period of eighteen months, such person shall be punished by a fine of not more than seven hundred fifty dollars or by imprisonment of not more than ninety days or by both such fine and imprisonment. Provided, however, the provisions of this subdivision shall not apply to a commercial motor vehicle as such term is defined in paragraph (a) of subdivision four of section five hundred one-a of this chapter.

(h) Notwithstanding the provisions of subdivisions (b) and (c) of this section, a person convicted of a traffic infraction for a violation of any ordinance, order, rule, regulation or local law adopted pursuant to one or more of the following provisions of this chapter: paragraphs two and nine of subdivision (a) of section sixteen hundred twenty-one; subdivision three of section sixteen hundred thirty; or subdivision five of section seventy-one of the transportation law, prohibiting the operation on a highway or parkway of a motor vehicle registered as a commercial vehicle and having a gross vehicle weight rating of at least ten thousand pounds but no more than twenty-six thousand pounds shall, for a first conviction thereof, be punished by a fine of not more than three hundred fifty dollars or by imprisonment of not more than fifteen days or by both such fine and imprisonment; for a conviction of a second violation, both of which were committed within a period of eighteen months, such person shall be punished by a fine of not more than seven hundred dollars or by imprisonment for not more than forty-five days or by both such fine and imprisonment; upon a conviction of a third or subsequent violation, all of which were committed within a period of eighteen months, such person shall be punished by a fine of not more than one thousand dollars or by imprisonment of not more than ninety days or by both such fine and imprisonment; provided, however, the provisions of this subdivision shall not apply to a commercial motor vehicle as such term is defined in paragraph (a) of subdivision four of section five hundred one-a of this chapter.

(i) Notwithstanding the provisions of subdivisions (b) and (c) of this section, a person convicted of a traffic infraction for a violation of any ordinance, order, rule, regulation or local law adopted pursuant to one or more of the following provisions of this chapter: paragraphs two and nine of subdivision (a) of section sixteen hundred twenty-one; subdivision three of section sixteen hundred thirty; or subdivision five of section seventy-one of the transportation law, prohibiting the operation on a highway or parkway of a commercial motor vehicle as defined in paragraph (a) of subdivision four of section five hundred one-a of this chapter, for a first conviction thereof, be punished by a fine of not more than seven hundred dollars or by imprisonment of not more than fifteen days or by both such fine and imprisonment; for a conviction of a second violation, both of which were committed within a period of eighteen months, such person shall be punished by a fine of not more than one thousand five hundred dollars or by imprisonment for not more than forty-five days or by both such fine and imprisonment; upon a conviction of a third or subsequent violation, all of which were committed within a period of eighteen months, such person shall be punished by a fine of not more than two thousand dollars or by imprisonment of not more than ninety days or by both such fine and imprisonment.

HISTORY:

Add, L 1959, ch 775, eff Oct 1, 1960, with substance transferred from former §§ 70(12), 1800; amd, L 1967, ch 783, § 3; L 1968, ch 186, § 1; L 1969, ch 1075, § 2; L 1970, ch 337, § 8, eff July 1, 1970; L 1981, ch 162, § 2; L 1983, ch 926, § 1; L 1983, ch 927, § 1; L 1989, ch 61, § 48, effective and applicable to violations committed on and after May 19, 1989; L 1993, ch 540, § 1, eff Nov 1, 1993; L 1995, ch 202, § 1, eff Aug 25, 1995; L 2003, ch 62, § 1 (Part C), eff May 15, 2003; L 2003, ch 203, § 1, eff Nov 1, 2003; L 2006, ch 574, § 2, eff Nov 1, 2006; L 2008, ch 221, § 1, eff Nov 1, 2008; L 2020, ch 58, § 1 (Part B), eff Sept 30, 2020.

§ 1809. Mandatory surcharge and crime victim assistance fee required in certain cases

1. [Eff until Sept 6, 2024] Whenever proceedings in an administrative tribunal or a court of this state result in a conviction for an offense under this chapter or a traffic infraction under this chapter, or a local law, ordinance, rule or regulation adopted pursuant to this chapter, other than a traffic infraction involving standing, stopping, or parking or violations by pedestrians or bicyclists, or other than an adjudication of liability of an owner for a violation of subdivision (d) of section eleven hundred eleven of this chapter in accordance with section eleven hundred eleven-a of this chapter, or other than an adjudication of liability of an owner for a violation of subdivision (d) of section eleven hundred eleven of this chapter in accordance with section eleven hundred eleven-b of this chapter, or other than an adjudication in accordance with section eleven hundred eleven-c of this chapter for a violation of a bus lane restriction as defined in such section, or other than an adjudication of liability of an owner for a violation of subdivision (d) of section eleven hundred eleven of this chapter in accordance with section eleven hundred eleven-d of this chapter, or other than an adjudication of liability of an owner for a violation of subdivision (b), (c), (d), (f) or (g) of section eleven hundred eighty of this chapter in accordance with section eleven hundred eighty-b of this chapter, or other than an adjudication of liability of an owner for a violation of subdivision (d) of section eleven hundred eleven of this chapter in accordance with section eleven hundred eleven-e of this chapter, or other than an adjudication of liability of an owner for a violation of section eleven hundred seventy-four of this chapter in accordance with section eleven hundred seventy-four-a of this chapter, or other than an adjudication of liability of an owner for a violation of subdivision (b), (c), (d), (f) or (g) of section eleven hundred eighty of this chapter in accordance with section eleven hundred eighty-d of this chapter, there shall be levied a crime victim assistance fee and a mandatory surcharge, in addition to any sentence required or permitted by law, in accordance with the following schedule:

(a) Whenever proceedings in an administrative tribunal or a court of this state result in a conviction for a traffic infraction pursuant to article nine of this chapter, there shall be levied a crime victim assistance fee in the amount of five dollars and a mandatory surcharge, in addition to any sentence required or permitted by law, in the amount of twenty-five dollars.

(b) Whenever proceedings in an administrative tribunal or a court of this state result in a conviction for a misdemeanor or felony pursuant to section eleven hundred ninety-two of this chapter, there shall be levied, in addition to any sentence required or permitted by law, a crime victim assistance fee in the amount of twenty-five dollars and a mandatory surcharge in accordance with the following schedule:

(i) a person convicted of a felony shall pay a mandatory surcharge of three hundred dollars;

(ii) a person convicted of a misdemeanor shall pay a mandatory surcharge of one hundred seventy-five dollars.

(c) Whenever proceedings in an administrative tribunal or a court of this state result in a conviction for an offense under this chapter other than a crime pursuant to section eleven hundred ninety-two of this chapter, or a traffic infraction under this chapter, or a local law, ordinance, rule or regulation adopted pursuant to this chapter, other than a traffic infraction involving standing, stopping, or parking or violations by pedestrians or bicyclists, or other than an adjudication of liability of an owner for a violation of subdivision (d) of section eleven hundred eleven of this chapter in accordance with section eleven hundred eleven-a of this chapter, or other than an adjudication of liability of an owner for a violation of subdivision (d) of section eleven hundred eleven of this chapter in accordance with section eleven hundred eleven-b of this chapter, or other than an adjudication of liability of an owner for a violation of subdivision (d) of section eleven hundred eleven of this chapter in accordance with section eleven hundred eleven-d of this chapter, or other than an infraction pursuant to article nine of this chapter or other than an adjudication of liability of an owner for a violation of toll collection regulations pursuant to section two thousand nine hundred eighty-five of the public authorities law or sections sixteen-a, sixteen-b and sixteen-c of chapter seven hundred seventy-four of the laws of nineteen hundred fifty or other than an adjudication in accordance with section eleven hundred eleven-c of this chapter for a violation of a bus lane restriction as defined in such section, or other than an adjudication of liability of an owner for a violation of subdivision (b), (c), (d), (f) or (g) of section eleven hundred eighty of this chapter in accordance with section eleven hundred eighty-b of this chapter, or other than an adjudication of liability of an owner for a violation of subdivision (d) of section eleven hundred eleven of this chapter in accordance with section eleven hundred eleven-e of this chapter, or other than an adjudication of liability of an owner for a violation of section eleven hundred seventy-four of this chapter in accordance with section eleven hundred seventy-four-a of this chapter, or other than an adjudication of liability of an owner for a violation of subdivision (b), (c), (d), (f) or (g) of section eleven hundred eighty of this chapter in accordance with section eleven hundred eighty-d of this chapter, there shall be levied a crime victim assistance fee in the amount of five dollars and a mandatory surcharge, in addition to any sentence required or permitted by law, in the amount of fifty-five dollars.

1. [Eff Sept 6, 2024; eff until Dec 1, 2024] Whenever proceedings in an administrative tribunal or a court of this state result in a conviction for an offense under this chapter or a traffic infraction under this chapter, or a local law, ordinance, rule or regulation adopted pursuant to this chapter, other than a traffic infraction involving standing, stopping, or parking or violations by pedestrians or bicyclists, or other than an adjudication of liability of an owner for a violation of subdivision (d) of section eleven hundred eleven of this chapter in accordance with section eleven hundred eleven-a of this chapter, or other than an adjudication of liability of an owner for a violation of subdivision (d) of section eleven hundred eleven of this chapter in accordance with section eleven hundred eleven-b of this chapter, or other than an adjudication in accordance with section eleven hundred eleven-c of this chapter for a violation of a bus lane restriction as defined in such section, or other than an adjudication of liability of an owner for a violation of subdivision (d) of section eleven hundred eleven of this chapter in accordance with section eleven hundred eleven-d of this chapter, or other than an adjudication of liability of an owner for a violation of subdivision (b), (c), (d), (f)

or (g) of section eleven hundred eighty of this chapter in accordance with section eleven hundred eighty-b of this chapter, or other than an adjudication of liability of an owner for a violation of subdivision (d) of section eleven hundred eleven of this chapter in accordance with section eleven hundred eleven-e of this chapter, or other than an adjudication of liability of an owner for a violation of section eleven hundred seventy-four of this chapter in accordance with section eleven hundred seventy-four-a of this chapter, there shall be levied a crime victim assistance fee and a mandatory surcharge, in addition to any sentence required or permitted by law, in accordance with the following schedule:

(a) Whenever proceedings in an administrative tribunal or a court of this state result in a conviction for a traffic infraction pursuant to article nine of this chapter, there shall be levied a crime victim assistance fee in the amount of five dollars and a mandatory surcharge, in addition to any sentence required or permitted by law, in the amount of twenty-five dollars.

(b) Whenever proceedings in an administrative tribunal or a court of this state result in a conviction for a misdemeanor or felony pursuant to section eleven hundred ninety-two of this chapter, there shall be levied, in addition to any sentence required or permitted by law, a crime victim assistance fee in the amount of twenty-five dollars and a mandatory surcharge in accordance with the following schedule:

(i) a person convicted of a felony shall pay a mandatory surcharge of three hundred dollars;

(ii) a person convicted of a misdemeanor shall pay a mandatory surcharge of one hundred seventy-five dollars.

(c) Whenever proceedings in an administrative tribunal or a court of this state result in a conviction for an offense under this chapter other than a crime pursuant to section eleven hundred ninety-two of this chapter, or a traffic infraction under this chapter, or a local law, ordinance, rule or regulation adopted pursuant to this chapter, other than a traffic infraction involving standing, stopping, or parking or violations by pedestrians or bicyclists, or other than an adjudication of liability of an owner for a violation of subdivision (d) of section eleven hundred eleven of this chapter in accordance with section eleven hundred eleven-a of this chapter, or other than an adjudication of liability of an owner for a violation of subdivision (d) of section eleven hundred eleven of this chapter in accordance with section eleven hundred eleven-b of this chapter, or other than an adjudication of liability of an owner for a violation of subdivision (d) of section eleven hundred eleven of this chapter in accordance with section eleven hundred eleven-d of this chapter, or other than an infraction pursuant to article nine of this chapter or other than an adjudication of liability of an owner for a violation of toll collection regulations pursuant to section two thousand nine hundred eighty-five of the public authorities law or sections sixteen-a, sixteen-b and sixteen-c of chapter seven hundred seventy-four of the laws of nineteen hundred fifty or other than an adjudication in accordance with section eleven hundred eleven-c of this chapter for a violation of a bus lane restriction as defined in such section, or other than an adjudication of liability of an owner for a violation of subdivision (b), (c), (d), (f) or (g) of section eleven hundred eighty of this chapter in accordance with section eleven hundred eighty-b of this chapter, or other than an adjudication of liability of an owner for a violation of subdivision (d) of section eleven hundred eleven of this chapter in accordance with section eleven hundred eleven-e of this chapter, or other than an adjudication of liability of an owner for a violation of section eleven hundred seventy-four of this chapter in accordance with section eleven hundred seventy-four-a of this chapter, there shall be levied a crime victim assistance fee in the amount of five dollars and a mandatory surcharge, in addition to any sentence required or permitted by law, in the amount of fifty-five dollars.

1. [Eff Sept 1, 2021, eff until Dec 1, 2024] Whenever proceedings in an administrative tribunal or a court of this state result in a conviction for a crime under this chapter or a traffic infraction under this chapter, or a local law, ordinance, rule or regulation adopted pursuant to this chapter, other than a traffic infraction involving standing, stopping, parking or motor vehicle equipment or violations by pedestrians or bicyclists, or other than an adjudication of liability of an owner for a violation of subdivision (d) of section eleven hundred eleven of this chapter in accordance with section eleven hundred eleven-a of this chapter, or other than an adjudication of liability of an owner

for a violation of subdivision (d) of section eleven hundred eleven of this chapter in accordance with section eleven hundred eleven-b of this chapter, or other than an adjudication in accordance with section eleven hundred eleven-c of this chapter for a violation of a bus lane restriction as defined in such section, or other than an adjudication of liability of an owner for a violation of subdivision (d) of section eleven hundred eleven of this chapter in accordance with section eleven hundred eleven-d of this chapter, or other than an adjudication of liability of an owner for a violation of subdivision (b), (c), (d), (f) or (g) of section eleven hundred eighty of this chapter in accordance with section eleven hundred eighty-b of this chapter, or other than an adjudication of liability of an owner for a violation of subdivision (b), (c), (d), (f) or (g) of section eleven hundred eighty of this chapter in accordance with section eleven hundred eighty-d of this chapter, or other than an adjudication of liability of an owner for a violation of subdivision (d) of section eleven hundred eleven of this chapter in accordance with section eleven hundred eleven-e of this chapter, or other than an adjudication of liability of an owner for a violation of section eleven hundred seventy-four of this chapter in accordance with section eleven hundred seventy-four-a of this chapter, there shall be levied a mandatory surcharge, in addition to any sentence required or permitted by law, in the amount of twenty-five dollars.

1. [Eff Dec 1, 2024; eff until Sept 20, 2025] Whenever proceedings in an administrative tribunal or a court of this state result in a conviction for a crime under this chapter or a traffic infraction under this chapter other than a traffic infraction involving standing, stopping, parking or motor vehicle equipment or violations by pedestrians or bicyclists, or other than an adjudication in accordance with section eleven hundred eleven-c of this chapter for a violation of a bus lane restriction as defined in such section, or other than an adjudication of liability of an owner for a violation of subdivision (d) of section eleven hundred eleven of this chapter in accordance with section eleven hundred eleven-d of this chapter, or other than an adjudication of liability of an owner for a violation of subdivision (b), (c), (d), (f) or (g) of section eleven hundred eighty of this chapter in accordance with section eleven hundred eighty-b of this chapter, or other than an adjudication of liability of an owner for a violation of subdivision (b), (c), (d), (f) or (g) of section eleven hundred eighty of this chapter in accordance with section eleven hundred eighty-d of this chapter, or other than an adjudication of liability of an owner for a violation of subdivision (d) of section eleven hundred eleven of this chapter in accordance with section eleven hundred eleven-e of this chapter, or other than an adjudication of liability of an owner for a violation of section eleven hundred seventy-four of this chapter in accordance with section eleven hundred seventy-four-a of this chapter, there shall be levied a mandatory surcharge, in addition to any sentence required or permitted by law, in the amount of seventeen dollars.

1. [Eff Sept 20, 2025; eff until July 1, 2022] Whenever proceedings in an administrative tribunal or a court of this state result in a conviction for a crime under this chapter or a traffic infraction under this chapter other than a traffic infraction involving standing, stopping, parking or motor vehicle equipment or violations by pedestrians or bicyclists, or other than an adjudication of liability of an owner for a violation of subdivision (b), (c), (d), (f) or (g) of section eleven hundred eighty of this chapter in accordance with section eleven hundred eighty-b of this chapter, or other than an adjudication of liability of an owner for a violation of subdivision (b), (c), (d), (f) or (g) of section eleven hundred eighty of this chapter in accordance with section eleven hundred eighty-d of this chapter, or other than an adjudication of liability of an owner for a violation of subdivision (d) of section eleven hundred eleven of this chapter in accordance with section eleven hundred eleven-d of this chapter, or other than an adjudication of liability of an owner for a violation of subdivision (d) of section eleven hundred eleven of this chapter in accordance with section eleven hundred eleven-e of this chapter, or other than an adjudication of liability of an owner for a violation of section eleven hundred seventy-four of this chapter in accordance with section eleven hundred seventy-four-a of this chapter, there shall be levied a mandatory surcharge, in addition to any sentence required or permitted by law, in the amount of seventeen dollars.

1. [Eff July 1, 2022; eff until Dec 1, 2024] Whenever proceedings in an administrative tribunal or a court of this state result in a conviction for a crime under this chapter or a traffic infraction under this chapter other than a traffic infraction involving

standing, stopping, parking or motor vehicle equipment or violations by pedestrians or bicyclists, or other than an adjudication of liability of an owner for a violation of subdivision (b), (c), (d), (f) or (g) of section eleven hundred eighty of this chapter in accordance with section eleven hundred eighty-d of this chapter, or other than an adjudication of liability of an owner for a violation of subdivision (d) of section eleven hundred eleven of this chapter in accordance with section eleven hundred eleven-d of this chapter, or other than an adjudication of liability of an owner for a violation of subdivision (d) of section eleven hundred eleven of this chapter in accordance with section eleven hundred eleven-e of this chapter, or other than an adjudication of liability of an owner for a violation of section eleven hundred seventy-four of this chapter in accordance with section eleven hundred seventy-four-a of this chapter, there shall be levied a mandatory surcharge, in addition to any sentence required or permitted by law, in the amount of seventeen dollars.

1. [Eff Dec 1, 2024; eff until Dec 1, 2024] Whenever proceedings in an administrative tribunal or a court of this state result in a conviction for a crime under this chapter or a traffic infraction under this chapter other than a traffic infraction involving standing, stopping, parking or motor vehicle equipment or violations by pedestrians or bicyclists, or other than an adjudication of liability of an owner for a violation of subdivision (b), (c), (d), (f) or (g) of section eleven hundred eighty of this chapter in accordance with section eleven hundred eighty-d of this chapter, or other than an adjudication of liability of an owner for a violation of subdivision (d) of section eleven hundred eleven of this chapter in accordance with section eleven hundred eleven-e of this chapter, or other than an adjudication of liability of an owner for a violation of section eleven hundred seventy-four of this chapter in accordance with section eleven hundred seventy-four-a of this chapter, there shall be levied a mandatory surcharge, in addition to any sentence required or permitted by law, in the amount of seventeen dollars.

1. [Eff Dec 1, 2024; eff until Dec 1, 2024] Whenever proceedings in an administrative tribunal or a court of this state result in a conviction for a crime under this chapter or a traffic infraction under this chapter other than a traffic infraction involving standing, stopping, parking or motor vehicle equipment or violations by pedestrians or bicyclists, or other than an adjudication of liability of an owner for a violation of subdivision (b), (c), (d), (f) or (g) of section eleven hundred eighty of this chapter in accordance with section eleven hundred eighty-d of this chapter, or other than an adjudication of liability of an owner for a violation of section eleven hundred seventy-four of this chapter in accordance with section eleven hundred seventy-four-a of this chapter, there shall be levied a mandatory surcharge, in addition to any sentence required or permitted by law, in the amount of seventeen dollars.

1. [Eff Dec 1, 2024] Whenever proceedings in an administrative tribunal or a court of this state result in a conviction for a crime under this chapter or a traffic infraction under this chapter other than a traffic infraction involving standing, stopping, parking or motor vehicle equipment or violations by pedestrians or bicyclists, there shall be levied a mandatory surcharge, in addition to any sentence required or permitted by law, in the amount of seventeen dollars.

2. [Eff until Sept 1, 2021] Where a person is convicted of two or more such crimes or traffic infractions committed through a single act or omission, or through an act or omission which in itself constituted one of the crimes or traffic infractions and also was a material element of the other, the court or administrative tribunal shall impose a crime victim assistance fee and a mandatory surcharge mandated by subdivision one of this section for each such conviction; provided however, that in no event shall the total amount of such crime victim assistance fees and mandatory surcharges imposed pursuant to paragraph (a) or (c) of subdivision one of this section exceed one hundred ninety-six dollars.

2. [Eff Sept 1, 2021] Where a person is convicted of two or more such crimes or traffic infractions committed through a single act or omission, or through an act or omission which in itself constituted one of the crimes or traffic infractions and also was a material element of the other, the court or administrative tribunal shall impose only one mandatory surcharge mandated by subdivision one of this section.

3. The mandatory surcharge provided for in subdivision one of this section shall be paid to the clerk of the court or administrative tribunal that rendered the conviction. Within the first ten days of the month following collection of the mandatory surcharge

the collecting authority shall determine the amount of mandatory surcharge collected and, if it is an administrative tribunal or a town or village justice court, it shall pay such money to the state comptroller who shall deposit such money in the state treasury pursuant to section one hundred twenty-one of the state finance law to the credit of the general fund. If such collecting authority is any other court of the unified court system, it shall, within such period, pay such money to the state commissioner of taxation and finance to the credit of the criminal justice improvement account established by section ninety-seven-bb of the state finance law. The crime victim assistance fee provided for in subdivision one of this section shall be paid to the clerk of the court or administrative tribunal that rendered the conviction. Within the first ten days of the month following collection of the crime victim assistance fee, the collecting authority shall determine the amount of crime victim assistance fee collected and, if it is an administrative tribunal or a town or village justice court, it shall pay such money to the state comptroller who shall deposit such money in the state treasury pursuant to section one hundred twenty-one of the state finance law to the credit of the criminal justice improvement account established by section ninety-seven-bb of the state finance law.

4. Any person who has paid a mandatory surcharge or crime victim assistance fee under the authority of this section which is ultimately determined not to be required by this section shall be entitled to a refund of such mandatory surcharge or crime victim assistance fee upon application to the state comptroller. The state comptroller shall require such proof as it is necessary in order to determine whether a refund is required by law.

5. When a person who is convicted of a crime or traffic infraction and sentenced to a term of imprisonment has failed to pay the mandatory surcharge or crime victim assistance fee required by this section, the clerk of the court or the administrative tribunal that rendered the conviction shall notify the superintendent or the municipal official of the facility where the person is confined. The superintendent or the municipal official shall cause any amount owing to be collected from such person during his term of imprisonment from moneys to the credit of an inmates' fund or such moneys as may be earned by a person in a work release program pursuant to section eight hundred sixty of the correction law. Such moneys shall be paid over to the state comptroller to the credit of the criminal justice improvement account established by section ninety-seven-bb of the state finance law, except that any such moneys collected which are surcharges or crime victim assistance fees levied in relation to convictions obtained in a town or village justice court shall be paid within thirty days after the receipt thereof by the superintendent or municipal official of the facility to the justice of the court in which the conviction was obtained. For the purposes of collecting such mandatory surcharge or crime victim assistance fee, the state shall be legally entitled to the money to the credit of an inmates' fund or money which is earned by an inmate in a work release program. For purposes of this subdivision, the term "inmates' fund" shall mean moneys in the possession of an inmate at the time of his admission into such facility, funds earned by him as provided for in section one hundred eighty-seven of the correction law and any other funds received by him or on his behalf and deposited with such superintendent or municipal official.

5-a. The provisions of subdivision four-a of section five hundred ten, subdivision three of section five hundred fourteen and subdivision three of section two hundred twenty-seven of this chapter governing actions which may be taken for failure to pay a fine or penalty shall be applicable to a mandatory surcharge or crime victim assistance fee imposed pursuant to this section.

6. Notwithstanding any other provision of this section, where a person has made restitution or reparation pursuant to section 60.27 of the penal law, such person shall not be required to pay a mandatory surcharge or crime victim assistance fee.

7. Notwithstanding any other provision of this section, where a mandatory surcharge or crime victim assistance fee is imposed pursuant to the provisions of section 60.35 of the penal law, no mandatory surcharge or crime victim assistance fee shall be imposed pursuant to the provisions of this section.

8. The provisions of this section shall only apply to offenses committed on or before September first, two thousand twenty-one.

9. Notwithstanding the provisions of subdivision one of this section, in the event a proceeding is in a town or village court, the court shall add an additional five dollars to the surcharges imposed by such subdivision one of this section.

10. For the purposes of this section, the term conviction means and includes the conviction of a felony or a misdemeanor for which a youthful offender finding was substituted and upon such a finding there shall be levied a mandatory surcharge and a crime victim assistance fee to the same extent and in the same manner and amount provided by this section for conviction of the felony or misdemeanor, as the case may be, for which such youthful offender finding was substituted.

HISTORY:

Add, L 1983, ch 15, § 52, eff April 1, 1983; amd, L 1983, ch 16, § 2; L 1983, ch 945, §§ 2, 3; L 1988, ch 746, § 13; L 1989, ch 62, § 85, eff April 19, 1989; L 1990, ch 190, § 318; L 1991, ch 166, §§ 337, 338, eff June 12, 1991; L 1991, ch 166, § 339, eff June 12, 1991; L 1992, ch 55, § 385, eff April 10, 1992; L 1992, ch 379, § 16, eff July 17, 1992; L 1994, ch 61, § 10, eff April 18, 1994, deemed eff April 1, 1994; L 1996, ch 309, § 70, eff Aug 31, 1996; L 1997, ch 435, § 65, eff Aug 20, 1997; L 1997, ch 452, § 3, eff Jan 1, 1998; L 1999, ch 385, § 5, eff July 27, 1999; L 1999, ch 452, §§ 13, 14, Sept 1, 1999, deemed eff on and after April 1, 1999; L 2000, ch 57, § 2 (Part L), eff May 15, 2000, deemed eff on and after April 1, 2000; L 2001, ch 95, § 17, eff July 13, 2001; L 2003, ch 16, § 16, eff March 31, 2003, deemed eff on and after March 31, 2003; L 2003, ch 62, §§ 2, 3 (Part M), eff Nov 11, 2003; L 2003, ch 261, § 4, eff July 29, 2003; L 2004, ch 56, § 3 (Part F), eff Feb 16, 2004; L 2005, ch 56, § 14 (Part D), eff April 12, 2005, deemed eff on and after April 1, 2005; L 2007, ch 56, § 14 (Part C), eff April 9, 2007, deemed eff on and after March 31, 2007; L 2008, ch 56, § 2 (Part DD), eff July 1, 2008; L 2009, ch 19, §§ 4, 5, eff May 28, 2009; L 2009, ch 20, § 17, 18, eff May 28, 2009; L 2009, ch 21, §§ 17, 18, eff May 28, 2009; L 2009, ch 22, §§ 17, 18, eff May 28, 2009; L 2009, ch 23, § 4, eff May 28, 2009; L 2009, ch 23, § 5; L 2009, ch 56, § 14 (Part U), eff April 7, 2009; L 2009, ch 59, § 1 (Part I), eff July 6, 2009; L 2009, ch 383, § 17, eff Sept 25, 2009; L 2009, ch 383, § 18; L 2010, ch 59, § 10 (Part II), eff Sept 20, 2010; L 2010, ch 59, §§ 10–a, 10–b (Part II); L 2011, ch 57, § 14 (Part A), eff March 31, 2011; L 2013, ch 55, § 6 (Part C), eff July 26, 2013; L 2013, ch 55, § 13 (Part E), eff March 28, 2013; L 2013, ch 189, §§ 11—11–c, eff Aug 30, 2013; L 2014, ch 43, §§ 3–3-d, eff July 25, 2014; L 2014, ch 99, §§ 10–10-d, eff Aug 21, 2014; L 2014, ch 101, §§ 10–10-d, eff Aug 21, 2014; L 2014, ch 123, §§ 10–10-d, eff Aug 21, 2014; L 2015, ch 55, § 13 (Part B), eff April 13, 2015; L 2015, ch 222, §§ 1–10-f, eff Sept 12, 2015; L 2017, ch 55, § 13 (Part A), eff April 20, 2017; L 2019, ch 55, § 13 (Part O), eff April 12, 2019; L 2019, ch 145, §§ 10–10-g, eff Sept 5, 2019; L 2019, ch 148, §§ 9–9-g, eff Sept 6, 2019; L 2020, ch 55, § 13 (Part A), eff April 3, 2020.

ALCOHOLIC BEVERAGE CONTROL LAW

Article 5—Special Provisions Relating to Liquor

§ 64-c. License to manufacture and sell alcoholic beverages in a premises commonly known as a restaurant-brewer

1. Any person may make an application to the state liquor authority for a license to operate a restaurant-brewer.

2. Such application shall be in such form and shall contain such information as shall be required by the liquor authority and shall be accompanied by a check or draft in the amount required by this section for such license.

3. [Repealed]

4. Section fifty-four of this chapter shall control so far as applicable the procedure in connection with such application.

5. Such restaurant-brewer license shall in form and in substance be a license to the person specifically licensed to operate a restaurant and sell liquor at retail to be consumed on the premises specifically licensed. Such license shall also be deemed to include a license to:

(a) sell wine and beer at retail to be consumed under the same terms and conditions, without the payment of any additional fee;

(b) sell beer brewed on the premises to other retail licensees, where such other retail license is held by the same person holding the restaurant-brewer license, or such other retail license is a commonly owned affiliate license, provided that such beer is sold through a New York state licensed beer wholesaler;

(c) sell no more than two thousand barrels of beer brewed on the premises to other retail licensees, where such other retail license is not held by the same person holding the restaurant-brewer license, and such other retail license is not a commonly owned affiliate license, provided that such beer is sold through a New York state licensed beer wholesaler; provided however such licensee may sell at wholesale without the use of a licensed beer wholesaler up to two hundred fifty barrels of those two thousand barrels to other retail licensees, where such other retail license is not held by the same person holding the restaurantbrewer license, and such other retail license is not a commonly owned affiliate license; and

(d) sell no more than two thousand barrels of beer brewed on the licensed premises at retail to a person for consumption in their home and at retail in bulk by the keg, cask or barrel for consumption and not for resale.

6. A license under this section may only be granted to a person who regularly and in a bona fide manner brews beer on the premises.

7. Not more than five licenses shall be granted to any person under this section.

8. A person holding one or more licenses under this section may brew, in the aggregate, no more than twenty thousand barrels of beer per year.

9. On or within thirty days of the effective date of this section, any person who holds a brewer's license under section fifty-one of this chapter as well as a license to sell beer, wine and liquor at retail for consumption on the premises may file an application with the liquor authority to convert those licenses into a license under this section. Such an application shall be granted by the authority except for good cause shown. The granting of such an application shall constitute conversion of said license into a restaurant-brewer license subject to the provisions of this chapter applicable to restaurant-brewers licenses issued under this section.

10.(a) For purposes of sections one hundred one and one hundred six of this chapter, a person licensed under this section shall be deemed a "retailer" as that term is defined within section three of this chapter. Notwithstanding any provision of this chapter to the contrary, a person licensed under this section may also be licensed (or interested directly or indirectly in a license) to sell liquor at retail to be consumed on or off the premises under section fifty-four, fifty-four-a, fifty-five, fifty-five-a, seventy-nine or eighty-one of this chapter or sections sixty-four, sixty-four-a, sixty-four-b and sixty-four-d of this article.

(b) No manufacturer or wholesaler of alcoholic beverages may be granted a license to operate a restaurant-brewer pursuant to this section. Any person who has an interest in premises eligible for conversion under subdivision nine of this section shall not be issued any license under this section unless and until a conversion application has been filed with and approved by the authority.

11.(a) No restaurant-brewer license shall be granted for any premises which shall be:

(i) on the same street or avenue and within two hundred feet of a building occupied exclusively as a school, church, synagogue or other place of worship; or

(ii) in a city, town or village having a population of twenty thousand or more within five hundred feet of three or more existing premises licensed and operating pursuant to the provisions of this section or sections sixty-four, sixty-four-a, sixty-four-b and/or sixty-four-d of this article; or

(iii) the measurements in subparagraphs (i) and (ii) of this paragraph are to be taken in straight lines from the center of the nearest entrance of the premises sought to be licensed to the center of the nearest entrance of such school, church, synagogue or other place of worship or to the center of the nearest entrance of each such premises licensed and operating pursuant to this section and sections sixty-four, sixty-four-a, sixty-four-b and/or sixty-four-d of this article; except that no license shall be denied to any premises at which a license under this chapter has been in existence continuously from a date prior to the date when a building on the same street or avenue and within two hundred feet of said premises has been occupied exclusively as a school, church, synagogue or other place of worship and except that no license shall be denied to any premises, which is within five hundred feet of three or more existing premises licensed and operating pursuant to this section and sections sixty-four, sixty-four-a, sixty-four-b and/or sixty-four-d of this article, at which a license under this chapter has been in existence continuously on or prior to November first, nineteen hundred ninety-three.

(b) Within the context of this subdivision, the word "entrance" shall mean a door of a school, of a house of worship, or premises licensed and operating pursuant to this section and sections sixty-four, sixty-four-a, sixty-four-b and/or sixty-four-d of this article or of the premises sought to be licensed, regularly used to give ingress to students of the school, to the general public attending the place of worship, and to patrons or guests of the premises licensed and operating pursuant to this section and sections sixty-four, sixty-four-a, sixty-four-b and/or sixty-four-d of this article or of the premises sought to be licensed, except that where a school or house of worship or premises licensed and operating pursuant to this section and sections sixty-four, sixty-four-a, sixty-four-b and/or sixty-four-d of this article is set back from a public thoroughfare, the walkway or stairs leading to any such door shall be deemed an entrance; and the measurement shall be taken to the center of the walkway or stairs at the point where it meets the building line or public thoroughfare. A door which has no exterior hardware, or which is used solely as an emergency or fire exit, or for maintenance purposes, or which leads directly to a part of a building not regularly used by the general public or patrons, is not deemed an "entrance".

(c) Notwithstanding the provisions of subparagraph (ii) of paragraph (a) of this subdivision, the authority may issue a license pursuant to this section for a premises which shall be within five hundred feet of three or more existing premises licensed and operating pursuant to this section and sections sixty-four, sixty-four-a, sixty-four-b and/or sixty-four-d of this article if, after consultation with the municipality or community board, it determines that granting such license would be in the public interest. Before it may issue any such license, the authority shall conduct a hearing, upon notice to the applicant and the municipality or community board, and shall state and file in its office its reasons therefor. The hearing may be rescheduled, adjourned or continued, and the authority shall give notice to the applicant and the municipality or community board of any such rescheduled, adjourned or continued hearing. Before the authority issues any said license, the authority or one or more of the commissioners thereof may, in addition to the hearing required by this paragraph, also conduct a public meeting regarding said license, upon notice to the applicant and the municipality or community board. The public meeting may be rescheduled, adjourned or continued, and the authority shall give notice to the applicant and the municipality or community board of any such rescheduled, adjourned or continued public meeting. Notice to the municipality or community board shall mean written notice mailed by the authority to such municipality or community board at least fifteen days in advance of any hearing scheduled pursuant to this paragraph. Upon the request of the authority, any municipality or community board may waive the fifteen day notice requirement. No premises having been granted a license pursuant to this section shall be denied a renewal of such license upon the grounds that such premises are within five hundred feet of a building or buildings wherein three or more premises are operating and licensed pursuant to this section or sections sixty-four, sixty-four-a, sixty-four-b and/or sixty-four-d of this article.

(d) Within the context of this subdivision, a building occupied as a place of worship does not cease to be "exclusively" occupied as a place of worship by incidental uses that are not of a nature to detract from the predominant character of the building as a place of worship, such uses which include, but which are not limited to: the conduct of legally authorized games of bingo or other games of chance held as a means of raising funds for the not-for-profit religious organization which conducts services at the place of worship or for other not-for-profit organizations or groups; use of the building for fund-raising performances by or benefitting the not-for-profit religious organization which conducts services at the place of worship or other not-for-profit organizations or groups; the use of the building by other religious organizations or groups for religious services or other purposes; the conduct of social activities by or for the benefit of the congregants; the use of the building for meetings held by organizations or groups providing bereavement counseling to persons having suffered the loss of a loved one, or providing advice or support for conditions or diseases including, but not limited to, alcoholism, drug addiction, cancer, cerebral palsy, Parkinson's disease, or Alzheimer's disease; the use of the building for blood drives, health screenings, health information meetings, yoga classes, exercise classes or other activities intended to promote the health of the congregants or other persons; and use of the building by non-congregant members of the community for private social functions. The building occupied as a place of worship does not cease to be "exclusively" occupied as a place of worship where the not-for-profit religious organization occupying the place of worship accepts the payment of funds to defray costs related to another party's use of the building.

12. The fee for an original and a renewal restaurant-brewer license shall be fifty-eight hundred fifty dollars in the counties of New York, Kings, Bronx and Queens; forty-three hundred fifty dollars in the county of Richmond and in cities having a population of more than one hundred thousand and less than one million; thirty-six hundred dollars in cities having a population of more than fifty thousand and less than one hundred thousand; and the sum of twenty-eight hundred fifty dollars elsewhere. Said license shall run for a period of three years. In addition to the license fees provided for in this subdivision, there shall be paid to the authority with each initial application a filing fee of two hundred dollars and with each renewal application a filing fee of one hundred dollars.

13.(a) A licensee or his or her employee may serve small samples of beer or malt beverages he or she produces at their licensed establishments.

(b) Each serving at such tasting shall be served only by the brewer or his or her employee and shall be limited to three ounces or less of a brand of beer or malt beverage produced by the brewer and no consumer of legal age shall be provided or given more than two servings of such brands offered for tasting.

(c) The authority is authorized and directed to promulgate such rules and regulations, as it deems necessary or appropriate to implement the provisions of this subdivision to protect the health, safety and welfare of the people of this state.

14. Notwithstanding the provisions of subdivision six of this section or of subdivision thirteen of section one hundred six of this chapter, the authority may issue a restaurant brewer's license pursuant to this section for a premises which shall be located wholly within the town of Ulster, county of Ulster, state of New York, bounded and described as follows:

ALL that certain plot, piece or parcel of land with the buildings and improvements thereon erected, situate, lying and being in the Town of Ulster, County of Ulster and the State of New York, bounded and described as follows:

BEGINNING at a point on the Northeasterly side of City View Terrace, said point being the Westerly corner of the lands of the State of New York and a Southwesterly corner of the herein described parcel; THENCE from said point of beginning along the Northeasterly side of City View Terrace, North 43 degrees 36 minutes 03 seconds West, 109.02 feet to a point on the Southeasterly side of Forest Hill Drive; THENCE along the Southeasterly side of Forest Hill Drive the following course and distances, North 16 degrees 32 minutes 34 seconds West, 92.62 feet to a point; THENCE North 10 degrees 38 minutes 26 seconds East, 70.45 feet to a point; THENCE North 35 degrees 53 minutes 26 seconds East, 122.45 feet to a point; THENCE North 46 degrees 30 minutes 26 seconds East, 203.40 feet to a point; THENCE North 62 degrees 37 minutes 26 seconds East; 115.94 feet to a point; THENCE North 79 degrees 39 minutes 26 seconds East, 47.82 feet to a point; THENCE North 45 degrees 16 minutes 41 seconds East, 63.33 feet to a recovered bar; THENCE along the bounds of lands of now or formerly Skytop Village Associates, L. 1916-P. 134, the following courses and distances, South 37 degrees 08 minutes 02 seconds East, 196.33 feet to a recovered bar; THENCE South 65 degrees 47 minutes 02 seconds East, 90.63 feet to a point; THENCE North 77 degrees 23 minutes 58 seconds East, 233.85 feet to a recovered bar; THENCE North 85 degrees 29 minutes 58 seconds East, 297.09 feet to a recovered bar; THENCE South 63 degrees 30 minutes 02 seconds East, 108.50 feet to a recovered bar; THENCE along the bounds of lands of now or formerly Robert D. Sabino, L. 1487-P. 397, and along a stone wall, South 32 degrees 24 minutes 04 seconds West, 353.51 feet to a point; THENCE leaving said stone and along the bounds of lands of now or formerly Stanley Amerling, L. 1440-P. 908, South 75 degrees 41 minutes 26 seconds West, 264.62 feet to a point; THENCE along the bounds of lands of Summit Properties, LLC, L. 2856-P. 82, the following courses and distances, North 41 degrees 29 minutes 34 seconds West, 50.00 feet to a point; THENCE South 71 degrees 10 minutes 26 seconds West, 89.84 feet to a point; THENCE South 59 degrees 51 minutes 26 seconds West, 251.72 feet to a point; THENCE South 13 degrees 15 minutes 34 seconds East, 90.20 feet to a point; THENCE along the bounds of lands of said State of New York, the following courses and distances, North 56 degrees 41 minutes 34 seconds West, 168.79 feet to a point; THENCE North 75 degrees 51 minutes 34 seconds West, 254.10 feet to the point and place of beginning. Being the same premises as conveyed to Skytop Motel, LLC by deed of Stewart Title, as agent of the grantor, Skytop Motel, Inc., dated April 29, 2003 and recorded in the office of the Ulster County Clerk on June 10, 2003 as document no. 2003-00016207, Receipt no. 48178, Bk-D VI 3621, pg-171.

15. Notwithstanding the provisions of subdivision six of this section or of subdivision thirteen of section one hundred six of this chapter, the authority may issue a restaurant brewer's license pursuant to this section for a premises which shall be located wholly within the city of Peekskill, county of Westchester, state of New York, bounded and described as follows:

Any such premises or business located on all that certain parcel of land situate in the City of Peekskill, County of Westchester and State of New York, that is a portion of Parcel I as it is shown on that certain map entitled, "Survey. .at Charles Point .." which was filed in the Westchester County Clerk's Office on October 23, 1980 as Map No. 20407 that is bounded and described as follows:

BEGINNING at a point on the easterly shoreline of the Hudson River and within the bounds of the said Parcel I as it is shown on the said Filed Map NO. 20407, which point occupies coordinate position:

North 464418.83 (y)

East 607401.00 (x)

of the New York State Coordinate System, East Zone and which point is distant, the following courses from the southerly corner of the Parcel shown on Map No. 20407 that occupies coordinate position

North 463520.804 (y)
East 608470.681 (x)
of the aforesaid New York State Coordinate System, East Zone:
North 47 degrees 30' 36 West 856.60 feet,
North 77 degrees 10' 53 West 488.18 feet,
North 41 degrees 17' 53 West 113.32 feet and
North 41 degrees 50' 16 East 169.08 feet;

THENCE from the said point of beginning along the said easterly shoreline (high water mark) of the east bank of the Hudson River:
Due North 16.17 feet,
North 53 degrees 58' 22 West 13.60 feet,
North 73 degrees 04' 21 West 24.04 feet,
North 63 degrees 26' 06 West 22.36 feet,
North 82 degrees 18' 14 West 37.34 feet,
North 64 degrees 47' 56 West 37.58 feet,
South 82 degrees 52' 30 West 16.12 feet,
North 61 degrees 41' 57 West 14.76 feet and
South 21 degrees 48' 05 West 9.71 feet;

THENCE leaving the high water mark and running across a peninsula of land and along the division line between Parcel I and Parcel II as shown on said Filed Map No. 20407, North 65 degrees 32' 43 West 30.18 feet to another point on the said easterly shoreline (high water mark) of the East Bank of the Hudson River;

THENCE northerly along the said high water mark, the following courses:
North 3 degrees 00' 46 West 17.54 feet,
North 13 degrees 45' 39 West 50.45 feet,
North 10 degrees 49' 23 West 69.23 feet,
North 0 degrees 47' 22 West 52.48 feet to a point which is the point of beginning of the hereinafter described 40 foot easement which point occupies coordinate position
North 464676.48 (y)
East 607189.28 (x)
of the New York State Coordinate System, East Zone;

THENCE continuing along the aforesaid easterly shoreline (high water mark) of the East Bank of the Hudson, the following courses:
North 10 degrees 18' 17 West 23.91 feet,
North 39 degrees 04' 58 West 21.39 feet,
North 20 degrees 13' 30 West 21.74 feet,
North 39 degrees 02' 08 West 95.27 feet,
North 13 degrees 08' 02 West 30.81 feet,
North 18 degrees 26' 06 West 53.76 feet,
North 28 degrees 10' 43 West 63.53 feet,
North 18 degrees 26' 06 West 50.60 feet,
North 37 degrees 14' 05 West 31.40 feet,
North 21 degrees 15' 02 West 96.57 feet,
North 32 degrees 00' 19 West 47.17 feet,
North 1 degree 18' 07 West 44.01 feet and
North 17 degrees 14' 29 East 29.32 feet to a point on the southerly line of lands under lease to the County of Westchester (Resco Site);

THENCE along the said County of Westchester (Resco Site) lands: Due East 432.31 feet to a point on the westerly line of an easement and a right-of-way leading to Charles Point Avenue;

THENCE along the said westerly and southwesterly line of the said right-of-way leading to Charles Point Avenue: Due South 241.16 feet and South 27 degrees 13' 00 East 406.90 feet to a point;

THENCE leaving the said easement and running along other lands now or formerly of The City of Peekskill Industrial Development Agency, South 41 degrees 50' 16 West 270.01 feet to the aforementioned easterly shoreline (high water mark) of the East Bank of the Hudson River and the point or place of beginning.

TOGETHER with an easement over all that parcel of land situate in the City of Peekskill, County of Westchester and State of New York that is more particularly bounded and described as follows:

BEGINNING at a point on the westerly line of Charles Point Avenue with the said westerly line is intersected by the line dividing the easement herein described on the south from lands under lease to the County of Westchester (Resco Site) on the north which point occupies coordinate position:

North 464719.99 (y)

East 608004.15 (x)

of the New York State Coordinate System, East Zone;

THENCE from the said point of beginning southerly along the said westerly line of Charles Point Avenue, South 14 degrees 54' 00 West 103.48 feet to a point;

THENCE westerly along other lands of the City of Peekskill Industrial Development Agency: Due West 396.44 feet to a point which is the easterly most corner of the lands of Point Associates, the grantee herein;

THENCE along the northeasterly line of the said Point Associates land, North 27 degrees 13' 00 West 406.90 feet and Due North 241.16 feet to a point on the southerly line of the aforementioned lands leased to the County of Westchester (Resco Site);

THENCE easterly along the said southerly line Due East 75.00 feet to a point;

THENCE southeasterly and easterly still along the said lands leased to the County of Westchester (Resco Site) the following courses:

Due South 223.00 feet,

South 27 degrees 13' 00 East 314.87 feet and

Due East 390.14 feet to the aforementioned westerly line of Charles Point Avenue and the point or place of BEGINNING.

TOGETHER WITH a non-exclusive easement for utilities, and ingress and egress over that certain right of way leading from Charles Point Avenue, now known as John E. Walsh Boulevard, in a westerly and northwesterly direction to the above described premises and as more fully described in the Declaration of Easement recorded in Liber 8888 cp 35.

HISTORY:

Add, L 1997, ch 538, § 1, eff Sept 3, 1997; amd, L 2006, ch 562, § 2, eff Sept 15, 2006; L 2007, ch 406, § 4, eff Nov 1, 2007; L 2008, ch 181, § 2, eff July 7, 2008; L 2010, ch 213, § 3, eff Jan 11, 2011; L 2011, ch 560, § 4, eff Sept 23, 2011; L 2012, ch 185, § 4, eff Jan 14, 2013; L 2012, ch 366, § 1, eff Aug 1, 2012; L 2016, ch 318, § 2, eff Sept 9, 2016; L 2019, ch 655, § 1, eff Jan 15, 2020; L 2020, ch 82, § 1, eff Jan 15, 2020.

Article 8—General Provisions

§ 100. Alcoholic beverages generally

1. No person shall manufacture for sale or sell at wholesale or retail any alcoholic beverage within the state without obtaining the appropriate license therefor required by this chapter.

1-a. No person shall sell, offer for sale, or otherwise provide for the consumption of any powdered or crystalline alcoholic product.

2. No manufacturer and no wholesaler shall sell, or agree to sell or deliver in this state any alcoholic beverage for the purposes of resale to any person who is not duly licensed pursuant to this chapter to sell such beverages, at wholesale or retail, as the case may be, at the time of such agreement and sale.

2-a. No retailer shall employ, or permit to be employed, or shall suffer to work, on any premises licensed for retail sale hereunder, any person under the age of eighteen years, as a hostess, waitress, waiter, or in any other capacity where the duties of such person require or permit such person to sell, dispense or handle alcoholic beverages; except that: (1) any person under the age of eighteen years and employed by any person holding a grocery or drug store beer license shall be permitted to handle and deliver beer and wine products for such licensee, (2) any person under the age of eighteen employed as a cashier by a person holding a grocery or drug store beer license shall be permitted to record and receive payment for beer and wine product sales when in the presence of and under the direct supervision of a person eighteen years of age or over, (2-a) any person under the age of eighteen years and employed by a person holding a grocery store or drug store beer license as either a cashier or in any other position to which handling of containers which may have held alcoholic beverages is necessary, shall be permitted to handle the containers if such have been presented for redemption in accordance with the provisions of title ten of article twenty-seven of the environmental conservation law, and (3) any person under the age of eighteen years employed as a dishwasher, busboy, or other such position as to which handling of containers which may have held alcoholic beverages is necessary shall be permitted to do so under the direct supervision of a person of legal age to purchase alcoholic beverages in the state.

2-b. Subject to the provisions of section ninety-nine-f of this chapter no retailer shall permit or suffer to appear as an entertainer, on any premises licensed for retail sale hereunder, any person under the age of eighteen years, except that a person under the age of eighteen years may appear as such entertainer, provided that:

(a) the parents or lawful guardian of such person expressly consent in writing to such appearance;

(b) the appearance is for a special function, occasion, or event;

(c) the appearance is approved by and made under the sponsorship of a primary or secondary school;

(d) the appearance takes place in the presence and under the direct supervision of a teacher of such school; and

(e) the appearance does not take place in a tavern. Failure to restrain such a person from so appearing shall be deemed to constitute permission.

3. Nothing contained in this chapter shall be construed to require that any food be sold or purchased with or in order to obtain any alcoholic beverage for consumption on the premises where sold.

4. Alcoholic beverages may be sold to be consumed on the premises at a bar, counter or similar contrivance. Only one such bar, counter or contrivance shall be permitted in any licensed premises, except that not more than two additional bars, counters or contrivances may be permitted by the liquor authority for good cause shown to it, and upon the payment to it of a fee, for each additional bar, equivalent to the amount of the annual license fee paid by the licensee or, in the case of an additional bar, counter or contrivance operated on a seasonal basis, a fee equivalent to the amount of the annual license fee paid by the licensee prorated for the number of months that the seasonal bar is in operation. Provided however that:

(a) if the licensed premises is a legitimate theatre or concert hall, or contiguous to and used in conjunction with a legitimate theatre or concert hall, additional bars, counters or contrivances may be permitted by the liquor authority upon payment to it of an annual fee of one hundred dollars for each such additional bar, counter or contrivance so permitted, in addition to the annual license fee paid by such licensee ;

(b) if such licensed premises be located at a baseball park, race track, or either outdoor or indoor athletic field, facility, arena or stadium, additional bars, counters or contrivances where beer shall be sold at retail for consumption on the premises may be permitted by the liquor authority, upon payment to it of the annual fee of thirty dollars for each such additional bar, counter or contrivance so permitted, in addition to the amount of the annual license fee paid by the licensee; and

(c) temporary portable bars, counters or contrivances shall be permitted in a ballroom, meeting room or private dining-room on the licensed premises of a hotel, restaurant or club during such time as said ballroom, meeting room or private dining-room is used for a private dinner, entertainment, meeting or similar affair to which members of the general public are not admitted.

4-a. At race meetings, authorized by the state racing commission, notwithstanding any inconsistent provision of law, additional bars, counters or contrivances where alcoholic beverages shall be sold at retail for consumption on the premises may be permitted by the liquor authority, upon payment to it of a fee equivalent to the amount of the annual or summer license fee paid by the licensee for each such additional bar, counter or contrivance so permitted in addition to the amount of the annual or summer license fee paid by the licensee.

4-b. Notwithstanding any inconsistent provision of law, for venues being operated or to be operated under a license to sell alcoholic beverages for consumption on the premises, and having a capacity for one thousand or more persons, the liquor authority may issue licenses for bars, counters, or similar contrivances in such numbers as the authority may determine in the exercise of its discretion.

5. No retail licensee for off-premises consumption shall sell, deliver or give away, or cause, permit or procure to be sold, delivered or given away any alcoholic beverage, other than as provided herein, on credit: a retail licensee for off-premises consumption, except a winery licensee, may accept third party credit cards for the sale of any alcoholic beverage for which it is licensed; a winery licensee having the right to sell wine at retail for off-premises consumption may accept third party credit cards for the sale of said beverages at the winery premises only; and any person duly authorized to sell wine at retail for consumption off the premises may sell on credit to any regularly organized church, synagogue or religious organization, wines to be used for sacramental purposes only. For purposes of this subdivision, beer and wine products that are delivered and left at the residence of a consumer without payment of the balance due thereon shall not constitute a sale on credit.

6. Notwithstanding any provision of law, rule or regulation to the contrary, a retail licensee for off-premises consumption may sell, deliver or give away, or cause, permit or procure to be sold, delivered or given away any alcoholic beverage on credit to a business or corporation, provided that the business or corporation is permitted to purchase from such retail licensee under this chapter. Such credit period shall not exceed thirty days.

7. No licensee shall sell or purchase any receipts, certificates, contracts or other documents issued for the storage of alcoholic beverages except as provided by the rules of the liquor authority. The liquor authority shall prescribe such rules for the purchase and sale of such receipts, certificates, contracts or other documents issued for the storage of alcoholic beverages which, in its opinion, will best accomplish

(1) Elimination of fraudulent and deceptive transactions;

(2) Protection of purchasers against defaults by sellers;

(3) The delivery of the alcoholic beverages represented by such receipts or documents, and

(4) The payment of all taxes due thereon to the state.

8. Within ten days after filing a new application to sell liquor at retail under section sixty-three of this chapter, a notice thereof, in the form prescribed by the authority, shall be posted by the applicant in a conspicuous place at the entrance to the proposed premises. The applicant shall make reasonable efforts to insure such notice shall remain posted throughout the pendency of the application. The provisions hereof shall apply only where no retail liquor license has previously been granted for the proposed premise and shall, specifically, not be applicable to a proposed sale of an existing business engaged in the retail sale of liquor. The authority may adopt such rules as it may deem necessary to carry out the purpose of this subdivision.

9.(a) Within ten days after filing a new application or an application for renewal to sell liquor under section sixty-four, sixty-four-a, sixty-four-b, sixty-four-c or sixty-four-d of this chapter, a notice thereof shall be posted by the applicant in a conspicuous place at the entrance to the establishment or proposed establishment where it can be easily read by passers-by. Said notice shall be in a form prescribed by the authority, provided however that said notice shall be either printed or highlighted in a pink ink of a neon, luminous or fluorescent variety. The notice shall specify the application date, the type of license, any identifying number assigned by the authority, if available at the time of posting such notice, and how to contact the state liquor authority to give a response to the application. The applicant shall make reasonable efforts to insure such notice shall remain posted throughout the pendency of such application. Additionally, within ten days of the applicant's receipt of a written request from the authority, the applicant shall re-post such notice. The authority may adopt such rules as it may deem necessary to carry out the purpose of this paragraph.

(b) Within ten days of the applicant's receipt of written notice of a hearing scheduled pursuant to section sixty-four, sixty-four-a or sixty-four-c of this chapter, the applicant shall post a copy of such notice in a conspicuous place at the entrance to the establishment or proposed establishment where it can be easily read by passers-by. This notice shall include in clear and concise language a statement of the use and capacity of the establishment. The applicant shall make reasonable efforts to insure such notice shall remain posted until the date of the hearing or public meeting specified in such notice. Additionally, within ten days of the applicant's receipt of a written request from the authority, the applicant shall re-post such notice. The authority may adopt such rules as it may deem necessary to carry out the purpose of this paragraph.

HISTORY:

Add, L 1934, ch 478, § 1, eff July 1, 1934; amd, L 1936, ch 651, eff Sept 1, 1936; amd, L 1939, ch 526, eff May 26, 1939; L 1939, ch 820; L 1940, ch 335; L 1941, ch 762, eff April 25, 1941; L 1948, ch 623; L 1950, ch 427; L 1954, ch 376; L 1954, ch 631; L 1961, ch 703; L 1963, ch 204, § 36; L 1964, ch 494; L 1966, ch 690; L 1968, ch 62; L 1969, ch 60; L 1969, ch 462; L 1971, ch 886; L 1976, ch 755; L 1976, ch 919; L 1976, ch 920; L 1977, ch 606; L 1978, ch 256, eff Aug 4, 1978; L 1978, ch 321, eff Aug 18, 1978; L 1980, ch 410, § 1; L 1984, ch 502, §§ 3, 4; L 1984, ch 614, § 1, eff July 27, 1984; L 1985, ch 564, § 2; L 1986, ch 18, § 1, eff March 31, 1986; L 1986, ch 797, § 1, eff Aug 2, 1986; L 2002, ch 249, § 1, eff July 30, 2002; L 2007, ch 447, § 1, eff November 1, 2007; L 2015, ch 231, § 2, eff Sept 13, 2015; L 2015, ch 466, § 1, eff Nov 20, 2015; L 2016, ch 423, § 1, eff Feb 12, 2017; L 2019, ch 724, § 1, eff March 19, 2020; L 2020, ch 39, § 1, eff March 19, 2020.

§ 106. Provisions governing licensees to sell at retail for consumption on the premises.

1. No retail license for on-premises consumption shall be granted for any premises, unless the applicant shall be the owner thereof, or shall be in possession of said premises under a lease, management agreement or other agreement giving the applicant control over the food and beverage at the premises, in writing, for a term not less than the license period except, however, that such license may thereafter be renewed without the requirement of a lease, management agreement or other agreement giving the applicant control over the food and beverage at the premises, as herein provided. This subdivision shall not apply to premises leased from government agencies, as defined under subdivision twelve-c of section three of this chapter; provided, however, that the appropriate administrator of such government agency provides some form of written documentation regarding the terms of occupancy under which the applicant is leasing said premises from the government agency for presentation to the state liquor authority at the time of the license application. Such documentation shall include the terms of occupancy between the applicant and the government agency, including, but not limited to, any short-term leasing agreements or written occupancy agreements.

2.(a) No retail licensee for on-premises consumption, except corporations operating railroad cars or aircraft being operated on regularly scheduled flights by a United States certificated airline or persons or corporations operating a hotel, as defined in subdivision fourteen of section three of this chapter, for exclusive use in the furnishing of room service in the manner prescribed by rule or regulation of the state liquor authority, shall keep upon the licensed premises any liquors and/or wines in any cask, barrel, keg, hogshead or other container, except in the original sealed package as received from the manufacturer or wholesaler. Such containers shall have affixed thereto such labels as may be required by the rules of the liquor authority, together with all necessary federal revenue and New York state excise stamps as required by law. No retail licensee for on-premises consumption shall reuse, refill, tamper with, intentionally adulterate, dilute or fortify the contents of any container of alcoholic beverages as received from the manufacturer or wholesaler.

(b) Notwithstanding the provisions of paragraph (a) of this subdivision, a retail licensee for on-premises consumption may prepare and keep drinks containing alcoholic beverages in dispensing machines, having capacities of not less than a gallon, which continually mix such drinks.

3. No retail licensee for on-premises consumption shall sell, deliver or give away, or cause or permit or procure to be sold, delivered or given away any liquors and/or wines for consumption off the premises where sold. The provisions of this subdivision shall not prohibit a licensed winery or farm winery from allowing a patron to leave the winery or farm winery with a partially consumed bottle of wine provided that the removal of the bottle is done in accordance with subdivision four of section eighty-one of this chapter.

4.(a) No liquors and/or wines shall be sold or served in premises licensed under section sixty-four or clause (a) of subdivision six of section sixty-four-a of this chapter, except at tables where food may be served and except as provided by subdivision four of section one hundred.

(b) No liquors and/or wines shall be sold or served in premises licensed under clause (b) of subdivision six of section sixty-four-a of this chapter, except at such times and upon such conditions and by the use of such facilities as the liquor authority, by regulation, may prescribe with due regard to the convenience of the public and the strict avoidance of sales prohibited by this chapter.

4-a. No beer shall be sold or served at a bar, counter or other similar contrivance unless a card, sign or plate, visible to the customer, upon which the name of the brewer is conspicuously and legibly displayed, is annexed or affixed to the tap or faucet from which the beer is drawn.

5. No alcoholic beverages shall be sold, offered for sale or given away upon any premises licensed to sell alcoholic beverages at retail for on-premises consumption, during the following hours:

(a) Except as provided in paragraph (c) of this subdivision, on Sunday, from four ante meridiem to ten o'clock a.m., except pursuant to a permit issued under section ninety-nine-h of this chapter.

(b) Except as provided in paragraph (c) of this subdivision, on any other day between four ante meridiem and eight ante meridiem.

(c) On any day between three ante meridian and six ante meridian, for a premises located within an international airport owned or operated by the Port Authority of New York and New Jersey. The provisions of this paragraph shall not be subject to change pursuant to subdivision eleven of section seventeen of this chapter.

Unless otherwise approved by the authority pursuant to subdivision eleven of section seventeen of this chapter, where any rule has been adopted in a county on or before April first, nineteen hundred ninety-five, further restricting the hours of sale for alcoholic beverages, such restricted hours shall be the hours, during which the sale of alcoholic beverages at retail for on-premises consumption shall not be permitted within such county.

Nor shall any person be permitted to consume any alcoholic beverages upon any such premises later than one-half hour after the start of the prohibited hours of sale provided for in this section.

6. No person licensed to sell alcoholic beverages shall suffer or permit any gambling on the licensed premises, or suffer or permit such premises to become disorderly. The use of the licensed premises, or any part thereof, for the sale of lottery tickets, playing of bingo or games of chance, or as a simulcast facility or simulcast theater pursuant to the racing, pari-mutuel wagering and breeding law, when duly authorized and lawfully conducted thereon, shall not constitute gambling within the meaning of this subdivision.

6-a. No retail licensee for on-premises consumption shall suffer or permit any person to appear on licensed premises in such manner or attire as to expose to view any portion of the pubic area, anus, vulva or genitals, or any simulation thereof, nor shall suffer or permit any female to appear on licensed premises in such manner or attire as to expose to view any portion of the breast below the top of the areola, or any simulation thereof.

6-b. No retail licensee for on-premises consumption shall suffer or permit any contest or promotion which endangers the health, safety, and welfare of any person with dwarfism. Any retail licensee in violation of this section shall be subject to the suspension or revocation of said licensee's license to sell alcoholic beverages for on-premises consumption. For the purposes of this section, the term "dwarfism" means a condition of being abnormally small which is caused by heredity, endocrine dysfunction, renal insufficiency or deficiency or skeletal diseases that result in disproportionate short stature and adult height of less than four feet ten inches.

6-c.(a) No retail licensee for on-premises consumption shall suffer, permit or promote an event on its premises wherein the contestants deliver, or are not forbidden by the applicable rules thereof from delivering kicks, punches or blows of any kind to the body of an opponent or opponents, whether or not the event consists of a professional match or exhibition, and whether or not the event or any such act, or both, is done for compensation.

(b) The prohibition contained in paragraph (a) of this subdivision, however, shall not be applied to any authorized combative sport.

(c) In addition to any other penalty provided by law, a violation of this subdivision shall constitute an adequate ground for instituting a proceeding to suspend, cancel or revoke the license of the violator in accordance with the applicable procedures specified in section one hundred nineteen of this article.

7. Except where a permit to do so is obtained pursuant to section 405.10 of the penal law, no retail licensee for on-premises consumption shall suffer, permit, or promote an event on its premises wherein any person shall use, explode, or cause to explode, any fireworks or other pyrotechnics in a building as defined in paragraph e of subdivision one of section 405.10 of the penal law, that is covered by such retail license or possess such fireworks or pyrotechnics for such purpose. In addition to any other penalty provided by law, a violation of this subdivision shall constitute an adequate ground for instituting a proceeding to suspend, cancel, or revoke the license of the violator in accordance with the applicable procedures specified in section one hundred nineteen of this article. Provided however, if more than one retail licensee is participating in a single event, upon approval by the authority, only one retail licensee must obtain such permit.

8. A club or a luncheon club licensed to sell alcoholic beverages for on-premises consumption shall be permitted to sell such beverages only to its members and to their guests accompanying them.

9. No restaurant and no premises licensed to sell liquors and/or wines for on-premises consumption under clause (a) of subdivision six of section sixty-four-a of this chapter shall be permitted to have any opening or means of entrance or passageway for persons or things between the licensed premises and any other room or place in the building containing the licensed premises, or any adjoining or abutting premises, unless such licensed premises are in a building used as a hotel and serves as a dining room for guests of such hotel, or unless such premises are a bona fide restaurant with such access for patrons and guests from any part of such building or adjoining or abutting premises as shall serve public convenience in a reasonable and suitable manner; or unless such licensed premises are in a building owned or operated by any county, town, city, village or public authority or agency, in a park or other similar place of public accommodation. All glass in any window or door on said licensed premises shall be clear and shall not be opaque, colored, stained or frosted.

10. A vessel licensed to sell liquors and/or wines for on-premises consumption shall not be permitted to sell any liquors and/or wines, while said vessel is moored to a pier or dock, except that vessels sailing on established schedules shall be permitted to sell liquors and/or wines for a period of three hours prior to the regular advertised sailing time.

11. A railroad car or aircraft being operated on regularly scheduled flights by a United States certificated airline licensed to sell liquors and/or wines for on-premises consumption shall be permitted to sell liquors and/or wines only to passengers and while in actual transit, except that a railroad operating licensed cars shall be allowed to sell liquors and/or wines from portable carts located on station platforms located at Penn Station, Grand Central Station, Jamaica, Hunterspoint Avenue or Flatbush from which such licensed railroad cars depart.

12. Each retail licensee for on-premises consumption shall keep and maintain upon the licensed premises, adequate records of all transactions involving the business transacted by such licensee which shall show the amount of alcoholic beverages, in gallons, purchased by such licensee together with the names, license numbers and places of business of the persons from whom the same were purchased, the amount involved in such purchases, as well as the sales of alcoholic beverages made by such licensee. The liquor authority is hereby authorized to promulgate rules and regulations permitting an on-premises licensee operating two or more premises separately licensed to sell alcoholic beverages for on-premises consumption to inaugurate or retain in this state methods or practices of centralized accounting, bookkeeping, control records, reporting, billing, invoicing or payment respecting purchases, sales or deliveries of alcoholic beverages, or methods and practices of centralized receipt or storage of alcoholic beverages within this state without segregation or earmarking for any such separately licensed premises, wherever such methods and practices assure the availability, at such licensee's central or main office in this state, of data reasonably needed for the enforcement of this chapter. Such records shall be available for inspection by any authorized representative of the liquor authority.

13.(a) No retail licensee for on-premises consumption shall be interested, directly or indirectly, in any premises where liquors, wines or beer are manufactured or sold at wholesale, by stock ownership, interlocking directors, mortgage or lien on any personal or real property or by any other means, except that liquors, wines or beer may be manufactured or sold wholesale by the person licensed as a manufacturer or wholesaler thereof:

(i) on real property owned by an interstate railroad corporation or a United States certificated airline with a retail license for on-premises consumption; or

(ii) on premises or with respect to a business constituting an overnight lodging and resort facility located wholly within the boundaries of the town of North Elba, county of Essex, township eleven, Richard's survey, great lot numbers two hundred seventy-eight, two hundred seventy-nine, two hundred eight, two hundred ninety-eight, two hundred ninety-nine, three hundred, three hundred eighteen, three hundred nineteen, three hundred twenty, three hundred thirty-five and three hundred thirty-six, and township twelve, Thorn's survey, great lot numbers one hundred six and one hundred thirteen, as shown on the Adirondack map, compiled by the conservation department of the state of New York - nineteen hundred sixty-four edition, in the Essex county atlas at page twenty-seven in the Essex county clerk's office, Elizabethtown, New York, provided that such facility maintains not less than two hundred fifty rooms and suites for overnight lodging; or

(iii) on premises or with respect to the operation of a restaurant in an office building located in a city having a population of five hundred thousand or more and in which is located the licensed premises of such manufacturer or wholesaler, provided that the building, the interior of the retail premise and the rental therefor fully comply with the criteria set forth in paragraph two of subdivision three of section one hundred one of this article; or

(iv) any such premises or business located on that tract or parcel of land, or any subdivision thereof, situate in the Village of Lake Placid, Town of North Elba, Essex County, New York; it being also a part of Lot No. 279, Township No. 11, Old Military Tract, Richard's Survey; it being also all of Lot No. 23 and part of Lot No. 22 as shown and designated on a certain map entitled "Map of Building Sites for Sale by B.R. Brewster" made by G.T. Chellis C.E. in 1892; also being PARCEL No. 1 on a certain map of lands of Robert J. Mahoney and wife made by G.C. Sylvester, P.E. & L.S. # 21300, dated August 4, 1964, and filed in the Essex County Clerk's Office on August 27, 1964, and more particularly bounded and described as follows; BEGINNING at the intersection of the northerly bounds of Shore Drive (formerly Mirror Street) with the westerly bounds of Park Place (formerly Rider Street) which point is also the northeast corner of Lot No. 23, from thence South 21°50' East in the westerly bounds of Park Place a distance of 119 feet, more or less, to a lead plug in the edge of the sidewalk marking the southeast corner of Lot No. 23 and the northeast corner of Lot No. 24; from thence South 68°00'50" West a distance of 50.05 feet to an iron pipe set in concrete at the corner of Lots 23 and 22; from thence South 65°10'50" West a distance of 7.94 feet along the south line of Lot No. 22 to an iron pipe for a corner; from thence North 23°21'40 West and at 17.84 feet along said line passing over a drill hole in a concrete sidewalk, and at 68.04 feet further along said line passing over an iron pipe at the southerly edge of another sidewalk, and at 1.22 feet further along said line passing over another drill hole in a sidewalk, a total distance of 119 feet, more or less, to the northerly line of Lot No. 22; from thence easterly in the northerly line of Lot 22 and 23 to the northeast corner of Lot No. 23 and the point of beginning. Also including the lands to the center of Shore Drive included between the northerly straight line continuation of the side lines of the above described parcel, and to the center of Park Place, where they abut the above described premises SUBJECT to the use thereof for street purposes. Being the same premises conveyed by Morestuff, Inc. to Madeline Sellers by deed dated June 30, 1992, recorded in the Essex County Clerk's Office on July 10, 1992 in Book 1017 of Deeds at Page 318; or

(v) any such premises or business located on that certain piece or parcel of land, or any subdivision thereof, situate, lying and being in the Town of Plattsburgh, County of Clinton, State of New York and being more particularly bounded and described as follows: Starting at an iron pipe found in the easterly bounds of the highway known as the Old Military Turnpike, said iron pipe being located 910.39 feet southeasterly, as measured along the easterly bounds of said highway, from the southerly bounds of the roadway known as Industrial Parkway West, THENCE running S 31° 54' 33" E along the easterly bounds of said Old Military Turnpike Extension, 239.88 feet to a point marking the beginning of a curve concave to the west; thence southerly along said curve, having a radius of 987.99 feet, 248.12 feet to an iron pipe found marking the point of beginning for the parcel herein being described, said point also marked the southerly corner of lands of Larry Garrow, et al, as described in Book 938 of Deeds at page 224; thence N 07° 45' 4" E along the easterly bounds of said Garrow, 748.16 feet to a 3"x4" concrete monument marking the northeasterly corner of said Garrow, the northwesterly corner of the parcel herein being described and said monument also marking the southerly bounds of lands of Salerno Plastic Corp. as described in Book 926 of Deeds at Page 186; thence S 81° 45' 28 E along a portion of the southerly bounds of said Salerno Plastic Corp., 441.32 feet to an iron pin found marking the northeasterly corner of the parcel herein being described and also marking the northwest corner of the remaining lands now or formerly owned by said Marx and Delaura; thence S 07° 45' 40'' W along the Westerly bounds of lands now of formerly of said Marx and DeLaura and along the easterly bounds of the parcel herein being described, 560.49 feet to an iron pin; thence N 83° 43' 21'' W along a portion of the remaining lands of said Marx and DeLaura, 41.51 feet to an iron pin; thence S 08° 31' 30'' W, along a portion of the remaining lands of said Marx and Delaura, 75.01 feet to an iron pin marking northeasterly corner of lands currently owned by the Joint Council for Economic Opportunity of Plattsburgh and Clinton County, Inc. as described in Book 963 of Deeds at Page 313; thence N 82° 20' 32'' W along a portion of the northerly bounds of said J.CEO, 173.50 feet to an iron pin; thence 61° 21' 12'' W, continuing along a portion of the northerly bounds of said J.CEO, 134.14 feet to an iron pin; thence S 07° 45' 42'' W along the westerly bounds of said J.CEO, 50 feet to an iron pin; thence S 66° 48' 56'' W along a portion of the northerly bounds of remaining lands of said Marx and DeLaura, 100.00 feet to an iron pipe found on the easterly bounds of the aforesaid highway, said from pipe also being located on a curve concave to the west; thence running and running northerly along the easterly bounds of the aforesaid highway and being along said curve, with the curve having a radius of 987.93 feet, 60.00 feet to the point of beginning and containing 6.905 acres of land. Being the same premises as conveyed to Ronald Marx and Alice Marx by deed of CIT Small Business Lending Corp., as agent of the administrator, U.S Small Business Administration, an agency of the United States Government dated September 10, 2001 and recorded in the office of the Clinton County Clerk on September 21, 2001 as Instrument #135020; or

(vi) any such premises or businesses located on that certain plot, piece or parcel of land, situate, lying and being in the Second Ward of the City of Schenectady, on the Northerly side of Union Street, bounded and described as follows: to wit; Beginning at the Southeasterly corner of the lands lately owned by Elisha L. Freeman and now by Albert Shear; and running from thence Easterly along the line of Union Street, 44 feet to the lands now owned by or in the possession of James G. Van Vorst; thence Northerly in a straight line along the last mentioned lands and the lands of the late John Lake, 102 feet to the lands of one Miss Rodgers; thence Westerly along the line of the last mentioned lands of said Rodgers to the lands of the said Shear; and thence Southerly along the lands of said Shear 101 feet, 6 inches to Union Street, the place of beginning.

Also all that tract or parcel of land, with the buildings thereon, situate in the City of Schenectady, County of Schenectady, and State of New York, situate in the First, formerly the Second Ward of the said City, on the Northerly side of Union Street, which was conveyed by William Meeker and wife to Elisha L. Freeman by deed dated the second day of December 1843, and recorded in the Clerk's Office of Schenectady County on December 5, 1843, in Book V of Deeds at page 392, which lot in said deed is bounded and described as follows: Beginning at a point in the Northerly line of Union Street where it is intersected by the Easterly line of property numbered 235 Union Street, which is hereby conveyed, and running thence Northerly along the Easterly line of said property, One Hundred Forty and Five-tenths (140.5) feet to a point sixteen (16) feet Southerly from the Southerly line of the new garage built upon land adjoining on the North; thence Westerly parallel with said garage, Forty-six and Seven-tenths (46.7) feet; thence Southerly One Hundred Forty and Eighty-tenths (140.8) feet to the

Northerly margin of Union Street; thence Easterly along the Northerly margin of Union Street, about Forty-eight and three-tenths (48.3) feet to the point or place of beginning.

The two above parcels are together more particularly described as follows:

All that parcel of land in the City of Schenectady beginning at a point in the northerly margin of Union Street at the southwesterly corner of lands now or formerly of Friedman (Deed Book 636 at page 423) which point is about 60 feet westerly of the westerly line of North College Street and runs thence N. 86 deg. 42' 20'' W. 92.30 feet to the southeasterly corner of other lands now or formerly of Friedman (Deed Book 798 at page 498); thence N. 04 deg. 06' 48'' E. 140.50 feet to the southwesterly corner of lands now or formerly of Stockade Associates (Deed Book 1038 at page 521); thence S. 87 deg. 05' 27'' E. 46.70 feet to lands now or formerly at McCarthy (Deed Book 1129 at page 281); thence along McCarthy S. 00 deg. 52' 02'' E. 3.69 feet to the northwesterly corner of lands now or formerly of SONYMA (Deed Book 1502 at page 621); thence along lands of SONYMA S. 02' 56'' W. 34.75 feet to a corner; thence still along lands of SONYMA and lands now or formerly of Magee (Deed Book 399 at page 165) S. 86 deg. 11' 52 E. 42.57 feet to a corner; thence still along lands of Magee and Lands of Friedman first above mentioned S. 03 deg. 10' 08'' W. 102.00 feet to the point of beginning.

Excepting and reserving all that portion of the above parcel lying easterly of a line described as follows:

All that tract or parcel of land, situated in the City of Schenectady and County of Schenectady and State of New York, on the Northerly side of Union Street bounded and described as follows:

Beginning at a point in the northerly line of Union Street, said point being in the division line between lands now or formerly of Electric Brew Pubs, Inc. (1506 of Deeds at page 763) on the West and lands now or formerly of Margaret Wexler and Donna Lee Wexler Pavlovic, as trustees under Will of Ruth F. Wexler (Street number 241 Union Street) on the East; thence North 03 deg. 04' 10'' East, along the building known as Street No. 241 Union Street, a distance of 30.50 feet to a point; thence North 88 deg. 45' 45'' West, along said building and building eve, a distance of 5.62 feet to a point; thence North 03 deg. 03' 30'' East, along said building eve of Street No. 241 Union Street, a distance of 32.74 feet; thence South 88 deg. 45' 45'' East, along said building eve, a distance of 1.2 feet to an intersection of building corner of Street No. 241 Union Street and a brick wall; thence north 03 deg. 37' 30'' East, along said brick wall, a distance of 14.47 feet to a point in the corner of the brick wall, thence South 86 deg. 46' 45'' East along said brick wall a distance of 4.42 feet to the intersection of brick wall with the boundary line between the Electric Brew Pubs, Inc. (aforesaid) on the West and lands of Margaret Wexler and Donna Lee Wexler Pavlovic, (aforesaid) on the East; thence North 03 deg 10' 08'' East a distance of 0.62 feet to the Northeast corner of lands belonging to Margaret Wexler and Donna Lee Wexler Pavlovic.

Also all that tract or parcel of land commonly known as the Union Street School, located on the Northeasterly corner of Union and North College Streets in the First Ward of the City and County of Schenectady and State of New York, more particularly bounded and described as follows: Beginning at a point in the Northerly street line of Union Street where it is intersected by the Easterly street line of North College Street, and runs thence Northerly along the Easterly street line of North College Street, one hundred seven and five-tenths (107.5) feet to a point, thence easterly at an angle of ninety (90) degrees, one hundred ninety-one and seventy-five hundredths (191.75) feet to a point in the Northwesterly street line of Erie Boulevard thence southwesterly along the Northwesterly street line of Erie Boulevard, one hundred twenty-three and eight-tenths (123.8) feet to its intersection with the Northerly street line of Union Street; thence Westerly along the Northerly street line of Union Street, one hundred twenty-four and fifty-five hundredths (124.55) feet to the point or place of beginning.

The above described parcel of property includes the Blue Line parcel of land, which is a portion of the abandoned Erie Canal Lands, located in the First Ward of the City of Schenectady, New York, and which Blue Line parcel lies between the Northwesterly line of Erie Boulevard as set forth in the above described premises and the Northeasterly lot line of the old Union Street School as it runs parallel with the Northwesterly line of Erie Boulevard as aforesaid.

The two above parcels are together more particularly described as follows: All that parcel of land in the City of Schenectady beginning at a point in the northerly margin of Union Street and the northwesterly margin of Erie Boulevard and runs thence along Union Street N. 86 deg. 42' 20" W. 124.55 feet to the easterly margin of North College Street; thence along North College Street N. 05 deg 04' 40" E. 107.50 feet to the southeasterly corner of lands now or formerly of McCarthy (Deed Book 1129 at page 279); thence along McCarthy, Cottage Alley and lands now or formerly of McGregor (Deed Book 912 at page 624) S. 84 deg. 55' 20" E. 191.75 feet to the northwesterly margin of Erie Boulevard; thence along Erie Boulevard S. 38 deg. 03' 53" W. 123.54 feet to the point of beginning;

(vii) any such premises or businesses located on that tract or parcel of land situate in the Town of Hopewell, Ontario County, State of New York, bounded and described as follows: Commencing at a 5/8" rebar found on the division line between lands now or formerly of Ontario County - Finger Lakes Community College (Liber 698 of Deeds, Page 466) on the north and lands now or formerly of James W. Baird (Liber 768 of Deeds, Page 1109) on the south; thence, North 43°-33'-40" West, on said division line, a distance of 77.32 feet to the Point of Beginning. Thence, North 43°-33'-40" West, continuing on said division line and through said lands of Ontario County, a distance of 520.45 feet to a point on the southeasterly edge of an existing concrete pad; thence, South 74°-19'-53" West, along said edge of concrete and the projection thereof, a distance of 198.78 feet to a point on the easterly edge of pavement of an existing campus drive; thence, the following two (2) courses and distances along said edge of pavement: Northeasterly on a curve to the left having a radius of 2221.65 feet, a chord bearing of North 30°-16'-39" East, a chord distance of 280.79, a central angle of 07°-14'-47", a length of 280.98 feet to a point of reverse curvature; thence, Northeasterly on a curve to the right having a radius of 843.42 feet, a chord bearing of North 45°-25'-09" East, a chord distance of 534.08, a central angle of 36°-55'-01", a length of 543.43 feet to a point; thence, South 30°-04'-59" East, a distance of 18.28 feet to the corner of the property acquired by Ontario County (Liber 766 of Deeds, Page 1112), as shown on a map recorded in the Ontario County Clerk's Office as Map No. 6313; thence, the following four (4) courses and distances along said property line: South 30°-04'-59" East, a distance of 177.17 feet to a point; thence, South 02°-20'-33" East, a distance of 147.53 feet to a point; thence, South 41°-31'-35" East, a distance of 200.93 feet to a point; thence, South 23°-48'-53" West, along said property line, and the projection thereof, through the first said lands of Ontario County - Finger Lakes Community College (Liber 698 of Deeds, Page 466), a distance of 517.96 feet to Point of Beginning. Said parcel containing 7.834 acres, more or less, as shown on a map entitled "Proposed Lease Area - Friends of the Finger Lakes Performing Arts Center, Hopewell, NY", prepared by Bergmann Associates, drawing LM-01, dated June 10, 2005, last revised August 17, 2005. The related PAC Properties are shown on the Map denominated "FLCC Campus Property, FLPAC Ground Lease, Parking, Vehicular & Pedestrian Access", recorded in the Ontario County Clerk's Office on December 10, 2009 in Book 1237 of Deeds at page 9 and are comprised of the areas separately labeled as Parking Lot 'A', Parking Lot 'G', the Ticket Booth area, the Sidewalks, and the Entry Roads;

(viii) any such premises or businesses located on all that certain piece or parcel of land situate in the City of Syracuse, County of Onondaga, State of New York, lying generally Northwesterly of the West Hiawatha Boulevard, and generally Northeasterly of the New York State Barge Canal, being a portion of Lot 11I and Lot 11J of the Carousel Center Subdivision as shown on a resubdivision plan of the Carousel Center Subdivision filed as Map No. 8743 in the Onondaga County Clerk's Office, and as of May 20, 2014 identified as space L323 in a lease between the liquor license applicant and property owner and on the third level of the shopping center thereon, such shopping center land being more particularly bounded and described as follows:

BEGINNING at the point of the intersection of the division line between the Northeasterly boundary of the New York State Barge Canal, Syracuse Terminal designated as "Parcel No. T-111" on the Southwest and Lot 11I of the Carousel Center Subdivision on the Northeast with the Northwesterly boundary of West Hiawatha Boulevard; thence North 50 deg. 26 min. 28 sec. West, along said division line, 690.72 feet; to a point; thence through Lot 11I and 11J of said subdivision the following thirty-five (35) courses and distances:

1) Thence North 40 deg. 22 min. 15 sec. East 191.79 feet to a point;

2) Thence South 82 deg. 04 min. 58 sec. East 294.58 feet to a point;

3) Thence North 07 deg. 52 min. 16 sec. East 314.89 feet to a point;
4) Thence South 82 deg. 07 min. 45 sec. East 53.96 feet to a point;
5) Thence North 07 deg. 52 min. 16 sec. East 70.18 feet to a point;
6) Thence South 82 deg. 07 min. 44 sec. East 40.81 feet to a point;
7) Thence North 07 deg. 52 min. 16 sec. East 35.49 feet to a point;
8) Thence South 82 deg. 07 min. 50 sec. East 1.52 feet to a point;
9) Thence North 07 deg. 52 min. 16 sec. East 45.53 feet to a point;
10) Thence South 82 deg. 07 min. 44 sec. East 92.67 feet to a point;
11) Thence North 07 deg. 52 min. 16 sec. East 194.00 feet to a point;
12) Thence North 82 deg. 07 min. 44 sec. West 121.00 feet to a point;
13) Thence North 07 deg. 52 min. 14 sec. East 408.67 feet to a point;
14) Thence South 82 deg. 07 min. 44 sec. East 168.50 feet to a point;
15) Thence North 07 deg. 52 min. 16 sec. East 34.33 feet to a point;
16) Thence South 82 deg. 07 min. 44 sec. East 15.33 feet to a point;
17) Thence North 07 deg. 52 min. 16 sec. East 341.67 feet to a point;
18) Thence North 82 deg. 07 min. 44 sec. West 199.44 feet to a point;
19) Thence North 07 deg. 52 min. 31 sec. East 0.97 feet to a point;
20) Thence North 52 deg. 50 min. 09 sec. East 11.22 feet to a point;
21) Thence North 07 deg. 52 min. 16 sec. East 20.77 feet to a point;
22) Thence North 37 deg. 05 min. 57 sec. West 30.86 feet to a point;
23) Thence North 82 deg. 07 min. 44 sec. West 21.02 feet to a point;
24) Thence South 52 deg. 13 min. 00 sec. West 5.85 feet to a point;
25) Thence North 82 deg. 07 min. 44 sec. West 7.41 feet to a point;
26) Thence North 07 deg. 52 min. 16 sec. East 108.15 feet to a point;
27) Thence South 82 deg. 07 min. 44 sec. East 0.75 feet to a point;
28) Thence North 07 deg. 52 min. 16 sec. East 22.46 feet to a point;
29) Thence North 82 deg. 07 min. 44 sec. West 0.75 feet to a point;
30) Thence North 07 deg. 52 min. 16 sec. East 43.48 feet to a point;
31) Thence North 52 deg. 52 min. 15 sec. East 7.78 feet to a point;
32) Thence North 07 deg. 52 min. 16 sec. East 47.79 feet to a point;
33) Thence North 37 deg. 07 min. 44 sec. West 7.78 feet to a point;
34) Thence North 07 deg. 52 min. 16 sec. East 198.11 feet to a point; and
35) Thence South 82 deg. 07 min. 44 sec. East 207.07 feet to a point on the westerly right of way line of Interstate Route 81, Thence along the westerly and southwesterly right of way line of Interstate Route 81, in a generally southeasterly direction, the following seven (7) courses and distances:

1) Thence South 18 deg. 26 min. 44 sec. East 44.24 feet to a point;
2) Thence South 31 deg. 26 min. 40 sec. East 70.85 feet to a point;
3) Thence South 37 deg. 56 min. 38 sec. East 377.51 feet to a point;
4) Thence South 33 deg. 48 min. 10 sec. East 129.69 feet to a point;
5) Thence South 32 deg. 22 min. 13 sec. East 213.26 feet to a point;
6) Thence South 42 deg. 27 min. 42 sec. East 58.65 feet to a point; and
7) Thence South 40 deg. 20 min. 45 sec. East 77.11 feet to its intersection with lands appropriated by the People of the State of New York described as Map 1401 Parcel 1831 in Book 5256 of Deeds at Page 686 and Book 5274 of Deeds at Page 836; Thence along the bounds of said Map 1401 Parcel 1831 the following fifteen (15) courses and distances:

1) South 07 deg. 30 min. 19 sec. East 39.16 feet to a point; thence
2) South 03 deg. 25 min. 41 sec. West 30.00 feet to a point; thence
3) South 12 deg. 49 min. 21 sec. West 30.00 feet to a point; thence
4) South 22 deg. 11 min. 30 sec. West 30.00 feet to a point; thence
5) South 31 deg. 35 min. 08 sec. West 30.00 feet to a point; thence
6) South 40 deg. 57 min. 25 sec. West 30.01 feet to a point; thence
7) South 48 deg. 44 min. 51 sec. West 20.00 feet to a point; thence
8) South 55 deg. 01 min. 19 sec. West 19.99 feet to a point; thence
9) South 65 deg. 30 min. 44 sec. West 8.49 feet to a point; thence
10) North 75 deg. 22 min. 31 sec. West 38.92 feet to a point; thence
11) North 29 deg. 08 min. 26 sec. West 25.83 feet to a point; thence
12) North 07 deg. 58 min. 33 sec. West 20.27 feet to a point; thence
13) North 07 deg. 40 min. 45 sec. East 100.00 feet to a point; thence

14) North 82 deg. 23 min. 04 sec. West 1.00 feet to a point; and

15) South 07 deg. 40 min. 49 sec. West 425.30 to its intersection with the northerly bounds of Map 1402 Parcel 1836 of said appropriation; Thence along the bounds of Map 1402 Parcel 1836 as described in Book 5256 of Deeds at Page 686 and Book 5274 of Deeds at Page 836 the following three (3) courses and distances:

1) South 07 deg. 40 min. 17 sec. West 70.35 feet to a point; thence

2) South 82 deg. 09 min. 26 sec. East 1.00 feet to a point; and

3) North 07 deg. 40 min. 37 sec. East 70.35 feet to its intersection with the bounds of the hereinabove described Map 1401 Parcel 1831; Thence along the bounds of said Map 1401 Parcel 1831 the following ten (10) courses and distances:

1) North 07 deg. 40 min. 37 sec. East 100.00 feet to a point; thence

2) North 40 deg. 32 min. 01 sec. East 61.06 feet to a point; thence

3) North 50 deg. 26 min. 34 sec. East 110.76 feet to a point; thence

4) North 55 deg. 51 min. 53 sec. East 43.02 feet to a point; thence

5) North 66 deg. 11 min. 17 sec. East 30.00 feet to a point; thence

6) North 79 deg. 28 min. 24 sec. East 30.00 feet to a point; thence

7) South 87 deg. 12 min. 02 sec. East 30.00 feet to a point; thence

8) South 73 deg. 54 min. 22 sec. East 30.00 feet to a point; thence

9) South 59 deg. 56 min. 49 sec. East 33.00 feet to a point; and

10) South 47 deg. 06 min. 38 sec. East 95.11 feet to its intersection with the division line between Lot 11J on the Northwest and the lands now or formerly of Woodstead Enterprises Co. as described in Book 3530 of Deeds at Page 257 on the Southeast (formerly lands of Rome Watertown and Oswego Railroad Company via Letters Patent, Book 292, Page 264); thence South 28 deg. 12 min. 27 sec. West along said division line and along the Northwesterly boundary of West Hiawatha Boulevard in part, 36.93 feet to its point of intersection with Northeasterly boundary of West Hiawatha Boulevard; thence North 61 deg. 43 min. 58 sec. West along said Northeasterly boundary 158.30 feet to its point of intersection with the Northwesterly boundary of said West Hiawatha Boulevard; thence West along said Northwesterly boundary the following three (3) courses: 1) South 30 deg. 39 min. 30 sec. West 599.46 feet to a point; thence 2) South 30 deg. 30 min. 42 sec. West 62.49 feet to a point; and 3) South 23 deg. 40 min. 55 sec. West 220.04 feet to its point of intersection with Southwesterly boundary of West Hiawatha Boulevard; thence South 49 deg. 30 min. 46 sec. East along said Southwesterly boundary, 0.30 feet to its point of intersection with the first hereinabove described Northwesterly boundary of West Hiawatha Boulevard; thence South 40 deg. 26 min. 20 sec. West, along said Northwesterly boundary, 98.08 feet to its point of intersection with the division line between Lot 11J on the Northeast and Lot 11H of the Carousel Center Subdivision on the Southwest; thence North 50 deg. 25 min. 12 sec. West, along said division line, 147.85 feet to the Northwest corner of Lot 11H; thence South 40 deg. 26 min. 20 sec. West 217.47 feet to the Southwest corner of lot 11H; thence South 49 deg. 49 min. 16 sec. East 147.83 feet to a point on the first hereinabove described Northwesterly boundary of West Hiawatha Boulevard; thence along said Northwesterly boundary of West Hiawatha Boulevard the following two (2) courses: 1) South 40 deg. 26 min. 20 sec. West 17.66 feet to a point; and 2) South 43 deg. 01 min. 50 sec. West 468.25 feet to the point of beginning.

Excepting the following piece or parcel of land appropriated by the People of the State of New York described as Map 1401 Parcel 1832 in Book 5256 of Deeds at Page 686 and Book 5274 of Deeds at Page 836: Commencing at the southwest corner of herein above described Map 1402 Parcel 1836 said point having a proceeding course of South 07 deg. 40 min. 17 sec. West 70.35 feet in the premises describe hereinabove; thence North 13 deg. 18 min. 48 sec. West 138.17 feet to the southeast corner of Map 1401 Parcel 1832; thence along the bounds of said Map 1401 Parcel 1832 the following four (4) courses and distances:

1) North 82 deg. 09 min. 26 sec. West 1.00 feet to a point; thence

2) North 07 deg. 53 min. 50 sec. East 353.36 feet to a point; thence

3) South 81 deg. 54 min. 58 sec. East 1.00 feet to a point, and

4) South 07 deg. 53 min. 54 sec. West 353.36 feet to the point of beginning; or such premises or businesses located on that tract or parcel of land situate lying and being in the Town of Oneonta, County of Otsego and State of New York and being a portion of Otsego County Tax Map Department Parcel Number 287.00-1-33 and

bounded and described as follows: Beginning at a point 2.12 feet off the northeasterly corner of a one story building on the lands, now or formerly, of Abner Doubleday, LLC, aka Cooperstown All Star Village, LLC, as owned by Martin and Brenda Patton, which point lies N 87°55'13" W a distance of 149.37' from the northeast corner of the Patton lands; thence N 74°30'18" W a distance of 51.50 feet to a point; thence S 15°29'42" W a distance of 2.00 feet to a point; thence N 74°30' 18" W a distance of 14.00 feet to a point; thence S 15°29'42" W a distance of 19.20 feet to a point; thence S 74°30'18" E a distance of 14.20 feet to a point; thence S 15°29'42" W a distance of 4.20 feet; thence S 74°30'18" E a distance of 51.30 feet to a point; thence N 15°29'42" E a distance of 25.40 feet to a point to the point and place of beginning; or

(ix) on premises or with respect to a business constituting the overnight lodging facility located wholly within the boundaries of that tract or parcel of land situated in the borough of Manhattan, city and county of New York, beginning at a point on the northerly side of west fifty-fourth street at a point one hundred feet easterly from the intersection of the said northerly side of west fifty-fourth street and the easterly side of seventh avenue; running thence northerly and parallel with the easterly side of seventh avenue one hundred feet five inches to the center line of the block; running thence easterly and parallel with the northerly side of west fifty-fourth street and along the center line of the block fifty feet to a point; running thence northerly and parallel with the easterly side of seventh avenue one hundred feet five inches to the southerly side of west fifty-fifth street at a point distant one hundred fifty feet easterly from the intersection of the said southerly side of west fifty-fifth street and the easterly side of seventh avenue; running thence easterly along the southerly side of west fifty-fifth street thirty-one feet three inches to a point; running thence southerly and parallel with the easterly side of the seventh avenue one hundred feet five inches to the center line of the block; running thence easterly along the center line of the block and parallel with the southerly side of west fifty-fifth street, one hundred feet; running thence northerly and parallel with the easterly side of seventh avenue one hundred feet five inches to the southerly side of west fifty-fifth street; running thence easterly along the southerly side of west fifty-fifth street twenty-one feet ten and one-half inches to a point; running thence southerly and parallel with the easterly side of seventh avenue one hundred feet five inches to the center line of the block; running thence westerly along the center line of the block and parallel with the northerly side of west fifty-fourth street three feet one and one-half inches; running thence southerly and parallel with the easterly side of seventh avenue one hundred feet five inches to the northerly side of west fifty-fourth street at a point distant three hundred feet easterly from the intersection of the said northerly side of west fifty-fourth street and the easterly side of seventh avenue; running thence westerly and along the northerly side of west fifty-fourth street two hundred feet to the point or place of beginning, provided that such facility maintains not less than four hundred guest rooms and suites for overnight lodging; or

(x) on such premises or business located on any of the following four parcels:

Parcel A

any such premises or business constituting the overnight lodging and resort facility located wholly within the boundaries of the Village of Altmar, County of Oswego, Great Lot 19 beginning at a point on centerline of Pulaski Street at its intersection with the division line between the lands now or formerly of Altmar Parish Williamstown Central School District (APW CSD) as described in Book 378 of Deeds at Page 118 on the northwest and the lands now or formerly of Tostanoski as described in Book 1356 of Deeds at Page 55 on the southeast; Thence along said centerline the following two (2) courses: 1) North 37 deg. 35 min. 00 sec. West, a distance of 803.88 ft. to a point and 2). North 45 deg. 48 min. 13 sec. West, a distance of 132.33 ft. to its intersection with the division line between the said lands of APW CSD on the southeast and the lands now or formerly of Hayward as described in Book 894 of Deeds at Page 211 & Doc. #2006-9318 on the northwest; Thence North 23 deg. 48 min. 43 sec. East along said division, a distance of 131.66 ft. to its intersection with the division line between the said lands of APW CSD on the north and the said lands of Hayward on the south; Thence South 73 deg. 16 min. 17 sec. West along the said division line, a distance of 131.66 ft. to its intersection with the division line between the said lands of APW CSD and the lands now or formerly of National Grid as described in Book 282 of Deeds at

Page 552; Thence along said division line to the following six (6) courses: 1) North 23 deg. 43 min. 38 sec. East, a distance of 158.73 ft. to a point; thence 2) North 83 deg. 39 min. 24 sec. West, a distance of 190.48 ft. to a point; thence 3) North 25 deg. 39 min. 08 sec. East, a distance of 24.15 ft. to a point; thence 4) North 53 deg. 32 min. 01 sec. East, a distance of 265.18 ft. to a point; thence 5) North 81 deg. 24 min. 54 sec. East a distance of 475.00 ft. to a point; and 6) North 81 deg. 24 min. 54 sec. East, a distance of +/- 522 ft. to its intersection with the center of Salmon River; Thence upstream along said center, and in a generally southerly direction, a distance of +/- 1,455 ft. to its intersection with the division line between the said lands of APW CSD on the northwest and the lands now or formerly of Bennett as described in Book 927 of Deeds at Page 65 on the southeast; Thence South 52 deg. 19 min. 00 sec. West along said division line, a distance of +/- 170 ft. to a point; Thence South 52 deg. 19 min. 00 sec. West, continuing along said division line, a distance of 400.00 ft. to its intersection with the centerline of Pulaski Street; Thence North 37 deg. 35 min. 00 sec. West along said centerline, a distance of 53.65 ft. to its intersection with the division line between the said lands of APW CSD on the southeast and the lands now or formerly of Pfluger as described in Book 922 of Deeds at Page 187 on the northwest; Thence North 52 deg. 25 min. 00 sec. East along said division line, a distance of 330.00 ft. to its intersection with the division line between the said lands of APW CSD on the northeast and the said lands of Pfluger, the lands now or formerly of Endsley as described in Book 1520 of Deeds at page 5, and the hereinabove said lands of Tostanoski, in part by each, on the southwest; Thence North 37 deg. 35 min. 00 sec. West along said division line, a distance of 247.50 ft. to its intersection with the division line between the said lands of APW CSD on the northwest and the said lands of Tostanoski on the southeast; Thence South 52 deg. 25 min. 000 sec. West along said division line, a distance of 330.00 ft. to the POINT OF BEGINNING; or

Parcel B

any such premises or business constituting the overnight lodging and resort facility located wholly within the boundaries of that tract or parcel of land situate in the city of Syracuse, County of Onondaga and State of New York, being part of Block 366 in said City and more particularly bounded and described as follows: beginning at a point at the intersection of the southerly line of East Genesee Street with the westerly line of University Avenue; running thence: South 00° 30' 30" West, along said Westerly line of University Avenue, a distance of 75.16 feet to a point therein; Thence North 89° 49' 00" West, a distance of 140.00 feet to a point; thence South 00° 30' 30" West, a distance of 271.55 feet to a point; Thence North 89° 49' 00" West, a distance of 103.01 feet to a point; Thence South 00° 11' 00" West, a distance of 132.00 feet to a point in the northerly line of Madison Street; Thence North 89° 49' 0" West along said northerly line, a distance of 141.36 feet to a point; Thence North 00° 25' 10" East, a distance of 50 feet to a point in the westerly line of Farm Lot 200 of the Salt Springs Reservation; Thence North 03° 26' 10" West along said westerly line, a distance of 415.12 feet to a point in the southerly line of East Genesee Street; Thence North 88° 11' 00" East, along said southerly line, a distance of 412.50 feet to the point of beginning. The premises are also described as follows: All that tract or parcel of land, situate in the City of Syracuse, County of Onondaga and State of New York, being known as new Lot 1A as is more particularly shown on a Resubdivision Map of Part of Block 366 made by Christopherson Land Surveying and filed in the Onondaga County Clerk's Office October 8, 2002 as Map No. 9498; or

Parcel C

any such premises or business constituting the overnight lodging and resort facility located wholly within the boundaries of all that tract or parcel of land situate in the city of Syracuse, County of Onondaga and State of New York, being a part of Lots 200 and 201, Lots 2, 6, and 7, Block 368 in the City of Syracuse and being further described as follows: Beginning at a drill hole set at the intersection of the easterly street margin of South Crouse Avenue and the southerly street margin of Harrison Street; Thence S. 89° 51' 36" E. (S 89° 49' 40" E measured), along the southerly street margin of Harrison Street, a distance of 395.30 feet to a capped iron rod set at the westerly line of a parcel of land conveyed to Syracuse University; Thence S. 00° 28' 34" W. (S 00° 30' 30" W measured), along the westerly line of those parcels of land conveyed to Syracuse University, a distance of 132.00 feet to a capped iron rod set; Thence N. 89° 51' 36" W.

(N 89° 49' 40" W measured), along the northerly line of a parcel of land conveyed to Syracuse University, a distance of 132.00 feet to a capped iron rod set; Thence N. 89° 51' 36" W. (N 89° 49' 40" W measured), along the northerly line of a parcel of land conveyed to Syracuse University, a distance of 66.00 feet to a capped iron rod set; Thence S. 00° 28' 34" W. (S 00° 30' 30" W measured), along the westerly line of that Syracuse University Property, a distance of 71.25 feet to a capped iron rod set; Thence N 89° 55' 36" W. (89° 53' 39" W measured), a distance of 130.40 feet to a capped iron rod set at the easterly line of that parcel of land conveyed to Crouse Health Systems, Inc. by deed recorded in the Onondaga County Clerk's Office in Liber 4800 at Page 730; Thence N. 03° 44' 23" W. (03° 42' 26" W measured), along the easterly line of the Crouse Health System, Inc. property, a distance of 37.99 feet to a magnetic nail set at the northeast corner of the aforementioned Crouse Health System, Inc.; Thence N. 89° 51' 36" W. (N 89° 49' 40" W measured), along the northerly line of the Crouse Health System, Inc. Property, a distance of 195.85 feet to a capped iron rod set at the easterly street margin of South Crouse Avenue; Thence N. 00° 23' 14" E. (N 00° 25' 10" E measured), along the easterly street margin of South Crouse Avenue, a distance of 165.50 feet to the point of beginning. Together with all the right, title and interest in and to strops and gores of land, if any, adjoining or adjacent to said premises and to the lands lying in the bed of any street, road land or right of way, as they now exist, or formerly existed in, in front of, or adjoining the premises above described or used in connection with said above described premises. Containing 1.55 acres of land more or less. It being the intent of this survey description to describe those parcels of land conveyed by Temple Adath Yeshurun, also known as the Congregation Adath Yeshurun, to the Syracuse Urban Renewal Agency, by a Warranty Deed dated September 21, 1972, that was duly recorded in the Onondaga County Clerk's Office on October 10, 1972 in Deed Book 2486 at Page 1137. Being a portion of the premises conveyed at Hotel Skylar, LLC, f/k/a 908 Harrison St., LLC, by deed dated June 5, 2007, and recorded in the Onondaga County Clerk's Office on June 14, 2007 in Deed Book 04998 at Page 0795 (Instrument: 0687909); or

Parcel D

any such premises or business constituting the overnight lodging and resort facility located wholly within the boundaries of all that tract or parcel of land situate in the city of Syracuse, County of Onondaga, being part of Lots 13, 14 and 15 of Block 233 in said City, more particularly bounded and described as follows: beginning at a point in the northerly line of East Genesee Street, a distance of 232.5 feet easterly, measured along said northerly line, from the easterly line of Almond Street; Running thence the following 8 courses and distances: (1.) S 89° 30' 50" E, along said northerly line of East Genesee Street, a distance of 109.5 feet; (2.) N 00° 20' E, parallel with said easterly line of Almond Street, a distance of 158.69 feet to the southerly line of Orange Alley; (3.) N 89° 30' 50" W, along said southerly line of Orange Alley, a distance of 66 feet to a point; (4.) N 00° 20' E, parallel with said easterly line of Almond Street, 20 feet to the northerly line of Orange Alley; (5.) N 89° 30' 50" W, along said northerly line of Orange Alley, a distance of 9 feet; (6.) S 00° 20' W, parallel with said easterly line of Almond Street, a distance of 13.5 feet to a point; (7.) N 89° 30' 50" W, parallel with the aforesaid northerly line of East Genesee Street, a distance of 3 feet to a point; and, (8.) S 00° 20' W, parallel with said easterly line of Almond Street, a distance of 165.19 feet to the point of beginning, containing 17,781+/- sq. ft. (0.41+/- Acres of Land) and; Parcel II (#716-718 East Fayette Street), All that tract or parcel of land situate in the City of Syracuse, County of Onondaga and State of New York, being Lot 3 and part of lots 4 and 9 of Block 233 beginning in the southerly line of East Fayette Street, a distance of 132 feet westerly, measured along said southerly line, from the westerly line of Forman Avenue; Running thence the following 4 courses and distances: (1.) N 89° 30' 50" W, along said southerly line of East Fayette Street, a distance of 97 feet; (2.) S 00° 20' 20" W, parallel with said westerly line of Forman Avenue, a distance of 178.69 feet to the northerly line of Orange Alley; (3.) S 89° 30' 50" E, along said northerly line of Orange Alley, a distance of 97 feet to a point; and, (4.) N 00° 20' 10" E, parallel with said westerly line of Forman Avenue, a distance of 178.69 feet to the point of beginning; or

(xi) with respect to any premises or business located on all that certain parcel of land situate in the City of Peekskill, County of Westchester and State of New York, that is a portion of Parcel I as it is shown on that certain map entitled, "Survey .. at Charles

Point.." which was filed in the Westchester County Clerk's Office on October 23, 1980 as Map No. 20407 that is bounded and described as follows:

BEGINNING at a point on the easterly shoreline of the Hudson River and within the bounds of the said Parcel I as it is shown on the said Filed Map No. 20407, which point occupies coordinate position:

North 464418.83 (y)

East 607401.00 (x)

of the New York State Coordinate System, East Zone and which point is distant, the following courses from the southerly corner of the Parcel shown on Map No. 20407 that occupies coordinate position

North 463520.804 (y)

East 608470.681 (x)

of the aforesaid New York State Coordinate System, East Zone:

North 47 degrees 30' 36'' West 856.60 feet,

North 77 degrees 10' 53'' West 488.18 feet,

North 41 degrees 17' 53'' West 113.32 feet and

North 41 degrees 50' 16'' East 169.08 feet;

THENCE from the said point of beginning along the said easterly shoreline (high water mark) of the east bank of the Hudson River:

Due North 16.17 feet,

North 53 degrees 58' 22'' West 13.60 feet,

North 73 degrees 04' 21'' West 24.04 feet,

North 63 degrees 26' 06'' West 22.36 feet,

North 82 degrees 18' 14'' West 37.34 feet,

North 64 degrees 47' 56'' West 37.58 feet,

South 82 degrees 52' 30'' West 16.12 feet,

North 61 degrees 41' 57'' West 14.76 feet and

South 21 degrees 48' 05'' West 9.71 feet;

THENCE leaving the high water mark and running across a peninsula of land and along the division line between Parcel I and Parcel II as shown on said Filed Map No. 20407, North 65 degrees 32' 43'' West 30.18 feet to another point on the said easterly shoreline (high water mark) of the East Bank of the Hudson River;

THENCE northerly along the said high water mark, the following courses:

North 3 degrees 00' 46'' West 17.54 feet,

North 13 degrees 45' 39'' West 50.45 feet,

North 10 degrees 49' 23'' West 69.23 feet,

North 0 degrees 47' 22'' West 52.48 feet to a point which is the point of beginning of the hereinafter described 40 foot easement which point occupies coordinate position

North 464676.48 (y)

East 607189.28 (x)

of the New York State Coordinate System, East Zone;

THENCE continuing along the aforesaid easterly shoreline (high water mark) of the East Bank of the Hudson, the following courses:

North 10 degrees 18' 17'' West 23.91 feet,

North 39 degrees 04' 58'' West 21.39 feet,

North 20 degrees 13' 30'' West 21.74 feet,

North 39 degrees 02' 08'' West 95.27 feet,

North 13 degrees 08' 02'' West 30.81 feet,

North 18 degrees 26' 06'' West 53.76 feet,

North 28 degrees 10' 43'' West 63.53 feet,

North 18 degrees 26' 06'' West 50.60 feet,

North 37 degrees 14' 05'' West 31.40 feet,

North 21 degrees 15' 02'' West 96.57 feet,

North 32 degrees 00' 19'' West 47.17 feet,

North 1 degree 18' 07'' West 44.01 feet and

North 17 degrees 14' 29'' East 29.32 feet to a point on the southerly line of lands under lease to the County of Westchester (Resco Site);

THENCE along the said County of Westchester (Resco Site) lands: Due East 432.31 feet to a point on the westerly line of an easement and a right-of-way leading to Charles Point Avenue;

THENCE along the said westerly and southwesterly line of the said right-of-way leading to Charles Point Avenue: Due South 241.16 feet and South 27 degrees 13' 00" East 406.90 feet to a point;

THENCE leaving the said easement and running along other lands now or formerly of The City of Peekskill Industrial Development Agency, South 41 degrees 50' 16" West 270.01 feet to the aforementioned easterly shoreline (high water mark) of the East Bank of the Hudson River and the point or place of beginning.

TOGETHER with an easement over all that parcel of land situate in the City of Peekskill, County of Westchester and State of New York that is more particularly bounded and described as follows:

BEGINNING at a point on the westerly line of Charles Point Avenue with the said westerly line is intersected by the line dividing the easement herein described on the south from lands under lease to the County of Westchester (Resco Site) on the north which point occupies coordinate position:

North 464719.99 (y)

East 608004.15 (x)

of the New York State Coordinate System, East Zone;

THENCE from the said point of beginning southerly along the said westerly line of Charles Point Avenue, South 14 degrees 54' 00" West 103.48 feet to a point;

THENCE westerly along other lands of the City of Peekskill Industrial Development Agency: Due West 396.44 feet to a point which is the easterly most corner of the lands of Point Associates, the grantee herein;

THENCE along the northeasterly line of the said Point Associates' land, North 27 degrees 13' 00" West 406.90 feet and Due North 241.16 feet to a point on the southerly line of the aforementioned lands leased to the County of Westchester (Resco Site);

THENCE easterly along the said southerly line Due East 75.00 feet to a point;

THENCE southeasterly and easterly still along the said lands leased to the County of Westchester (Resco Site) the following courses:

Due South 223.00 feet,

South 27 degrees 13' 00" East 314.87 feet and

Due East 390.14 feet to the aforementioned westerly line of Charles Point Avenue and the point or place of BEGINNING.

TOGETHER WITH a non-exclusive easement for utilities, and ingress and egress over that certain right of way leading from Charles Point Avenue, now known as John E. Walsh Boulevard, in a westerly and northwesterly direction to the above described premises and as more fully described in the Declaration of Easement recorded in Liber 8888 cp 35; or

(xii) all those tracts or parcels of land, situate in the Tenth Ward of the City of Troy, County of Rensselaer and State of New York, known as Lots Number Seven (7), A Seven (A7), Six (6), A Six (A6), Five (5), A Five (A5) and the southerly portions of Lots Four (4) and A Four (A4), as the same are laid down and described on a certain Map made by Frederick W. Orr, dated August 15, 1918, filed in the Office of the Clerk of the County of Rensselaer as Map No. 29 1/2, Drawer 18. The said premises hereby intended to be conveyed are bounded and described as follows:

COMMENCING at an iron rod in the westerly side of River Street at the most southeasterly corner of premises heretofore conveyed by Harry Goldberg and Norman Goldberg to Arthur E. Collins and another, by Deed dated November 8, 1940, recorded November 12, 1940 In the Office of the Clerk of the County of Rensselaer in Book 633 of Deeds at page 400 and running thence southerly along the westerly line of River Street 215.6 feet to a pipe in the most southeasterly corner of Lot No. A7; thence westerly along the southerly line of Lots Nos. A7 and 7, 163 feet more or less to the easterly shore of the Hudson River; thence northerly along the easterly shore of the Hudson River 216 feet more or less to the most southwesterly corner of land heretofore conveyed by the said Harry Goldberg and Norman Goldberg to Arthur E. Collins and another hereinbefore recited; thence along the southerly line of lands heretofore conveyed to said Collins and another easterly 31.75 feet; thence northerly 6.33 feet; thence easterly 18 feet; thence southerly 6.33 feet; thence easterly 150.57 feet to the point or place of beginning.

EXCEPTING THEREFROM that portion of the above described premises as were conveyed by John B. Garrett, Inc. to Cahill Orthopedic Laboratory, Inc. by deed dated June 22, 1993 and recorded in the Rensselaer County Clerk's Office on June 24, 1993 in Book 1960 of Deeds at Page 215, Containing 17,600 square feet of land more or less.

BEARINGS refer to the magnetic meridian of 1993. Said premises are also described as follows: Ward & Plate: 1005500 669 RIVER ST: frontage and depth 115.60 x 220.00 being the same premises described in Book 6534 of Deeds at Page 256 in the Rensselaer County Clerk's Office and being the same premises in the 2009 City of Troy Assessment Rolls and 90.78-3-2.1 In Rem Serial No. AY0054 (RIVERVIEW PROPERTIES INC; CORINA, ANGELO; MCLAUGHLIN, JOHN D & VASIL, SCOTT); and being further bounded and described as follows: BEGINNING at a point marked by a capped iron rod where the division line between lands now or formerly of Walter Snyder Printer, Inc. (Liber 1334, Page 861) on the northeast and lands herein described on the southwest intersects the northwesterly side of River Street; running thence South 40° 01' 52" West along the northwesterly side of River Street a distance of 100.00 feet to a point; thence North 49° 45' 31" West a distance of 41.97 feet to a point at the southwesterly corner of the building located on the herein described premises, said point also being the northeasterly corner of the building located on the property adjoining on the southwest; thence North 60° 59' 40" West along the building wall located on the property adjoining on the southwest and the northwesterly continuation of same a distance of 140.88 feet to the easterly shore of the Hudson River; thence North 30° 16' 52" East along the shore of the Hudson River a distance of 90.90 feet to a point; thence South 60° 44' 08" East along lands now or formerly of Walter Snyder Printer, Inc. (Liber 1334, Page 861) a distance of 31.75 feet to a point; thence North 30° 16' 52" East continuing along lands now or formerly of Walter Snyder Printer, Inc. a distance of 6.33 feet to a point; thence South 60° 44' 08" East continuing along lands now or formerly of Walter Snyder Printer, Inc a distance of 18.00 feet to a point; thence South 30° 16' 52" West continuing along lands now or formerly of Walter Snyder Printer, Inc. a distance of 6.33 feet to a point; thence South 60° 44' 08 East continuing along lands now or formerly of Walter Snyder Printer, Inc. a distance of 149.40 feet to the point and place of beginning. Be the aforesaid dimensions in this clause more or less and encompassing lands considered to be a single contiguous parcel.

(xii) all those tracts or parcels of land, situate in the Tenth Ward of the City of Troy, County of Rensselaer and State of New York, known as Lots Number Seven (7), A Seven (A7), Six (6), A Six (A6), Five (5), A Five (A5) and the southerly portions of Lots Four (4) and A Four (A4), as the same are laid down and described on a certain Map made by Frederick W. Orr, dated August 15, 1918, filed in the Office of the Clerk of the County of Rensselaer as Map No. 29 1/2, Drawer 18. The said premises hereby intended to be conveyed are bounded and described as follows:

COMMENCING at an iron rod in the westerly side of River Street at the most southeasterly corner of premises heretofore conveyed by Harry Goldberg and Norman Goldberg to Arthur E. Collins and another, by Deed dated November 8, 1940, recorded November 12, 1940 In the Office of the Clerk of the County of Rensselaer in Book 633 of Deeds at page 400 and running thence southerly along the westerly line of River Street 215.6 feet to a pipe in the most southeasterly corner of Lot No. A7; thence westerly along the southerly line of Lots Nos. A7 and 7, 163 feet more or less to the easterly shore of the Hudson River; thence northerly along the easterly shore of the Hudson River 216 feet more or less to the most southwesterly corner of land heretofore conveyed by the said Harry Goldberg and Norman Goldberg to Arthur E. Collins and another hereinbefore recited; thence along the southerly line of lands heretofore conveyed to said Collins and another easterly 31.75 feet; thence northerly 6.33 feet; thence easterly 18 feet; thence southerly 6.33 feet; thence easterly 150.57 feet to the point or place of beginning.

EXCEPTING THEREFROM that portion of the above described premises as were conveyed by John B. Garrett, Inc. to Cahill Orthopedic Laboratory, Inc. by deed dated June 22, 1993 and recorded in the Rensselaer County Clerk's Office on June 24, 1993 in Book 1960 of Deeds at Page 215, Containing 17,600 square feet of land more or less.

BEARINGS refer to the magnetic meridian of 1993. Said premises are also described as follows: Ward & Plate: 1005500 669 RIVER ST: frontage and depth 115.60 x 220.00 being the same premises described in Book 6534 of Deeds at Page 256 in the Rensselaer

County Clerk's Office and being the same premises in the 2009 City of Troy Assessment Rolls and 90.78-3-2.1 In Rem Serial No. AY0054 (RIVERVIEW PROPERTIES INC; CORINA, ANGELO; MCLAUGHLIN, JOHN D & VASIL, SCOTT); or

(xiii) [There are two subparagraphs (xiii)] ALSO ALL THOSE TRACTS OR PARCEL OF LAND, situate in the City of Saratoga Springs, Saratoga County, New York, bounded and described as follows: Beginning at a point 55 feet south on Beekman Street, from where the west line of Beekman Street intersects the south line of Congress Street, and running thence southerly along the west line of Beekman Street 55 feet, more or less, to the north line of the premises now or formerly owned or occupied by Henry Curtis; thence westerly along said Curtis' north line 65 feet, more or less, to the east line of the premises heretofore conveyed to Edward M. Merritt; thence northerly along said Merritt's east line 55 feet, more or less, to a point 55 feet south of the south line of Congress Street; thence easterly on a line parallel with the south line of Congress Street 65 feet, more or less, to the point and place of beginning; and being further bounded and described as follows: BEGINNING at a point in the Southerly line Grand Avenue at the intersection of the Westerly line of Beekman Street, said point also being the Northeast comer of lands now or formerly of Dublin Underground, LLC as conveyed in Book 1769 of Deeds at Page 657,thence along said Westerly line of Beekman Street, South 01°02'45" West, SS.00 feet to a point at the intersection of the common division line between lands now or formerly of Haggerty as conveyed in Book 1595 of Deeds at Page 480 on the South and lands of said Dublin Underground LLC on the North, thence along said division line, North 88°57'15" West, 65.00 feet to a point at the intersection of the common division line between lands now or formerly of Haynes as conveyed in Book 1630 of Deeds at Page 727 on the West and said lands of Dublin Underground UC on the East, thence along said division line, North 01°02'45" East, 55.00 feet to a point in the Southerly line of Grand Avenue, thence along said Southerly line, South 88°57'15" East, 65.00 feet to the point or place of beginning and containing 3576 ± square feet of land; and being further bounded and described as follows: BEGINNING at a point where the east line of an alley intersects the south line of Grand Avenue, running thence easterly fifty-five (55) feet, more or less, to the west line of property now or formerly owned by one Desidora; thence southerly one hundred ten (110) feet, more or less, to the northerly line of property now or formerly owned by one Gutierresl thence westerly fifty-five (55) feet, more or less to the easterly line of an alley; thence northerly one hundred ten (110) feet, more or less to the point or place of beginning. Be the aforesaid dimensions in this clause more or less and encompassing lands considered to be a single contiguous parcel.

(xiii) [There are two subparagraphs (xiii)] any such premises or business located on that certain piece or parcel of land, or any subdivision thereof, situate, lying and being in the Village of Suffern, Town of Ramapo, County of Rockland and State of New York, addressed as 97-99 Lafayette Avenue, Suffern, New York, identified for tax purposes by the Town of Ramapo - 2000 County/Town Tax Bill, Tax Map No. 07/016-B-0239-B-0000 and New Parcel Tax Identification No. 54.35-2-54, bounded and described as follows:

BEGINNING at a point on the Westerly side of Washington Avenue, where the same is intersected by the Northerly line of lands now or formerly of the Village of Suffern (Sect. 168, Lot 284), said point also being the Southeasterly corner of the premises herein intended to be described.

RUNNING THENCE North 76 degrees 15 minutes West along the Northerly line of lands now or formerly of the Village of Suffern a distance of 210.30 feet to a point; THENCE South 13 degrees 45 minutes West along the Westerly line of lands now or formerly of the Village of Suffern a distance of 78.75 feet to a point; THENCE North 76 degrees 28 minutes West along the Northerly line of lands now or formerly of the Village of Suffern a distance of 96.30 feet to a point; THENCE North 13 degrees 32 minutes East a distance of 117.60 feet to a point; THENCE South 76 degrees 15 minutes East a distance of 6.00 feet to a point; THENCE North 13 degrees 32 minutes East a distance of 54.80 feet to a point; THENCE South 76 degrees 15 minutes East a distance of 91.00 feet to a point; THENCE North 13 degrees 45 minutes East along the Easterly line of lands now or formerly of Mirando (Sect. 168. Lot 239A) a distance of 123.25 feet to a point on the Southerly side of Lafayette Avenue; THENCE South 59 degrees 56 minutes 42 seconds East along the Southerly side of Lafayette Avenue a distance of 176.92 feet to a point; THENCE Southeasterly along the Southerly side of Lafayette Avenue, on a curve to the right having a radius of 58.97 feet an arc distance of 76.88 feet to a point; THENCE South 14 degrees 45 minutes West along the Westerly side of Washington Avenue a distance of 109.22 feet to the point or place of BEGINNING.

Being the same premises described in a deed dated June 11, 1999 from Westchester Realty Group LLC to Marandy Realty Associates, LLC and recorded in the Rockland County Clerk's Office on June 24, 1999 Instrument ID # 1999-00033893.

The premises described above are more particularly described after field survey by A.R. Sparaco, Jr., P.L.S. dated June 13, 2000, as follows:

ALL THAT TRACT, piece or parcel of land with the buildings and improvements thereon in the Village of Suffern, Town of Ramapo, Rockland County, New York, Tax Map Reference Section 16B; Lots 239 B and 254, bounded and described as follows:

BEGINNING at a cross-cut in the westerly line of Washington Ave. (50 feet wide) where the same is intersected by the northerly line of lands of the Village of Suffern (formerly Washington Ave. School) and running thence; North 78° 42' 52" West 211.11' along the northerly line of lands of the Village of Suffern to an iron pipe; thence, South 11° 03' 40" West 78.38' continuing along said lands to a PK nail; thence, North 79° 21' 20" West 96.30' continuing along said lands to an iron pipe; thence, North 10° 21' 09" E 117.12' along lands now or formerly of Meadows to a point; thence, South 79°00'00" East 6.00' to a point in the centerline of an old right of way; thence, North 12°50'10" East 55.32' along the centerline of an old right of way to an iron pipe; thence, South 79°00'00" East 91.04' crossing through said right of way and continuing along the southerly line of lands now or formerly of Miranda to a cross cut; thence, North 11°15'34" East 123.37' along the easterly line of said lands to a cross cut in the southerly line of Lafayette Ave.; thence, South 62°34'00" East 165.97' along the assumed southerly line of Lafayette Ave. to a point of curvature; thence, Southeasterly along a curve to the right having a radius of 72.00' and an arc distance of 93.43' continuing along the same to a point of tangency in the westerly line of Washington Ave; thence, South 11°47'00" West 100.86' along the westerly line of Washington Ave. to the point or place of BEGINNING.

Containing 1.267 acres of land more or less.

SUBJECT to utility easements described in Uber 1016, page 487, Liber 1038, page 977, Book 340, page 1277.

SUBJECT TO a 6' wide easement for ingress and egress as described in Liber 318, page 4.

TOGETHER with a 6' wide and 12' wide right of way as described in Liber 318, page 4.

SUBJECT TO any other easements, rights of ways or restrictions of record.

Being the same premises described in a deed dated June 11, 1999 from Westchester Realty Group LLC to Marandy Realty Associates, LLC and recorded in the Rockland County Clerk's Office on June 24, 1999 Instrument ID #1999-00033893.

(xiv) ALSO ALL THOSE TRACTS OR PARCEL OF LAND, situate in the City of Saratoga Springs, County of Saratoga and State of New York, bounded and described as follows: Starting at an iron pipe on the southerly side of New York State Highway 9P at the intersection of the lands now of formerly of Ernst and one Walbridge and runs thence along the said highway S 64 degrees 25' E 72.4 feet to a concrete state monument; thence S 35 degrees 9' E 135.6 feet to an iron pipe on the Westerly side of an 18 foot wide Right of Way extending from the aforementioned highway to the Low Water Mark of Saratoga Lake; thence along the said Right of Way S 17 degrees 20' W 115 feet to an iron pipe, the place of beginning; thence in the same straight line along the said Right of Way 78.4 feet to an iron pipe; thence still along the said Right of Way S 38 degrees 9' W 208 feet to an iron pipe; thence N 51 degrees 51' W 81 feet to an iron pipe; thence N 14 degrees 34' E 54.2 feet to an iron pipe; thence N 56 degrees 0' E 242.8 feet to the place of beginning, the aforementioned dimensions more or less; and being further bounded and described as follows: BEGINNING at an iron pipe of the southerly side of New York State Highway 9P at the intersection of the lands now of formerly of Ernst and one Walbridge and runs thence along said highway S. 64 degrees 25' E. 72.4 feet to a concrete state monument; thence still along the said highway S. 35 degrees 9' E. 135.6 feet to an iron pipe on the westerly side of a Right of Way 18 feet wide running from the beforementioned highway to the Low Water Mark of Saratoga Lake; thence across the said Right of Way S. 26 degrees E. 21.15 feet to the Easterly side of the said Right of Way, the place of beginning; thence along the said Right of Way S. 17 degrees

20' W. 171.1 feet to a point; thence still along the said Right of Way S. 38 degrees 9' W. to the Low Water Mark of Saratoga Lake; thence along the Low Water Mark of the said lake to an iron pipe on the Westerly side of the said Highway which point is about 435 feet Easterly at right angles from the Easterly side of the beforementioned Right of Way; thence along the said Highway N. 10 degrees 57' W. 653.5 feet to a concrete monument; thence N. 26 degrees 10' W. 9.85 feet to the place of beginning. Be the aforesaid dimensions in this clause more or less and encompassing lands considered to be a single parcel.

(a-1) The provisions of paragraph (a) of this subdivision shall not apply to the holder of a retail on-premises consumption license issued for a premises located in the borough of Manhattan, city, county and state of New York, bounded and described as follows: Beginning at a point on the northerly side of 52nd Street, distant 375 feet westerly from the northwesterly corner of 52nd Street and Fifth Avenue; running thence northerly parallel with Fifth Avenue and part of the way through a party wall, 75 feet 5 inches; thence westerly parallel with the northerly side of 52nd Street, 11 feet 2-3/4 inches; thence northerly parallel with Fifth Avenue, 25 feet to the center line of the block; thence easterly along said center line of the block, 71 feet 2-3/4 inches; thence southerly parallel with Fifth Avenue and part of the way through a party wall, 100 feet 5 inches to the northerly side of 52nd Street; thence westerly along the northerly side of 52nd Street, 60 feet to the point or place of beginning. Provided, however, that with respect to such retail licensee's interest in a business engaged in the manufacture or sale at wholesale of alcoholic beverages described in subdivision 1-a of section one hundred one of this article: such interest must have been acquired prior to the effective date of the chapter of the laws of two thousand nineteen which added this paragraph; (ii) such retail licensee may not purchase alcoholic beverages directly from any such manufacturer or wholesaler; and (iii) no more than fifteen percent of the annual dollar value of alcoholic beverages purchased by such retail licensee for sale on the premises may be produced by any such manufacturer.

(b) Any lien, mortgage or other interest or estate now held by said retail licensee on or in the personal or real property of such manufacturer or wholesaler, which mortgage, lien, interest or estate was acquired on or before December thirty-first, nineteen hundred thirty-two, shall not be included within the provisions of this subdivision; provided, however, the burden of establishing the time of the accrual of the interest, comprehended by this subdivision shall be upon the person who claims to be entitled to the protection and exemption afforded hereby.

14. No retail licensee for on-premises consumption shall make or cause to be made any loan to any person engaged in the manufacture or sale of liquors, wines or beer at wholesale.

15. All retail licensed premises shall be subject to inspection by any peace officer, acting pursuant to his or her special duties, or police officer and by the duly authorized representatives of the liquor authority, during the hours when the said premises are open for the transaction of business.

16. [Repealed]

17. Notwithstanding any other provision of law, a retail licensee for on-premises consumption that is a person or corporation operating a hotel shall be permitted to sell liquors, beer, and/or wines through a mechanical device or vending machine placed in the lodger's rooms and to which access to such device or machine is restricted by means of a locking device which requires the use of a key, magnetic card or similar device provided, however, that no such key, card or similar device shall be provided to any person under the age of twenty-one or to any person who is visibly intoxicated.

HISTORY:

Add, L 1934, ch 478, § 1, eff July 1, 1934; amd, L 1936, ch 111; L 1936, ch 572, eff May 19, 1936; L 1937, ch 449; L 1940, ch 72; L 1940, ch 77; L 1940, ch 320; L 1940, ch 551; L 1941, ch 113; L 1941, ch 384; L 1941, ch 393; L 1941, ch 493; L 1944, ch 621; L 1950, ch 97, eff March 13, 1950; L 1950, ch 506, eff April 8, 1950; L 1955, ch 467; L 1958, ch 704; L 1964, ch 531, § 16, eff June 1, 1964; L 1965, ch 1016; L 1967, ch 632; L 1968, ch 789; L 1969, ch 673, eff May 21, 1969; L 1971, ch 36, eff March 16, 1971; L 1971, ch 235; L 1973, ch 372; L 1974, ch 76; L 1974, ch 466, eff May 23, 1974; L 1974, ch 1036, eff June 15, 1974; L 1977, ch 321, eff July 28, 1977; L 1978, ch 574, § 14; L 1980, ch 843, § 108, eff Sept 1, 1980; L 1983, ch 445, § 1; L 1985, ch 48, § 3, eff June 16, 1985; L 1985, ch 545, § 1, eff

July 24, 1985; L 1986, ch 919, § 22, eff Dec 29, 1986; L 1988, ch 64, § 20, eff April 24, 1988; L 1988, ch 209, § 3, eff July 1, 1988; L 1989, ch 217, § 1, eff June 26, 1989; L 1990, ch 759, § 1, eff Aug 21, 1990; L 1995, ch 83, §§ 155, 156, eff June 20, 1995; L 1995, ch 185, § 2; L 1996, ch 675, § 2; L 1998, ch 40, §§ 1–5; L 2000, ch 512, § 1, eff Nov 3, 2000; L 2001, ch 254, § 1, eff Sept 5, 2001; L 2002, ch 105, § 2, eff June 28, 2002; L 2006, ch 655, § 1, eff Sept 13, 2006; L 2010, ch 390, § 2, eff Aug 13, 2010; L 2011, ch 22, § 2, eff May 17, 2011; L 2011, ch 196, § 2, eff Jan 16, 2012; L 2013, ch 224, § 1, eff July 31, 2013; L 2014, ch 282, § 1, eff Aug 11, 2014; L 2014, ch 301, § 2, eff Aug 11, 2014; L 2016, ch 32, § 9, eff Sept 1, 2016; L 2016, ch 297, § 12, eff Sept 7, 2016; L 2016, ch 303, § 2, eff Sept 9, 2016; L 2016, ch 318, § 3, eff Sept 9, 2016; L 2018, ch 453, § 3, eff Dec 21, 2018; L 2019, ch 429, § 2, eff Oct 29, 2019; L 2019, ch 549, § 1, eff Nov 25, 2019; L 2019, ch 611, § 3, eff Dec 6, 2019; L 2020, ch 55, § 1 (Part FF), eff April 3, 2020.

EXECUTIVE LAW

Article 22 Office of Victim Services

Article 35 Division of Criminal Justice Services

Article 22—Office of Victim Services

§ 621. Definitions

For the purposes of this article:

1. "Office" shall mean the office of victim services.
2. "Claimant" shall mean the person filing a claim pursuant to this article.
3. "Crime" shall mean

(a) an act committed in New York state which would, if committed by a mentally competent criminally responsible adult, who has no legal exemption or defense, constitute a crime as defined in and proscribed by law; or

(b) an act committed outside the state of New York against a resident of the state of New York which would be compensable had it occurred within the state of New York and which occurred in a state which does not have an eligible crime victim compensation program as such term is defined in the federal victims of crime act of 1984; or

(c) an act of terrorism, as defined in section 2331 of title 18, United States Code, committed outside of the United States against a resident of New York state.

4. "Family", when used with reference to a person, shall mean (a) any person related to such person within the third degree of consanguinity or affinity, (b) any person maintaining a sexual relationship with such person, or (c) any person residing in the same household with such person.
5. "Victim" shall mean (a) a person who suffers personal physical injury as a direct result of a crime; (b) a person who is the victim of either the crime of (1) unlawful imprisonment in the first degree as defined in section 135.10 of the penal law, (2) kidnapping in the second degree as defined in section 135.20 of the penal law, (3) kidnapping in the first degree as defined in section 135.25 of the penal law, (4) menacing in the first degree as defined in section 120.13 of the penal law, (5) criminal obstruction of breathing or blood circulation as defined in section 121.11 of the penal law, (6) harassment in the second degree as defined in section 240.26 of the penal law, (7) harassment in the first degree as defined in section 240.25 of the penal law, (8) aggravated harassment in the second degree as defined in subdivision three or five of section 240.30 of the penal law, (9) aggravated harassment in the first degree as defined in subdivision two of section 240.31 of the penal law, (10) criminal contempt in the first degree as defined in subdivision (b) or subdivision (c) of section 215.51 of the penal law, (11) stalking in the fourth, third, second or first degree as defined in sections 120.45, 120.50, 120.55 and 120.60 of the penal law, (12) labor trafficking as defined in section 135.35 of the penal law, (13) sex trafficking as defined in section 230.34 of the penal law; or (14) sex trafficking of a child as defined in section 230.34-a of the penal law; a vulnerable elderly person or an incompetent or physically disabled person as defined in section 260.31 of the penal law who incurs a loss of savings as defined in subdivision twenty-four of this section; or a person who has had a frivolous lawsuit filed against them.

6. "Representative" shall mean one who represents or stands in the place of another person, including but not limited to an agent, an assignee, an attorney, a guardian, a committee, a conservator, a partner, a receiver, an administrator, an executor or an heir of another person, or a parent of a minor.

7. "Good samaritan" shall mean a person who, other than a law enforcement officer, acts in good faith (a) to apprehend a person who has committed a crime in his presence or who has in fact committed a felony, (b) to prevent a crime or an attempted crime from occurring, or (c) to aid a law enforcement officer in effecting an arrest.

8. "Essential personal property" shall mean articles of personal property necessary and essential to the health, welfare or safety of the victim.

9. "Elderly victim" shall mean a person sixty years of age or older who suffers loss, or damage as a direct result of a crime.

10. "Disabled victim" shall mean a person who has (a) physical, mental or medical impairment from anatomical, physiological or neurological conditions which prevents the exercise of a normal bodily function or is demonstrable by medically accepted clinical or laboratory diagnostic techniques or (b) a record of such an impairment or (c) a condition regarded by others as such an impairment.

11. For purposes of this article "child victim" shall mean a person less than eighteen years of age who suffers physical, mental or emotional injury, or loss or damage, as a direct result of a crime or any violation listed in subdivision twelve of section six hundred thirty-one of this article, or as a result of witnessing a crime or any violation listed in subdivision twelve of section six hundred thirty-one of this article.

12. "Frivolous lawsuit" shall mean a lawsuit brought by the individual who committed a crime against the victim of the crime, found to be frivolous, meritless and commenced to harass, intimidate or menace the victim by a court and costs were imposed upon the plaintiff pursuant to section eighty-three hundred three-a of the civil practice law and rules.

13. "Crime scene cleanup" shall mean removing, or attempting to remove from the crime scene, blood, dirt, stains, debris, odors, or other impurities caused by the crime or the processing of the crime scene and the repair or replacement of permanent fixtures and floor coverings, soiled, damaged, or rendered unusable or uncleanable by the crime, the processing of the crime scene, or by being taken into evidence.

14. "Securing a crime scene" shall mean taking immediate, emergency steps to return the residence where the crime occurred to the level of safety present prior to the crime. It shall include, but not be limited to, the repair or replacement of doors, windows, screens and locks or other points of entry damaged or rendered unusable by the crime.

15. "Livery" shall mean a for-hire vehicle duly licensed by the appropriate local licensing authority, designed to carry no more than five passengers for direct cash payment by such passenger and which is affiliated with a livery car base. The term "livery" shall not include a vehicle driven by a "black car operator", as defined in section one hundred sixty-cc of this chapter.

16. "Livery car base" shall mean a central facility, wherever located, that dispatches the livery operator to both pick-up and discharge passengers in the state.

17. "Livery operator" shall mean the registered owner of a livery, or a driver designated by such registered owner to operate the registered owner's livery as the registered owner's authorized designee, whose status as a livery operator victim arose out of and in the course of providing services while affiliated with a livery car base. The term "livery operator" shall not include a "black car operator", as defined in section one hundred sixty-cc of this chapter.

18. "Livery operator victim" shall mean a livery operator homicide victim or a livery operator assault victim.

19. "Livery operator assault victim" shall mean a livery operator who is the victim of a violent felony offense, as defined in subdivision one of section 70.02 of the penal law, which offense directly results in a serious physical injury, as defined in subdivision ten of section 10.00 of the penal law.

20. "Livery operator homicide victim" shall mean a livery operator who is the victim of a homicide, as defined in article one hundred twenty-five of the penal law.

21. "Local licensing authority" shall mean the governmental agency in the state, if any, that is authorized to license a livery and/or a livery car base.

22. "Financial counselling" shall mean financial services provided by an experienced financial counsellor or adviser which may include, but are not limited to: analysis of a victim's financial situation such as income producing capacity and crime related financial obligations, assistance with restructuring budget and debt, assistance in accessing insurance, public assistance and other benefits, assistance in completing the financial aspects of victim impact statements, and assistance in settling estates and handling guardianship matters.

23. "Relocation expenses" shall mean the cost of relocating a crime victim, when relocation is necessary for the health or safety of the victim. An award for relocation expenses of a victim shall include the reasonable cost of moving and transportation expenses for (a) the victim, which may include the relocation expenses of their spouse and any other person dependent for his or her principal support upon the victim or spouse who lives in the same residence as the victim, or (b) if the victim is a child victim eligible for such an award pursuant to this article, the child victim, which may include the relocation expenses of their parent, stepparent, guardian and any other person dependent for his or her principal support upon such parent, stepparent, and guardian who lives in the same residence as the child victim.

24. "Loss of savings" shall mean the result of any act or series of acts of larceny as defined in article one hundred fifty-five of the penal law, indicated by a criminal justice agency as defined in subdivision one of section six hundred thirty-one of this article, in which cash is stolen from a vulnerable elderly person or an incompetent or physically disabled person as defined in section 260.31 of the penal law.

25. "Domestic partner" shall mean a person who, with respect to another person:

(a) is formally a party in a domestic partnership or similar relationship with the other person, entered into pursuant to the laws of the United States or of any state, local or foreign jurisdiction, or registered as the domestic partner of the other person with any registry maintained by the employer of either party or any state, municipality, or foreign jurisdiction; or

(b) is formally recognized as a beneficiary or covered person under the other person's employment benefits or health insurance; or

(c) is dependent or mutually interdependent on the other person for support, as evidenced by the totality of the circumstances indicating a mutual intent to be a domestic partner including but not limited to: common ownership or joint leasing of real or personal property; common householding, shared income or shared expenses; children in common; signs of intent to marry or become a domestic partner under paragraph (a) or (b) of this subdivision; or the length of the personal relationship of the persons.

Each party to a domestic partnership shall be considered to be the domestic partner of the other party. "Domestic partner" shall not include a person who is related to the other person by blood in a manner that would bar marriage to the other person in New York state. "Domestic partner" also shall not include any person who is less than eighteen years of age or who is the adopted child of the other person or who is related by blood in a manner that would bar marriage in New York state to a person who is the lawful spouse of the other person.

HISTORY:

Add, L 1966, ch 894, § 1, eff Aug 1, 1966; amd, L 1981, ch 445, § 1, eff July 7, 1981; L 1982, ch 17, § 1, eff March 15, 1982; L 1982, ch 351, § 1, eff June 21, 1982, and applicable to all claims filed on or after the date on which it shall have become a law; L 1983, ch 197, § 1, eff May 31, 1983, and applicable to claims submitted and based upon crimes committed on or after such date; L 1985, ch 688, §§ 8, 9; L 1986, ch 263, § 2; L 1988, ch 56, § 1, eff Nov 1, 1988; L 1989, ch 163, § 1, eff June 17, 1989; L 1995, ch 543, § 1, eff Aug 2, 1995; L 1996, ch 710, § 1, eff Oct 9, 1996; L 1997, ch 620, §§ 1, 2, eff Nov 1, 1997; L 1998, ch 81, § 1, eff June 2, 1998; L 2000, ch 148, § 1, eff July 12, 2000, deemed eff on and after Jan 1, 2000; L 2003, ch 391, § 1, eff Aug 19, 2003; L 2005, ch 377, § 1, eff Aug 2, 2005; L 2007, ch 74, § 12, eff Nov 1, 2007; L 2010, ch 56, § 6 (Part A–1), eff June 22, 2010; L 2013, ch 261, § 1, eff Aug 30, 2013; L 2017, ch 55, §§ 1, 2 (Part H), eff Oct 17, 2017; L 2018, ch 189, § 21, eff Nov 13, 2018; L 2019, ch 178, § 1, eff Feb 17, 2020; L 2020, ch 70, § 2, eff Dec 20, 2019.

§ 624. Eligibility

1. Except as provided in subdivision two of this section, the following persons shall be eligible for awards pursuant to this article:

(a) a victim of a crime;

(b) a surviving spouse, domestic partner, grandparent, parent, stepparent, guardian, brother, sister, stepbrother, stepsister, child, stepchild or grandchild of a victim of a crime who died as a direct result of such crime;

(c) any other person dependent for his principal support upon a victim of a crime who died as a direct result of such crime;

(d) any person or business represented by a person who has paid for or incurred the burial expenses of a victim who died as a direct result of such crime, except such person shall not be eligible to receive an award for other than burial expenses unless otherwise eligible under paragraph (a), (b) or (c) of this subdivision;

(e) an elderly victim of a crime;

(f) a disabled victim of a crime;

(g) a child victim of a crime;

(h) a parent, stepparent, grandparent, guardian, brother, sister, stepbrother or stepsister of a child victim of a crime;

(i) a surviving spouse of a crime victim who died from causes not directly related to the crime when such victim died prior to filing a claim with the office or subsequent to filing a claim but prior to the rendering of a decision by the office. Such award shall be limited to out-of-pocket loss incurred as a direct result of the crime; and

(j) a spouse, child or stepchild of a victim of a crime who has sustained personal physical injury as a direct result of a crime.

(k) a surviving spouse, grandparent, parent, stepparent, guardian, brother, sister, stepbrother, stepsister, child, stepchild, or grandchild of a victim of a crime who died as a direct result of such crime and where such crime occurred in the residence shared by such family member or members and the victim.

1-a. For the purposes of this section, "domestic partner" means a person who, with respect to another person:

(a) is formally a party in a domestic partnership or similar relationship with the other person, entered into pursuant to the laws of the United States or of any state, local or foreign jurisdiction, or registered as the domestic partner of the other person with any registry maintained by the employer of either party or any state, municipality, or foreign jurisdiction; or

(b) is formally recognized as a beneficiary or covered person under the other person's employment benefits or health insurance; or

(c) is dependent or mutually interdependent on the other person for support, as evidenced by the totality of the circumstances indicating a mutual intent to be a domestic partner including but not limited to: common ownership or joint leasing of real or personal property; common householding, shared income or shared expenses; children in common; signs of intent to marry or become a domestic partner under paragraph (a) or (b) of this subdivision; or the length of the personal relationship of the persons.

2. A person who is criminally responsible for the crime upon which a claim is based or an accomplice of such person shall not be eligible to receive an award with respect to such claim. A member of the family of a person criminally responsible for the crime upon which a claim is based or a member of the family of an accomplice of such person, shall be eligible to receive an award, unless the office determines pursuant to regulations promulgated to carry out the provisions and purposes of this article, that the person criminally responsible will receive substantial economic benefit or unjust enrichment from the compensation. In such circumstances the award may be reduced or structured in such way as to remove the substantial economic benefit or unjust enrichment to such person or the claim may be denied.

HISTORY:

Add, L 1966, ch 894, § 1, eff Aug 1, 1966; amd, L, 1982, ch 205, § 1, L 1983, ch 197, § 2; L 1968, ch 661, § 1; L 1983, ch 805, § 2; L 1983, ch 811, § 1; L 1984, ch 729, § 1; L 1986, ch 74, § 3; L 1986, ch 263, § 3; L 1989, ch 307, § 1, eff July 10, 1989; L 1990, ch 859, § 1, eff Oct 1, 1990 (see 1990 note); L 1998, ch 276, § 1, eff July 10, 1998 (see 1998 note); L 1999, ch 427, § 1, eff Aug 31, 1999 (see 1999 note); L 2010, ch

56, § 9 (Part A–1), eff June 22, 2010; L 2012, ch 233, § 1, eff July 18, 2012; L 2013, ch 119, § 1, eff Aug 11, 2013 (see 2013 note); L 2015, ch 104, § 1, eff Aug 13, 2015; L 2016, ch 243, § 1, eff Aug 18, 2016; L 2017, ch 117, § 1, eff Jan 21, 2018; L 2020, ch 70, § 1, eff Dec 20, 2019; L 2019, ch 690, § 1, § 2, eff June 17, 2020.

§ 624. Eligibility

1. Except as provided in subdivision two of this section, the following persons shall be eligible for awards pursuant to this article:

(a) a victim of a crime;

(b) a surviving spouse, grandparent, parent, stepparent, guardian, brother, sister, stepbrother, stepsister, child, stepchild or grandchild of a victim of a crime who died as a direct result of such crime;

(c) any other person dependent for his principal support upon a victim of a crime who died as a direct result of such crime;

(d) any person or business represented by a person who has paid for or incurred the burial expenses of a victim who died as a direct result of such crime, except such person shall not be eligible to receive an award for other than burial expenses unless otherwise eligible under paragraph (a), (b) or (c) of this subdivision;

(e) an elderly victim of a crime;

(f) a disabled victim of a crime;

(g) a child victim of a crime;

(h) a parent, stepparent, grandparent, guardian, brother, sister, stepbrother or stepsister of a child victim of a crime;

(i) a surviving spouse of a crime victim who died from causes not directly related to the crime when such victim died prior to filing a claim with the office or subsequent to filing a claim but prior to the rendering of a decision by the office. Such award shall be limited to out-of-pocket loss incurred as a direct result of the crime; and

(j) a spouse, child or stepchild of a victim of a crime who has sustained personal physical injury as a direct result of a crime.

(k) a surviving spouse, grandparent, parent, stepparent, guardian, brother, sister, stepbrother, stepsister, child, stepchild, or grandchild of a victim of a crime who died as a direct result of such crime and where such crime occurred in the residence shared by such family member or members and the victim.

2. A person who is criminally responsible for the crime upon which a claim is based or an accomplice of such person shall not be eligible to receive an award with respect to such claim. A member of the family of a person criminally responsible for the crime upon which a claim is based or a member of the family of an accomplice of such person, shall be eligible to receive an award, unless the office determines pursuant to regulations promulgated to carry out the provisions and purposes of this article, that the person criminally responsible will receive substantial economic benefit or unjust enrichment from the compensation. In such circumstances the award may be reduced or structured in such way as to remove the substantial economic benefit or unjust enrichment to such person or the claim may be denied.

HISTORY:

Add, L 1966, ch 894, § 1, eff Aug 1, 1966; amd, L, 1982, ch 205, § 1, L 1983, ch 197, § 2; L 1968, ch 661, § 1; L 1983, ch 805, § 2; L 1983, ch 811, § 1; L 1984, ch 729, § 1; L 1986, ch 74, § 3; L 1986, ch 263, § 3; L 1989, ch 307, § 1, eff July 10, 1989; L 1990, ch 859, § 1, eff Oct 1, 1990 (see 1990 note); L 1998, ch 276, § 1, eff July 10, 1998 (see 1998 note); L 1999, ch 427, § 1, eff Aug 31, 1999 (see 1999 note); L 2010, ch 56, § 9 (Part A–1), eff June 22, 2010; L 2012, ch 233, § 1, eff July 18, 2012; L 2013, ch 119, § 1, eff Aug 11, 2013 (see 2013 note); L 2015, ch 104, § 1, eff Aug 13, 2015; L 2016, ch 243, § 1, eff Aug 18, 2016; L 2017, ch 117, § 1, eff Jan 21, 2018; L 2020, ch 70, § 1, eff Dec 20, 2019.

§ 626. Out-of-pocket loss; definition

1. Out-of-pocket loss shall mean unreimbursed and unreimbursable expenses or indebtedness reasonably incurred for medical care or other services necessary as a result of the injury upon which such claim is based, including such expenses incurred as a result of the exacerbation of a pre-existing disability or condition directly resulting from the crime or causally related to the crime. Such expenses or indebtedness shall include the cost of counseling for the eligible spouse, domestic partner, grandparents, parents, stepparents, guardians, brothers, sisters, stepbrothers, stepsisters, children,

stepchildren or grandchildren of a homicide victim, and crime victims who have sustained a personal physical injury as the direct result of a crime and the spouse, children or stepchildren of such physically injured victim. For the purposes of this subdivision, the victim of a sex offense as defined in article one hundred thirty of the penal law is presumed to have suffered physical injury. Such counseling may be provided by local victim service programs, where available. It shall also include the cost of residing at or utilizing services provided by shelters for battered spouses and children who are eligible pursuant to subdivision two of section six hundred twenty-four of this article, and the cost of reasonable attorneys' fees for representation before the office and/or before the appellate division upon judicial review not to exceed one thousand dollars.

2. Out-of-pocket loss shall also include the cost of counseling for a child victim and the parent, stepparent, grandparent, guardian, brother, sister, stepbrother or stepsister of such victim, pursuant to regulations promulgated to carry out the provisions and purposes of this article.

3. [Repealed]

4. Out-of-pocket loss shall also include the cost of counseling for surviving family members of homicide victims who are otherwise eligible pursuant to paragraph (b) of subdivision one of section six hundred twenty-four of this article.

HISTORY:

Add, L 1966, ch 894, § 1; amd, L 1976, ch 952, § 3; L 1983, ch 198, § 1; L 1985, ch 688, § 1 (see 1985 note); L 1986, ch 263, § 4, eff Jan 1, 1987; L 1986, ch 312, § 1, eff Nov 14, 1986; L 1989, ch 324, § 1, eff Nov 7, 1989 (see 1989 note); L 1998, ch 276, § 2, eff July 10, 1998 (see 1998 note); L 1999, ch 427, § 2, eff Aug 31, 1999 (see 1999 note); L 2005, ch 408, § 1, eff Aug 2, 2005; L 2007, ch 21, § 1, eff April 17, 2007 (see 2007 note); L 2010, ch 56, § 17 (Part A–1), eff June 22, 2010; L 2015, ch 104, § 2, eff Aug 13, 2015; L 2020, ch 70, §§ 3, 4, eff June 17, 2020.

§ 631. Awards.

1. No award shall be made unless the office finds that (a) a crime was committed, (b) such crime directly resulted in personal physical injury to or the exacerbation of a preexisting disability, or condition, or death of, the victim, and (c) criminal justice agency records show that such crime was promptly reported to the proper authorities; and in no case may an award be made where the criminal justice agency records show that such report was made more than one week after the occurrence of such crime unless the office, for good cause shown, finds the delay to have been justified. Notwithstanding the foregoing provisions of this subdivision, in cases involving an alleged sex offense as contained in article one hundred thirty of the penal law or incest as defined in section 255.25, 255.26 or 255.27 of the penal law or labor trafficking as defined in section 135.35 of the penal law or sex trafficking as defined in sections 230.34 and 230.34-a of the penal law or an offense chargeable as a family offense as described in section eight hundred twelve of the family court act or section 530.11 of the criminal procedure law, the criminal justice agency report need only be made within a reasonable time considering all the circumstances, including the victim's physical, emotional and mental condition and family situation. For the purposes of this subdivision, "criminal justice agency" shall include, but not be limited to, a police department, a district attorney's office, and any other governmental agency having responsibility for the enforcement of the criminal laws of the state provided, however, that in cases involving such sex offense or family offense a criminal justice agency shall also mean a family court, a governmental agency responsible for child and/or adult protective services pursuant to title six of article six of the social services law and/or title one of article nine-B of the social services law, and any medical facility established under the laws of the state that provides a forensic physical examination for victims of rape and sexual assault.

1-a. No award shall be made for a frivolous lawsuit unless the office finds that the victim has been awarded costs pursuant to section eighty-three hundred three-a of the civil practice law and rules and the individual responsible for the payment of costs is unable to pay such costs provided, however, that in no event shall the amount of such costs exceed two thousand five hundred dollars.

2. Any award made pursuant to this article shall be in an amount not exceeding out-of-pocket expenses, including indebtedness reasonably incurred for medical or

other services necessary as a result of the injury upon which the claim is based; loss of earnings or support resulting from such injury not to exceed thirty thousand dollars; loss of savings not to exceed thirty thousand dollars; burial expenses not exceeding six thousand dollars of a victim who died on or after November first, nineteen ninety-six as a direct result of a crime; the costs of crime scene cleanup and securing of a crime scene not exceeding twenty-five hundred dollars; reasonable relocation expenses not exceeding twenty-five hundred dollars; and the unreimbursed cost of repair or replacement of articles of essential personal property lost, damaged or destroyed as a direct result of the crime. An award for loss of earnings shall include earnings lost by a parent or guardian as a result of the hospitalization of a child victim under age eighteen for injuries sustained as a direct result of a crime. In addition to the medical or other services necessary as a result of the injury upon which the claim is based, an award may be made for rehabilitative occupational training for the purpose of job retraining or similar employment-oriented rehabilitative services based upon the claimant's medical and employment history. For the purpose of this subdivision, rehabilitative occupational training shall include but not be limited to educational training and expenses. An award for rehabilitative occupational training may be made to a victim, or to a family member of a victim where necessary as a direct result of a crime.

3. Any award made for loss of earnings or support shall, unless reduced pursuant to other provisions of this article, be in an amount equal to the actual loss sustained, provided, however, that no such award shall exceed six hundred dollars for each week of lost earnings or support. Awards with respect to livery operator victims pursuant to paragraphs (f) and (g) of subdivision one of section six hundred twenty-seven of this article shall be granted in the amount and in the manner provided therein. The aggregate award for all such losses pursuant to this subdivision, including any awards made pursuant to paragraphs (f) and (g) of subdivision one of section six hundred twenty-seven of this article, shall not exceed thirty thousand dollars. If there are two or more persons entitled to an award as a result of the death of a person which is the direct result of a crime, the award shall be apportioned by the office among the claimants.

3-a. Any award made for loss of savings shall, unless reduced pursuant to other provisions of this article, be in an amount equal to the actual loss sustained.

4. Any award made pursuant to this article shall be reduced by the amount of any payments received or to be received by the claimant as a result of the injury (a) from or on behalf of the person who committed the crime, (b) under insurance programs mandated by law, (c) from public funds, (d) under any contract of insurance wherein the claimant is the insured or beneficiary, (e) as an emergency award pursuant to section six hundred thirty of this article. Notwithstanding the foregoing, where the person injured is a livery operator victim, because undue hardship may result to the claimant if immediate payment is not made, any award pursuant to paragraphs (f) and (g) of subdivision one of section six hundred twenty-seven of this article shall be granted without reduction for workers' compensation benefits to be received, if any.

5.(a) In determining the amount of an award, the office shall determine whether, because of his conduct, the victim of such crime contributed to the infliction of his injury, and the office shall reduce the amount of the award or reject the claim altogether, in accordance with such determination.

(b) Notwithstanding the provisions of paragraph (a) of this subdivision, the office shall disregard for this purpose the responsibility of the victim for his own injury where the record shows that the person injured was acting as a good samaritan, as defined in this article.

(c) Notwithstanding any inconsistent provision of this article, where the person injured acted as a good samaritan, the office may, without regard to the financial difficulty of the claimant, make an award for out-of-pocket losses. Such award may also include compensation for any loss of property up to five thousand dollars suffered by the victim during the course of his actions as a good samaritan.

(d) Notwithstanding any inconsistent provision of this article, where a person acted as a good samaritan, and was killed as a direct result of the crime, the office may, without regard to the financial difficulty of the claimant, make a lump sum award to such claimant for actual loss of support not to exceed thirty thousand dollars.

(e) Notwithstanding any inconsistent provision of this article, where a police officer or firefighter, both paid and volunteer, dies from injuries received in the line of duty as a direct result of a crime, the office may, without regard to the financial difficulty of the claimant, make an award for the unreimbursed counseling expenses of the eligible spouse, parents, brothers, sisters or children of such victim, and/or the reasonable burial expenses incurred by the claimant.

(f) Notwithstanding the provisions of paragraph (a) of this subdivision, the office shall disregard for this purpose the responsibility of the victim for his or her own loss of savings.

(g) Notwithstanding the provisions of paragraph (a) of this subdivision, if the crime upon which the claim is based resulted in the death of the victim, the office shall determine whether, because of his or her conduct, the victim of such crime contributed to the infliction of his or her injury, and the office may reduce the amount of the award by no more than fifty percent, in accordance with such determination.

6.(a) Claims may be approved only if the office finds that unless the claimant's award is approved he or she will suffer financial difficulty. However, no finding of financial difficulty is required for a claim for an emergency award or an award less than ten thousand dollars. In determining financial difficulty, the office shall consider all relevant factors, including but not limited to:

(1) the number of claimant's dependents;

(2) reasonable living expenses of the claimant and his family;

(3) any special health, rehabilitative or educational needs of the claimant and his dependents;

(4) the claimant's employment situation including income and potential earning capacity;

(5) the claimant's net financial resources after authorized deduction as provided in paragraphs (b) and (c) of this subdivision;

(6) whether claimant's financial resources will become exhausted during his lifetime; and

(7) the nature and the amount of claimant's total debt and liabilities, including the amount of debt incurred or to be incurred to pay for losses and expenses of the crime, and the extent to which claimant's essential assets will have to be liquidated.

(b) Claimant's net financial resources do not include the present value of future earnings, and shall be determined by the office by deducting from his total financial resources the value, within reasonable limits, of the following items:

(1) a homestead, not exceeding five hundred thousand dollars, or a total of ten years' rent for a renter;

(2) personal property consisting of clothing and strictly personal effects;

(3) household furniture, appliances and equipment;

(4) tools and equipment necessary for the claimant's trade, occupation or business;

(5) a family automobile;

(6) life insurance, except in death claims; and

(7) retirement, education and health plans or contributions to a retirement or pension program including but not limited to contributions to: (i) employee profit sharing plans, (ii) employee money purchase plans, (iii) 401 (k) plans, (iv) simplified employee pensions (SEP), (v) individual retirement accounts (IRA), (vi) 403 (b) plans, (vii) 457 plans, (viii) Keogh plans, (self employed), and (ix) any other plan or account for which contributions are made primarily for retirement purposes.

(c) The office, after taking into consideration the claimant's financial resources, may exempt that portion of the victim's or claimant's annual income required to meet reasonable living expenses and the value of inventory or other property necessary for the claimant's business or occupation or the production of income required to meet reasonable living expenses. In no event shall the aggregate value of exemptions under this paragraph exceed one hundred thousand dollars.

(d) Nothing contained in this subdivision shall be construed to mean that the office must maintain the same standard of living enjoyed by the claimant prior to the death or injury.

(e) The director shall promulgate such rules and regulations as are necessary for the implementation of this section.

7. Notwithstanding the provisions of subdivision six of this section, an award shall include out-of-pocket expenses, including indebtedness reasonably incurred by the victim of a sex offense or the person responsible for the victim of such sex offense, as such sex offense is defined in article one hundred thirty of the penal law, for a hospital or medical examination in connection with the investigation or prosecution of any such offense.

8. Notwithstanding the provisions of subdivisions one, two and three of this section, an elderly or disabled victim who has not been physically injured as a direct result of a crime, shall only be eligible for an award that includes the unreimbursed cost of repair or replacement of essential personal property that has been lost, damaged or destroyed as a direct result of a crime, transportation expenses incurred for necessary court appearances in connection with the prosecution of such crimes and the unreimbursed cost of counselling provided to the elderly or disabled victim on account of mental or emotional stress or financial counselling provided to the elderly or disabled victim on account of financial difficulty resulting from the incident in which the crime occurred if such counselling or financial counselling is commenced within one year from the date of the incident. For purposes of this subdivision, "necessary court appearances" shall include, but not be limited to, any part of trial from arraignment through sentencing, pre and post trial hearings and grand jury hearings.

8-a. Notwithstanding the provisions of subdivision one of this section, a vulnerable elderly person or an incompetent or physically disabled person, as defined in section 260.31 of the penal law, who has not been physically injured as a direct result of a crime, shall be eligible for an award that includes loss of savings.

9. Any award made for the cost of repair or replacement of essential personal property, including cash losses of essential personal property, shall be limited to an amount of five hundred dollars, except that all cash losses of essential personal property shall be limited to the amount of one hundred dollars. In the case of medically necessary life-sustaining equipment which was lost or damaged as the direct result of a crime, the award shall be limited to the amount of ten thousand dollars.

10. Notwithstanding any contrary provision of law, an award shall include reasonable transportation expenses incurred for necessary court appearances in connection with the prosecution of such crimes upon which the claim is based. For purposes of this subdivision, "necessary court appearances" shall include but not be limited to any part of a proceeding from arraignment through sentencing, pre and post trial hearings and grand jury hearings.

11. Notwithstanding the provisions of subdivisions one, two and three of this section, an individual who was a victim of either the crime of: menacing in the second degree as defined in subdivision one of section 120.14 of the penal law; menacing in the third degree as defined in section 120.15 of the penal law; unlawful imprisonment in the first degree as defined in section 135.10 of the penal law; kidnapping in the second degree as defined in section 135.20 of the penal law; kidnapping in the first degree as defined in section 135.25 of the penal law; criminal mischief in the fourth degree as defined in subdivision four of section 145.00 of the penal law; robbery in the third degree as defined in section 160.05 of the penal law; robbery in the second degree as defined in subdivision one, paragraph (b) of subdivision two or subdivision three of section 160.10 of the penal law; robbery in the first degree as defined in subdivisions two, three and four of section 160.15 of the penal law; unlawful surveillance in the second degree as defined in section 250.45 of the penal law; or unlawful surveillance in the first degree as defined in section 250.50 of the penal law who has not been physically injured as a direct result of such crime shall only be eligible for an award that includes loss of earnings and the unreimbursed costs of counseling provided to such victim on account of mental or emotional stress resulting from the incident in which the crime occurred.

12. Notwithstanding the provisions of subdivisions one, two and three of this section, an individual who was a victim of either the crime of menacing in the second degree as defined in subdivision two or three of section 120.14 of the penal law, menacing in the first degree as defined in section 120.13 of the penal law, criminal obstruction of breathing or blood circulation as defined in section 121.11 of the penal law, harassment in the second degree as defined in section 240.26 of the penal law, harassment in the first degree as defined in section 240.25 of the penal law, aggravated

harassment in the second degree as defined in subdivision three or five of section 240.30 of the penal law, aggravated harassment in the first degree as defined in subdivision two of section 240.31 of the penal law, criminal contempt in the first degree as defined in subdivision (b) or subdivision (c) of section 215.51 of the penal law, or stalking in the fourth, third, second or first degree as defined in sections 120.45, 120.50, 120.55 and 120.60 of the penal law, respectively, or dissemination of an unlawful surveillance image in the second or first degree as defined in sections 250.55 and 250.60, respectively, or a hate crime as defined in section 485.05 of the penal law who has not been physically injured as a direct result of such crime shall only be eligible for an award that includes loss of earning or support, the unreimbursed cost of repair or replacement of essential personal property that has been lost, damaged or destroyed as a direct result of such crime, the unreimbursed cost for security devices to enhance the personal protection of such victim, the cost of residing at or utilizing services provided by shelters for battered spouses and children as provided in subdivision one of section six hundred twenty-six of this article, transportation expenses incurred for necessary court appearances in connection with the prosecution of such crime, the unreimbursed costs of counseling provided to such victim on account of mental or emotional stress resulting from the incident in which the crime occurred, the unreimbursed cost of crime scene cleanup and securing a crime scene, reasonable relocation expenses, and for occupational or job training. For purposes of this subdivision, "necessary court appearances" shall include, but not be limited to, any part of trial from arraignment through sentencing, pre and post trial hearings and grand jury hearings.

13.(a) Notwithstanding any other provision of law, rule, or regulation to the contrary, when any New York state accredited hospital, accredited sexual assault examiner program, or licensed health care provider furnishes services to any sexual assault survivor, including but not limited to a health care forensic examination in accordance with the sex offense evidence collection protocol and standards established by the department of health, such hospital, sexual assault examiner program, or licensed healthcare provider shall provide such services to the person without charge and shall bill the office directly. The office, in consultation with the department of health, shall define the specific services to be covered by the sexual assault forensic exam reimbursement fee, which must include at a minimum forensic examiner services, hospital or healthcare facility services related to the exam, and any necessary related laboratory tests or pharmaceuticals; including but not limited to HIV post-exposure prophylaxis provided by a hospital emergency room at the time of the forensic rape examination pursuant to paragraph (c) of subdivision one of section twenty-eight hundred five-i of the public health law. For a person eighteen years of age or older, follow-up HIV post-exposure prophylaxis costs shall continue to be reimbursed according to established office procedure. The office, in consultation with the department of health, shall also generate the necessary regulations and forms for the direct reimbursement procedure.

(b) The rate for reimbursement shall be the amount of itemized charges, to be reimbursed at the Medicaid rate and which shall cumulatively not exceed (1) eight hundred dollars for an exam of a sexual assault survivor where no sexual offense evidence collection kit is used; (2) one thousand two hundred dollars for an exam of a sexual assault survivor where a sexual offense evidence collection kit is used; (3) one thousand five hundred dollars for an exam of a sexual assault survivor who is eighteen years of age or older, with or without the use of a sexual offense evidence collection kit, and with the provision of a necessary HIV post-exposure prophylaxis seven day starter pack; and (4) two thousand five hundred dollars for an exam of a sexual assault survivor who is less than eighteen years of age, with or without the use of a sexual offense evidence collection kit, and with the provision of the full regimen of necessary HIV post-exposure prophylaxis. The hospital, sexual assault examiner program, or licensed health care provider must accept this fee as payment in full for these specified services. No additional billing of the survivor for said services is permissible. A sexual assault survivor may voluntarily assign any private insurance benefits to which she or he is entitled for the healthcare forensic examination, in which case the hospital or healthcare provider may not charge the office; provided, however, in the event the sexual assault survivor assigns any private health insurance benefit, such coverage shall not be subject to annual deductibles or coinsurance or balance billing by the hospital, sexual assault examiner program or licensed health care provider. A hospital, sexual assault examiner program or licensed health care provider shall, at the time of the initial visit, request assignment of any private health insurance benefits to which the sexual assault survivor is entitled on a form prescribed by the office; provided, however, such sexual assault survivor shall be advised orally and in writing that he or she may decline to provide such information regarding private health insurance benefits if he or she believes that the provision of such information would substantially interfere with his or her personal privacy or safety and in such event, the sexual assault forensic exam fee shall be paid by the office. Such sexual assault survivor shall also be advised that providing such information may provide additional resources to pay for services to other sexual assault victims. Such sexual assault survivor shall also be advised that the direct reimbursement program established by this subdivision does not automatically make them eligible for any other compensation benefits available from the office including, but not limited to, reimbursement for mental health counseling expenses, relocation expenses, and loss of earnings, and that such compensation benefits may only be made available to them should the sexual assault survivor or other person eligible to file pursuant to section six hundred twenty-four of this article, file a compensation application with the office. If he or she declines to provide such health insurance information, he or she shall indicate such decision on the form provided by the hospital, sexual assault examiner program or licensed health care provider, which form shall be prescribed by the office.

14. Notwithstanding any inconsistent provision of this article, where a victim dies from injuries received as a direct result of the World Trade Center terrorist attacks on September eleventh, two thousand one, the office may make an award for the unreimbursed and unreimbursable expense or indebtedness reasonably incurred for the cost of counseling for the eligible spouse, grandparents, parents, stepparents, guardians, brothers, sisters, stepbrothers, stepsisters, children, or stepchildren of such victim. Any award for such expense incurred on or before December thirty-first, two thousand seven, shall be made without regard to the financial difficulty of the claimant.

15. Notwithstanding any inconsistent provision of this article, where a victim is injured as a direct result of the World Trade Center terrorist attacks on September eleventh, two thousand one, the office may make an award for the unreimbursed and unreimbursable expense or indebtedness reasonably incurred by the claimant for medical care or counseling services necessary as a result of such injury. Any award for such expense or indebtedness incurred on or before December thirty-first, two thousand seven, shall be made without regard to the financial difficulty of the claimant.

16. Notwithstanding any inconsistent provision of this article, and without regard to the financial difficulty of the claimant, where a victim dies from injuries received as a direct result of the World Trade Center terrorist attacks on September eleventh, two thousand one, the office may make an award of reasonable burial expenses for such victim.

17. Notwithstanding the provisions of subdivision one of this section, where a child victim has not been physically injured as a direct result of a crime or any violation listed in subdivision twelve of this section, or has witnessed a crime or any violation listed in subdivision twelve of this section in which no physical injury occurred, the claimant shall only be eligible for an award that includes the unreimbursed cost of repair or replacement of essential personal property of the child victim that has been lost, damaged or destroyed as a direct result of a crime or any violation listed in subdivision twelve of this section, transportation expenses incurred by the claimant for necessary court appearances of the child victim in connection with the prosecution of such crimes, and, if counseling is commenced within one year from the date of the incident or its discovery, (1) the unreimbursed cost of counseling provided to the child victim on account of mental or emotional stress resulting from the incident in which the crime or any violation listed in subdivision twelve of this section occurred, and/or (2) the unreimbursed cost of counseling provided to the claimant eligible under paragraph (h) of subdivision one of section six hundred twenty-four of this article and resulting from the incident in which the crime or any violation listed in subdivision twelve of this section occurred.

18. Notwithstanding any inconsistent provision of this article and subject to any applicable maximum award limitations contained in this section, where a victim has died as a direct result of the crime upon which the claim is based and the crime occurred in the residence of a person eligible pursuant to paragraph (k) of subdivision one of section six hundred twenty-four of this article, the office may make no more than one award for crime scene clean-up related to such residence.

HISTORY:

Add, L 1966, ch 894, § 1, eff Aug 1, 1966; amd, L 1970, ch 376, § 1; L 1974, ch 392, § 1; L 1976, ch 952, § 6; L 1977, ch 693, § 1; L 1979, ch 418, § 1, eff July 5, 1979; L 1982, ch 351, § 2, eff June 21, 1982; L 1982, ch 885, § 1; L 1983, ch 85, § 1; L 1983, ch 197, § 3,4, eff May 31, 1983; L 1983, ch 810, § 1, eff Sept 28, 1983; L 1985, ch 688, §§ 6, 7, 10; L 1986, ch 74, § 5, eff May 12, 1986; L 1986, ch 309, § 1; L 1986, ch 327, § 1; L 1986, ch 465, § 1; L 1988, ch 368, § 1; L 1989, ch 345, § 1; L 1990, ch 720, § 1, eff July 22, 1990; L 1990, ch 763, § 1, eff July 22, 1990; L 1991, ch 166, §§ 364–367; L 1991, ch 400, § 1, eff July 15, 1991; L 1992, ch 55, §§ 295–298, eff April 10, 1992; L 1994, ch 244, § 1, eff July 6, 1994; L 1995, ch 543, § 2, eff Aug 2, 1995; L 1996, ch 141, § 1, eff Nov 1, 1996; L 1996, ch 309, §§ 55–60, eff July 13, 1996; L 1997, ch 620, § 4, eff Nov 1, 1997; L 1998, ch 58, § 30 (Part E), eff May 28, 1998; L 1998, ch 81, § 2, eff June 2, 1998; L 1998, ch 443, § 1, eff July 22, 1998; L 1999, ch 635, § 6, eff Dec 1, 1999; L 2000, ch 1, § 28, eff Feb 1, 2001; L 2000, ch 148, §§ 3, 4, eff July 12, 2000, deemed eff on and after Jan 1, 2000; L 2000, ch 434, § 2, eff Oct 20, 2000; L 2003, ch 264, § 68, eff April 1, 2005; L 2003, ch 391, § 2, eff Aug 19, 2003; L 2005, ch 322, § 1, eff July 26, 2005; L 2005, ch 377, § 2, eff Aug 2, 2005; L 2005, ch 408, § 4, eff Aug 2, 2005; L 2006, ch 320, § 24, eff Nov 1, 2006; L 2007, ch 21, § 2, eff April 17, 2007; L 2007, ch 74, § 13, eff Nov 1, 2007; L 2008, ch 162, § 1, eff Sept 1, 2008; L 2009, ch 56, § 1 (Part E), eff April 7, 2009; L 2009, ch 272, § 1, eff July 28, 2009; L 2010, ch 56, § 22 (Part A–1), eff June 22, 2010; L 2011, ch 534, § 1, eff Dec 22, 2011; L 2012, ch 39, § 2, eff Nov 27, 2012; L 2013, ch 119, § 2, eff Aug 11, 2013; L 2014, ch 188, § 2, eff July 23, 2014; L 2014, ch 487, § 1, eff Jan 1, 2015; L 2015, ch 263, § 1, eff Sept 25, 2015; L 2017, ch 55, § 1 (Part G), eff Oct 17, 2017; L 2017, ch 55, §§ 3-6 (Part H), eff Oct 17, 2017; L 2017, ch 416, § 1, eff Nov 29, 2017; L 2018, ch 57, § 3 (Part HH), eff April 12, 2018; L 2018, ch 189, § 22, eff Nov 13, 2018; L 2018, ch 204, § 1, eff Feb 18, 2019; L 2018, ch 295, § 1, eff Oct 31, 2018; L 2018, ch 494, §§ 2, 3, eff June 26, 2019; L 2019, ch 178, § 2, eff Feb 17, 2020; L 2019, ch 179, §§ 1, 2, eff Feb 17, 2020; L 2019, ch 681, § 2, eff June 15, 2020; L 2020, ch 55, § 3 (Part XX, Subpart S), eff June 15, 2020.

§ 631-b. Safe way home transportation program. [Repealed]

HISTORY:

L 2019, ch 737, § 2, eff March 22, 2020; repealed by repealed, L 2020, ch 55, § 1 (Part XX, Subpart A), eff March 22, 2020.

Article 35—Division of Criminal Justice Services

§ 837. Functions, powers and duties of division

The division shall have the following functions, powers and duties:

1. Advise and assist the governor in developing policies, plans and programs for improving the coordination, administration and effectiveness of the criminal justice system;

2. Make recommendations to agencies in the criminal justice system for improving their administration and effectiveness:

3. Act as the official state planning agency pursuant to the federal acts; in accordance therewith, prepare, evaluate and revise statewide crime control and juvenile delinquency prevention and control plans; and receive and disburse funds from the federal government;

4. In cooperation with the state administrator of the unified court system as well as any other public or private agency,

(a) through the central data facility collect, analyze, evaluate and disseminate statistical and other information and data; and

(b) undertake research, studies and analyses and act as a central repository, clearinghouse and disseminator of research studies, in respect to criminal justice functions and any agency responsible for a criminal justice function, with specific attention to the effectiveness of existing programs and procedures for the efficient and just processing and disposition of criminal cases; and (b-1) collect data and undertake research, studies and analyses of judicial diversion programs including but not limited to the judicial diversion program described in article two hundred sixteen of the criminal procedure law; and

(c) collect and analyze statistical and other information and data with respect to the number of crimes reported or known to police officers or peace officers, the number of persons arrested for the commission of offense, the offense for which the person was arrested, the county within which the arrest was made and the accusatory instrument filed, the disposition of the accusatory instrument including, but not limited to, as the case may be, dismissal, acquittal, the offense to which the defendant pled guilty, the offense the defendant was convicted of after trial, and the sentence; and where a firearm as defined in section 265.00 of the penal law or machine gun, rifle or shotgun comes into the custody of police officers or peace officers in the course of an investigation of such crime or offense, the make, model type, caliber and magazine or cylinder capacity of any such firearm and whether possession of such firearm by the defendant is licensed or unlicensed and if confiscated at arrest, the style and manufacturer of any ammunition; and

(d) Supply data, upon request, to federal bureaus or departments engaged in collecting national criminal statistics; and

(e) Supply data, including confidential and sealed criminal history record information, for bona fide research purposes. Such information shall be disseminated in accordance with procedures established by the division to assure the security and privacy of identification and information data, which shall include the execution of an agreement which protects the confidentiality of the information and reasonably protects against data linkage to individuals; and

(f) Accomplish all of the functions, powers, and duties set forth in paragraphs (a), (b), (c) and (d) of this subdivision with respect to the processing and disposition of cases involving violent felony offenses specified in subdivision one of section 70.02 of the penal law.

4-a. In cooperation with the state administrator of the unified court system as well as any other public or private agency, collect and analyze statistical and all other information and data with respect to the number of environmental crimes and offenses in violation of articles twenty-seven, thirty-seven and forty, and titles twenty-seven and thirty-seven of article seventy-one of the environmental conservation law reported or known to the department of environmental conservation, the division of state police, and all other police or peace officers, the number of persons arrested for the commission of said violation, the offense for which the person was arrested, the county within which the arrest was made and the accusatory instrument filed, the disposition of the accusatory instrument filed, including, but not limited to, as the case may be, dismissal, acquittal, the offense to which the defendant pled guilty, the offense the defendant was convicted of after trial, and the sentence or monetary penalty levied, or the civil disposition of the offense if such offense was adjudicated by civil means.

4-b. In cooperation with any public or private agency or entity, collect and analyze statistical data and all other information and data with respect to the number of crimes and offenses committed against employees of the city of New York responsible for enforcing certain regulations in such city, while such employees were enforcing or attempting to enforce such regulations and reported or known to any law enforcement agency, the number of persons arrested for the commission of said offenses, the offense for which the person was arrested, the county within which the arrest was made and the accusatory instrument filed, the disposition of the accusatory instrument filed, including but not limited to, as the case may be, dismissal, acquittal, the offense to which the defendant pled guilty, the offense the defendant was convicted of after trial, and the sentence or other penalty levied. For the purposes of this subdivision, an employee of the city of New York responsible for enforcing certain regulations in such city shall mean a traffic enforcement agent or an employee of the department of sanitation who is authorized to issue notices of violation, summons or appearance tickets.

4-c. In cooperation with the chief administrator of the courts as well as any other public or private agency, including law enforcement agencies, collect and analyze statistical and all other information and data with respect to the number of hate crimes reported to or investigated by the division of state police, and all other police or peace officers, the number of persons arrested for the commission of such crimes, the offense for which the person was arrested, the county within which the arrest was made and the accusatory instrument filed, the disposition of the accusatory instrument filed, including, but not limited to, as the case may be, dismissal, acquittal, the offense to which the defendant pled guilty, the offense the defendant was convicted of after trial, and the sentence imposed. The division shall include the statistics and other information required by this subdivision in the annual report submitted to the governor and legislature pursuant to subdivision twelve of this section.

5. Conduct studies and analyses of the administration or operations of any criminal justice agency when requested by the head of such agency, and make the results thereof available for the benefit of such agency;

5-a. Undertake to furnish or make available to the district attorneys of the state such supportive services and technical assistance as the commissioner and any one or more of the district attorneys shall agree are appropriate to promote the effective performance of his or their prosecutorial functions.

6. Establish, through electronic data processing and related procedures, a central data facility with a communication network serving qualified agencies anywhere in the state, so that they may, upon such terms and conditions as the commissioner, and the appropriate officials of such qualified agencies shall agree, contribute information and, except as provided in subdivision two of section 306.2 of the family court act, have access to information contained in the central data facility, which shall include but not be limited to such information as criminal record, personal appearance data, fingerprints, photographs, and handwriting samples;

6-a. Upon request, provide an inmate of the state or local correctional facility, at no charge, with a copy of all criminal history information maintained on file by the division pertaining to such inmate.

7. Receive, process and file fingerprints, photographs and other descriptive data for the purpose of establishing identity and previous criminal record;

7-a. Receive, process and file orders granting a change of name to persons convicted of a felony subject to the provisions of subdivision two of section sixty-one of the civil rights law;

8. Adopt appropriate measures to assure the security and privacy of identification and information data;

8-a. Charge a fee when, pursuant to statute or the regulations of the division, it conducts a search of its criminal history records and returns a report thereon in connection with an application for employment or for a license or permit. The division shall adopt and may, from time to time, amend a schedule of such fees which shall be in amounts determined by the division to be reasonably related to the cost of conducting such searches and returning reports thereon but, in no event, shall any such fee exceed twenty-five dollars and an additional surcharge of fifty dollars. The comptroller is hereby authorized to deposit such fees into the general fund, provided, however, that the monies received by the division of criminal justice services for payment of the additional surcharge shall be deposited in equal amounts to the general fund and to the fingerprint identification and technology account. Notwithstanding the foregoing, the division shall not request or accept any fee for searching its records and supplying a criminal history report pursuant to section two hundred fifty-one-b of the general business law relating to participating in flight instruction at any aeronautical facility, flight school or institution of higher learning.

8-b. Notwithstanding any other provision of law to the contrary, charge a fee for the provision of agency materials and publications, conferences, criminal history record reviews, legal services, the provision of services to analyze or prepare data that is not prepared in the ordinary course of business, the provision of information in a computerized format, the application for approval and renewal of security guard training schools and the certification and renewal certification of security guard instructors, the service and repair of municipal law enforcement agency equipment and collect reimbursement and other moneys. Such fees shall be reasonably related to the actual costs incurred, including the costs of salaries, computer time, shipping and handling, as appropriate. The comptroller is hereby authorized to deposit such fees into the general fund effective August thirty-first, nineteen hundred ninety-six.

8-c. Notwithstanding the provisions of section one hundred three of the general municipal law, section one hundred seventy-four of the state finance law and any other general, special or local law to the contrary, any officer, board or agency of a political subdivision or state agency authorized to make purchases of materials, equipment or supplies, may make such purchases of statewide automated fingerprint identification system-related materials, equipment or supplies, through the agreement executed between the division and North American Morpho Systems, Inc. Notwithstanding any other law to the contrary, the division shall be authorized to enter into voluntary cost-sharing arrangements with local criminal justice agencies for expanded facsimile services and criminal justice information access through the criminal justice data communications network.

9. Accept, agree to accept and contract as agent of the state, with the approval of the governor, any grant, including federal grants, or any gift for any of the purposes of this article;

10. Accept, with the approval of the governor, as agent of the state, any gift, grant, devise or bequest, whether conditional or unconditional (notwithstanding the provisions of section eleven of the state finance law), including federal grants, for any of the purposes of this article. Any monies so received may be expended by the division to effectuate any purpose of this article, subject to the same limitations as to approval of expenditures and audit as are prescribed for state monies appropriated for the purposes of this article;

11. Enter into contracts with any person, firm, corporation, municipality, or governmental agency;

12. Make an annual report to the governor and legislature concerning its work during the preceding year, and such further interim reports to the governor, or to the governor and legislature, as it shall deem advisable, or as shall be required by the governor;

13. Adopt, amend or rescind such rules and regulations as may be necessary or convenient to the performance of the functions, powers and duties of the division;

14. Do all other things necessary or convenient to carry out the functions, powers and duties expressly set forth in this article.

15. Promulgate, in consultation with the superintendent of state police and the state office for the prevention of domestic violence, and in accordance with paragraph (f) of subdivision three of section eight hundred forty of this article, a standardized "domestic violence incident report form" for use by state and local law enforcement agencies in the reporting, recording and investigation of all alleged incidents of domestic violence, regardless of whether an arrest is made as a result of such investigation. Such form shall be prepared in multiple parts, one of which shall be immediately provided to the victim, and shall include designated spaces for: the recordation of the results of the investigation by the law enforcement agency and the basis for any action taken; the recordation of a victim's allegations of domestic violence; the age and gender of the victim and the alleged offender or offenders; and immediately thereunder a space on which the victim may sign and verify such victim's allegations. Such form shall also include, but not be limited to spaces to identify:

(a) what other services or agencies, including but not limited to medical, shelter, advocacy and other supportive services are or have previously been involved with the victim; and

(b) whether the victim has been provided with the written notice described in subdivision five of section eight hundred twelve of the family court act and subdivision six of section 530.11 of the criminal procedure law.

16. Operate a toll-free twenty-four hour telephone number that members of the public may call to obtain information as to resources available to the public to assist in the location and recovery of missing persons. Such toll-free telephone line may be operated by the division as part of the toll-free telephone line established pursuant to section eight hundred thirty-seven-f of this article. Furthermore, all such information relating to the locating and recovery of missing persons may be included on the division homepage established pursuant to section eight hundred forty-three of this article.

17. In consultation with the district attorneys, develop and operate a witness protection program. Within the amounts available by appropriation, such program shall provide assistance to district attorneys in protecting witnesses and victims, including their family members, who may suffer physical or emotional harm, intimidation or retaliatory violence as a result of the cooperation of the witness or victim with law enforcement, with a particular emphasis on vulnerable witnesses and victims, including witnesses to and victims of domestic violence and sexual exploitation and witnesses and victims testifying against violent or dangerous defendants. Such assistance may include, but not be limited to, administrative measures to: (a) facilitate name changes and receipt of new identification documents for witnesses and victims in appropriate cases; and (b) provide a range of protective services, including, when necessary, relocating victims and witnesses, and their family members. The division may enter into contracts with any person, firm, corporation, not-for-profit entity or governmental agency to provide administrative oversight and assistance in the operation of this program, may issue appropriate guidelines and may adopt, amend or rescind any rules and regulations as may be necessary or convenient to the operation of the program. These guidelines and regulations shall include a process by which district attorneys may apply for reimbursement of the costs of providing witness protection services.

18. In cooperation with any public or private agency or entity, undertake to make and furnish an instructional video relating to how sexual predators lure children. The video shall be geared toward parental information and education. The division shall distribute a copy of the video to all public libraries and police departments for public use and viewing.

19. Receive names and other non-clinical identifying information pursuant to section 9.46 of the mental hygiene law; provided, however, any such information shall be destroyed five years after such receipt, or pursuant to a proceeding brought under article seventy-eight of the civil practice law and rules determining that an individual is eligible for a license pursuant to section 400.00 of the penal law and otherwise permitted to possess a firearm.

20. To assist the department of agriculture and markets in developing information about animal cruelty and protection laws pursuant to subdivision forty-eight of section sixteen of the agriculture and markets law.

21. Promulgate a standardized and detailed written protocol that is grounded in evidence-based principles for the administration of photographic array and live lineup identification procedures for police agencies and standardized forms for use by such agencies in the reporting and recording of such identification procedure. The protocol shall address the following topics:

(a) the selection of photographic array and live lineup filler photographs or participants;

(b) instructions given to a witness before conducting a photographic array or live lineup identification procedure;

(c) the documentation and preservation of results of a photographic array or live lineup identification procedure;

(d) procedures for eliciting and documenting the witness's confidence in his or her identification following a photographic array or live lineup identification procedure, in the event that an identification is made; and

(e) procedures for administering a photographic array or live lineup identification procedure in a manner designed to prevent opportunities to influence the witness.

22.(a) Maintain and annually update a list of offenses in states and territories of the United States other than New York that include all of the essential elements of a serious offense as defined by subdivision seventeen of section 265.00 of the penal law, to assist courts, licensing authorities and others in determining which offenses in such other states and territories qualify as a serious offense for purposes of article two hundred sixty-five of the penal law, subdivision seventeen of section 265.00 of the penal law, and subdivision one-a of section 400.00 of the penal law. The division shall append to such list of offenses a disclaimer that such list shall be for informational purposes only and is not intended to be a substitute for the advice of an attorney or counselor-at-law.

(b) Such updated list shall be prominently posted on the website maintained by the division. Each list shall bear the date of posting, and each posted and dated listing shall be separately maintained by the division as a record available to the public. The first list compiled under this subdivision shall be prominently posted by the division no later than nine months after the effective date of this subdivision.

HISTORY:

Formerly § 824, add, L 1972, ch 399, § 1, with substance transferred from § 603; renumbered § 837, L 1973, ch 603, §§ 13, 16; L 1974, ch 654, § 3, with substance derived from Correction Law § 616; L 1975, ch 831, § 1, eff Aug 9, 1975; L 1976, ch 548, § 1; L 1978, ch 481, § 20; L 1981, ch 103, § 125; L 1987, ch 631, § 1, eff Nov 1, 1987; L 1989, ch 779, § 2; L 1990, ch 1, § 2, eff July 1, 1990; L 1992, ch 55, § 151, eff April 10, 1992; L 1994, ch 169, §§ 82–85, eff June 9, 1994, deemed eff April 1, 1994; L 1994, ch 222, § 27, eff Jan 1, 1995; L 1995, ch 512, § 1, eff Oct 31, 1995; L 1996, ch 309, §§ 67, 68, eff Aug 31, 1996; L 1996, 645, § 5, eff Sept 13, 1996; L 1997, ch 626, § 3, eff Sept 17, 1997; L 2000, ch 107, § 8, eff Oct 8, 2000; L 2003, ch 62, § 1 (Part G), eff May 15, 2003; L 2006, ch 561, § 2, eff Oct 15, 2006; L 2008, ch 56, § 1 (Part D), eff April 23, 2008; L 2008, ch 289, § 1, eff July 21, 2008; L 2009, ch 56, § 1 (Part G), eff April 7, 2009; L 2009, ch 56, § 14-a (Part AAA), eff April 7, 2009; L 2010, ch 56, § 4 (Part OO), eff July 22, 2010; L 2013, ch 1, § 16, eff March 16, 2013; L 2015, ch 384, § 2, eff Oct 26, 2015; L 2015, ch 432, § 3, eff Feb 18, 2016; L 2017, ch 59, § 9 (Part VVV), eff July 1, 2017; L 2020, ch 55, § 3 (Part N), eff April 3, 2020.

§ 837-u. The division of criminal justice services, in conjunction with the chief administrator of the courts, shall collect data and report annually regarding pretrial release and detention [Effective July 2, 2020]

Such data and report shall contain information categorized by gender, racial and ethnic background; regarding the nature of the criminal offenses, including the top charge of each case; the number and type of charges in each defendant's criminal record; the number of individuals released on recognizance; the number of individuals released on non-monetary conditions, including the conditions imposed; the number of individuals committed to the custody of a sheriff prior to trial; the rates of failure to appear and rearrest; the outcome of such cases or dispositions; whether the defendant was represented by counsel at every court appearance regarding the defendant's securing order; the length of the pretrial detention stay and any other such information as the chief administrator and the division of criminal justice services may find necessary and appropriate. Such annual report shall aggregate the data collected by county; court, including city, town and village courts; and judge. The data shall be disaggregated in order to protect the identity of individual defendants. The report shall be released publicly and published on the websites of the office of court administration and the division of criminal justice services. The first report shall be published eighteen months after this section shall have become a law, and shall include data from the first twelve months following the enactment of this section. Reports for subsequent years shall be published annually on or before that date thereafter.

HISTORY:

L 2020, ch 56, § 6 (Part UU), eff July 2, 2020.

§ 840. Functions, powers and duties of council

1. The council may recommend to the governor rules and regulations with respect to:

(a) The approval, or revocation thereof, of police training schools administered by municipalities;

(b) Minimum courses of study, attendance requirements, and equipment and facilities to be required at approved municipal police training schools;

(c) Minimum qualifications for instructors at approved police training schools;

(d) The requirements of minimum basic training which police officers appointed to probationary terms shall complete before being eligible for permanent appointment, and the time within which such basic training must be completed following such appointment to a probationary term;

(e) The requirements of minimum basic training which police officers not appointed for probationary terms but appointed on other than a permanent basis shall complete in order to be eligible for continued employment or permanent appointment, and the time within which such basic training must be completed following such appointment on a non-permanent basis;

(f) The requirements of minimum basic training which peace officers must complete before being eligible for certification as peace officers, pursuant to section 2.30 of the criminal procedure law;

(g) Categories or classifications of advanced in-service training programs and minimum courses of study and attendance requirements with respect to such categories or classifications; and

(h) Exemptions from particular provisions of this article in the case of any city having a population of one million or more, or in the case of the state department of corrections and community supervision if in its opinion the standards of police officer or peace officer training established and maintained by such city or department are higher than those established pursuant to this article; or revocation in whole or in part of such exemption, if in its opinion the standards of police officer or peace officer training established and maintained by such city or department are lower than those established pursuant to this article.

(i) The establishment, in cooperation with the division of state police, of a formalized consumer product tampering training program for all law enforcement personnel.

(j) (1) Development, maintenance and dissemination of written policies and procedures pursuant to title six of article six of the social services law and applicable provisions of article ten of the family court act, regarding the mandatory reporting of child abuse or neglect, reporting procedures and obligations of persons required to report, provisions for taking a child into protective custody, mandatory reporting of deaths, immunity from liability, penalties for failure to report and obligations for the provision of services and procedures necessary to safeguard the life or health of the child; (2) establishment and implementation on an ongoing basis, of a training program for all current and new police officers regarding the policies and procedures established pursuant to this paragraph; and (3) establishment of a training program for police officers whose main responsibilities are juveniles and the laws pertaining thereto, which training program shall be successfully completed before such officers are accredited pursuant to section eight hundred forty-six-h of this chapter.

(k) Development, maintenance and dissemination, in consultation with the department of agriculture and markets, of written policies and procedures pursuant to animal cruelty and protection laws, including, but not limited to, article twenty-six of the agriculture and markets law, section 352.3 of the family court act as it applies to companion animals, and applicable provisions of the penal law, regarding the investigation and prevention of any act of cruelty to animals. The council shall make provisions in such policies and procedures for the education and training in enforcement of such animal cruelty and protection laws.

(l) Exemptions from particular provisions of this article in the case of peace officers appointed by the superintendent of state police if in its opinion the standards of peace officer training provided by the division of state police exceed those established pursuant to this article.

(m) Establishment and implementation on an ongoing basis, of a training program for all current and new police officers and peace officers regarding the policies and procedures established pursuant to paragraph (k) of this subdivision.

2. The council shall promulgate, and may from time to time amend, such rules and regulations prescribing height, weight and physical fitness requirements for eligibility of persons for provisional or permanent appointment in the competitive class of the civil service as police officers of any county, city, town, village or police district as it deems necessary and proper for the efficient performance of police duties.

2-a. The council, in consultation with the state commission of correction, shall promulgate rules and regulations with respect to:

(a) The approval, or revocation thereof, of basic and other correctional training programs administered by municipalities;

(b) Minimum courses of study, attendance requirements, and equipment and facilities to be required at approved basic and other correctional training programs;

(c) Minimum qualifications for instructors at approved basic and other correctional training programs; and

(d) The requirements of a minimum basic correctional training program required by subdivision nine of section eight hundred thirty-seven-a of this article.

3. The council shall, in addition:

(a) Consult with, advise and make recommendations to the commissioner with respect to the exercise of his or her functions, powers and duties as set forth in section eight hundred forty-one of this article;

(b) Recommend studies, surveys and reports to be made by the commissioner regarding the carrying out of the objectives and purposes of this section;

(c) Visit and inspect any police training school and correctional training programs approved by the commissioner or for which application for such approval has been made;

(d) Make recommendations, from time to time, to the commissioner, the governor and the legislature, regarding the carrying out of the purposes of this section;

(e) Perform such other acts as may be necessary or appropriate to carry out the functions of the council;

(f) Develop, maintain and disseminate, in consultation with the state office for the prevention of domestic violence, written policies and procedures consistent with article eight of the family court act and applicable provisions of the criminal procedure and domestic relations laws, regarding the investigation of and intervention by new and veteran police officers in incidents of family offenses. Such policies and procedures shall make provisions for education and training in the interpretation and enforcement of New York's family offense laws, including but not limited to:

(1) intake and recording of victim statements, and the prompt translation of such statements if made in a language other than English, in accordance with subparagraph three of this paragraph, on a standardized "domestic violence incident report form" promulgated by the division of criminal justice services in consultation with the superintendent of state police, representatives of local police forces and the state office for the prevention of domestic violence, and the investigation thereof so as to ascertain whether a crime has been committed against the victim by a member of the victim's family or household as such terms are defined in section eight hundred twelve of the family court act and section 530.11 of the criminal procedure law; and

(2) the need for immediate intervention in family offenses including the arrest and detention of alleged offenders, pursuant to subdivision four of section 140.10 of the criminal procedure law, and notifying victims of their rights, in their native language, if identified as other than English, in accordance with subparagraph three of this paragraph, including but not limited to immediately providing the victim with the written notice required in subdivision six of section 530.11 of the criminal procedure law and subdivision five of section eight hundred twelve of the family court act;

(3) determine, in consultation with the superintendent of state police and the office for the prevention of domestic violence, the languages in which such translation required by subparagraph one of this paragraph, and the notification required by subparagraph two of this paragraph, shall be provided. Such determination shall be based on the size of the New York state population that speaks each language and any other relevant factor. Such written notice required pursuant to subparagraph two of this paragraph shall be made available to all local law enforcement agencies throughout the state. Nothing in this paragraph shall prevent the council from using the determinations made by the superintendent of state police pursuant to subdivision (c) of section two hundred fourteen-b of this chapter;

(f-1) Develop, maintain and disseminate, in consultation with the office of temporary and disability assistance and the division of criminal justice services, written policies and procedures regarding human trafficking victims. Such policies and procedures shall include, but not be limited to the following: (1) the identification of potential victims of human trafficking, as defined under section four hundred eighty-three-aa of the social services law; and (2) information and/or referral to appropriate social and legal services for victims of human trafficking in accordance with section four hundred eighty-three-bb of the social services law;

(g) Develop, maintain and disseminate, in consultation with the state division of human rights and the state civil service department, written policies and procedures to enhance police and correctional officer recruitment efforts and to increase police and correctional officer awareness of racial, ethnic, religious and gender differences, and other diversity issues, in communities served by such police and in correctional facilities; and

(h) Consult with the state commission of correction regarding correctional training programs.

4. The council shall, in addition:

(a) Develop, maintain and disseminate, in consultation with rape crisis centers experienced in assisting victims in this state, written policies and procedures consistent with applicable provisions of the family court act, domestic relations law, criminal procedure law and the penal law, regarding the investigation of and intervention by new and veteran police officers in crimes involving sexual assault. Such policies and procedures shall make provisions for education and training of new and veteran police officers in the investigation and enforcement of crimes involving sexual assault under state law, including but not limited to:

(1) techniques for interviewing sexual assault victims,

(2) fair treatment standards for crime victims pursuant to article twenty-three of this chapter,

(3) evidence gathering and evidence preservation, and

(4) dissemination of information concerning availability of local services for the victims of such crimes; and

(b) Recommend to the governor, rules and regulations with respect to establishment and implementation on an ongoing basis of a training program for all current and new police officers regarding the policies and procedures established pursuant to this subdivision, along with recommendations for periodic retraining of police officers.

(c) Disseminate the written policies and procedures promulgated in accordance with subdivision twenty-one of section eight hundred thirty-seven of this article to all police departments in this state and implement a training program for all current and new police officers regarding the policies and procedures established pursuant to such subdivision.

(d)(1) Establish and regularly update a model law enforcement use of force policy suitable for adoption by any agency that employs police or peace officers.

(2) The model law enforcement use of force policy shall include, but is not limited to:

(i) information on current law as it relates to the use of force by police and peace officers;

(ii) guidelines regarding when use of force is permitted;

(iii) requirements for documenting use of force;

(iv) procedures for investigating use of force incidents;

(v) guidelines regarding excessive use of force including duty to intervene, reporting, and timely medical treatment for injured persons;

(vi) standards for failure to adhere to use of force guidelines;

(vii) training mandates on use of force, conflict prevention, conflict resolution and negotiation, de-escalation techniques and strategies, including, but not limited to, interacting with persons presenting in an agitated condition; and

(viii) prohibited uses of force.

(3) The person in charge of every local police department, local correctional facility, each county sheriff, the superintendent of the division of the state police, the commissioner of the department of corrections and community supervision, and the person in charge of every agency that employs a peace officer in this state shall adopt and implement a use of force policy in the agency of which they are in charge. Such use of force policy shall be consistent with the model law enforcement use of force policy established pursuant to this subdivision, except that such departments, county sheriffs, superintendent, commissioner and agencies that employ a peace officer may impose further and additional restrictions on the use of force, in such use of force policy or otherwise.

(4) The model law enforcement use of force policy and every use of force policy established pursuant to subparagraph three of this paragraph shall be a public document, and shall be made available without charge to any member of the public promptly upon request. Each such current use of force policy shall be conspicuously posted on the public website of the agency that adopted it. Revisions to such use of force

policies shall be updated on the agency's public website within seventy-two hours of approval of any amendment.

5. The council shall, in addition:

(a) Develop, maintain and disseminate, in consultation with the commissioner of the office for people with developmental disabilities, written policies and procedures consistent with section 13.43 of the mental hygiene law, regarding the handling of emergency situations involving individuals with autism spectrum disorder and other developmental disabilities. Such policies and procedures shall make provisions for the education and training of new and veteran police officers on the handling of emergency situations involving individuals with autism spectrum disorder and other developmental disabilities; and

(b) Recommend to the governor, rules and regulations with respect to the establishment and implementation on an ongoing basis of a training program for all current and new police officers regarding the policies and procedures established pursuant to this subdivision, along with recommendations for periodic retraining of police officers.

6. The council shall, in addition:

(a) Develop, maintain and disseminate, in consultation with the division of human rights and the hate crime task force established pursuant to section two hundred sixteen of this chapter, written policies and procedures regarding the recognition of and response to hate crimes, as defined in article four hundred eighty-five of the penal law. Such policies and procedures shall make provisions for the education and training of new and veteran police officers on the recognition of and response to hate crimes; and

(b) Recommend to the governor, rules and regulations with respect to the establishment and implementation on an ongoing basis of a training program for all current and new police officers regarding the policies and procedures established pursuant to this subdivision, along with recommendations for periodic retraining of police officers. Such recommended rules and recommendations shall also be submitted to the temporary president of the senate and the speaker of the assembly.

HISTORY:

Formerly § 828, add, L 1972, ch 399, § 1, with substance transferred from § 485; renumbered § 840, L 1973, ch 603, § 13, eff Sept 1, 1973; L 1973, ch 66, § 3, eff Jan 1, 1974; L 1975, ch 459, § 4, eff July 24, 1975; L 1980, ch 843, § 4, eff Sept 1, 1980; L 1987, ch 324, § 2, eff Nov 17, 1987; L 1988, ch 504, § 6; L 1990, ch 617, § 1, eff Nov 15, 1990; L 1991, ch 166, § 342; L 1994, ch 222, § 28; L 1994, ch 224, §§ 4, 5, eff Jan 1, 1995; L 2008, ch 155, § 1, eff Jan 1, 2009; L 2009, ch 56, § 5 (Part Q), eff Oct 4, 2009; L 2009, ch 492, § 1, eff Oct 28, 2009; L 2011, ch 62, § 103 (Part C, Subpart B), eff March 31, 2011; L 2011, ch 506, § 1, eff Dec 22, 2011; L 2015, ch 368, § 42, eff Jan 19, 2016; L 2015, ch 384, § 1, eff Oct 26, 2015; L 2015, ch 432, § 2, eff Feb 18, 2016; L 2017, ch 59, § 10 (Part VVV), eff July 1, 2017; L 2018, ch 57, § 4 (Part JJ), eff Oct 9, 2018; L 2019, ch 55, § 1 (Part ZZ), eff June 11, 2019; L 2019, ch 552, § 1, eff Feb 23, 2020.

PUBLIC HEALTH LAW

Article 33—Controlled Substances

Title I
General Provisions

§ 3302. Definitions of terms of general use in this article

Except where different meanings are expressly specified in subsequent provisions of this article, the following terms have the following meanings:

1. "Addict" means a person who habitually uses a controlled substance for a non-legitimate or unlawful use, and who by reason of such use is dependent thereon.

2. "Administer" means the direct application of a controlled substance, whether by injection, inhalation, ingestion, or any other means, to the body of a patient or research subject.

3. "Agent" means an authorized person who acts on behalf of or at the direction of a manufacturer, distributor, or dispenser. No person may be authorized to so act if under title VIII of the education law such person would not be permitted to engage in such conduct. It does not include a common or contract carrier, public warehouseman, or employee of the carrier or warehouseman when acting in the usual and lawful course of the carrier's or warehouseman's business.

4. "Concentrated Cannabis" means

(a) the separated resin, whether crude or purified, obtained from a plant of the genus Cannabis; or

(b) a material, preparation, mixture, compound or other substance which contains more than two and one-half percent by weight of delta-9 tetrahydrocannabinol, or its isomer, delta-8 dibenzopyran numbering system, or delta-1 tetrahydrocannabinol or its isomer, delta 1 (6) monoterpene numbering system.

5. "Controlled substance" means a substance or substances listed in section thirty-three hundred six of this chapter.

6. "Commissioner" means commissioner of health of the state of New York.

7. "Deliver" or "delivery" means the actual, constructive or attempted transfer from one person to another of a controlled substance, whether or not there is an agency relationship.

8. "Department" means the department of health of the state of New York.

9. "Dispense" means to deliver a controlled substance to an ultimate user or research subject by lawful means, including by means of the internet, and includes the packaging, labeling, or compounding necessary to prepare the substance for such delivery.

10. "Distribute" means to deliver a controlled substance, including by means of the internet, other than by administering or dispensing.

11. "Distributor" means a person who distributes a controlled substance.

12. "Diversion" means manufacture, possession, delivery or use of a controlled substance by a person or in a manner not specifically authorized by law.

13. "Drug" means

(a) substances recognized as drugs in the official United States Pharmacopoeia, official Homeopathic Pharmacopoeia of the United States, or official National Formulary, or any supplement to any of them;

(b) substances intended for use in the diagnosis, cure, mitigation, treatment, or prevention of disease in man or animals; and

(c) substances (other than food) intended to affect the structure or a function of the body of man or animal. It does not include devices or their components, parts, or accessories.

14. "Federal agency" means the Drug Enforcement Administration, United States Department of Justice, or its successor agency.

15. "Federal controlled substances act" means the Comprehensive Drug Abuse Prevention and Control Act of 1970, Public Law 91-513, and any act or acts amendatory or supplemental thereto or regulations promulgated thereunder.

16. "Federal registration number" means such number assigned by the Federal agency to any person authorized to manufacture, distribute, sell, dispense or administer controlled substances.

17. "Habitual user" means any person who is, or by reason of repeated use of any controlled substance for non-legitimate or unlawful use is in danger of becoming, dependent upon such substance.

18. "Institutional dispenser" means a hospital, veterinary hospital, clinic, dispensary, maternity home, nursing home, mental hospital or similar facility approved and certified by the department as authorized to obtain controlled substances by distribution and to dispense and administer such substances pursuant to the order of a practitioner.

19. "License" means a written authorization issued by the department or the New York state department of education permitting persons to engage in a specified activity with respect to controlled substances.

20. "Manufacture" means the production, preparation, propagation, compounding, cultivation, conversion or processing of a controlled substance, either directly or indirectly or by extraction from substances of natural origin, or independently by means of chemical synthesis, or by a combination of extraction and chemical synthesis, and includes any packaging or repackaging of the substance or labeling or relabeling of its container, except that this term does not include the preparation, compounding, packaging or labeling of a controlled substance:

(a) by a practitioner as an incident to his administering or dispensing of a controlled substance in the course of his professional practice; or

(b) by a practitioner, or by his authorized agent under his supervision, for the purpose of, or as an incident to, research, teaching, or chemical analysis and not for sale; or

(c) by a pharmacist as an incident to his dispensing of a controlled substance in the course of his professional practice.

21. "Marihuana" means all parts of the plant of the genus Cannabis, whether growing or not; the seeds thereof; the resin extracted from any part of the plant; and every compound, manufacture, salt, derivative, mixture, or preparation of the plant, its seeds or resin. The term "marihuana" shall not include:

(a) the mature stalks of the plant, fiber produced from the stalks, oil or cake made from the seeds of the plant, any other compound, manufacture, salt, derivative, mixture, or preparation of the mature stalks (except the resin extracted therefrom), fiber, oil, or cake, or the sterilized seed of the plant which is incapable of germination;

(b) hemp, as defined in subdivision one of section five hundred five of the agriculture and markets law;

(c) cannabinoid hemp as defined in subdivision two of section thirty-three hundred ninety-eight of this chapter; or

(d) hemp extract as defined in subdivision five of section thirty-three hundred ninety-eight of this chapter.

22. "Narcotic drug" means any of the following, whether produced directly or indirectly by extraction from substances of vegetable origin, or independently by means of chemical synthesis, or by a combination of extraction and chemical synthesis:

(a) opium and opiate, and any salt, compound, derivative, or preparation of opium or opiate;

(b) any salt, compound, isomer, derivative, or preparation thereof which is chemically equivalent or identical with any of the substances referred to in subdivision (a), but not including the isoquinoline alkaloids of opium;

(c) opium poppy and poppy straw.

23. "Opiate" means any substance having an addiction-forming or addiction-sustaining liability similar to morphine or being capable of conversion into a drug having addiction-forming or addiction-sustaining liability. It does not include, unless

specifically designated as controlled under section 3306 of this article, the dextrorotatory isomer of 3-methoxy-n-methylmorphinan and its salts (dextromethorphan). It does include its racemic and levorotatory forms.

24. "Opium poppy" means the plant of the species Papaver somniferum L., except its seeds.

25. "Person" means individual, institution, corporation, government or governmental subdivision or agency, business trust, estate, trust, partnership or association, or any other legal entity.

26. "Pharmacist" means any person licensed by the state department of education to practice pharmacy.

27. "Pharmacy" means any place registered as such by the New York state board of pharmacy and registered with the Federal agency pursuant to the federal controlled substances act.

28. "Poppy straw" means all parts, except the seeds, of the opium poppy, after mowing.

29. "Practitioner" means:

A physician, dentist, podiatrist, veterinarian, scientific investigator, or other person licensed, or otherwise permitted to dispense, administer or conduct research with respect to a controlled substance in the course of a licensed professional practice or research licensed pursuant to this article. Such person shall be deemed a "practitioner" only as to such substances, or conduct relating to such substances, as is permitted by his license, permit or otherwise permitted by law.

30. "Prescribe" means a direction or authorization, by prescription, permitting an ultimate user lawfully to obtain controlled substances from any person authorized by law to dispense such substances.

31. "Prescription" shall mean an official New York state prescription, an electronic prescription, an oral prescription, an out-of-state prescription, or any one.

32. "Sell" means to sell, exchange, give or dispose of to another, or offer or agree to do the same.

33. "Ultimate user" means a person who lawfully obtains and possesses a controlled substance for his own use or the use by a member of his household or for an animal owned by him or in his custody. It shall also mean and include a person designated, by a practitioner on a prescription, to obtain such substance on behalf of the patient for whom such substance is intended.

34. "Internet" means collectively computer and telecommunications facilities which comprise the worldwide network of networks that employ a set of industry standards and protocols, or any predecessor or successor protocol to such protocol, to exchange information of all kinds. "Internet," as used in this article, also includes other networks, whether private or public, used to transmit information by electronic means.

35. "By means of the internet" means any sale, delivery, distribution, or dispensing of a controlled substance that uses the internet, is initiated by use of the internet or causes the internet to be used.

36. "Online dispenser" means a practitioner, pharmacy, or person in the United States that sells, delivers or dispenses, or offers to sell, deliver, or dispense, a controlled substance by means of the internet.

37. "Electronic prescription" means a prescription issued with an electronic signature and transmitted by electronic means in accordance with regulations of the commissioner and the commissioner of education and consistent with federal requirements. A prescription generated on an electronic system that is printed out or transmitted via facsimile is not considered an electronic prescription and must be manually signed.

38. "Electronic" means of or relating to technology having electrical, digital, magnetic, wireless, optical, electromagnetic or similar capabilities. "Electronic" shall not include facsimile.

39. "Electronic record" means a paperless record that is created, generated, transmitted, communicated, received or stored by means of electronic equipment and includes the preservation, retrieval, use and disposition in accordance with regulations of the commissioner and the commissioner of education and in compliance with federal law and regulations.

40. "Electronic signature" means an electronic sound, symbol, or process, attached to or logically associated with an electronic record and executed or adopted by a person with the intent to sign the record, in accordance with regulations of the commissioner and the commissioner of education.

41. "Registry" or "prescription monitoring program registry" means the prescription monitoring program registry established pursuant to section thirty-three hundred forty-three-a of this article.

42. "Compounding" means the combining, admixing, mixing, diluting, pooling, reconstituting, or otherwise altering of a drug or bulk drug substance to create a drug with respect to an outsourcing facility under section 503B of the federal Food, Drug and Cosmetic Act and further defined in this section.

43. "Outsourcing facility" means a facility that:

(a) is engaged in the compounding of sterile drugs as defined in section sixty-eight hundred two of the education law;

(b) is currently registered as an outsourcing facility pursuant to article one hundred thirty-seven of the education law; and

(c) complies with all applicable requirements of federal and state law, including the Federal Food, Drug and Cosmetic Act.

Notwithstanding any other provision of law to the contrary, when an outsourcing facility distributes or dispenses any drug to any person pursuant to a prescription, such outsourcing facility shall be deemed to be providing pharmacy services and shall be subject to all laws, rules and regulations governing pharmacies and pharmacy services.

HISTORY:

Add, L 1972, ch 878, § 2, eff April 1, 1973; amd, L 1973, ch 163, §§ 1–3, eff April 1, 1973; L 1998, ch 537, § 3, eff Nov 1, 1998; L 2004, ch 58, § 4 (Part A), eff Oct 20, 2004; L 2010, ch 178, §§ 1, 2, eff July 15, 2010; L 2012, ch 447, § 6 (Part A), eff Aug 27, 2013; L 2014, ch 60, § 13 (Part D), eff June 29, 2014; L 2020, ch 1, § 3, eff March 8, 2020.

§ 3306. Schedules of controlled substances [Effective until July 2, 2020]

There are hereby established five schedules of controlled substances, to be known as schedules I, II, III, IV and V respectively. Such schedules shall consist of the following substances by whatever name or chemical designation known:

Schedule I.

(a) Schedule I shall consist of the drugs and other substances, by whatever official name, common or usual name, chemical name, or brand name designated, listed in this section.

(b) Opiates. Unless specifically excepted or unless listed in another schedule, any of the following opiates, including their isomers, esters, ethers, salts, and salts of isomers, esters, and ethers, whenever the existence of such isomers, esters, ethers and salts is possible within the specific chemical designation (for purposes of 3-methylfentanyl only, the term isomer includes the optical and geometric isomers):

(1) Acetyl-alpha-methylfentanyl (N-[1-(-methyl-2-phenethyl) -4-piperidinyl] -N-phenylacetamide.

(2) Acetylmethadol.

(3) Allylprodine.

(4) Alphacetylmethadol (except levo-alphacetylmethadol also known as levo-alpha-acetylmethadol, levomethadyl acetate or LAAM).

(5) Alphameprodine.

(6) Alphamethadol.

(7) Alpha-methylfentanyl (N-[1-(alpha-methyl-beta-phenyl) ethyl-4-piperidyl] propionanilide; 1-(1-methyl-2-phenylethyl) -4-(N-propanilido) piperidine).

(8) Alpha-methylthiofentanyl (N-[1-methyl-2)2-thienyl) ethyl-4-piperidinyl] -N-phenylpropanamide).

(9) Beta-hydroxyfentanyl (N-[1-2 (2-hydroxy-2-phenethyl)- 4-piperidinyl] -N-phenylpropanamide).

(10) Beta-hydroxy-3-methylfentanyl (other name: N-[1- (2-hydroxy-2-phenethyl) -3-methyl-4-piperidinyl] -N-phenylpropanamide.

(11) Benzethidine.

(12) Betacetylmethadol.
(13) Betameprodine.
(14) Betamethadol.
(15) Betaprodine.
(16) Clonitazene.
(17) Dextromoramide.
(18) Diampromide.
(19) Diethylthiambutene.
(20) Difenoxin.
(21) Dimenoxadol.
(22) Dimepheptanol.
(23) Dimethylthiambutene.
(24) Dioxaphetyl butyrate.
(25) Dipipanone.
(26) Ethylmethylthiambutene.
(27) Etonitazene.
(28) Etoxeridine.
(29) Furethidine.
(30) Hydroxypethidine.
(31) Ketobemidone.
(32) Levomoramide.
(33) Levophenacylmorphan.
(34) 3-Methylfentanyl (N-[3-methyl-1- (2- phenylethyl -4-piperidyl] -N-phenylpropanamide).
(35) 3-Methylthiofentanyl (N-[3-methyl-1- (2-thienyl)ethyl -4-piperidinyl] -N-phenylpropanamide).
(36) Morpheridine.
(37) MPPP (1-methyl -4-phenyl -4-propionoxypiperidine).
(38) Noracymethadol.
(39) Norlevorphanol.
(40) Normethadone.
(41) Norpipanone.
(42) Para-fluorofentanyl (N- (4-fluorophenyl) -N-[1- (2-phenethyl) -4-piperidinyl] -propanamide.
(43) PEPAP (1- (-2-phenethyl) -4-phenyl -4-acetoxypiperidine.
(44) Phenadoxone.
(45) Phenampromide.
(46) Phenomorphan.
(47) Phenoperidine.
(48) Piritramide.
(49) Proheptazine.
(50) Properidine.
(51) Propiram.
(52) Racemoramide.
(53) Thiofentanyl (N-phenyl-N-[1- (2-thienyl) ethyl -4- piperidinyl] -propanamide.
(54) Tilidine.
(55) Trimeperidine.
(56) 3,4-dichloro-N-{(1-dimethylamino) cyclohexylmethyl}benzamide. Some trade or other names: AH-7921.
(57) N-(1-phenethylpiperidin-4-yl)-N-phenylacetamide (Acetyl Fentanyl).

(c) Opium derivatives. Unless specifically excepted or unless listed in another schedule, any of the following opium derivatives, its salts, isomers, and salts of isomers whenever the existence of such salts, isomers, and salts of isomers is possible within the specific chemical designation:
(1) Acetorphine.
(2) Acetyldihydrocodeine.
(3) Benzylmorphine.
(4) Codeine methylbromide.
(5) Codeine-N-oxide.
(6) Cyprenorphine.

(7) Desomorphine.
(8) Dihydromorphine.
(9) Drotebanol.
(10) Etorphine (except hydrochloride salt).
(11) Heroin.
(12) Hydromorphinol.
(13) Methyldesorphine.
(14) Methyldihydromorphine.
(15) Morphine methylbromide.
(16) Morphine methylsulfonate.
(17) Morphine-N-oxide.
(18) Myrophine.
(19) Nicocodeine.
(20) Nicomorphine.
(21) Normorphine.
(22) Pholcodine.
(23) Thebacon.

(d) Hallucinogenic substances. Unless specifically excepted or unless listed in another schedule, any material, compound, mixture, or preparation, which contains any quantity of the following hallucinogenic substances, or which contains any of its salts, isomers, and salts of isomers whenever the existence of such salts, isomers, and salts of isomers is possible within the specific chemical designation (for purposes of this paragraph only, the term "isomer" includes the optical, position and geometric isomers):

(1) 4-bromo-2, 5-dimethoxy-amphetamine Some trade or other names: 4-bromo-2, 5-dimethoxy-α-methylphenethylamine; 4-bromo-2, 5-DMA.

(2) 2, 5-dimethoxyamphetamine Some trade or other names: 2, 5-dimethoxy-α-methylphenethylamine; 2, 5-DMA.

(3) 4-methoxyamphetamine Some trade or other names: 4-methoxy-α-methylphenethylamine; paramethoxyamphetamine, PMA.

(4) 5-methoxy-3, 4-methylenedioxy-amphetamine.

(5) 4-methyl-2, 5-dimethoxy-amphetamine Some trade and other names: 4-methyl-2, 5-dimethoxy-α-methylphenethylamine; "DOM"; and "STP".

(6) 3, 4-methylenedioxy amphetamine.

(7) 3, 4, 5-trimethoxy amphetamine.

(8) Bufotenine Some trade and other names: 3-(β-dimethylaminoethyl)-5 Hydroxindole; 3-(2-dimethylaminoethyl)-5-indolol; N, N-dimethylserotonin; -5-hydroxy-N, N-dimethyltryptamine; mappine.

(9) Diethyltryptamine Some trade and other names: N, N-diethyltryptamine; DET.

(10) Dimethyltryptamine Some trade or other names: DMT.

(11) Ibogane Some trade and other names: 7-ethyl-6, 6β, 7, 8, 9, 10, 12, 13-octahydro-2-methoxy-6, 9-methano-5h-pyrido [1', 2': 1,2] azepino [5,4-b] indole: tabernanthe iboga.

(12) Lysergic acid diethylamide.

(13) Marihuana.

(14) Mescaline.

(15) Parahexyl. Some trade or other names: 3-Hexyl-1-hydroxy-7, 8, 9, 10-tetra hydro-6, 6, 9-trimethyl-6H-dibenfo[b,d] pyran.

(16) Peyote. Meaning all parts of the plant presently classified botanically as Lophophora williamsii Lemaire, whether growing or not, the seeds thereof, any extract from any part of such plant, and every compound, manufacture, salts, derivative, mixture, or preparation of such plant, its seeds or extracts.

(17) N-ethyl-3-piperidyl benzilate.

(18) N-methyl-3-piperidyl benzilate.

(19) Psilocybin.

(20) Psilocyn.

(21) Tetrahydrocannabinols. Synthetic equivalents of the substances contained in the plant, or in the resinous extractives of cannabis, sp. and/or synthetic substances, derivatives, and their isomers with similar chemical structure and pharmacological activity such as the following:

δ^1 cis or trans tetrahydrocannabinol, and their optical isomers

δ^6 cis or trans tetrahydrocannabinol, and their optical isomers

$\delta^{3,4}$ cis or trans tetrahydrocannabinol, and its optical isomers (since nomenclature of these substances is not internationally standardized, compounds of these structures, regardless of numerical designation of atomic positions covered).

(22) Ethylamine analog of phencyclidine. Some trade or other names: N-ethyl-1-phenylcyclohexylamine, (1-phenylcyclohexyl) ethylamine, N-(1-phenylcyclohexyl) ethylamine cyclohexamine, PCE.

(23) Pyrrolidine analog of phencyclidine. Some trade or other names 1-(1-phenylcyclohexyl)-pyrrolidine; PCPy, PHP.

(24) Thiophene analog of phencyclidine. Some trade or other names: 1-[1-(2-thienyl)-cyclohexyl]-piperidine, 2-thienylanalog of phencyclidine, TPCP, TCP.

(25) 3,4-methylenedioxymethamphetamine (MDMA).

(26) 3,4-methylendioxy-N-ethylamphetamine (also known as N-ethyl-alpha-methyl-3,4 (methylenedioxy) phenethylamine, N-ethyl MDA, MDE, MDEA.

(27) N-hydroxy-3,4-methylenedioxyamphetamine (also known as N-hydroxy-alpha-methyl-3,4 (methylenedioxy) phenethylamine, and N-hydroxy MDA.

(28) 1-[1- (2-thienyl) cyclohexyl] pyrrolidine. Some other names: TCPY.

(29) Alpha-ethyltryptamine. Some trade or other names: etryptamine; Monase; Alpha-ethyl-1H-indole-3-ethanamine; 3- (2-aminobutyl) indole; Alpha-ET or AET.

(30) 2,5-dimethoxy-4-ethylamphetamine. Some trade or other names: DOET.

(31) 4-Bromo-2,5-dimethoxyphenethylamine. Some trade or other names: 2-(4-bromo-2,5-dimethoxyphenyl)-1-aminoethane; alpha-desmethyl DOB; 2C-B, Nexus.

(32) 2,5-dimethoxy-4-(n)-propylthiophenethylamine (2C-T-7), its optical isomers, salts and salts of isomers.

(33) 2-(4-iodo-2,5-dimethoxyphenyl)-N-(2-methoxybenzyl)ethanamine, also known as 25I-NBOMe; 2C-I-NBOMe; 25I; or Cimbi-5.

(34) 2-(4-chloro-2,5-dimethoxyphenyl)-N-(2-methoxybenzyl) ethanamine, also known as 25 CNBOMe; 2C-C-NBOMe; 25C; or Cimbi-82.

(35) 2-(4-bromo-2,5-dimethoxyphenyl)-N-(2-methoxybenzyl) ethanamine, also known as, 25 BNBOMe; 2C-B-NBOMe; Cimbi-36.

(36) 5-methoxy-N,N-dimethyltryptamine.

(37) Alpha-methyltryptamine. Some trade or other names: AMT.

(38) 5-methoxy-N,N-diisopropyltryptamine. Some trade or other names: 5-MeO-DIPT.

(e) Depressants. Unless specifically excepted or unless listed in another schedule, any material, compound, mixture, or preparation which contains any quantity of the following substances having a depressant effect on the central nervous system, including its salts, isomers, and salts of isomers whenever the existence of such salts, isomers, and salts of isomers is possible within the specific chemical designation:

(1) Mecloqualone.

(2) Methaqualone.

(3) Phencyclidine.

(4) Gamma hydroxybutyric acid, and salt, hydroxybutyric compound, derivative or preparation of gamma hydroxybutyric acid, including any isomers, esters and ethers and salts of isomers, esters and ethers of gamma hydroxybutyric acid, except gamma-butyrolactone, whenever the existence of such isomers, esters and ethers and salts is possible within the specific chemical.

(5) Gamma-butyrolactone, including butyrolactone; butyrolactone gamma; 4-butyrolactone; 2(3H)-furanone dihydro; dihydro-2(3H)-furanone; tetrahydro-2-furanone; 1,2-butanolide; 1,4-butanolide; 4-butanolide; gamma-hydroxybutyric acid lactone; 3-hydroxybutyric acid lactone and 4-hydroxybutanoic acid lactone with Chemical Abstract Service number (96-48-0) when any such substance is intended for human consumption.

(6) 1,4 butanediol, including butanediol; butane-1,4-diol; 1,4-butylene glyco; butylene glycol; 1,4-dihydroxybutane; 1,4-tetramethyleneglycol; tetramethylene glycol; tetramethylene Abstract Service number (110-63-4) when any such substance is intended for human consumption.

(f) Stimulants. Unless specifically excepted or unless listed in another schedule, any material, compound, mixture, or preparation which contains any quantity of the following substances having a stimulant effect on the central nervous system, including its salts, isomers, and salts of isomers:

(1) Fenethylline.
(2) N-ethylamphetamine.
(3) (+ -)cis-4-methylaminorex ((+ -)cis-4,5-dihydro-4-methyl -5-phenyl -2-oxazolamine).
(4) N,N-dimethylamphetamine (also known as N,N-alpha- trimethyl-benzeneethanamine; N,N-alpha- trimethylphenethylamine).
(5) Methcathinone (some other names: 2-(methylamino) - propiophenone; alpha-(methylamino) propiophenone; 2-(methylamino) -1-phenylpropan- 1 -one; alpha-N-methylaminopropiophenone; monomethylpropion; ephedrone, N-methylcathinone, methylcathinone; AL-464; AL-422; AL-463 and UR1432), its salts, optical isomers and salts of optical isomers.
(6) Aminorex. Some other names: aminoxaphen; 2-amino-5-phenyl -2-oxazoline; or 4,5-dihydro-5-phenyl-2-oxazolamine.
(7) Cathinone. Some trade or other names: 2-amino-1-phenyl-1-propanone, alpha-aminopropiophenone, 2-aminopropiophenone, and norephedrone.
(8) N-benzylpiperazine (some other names: BZP; 1-benzylpiperazine), its optical isomers, salts and salts of isomers.
(9) 4-methyl-N-methylcathinone or 4-Methylmethcathinone, also known as Mephedrone.
(10) 3,4-methylenedioxypyrovalerone or Methylenedioxypyrovalerone, also known as MDPV.
(11) 3,4-methylenedioxy-N-methylcathinone (some other names: methylone).
(12) 4-Methoxymethcathinone.
(13) 3-Fluoromethcathinone.
(14) 4-Fluoromethcathinone.
(15) Ethylpropion (Ethcathinone).
(16) 2-(2,5-Dimethoxy-4-ethylphenyl)ethanamine (2C-E).
(17) 2-(2,5-Dimethoxy-4-methylphenyl)ethanamine (2C-D).
(18) 2-(4-Chloro-2,5-dimethoxyphenyl)ethanamine (2C-C).
(19) 2-(4-Iodo-2,5-dimethoxyphenyl)ethanamine (2C-I).
(20) 2-[4-(Ethylthio)-2,5-dimethoxyphenyl]ethanamine (2C-T-2).
(21) 2-[4-(Isopropylthio)-2,5-dimethoxyphenyl]ethanamine (2C-T-4).
(22) 2-(2,5-Dimethoxyphenyl)ethanamine (2C-H).
(23) 2-(2,5-Dimethoxy-4-nitro-phenyl)ethanamine (2C-N).
(24) 2-(2,5-Dimethoxy-4-(n)-propylphenyl)ethanamine (2C-P).

(g) Synthetic cannabinoids. Unless specifically excepted or unless listed in another schedule, any material, compound, mixture, or preparation, which contains any quantity of the following synthetic cannabinoid substances, or which contains any of its salts, isomers, and salts of isomers whenever the existence of such salts, isomers, and salts of isomers is possible within the specific chemical designation (for purposes of this paragraph only, the term "isomer" includes the optical, position and geometric isomers):
(1) (1 pontyl-1H-indol-3-yl)(2,2,3,3-tetramethylcyclopropyl) methanone. Some trade or other names: UR-144.
(2) {1-(5-fluro-pentyl)-1H-indol-3-yl}(2,2,3,3-tetramethylcyclopropyl) methanone. Some trade names or other names: 5-fluoro-UR-144, XLR11.
(3) N-(1-adamantyl)-1-pentyl-1H-indazole-3-carboxamide. Some trade or other names: APINACA, AKB48.
(4) quinolin-8-yl 1-pentyl-1H-indole-3-carboxylate. Some trade or other names: PB-22; QUPIC.
(5) quinolin-8-yl 1-(5-fluoropentyl)-1H-indole-3-carboxylate. Some trade or other names: 5-fluoro-PB-22; 5F-PB-22.
(6) N-(1-amino-3-methyl-1-oxobutan-2-yl)-1-(4-fluorobenzyl)-1H-indazole-3-carboxamide. Some trade or other names: AB-FUBINACA.
(7) N-(1-amino-3,3-dimethyl-1-oxobutan-2-yl) -1-pentyl-1H-indazole-3-carboxamide. Some trade or other names: ADB-PINACA.
(8) N-(1-amino-3-methyl-1-oxobutan-2-yl) -1-(cyclohexylmethyl)- 1H-indazole-3-carboxamide. Some trade or other names: AB-CHMINACA.
(9) N-(1-amino-3-methyl-1-oxobutan-2-yl) -1-pentyl-1H-indazole-3-carboxamide. Some trade or other names: AB-PINACA.

(10) {1-(5-fluoropentyl)-1H-indazol-3-yl}(naphthalen-1-yl)methanone. Some trade or other names: THJ-2201.

(h)(1) Cannabimimetic agents. Unless specifically exempted or unless listed in another schedule, any material, compound, mixture, or preparation that is not approved by the federal food and drug administration (FDA) which contains any quantity of cannabimimetic agents, or which contains their salts, isomers, and salts of isomers whenever the existence of such salts, isomers, and salts of isomers is possible within the specific chemical designation.

(2) As used in this subdivision, the term "cannabimimetic agents" means any substance that is a cannabinoid receptor type 1 (CB1 receptor) agonist as demonstrated by binding studies and functional assays within any of the following structural classes:

(i) 2-(3-hydroxycyclohexyl)phenol with substitution at the 5-position of the phenolic ring by alkyl or alkenyl, whether or not substituted on the cyclohexyl ring to any extent.

(ii) 3-(1-naphthoyl)indole or 3-(1-naphthylmethane)indole by substitution at the nitrogen atom of the indole ring, whether or not further substituted on the indole ring to any extent, whether or not substituted on the naphthoyl or naphthyl ring to any extent.

(iii) 3-(1-naphthoyl)pyrrole by substitution at the nitrogen atom of the pyrrole ring, whether or not further substituted in the pyrrole ring to any extent, whether or not substituted on the naphthoyl ring to any extent.

(iv) 1-(1-naphthylmethylene)indene by substitution of the 3-position of the indene ring, whether or not further substituted in the indene ring to any extent, whether or not substituted on the naphthyl ring to any extent.

(v) 3-phenylacetylindole or 3-benzoylindole by substitution at the nitrogen atom of the indole ring, whether or not further substituted in the indole ring to any extent, whether or not substituted on the phenyl ring to any extent.

(3) Such term includes:

(i) 5-(1,1-dimethylheptyl)-2-{(1R,3S)-3-hydroxycyclohexyl}-phenol (CP-47,497);

(ii) 5-(1,1-dimethyloctyl)-2-{(1R,3S)-3-hydroxycyclohexyl}-phenol (cannabicyclohexanol or CP-47,497 C8-homolog);

(iii) 1-pentyl-3-(1-naphthoyl)indole (JWH-018 and AM678);

(iv) 1-butyl-3-(1-naphthoyl)indole (JWH-073);

(v) 1-hexyl-3-(1-naphthoyl)indole (JWH-019);

(vi) 1-{2-(4-morpholinyl)ethyl}-3-(1-naphthoyl)indole (JWH-200);

(vii) 1-pentyl-3-(2-methoxyphenylacetyl)indole (JWH-250);

(viii) 1-pentyl-3-{1-(4-methoxynaphthoyl)}indole (JWH-081);

(ix) 1-pentyl-3-(4-methyl-1-naphthoyl)indole (JWH-122);

(x) 1-pentyl-3-(4-chloro-1-naphthoyl)indole (JWH-398);

(xi) 1-(5-fluoropentyl)-3-(1-naphthoyl)indole (AM2201);

(xii) 1-(5-fluoropentyl)-3-(2-iodobenzoyl)indole (AM694);

(xiii) 1-pentyl-3-{(4-methoxy)-benzoyl}indole (SR-19 and RCS-4);

(xiv) 1-cyclohexylethyl-3-(2-methoxyphenylacetyl)indole (SR-18 and RCS-8); and

(xv) 1-pentyl-3-(2-chlorophenylacetyl)indole (JWH-203).

Schedule II.

(a) Schedule II shall consist of the drugs and other substances, by whatever official name, common or usual name, chemical name, or brand name designated, listed in this section.

(b) Substances, vegetable origin or chemical synthesis. Unless specifically excepted or unless listed in another schedule, any of the following substances whether produced directly or indirectly by extraction from substances of vegetable origin, or independently by means of chemical synthesis, or by a combination of extraction and chemical synthesis:

(1) Opium and opiate, and any salt, compound, derivative, or preparation of opium or opiate, excluding apomorphine, dextrorphan, nalbuphine, nalmefene, naloxone, and naltrexone, and their respective salts, but including the following:

1. Raw opium.
2. Opium extracts.
3. Opium fluid.
4. Powdered opium.
5. Granulated opium.

6. Tincture of opium.
7. Codeine.
8. Ethylmorphine.
9. Etorphine hydrochloride.
10. Hydrocodone (also known as dihydrocodeinone).
11. Hydromorphone.
12. Metopon.
13. Morphine.
14. Oxycodone.
15. Oxymorphone.
16. Thebaine.
17. Dihydroetorphine.
18. Oripavine.

(2) Any salt, compound, derivative, or preparation thereof which is chemically equivalent or identical with any of the substances referred to in this section, except that these substances shall not include the isoquinoline alkaloids of opium.

(3) Opium poppy and poppy straw.

(4) Coca leaves and any salt, compound, derivative, or preparation of coca leaves, and any salt, compound, derivative, or preparation thereof which is chemically equivalent or identical with any of these substances including cocaine and ecgonine, their salts, isomers, and salts of isomers, except that the substances shall not include: (A) decocainized coca leaves or extraction of coca leaves, which extractions do not contain cocaine or ecgonine; or (B) {123I} ioflupane.

(5) Concentrate of poppy straw (the crude extract of poppy straw in either liquid, solid or powder form which contains the phenanthrene alkaloids of the opium poppy).

(6) [Repealed]

(b-1) Unless specifically excepted or unless listed in another schedule, any material, compound, mixture, or preparation containing any of the following, or their salts calculated as the free anhydrous base or alkaloid, in limited quantities as set forth below:

(1) Not more than three hundred milligrams of dihydrocodeinone (hydrocodone) per one hundred milliliters or not more than fifteen milligrams per dosage unit, with a fourfold or greater quantity of an isoquinoline alkaloid of opium.

(2) Not more than three hundred milligrams of dihydrocodeinone (hydrocodone) per one hundred milliliters or not more than fifteen milligrams per dosage unit, with one or more active nonnarcotic ingredients in recognized therapeutic amounts.

(c) Opiates. Unless specifically excepted or unless in another schedule any of the following opiates, including its isomers, esters, ethers, salts and salts of isomers, esters and ethers whenever the existence of such isomers, esters, ethers, and salts is possible within the specific chemical designation, dextrorphan and levopropoxyphene excepted:

(1) Alfentanil.
(2) Alphaprodine.
(3) Anileridine.
(4) Bezitramide.
(5) Bulk dextropropoxyphene (non-dosage forms).
(6) Carfentanil.
(7) Dihydrocodeine.
(8) Diphenoxylate.
(9) Fentanyl.
(10) Isomethadone.
(11) Levo-alphacetylmethadol (also known as levo-alpha-acetylmethadol, levomethadyl acetate or LAAM).
(12) Levomethorphan.
(13) Levorphanol.
(14) Metazocine.
(15) Methadone.
(16) Methadone-intermediate, 4-cyano-2-dimethylamino-4, 4-diphenyl butane.
(17) Moramide-intermediate, 2-methyl-3-morpholino-1, 1-diphenylpropane-carboxylic acid.
(18) Pethidine (meperidine).

(19) Pethidine-intermediate-A, 4-cyano-1-methyl-4-phenylpiperidine.
(20) Pethidine-intermediate-B, ethyl-4-phenylpiperidine-4-carboxylate.
(21) Pethidine-intermediate-C, 1-methyl-4- phenylpiperidine-4-carboxylic acid.
(22) Phenazocine.
(23) Piminodine.
(24) Racemethorphan.
(25) Racemorphan.
(26) Sufentanil.
(27) Remifentanil.
(28) Tapentadol.

(d) Stimulants. Unless specifically excepted or unless listed in another schedule, any material, compound, mixture, or preparation which contains any quantity of the following substances having a stimulant effect on the central nervous system, including its salts, isomers, and salts of isomers:

(1) Amphetamine.
(2) Methamphetamine.
(3) Phenmetrazine.
(4) Methylphenidate.
(5) Lisdexamfetamine.

(e) Depressants. Unless specifically excepted or unless listed in another schedule, any material, compound, mixture, or preparation which contains any quantity of the following substances having a depressant effect on the central nervous system, including its salts, isomers, and salts of isomers whenever the existence of such salts, isomers, and salts of isomers is possible within the specific chemical designation:

(1) Amobarbital.
(2) Glutethimide.
(3) Pentobarbital.
(4) Secobarbital.

(f) Hallucinogenic substances.

Nabilone: Another name for nabilone: (+,-)- trans- 3-(1,1-dimethylheptyl)-6, 6a, 7, 8, 10, 10a-hexahydro-1-hydroxy-6, 6-dimethyl-9H-dibenzo [b,d] pyran-9-one.

(g) Immediate precursors. Unless specifically excepted or unless listed in another schedule, any material, compound, mixture or preparation which contains any quantity of the following substances:

(1) Immediate precursor to amphetamine and methamphetamine:

(i) Phenylacetone Some trade or other names: phenyl-2-propanone; P2P; benzyl methyl ketone; methyl benzyl ketone;

(2) Immediate precursors to phencyclidine (PCP):

(i) 1-phenylcyclohexylamine;

(ii) 1-piperidinocyclohexanecarbonitrile (PCC).

(3) Immediate precursor to fentanyl:

(i) 4-anilino-N-phenethyl-4-piperidine (ANPP).

(h) Anabolic steroids. Unless specifically excepted or unless listed in another schedule, "anabolic steroid" shall mean any drug or hormonal substance, chemically and pharmacologically related to testosterone (other than estrogens, progestins, corticosteroids and dehydroepiandrosterone) and includes:

(1) 3[beta], 17-dihydroxy-5a-androstane.
(2) 3[alpha], 17[beta]-dihydroxy-5a-androstane.
(3) 5[alpha]-androstan-3,17-dione.
(4) 1-androstenediol (3[beta],17[beta]-dihydroxy-5[alpha]-androst-1-ene).
(5) 1-androstenediol (3[alpha],17[beta]-dihydroxy-5[alpha]-androst-1-ene).
(6) 4-androstenediol (3[beta], 17[beta]-dihydroxy-androst-4-ene).
(7) 5-androstenediol (3[beta], 17[beta]-dihydroxy-androst-5-ene).
(8) 1-androstenedione ([5[alpha]]-androst-1-en-3,17-dione).
(9) 4-androstenedione (androst-4-en-3,17-dione).
(10) 5-androstenedione (androst-5-en-3,17-dione).
(11) Bolasterone (7[alpha],17[alpha]-dimethyl-17[beta]-hydroxyandrost-4-en-3-one).
(12) Boldenone (17[beta]-hydroxyandrost-1, 4,-diene-3-one).
(13) Boldione (androsta-1,4-diene-3,17-dione).

(14) Calusterone (7[beta], 17[alpha]-dimethyl-17[beta]-hydroxyandrost-4-en-3-one).
(15) Clostebol (4-chloro-17[beta]-hydroxyandrost-4-en-3-one).
(16) Dehydrochloromethyltestosterone (4-chloro-17[beta]-hydroxy-17 [alpha]-methyl-androst-1, 4-dien-3-one).
(17) [Delta] 1-dihydrotestosterone (a.k.a. '1-testosterone') (17 [beta]-hydroxy-5[alpha]-androst-1-en-3-one).
(18) 4-dihydrotestosterone (17[beta]-hydroxy-androstan-3-one).
(19) Drostanolone (17[beta]-hydroxy-2[alpha]-methyl-5[alpha]-androstan-3-one).
(20) Ethylestrenol (17[alpha]-ethyl-17[beta]-hydroxyestr-4-ene).
(21) Fluoxymesterone (9-fluoro-17[alpha]-methyl-11[beta], 17[beta]-dihydroxyandrost-4-en-3-one).
(22) Formebolone (2-formyl-17[alpha]-methyl-11[alpha], 17[beta]-dihydroxyandrost-1, 4-dien-3-one).
(23) Furazabol (17[alpha]-methyl-17[beta]-hydroxyandrostano [2, 3-c]-furazan).
(24) 13[beta]-ethyl-17[beta]-hyroxygon-4-en-3-one.
(25) 4-hydroxytestosterone (4, 17[beta]-dihydroxy-androst-4-en-3-one).
(26) 4-hydroxy-19-nortestosterone (4,17[beta]-dihydroxy-estr-4-en-3-one).
(27) desoxymethyltestosterone (17[alpha]-methyl-5[alpha]-androst-2-en-17[beta]-ol) (a.k.a., madol).
(28) Mestanolone (17[alpha]-methyl-17[beta]-hydroxy-5-androstan-3-one).
(29) Mesterolone (1[alpha]methyl-17[beta]-hydroxy-[5[alpha]]-androstan-3-one).
(30) Methandienone (17[alpha]-methyl-17[beta]-hydroxyandrost-1, 4-dien-3-one).
(31) Methandriol (17[alpha]-methyl-3[beta],17[beta]-dihydroxyandrost-5-ene).
(32) Methenolone (1-methyl-17[beta]-hydroxy-5[alpha]-androst-1-en-3-one).
(33) 17[alpha]-methyl-3[beta], 17[beta]-dihydroxy-5a-androstane.
(34) 17[alpha]-methyl-3[alpha], 17[beta]-dihydroxy-5a-androstane.
(35) 17[alpha]-methyl-3[beta], 17[beta]-dihydroxyandrost-4-ene.
(36)
17[alpha]-methyl-4-hydroxynandrolone(17[alpha]-methyl-4-hydroxy-17[beta]-hydroxyestr-4-en-3-one).
(37) Methyldienolone (17[alpha]-methyl-17[beta]-hydroxyestra-4,9(10)-dien-3-one).
(38) Methyltrienolone (17[alpha]-methyl-17[beta]-hydroxyestra-4, 9-11-trien-3-one).
(39) Methyltestosterone (17[alpha]-methyl-17[beta]-hydroxyandrost- 4-en-3-one).
(40) Mibolerone (7[alpha],17[alpha]-dimethyl-17[beta]-hydroxyestr- 4-en-3-one).
(41) 17[alpha]-methyl-[Delta] 1-dihydrotestosterone(17b[beta]-hydroxy-17[alpha]-methyl-5[alpha]-androst-1-en-3-one)(a.k.a. '17-[alpha]-methyl-1-testosterone').
(42) Nandrolone(17[beta]-hydroxyestr-4-en-3-one).
(43) 19-nor-4-androstenediol (3[beta],17[beta]-dihydroxyestr-4-ene).
(44) 19-nor-4-androstenediol (3[alpha],17[beta]-dihydroxyestr-4-ene).
(45) 19-nor-5-androstenediol (3[beta],17[beta]-dihydroxyestr-5-ene).
(46) 19-nor-5-androstenediol (3[alpha],17[beta]-dihydroxyestr-5-ene)
(47) 19-nor-4,9(10)-androstadienedione (estra-4,9(10)-diene-3,17-dione).
(48) 19-nor-4-androstenedione (estr-4-en-3,17-dione).
(49) 19-nor-5-androstenedione (estr-5-en-3,17-dione).
(50) Norbolethone (13[beta], 17[alpha]-diethyl-17[beta]-hydroxygon-4-en-3-one).
(51) Norclostebol (4-chloro-17[beta]-hydroxyestr-4-en-3-one).
(52) Norethandrolone (17[alpha]-ethyl-17[beta]-hydroxyestr-4-en-3-one).
(53) Normethandrolone (17[alpha]-methyl-17[beta]-hydroxyestr-4-en-3-one).
(54) Oxandrolone (17[alpha]-methyl-17[beta]-hydroxy-2-oxa-[5[alpha]]-androstan-3-one).
(55) Oxymesterone (17[alpha]-methyl-4, 17[beta]-dihydroxy androst-4-en-3-one).
(56) Oxymetholone (17[alpha]-methyl-2-hydroxymethylene-17[beta]-hydroxy-[5[alpha]]- androstan-3-one).
(57) Stanozolol (17[alpha]-methyl-17[beta]-hydroxy-[5[alpha]]-androst-2-eno[3, 2-c]-pyrazole).
(58) Stenbolone (17[beta]-hydroxy-2-methyl-[5[alpha]]-androst-1-en-3-one).
(59) Testolactone (13-hydroxy-3-oxo-13, 17-secoandrosta-1, 4-dien-17-oic acid lactone).
(60) Testosterone (17[beta]-hydroxyandrost-4-en-3-one).

(61) Tetrahydrogestrinone (13[beta], 17[alpha]-diethyl-17[beta]-hydroxygon-4, 9, 11-trien-3-one).

(62) Trenbolone (17[beta]-hydroxyestr-4, 9, 11-trien-3-one).

(63) Any salt, ester or ether of a drug or substance described or listed in this subdivision.

(i) Subdivision (h) of this section shall not include any substance containing anabolic steroids expressly intended for administration through implants to cattle or other nonhuman species and that are approved by the federal food and drug administration solely for such use. Any individual who knowingly and willfully administers to himself or another person, prescribes, dispenses or distributes such substances for other than implantation to cattle or nonhuman species shall be subject to the same penalties as a practitioner who violates the provisions of this section or any other penalties prescribed by law.

(j) [Repealed]

Schedule III.

(a) Schedule III shall consist of the drugs and other substances, by whatever official name, common or usual name, chemical name, or brand name designated, listed in this section.

(b) Stimulants. Unless specifically excepted or unless listed in another schedule, any material, compound, mixture, or preparation which contains any quantity of the following substances having a stimulant effect on the central nervous system, including its salts, isomers (whether optical, position, or geometric), and salts of such isomers whenever the existence of such salts, isomers, and salts of isomers is possible within the specific chemical designation:

(1) Those compounds, mixtures, or preparations in dosage unit form containing any stimulant substances listed in schedule II which compounds, mixtures, or preparations were listed on August twenty-five, nineteen hundred seventy-one, as excepted compounds under title twenty-one, section 308.32 of the code of federal regulations and any other drug of the quantitive composition shown in that list for those drugs or which is the same except that it contains a lesser quantity of controlled substances.

(2) Benzphetamine.

(3) Chlorphentermine.

(4) Clortermine.

(5) [Repealed]

(6) Phendimetrazine.

(c) Depressants. Unless specifically excepted or unless listed in another schedule, any material, compound, mixture, or preparation which contains any quantity of the following substances having a depressant effect on the central nervous system, including its salts, isomers, and salts of isomers:

(1) Any compound, mixture or preparation containing:

(i) Amobarbital;

(ii) Secobarbital;

(iii) Pentobarbital;

or any salt thereof and one or more other active medicinal ingredients which are not listed in any schedule.

(2) Any suppository dosage form containing:

(i) Amobarbital;

(ii) Secobarbital;

(iii) Pentobarbital;

or any salt of any of these drugs and approved by the federal food and drug administration for marketing only as a suppository.

(3) Any substance which contains any quantity of a derivative of barbituric acid or any salt thereof.

(4) Chlorhexadol.

(5) Lysergic acid.

(6) Lysergic acid amide.

(7) Methyprylon.

(8) Sulfondiethylmethane.

(9) Sulfonethylmethane.

(10) Sulfonmethane.

(11) Tiletamine and zolazepam or any salt thereof. Some trade or other names for a tiletamine-zolazepam combination product: Telazol. Some trade or other names for tiletamine: 2-(ethylamino) -2-(2-thienyl) -cyclohexanone. Some trade or other names for zolazepam: 4-(2-fluorophenyl) -6,8-dihydro -1, 3, 8i-trimethylpyrazolo-[3,4-e] [1,4]-diazepin-7(1H)-one, flupyrazapon.

(12) Gamma hydroxybutyric acid, and salt, hydroxybutyric compound, derivative or preparation of gamma hydroxybutyric acid, including any isomers, esters and ethers and salts of isomers, esters and ethers of gamma hydroxybutyric acid, contained in a drug product for which an application has been approved under section 505 of the federal food, drug and cosmetic act.

(13) Ketamine, its salts, isomers and salts of isomers (some other names for ketamine: (±)-2-(2-chlorophenyl)-2-(methylamino)-cyclohexanone).

(14) Embutramide.

(d) Nalorphine.

(e) Narcotic drugs. Unless specifically excepted or unless listed in another schedule, any material, compound, mixture, or preparation containing any of the following narcotic drugs, or their salts calculated as the free anhydrous base or alkaloid, in limited quantities as set forth below:

(1) Not more than 1.8 grams of codeine per one hundred milliliters or not more than ninety milligrams per dosage unit, with an equal or greater quantity of an isoquinoline alkaloid of opium.

(2) Not more than 1.8 grams of codeine per one hundred milliliters or not more than ninety milligrams per dosage unit, with one or more active, nonnarcotic ingredients in recognized therapeutic amounts.

(3) Not more than 1.8 grams of dihydrocodeine per one hundred milliliters or not more than ninety milligrams per dosage unit, with one or more active nonnarcotic ingredients in recognized therapeutic amounts.

(4) Not more than three hundred milligrams of ethylmorphine per one hundred milliliters or not more than fifteen milligrams per dosage unit, with one or more active, nonnarcotic ingredients in recognized therapeutic amounts.

(5) Not more than five hundred milligrams of opium per one hundred milliliters or per one hundred grams or not more than twenty-five milligrams per dosage unit, with one or more active, nonnarcotic ingredients in recognized therapeutic amounts.

(6) Not more than fifty milligrams of morphine per one hundred milliliters or per one hundred grams, with one or more active, nonnarcotic ingredients in recognized therapeutic amounts.

(7) Buprenorphine in any quantities.

(8), (9) [Redesignated]

(f) Dronabinol (synthetic) in sesame oil and encapsulated in a soft gelatin capsule in a U.S. Food and Drug Administration approved product.

Some other names for dronabinol include: (6aR-trans)-6a, 7, 8, 10a-tetrahydro-6, 6, 9-trimethyl-3-pentyl-6H-dibenzo[b,d] pyran-1-o1, or (-)-delta-9-(trans) - tetrahydrocannabinol.

(g) Chorionic gonadotropin.

(1) Unless specifically excepted or unless listed in another schedule any material, compound, mixture, or preparation which contains any amount of chorionic gonadotropin.

(2) Paragraph one of this subdivision shall not include any substance containing chorionic gonadotropin expressly intended for administration through implants or injection to cattle or other nonhuman species and that are approved by the federal food and drug administration solely for such use. Any individual who knowingly and willfully administers to himself or another person, prescribes, dispenses or distributes such substances for other than implantation or injection to cattle or nonhuman species shall be subject to the same penalties as a practitioner who violates the provisions of this section or any other penalties prescribed by law.

Schedule IV.

(a) Schedule IV shall consist of the drugs and other substances, by whatever official name, common or usual name, chemical name, or brand name designated, listed in this section.

(b) Narcotic drugs. Unless specifically excepted or unless listed in another schedule, any material, compound, mixture, or preparation containing any of the following narcotic drugs, or their salts calculated as the free anhydrous base or alkaloid, in limited quantities as set forth below:

(1) Not more than one milligram of difenoxin and not less than twenty-five micrograms of atropine sulfate per dosage unit.

(2) Dextropropoxyphene (alpha-(+)-4-dimethylamino-1, 2-diphenyl-3-methyl-2-propionoxybutane).

(c) Depressants. Unless specifically excepted or unless listed in another schedule, any material, compound, mixture, or preparation which contains any quantity of the following substances, including its salts, isomers, and salts of isomers whenever the existence of such salts, isomers, and salts of isomers is possible within the specific chemical designation:

(1) Alprazolam.
(2) Barbital.
(3) Bromazepam.
(4) Camazepam.
(5) Chloral betaine.
(6) Chloral hydrate.
(7) Chlordiazepoxide.
(8) Clobazam.
(9) Clonazepam.
(10) Clorazepate.
(11) Clotiazepam.
(12) Cloxazolam.
(13) Delorazepam.
(14) Diazepam.
(15) Estazolam.
(16) Ethchlorvynol.
(17) Ethinamate.
(18) Ethyl Loflazepate.
(19) Fludiazepam.
(20) Flunitrazepam.
(21) Flurazepam.
(22) Halazepam.
(23) Haloxazolam.
(24) Ketazolam.
(25) Loprazolam.
(26) Lorazepam.
(27) Lormetazepam.
(28) Mebutamate.
(29) Medazepam.
(30) Meprobamate.
(31) Methohexital.
(32) Methylphenobarbital (mephobarbital).
(33) Nimetazepam.
(34) Nitrazepam.
(35) Nordiazepam.
(36) Oxazepam.
(37) Oxazolam.
(38) Paraldehyde.
(39) Petrichoral.
(40) Phenobarbital.
(41) Pinazepam.
(42) Prazepam.
(43) Temazepam.
(44) Tetrazepam.
(45) Triazolam.
(46) Midazolam.
(47) Quazepam.

(48) Zolpidem.
(49) Dichloralphenazone.
(50) Zaleplon.
(51) Zopiclone (eszopiclone).
(52) Fospropofol.
(53) Carisoprodol.
(d) [Deleted]

(e) Stimulants. Unless specifically excepted or unless listed in another schedule, any material, compound, mixture, or preparation which contains any quantity of the following substances having a stimulant effect on the central nervous system, including its salts, isomers, and salts of such isomers:

(1) Cathine ((+) - norpseudoephedrine).
(2) Diethylpropion.
(3) Fencamfamin.
(4) Fenproporex.
(5) Mazindol.
(6) Mefenorex.
(7) Pemoline (including organometallic complexes and chelates thereof).
(8) Phentermine.
(9) Pipradrol.
(10) SPA ((-))-1-dimethylamino-1, 2-diphenylethane).
(11) Modafinil.
(12) Sibutramine.

(f) Other substances. Unless specifically excepted or unless listed in another schedule, any material, compound, mixture or preparation which contains any quantity of the following substances, including its salts:

(1) Pentazocine.
(2) Butorphanol (including its optical isomers).
(3) Tramadol in any quantities.

Schedule V.

(a) Schedule V shall consist of the drugs and other substances, by whatever official name, common or usual name, chemical name, or brand name designated, listed in this section.

(b) Narcotic drugs containing nonnarcotic active medicinal ingredients. Any compound, mixture, or preparation containing any of the following narcotic drugs, or their salts calculated as the free anhydrous base or alkaloid, in limited quantities as set forth below, which shall include one or more nonnarcotic active medicinal ingredients in sufficient proportion to confer upon the compound, mixture, or preparation valuable medicinal qualities other than those possessed by narcotic drugs alone:

(1) Not more than two hundred milligrams of codeine per one hundred milliliters or per one hundred grams.

(2) Not more than one hundred milligrams of dihydrocodeine per one hundred milliliters or per one hundred grams.

(3) Not more than one hundred milligrams of ethylmorphine per one hundred milliliters or per one hundred grams.

(4) Not more than 2.5 milligrams of diphenoxylate and not less than twenty-five micrograms of atropine sulfate per dosage unit.

(5) Not more than one hundred milligrams of opium per one hundred milliliters or per one hundred grams.

(6) Not more than 0.5 milligram of difenoxin and not less than twenty-five micrograms of atropine sulfate per dosage unit.

(c) Stimulants. Unless specifically exempted or excluded or unless listed in another schedule, any material, compound, mixture, or preparation which contains any quantity of the following substances having a stimulant effect on the central nervous system, including its salts, isomers and salts of isomers:

(1) Pyrovalerone.

(d) Depressants. Unless specifically exempted or excluded or unless listed in another schedule, any material, compound, mixture, or preparation which contains any quantity of the following substances having a depressant effect on the central nervous system, including its salts, isomers, and salts of isomers:

(1) Ezogabine [N-[2-amino-4-(4-fluorobenzylamino)-phenyl]-carbamic acid ethyl ester].

(2) Lacosamide [(R)-2-acetoamido-N-benzyl-3-methoxy-propionamide].

(3) Pregabalin[(S)-3-(aminomethyl)-5-methylhexanoic acid].

HISTORY:

Add, L 1985, ch 664, § 1, eff Nov 1, 1985; amd, L 1986, ch 826, § 1, eff Sept 1, 1986; L 1987, ch 44, §§ 1, 2, eff April 21, 1987; L 1989, ch 418, § 1; L 1990, ch 640, §§ 1, 2; L 1992, ch 115, § 1, eff June 1, 1992; L 1993, ch 473, § 1, eff July 26, 1993; L 1995, ch 452, §§ 1, 2; L 1996, ch 443, § 1, eff Aug 2, 1996; L 1996, ch 589, §§ 1–10, eff Feb 4, 1997; L 1997, ch 635, § 2, eff Jan 22, 1998; L 2000, ch 1, §§ 29, 30, eff Feb 1, 2001; L 2001, ch 565, § 1, eff Jan 1, 2002; L 2001, ch 575, §§ 1–3, eff Dec 19, 2001; L 2003, ch 264, §§ 56, 57, eff Nov 1, 2003; L 2003, ch 591, §§ 1, 2, eff Sept 22, 2003; L 2006, ch 457, §§ 1–15, eff Aug 16, 2006; L 2010, ch 178, §§ 13–18, eff Oct 13, 2010; L 2011, ch 130, § 1, eff Aug 14, 2011; L 2012, ch 447, §§ 1, 4–9, 11–13, 16 (Part C), eff Nov 25, 2012; L 2012, ch 447, §§ 2, 10, 14 (Part C), eff Feb 23, 2013; L 2012, ch 447, § 15 (Part C), eff Aug 27, 2012; L 2013, ch 341, § 1, eff Dec 11, 2013; L 2015, ch 370, § 1, eff Oct 26, 2015; L 2016, ch 244, § 1, eff Aug 18, 2016; L 2018, ch 57, §§ 4, 5, 7 (Part BB), eff July 11, 2018; L 2018, ch 428, § 1, eff June 19, 2019.

§ 3306. Schedules of controlled substances [Effective July 2, 2020]

There are hereby established five schedules of controlled substances, to be known as schedules I, II, III, IV and V respectively. Such schedules shall consist of the following substances by whatever name or chemical designation known:

Schedule I.

(a) Schedule I shall consist of the drugs and other substances, by whatever official name, common or usual name, chemical name, or brand name designated, listed in this section.

(b) Opiates. Unless specifically excepted or unless listed in another schedule, any of the following opiates, including their isomers, esters, ethers, salts, and salts of isomers, esters, and ethers, whenever the existence of such isomers, esters, ethers and salts is possible within the specific chemical designation (for purposes of 3-methylfentanyl only, the term isomer includes the optical and geometric isomers):

(1) Acetyl-alpha-methylfentanyl (N-[1-(-methyl-2-phenethyl) -4-piperidinyl] -N-phenylacetamide.

(2) Acetylmethadol.

(3) Allylprodine.

(4) Alphacetylmethadol (except levo-alphacetylmethadol also known as levo-alpha-acetylmethadol, levomethadyl acetate or LAAM).

(5) Alphameprodine.

(6) Alphamethadol.

(7) Alpha-methylfentanyl (N-[1-(alpha-methyl-beta-phenyl) ethyl-4-piperidyl] propionanilide; 1-(1-methyl-2-phenylethyl) -4-(N-propanilido) piperidine).

(8) Alpha-methylthiofentanyl (N-[1-methyl-2)2-thienyl) ethyl-4-piperidinyl] -N-phenylpropanamide).

(9) Beta-hydroxyfentanyl (N-[1-2 (2-hydroxy-2-phenethyl)- 4-piperidinyl] -N-phenylpropanamide).

(10) Beta-hydroxy-3-methylfentanyl (other name: N-[1- (2-hydroxy-2-phenethyl) -3-methyl-4-piperidinyl] -N-phenylpropanamide.

(11) Benzethidine.

(12) Betacetylmethadol.

(13) Betameprodine.

(14) Betamethadol.

(15) Betaprodine.

(16) Clonitazene.

(17) Dextromoramide.

(18) Diampromide.

(19) Diethylthiambutene.

(20) Difenoxin.

(21) Dimenoxadol.

(22) Dimepheptanol.
(23) Dimethylthiambutene.
(24) Dioxaphetyl butyrate.
(25) Dipipanone.
(26) Ethylmethylthiambutene.
(27) Etonitazene.
(28) Etoxeridine.
(29) Furethidine.
(30) Hydroxypethidine.
(31) Ketobemidone.
(32) Levomoramide.
(33) Levophenacylmorphan.
(34) 3-Methylfentanyl (N-[3-methyl-1- (2- phenylethyl -4-piperidyl] -N-phenylpropanamide).
(35) 3-Methylthiofentanyl (N-[3-methyl-1- (2-thienyl)ethyl -4-piperidinyl] -N-phenylpropanamide).
(36) Morpheridine.
(37) MPPP (1-methyl -4-phenyl -4-propionoxypiperidine).
(38) Noracymethadol.
(39) Norlevorphanol.
(40) Normethadone.
(41) Norpipanone.
(42) Para-fluorofentanyl (N- (4-fluorophenyl) -N-[1- (2-phenethyl) -4-piperidinyl] -propanamide.
(43) PEPAP (1- (-2-phenethyl) -4-phenyl -4-acetoxypiperidine.
(44) Phenadoxone.
(45) Phenampromide.
(46) Phenomorphan.
(47) Phenoperidine.
(48) Piritramide.
(49) Proheptazine.
(50) Properidine.
(51) Propiram.
(52) Racemoramide.
(53) Thiofentanyl (N-phenyl-N-[1- (2-thienyl) ethyl -4- piperidinyl] -propanamide.
(54) Tilidine.
(55) Trimeperidine.
(56) 3,4-dichloro-N-{(1-dimethylamino)cyclohexylmethyl}benzamide. Some trade or other names: AH-7921.
(57) N-(1-phenethylpiperidin-4-yl)-N-phenylacetamide. Some trade or other names: Acetyl Fentanyl.

(c) Opium derivatives. Unless specifically excepted or unless listed in another schedule, any of the following opium derivatives, its salts, isomers, and salts of isomers whenever the existence of such salts, isomers, and salts of isomers is possible within the specific chemical designation:
(1) Acetorphine.
(2) Acetyldihydrocodeine.
(3) Benzylmorphine.
(4) Codeine methylbromide.
(5) Codeine-N-oxide.
(6) Cyprenorphine.
(7) Desomorphine.
(8) Dihydromorphine.
(9) Drotebanol.
(10) Etorphine (except hydrochloride salt).
(11) Heroin.
(12) Hydromorphinol.
(13) Methyldesorphine.
(14) Methyldihydromorphine.
(15) Morphine methylbromide.

(16) Morphine methylsulfonate.
(17) Morphine-N-oxide.
(18) Myrophine.
(19) Nicocodeine.
(20) Nicomorphine.
(21) Normorphine.
(22) Pholcodine.
(23) Thebacon.

(d) Hallucinogenic substances. Unless specifically excepted or unless listed in another schedule, any material, compound, mixture, or preparation, which contains any quantity of the following hallucinogenic substances, or which contains any of its salts, isomers, and salts of isomers whenever the existence of such salts, isomers, and salts of isomers is possible within the specific chemical designation (for purposes of this paragraph only, the term "isomer" includes the optical, position and geometric isomers):

(1) 4-bromo-2, 5-dimethoxy-amphetamine Some trade or other names: 4-bromo-2, 5-dimethoxy-α-methylphenethylamine; 4-bromo-2, 5-DMA.

(2) 2, 5-dimethoxyamphetamine Some trade or other names: 2, 5-dimethoxy-α-methylphenethylamine; 2, 5-DMA.

(3) 4-methoxyamphetamine Some trade or other names: 4-methoxy-α-methylphenethylamine; paramethoxyamphetamine, PMA.

(4) 5-methoxy-3, 4-methylenedioxy-amphetamine.

(5) 4-methyl-2, 5-dimethoxy-amphetamine Some trade and other names: 4-methyl-2, 5-dimethoxy-α-methylphenethylamine; "DOM"; and "STP".

(6) 3, 4-methylenedioxy amphetamine.

(7) 3, 4, 5-trimethoxy amphetamine.

(8) Bufotenine Some trade and other names: 3-(β-dimethylaminoethyl)-5 Hydroxindole; 3-(2-dimethylaminoethyl)-5-indolol; N, N-dimethylserotonin; -5-hydroxy-N, N-dimethyltryptamine; mappine.

(9) Diethyltryptamine Some trade and other names: N, N-diethyltryptamine; DET.

(10) Dimethyltryptamine Some trade or other names: DMT.

(11) Ibogane Some trade and other names: 7-ethyl-6, 6β, 7, 8, 9, 10, 12, 13-octahydro-2-methoxy-6, 9-methano-5h-pyrido [1', 2': 1,2] azepino [5,4-b] indole: tabernanthe iboga.

(12) Lysergic acid diethylamide.

(13) Marihuana.

(14) Mescaline.

(15) Parahexyl. Some trade or other names: 3-Hexyl-1-hydroxy-7, 8, 9, 10-tetra hydro-6, 6, 9-trimethyl-6H-dibenfo[b,d] pyran.

(16) Peyote. Meaning all parts of the plant presently classified botanically as Lophophora williamsii Lemaire, whether growing or not, the seeds thereof, any extract from any part of such plant, and every compound, manufacture, salts, derivative, mixture, or preparation of such plant, its seeds or extracts.

(17) N-ethyl-3-piperidyl benzilate.

(18) N-methyl-3-piperidyl benzilate.

(19) Psilocybin.

(20) Psilocyn.

(21) Tetrahydrocannabinols. Synthetic equivalents of the substances contained in the plant, or in the resinous extractives of cannabis, sp. and/or synthetic substances, derivatives, and their isomers with similar chemical structure and pharmacological activity such as the following:

δ^1 cis or trans tetrahydrocannabinol, and their optical isomers

δ^6 cis or trans tetrahydrocannabinol, and their optical isomers

$\delta^{3,4}$ cis or trans tetrahydrocannabinol, and its optical isomers (since nomenclature of these substances is not internationally standardized, compounds of these structures, regardless of numerical designation of atomic positions covered).

(22) Ethylamine analog of phencyclidine. Some trade or other names: N-ethyl-1-phenylcyclohexylamine, (1-phenylcyclohexyl) ethylamine, N-(1-phenylcyclohexyl) ethylamine cyclohexamine, PCE.

(23) Pyrrolidine analog of phencyclidine. Some trade or other names 1-(1-phenylcyclohexyl)-pyrrolidine; PCPy, PHP.

(24) Thiophene analog of phencyclidine. Some trade or other names: 1-[1-(2-thienyl)-cyclohexyl]-piperidine, 2-thienylanalog of phencyclidine, TPCP, TCP.

(25) 3,4-methylenedioxymethamphetamine (MDMA).

(26) 3,4-methylendioxy-N-ethylamphetamine (also known as N-ethyl-alpha-methyl-3,4 (methylenedioxy) phenethylamine, N-ethyl MDA, MDE, MDEA.

(27) N-hydroxy-3,4-methylenedioxyamphetamine (also known as N-hydroxy-alpha-methyl-3,4 (methylenedioxy) phenethylamine, and N-hydroxy MDA.

(28) 1-[1- (2-thienyl) cyclohexyl] pyrrolidine. Some other names: TCPY.

(29) Alpha-ethyltryptamine. Some trade or other names: etryptamine; Monase; Alpha-ethyl-1H-indole-3-ethanamine; 3- (2-aminobutyl) indole; Alpha-ET or AET.

(30) 2,5-dimethoxy-4-ethylamphetamine. Some trade or other names: DOET.

(31) 4-Bromo-2,5-dimethoxyphenethylamine. Some trade or other names: 2-(4-bromo-2,5-dimethoxyphenyl)-1-aminoethane; alpha-desmethyl DOB; 2C-B, Nexus.

(32) 2,5-dimethoxy-4-(n)-propylthiophenethylamine (2C-T-7), its optical isomers, salts and salts of isomers.

(33) 2-(4-iodo-2,5-dimethoxyphenyl)-N-(2-methoxybenzyl)ethanamine, also known as 25I-NBOMe; 2C-I-NBOMe; 25I; or Cimbi-5.

(34) 2-(4-chloro-2,5-dimethoxyphenyl)-N-(2-methoxybenzyl) ethanamine, also known as 25 CNBOMe; 2C-C-NBOMe; 25C; or Cimbi-82.

(35) 2-(4-bromo-2,5-dimethoxyphenyl)-N-(2-methoxybenzyl) ethanamine, also known as, 25 BNBOMe; 2C-B-NBOMe; Cimbi-36.

(36) 5-methoxy-N,N-dimethyltryptamine.

(37) Alpha-methyltryptamine. Some trade or other names: AMT.

(38) 5-methoxy-N,N-diisopropyltryptamine. Some trade or other names: 5-MeO-DIPT.

(e) Depressants. Unless specifically excepted or unless listed in another schedule, any material, compound, mixture, or preparation which contains any quantity of the following substances having a depressant effect on the central nervous system, including its salts, isomers, and salts of isomers whenever the existence of such salts, isomers, and salts of isomers is possible within the specific chemical designation:

(1) Mecloqualone.

(2) Methaqualone.

(3) Phencyclidine.

(4) Gamma hydroxybutyric acid, and salt, hydroxybutyric compound, derivative or preparation of gamma hydroxybutyric acid, including any isomers, esters and ethers and salts of isomers, esters and ethers of gamma hydroxybutyric acid, except gamma-butyrolactone, whenever the existence of such isomers, esters and ethers and salts is possible within the specific chemical.

(5) Gamma-butyrolactone, including butyrolactone; butyrolactone gamma; 4-butyrolactone; 2(3H)-furanone dihydro; dihydro-2(3H)-furanone; tetrahydro-2-furanone; 1,2-butanolide; 1,4-butanolide; 4-butanolide; gamma-hydroxybutyric acid lactone; 3-hydroxybutyric acid lactone and 4-hydroxybutanoic acid lactone with Chemical Abstract Service number (96-48-0) when any such substance is intended for human consumption.

(6) 1,4 butanediol, including butanediol; butane-1,4-diol; 1,4-butylene glyco; butylene glycol; 1,4-dihydroxybutane; 1,4-tetramethyleneglycol; tetramethylene glycol; tetramethylene Abstract Service number (110-63-4) when any such substance is intended for human consumption.

(f) Stimulants. Unless specifically excepted or unless listed in another schedule, any material, compound, mixture, or preparation which contains any quantity of the following substances having a stimulant effect on the central nervous system, including its salts, isomers, and salts of isomers:

(1) Fenethylline.

(2) N-ethylamphetamine.

(3) (+ -)cis-4-methylaminorex ((+ -)cis-4,5-dihydro-4-methyl -5-phenyl -2-oxazolamine).

(4) N,N-dimethylamphetamine (also known as N,N-alpha- trimethyl-benzeneethanamine; N,N-alpha- trimethylphenethylamine).

(5) Methcathinone (some other names: 2-(methylamino) - propiophenone; alpha-(methylamino) propiophenone; 2-(methylamino) -1-phenylpropan- 1 -one; alpha-N-

methylaminopropiophenone; monomethylpropion; ephedrone, N-methylcathinone, methylcathinone; AL-464; AL-422; AL-463 and UR1432), its salts, optical isomers and salts of optical isomers.

(6) Aminorex. Some other names: aminoxaphen; 2-amino-5-phenyl -2-oxazoline; or 4,5-dihydro-5-phenyl-2-oxazolamine.

(7) Cathinone. Some trade or other names: 2-amino-1-phenyl-1-propanone, alpha-aminopropiophenone, 2-aminopropiophenone, and norephedrone.

(8) N-benzylpiperazine (some other names: BZP; 1-benzylpiperazine), its optical isomers, salts and salts of isomers.

(9) 4-methyl-N-methylcathinone or 4-Methylmethcathinone, also known as Mephedrone.

(10) 3,4-methylenedioxypyrovalerone or Methylenedioxypyrovalerone, also known as MDPV.

(11) 3,4-methylenedioxy-N-methylcathinone (some other names: methylone).

(12) 4-Methoxymethcathinone.

(13) 3-Fluoromethcathinone.

(14) 4-Fluoromethcathinone.

(15) Ethylpropion (Ethcathinone).

(16) 2-(2,5-Dimethoxy-4-ethylphenyl)ethanamine (2C-E).

(17) 2-(2,5-Dimethoxy-4-methylphenyl)ethanamine (2C-D).

(18) 2-(4-Chloro-2,5-dimethoxyphenyl)ethanamine (2C-C).

(19) 2-(4-Iodo-2,5-dimethoxyphenyl)ethanamine (2C-I).

(20) 2-[4-(Ethylthio)-2,5-dimethoxyphenyl]ethanamine (2C-T-2).

(21) 2-[4-(Isopropylthio)-2,5-dimethoxyphenyl]ethanamine (2C-T-4).

(22) 2-(2,5-Dimethoxyphenyl)ethanamine (2C-H).

(23) 2-(2,5-Dimethoxy-4-nitro-phenyl)ethanamine (2C-N).

(24) 2-(2,5-Dimethoxy-4-(n)-propylphenyl)ethanamine (2C-P).

(g) Synthetic cannabinoids. Unless specifically excepted or unless listed in another schedule, any material, compound, mixture, or preparation, which contains any quantity of the following synthetic cannabinoid substances, or which contains any of its salts, isomers, and salts of isomers whenever the existence of such salts, isomers, and salts of isomers is possible within the specific chemical designation (for purposes of this paragraph only, the term "isomer" includes the optical, position and geometric isomers):

(1) (1-pentyl-1H-indol-3-yl)(2,2,3,3-tetramethylcyclopropyl) methanone. Some trade or other names: UR-144.

(2) {1-(5-fluro-pentyl)-1H-indol-3-yl}(2,2,3,3-tetramethylcyclopropyl) methanone. Some trade names or other names: 5-fluoro-UR-144, XLR11.

(3) N-(1-adamantyl)-1-pentyl-1H-indazole-3-carboxamide. Some trade or other names: APINACA, AKB48.

(4) quinolin-8-yl 1-pentyl-1H-indole-3-carboxylate. Some trade or other names: PB-22; QUPIC.

(5) quinolin-8-yl 1-(5-fluoropentyl)-1H-indole-3-carboxylate. Some trade or other names: 5-fluoro-PB-22; 5F-PB-22.

(6) N-(1-amino-3-methyl-1-oxobutan-2-yl)-1-(4-fluorobenzyl)-1H-indazole-3-carboxamide. Some trade or other names: AB-FUBINACA.

(7) N-(1-amino-3,3-dimethyl-1-oxobutan-2-yl) -1-pentyl-1H-indazole-3-carboxamide. Some trade or other names: ADB-PINACA.

(8) N-(1-amino-3-methyl-1-oxobutan-2-yl) -1-(cyclohexylmethyl)- 1H-indazole-3-carboxamide. Some trade or other names: AB-CHMINACA.

(9) N-(1-amino-3-methyl-1-oxobutan-2-yl) -1-pentyl-1H-indazole-3-carboxamide. Some trade or other names: AB-PINACA.

(10) {1-(5-fluoropentyl)-1H-indazol-3-yl}(naphthalen-1-yl)methanone. Some trade or other names: THJ-2201.

(h)(1) Cannabimimetic agents. Unless specifically exempted or unless listed in another schedule, any material, compound, mixture, or preparation that is not approved by the federal food and drug administration (FDA) which contains any quantity of cannabimimetic agents, or which contains their salts, isomers, and salts of isomers whenever the existence of such salts, isomers, and salts of isomers is possible within the specific chemical designation.

(2) As used in this subdivision, the term "cannabimimetic agents" means any substance that is a cannabinoid receptor type 1 (CB1 receptor) agonist as demonstrated by binding studies and functional assays within any of the following structural classes:

(i) 2-(3-hydroxycyclohexyl)phenol with substitution at the 5-position of the phenolic ring by alkyl or alkenyl, whether or not substituted on the cyclohexyl ring to any extent.

(ii) 3-(1-naphthoyl)indole or 3-(1-naphthylmethane)indole by substitution at the nitrogen atom of the indole ring, whether or not further substituted on the indole ring to any extent, whether or not substituted on the naphthoyl or naphthyl ring to any extent.

(iii) 3-(1-naphthoyl)pyrrole by substitution at the nitrogen atom of the pyrrole ring, whether or not further substituted in the pyrrole ring to any extent, whether or not substituted on the naphthoyl ring to any extent.

(iv) 1-(1-naphthylmethylene)indene by substitution of the 3-position of the indene ring, whether or not further substituted in the indene ring to any extent, whether or not substituted on the naphthyl ring to any extent.

(v) 3-phenylacetylindole or 3-benzoylindole by substitution at the nitrogen atom of the indole ring, whether or not further substituted in the indole ring to any extent, whether or not substituted on the phenyl ring to any extent.

(3) Such term includes:

(i) 5-(1,1-dimethylheptyl)-2-{(1R,3S)-3-hydroxycyclohexyl}-phenol (CP-47,497);

(ii) 5-(1,1-dimethyloctyl)-2-{(1R,3S)-3-hydroxycyclohexyl}-phenol (cannabicyclohexanol or CP-47,497 C8-homolog);

(iii) 1-pentyl-3-(1-naphthoyl)indole (JWH-018 and AM678);

(iv) 1-butyl-3-(1-naphthoyl)indole (JWH-073);

(v) 1-hexyl-3-(1-naphthoyl)indole (JWH-019);

(vi) 1-{2-(4-morpholinyl)ethyl}-3-(1-naphthoyl)indole (JWH-200);

(vii) 1-pentyl-3-(2-methoxyphenylacetyl)indole (JWH-250);

(viii) 1-pentyl-3-{1-(4-methoxynaphthoyl)}indole (JWH-081);

(ix) 1-pentyl-3-(4-methyl-1-naphthoyl)indole (JWH-122);

(x) 1-pentyl-3-(4-chloro-1-naphthoyl)indole (JWH-398);

(xi) 1-(5-fluoropentyl)-3-(1-naphthoyl)indole (AM2201);

(xii) 1-(5-fluoropentyl)-3-(2-iodobenzoyl)indole (AM694);

(xiii) 1-pentyl-3-{(4-methoxy)-benzoyl}indole (SR-19 and RCS-4);

(xiv) 1-cyclohexylethyl-3-(2-methoxyphenylacetyl)indole (SR-18 and RCS-8); and

(xv) 1-pentyl-3-(2-chlorophenylacetyl)indole (JWH-203).

Schedule II.

(a) Schedule II shall consist of the drugs and other substances, by whatever official name, common or usual name, chemical name, or brand name designated, listed in this section.

(b) Substances, vegetable origin or chemical synthesis. Unless specifically excepted or unless listed in another schedule, any of the following substances whether produced directly or indirectly by extraction from substances of vegetable origin, or independently by means of chemical synthesis, or by a combination of extraction and chemical synthesis:

(1) Opium and opiate, and any salt, compound, derivative, or preparation of opium or opiate, excluding apomorphine, dextrorphan, nalbuphine, nalmefene, naloxone, and naltrexone, and their respective salts, but including the following:

1. Raw opium.
2. Opium extracts.
3. Opium fluid.
4. Powdered opium.
5. Granulated opium.
6. Tincture of opium.
7. Codeine.
8. Ethylmorphine.
9. Etorphine hydrochloride.
10. Hydrocodone (also known as dihydrocodeinone).
11. Hydromorphone.
12. Metopon.
13. Morphine.

14. Oxycodone.
15. Oxymorphone.
16. Thebaine.
17. Dihydroetorphine.
18. Oripavine.

(2) Any salt, compound, derivative, or preparation thereof which is chemically equivalent or identical with any of the substances referred to in this section, except that these substances shall not include the isoquinoline alkaloids of opium.

(3) Opium poppy and poppy straw.

(4) Coca leaves and any salt, compound, derivative, or preparation of coca leaves, and any salt, compound, derivative, or preparation thereof which is chemically equivalent or identical with any of these substances including cocaine and ecgonine, their salts, isomers, and salts of isomers, except that the substances shall not include: (A) decocainized coca leaves or extraction of coca leaves, which extractions do not contain cocaine or ecgonine; or (B) {123I} ioflupane.

(5) Concentrate of poppy straw (the crude extract of poppy straw in either liquid, solid or powder form which contains the phenanthrene alkaloids of the opium poppy).

(6) [Repealed]

(b-1) Unless specifically excepted or unless listed in another schedule, any material, compound, mixture, or preparation containing any of the following, or their salts calculated as the free anhydrous base or alkaloid, in limited quantities as set forth below:

(1) Not more than three hundred milligrams of dihydrocodeinone (hydrocodone) per one hundred milliliters or not more than fifteen milligrams per dosage unit, with a fourfold or greater quantity of an isoquinoline alkaloid of opium.

(2) Not more than three hundred milligrams of dihydrocodeinone (hydrocodone) per one hundred milliliters or not more than fifteen milligrams per dosage unit, with one or more active nonnarcotic ingredients in recognized therapeutic amounts.

(c) Opiates. Unless specifically excepted or unless in another schedule any of the following opiates, including its isomers, esters, ethers, salts and salts of isomers, esters and ethers whenever the existence of such isomers, esters, ethers, and salts is possible within the specific chemical designation, dextrorphan and levopropoxyphene excepted:

(1) Alfentanil.
(2) Alphaprodine.
(3) Anileridine.
(4) Bezitramide.
(5) Bulk dextropropoxyphene (non-dosage forms).
(6) Carfentanil.
(7) Dihydrocodeine.
(8) Diphenoxylate.
(9) Fentanyl.
(10) Isomethadone.
(11) Levo-alphacetylmethadol (also known as levo-alpha-acetylmethadol, levomethadyl acetate or LAAM).
(12) Levomethorphan.
(13) Levorphanol.
(14) Metazocine.
(15) Methadone.
(16) Methadone-intermediate, 4-cyano-2-dimethylamino-4, 4-diphenyl butane.
(17) Moramide-intermediate, 2-methyl-3-morpholino-1, 1-diphenylpropane-carboxylic acid.
(18) Pethidine (meperidine).
(19) Pethidine-intermediate-A, 4-cyano-1-methyl-4-phenylpiperidine.
(20) Pethidine-intermediate-B, ethyl-4-phenylpiperidine-4-carboxylate.
(21) Pethidine-intermediate-C, 1-methyl-4- phenylpiperidine-4-carboxylic acid.
(22) Phenazocine.
(23) Piminodine.
(24) Racemethorphan.
(25) Racemorphan.
(26) Sufentanil.

(27) Remifentanil.
(28) Tapentadol.
(29) Thiafentanil.

(d) Stimulants. Unless specifically excepted or unless listed in another schedule, any material, compound, mixture, or preparation which contains any quantity of the following substances having a stimulant effect on the central nervous system, including its salts, isomers, and salts of isomers:

(1) Amphetamine.
(2) Methamphetamine.
(3) Phenmetrazine.
(4) Methylphenidate.
(5) Lisdexamfetamine.

(e) Depressants. Unless specifically excepted or unless listed in another schedule, any material, compound, mixture, or preparation which contains any quantity of the following substances having a depressant effect on the central nervous system, including its salts, isomers, and salts of isomers whenever the existence of such salts, isomers, and salts of isomers is possible within the specific chemical designation:

(1) Amobarbital.
(2) Glutethimide.
(3) Pentobarbital.
(4) Secobarbital.

(f) Hallucinogenic substances.

Nabilone: Another name for nabilone: (+,-)- trans- 3-(1,1-dimethylheptyl)-6, 6a, 7, 8, 10, 10a-hexahydro-1-hydroxy-6, 6-dimethyl-9H-dibenzo [b,d] pyran-9-one.

(g) Immediate precursors. Unless specifically excepted or unless listed in another schedule, any material, compound, mixture or preparation which contains any quantity of the following substances:

(1) Immediate precursor to amphetamine and methamphetamine:

(i) Phenylacetone Some trade or other names: phenyl-2-propanone; P2P; benzyl methyl ketone; methyl benzyl ketone;

(2) Immediate precursors to phencyclidine (PCP):

(i) 1-phenylcyclohexylamine;

(ii) 1-piperidinocyclohexanecarbonitrile (PCC).

(3) Immediate precursor to fentanyl:

(i) 4-anilino-N-phenethyl-4-piperidine (ANPP).

(h) Anabolic steroids. Unless specifically excepted or unless listed in another schedule, "anabolic steroid" shall mean any drug or hormonal substance, chemically and pharmacologically related to testosterone (other than estrogens, progestins, corticosteroids and dehydroepiandrosterone) and includes:

(1) 3[beta], 17-dihydroxy-5a-androstane.
(2) 3[alpha], 17[beta]-dihydroxy-5a-androstane.
(3) 5[alpha]-androstan-3,17-dione.
(4) 1-androstenediol (3[beta],17[beta]-dihydroxy-5[alpha]-androst-1-ene).
(5) 1-androstenediol (3[alpha],17[beta]-dihydroxy-5[alpha]-androst-1-ene).
(6) 4-androstenediol (3[beta], 17[beta]-dihydroxy-androst-4-ene).
(7) 5-androstenediol (3[beta], 17[beta]-dihydroxy-androst-5-ene).
(8) 1-androstenedione ([5[alpha]]-androst-1-en-3,17-dione).
(9) 4-androstenedione (androst-4-en-3,17-dione).
(10) 5-androstenedione (androst-5-en-3,17-dione).
(11) Bolasterone (7[alpha],17[alpha]-dimethyl-17[beta]-hydroxyandrost-4-en-3-one).
(12) Boldenone (17[beta]-hydroxyandrost-1, 4,-diene-3-one).
(13) Boldione (androsta-1,4-diene-3,17-dione).
(14) Calusterone (7[beta], 17[alpha]-dimethyl-17[beta]-hydroxyandrost-4-en-3-one).
(15) Clostebol (4-chloro-17[beta]-hydroxyandrost-4-en-3-one).
(16) Dehydrochloromethyltestosterone (4-chloro-17[beta]-hydroxy-17 [alpha]-methyl-androst-1, 4-dien-3-one).
(17) [Delta] 1-dihydrotestosterone (a.k.a. '1-testosterone') (17 [beta]-hydroxy-5[alpha]-androst-1-en-3-one).
(18) 4-dihydrotestosterone (17[beta]-hydroxy-androstan-3-one).

(19) Drostanolone (17[beta]-hydroxy-2[alpha]-methyl-5[alpha]-androstan-3-one).

(20) Ethylestrenol (17[alpha]-ethyl-17[beta]-hydroxyestr-4-ene).

(21) Fluoxymesterone (9-fluoro-17[alpha]-methyl-11[beta], 17[beta]-dihydroxyandrost-4-en-3-one).

(22) Formebolone (2-formyl-17[alpha]-methyl-11[alpha], 17[beta]-dihydroxyandrost-1, 4-dien-3-one).

(23) Furazabol (17[alpha]-methyl-17[beta]-hydroxyandrostano [2, 3-c]-furazan).

(24) 13[beta]-ethyl-17[beta]-hyroxygon-4-en-3-one.

(25) 4-hydroxytestosterone (4, 17[beta]-dihydroxy-androst-4-en-3-one).

(26) 4-hydroxy-19-nortestosterone (4,17[beta]-dihydroxy-estr-4-en-3-one).

(27) desoxymethyltestosterone (17[alpha]-methyl-5[alpha]-androst-2-en-17[beta]-ol) (a.k.a., madol).

(28) Mestanolone (17[alpha]-methyl-17[beta]-hydroxy-5-androstan-3-one).

(29) Mesterolone (1[alpha]methyl-17[beta]-hydroxy-[5[alpha]]-androstan-3-one).

(30) Methandienone (17[alpha]-methyl-17[beta]-hydroxyandrost-1, 4-dien-3-one).

(31) Methandriol (17[alpha]-methyl-3[beta],17[beta]-dihydroxyandrost-5-ene).

(32) Methenolone (1-methyl-17[beta]-hydroxy-5[alpha]-androst-1-en-3-one).

(33) 17[alpha]-methyl-3[beta], 17[beta]-dihydroxy-5a-androstane.

(34) 17[alpha]-methyl-3[alpha], 17[beta]-dihydroxy-5a-androstane.

(35) 17[alpha]-methyl-3[beta], 17[beta]-dihydroxyandrost-4-ene.

(36) 17[alpha]-methyl-4-hydroxynandrolone(17[alpha]-methyl-4-hydroxy-17[beta]-hydroxyestr-4-en-3-one).

(37) Methyldienolone (17[alpha]-methyl-17[beta]-hydroxyestra-4,9(10)-dien-3-one).

(38) Methyltrienolone (17[alpha]-methyl-17[beta]-hydroxyestra-4, 9-11-trien-3-one).

(39) Methyltestosterone (17[alpha]-methyl-17[beta]-hydroxyandrost- 4-en-3-one).

(40) Mibolerone (7[alpha],17[alpha]-dimethyl-17[beta]-hydroxyestr- 4-en-3-one).

(41) 17[alpha]-methyl-[Delta] 1-dihydrotestosterone(17b[beta]-hydroxy-17[alpha]-methyl-5[alpha]-androst-1-en-3-one)(a.k.a. '17-[alpha]-methyl-1-testosterone').

(42) Nandrolone(17[beta]-hydroxyestr-4-en-3-one).

(43) 19-nor-4-androstenediol (3[beta],17[beta]-dihydroxyestr-4-ene).

(44) 19-nor-4-androstenediol (3[alpha],17[beta]-dihydroxyestr-4-ene).

(45) 19-nor-5-androstenediol (3[beta],17[beta]-dihydroxyestr-5-ene).

(46) 19-nor-5-androstenediol (3[alpha],17[beta]-dihydroxyestr-5-ene).

(47) 19-nor-4,9(10)-androstadienedione (estra-4,9(10)-diene-3,17-dione).

(48) 19-nor-4-androstenedione (estr-4-en-3,17-dione).

(49) 19-nor-5-androstenedione (estr-5-en-3,17-dione).

(50) Norbolethone (13[beta], 17[alpha]-diethyl-17[beta]-hydroxygon-4-en-3-one).

(51) Norclostebol (4-chloro-17[beta]-hydroxyestr-4-en-3-one).

(52) Norethandrolone (17[alpha]-ethyl-17[beta]-hydroxyestr-4-en-3-one).

(53) Normethandrolone (17[alpha]-methyl-17[beta]-hydroxyestr-4-en-3-one).

(54) Oxandrolone (17[alpha]-methyl-17[beta]-hydroxy-2-oxa-[5[alpha]]-androstan-3-one).

(55) Oxymesterone (17[alpha]-methyl-4, 17[beta]-dihydroxy androst-4-en-3-one).

(56) Oxymetholone (17[alpha]-methyl-2-hydroxymethylene-17[beta]-hydroxy-[5[alpha]]- androstan-3-one).

(57) Stanozolol (17[alpha]-methyl-17[beta]-hydroxy-[5[alpha]]-androst-2-eno[3, 2-c]-pyrazole).

(58) Stenbolone (17[beta]-hydroxy-2-methyl-[5[alpha]]-androst-1-en-3-one).

(59) Testolactone (13-hydroxy-3-oxo-13, 17-secoandrosta-1, 4-dien-17-oic acid lactone).

(60) Testosterone (17[beta]-hydroxyandrost-4-en-3-one).

(61) Tetrahydrogestrinone (13[beta], 17[alpha]-diethyl-17[beta]-hydroxygon-4, 9, 11-trien-3-one).

(62) Trenbolone (17[beta]-hydroxyestr-4, 9, 11-trien-3-one).

(63) Any salt, ester or ether of a drug or substance described or listed in this subdivision.

(i) Subdivision (h) of this section shall not include any substance containing anabolic steroids expressly intended for administration through implants to cattle or other nonhuman species and that are approved by the federal food and drug administration solely for such use. Any individual who knowingly and willfully administers to himself or another person, prescribes, dispenses or distributes such substances for other than implantation to cattle or nonhuman species shall be subject to the same penalties as a practitioner who violates the provisions of this section or any other penalties prescribed by law.

(j) [Repealed]

Schedule III.

(a) Schedule III shall consist of the drugs and other substances, by whatever official name, common or usual name, chemical name, or brand name designated, listed in this section.

(b) Stimulants. Unless specifically excepted or unless listed in another schedule, any material, compound, mixture, or preparation which contains any quantity of the following substances having a stimulant effect on the central nervous system, including its salts, isomers (whether optical, position, or geometric), and salts of such isomers whenever the existence of such salts, isomers, and salts of isomers is possible within the specific chemical designation:

(1) Those compounds, mixtures, or preparations in dosage unit form containing any stimulant substances listed in schedule II which compounds, mixtures, or preparations were listed on August twenty-five, nineteen hundred seventy-one, as excepted compounds under title twenty-one, section 308.32 of the code of federal regulations and any other drug of the quantitive composition shown in that list for those drugs or which is the same except that it contains a lesser quantity of controlled substances.

(2) Benzphetamine.

(3) Chlorphentermine.

(4) Clortermine.

(5) [Repealed]

(6) Phendimetrazine.

(c) Depressants. Unless specifically excepted or unless listed in another schedule, any material, compound, mixture, or preparation which contains any quantity of the following substances having a depressant effect on the central nervous system, including its salts, isomers, and salts of isomers:

(1) Any compound, mixture or preparation containing:

(i) Amobarbital;

(ii) Secobarbital;

(iii) Pentobarbital;

or any salt thereof and one or more other active medicinal ingredients which are not listed in any schedule.

(2) Any suppository dosage form containing:

(i) Amobarbital;

(ii) Secobarbital;

(iii) Pentobarbital;

or any salt of any of these drugs and approved by the federal food and drug administration for marketing only as a suppository.

(3) Any substance which contains any quantity of a derivative of barbituric acid or any salt thereof.

(4) Chlorhexadol.

(5) Lysergic acid.

(6) Lysergic acid amide.

(7) Methyprylon.

(8) Sulfondiethylmethane.

(9) Sulfonethylmethane.

(10) Sulfonmethane.

(11) Tiletamine and zolazepam or any salt thereof. Some trade or other names for a tiletamine-zolazepam combination product: Telazol. Some trade or other names for tiletamine: 2-(ethylamino) -2-(2-thienyl) -cyclohexanone. Some trade or other names for zolazepam: 4-(2-fluorophenyl) -6,8-dihydro -1, 3, 8i-trimethylpyrazolo-[3,4-e] [1,4]-diazepin-7(1H)-one, flupyrazapon.

(12) Gamma hydroxybutyric acid, and salt, hydroxybutyric compound, derivative or preparation of gamma hydroxybutyric acid, including any isomers, esters and ethers

and salts of isomers, esters and ethers of gamma hydroxybutyric acid, contained in a drug product for which an application has been approved under section 505 of the federal food, drug and cosmetic act.

(13) Ketamine, its salts, isomers and salts of isomers (some other names for ketamine: (±)-2-(2-chlorophenyl)-2-(methylamino)-cyclohexanone).

(14) Embutramide.

(d) Nalorphine.

(e) Narcotic drugs. Unless specifically excepted or unless listed in another schedule, any material, compound, mixture, or preparation containing any of the following narcotic drugs, or their salts calculated as the free anhydrous base or alkaloid, in limited quantities as set forth below:

(1) Not more than 1.8 grams of codeine per one hundred milliliters or not more than ninety milligrams per dosage unit, with an equal or greater quantity of an isoquinoline alkaloid of opium.

(2) Not more than 1.8 grams of codeine per one hundred milliliters or not more than ninety milligrams per dosage unit, with one or more active, nonnarcotic ingredients in recognized therapeutic amounts.

(3) Not more than 1.8 grams of dihydrocodeine per one hundred milliliters or not more than ninety milligrams per dosage unit, with one or more active nonnarcotic ingredients in recognized therapeutic amounts.

(4) Not more than three hundred milligrams of ethylmorphine per one hundred milliliters or not more than fifteen milligrams per dosage unit, with one or more active, nonnarcotic ingredients in recognized therapeutic amounts.

(5) Not more than five hundred milligrams of opium per one hundred milliliters or per one hundred grams or not more than twenty-five milligrams per dosage unit, with one or more active, nonnarcotic ingredients in recognized therapeutic amounts.

(6) Not more than fifty milligrams of morphine per one hundred milliliters or per one hundred grams, with one or more active, nonnarcotic ingredients in recognized therapeutic amounts.

(7) Buprenorphine in any quantities.

(8), (9) [Redesignated]

(f) Dronabinol (synthetic) in sesame oil and encapsulated in a soft gelatin capsule in a U.S. Food and Drug Administration approved product.

Some other names for dronabinol include: (6aR-trans)-6a, 7, 8, 10a-tetrahydro-6, 6, 9-trimethyl-3-pentyl-6H-dibenzo[b,d] pyran-1-o1, or (-)-delta-9-(trans) - tetrahydrocannabinol.

(g) Chorionic gonadotropin.

(1) Unless specifically excepted or unless listed in another schedule any material, compound, mixture, or preparation which contains any amount of chorionic gonadotropin.

(2) Paragraph one of this subdivision shall not include any substance containing chorionic gonadotropin expressly intended for administration through implants or injection to cattle or other nonhuman species and that are approved by the federal food and drug administration solely for such use. Any individual who knowingly and willfully administers to himself or another person, prescribes, dispenses or distributes such substances for other than implantation or injection to cattle or nonhuman species shall be subject to the same penalties as a practitioner who violates the provisions of this section or any other penalties prescribed by law.

Schedule IV.

(a) Schedule IV shall consist of the drugs and other substances, by whatever official name, common or usual name, chemical name, or brand name designated, listed in this section.

(b) Narcotic drugs. Unless specifically excepted or unless listed in another schedule, any material, compound, mixture, or preparation containing any of the following narcotic drugs, or their salts calculated as the free anhydrous base or alkaloid, in limited quantities as set forth below:

(1) Not more than one milligram of difenoxin and not less than twenty-five micrograms of atropine sulfate per dosage unit.

(2) Dextropropoxyphene (alpha-(+)-4-dimethylamino-1, 2-diphenyl-3-methyl-2-propionoxybutane).

(c) Depressants. Unless specifically excepted or unless listed in another schedule, any material, compound, mixture, or preparation which contains any quantity of the following substances, including its salts, isomers, and salts of isomers whenever the existence of such salts, isomers, and salts of isomers is possible within the specific chemical designation:

(1) Alprazolam.
(2) Barbital.
(3) Bromazepam.
(4) Camazepam.
(5) Chloral betaine.
(6) Chloral hydrate.
(7) Chlordiazepoxide.
(8) Clobazam.
(9) Clonazepam.
(10) Clorazepate.
(11) Clotiazepam.
(12) Cloxazolam.
(13) Delorazepam.
(14) Diazepam.
(15) Estazolam.
(16) Ethchlorvynol.
(17) Ethinamate.
(18) Ethyl Loflazepate.
(19) Fludiazepam.
(20) Flunitrazepam.
(21) Flurazepam.
(22) Halazepam.
(23) Haloxazolam.
(24) Ketazolam.
(25) Loprazolam.
(26) Lorazepam.
(27) Lormetazepam.
(28) Mebutamate.
(29) Medazepam.
(30) Meprobamate.
(31) Methohexital.
(32) Methylphenobarbital (mephobarbital).
(33) Nimetazepam.
(34) Nitrazepam.
(35) Nordiazepam.
(36) Oxazepam.
(37) Oxazolam.
(38) Paraldehyde.
(39) Petrichoral.
(40) Phenobarbital.
(41) Pinazepam.
(42) Prazepam.
(43) Temazepam.
(44) Tetrazepam.
(45) Triazolam.
(46) Midazolam.
(47) Quazepam.
(48) Zolpidem.
(49) Dichloralphenazone.
(50) Zaleplon.
(51) Zopiclone (eszopiclone).
(52) Fospropofol.
(53) Carisoprodol.

(d) [Deleted]

(e) Stimulants. Unless specifically excepted or unless listed in another schedule, any material, compound, mixture, or preparation which contains any quantity of the following substances having a stimulant effect on the central nervous system, including its salts, isomers, and salts of such isomers:

(1) Cathine ((+) - norpseudoephedrine).

(2) Diethylpropion.

(3) Fencamfamin.

(4) Fenproporex.

(5) Mazindol.

(6) Mefenorex.

(7) Pemoline (including organometallic complexes and chelates thereof).

(8) Phentermine.

(9) Pipradrol.

(10) SPA ((-))-1-dimethylamino-1, 2-diphenylethane).

(11) Modafinil.

(12) Sibutramine.

(f) Other substances. Unless specifically excepted or unless listed in another schedule, any material, compound, mixture or preparation which contains any quantity of the following substances, including its salts:

(1) Pentazocine.

(2) Butorphanol (including its optical isomers).

(3) Tramadol in any quantities.

Schedule V.

(a) Schedule V shall consist of the drugs and other substances, by whatever official name, common or usual name, chemical name, or brand name designated, listed in this section.

(b) Narcotic drugs containing nonnarcotic active medicinal ingredients. Any compound, mixture, or preparation containing any of the following narcotic drugs, or their salts calculated as the free anhydrous base or alkaloid, in limited quantities as set forth below, which shall include one or more nonnarcotic active medicinal ingredients in sufficient proportion to confer upon the compound, mixture, or preparation valuable medicinal qualities other than those possessed by narcotic drugs alone:

(1) Not more than two hundred milligrams of codeine per one hundred milliliters or per one hundred grams.

(2) Not more than one hundred milligrams of dihydrocodeine per one hundred milliliters or per one hundred grams.

(3) Not more than one hundred milligrams of ethylmorphine per one hundred milliliters or per one hundred grams.

(4) Not more than 2.5 milligrams of diphenoxylate and not less than twenty-five micrograms of atropine sulfate per dosage unit.

(5) Not more than one hundred milligrams of opium per one hundred milliliters or per one hundred grams.

(6) Not more than 0.5 milligram of difenoxin and not less than twenty-five micrograms of atropine sulfate per dosage unit.

(c) Stimulants. Unless specifically exempted or excluded or unless listed in another schedule, any material, compound, mixture, or preparation which contains any quantity of the following substances having a stimulant effect on the central nervous system, including its salts, isomers and salts of isomers:

(1) Pyrovalerone.

(d) Depressants. Unless specifically exempted or excluded or unless listed in another schedule, any material, compound, mixture, or preparation which contains any quantity of the following substances having a depressant effect on the central nervous system, including its salts, isomers, and salts of isomers:

(1) Ezogabine [N-[2-amino-4-(4-fluorobenzylamino)-phenyl]-carbamic acid ethyl ester].

(2) Lacosamide [(R)-2-acetoamido-N-benzyl-3-methoxy-propionamide].

(3) Pregabalin[(S)-3-(aminomethyl)-5-methylhexanoic acid].

HISTORY:

Add, L 1985, ch 664, § 1, eff Nov 1, 1985; amd, L 1986, ch 826, § 1, eff Sept 1, 1986; L 1987, ch 44, §§ 1, 2, eff April 21, 1987; L 1989, ch 418, § 1; L 1990, ch 640, §§ 1, 2; L 1992, ch 115, § 1, eff June 1, 1992; L 1993, ch 473, § 1, eff July 26, 1993; L 1995, ch 452, §§ 1, 2; L 1996, ch 443, § 1, eff Aug 2, 1996; L 1996, ch 589, §§ 1–10, eff Feb 4, 1997; L 1997, ch 635, § 2, eff Jan 22, 1998; L 2000, ch 1, §§ 29, 30, eff Feb 1, 2001; L 2001, ch 565, § 1, eff Jan 1, 2002; L 2001, ch 575, §§ 1–3, eff Dec 19, 2001; L 2003, ch 264, §§ 56, 57, eff Nov 1, 2003; L 2003, ch 591, §§ 1, 2, eff Sept 22, 2003; L 2006, ch 457, §§ 1–15, eff Aug 16, 2006; L 2010, ch 178, §§ 13–18, eff Oct 13, 2010; L 2011, ch 130, § 1, eff Aug 14, 2011; L 2012, ch 447, §§ 1, 4–9, 11–13, 16 (Part C), eff Nov 25, 2012; L 2012, ch 447, §§ 2, 10, 14 (Part C), eff Feb 23, 2013; L 2012, ch 447, § 15 (Part C), eff Aug 27, 2012; L 2013, ch 341, § 1, eff Dec 11, 2013; L 2015, ch 370, § 1, eff Oct 26, 2015; L 2016, ch 244, § 1, eff Aug 18, 2016; L 2018, ch 57, §§ 4, 5, 7 (Part BB), eff July 11, 2018; L 2018, ch 428, § 1, eff June 19, 2019; L 2020, ch 56, §§ 1, 3 (Part CC), eff July 2, 2020.

§ 3309. Opioid overdose prevention

1. The commissioner is authorized to establish standards for approval of any opioid overdose prevention program, and opioid antagonist prescribing, dispensing, distribution, possession and administration pursuant to this section which may include, but not be limited to, standards for program directors, appropriate clinical oversight, training, record keeping and reporting.

2. Notwithstanding any inconsistent provisions of section sixty-five hundred twelve of the education law or any other law, the purchase, acquisition, possession or use of an opioid antagonist pursuant to this section shall not constitute the unlawful practice of a profession or other violation under title eight of the education law or this article.

3.(a) As used in this section:

(i) "Opioid antagonist" means a drug approved by the Food and Drug Administration that, when administered, negates or neutralizes in whole or in part the pharmacological effects of an opioid in the body. "Opioid antagonist" shall be limited to naloxone and other medications approved by the department for such purpose.

(ii) "Health care professional" means a person licensed, registered or authorized pursuant to title eight of the education law to prescribe prescription drugs.

(iii) "Pharmacist" means a person licensed or authorized to practice pharmacy pursuant to article one hundred thirty-seven of the education law.

(iv) "Opioid antagonist recipient" or "recipient" means a person at risk of experiencing an opioid-related overdose, or a family member, friend or other person in a position to assist a person experiencing or at risk of experiencing an opioid-related overdose, or an organization registered as an opioid overdose prevention program pursuant to this section or a school district, public library, board of cooperative educational services, county vocational education and extension board, charter school, non-public elementary and/or secondary school in this state or any person employed by such district, library board or school.

(b)(i) A health care professional may prescribe by a patient-specific or non-patient-specific prescription, dispense or distribute, directly or indirectly, an opioid antagonist to an opioid antagonist recipient.

(ii) A pharmacist may dispense an opioid antagonist, through a patient-specific or non-patient-specific prescription pursuant to this paragraph, to an opioid antagonist recipient.

(iii) An opioid antagonist recipient may possess an opioid antagonist obtained pursuant to this paragraph, may distribute such opioid antagonist to a recipient, and may administer such opioid antagonist to a person the recipient reasonably believes is experiencing an opioid overdose.

(iv) The provisions of this paragraph shall not be deemed to require a prescription for any opioid antagonist that does not otherwise require a prescription; nor shall it be deemed to limit the authority of a health care professional to prescribe, dispense or distribute, or of a pharmacist to dispense, an opioid antagonist under any other provision of law.

(v) Any pharmacy with twenty or more locations in the state, shall either: (1) pursue or maintain a non-patient-specific prescription with an authorized health care professional to dispense an opioid antagonist to a consumer upon request, as authorized by this section; or (2) register with the department as an opioid overdose prevention program.

3-a. Any distribution of opioid antagonists through this program shall include an informational card or sheet. The informational card or sheet shall include, at a minimum, information on:

(a) how to recognize symptoms of an opioid overdose;

(b) steps to take prior to and after an opioid antagonist is administered, including calling first responders;

(c) the number for the toll free office of alcoholism and substance abuse services HOPE line;

(d) how to access the office of alcoholism and substance abuse services' website;

(e) the application of good samaritan protections provided in section three thousand-a of this chapter; and

(f) any other information deemed relevant by the commissioner.

The educational card shall be provided in languages other than English as deemed appropriate by the commissioner. The department shall make such informational cards available to the opioid overdose prevention programs.

4. Use of an opioid antagonist pursuant to this section shall be considered first aid or emergency treatment for the purpose of any statute relating to liability.

A recipient, opioid overdose prevention program, school district, public library, board of cooperative educational services, county vocational education and extension board, charter school, non-public elementary school and/or secondary school in the state, or any person employed by such district, public library, board or school under this section, acting reasonably and in good faith in compliance with this section, shall not be subject to criminal, civil or administrative liability solely by reason of such action.

5. The commissioner shall publish findings on statewide opioid overdose data that reviews overdose death rates and other information to ascertain changes in the cause and rates of opioid overdoses, including fatal opioid overdoses. The report shall be submitted annually, on or before October first, to the governor, the temporary president of the senate, the speaker of the assembly and the chairs of the senate and assembly health committees, and shall be made public on the department's internet website. The report shall include, at a minimum, the following information on a county basis:

(a) information on opioid overdoses and opioid overdose deaths, including age, gender, ethnicity, and geographic location;

(b) data on emergency room utilization for the treatment of opioid overdose;

(c) data on utilization of pre-hospital services;

(d) data on the dispensing and utilization of opioid antagonists; and

(e) any other information necessary to ascertain the success of the program, areas of the state which are experiencing particularly high rates of overdoses, ways to determine if services, resources and responses in particular areas of the state are having a positive impact on reducing overdoses, and ways to further reduce overdoses.

6. [Expires and deemed repealed March 31, 2021] The commissioner shall provide the current information and data specified in subdivision five of this section to each county every three months. Such information and data may be utilized by a county or any combination thereof as it works to address the opioid epidemic.

HISTORY:

Add, L 2005, ch 413, § 1, eff April 1, 2006; L 2014, ch 34, § 1, eff June 23, 2014; amd, L 2014, ch 42, § 1, eff June 24, 2014; L 2015, ch 57, §§ 1–3 (Part V), eff Aug 11, 2015; L 2016, ch 65, § 1, eff June 22, 2016; L 2016, ch 66, § 1, eff June 22, 2016; L 2016, ch 68, §§ 1, 2, eff June 22, 2016; L 2016, ch 70, § 1 (Part B), eff June 22, 2016; L 2019, ch 504, § 1, eff Jan 19, 2020.

SOCIAL SERVICES LAW

Article 11—Protection of People With Special Needs

§ 488. Definitions [Effective until July 2, 2020]

As used in this article, the following terms shall have the following meanings:

1. "Reportable incident" shall mean the following conduct that a mandated reporter is required to report to the vulnerable persons' central register:

(a) "Physical abuse," which shall mean conduct by a custodian intentionally or recklessly causing, by physical contact, physical injury or serious or protracted impairment of the physical, mental or emotional condition of a service recipient or causing the likelihood of such injury or impairment. Such conduct may include but shall not be limited to: slapping, hitting, kicking, biting, choking, smothering, shoving, dragging, throwing, punching, shaking, burning, cutting or the use of corporal punishment. Physical abuse shall not include reasonable emergency interventions necessary to protect the safety of any person.

(b) "Sexual abuse," which shall mean any conduct by a custodian that subjects a person receiving services to any offense defined in article one hundred thirty or section 255.25, 255.26 or 255.27 of the penal law; or any conduct or communication by such custodian that allows, permits, uses or encourages a service recipient to engage in any act described in articles two hundred thirty or two hundred sixty-three of the penal law. For purposes of this paragraph only, a person with a developmental disability who is or was receiving services and is also an employee or volunteer of a service provider shall not be considered a custodian if he or she has sexual contact with another service recipient who is a consenting adult who has consented to such contact.

(c) "Psychological abuse," which shall mean conduct by a custodian intentionally or recklessly causing, by verbal or non-verbal conduct, a substantial diminution of a service recipient's emotional, social or behavioral development or condition, supported by a clinical assessment performed by a physician, psychologist, psychiatric nurse practitioner, licensed clinical or master social worker or licensed mental health counselor, or causing the likelihood of such diminution. Such conduct may include but shall not be limited to intimidation, threats, the display of a weapon or other object that could reasonably be perceived by a service recipient as a means for infliction of pain or injury, in a manner that constitutes a threat of physical pain or injury, taunts, derogatory comments or ridicule.

(d) "Deliberate inappropriate use of restraints," which shall mean the use of a restraint when the technique that is used, the amount of force that is used or the situation in which the restraint is used is deliberately inconsistent with a service recipient's individual treatment plan or behavioral intervention plan, generally accepted treatment practices and/or applicable federal or state laws, regulations or policies, except when the restraint is used as a reasonable emergency intervention to prevent imminent risk of harm to a person receiving services or to any other person. For purposes of this subdivision, a "restraint" shall include the use of any manual, pharmacological or mechanical measure or device to immobilize or limit the ability of a person receiving services to freely move his or her arms, legs or body.

(e) "Use of aversive conditioning," which shall mean the application of a physical stimulus that is intended to induce pain or discomfort in order to modify or change the behavior of a person receiving services in the absence of a person-specific authorization by the operating, licensing or certifying state agency pursuant to governing state agency regulations. Aversive conditioning may include but is not limited to, the use of physical stimuli such as noxious odors, noxious tastes, blindfolds, the withholding of meals and the provision of substitute foods in an unpalatable form and movement limitations used as punishment, including but not limited to helmets and mechanical restraint devices.

(f) "Obstruction of reports of reportable incidents," which shall mean conduct by a custodian that impedes the discovery, reporting or investigation of the treatment of a service recipient by falsifying records related to the safety, treatment or supervision of a service recipient, actively persuading a mandated reporter from making a report of a reportable incident to the statewide vulnerable persons' central register with the intent to suppress the reporting of the investigation of such incident, intentionally making a false statement or intentionally withholding material information during an investigation into such a report; intentional failure of a supervisor or manager to act upon such a report in accordance with governing state agency regulations, policies or procedures; or, for a mandated reporter who is a custodian as defined in subdivision two of this section, failing to report a reportable incident upon discovery.

(g) "Unlawful use or administration of a controlled substance," which shall mean any administration by a custodian to a service recipient of: a controlled substance as defined by article thirty-three of the public health law, without a prescription; or other medication not approved for any use by the federal food and drug administration. It also shall include a custodian unlawfully using or distributing a controlled substance as defined by article thirty-three of the public health law, at the workplace or while on duty.

(h) "Neglect," which shall mean any action, inaction or lack of attention that breaches a custodian's duty and that results in or is likely to result in physical injury or serious or protracted impairment of the physical, mental or emotional condition of a service recipient. Neglect shall include, but is not limited to: (i) failure to provide proper supervision, including a lack of proper supervision that results in conduct between persons receiving services that would constitute abuse as described in paragraphs (a) through (g) of this subdivision if committed by a custodian; (ii) failure to provide adequate food, clothing, shelter, medical, dental, optometric or surgical care, consistent with the rules or regulations promulgated by the state agency operating, certifying or supervising the facility or provider agency, provided that the facility or provider agency has reasonable access to the provision of such services and that necessary consents to any such medical, dental, optometric or surgical treatment have been sought and obtained from the appropriate individuals; or (iii) failure to provide access to educational instruction, by a custodian with a duty to ensure that an individual receives access to such instruction in accordance with the provisions of part one of article sixty-five of the education law and/or the individual's individualized education program.

(i) "Significant incident" shall mean an incident, other than an incident of abuse or neglect, that because of its severity or the sensitivity of the situation may result in, or has the reasonably foreseeable potential to result in, harm to the health, safety or welfare of a person receiving services and shall include but shall not be limited to:

(1) conduct between persons receiving services that would constitute abuse as described in paragraphs (a) through (g) of this subdivision if committed by a custodian; or

(2) conduct on the part of a custodian, which is inconsistent with a service recipient's individual treatment plan or individualized educational program, generally accepted treatment practices and/or applicable federal or state laws, regulations or policies and which impairs or creates a reasonably foreseeable potential to impair the health, safety or welfare of a person receiving services, including but not limited to:

(A) unauthorized seclusion, which shall mean the placement of a person receiving services in a room or area from which he or she cannot, or perceives that he or she cannot, leave at will;

(B) unauthorized use of time-out, which shall mean the use of a procedure in which a person receiving services is removed from regular programming and isolated in a room or area for the convenience of a custodian, or as a substitute for programming but shall not include the use of a time-out as an emergency intervention to protect the health or safety of the individual or other persons;

(C) except as provided for in paragraph (g) of subdivision one of this section, the administration of a prescribed or over-the-counter medication, which is inconsistent with a prescription or order issued for a service recipient by a licensed, qualified health care practitioner, and which has an adverse effect on a service recipient. For purposes of this paragraph, "adverse effect" shall mean the unanticipated and undesirable side effect from the administration of a particular medication which unfavorably affects the well-being of a service recipient;

(D) inappropriate use of restraints, which shall mean the use of a restraint when the technique that is used, the amount of force that is used or the situation in which the restraint is used is inconsistent with a service recipient's individual plan, generally accepted treatment practices and/or applicable federal or state laws, regulations or policies. For the purposes of this subdivision, a "restraint" shall include the use of any manual, pharmacological or mechanical measure or device to immobilize or limit the ability of a person receiving services to freely move his or her arms, legs or body; or

(3) any other conduct identified in regulations of the state oversight agency, pursuant to guidelines or standards established by the executive director.

2. "Custodian" means a director, operator, employee or volunteer of a facility or provider agency; or a consultant or an employee or volunteer of a corporation, partnership, organization or governmental entity which provides goods or services to a facility or provider agency pursuant to contract or other arrangement that permits such person to have regular and substantial contact with individuals who are cared for by the facility or provider agency.

3. "Executive director" shall mean the executive director of the justice center for the protection of people with special needs as established by article twenty of the executive law.

4. "Facility" or "provider agency" shall mean:

(a) a facility or program in which services are provided and which is operated, licensed or certified by the office of mental health, the office for people with developmental disabilities or the office of alcoholism and substance abuse services, including but not limited to psychiatric centers, inpatient psychiatric units of a general hospital, developmental centers, intermediate care facilities, community residences, group homes and family care homes, provided, however, that such term shall not include a secure treatment facility as defined in section 10.03 of the mental hygiene law, services defined in subparagraph four of subdivision (a) of section 16.03 of the mental hygiene law, or services provided in programs or facilities that are operated by the office of mental health and located in state correctional facilities under the jurisdiction of the department of corrections and community supervision;

(b) any program or facility that is operated by the office of children and family services for juvenile delinquents or juvenile offenders placed in the custody of the commissioner of such office and any residential programs or facilities licensed or certified by the office of children and family services, excluding foster family homes and residential programs for victims of domestic violence;

(c) adult care facilities, which shall mean adult homes or enriched housing programs licensed pursuant to article seven of this chapter: (i) (A) that have a licensed capacity of eighty or more beds; and (B) in which at least twenty-five percent of the residents are persons with serious mental illness as defined by subdivision fifty-two of section 1.03 of the mental hygiene law; (ii) but not including an adult home or enriched housing program which is authorized to operate fifty-five percent or more of its total licensed capacity of beds as assisted living program beds pursuant to section four hundred sixty-one-l of this chapter;

(d) any overnight, summer day and traveling summer day camps for children with developmental disabilities as defined in regulations promulgated by the commissioner of health; or

(e) the New York state school for the blind and the New York state school for the deaf, which operate pursuant to articles eighty-seven and eighty-eight of the education law; an institution for the instruction of the deaf and the blind which has a residential component and is subject to the visitation of the commissioner of education pursuant to article eighty-five of the education law with respect to its day and residential components; special act school districts serving students with disabilities; or in-state private schools which have been approved by the commissioner of education for special education services or programs, and which have a residential program.

4-a. "State oversight agency" shall mean the state agency that operates, licenses or certifies an applicable facility or provider agency; provided however that such term shall only include the following entities: the office of mental health, the office for people with developmental disabilities, the office of alcoholism and substance abuse services, the office of children and family services, the department of health and the state education department. "State oversight agency" does not include agencies that are certification agencies pursuant to federal law or regulation.

5. "Mandated reporter" shall mean a custodian or a human services professional, but shall not include a service recipient.

5-a. "Human services professional" shall mean any: physician; registered physician assistant; surgeon; medical examiner; coroner; dentist; dental hygienist; osteopath; optometrist; chiropractor; podiatrist; resident; intern; psychologist; registered nurse; licensed practical nurse; nurse practitioner; social worker; emergency medical technician; licensed creative arts therapist; licensed marriage and family therapist; licensed mental health counselor; licensed psychoanalyst; licensed behavior analyst; certified behavior analyst assistant; licensed speech/language pathologist or audiologist; licensed physical therapist; licensed occupational therapist; hospital personnel engaged in the admission, examination, care or treatment of persons; Christian Science practitioner; school official, which includes but is not limited to school teacher, school guidance counselor, school psychologist, school social worker, school nurse, school administrator or other school personnel required to hold a teaching or administrative license or certificate; full or part-time compensated school employee required to hold a temporary coaching license or professional coaching certificate; social services worker; any other child care or foster care worker; mental health professional; person credentialed by the office of alcoholism and substance abuse services; peace officer; police officer; district attorney or assistant district attorney; investigator employed in the office of a district attorney; or other law enforcement official.

6. "Physical injury" and "impairment of physical condition" shall mean any confirmed harm, hurt or damage resulting in a significant worsening or diminution of an individual's physical condition.

7. "Delegate investigatory entity" shall mean a facility or provider agency, or any other entity authorized by the regulations of a state oversight agency or the justice center for the protection of people with special needs to conduct an investigation of a reportable incident.

8. "Justice center" shall mean the justice center for the protection of people with special needs.

9. "Person receiving services," or "service recipient" shall mean an individual who resides or is an inpatient in a residential facility or who receives services from a facility or provider agency.

10. "Personal representative" shall mean a person authorized under state, tribal, military or other applicable law to act on behalf of a vulnerable person in making health care decisions or, for programs that serve children under the jurisdiction of the state education department or the office of children and family services, the service recipient's parent, guardian or other person legally responsible for such person.

11. "Abuse or neglect" shall mean the conduct described in paragraphs (a) through (h) of subdivision one of this section.

12. "Subject of the report" shall mean a custodian, as defined in subdivision two of this section, who is reported to the vulnerable persons' central register for the alleged abuse or neglect of a vulnerable person as defined in subdivision eleven of this section.

13. "Other persons named in the report" shall mean and be limited to the following persons who are named in a report to the vulnerable persons' central register other than the subject of the report: the service recipient whose care and treatment is the concern of a report to the vulnerable persons' central register, and the personal representative, if any, as defined in subdivision ten of this section.

14. "Vulnerable persons' central register" shall mean the statewide central register of reportable incidents involving vulnerable persons, which shall operate in accordance with section four hundred ninety-two of this article.

15. "Vulnerable person" shall mean a person who, due to physical or cognitive disabilities, or the need for services or placement, is receiving services from a facility or provider agency.

16. "Intentionally" and "recklessly" shall have the same meanings as provided in subdivisions one and three of section 15.05 of the penal law.

HISTORY:

Add, L 2012, ch 501, § 1 (Part B), eff June 30, 2013; amd, L 2013, ch 83, § 2, eff June 30, 2013; L 2014, ch 8, § 1, eff July 1, 2014; L 2014, ch 126, § 11, eff July 22, 2014; L 2014, ch 205, § 2, eff July 1, 2015; L 2015, ch 58, § 2 (Part MM), eff April 13, 2015.

§ 488. Definitions [Effective July 2, 2020]

As used in this article, the following terms shall have the following meanings:

1. "Reportable incident" shall mean the following conduct that a mandated reporter is required to report to the vulnerable persons' central register:

(a) "Physical abuse," which shall mean conduct by a custodian intentionally or recklessly causing, by physical contact, physical injury or serious or protracted impairment of the physical, mental or emotional condition of a service recipient or causing the likelihood of such injury or impairment. Such conduct may include but shall not be limited to: slapping, hitting, kicking, biting, choking, smothering, shoving, dragging, throwing, punching, shaking, burning, cutting or the use of corporal punishment. Physical abuse shall not include reasonable emergency interventions necessary to protect the safety of any person.

(b) "Sexual abuse," which shall mean any conduct by a custodian that subjects a person receiving services to any offense defined in article one hundred thirty or section 255.25, 255.26 or 255.27 of the penal law; or any conduct or communication by such custodian that allows, permits, uses or encourages a service recipient to engage in any act described in articles two hundred thirty or two hundred sixty-three of the penal law. For purposes of this paragraph only, a person with a developmental disability who is or was receiving services and is also an employee or volunteer of a service provider shall not be considered a custodian if he or she has sexual contact with another service recipient who is a consenting adult who has consented to such contact.

(c) "Psychological abuse," which shall mean conduct by a custodian intentionally or recklessly causing, by verbal or non-verbal conduct, a substantial diminution of a service recipient's emotional, social or behavioral development or condition, supported by a clinical assessment performed by a physician, psychologist, psychiatric nurse practitioner, licensed clinical or master social worker or licensed mental health counselor, or causing the likelihood of such diminution. Such conduct may include but shall not be limited to intimidation, threats, the display of a weapon or other object that could reasonably be perceived by a service recipient as a means for infliction of pain or injury, in a manner that constitutes a threat of physical pain or injury, taunts, derogatory comments or ridicule.

(d) "Deliberate inappropriate use of restraints," which shall mean the use of a restraint when the technique that is used, the amount of force that is used or the situation in which the restraint is used is deliberately inconsistent with a service recipient's individual treatment plan or behavioral intervention plan, generally accepted treatment practices and/or applicable federal or state laws, regulations or policies, except when the restraint is used as a reasonable emergency intervention to prevent imminent risk of harm to a person receiving services or to any other person. For purposes of this subdivision, a "restraint" shall include the use of any manual, pharmacological or mechanical measure or device to immobilize or limit the ability of a person receiving services to freely move his or her arms, legs or body.

(e) "Use of aversive conditioning," which shall mean the application of a physical stimulus that is intended to induce pain or discomfort in order to modify or change the behavior of a person receiving services in the absence of a person-specific authorization by the operating, licensing or certifying state agency pursuant to governing state agency regulations. Aversive conditioning may include but is not limited to, the use of physical stimuli such as noxious odors, noxious tastes, blindfolds, the withholding of meals and the provision of substitute foods in an unpalatable form and movement limitations used as punishment, including but not limited to helmets and mechanical restraint devices.

(f) "Obstruction of reports of reportable incidents," which shall mean conduct by a custodian that impedes the discovery, reporting or investigation of the treatment of a service recipient by falsifying records related to the safety, treatment or supervision of a service recipient, actively persuading a mandated reporter from making a report of a reportable incident to the statewide vulnerable persons' central register with the intent to suppress the reporting of the investigation of such incident, intentionally making a false statement or intentionally withholding material information during an investigation into such a report; intentional failure of a supervisor or manager to act upon such a report in accordance with governing state agency regulations, policies or procedures; or, for a mandated reporter who is a custodian as defined in subdivision two of this section, failing to report a reportable incident upon discovery.

(g) "Unlawful use or administration of a controlled substance," which shall mean any administration by a custodian to a service recipient of: a controlled substance as defined by article thirty-three of the public health law, without a prescription; or other medication not approved for any use by the federal food and drug administration. It also shall include a custodian unlawfully using or distributing a controlled substance as defined by article thirty-three of the public health law, at the workplace or while on duty.

(h) "Neglect," which shall mean any action, inaction or lack of attention that breaches a custodian's duty and that results in or is likely to result in physical injury or serious or protracted impairment of the physical, mental or emotional condition of a service recipient. Neglect shall include, but is not limited to: (i) failure to provide proper supervision, including a lack of proper supervision that results in conduct between persons receiving services that would constitute abuse as described in paragraphs (a) through (g) of this subdivision if committed by a custodian; (ii) failure to provide adequate food, clothing, shelter, medical, dental, optometric or surgical care, consistent with the rules or regulations promulgated by the state agency operating, certifying or supervising the facility or provider agency, provided that the facility or provider agency has reasonable access to the provision of such services and that necessary consents to any such medical, dental, optometric or surgical treatment have been sought and obtained from the appropriate individuals; or (iii) failure to provide access to educational instruction, by a custodian with a duty to ensure that an individual receives access to such instruction in accordance with the provisions of part one of article sixty-five of the education law and/or the individual's individualized education program.

(i) "Significant incident" shall mean an incident, other than an incident of abuse or neglect, that because of its severity or the sensitivity of the situation may result in, or has the reasonably foreseeable potential to result in, harm to the health, safety or welfare of a person receiving services and shall include but shall not be limited to:

(1) conduct between persons receiving services that would constitute abuse as described in paragraphs (a) through (g) of this subdivision if committed by a custodian; or

(2) conduct on the part of a custodian, which is inconsistent with a service recipient's individual treatment plan or individualized educational program, generally accepted treatment practices and/or applicable federal or state laws, regulations or policies and which impairs or creates a reasonably foreseeable potential to impair the health, safety or welfare of a person receiving services, including but not limited to:

(A) unauthorized seclusion, which shall mean the placement of a person receiving services in a room or area from which he or she cannot, or perceives that he or she cannot, leave at will;

(B) unauthorized use of time-out, which shall mean the use of a procedure in which a person receiving services is removed from regular programming and isolated in a room or area for the convenience of a custodian, or as a substitute for programming but shall not include the use of a time-out as an emergency intervention to protect the health or safety of the individual or other persons;

(C) except as provided for in paragraph (g) of subdivision one of this section, the administration of a prescribed or over-the-counter medication, which is inconsistent with a prescription or order issued for a service recipient by a licensed, qualified health care practitioner, and which has an adverse effect on a service recipient. For purposes of this paragraph, "adverse effect" shall mean the unanticipated and undesirable side effect from the administration of a particular medication which unfavorably affects the well-being of a service recipient;

(D) inappropriate use of restraints, which shall mean the use of a restraint when the technique that is used, the amount of force that is used or the situation in which the restraint is used is inconsistent with a service recipient's individual plan, generally accepted treatment practices and/or applicable federal or state laws, regulations or policies. For the purposes of this subdivision, a "restraint" shall include the use of any manual, pharmacological or mechanical measure or device to immobilize or limit the ability of a person receiving services to freely move his or her arms, legs or body; or

(3) any other conduct identified in regulations of the state oversight agency, pursuant to guidelines or standards established by the executive director.

2. "Custodian" means a director, operator, employee or volunteer of a facility or provider agency; or a consultant or an employee or volunteer of a corporation, partnership, organization or governmental entity which provides goods or services to a facility or provider agency pursuant to contract or other arrangement that permits such person to have regular and substantial contact with individuals who are cared for by the facility or provider agency.

3. "Executive director" shall mean the executive director of the justice center for the protection of people with special needs as established by article twenty of the executive law.

4. "Facility" or "provider agency" shall mean:

(a) a facility or program in which services are provided and which is operated, licensed or certified by the office of mental health, the office for people with developmental disabilities or the office of addiction services and supports, including but not limited to psychiatric centers, inpatient psychiatric units of a general hospital, developmental centers, intermediate care facilities, community residences, group homes and family care homes, provided, however, that such term shall not include a secure treatment facility as defined in section 10.03 of the mental hygiene law, services defined in paragraphs four and five of subdivision (a) of section 16.03 of the mental hygiene law, or services provided in programs or facilities that are operated by the office of mental health and located in state correctional facilities under the jurisdiction of the department of corrections and community supervision;

(b) any program or facility that is operated by the office of children and family services for juvenile delinquents or juvenile offenders placed in the custody of the commissioner of such office and any residential programs or facilities licensed or certified by the office of children and family services, excluding foster family homes and residential programs for victims of domestic violence;

(c) adult care facilities, which shall mean adult homes or enriched housing programs licensed pursuant to article seven of this chapter: (i) (A) that have a licensed capacity of eighty or more beds; and (B) in which at least twenty-five percent of the residents are persons with serious mental illness as defined by subdivision fifty-two of section 1.03 of the mental hygiene law; (ii) but not including an adult home or enriched housing program which is authorized to operate fifty-five percent or more of its total licensed capacity of beds as assisted living program beds pursuant to section four hundred sixty-one-l of this chapter;

(d) any overnight, summer day and traveling summer day camps for children with developmental disabilities as defined in regulations promulgated by the commissioner of health; or

(e) the New York state school for the blind and the New York state school for the deaf, which operate pursuant to articles eighty-seven and eighty-eight of the education law; an institution for the instruction of the deaf and the blind which has a residential component and is subject to the visitation of the commissioner of education pursuant to article eighty-five of the education law with respect to its day and residential components; special act school districts serving students with disabilities; or in-state private schools which have been approved by the commissioner of education for special education services or programs, and which have a residential program.

4-a. "State oversight agency" shall mean the state agency that operates, licenses or certifies an applicable facility or provider agency; provided however that such term shall only include the following entities: the office of mental health, the office for people with developmental disabilities, the office of alcoholism and substance abuse services, the office of children and family services, the department of health and the state education department. "State oversight agency" does not include agencies that are certification agencies pursuant to federal law or regulation.

5. "Mandated reporter" shall mean a custodian or a human services professional, but shall not include a service recipient.

5-a. "Human services professional" shall mean any: physician; registered physician assistant; surgeon; medical examiner; coroner; dentist; dental hygienist; osteopath; optometrist; chiropractor; podiatrist; resident; intern; psychologist; registered nurse; licensed practical nurse; nurse practitioner; social worker; emergency medical technician; licensed creative arts therapist; licensed marriage and family therapist; licensed mental health counselor; licensed psychoanalyst; licensed behavior analyst; certified behavior analyst assistant; licensed speech/language pathologist or audiologist; licensed physical therapist; licensed occupational therapist; hospital personnel engaged in the admission, examination, care or treatment of persons; Christian Science practitioner; school official, which includes but is not limited to school teacher, school guidance counselor, school psychologist, school social worker, school nurse, school administrator or other school personnel required to hold a teaching or administrative license or certificate; full or part-time compensated school employee required to hold a temporary coaching license or professional coaching certificate; social services worker; any other child care or foster care worker; mental health professional; person credentialed by the office of alcoholism and substance abuse services; peace officer; police officer; district attorney or assistant district attorney; investigator employed in the office of a district attorney; or other law enforcement official.

6. "Physical injury" and "impairment of physical condition" shall mean any confirmed harm, hurt or damage resulting in a significant worsening or diminution of an individual's physical condition.

7. "Delegate investigatory entity" shall mean a facility or provider agency, or any other entity authorized by the regulations of a state oversight agency or the justice center for the protection of people with special needs to conduct an investigation of a reportable incident.

8. "Justice center" shall mean the justice center for the protection of people with special needs.

9. "Person receiving services," or "service recipient" shall mean an individual who resides or is an inpatient in a residential facility or who receives services from a facility or provider agency.

10. "Personal representative" shall mean a person authorized under state, tribal, military or other applicable law to act on behalf of a vulnerable person in making health care decisions or, for programs that serve children under the jurisdiction of the state education department or the office of children and family services, the service recipient's parent, guardian or other person legally responsible for such person.

11. "Abuse or neglect" shall mean the conduct described in paragraphs (a) through (h) of subdivision one of this section.

12. "Subject of the report" shall mean a custodian, as defined in subdivision two of this section, who is reported to the vulnerable persons' central register for the alleged abuse or neglect of a vulnerable person as defined in subdivision eleven of this section.

13. "Other persons named in the report" shall mean and be limited to the following persons who are named in a report to the vulnerable persons' central register other than the subject of the report: the service recipient whose care and treatment is the concern of a report to the vulnerable persons' central register, and the personal representative, if any, as defined in subdivision ten of this section.

14. "Vulnerable persons' central register" shall mean the statewide central register of reportable incidents involving vulnerable persons, which shall operate in accordance with section four hundred ninety-two of this article.

15. "Vulnerable person" shall mean a person who, due to physical or cognitive disabilities, or the need for services or placement, is receiving services from a facility or provider agency.

16. "Intentionally" and "recklessly" shall have the same meanings as provided in subdivisions one and three of section 15.05 of the penal law.

HISTORY:

Add, L 2012, ch 501, § 1 (Part B), eff June 30, 2013; amd, L 2013, ch 83, § 2, eff June 30, 2013; L 2014, ch 8, § 1, eff July 1, 2014; L 2014, ch 126, § 11, eff July 22, 2014; L 2014, ch 205, § 2, eff July 1, 2015; L 2015, ch 58, § 2 (Part MM), eff April 13, 2015; L 2020, ch 58, § 4 (Part RRR), eff July 2, 2020.

NEW YORK CITY CODE AND RULES

ADMINISTRATIVE CODE OF THE CITY OF NEW YORK

TITLE 10
PUBLIC SAFETY

Chapter 3
FIREARMS
(Selected Sections)

§ 10-301. Control and regulation of the disposition, purchase and possession of firearms, rifles, shotguns and assault weapons

Definitions. Whenever used in this chapter the following terms shall mean and include:

1. "Firearm." (a) Any pistol or revolver; (b) a shotgun having one or more barrels less than eighteen inches in length; or (c) a rifle having one or more barrels less than sixteen inches in length; or (d) any weapon made from a shotgun or rifle whether by alteration, modification, or otherwise if such weapon as altered, modified, or otherwise has an overall length of less than twenty-six inches. For the purpose of this subdivision the length of the barrel on a shotgun or rifle shall be determined by measuring the distance between the muzzle and the face of the bolt, breech, or breechlock when closed and when the shotgun or rifle is cocked; the overall length of a weapon made from a shotgun or rifle is the distance between the extreme ends of the weapon measured along a line parallel to the center line of the bore. Firearm does not include an antique firearm. The provisions of this chapter relating to firearms shall not apply to assault weapons except as specifically provided.

2. "Rifle." A weapon designed or redesigned, made or remade, and intended to be fired from the shoulder, and, even if not designed or redesigned, made or remade, and intended to be fired from the shoulder, is not a firearm as defined in subdivision one of this section, and designed or redesigned and made or remade to use the energy of the explosive in a fixed metallic cartridge to fire only a single projectile through a rifled bore for each pull of the trigger. The provisions of this chapter relting to rifles shall not apply to assault weapons except as specifically provided.

3. "Shotgun." A weapon designed or redesigned, made or remade, and intended to be fired from the shoulder, and, even if not designed or redesigned, made or remade, and intended to be fired from the shoulder, is not a firearm as defined in subdivision one of this section, and designed or redesigned and made or remade to use the energy of the explosive in a fixed shotgun shell, to fire through a smooth bore either a number of ball shot or a single projectile for each single pull of the trigger. The provisions of this chapter relating to shotguns shall not apply to assault weapons except as specifically provided.

4. "Gunsmith." Any person, firm, partnership, corporation, or company who engages in the business of repairing, altering, assembling, manufacturing, cleaning, polishing,

engraving, or trueing, or who in the course of such business performs any mechanical operation on any rifle, shotgun, firearm, assault weapon or machine gun.

5. "Dealer in firearms." Any person, firm, partnership, corporation or company who engages in the business of purchasing, selling, keeping for sale, loaning, leasing, or in any manner disposing of any pistol or revolver or other firearms which may be concealed upon the person. Dealer in firearms shall not include a wholesale dealer.

6. "Dealer in rifles and shotguns." Any person, firm, partnership, corporation or company who engages in the business of purchasing, selling, keeping for sale, loaning, leasing, or in any manner disposing of any rifle, or shotgun. Dealer in rifles and shotguns shall not include a wholesale dealer.

7. "Ammunition." Explosives suitable to be fired from a firearm, machine gun, pistol, revolver, rifle, shotgun, assault weapon or other dangerous weapon.

8. "Dispose of." To dispose of, give away, give, lease, loan, keep for sale, offer, offer for sale, sell, transfer and otherwise dispose of.

9. "Deface." To remove, deface, cover, alter, or destroy the manufacturer's serial number or any other distinguishing number or identification mark.

10. "Commissioner." The police commissioner of the city of New York or the commissioner's designee.

11. "Permit." The permit for purchase and possession of rifles and shotguns issued by the commissioner.

12. "Certificate." The certificate of registration for possession of rifles and shotguns.

13. "Serious offense." A serious offense as defined in subdivision seventeen of section 265.00 of the penal law.

14. "Business enterprise." Any proprietorship, company, partnership, corporation, association, cooperative, nonprofit organization or other entity engaged or seeking to engage in the activities regulated pursuant to section 10-302 of this chapter.

15. "Semiautomatic." Any firearm, rifle or shotgun that uses part of the energy of a fired cartridge to expel the case of the fired cartridge and load another cartridge into the firing chamber, and which requires a separate pull of the trigger to fire each cartridge.

16. "Assault weapon."

(a) Any semiautomatic centerfire or rimfire rifle or semiautomatic shotgun which has one or more of the following features:

1. folding or telescoping stock or no stock;
2. pistol grip that protrudes conspicuously beneath the action of the weapon;
3. bayonet mount;
4. flash suppressor or threaded barrel designed to accommodate a flash suppressor;
5. barrel shroud;
6. grenade launcher; or
7. modifications of such features, or other features, determined by rule of the commissioner to be particularly suitable for military and not sporting purposes. In addition, the commissioner shall, by rule, designate specific semiautomatic centerfire or rimfire rifles or semiautomatic shotguns, identified by make, model and/or manufacturer's name, as within the definition of assault weapon, if the commissioner determines that such weapons are particularly suitable for military and not sporting purposes. The commissioner shall inspect such specific designated semiautomatic centerfire or rimfire rifles or semiautomatic shotguns at least three times per year, and shall revise or update such designations as he or she deems appropriate.

(b) Any shotgun with a revolving-cylinder magazine.

(c) Any part, or combination of parts, designed or redesigned or intended to readily convert a rifle or shotgun into an assault weapon.

(d) "Assault weapon" shall not include any rifle or shotgun modified to render it permanently inoperative.

17. "Ammunition feeding device." Magazines, belts, feedstrips, drums or clips capable of being attached to or utilized with firearms, rifles, shotguns or assault weapons.

18. "Antique firearm." Any unloaded muzzle loading pistol or revolver with a matchlock, flintlock, percussion cap, or similar type of ignition system, or a pistol or revolver which uses fixed cartridges which are no longer available in the ordinary channels of commercial trade.

19. "Special theatrical dealer." Any person, firm, partnership, corporation or company who possesses assault weapons exclusively for the purpose of leasing such assault weapons to special theatrical permittees within the city and for theatrical purposes outside the city.

20. "Acquire." To gain possession of or title to a weapon through purchase, gift, lease, loan, or otherwise.

21. "Frame or receiver." Part of a firearm, rifle, shotgun or assault weapon that provides housing for the hammer, bolt or breechblock, and firing mechanism, and that is usually threaded at its forward portion to receive the barrel.

22. "Unfinished frame or receiver." A piece of any material that does not constitute the frame or receiver of a firearm, rifle, shotgun or assault weapon but that has been shaped or formed in any way for the purpose of becoming the frame or receiver of a firearm, rifle, shotgun or assault weapon with modification by the user and that is not engraved with a serial number that meets or exceeds requirements pursuant to subsection (i) of section 923 of title 18 of the United States code and regulations issued pursuant thereto.

HISTORICAL NOTES:

Section heading amended L.L. 78/1991 § 5, eff. Sept. 30, 1991.

Section added chap 907/1985 § 1.

Subds. 1, 2, 3, 4, 7, 10 amended L.L. 78/1991 § 5, eff. Sept. 30, 1991.

Subd. 15 added L.L. 78/1991 § 6, eff. Sept. 30, 1991.

Subd. 16 added L.L. 78/1991 § 6, eff. Sept. 30, 1991.

Subd. 16 par (a) subpar 7 amended L.L. 8/2005 § 1, eff. Apr. 18, 2005.

Subds. 17-18 added L.L. 78/1991 § 6, eff. Sept. 30, 1991.

Subd. 19 added L.L. 22/1992 § 2, eff. Apr. 10, 1992.

Subd. 20 added L.L. 31/2006 § 2, eff. Nov. 24, 2006. [See § 10-302.1]

Subd. 21, 22 added L.L. 187/2019 § 1, eff. Feb. 23, 2020.

§ 10-314. Prohibition on unfinished frames or receivers

a. Restriction of possession. Notwithstanding any other provision of this chapter, no person shall dispose of or possess an unfinished frame or receiver.

b. Penalties. The violation of this section constitutes a class A misdemeanor for each prohibited item disposed of or possessed.

HISTORICAL NOTE:

Section added L.L. 187/2019 § 2, eff. Feb. 23, 2020.

TITLE 17
HEALTH

CHAPTER 3
LICENSES AND PERMITS

SUBCHAPTER 2
FOOD VENDORS
(Selected Section)

§ 17-315. Restrictions on the placement of vehicles and pushcarts; vending in certain areas restricted or prohibited

a. No pushcart shall be placed upon any sidewalk unless said sidewalk has at least a twelve foot clear pedestrian path to be measured from the boundary of any private property to any obstruction in or on the sidewalk, or if there are no obstructions, to the curb. In no event shall any pushcart be placed on any part of a sidewalk other than that which abuts the curb.

b. No vending vehicle or pushcart or any other item related to the operation of a food vendor's business shall touch, lean against or be affixed permanently or temporarily in any building or structure including, but not limited to, lamp posts, parking meters, mail boxes, traffic signal stanchions, fire hydrants, tree boxes, benches, bus shelters, taxi stands, refuse baskets or traffic barriers.

c. All items relating to the operation of a food vending business shall be kept in or under the vending vehicle or pushcart, except that samples of the non-perishable items sold may be displayed on the vending vehicle or pushcart. No items relating to the operation of a food vending business other than an adjoining acceptable waste container shall be placed upon any public space adjacent to the vending vehicle or pushcart, and no food shall be sold except from an authorized vehicle or pushcart.

d. No vending pushcart shall be located against display windows of fixed location businesses, nor shall they be within twenty feet of any entranceway to any building, store, theatre, movie house, sports arena or other place of public assembly, or within twenty feet from exits, including service exits, to buildings that are exclusively residential at the street level.

e. No food vendor shall vend within any bus stop, taxi stand, within the portion of the sidewalk abutting any no standing zone adjacent to a hospital as defined in subdivision one of section 2801 of the New York state public health law, within ten feet of any driveway, any subway entrance or exit, or any crosswalk at any intersection.

f. Each food vendor who vends from a pushcart or vehicle in the roadway shall obey all traffic and parking laws, rules and regulations as now exist or as may be promulgated, but in no case shall a food vendor vend so as to restrict the continued maintenance of a clear passageway for vehicles.

g. Repealed.

h. No food vendor shall vend on the median strip of a divided roadway unless such strip is intended for use as a pedestrian mall or plaza.

i. No vendor shall vend within areas under the jurisdiction of the department of parks and recreation unless written authorization therefor has been obtained from the commissioner of such department, but nothing therein contained shall exempt any vendor from obtaining a license and permit in accordance with this subchapter.

j. Where exigent circumstances exist and a police officer or other authorized officer or employee of the city gives notice to a food vendor to temporarily move from a location such vendor shall not vend from such location. For the purpose of this subdivision, exigent circumstances shall include but not be limited to, unusually heavy pedestrian or vehicular traffic, existence of any obstructions in the public space at or near such location, an accident, fire or other emergency situation at or near such location, or a parade, demonstration, or other such event or occurrence at or near such location.

k. No food vendor shall vend on any street at any time where and when the operation of any food vending business is prohibited pursuant to either local law or section 20-465.1 of the code and any rules promulgated pursuant thereto.

1. No food vendor shall vend in the area including and bounded on the east by the easterly side of Broadway, on the south by the southerly side of Liberty Street, on the west by the westerly side of West Street and on the north by the southerly side of Barclay Street. In addition:

(a) No food vendor shall vend on the easterly or westerly side of Greenwich Street between Liberty Street and Thames Street;

(b) No food vendor shall vend on the easterly side of West Broadway between Barclay Street and Park Place;

(c) No food vendor shall vend on the northerly or southerly side of Liberty Street between Trinity Place to West Street;

(d) No food vendor shall vend on the easterly side of West Street between Liberty Street and Cedar Street;

(e) No food vendor shall vend on the westerly side of Trinity Place between Liberty Street and Thames Street; and

(f) Notwithstanding the restriction described in paragraph 1 of subdivision k, food vending shall be permitted on the following streets provided that food vendors comply with all applicable laws and rules:

(1) The easterly and westerly side of Broadway between Barclay Street and Vesey Street;

(2) The easterly side of West Street between Barclay Street and Vesey Street; and

(3) The southerly side of Barclay Street between Church Street and Broadway.

2. Food vendors shall be prohibited from vending on the following streets at the following days and times:

BOROUGH OF MANHATTAN

Third Avenue: East 40th to East 57th Street, Monday through Friday, 8 am to 6 pm; East 58th to East 60th Street, Monday through Saturday, 8 am to 9 pm; Lexington Avenue: East 40th to East 57th Street, Monday through Saturday, 8 am to 7 pm; East 58th to East 60th Street, Monday through Saturday, 8 am to 9 pm; East 61st to East 69th Street, Monday through Saturday, 8 am to 6 pm; Park Avenue: East 34th to East 42nd Street, Monday through Friday, 8 am to 7 pm; East 55th to East 59th Street, Monday through Friday, 10 am to 7 pm; Vanderbilt Avenue: East 42nd to East 45th Street, Monday through Friday, 8 am to 7 pm; Madison Avenue: East 34th to East 45th Street, Monday through Friday, 8 am to 6 pm; East 46th to East 59th Street, Monday through Saturday, 10 am to 7 pm; Fifth Avenue: 32nd to 59th Street, Monday through Saturday, 8 am to 7 pm; Avenue of the Americas: West 32nd to West 59th Street, Monday through Saturday, 8 am to 7 pm; Broadway: West 32nd to West 52nd Street, Everyday, 8 am to 8 pm; Seventh Avenue: West 33rd to West 34th Street, Monday through Saturday, 8 am to 6 pm; West 35th to West 45th Street, Monday through Saturday, 8 am to midnight; West 46th to West 52nd Street, Monday through Saturday, 2 pm to 7 pm; Fourteenth Street: Broadway to Seventh Avenue, Monday through Saturday, noon to 8 pm; West Thirty-fourth Street: Fifth Avenue to Seventh Avenue, Monday through Saturday, 8 am to 7 pm; Forty-second Street: Third Avenue to Eighth Avenue, Monday through Saturday, 8 am to 7 pm; West Forty-third Street: Broadway to Eighth Avenue, Wednesday and Saturday, noon to 11 pm; Sunday, noon to 6 pm; Other days, 7 pm to 11 pm; West Forty-fourth Street: Broadway to Eighth Avenue, Wednesday and Saturday, noon to 11 pm; Sunday, noon to 6 pm; Other days, 7 pm to 11 pm; West Forty-fifth Street: Broadway to Eighth Avenue, Wednesday and Saturday, noon to 11 pm; Sunday, noon to 6 pm; Other days, 7 pm to 11 pm; West Forty-sixth Street: Seventh to Eighth Avenues, Wednesday and Saturday, noon to 11 pm; Sunday, noon to 6 pm; Other days, 7 pm to 11 pm; West Forty-seventh Street: Fifth to Eighth Avenues, Wednesday and Saturday, noon to 11 pm; Sunday, noon to 6 pm; Other days, 7 pm to 11 pm; West Forty-eighth Street: Broadway to Eighth Avenues, Wednesday and Saturday, noon to 11 pm; Sunday, noon to 6 pm; Other days, 7 pm to 11 pm; West Forty-ninth Street: Broadway to Eighth Avenues, Wednesday and Saturday, noon to 11 pm; Sunday, noon to 6 pm; Other days, 7 pm to 11 pm; West Fiftieth Street: Broadway to Eighth Avenues, Wednesday and Saturday, noon to 11 pm; Sunday, noon to 6 pm; Other days, 7 pm to 11 pm; West Fifty-first Street: Broadway to Eighth Avenues, Wednesday and Saturday, noon to 11 pm; Sunday, noon to 6 pm; Other days, 7 pm to 11 pm; West Fifty-second Street: Broadway to Eighth Avenues, Wednesday and Saturday, noon to 11 pm; Sunday, noon to 6 pm; Other days, 7 pm to 11 pm; West Fifty-third Street: Broadway to Eighth Avenues, Wednesday and Saturday, noon to 11 pm; Sunday, noon to 6 pm; Other days, 7 pm to 11 pm.

BOROUGH OF QUEENS

Main Street: Northern Boulevard to Sanford Avenue, every day, noon to midnight; 38th Avenue: Prince Street to 138th Street, every day, noon to midnight; Prince Street: 38th Avenue to 39th Avenue, every day, noon to midnight; 39th Avenue: College Point Boulevard to Union Street, every day, noon to midnight; Lippman Plaza: 39th Avenue to Roosevelt Avenue, every day, noon to midnight; Roosevelt Avenue: College Point Boulevard to Union Street, every day, noon to midnight; 41st Avenue: College Point Boulevard to Union Street, every day, noon to midnight; Kissena Boulevard: 41st Avenue to Barclay Avenue, every day, noon to midnight; Sanford Avenue: Frame Place to Main Street, every day, noon to midnight.

3. No food vendor shall vend beginning on Thanksgiving until New Year's Day of the following year in the area including and bounded on the west by the westerly side of 10th avenue, on the south by the southerly side of 86th street, on the east by the easterly side of 13th avenue and on the north by the northerly side of 81st street, between the hours of midnight to 6:00 a.m. and between the hours of 2:00 p.m. to midnight, in the borough of Brooklyn.

HISTORICAL NOTES:

Section added chap 907/1985 § 1.

Subd. b amended L.L. 17/2013 § 1, eff. July 16, 2013.

Subd. c amended L.L. 39/2006 § 2, eff. Dec 16, 2006.

Subd. d amended L.L. 18/2013 § 1, eff. June 16, 2013.

Subd. e separately amended L.L. 17/2013 § 1, eff. July 16, 2013.

Subd. e separately amended L.L. 19/2013 § 1, eff. June 16, 2013.

Subd. g repealed L.L. 14/1995 § 1, eff. Feb. 3, 1995.

Subd. k amended (incorporating subd. l as par 2) L.L. 180/2018 § 1, eff. Dec. 26, 2018.

Subd. k par 2 separately amended L.L. 181/2018 § 1, eff. Apr. 25, 2019.

Subd. k par 3 added L.L. 191/2019 § 1, eff. Nov. 17, 2019.

RULES OF THE CITY OF NEW YORK

TITLE 34
DEPARTMENT OF TRANSPORTATION

CHAPTER 4
TRAFFIC RULES AND REGULATIONS
(Selected Sections)

§ 4-07. Other Restrictions on Movement

(a) Yield signs. The operator of a vehicle approaching a YIELD or YIELD-RIGHT-OF-WAY sign shall slow to a reasonable speed for existing conditions of traffic and visibility, stopping if necessary, and shall yield the right-of-way to all traffic on the intersecting street which is so close as to constitute an immediate hazard. Proceeding past such sign with resultant collision or other impediment or interference with traffic on the intersecting street shall be deemed prima facie evidence of a violation of this rule.

(b) Obstruction of traffic.

(1) Traffic lane. No person shall operate a vehicle in a manner which obstructs traffic in lanes specifically designated for the movement of traffic. Such lanes include, but are not limited to, no standing zones and no stopping zones.

(2) Spillback. No operator shall enter an intersection and its crosswalks unless there is sufficient unobstructed space beyond the intersection and its crosswalks in the lane in which he/she is traveling to accommodate the vehicle, notwithstanding any traffic control signal indication to proceed.

(c) Restrictions on crossing sidewalks.

(1) Driveways. No person shall drive within any sidewalk area except at a permanent or temporary driveway.

(2) Avoiding intersections. No person shall drive across a sidewalk or upon a driveway in order to avoid an intersection.

(3) Bicycles and limited use vehicles.

(i) No person shall ride or operate a bicycle upon any sidewalk area unless permitted by sign. This prohibition shall not apply to the operation of bicycles with wheels of less than 26 inches in diameter upon the sidewalk by children of 12 years or less in age.

(ii) No person shall ride, park or operate a limited use vehicle within any sidewalk area except where permitted by sign. This prohibition shall not apply to the pushing of a limited use vehicle within a sidewalk area or to the pushing of such a vehicle to an authorized parking area.

(d) Restrictions on backing. No person shall back a vehicle into an intersection or over a crosswalk and shall not in any event or at any place back a vehicle unless such movement can be made in safety.

(e) Play streets. Whenever authorized signs are erected indicating any street or part thereof as a play street or play area, no person shall drive a vehicle upon any such street or area between 8 a.m. and one-half hour after sunset, unless other hours are prescribed by signs, except operators of vehicles having business or whose residences are within such restricted area. Any such operator shall exercise the greatest care in driving upon any such street.

(f) Restrictions on learners.

(1) An operator with a learner's permit shall not operate a motor vehicle in any park, on any play street, or along any block in which there is an entrance to a public playground or park.

(2) The licensed operator accompanying an operator with a learner's permit shall not permit such learner to violate paragraph (f)(1), above.

(g) Following emergency vehicles prohibited. The operator of any vehicle other than one on official public business shall not follow any emergency vehicle traveling in response to an emergency call closer than 200 feet, nor drive into nor park such vehicle within the block where such emergency work is in progress.

(h) Driving on divided highways.

(1) Whenever any highway is divided into two or more roadways by an intervening space, physical barrier, or clearly indicated dividing section so constructed as to impede vehicular traffic, every vehicle shall be driven only upon the right-hand roadway unless directed or permitted to use another roadway by official traffic control devices or law enforcement officers. No vehicle shall be driven over, across or within any such dividing space, barrier or section, except through an opening in such physical barrier or dividing section or space or at a crossover or intersection, as established, unless specifically authorized by public authority.

(2) No vehicle shall make a U-turn on a divided highway, except where permitted by sign or at the direction of a law enforcement officer.

(i) Towing of vehicles on parkways, expressways, drives, highways, interstate routes, thruways, and bridges.

(1) Restrictions. No person shall cause or permit a disabled vehicle to be towed except by a tow truck under permit issued by the commissioner of the Police Department, or by a Police Department tow truck and then only by such tow truck on the main roadway, including the berm or shoulder adjacent to said roadways or entrances and exits of the following parkways, expressways, thruways, and bridges:

Belt Parkway System
Bronx River Parkway
Cross Island Parkway
Grand Central Parkway
Henry Hudson Parkway
Hutchinson River Parkway
Jackie Robinson Parkway
Laurelton Parkway
Mosholu Parkway Extension
Richmond Parkway
Shore Parkway
Southern Parkway
Brooklyn-Queens Expressway
Bruckner Expressway
Clearview Expressway
Cross Bronx Expressway and Extension
Franklin Delano Roosevelt Drive
Gowanus Expressway
Harlem River Drive
Long Island Expressway
Major Deegan Expressway
Martin Luther King Expressway
Miller Highway
Nassau Expressway
Governor Thomas E. Dewey Thruway (New England Section)
Prospect Expressway
Route 25A (Elevated Section) from 112th Place to 126th Street

Sheridan Expressway
Staten Island Expressway
Throgs Neck Expressway
Van Wyck Expressway and Extension
West Shore Expressway
Whitestone Expressway
Brooklyn Bridge
Manhattan Bridge
Queensboro Bridge
Williamsburg Bridge
Alexander Hamilton Bridge
Eastern Boulevard (Bruckner Boulevard) Bridge
Hutchinson River Parkway Extension Bridge
Kosciuszko Bridge
Midtown Highway Bridge
Mill Basin Bridge
Third Avenue Bridge between Manhattan and Bronx
Unionport Bridge
Whitestone Expressway Bridge
Willis Avenue Bridge

(2) Police commissioner may waive requirements. The commissioner of the Police Department in his/her discretion may waive and reimpose the requirement for a permit in the case of any specific bridge, highway, parkway, expressway, drive, interstate route and thruway.

(3) Road service and towing rates. For the pupose of this paragraph, road service shall mean service performed that will enable a vehicle to continue under it's own power.

(i) Road service, all vehicles

(A) Gasoline delivery, not including cost of gas $25.00

(B) Removing each flat tire and replacing each with spare tire $25.00

(C) Battery charge $25.00

(ii) Passenger cars, hoist and tow, per mile and storage fees. Hoist and tow fees, per mile fees, and storage fees for all passenger cars towed pursuant to arterial tow service permits in the City of New York, shall be those provided for such services in subdivisions a and b of §2-368 of subchapter EE of title 6 of the rules of the city of New York.

(iii) Vehicles other than passenger cars

(A) Any vehicle with a maximum gross vehicle weight over 4,500 lbs. and under 10,000 lbs.

(a) Preparation, hoist and tow, including first mile or fraction thereof $125.00

(b) Each additional mile $5.00

(c) Storage per 24-hour period $35.00

(B) Any two axle truck or bus with a maximum gross vehicle weight from 10,000 to 18,000 lbs.

(a) Preparation, hoist and tow, including first mile or fraction thereof $175.00

(b) Each additional mile $10.00

(c) Use of under-lift $50.00

(d) Storage per 24-hour period $50.00

(C) Any two axle truck or bus with a maximum gross vehicle weight from 18,000 to 26,000 lbs.

(a) Preparation, hoist and tow, including first mile or fraction thereof $250.00

(b) Each additional mile $10.00

(c) Use of under-lift $50.00

(d) Storage per 24-hour period $50.00

(D) Any truck, bus or tractor trailer with a maximum gross vehicle weight above 26,000 lbs.

(a) Preparation, hoist and tow, including first mile or fraction thereof $300.00

(b) Each additional mile $10.00
(c) Use of under-lift $100.00
(d) Storage for tractor, per 24-hour period $50.00
(e) Storage for bus or trailer, per 24-hour period $75.00
(E) Labor per 1/4 hour per truck or per person or tow operator $50.00

Applies only to vehicles over 4,500 lbs. in the following situations: overturned, wedged on guardrails, off-road recovery (embankment) and may apply to jackknifed, wedged under overpass/bridge, or broken/defective axle in which recovery (off-loading or positioning) must be performed prior to actual tow.

(F) Special equipment such as fork lifts, cranes, loading equipment, trailer, tractor, front end loaders and dump trucks will be considered rented equipment. The cost for such equipment will be billed on a daily basis with the approval of the Department.

(G) Tire service. If subcontracting to a tire company is required for on-road service, the tow vehicle must remain on the scene. Billing will be calculated for actual work time at $100.00 per hour. Subcontracting for off-roadway service, no tow truck required to remain on scene: a one-time charge of $55.00.

(j) Yearly and single issue permits for use of roadways.

(1) General information. Vehicles normally prohibited from roadways may be issued yearly or single-use permits by the Department of Transportation upon application in writing. Such permits must be displayed so that they are visible through the windshield. The Commissioner or his/her designee may charge a fee for such permits equal to the cost of administering the permit program.

(2) Eligible groups and vehicles. Yearly permits are available to the following, as well as to any other groups or vehicles specified by the Commissioner or his/her designee:

(i) companies that transport passengers to and from airports;
(ii) commuter and shuttle services;
(iii) ambulettes;
(iv) school bus companies;
(v) buses;
(vi) medical, blood and human service programs;
(vii) not-for-profit groups going to and from special events;
(viii) vehicles that service businesses accessible only by use of parkways; and
(ix) service vehicles that repair and maintain highways and highway facilities.

(3) Authorized roadways. Yearly and single issue permits will be granted only for the following parkways or any other area designated by the Department of Transportation:

(i) Belt Parkway
(ii) Bronx River Parkway
(iii) Cross Island Parkway
(iv) Eastern Parkway
(v) Grand Central Parkway: Between the TriBoro Bridge and the Van Wyck Expressway
(vi) Harlem River Drive
(vii) Henry Hudson Parkway
(viii) Hutchinson River Parkway
(ix) Mosholu Parkway
(x) Pelham Parkway
(xi) Richmond Parkway
(xii) Willowbrook Parkway

For reasons of safety, the use of these roadways may be limited.

(4) Duration. Permits are issued for the minimum hours and days essential for the activity. Bus permits are valid only while transporting passengers. Yearly permits are issued on an annual basis on dates determined by the Department of Transportation. These permits are renewable by reapplication in writing to the Department of Transportation. The Commissioner or his/her designee may, at his/her discretion, issue, extend or revoke any permit.

(k) Express lanes.

(1) Restrictions. Wherever signs are erected on highways or bridges giving notice of express lanes, except as otherwise posted, no person shall operate a vehicle other than a vehicle as specified in paragraph (2) of this subdivision, an emergency vehicle as specified in paragraph (4) of this subdivision, or a vehicle classified as an HOV, with or without EZPASS as specified on such sign, within a designated express lane on a highway or bridge during the hours specified on such signs.

(2) Buses and Access-A-Ride vehicles. Vehicles registered as buses in New York State, vehicles registered out-of-state that are equivalent to New York State registered buses, Access-A-Ride vehicles and motorcycles shall be eligible to use express lanes on highways or bridges pursuant to this subdivision.

(3) Taxis and for-hire vehicles. Medallion taxis and for-hire vehicles duly licensed by the New York City Taxi and Limousine Commission carrying at least one passenger shall be allowed to use express lanes on highways or bridges. Medallion taxis and for-hire vehicles without passengers shall not be allowed to use express lanes on highways or bridges. Medallion taxis and for-hire vehicles without passengers shall not be allowed to use express lanes on highways or bridges.

(4) Emergency vehicles. Emergency vehicles responding to emergencies shall be allowed to use express lanes on highways or bridges. Emergency vehicles not responding to emergencies shall not be allowed to use express lanes on highways or bridges.

(*l*) Use of the Grand Central Parkway by certain vehicles. Notwithstanding any other provision of these rules to the contrary, single-unit vehicles with no more than three axles and ten tires may operate in both directions on the roadway of the Grand Central Parkway, between the Triborough Bridge and the western leg of the Brooklyn-Queens Expressway. Buses will continue to be prohibited from operating on the Grand Central Parkway without consent.

(m) Use of the Korean War Veterans Parkway by certain vehicles. Notwithstanding any other provision of these rules to the contrary, not more than forty-ton motor vehicles commonly classified as construction trucks owned and/or operated by the Department of Environmental Protection of the City of New York, its agents or contractors shall be permitted the use of the Korean War Veterans Parkway during remediation of the Brookfield landfill in Staten Island for the purpose of the remediation of such landfill, provided that such trucks comply with all other provisions of applicable state and local law, including but not limited to §4-15 of these rules.

HISTORICAL NOTES:

Section repealed and added City Record Apr. 22, 1992 eff. May 22, 1992.

Subd. (i) par (1) amended City Record Dec. 11, 1998 eff. Jan. 10, 1999.

Subd. (i) par (2) amended City Record Dec. 11, 1998 eff. Jan. 10, 1999.

Subd. (i) par (3) subpar (i) amended City Record July 25, 1996 eff. Aug. 24, 1996.

Subd. (i) par (3) subpar (iii) repealed and added City Record July 25, 1996 eff. Aug. 24, 1996.

Subd. (j) par (3) subpar (i) amended City Record Jan. 10, 2020 §2, eff. Feb. 9, 2020.

Subd. (k) amended City Record Apr. 30, 2019 §2, eff. May 30, 2019.

Subd. (*l*) amended City Record Oct. 1, 2004 eff. Oct. 31, 2004.

Subd. (m) added City Record May 3, 2010 §1, eff. May 3, 2010 per City Record notice.

§ 4-11. Taxis, Commuter Vans, For-Hire and Certain Diplomatic and Consular Vehicles

(a) Standing. No operator of a taxi, while awaiting employment shall stand his/her vehicle in any street except:

(1) At an authorized taxi stand.

(2) In front of fire hydrants where standing or stopping is not prohibited by signs or rules, provided that the operator remains in the operator's seat ready for immediate operation of the taxi at all times and starts the motor on hearing the approach of fire

apparatus, and provided further, that the operator shall immediately remove the taxi from in front of the fire hydrant when instructed to do so by any member of the police, fire, or other municipal department acting in his/her official capacity.

(b) Cruising prohibited. An operator of a vehicle other than a taxi shall not operate his/her vehicle along a street for the purpose of soliciting passengers or searching for passengers.

(c) Pickup and discharge of passengers by taxis, commuter vans and for-hire vehicles. Operators of taxis, commuter vans and for-hire vehicles may, in the course of the lawful operation of such vehicles, temporarily stop their vehicles to expeditiously pick up or discharge passengers at the curb in areas where standing or parking is prohibited. Taxis, commuter vans and for-hire vehicles, while engaged in picking up or discharging passengers must be within 12 inches of the curb and parallel thereto, but may stop or stand to pick up or discharge passengers alongside a vehicle parked at the curb only if there is no unoccupied curb space available within 100 feet of the pickup or discharge location; however, picking up or discharging passengers shall not be made:

(1) Within a pedestrian crosswalk.

(2) Within an intersection, except on the side of a roadway opposite a street which intersects but does not cross such roadway.

(3) Alongside or opposite any street excavation when stopping to pick up or discharge passengers obstructs traffic.

(4) Under such conditions as to obstruct the movement of traffic and in no instance so as to leave fewer than 10 feet available for the free movement of vehicular traffic.

(5) Where stopping is prohibited.

(6) Within a bicycle lane.

(7) Within horse-drawn cab passenger boarding areas.

(d) Pickup and discharge of passengers by certain diplomatic and consular vehicles. A vehicle bearing "A", "C" or "D" series license plates issued by the U.S. Department of State and displaying a valid non-transferable service vehicle decal issued by the City of New York that is affixed to the inside of the operator's side of the windshield shall be treated like a for-hire vehicle while actively engaged in and for the purpose of expeditiously picking up or discharging passengers, in a manner that does not obstruct traffic, provided that the operator of such vehicle bearing such "A" "C" or "D" series license plates and displaying such non-transferable service vehicle decal:

(1) may not pick up or discharge passengers in a for-hire vehicle stop;

(2) remains in attendance at the vehicle; and

(3) shall immediately remove such vehicle when instructed to do so by any law enforcement officer.

HISTORICAL NOTES:

Section heading amended City Record May 9, 2003 §5, eff. June 8, 2003. [See T34 §4-08 Note 27]

Section repealed and added City Record Apr. 22, 1992 eff. May 22, 1992.

Section in original publication July 1, 1991.

Subd. (a) par (3) repealed City Record July 2, 2018 §14, eff. Aug. 1, 2018.

Subd. (c) amended City Record Oct. 7, 1996 eff. Nov. 6, 1996.

Subd. (c) par (7) amended City Record Jan. 4, 2019 §3, eff. Feb. 15, 2019.

Subd. (d) added City Record May 9, 2003 §6, eff. June 8, 2003.

OFFENSES AND THEIR CLASSIFICATIONS FOR THE PENAL LAW OF NEW YORK

(All references are to sections of the N.Y. Penal Law)

Offenses	Sections
1. CLASS A-I FELONIES	
Domestic Act of Terrorism Motivated by Hate-2nd Degree	490.27
Domestic Act of Terrorism Motivated by Hate-1st Degree	490.28
7. CLASS A MISDEMEANORS	
Harassment of a Rent Regulated Tenant-2nd Degree	241.02